Peter Norton's

Windows 3.0 Power Programming Techniques

Peter Norton's

Windows 3.0 Power Programming Techniques

Peter Norton
Paul L. Yao

BANTAM BOOKS
TORONTO · NEW YORK · LONDON · SYDNEY · AUCKLAND

PETER NORTON'S WINDOWS 3.0 POWER PROGRAMMING TECHNIQUES
A Bantam Book / December 1990

Produced by MicroText Productions
Composed by Context Publishing Services

ISBN 0-553-34940-6

Published simultaneously in the United States and Canada

Bantam Books are published by Bantam Books, a division of Bantam
Doubleday Dell Publishing Group Inc. Its trademark, consisting of the
words "Bantam Books" and the portrayal of a rooster, is registered in the
U.S. Patent and Trademark Office and in other countries. Marca Registrada,
Bantam Books, Inc., 666 Fifth Avenue, New York, New York 10103.

PRINTED IN THE UNITED STATES OF AMERICA

0 9 8 7 6 5 4 3 2 1

Dedication

To my wife, Rebecca.
P. L. Y.

To my wife, Eileen
P. N.

Preface

In the spring of 1989, we got word that Microsoft was planning to create its third major revision to Windows. The more we learned about it, the more we became convinced that this would be the version that would attract the critical mass of developers and users that would turn it into a hit. Events have proved our hunch correct: Microsoft shipped more than one million copies of Windows in the first three months after its announcement on May 22, 1990. Sales of the software development kit are said to be five times what had been expected.

This book was written to help experienced C programmers learn to program in Windows. There are a couple of resources that are invaluable when learning about a new environment. One is sample code that shows the basic techniques necessary to take advantage of the features of the environment. Another is the help of a guru who knows the ins and outs of the environment. This book provides you both.

This book has dozens of programs to demonstrate the use of different features in Windows. We have provided a complete listing of these programs, to give you a complete picture of the pieces that you will be working with. Someone once said that only one Windows program has ever been written. Every other Windows program has been cut and pasted from the very first one. Feel free to use any of the code in your Windows development projects. (These programs are available in machine-readable form. For more details, please see the inside back cover.)

To get started in programming for Windows, you're going to need the following:

- The Microsoft Software Development Kit (SDK)
- A Windows compatible C compiler (see the list in Chapter 2)
- Windows version 3

Although it's not a requirement, if you plan to run the Codeview debugger, you'll also want the following hardware, which will give Codeview its own output device:

- On computers equipped with an AT-style bus, an MDA card and a monochrome monitor. A Hercules-compatible graphics card can often be used in the place of an MDA card.
- On computers equipped with an MCA bus, you'll want to have an 8514/a adapter and a compatible display, in addition to a VGA-style monitor.

Intertwined with the discussion of Windows programming, this book describes the architecture and innerworkings of Windows. We've worked closely with the Windows development teams—both past and present—to create a picture that we hope you'll find complete and accurate. One thing is for certain: the more we learn about Windows, the more impressed we have become with the ingenuity with which the product has been created.

This book is divided into seven sections. In Section I, we provide a brief history of Windows, and describe the three challenges that new programmers face: mastering message-driven programming, creating and controlling graphical output, and learning how to use the various user-interface objects.

Section II dissects a minimum Windows program, and explores several fundamental topics in Windows programming. The focus of this section is understanding the basic structure that all Windows programs share.

Section III introduces topics relating to creating graphical output. Output is the domain of Windows' Graphic Device Interface (GDI), which provides device-independent graphic output on displays, printers and plotters. Chapter 6 describes basic concepts in graphic programming, such as drawing coordinates, GDI's device context, and clipping. From there, subsequent chapters cover the output of pixels, lines, filled areas, and text.

In Section IV, we cover three key user-interface objects: menus, windows, and dialog boxes. We describe the inner-workings of each type of object and all of the basics required to make them operational.

Section V is dedicated to getting user input. Windows is a message driven operating environment, so it is not surprising to find that keyboard and mouse input arrives in the form of messages. We describe the flow of data from the physical hardware, through the system buffers and into a Windows program.

We cover operating system considerations in Section VI. This covers two basic areas: memory and dynamic linking. One of the big news items of Windows 3 involves the improvements that have been made in memory use. To help you understand exactly what this means, we describe the inner workings of each of Windows' operating modes.

And finally, in Section VII, we return to topics in GDI programming. Chapter 20 describes scrolling and coordinate transformation. Scrolling describes the way a program helps the user to view a data object that is larger than a window. Coordinate transformation is a service provided by GDI to let you choose the type of coordinates that you wish to use. The default is pixels, but GDI also lets you draw using inches, millimeters, or your own, custom scaling factors. Chapter 21 introduces topics that relate to printing. To help in the creation of full-blown Windows programs, we provide complete source code to a printer configuration dialog box.

Acknowledgments

Researching and organizing the amount of information required for a book like this is impossible without the help of a lot of people. We are fortunate to be associated with a group of individuals who share an incredible commitment to the success of Windows.

We'd like to start off by thanking the development teams of Windows 1.x, 2.x and 3.0. In particular, we want to thank the developers and marketeers who gave of their time and energies to help us understand the subtle nuances of the way Windows works: Peter Belew, John Butler, Mark Cligget, Clark Cyr, Rick Dill, Marlin Eller, Ron Gery, Bob Gunderson, Paul Klinger, Scott MacGregor, Ed Mills, Walt Moore, Gabe Newell, Chris Peters, John Pollock, Rao Remala, Lin Shaw, Charles Simonyi, Tandy Trower, Manny Vellon, David Weise, and Steve Wood.

Within other divisions at Microsoft, thanks to the individuals who helped us and supported us in the creation of this book. At Microsoft University, we'd like to thank Kim Crouse, Mel Kanner, Sheila Keane, Bruce King, Janet Shepardigian, John Thorsen, Mark Ursino, and Ceil Wallick. A special word of thanks goes to David Durant, who is and always will be our first Windows programming instructor. Within the Application's Development Division, thanks to Jim Cash, for helping us solve the puzzle of making Windows programming comprehensible, and to Paul Klemond, a cracker-jack Windows application developer who helped us solve a few Windows programming riddles.

At Bantam Electronic Publishing, we'd like to thank our publisher, and the vice-president of publishing, Kenzi Shugihara. Thanks go to Stephen Guty, our editor, for his long hours and painstaking efforts. And thanks are also due to Lauralee Butler, Steve Gambini, and Tom Szalkiewicz, who handled the production of the book itself.

Thanks to Kevin Goldstein at Peter Norton Computing, who helped give the manuscript its cohesive direction.

Finally, we'd like to thank the staff at Waterside Productions, and especially their chief, Bill Gladstone, the literary agent for both Peter Norton and Paul Yao.

Contents

xvi Peter Norton's Windows 3 Power Programming Techniques

Part 1

An Introduction to Windows

1
An Introduction to Windows

Microsoft Windows is a graphical extension to the MS-DOS operating system. Windows extends DOS in several ways. DOS is built to support a single program at a time; Windows runs multiple programs concurrently. DOS has limited support for graphical output; Windows supports sophisticated, high-level graphics. DOS requires each program to provide its own user interface, which means that users must learn a different set of commands for every DOS program they use. A different command structure in different programs is like having a different steering mechanism and gear shift in different cars: Variety is nice, but a standard interface allows the user to operate any Windows program with a minimum of training. Windows provides a standard set of user interface objects like windows, menus, and icons. A common set of user interface objects means a consistent "look and feel" for all Windows programs, which helps make Windows programs easy to learn and easy to use.

Windows provides a multitasking, graphical user interface, or **GUI**, that fosters the creation of interactive programs. Windows represents a relatively new type of operating environment that is optimized for the interaction between human beings and computer programs, and these programs have a different structure from programs in more traditional environments. This structure has a lot in common with programs written for other GUI systems, like the Apple Macintosh and the OS/2 Presentation Manager. Programs that run in these environments are **event-driven**. That is to say, the structure and operation of these types of programs centers around user-generated events (like keystrokes and mouse clicks). The architecture of such programs has more in common with operating-system software and interrupt-management routines than with traditional application software.

Traditionally, application programs have been sequence driven and not event driven. That is to say, *the program* dictates the sequence that the user must follow to accomplish the goal of the program. Event-driven programs, on the other hand, allow the *user* to dictate the steps required to complete a given task. The change from sequence-driven programming to event-driven programming requires a new way of thinking. Helping you learn this new way of thinking is what this book is all about.

A History of Windows

All GUI systems trace their roots back to the work done at Xerox. In 1970, Xerox created the Palo Alto Research Center. Its charter was to create a new architecture for the way information is handled. Among its other accomplishments, PARC is credited with the development of laser printing, local area networks, graphical user interfaces, and object-oriented programming.

The researchers at PARC built several versions of a machine they dubbed "Alto." Over the years, several hundred of these internal research machines were built and were in widespread use. Built on the research of Alto, Xerox created a commercial GUI system: the Star 8010 workstation. Xerox introduced the Star in April of 1981, four months before the IBM PC was made public. This multitasking system came equipped with a mouse and a bitmapped graphical display on which were displayed icons, windows, and proportionally spaced text. Although its high price kept it from becoming a commercial success, the Star marks an important milestone as the first commercially available GUI system.

The story is told that Steve Jobs, a co-founder of Apple Computer, was taken on a tour of Xerox PARC in 1979 or so. He was so impressed by the various Alto systems that he saw, that he returned to Apple and pushed for research in the development of a similar system. Apple introduced its first GUI system in 1983: the Apple Lisa. Apple followed the Lisa with its second GUI system, the Apple Macintosh. For its announcement, Apple bought time during the Super Bowl in January of 1984 and aired a commercial that introduced the Macintosh as the computer to save the world from the nightmare of Big Brother described in George Orwell's novel *1984*. Although it took a few years to achieve success in the market, the importance of the Apple Macintosh is that it was the first commercially successful GUI system.

Microsoft started working on Windows in the spring of 1983. Eight years had passed since Microsoft's founders, Bill Gates and Paul Allen, wrote a BASIC interpreter for the world's first computer kit, the MITS Altair. And two years had passed since IBM introduced its personal computer, which came bundled with two Microsoft products: DOS and BASIC. Microsoft was just getting ready to ship version 2.0 of DOS, with its support for a hierarchical file system to support the hard disk of another new product, IBM's PC/XT computer.

At that time, there was talk at Microsoft of building a GUI system for the IBM personal computers, but no firm plans had been put in place. The primary reason was that the typical PC in those days had two floppy drives, 64K of RAM, and an 8088 CPU. For a GUI system to have acceptable performance, it was felt that more powerful hardware was needed. Hard disks would have to be available to provide fast access, more memory would be needed to accommodate both the sophisticated code and the memory hungry graphic data that such systems require. But something happened to spur Microsoft into GUI development.

In February 1983, VisiCorp, makers of the (then) popular spreadsheet VisiCalc, announced a GUI product for the IBM PC. Dubbed "VisiOn," it provided the motivation for Microsoft to begin working on its own GUI system. After all, if VisiOn caught on, it presented the possibility of taking software developers off the MS-DOS standard. And one thing was clear very early on at Microsoft: Software standards and compatibility would always be critical to the success of the microcomputer industry.

A team of developers that became known as the "Interactive Systems Group," or ISG, was assembled at Microsoft. Among the members of the team was a Xerox PARC alumnus, Scott MacGregor. Another Windows developer, Neil Konzen, had worked on porting Microsoft's spreadsheet, Multiplan, to the Macintosh. When the first version of Windows was introduced in November 1985, it had features that reflect the influence of Xerox PARC and the Apple Macintosh. But Windows itself was home-grown Microsoft, with features that anticipated the power of an operating system yet to be born: OS/2.

Figure 1.1   *Windows version 1.01*

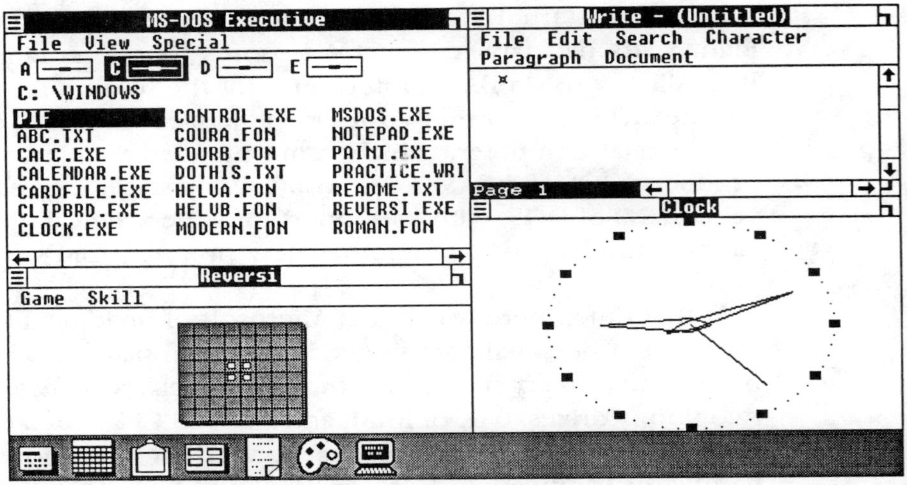

Version 1.01 of Windows started shipping in November 1985. As depicted in Figure 1.1, the first version of Windows provided automatic tiling of program windows. It was felt that the automatic arrangement of windows minimized the amount of work required of the user. This first version also supported overlapping or "popup" windows, which served primarily for the creation of dialog boxes. Windows 1 sported a "three-slice toaster," which provided access to the system menu. Some of the developers joked that this was actually a tiny vent that served to cool the screen lest it become overheated from the speed of the graphics.

The first version of Windows was built to run on a two-floppy drive IBM PC with 256K RAM and an Intel 8088 CPU. This, incidentally, was the configuration used by ISG team members themselves during the earliest days of Windows development. Only later were tools available that developers today take for granted: hard disks, high-speed local area networks with file servers and print servers. And while this slowed development somewhat, Microsoft knew that this was the equipment that application developers would someday use to create software that would run under Windows. Developing in this environment, then, helped to stress test its suitability for application development.

Figure 1.2 *Windows version 2*

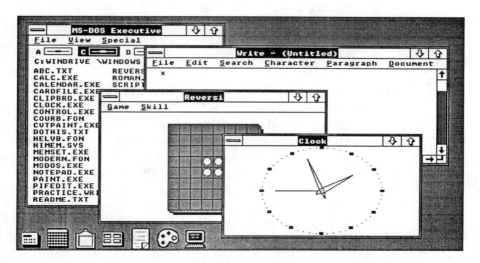

The next major revision of Windows was version 2, which started shipping in September 1987. Windows 2, shown in Figure 1.2, featured overlapping Windows. The primary reason for the change from automatic tiling was because Microsoft had received feedback from end users who did not appreciate the benefits of tiled windows, but who felt rather that tiling got in the way. The change away from automatic tiling was also part of an effort to make Windows consistent with another graphical environment that had been announced in April of that year: the OS/2 Presentation Manager.

The similarity between the Windows and the OS/2 user interface is intended to help users move easily from one environment to the other. In fact, the user interface shared by these two environments is part of a much larger IBM strategy to create software consistency that extends from the smallest personal computer up to the largest mainframe. This strategy is called **Systems Application Architecture**, or **SAA**. A primary goal of SAA is to allow a program written on one platform to be easily ported to another environment. For example, if SAA comes to complete fruition, you will someday see OS/2 Presentation Manager programs running on IBM mainframes, minicomputers, and, of course, on personal computers. The part of SAA that addresses user interface issues is known as **Common User Access**, or **CUA**. To help programmers create programs that respect this standard, Microsoft ships with its software development kit a document from IBM that defines the standard: *Systems Application Architecture, Common User Access, Advanced Interface Design Guide.*

Besides a new user interface, one of the key improvements introduced in Windows 2 was better use of memory in the form of support for expanded memory—memory made available according to the **Expanded Memory Specification (EMS)**. EMS describes a bank switching technique that allows additional memory to be available, although bank-switched memory is not *simultaneously* available. EMS under Windows 2 allowed more Windows programs to reside in memory at the same time, since each program was given a private EMS bank. EMS helped relieve the memory crunch that Windows 1 users had experienced, but didn't completely solve the memory shortage problem since Windows 2 only ran in Real Mode. Even on the powerful Intel 80286 and 80386 chips, for compatibility reasons, Intel gave these chips the same one megabyte address space as its less powerful siblings, the 8088 and 8086.

With much fanfare, Microsoft announced version 3 of Windows on May 22, 1990 and started shipping shrink-wrapped packages immediately. Within six weeks, Microsoft had shipped 500,000 copies of the new version, breaking every record for the sale of any software product in a six-week period. From a sales standpoint, industry watchers worldwide have found Windows 3 to be a smashing success.

Figure 1.3 shows the new Windows 3 user interface, created to give Windows a new look for the 90s. It features a proportional system font, to give Windows a more refined look and to make text easier to read. Three-dimensional shadowing, color icons, and redesigned applications combine to make Windows more appealing to the average user. Windows 3 also has better support for running DOS applications, which has prompted many to use it as the primary user interface for DOS-based computers.

From a programming point of view, Microsoft has provided an even richer set of capabilities into the user interface: Support for owner-draw menus, owner-draw listboxes, and owner-draw buttons gives programmers the capability to customize Windows more than ever before. Menus in the new Windows can be nested as deeply as programmers can make them, and tear-off menus give programmers the freedom to place menus anywhere they please. The MS-DOS

Figure 1.3 *Windows version 3*

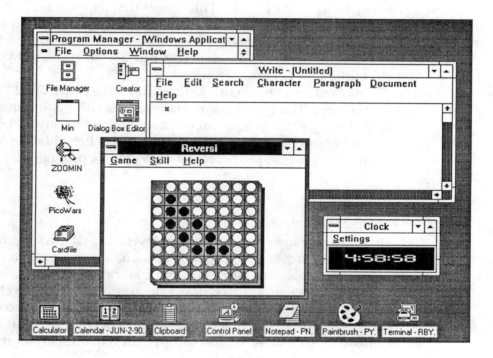

Executive, which was so familiar to users of earlier versions, has been fired and replaced by a set of programs that manage programs and files: the **Program Manager**, the **Task List** and the **File Manager**.

Internally, the most significant feature of Windows 3 is support for extended memory. Under Windows 3, Windows programs can access up to 16 megabytes of RAM. And when an 80386 or higher CPU is present, Windows uses the memory management features of these chips to provide virtual memory. In its 386-Enhanced mode, virtual memory up to four times the installed physical memory is available. For example, with 16 megabytes of physical memory (and enough room on the swap disk) Windows 386 provides a 64-megabyte address space!

Windows 3 also has better network support than earlier versions, making it easy to connect network file servers and print servers. It supports a device-independent bitmap format that provides a standard for sharing color bitmaps among devices; and on devices that support more than 256 colors, applications are even given access to the hardware color palette. This means that support for picture-perfect images, such as those that a multimedia system might use, can now be supported in Windows. Another new feature is a built-in, sophisticated help facility that you can use to provide hyper text help to the users of your programs.

Windows has a cousin that is married to OS/2: the OS/2 Presentation Manager. The Presentation Manager is a GUI system that has an applications programming interface similar to Windows'. Let's take a moment to consider the impact of the OS/2 Presentation Manager on you as you begin your career as a Windows programmer.

The OS/2 Presentation Manager

It seems that every company that develops a GUI system has gone on to build a "new and improved" version. Xerox first built the Alto, then went on to create the Star. Apple started with its Lisa and later built the Macintosh. Created under the terms of a joint development agreement between IBM and Microsoft, Microsoft's second GUI system is the OS/2 Presentation Manager. The product was first announced in April of 1987, and shipped on schedule in October 1988 as a part of OS/2 version 1.1.

The Presentation Manager's application programming interface (API) is a full participant in IBM's SAA architecture. The idea is to provide a programming interface to allow programmers to write code that will work on microcomputers, mini's, and mainframes. The development of this architecture is just beginning, so it is too early to tell how successful it will be. But even if it only delivers a fraction of what is promised, SAA will create a real revolution in programming. Not only will Presentation Manager programs be able to run across a wide spectrum of computers, but they will all have the same high-level, interactive user interface on a wide spectrum of computers.

Windows and Presentation Manager have a lot in common. For one thing, they share a common user interface. This allows users to move between the two environments with little or no retraining. They also share a common programming model, so programmers who are familiar with Windows usually find the OS/2 Presentation Manager easy to learn. But while the programming interfaces are architecturally the same, they are different enough to make porting between the two environments a tedious task.

Where does this leave Windows programmers? In a joint press release at Fall Comdex '89, IBM and Microsoft announced that they would "provide support through tools, seminars, and technical assistance" to help migrate Windows programs to the OS/2 Presentation Manager. In early 1990, Microsoft announced the release of a tool kit, called the **Software Migration Kit**, or **SMK**, that allows a Windows program to be quickly and easily ported to run under OS/2 version. It is not uncommon for the porting of an application to take just a few days. And OS/2, version 2.0, will be binary compatible with Windows programs. From this, it should be clear that writing Windows programs today is the best way to make sure your programs will run in two environments: Windows *and* OS/2.

Now that you know where Windows has come from, and have an idea about where it's going, the time has come to discuss the major obstacles that you will encounter as you learn to program in Windows. It is important to be aware of the required effort, because it is easy to look at Windows' flexible user interface and conclude (incorrectly) that the programming interface is just as easy to work with.

In fact, the challenge to Windows programmers is to understand the fundamental principles and models embodied in its architecture. Once you understand the "Windows-way" of thinking, you'll find that Windows programming is as easy to tackle as any other type of programming that you have done. Incidentally, if you have programmed with any other GUI system, such as the Apple Macintosh, the OS/2 Presentation Manager, or the various X-Windows systems, you'll find much that is familiar in Windows. Let's consider, then, the challenges that lie ahead.

The Windows Programming Challenges

Consider the following scenario. It is Friday afternoon, and on your way out of the office you run into your boss. He has good news: The proposal that you made for the Windows development project has been approved. This means that you, and the crack team of programmers who work for you, are going to get to build your company's first Windows program. One of the first things you'll have to do is make sure that everyone on your team is up to speed on Windows. What challenges will be faced by the programmers who work for you who have no previous Windows programming experience?

Assuming that a programmer is proficient in C, the three primary challenges are understanding message-driven programming, controlling graphical output, and using the various user interface objects like windows, menus, dialog boxes, etc. Incidentally, if a programmer has been exposed to one or more of these areas, it makes it easier to learn Windows programming.

Before we discuss each of these areas in detail, one suggestion we'd like to make is that you become a full-time Windows user. There are subtleties in the Windows user interface that only become evident when you have spent time as an *end-user*. For example, the way the keyboard and mouse work together, the ways that menus and accelerator keys operate, and the operation of the various types of dialog box controls. If you become a full-time Windows user, it will help you to become a better Windows programmer. At the very least, try to find one Windows program that you use on a daily basis: It might be a word processing program, a drawing package, terminal emulation software, or even a game.

Let's take a look at the three challenges that every new Windows programmer faces, starting with message-driven programming.

Challenge 1: Message-Driven Programming

Most programmers are used to writing code that runs in a sequential, procedure-driven manner. Such a program has a well-defined beginning, middle, and end. Consider, for example, a program that displays a series of data entry screens for the creation of some written document, which might be an airplane ticket or a company purchase order. The flowchart in Figure 1.4 depicts the strict sequence in which such a program might operate.

For the sake of this discussion, let's say that this flow chart represents a program used by travel agents to issue airplane tickets. The first entry screen accepts passenger information: name, address, etc. The second screen allows the input of flight information and provides fares and scheduling information. And finally, the third screen accepts payment information based on the fares in the previous screen. Each data entry screen must be correctly filled in before the travel agent can proceed to the next step, and all three screens must have correct information to issue a ticket.

Figure 1.4 *A sequence-driven program*

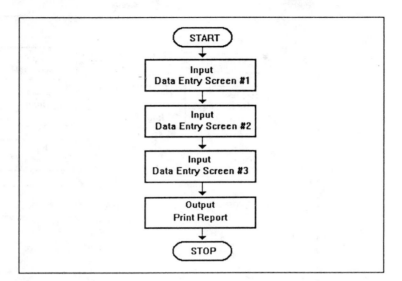

At first glance, this seems like a reasonable way for such a program to proceed. After all, the job of the computer program is not only to issue tickets, but to make sure that correct passenger information has been received and that the payment provided agrees with the currently available fares. There are limitations to this approach, however, that are a direct result of this sequence-driven orientation.

For example, since the program dictates the sequence of operation, a travel agent cannot get to the second screen—for fare and flight information—without first entering complete passenger information. While a travel agency might like this feature, since it allows them to avoid giving away free information, the net result is the creation of unnecessary steps.

While the program insures that all required information has been entered, it doesn't take into account real-world exceptions. For example, if a travel agent were to sell a group of tickets—perhaps to a family that is going on vacation—the travel agent must traverse all three screens for every ticket that is issued. Once again, the program does its job of insuring that all the necessary information has been collected, but at a cost to the travel agent in the form of the additional work required.

Figure 1.5   *An event-driven program*

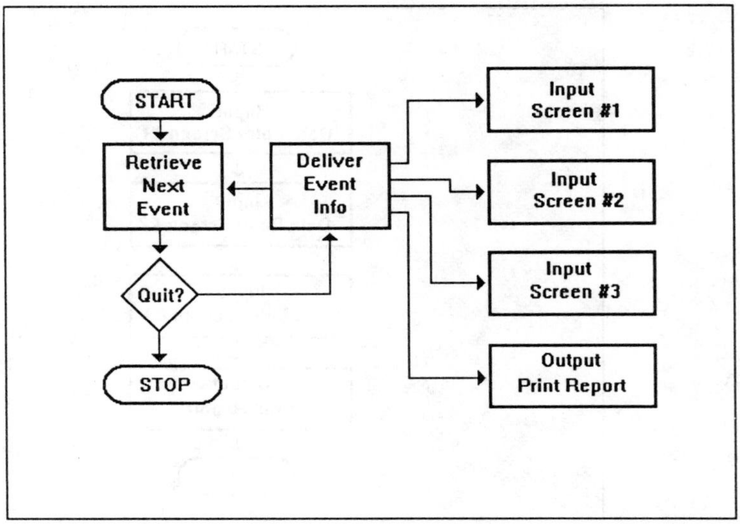

An event-driven program, on the other hand, allows a travel agent to enter the data in whatever order seems appropriate. Perhaps an agent would choose the same order that the sequence-driven program dictated. However, an agent would be free to perform the necessary tasks in a sequence that fit the requirements of different customers. Figure 1.5 gives a rough idea of how an event-driven approach might change the traditional, sequence-driven program that we described earlier.

And yet, this is only one aspect of the way that an event-driven program differs from a sequence-driven program. An event-driven operating system like Windows goes even further so that; for example, within the data entry screens, the travel agent would have a tremendous amount of flexibility in the order in which fields were entered.

A sequence-driven program is built on an awkwardly arranged set of **modes**. A mode is a state of a program in which user actions are interpreted in a specific way and produce a specific set of results. In a reaction against sequence-driven programs, some GUI programmers may tell you that modes are bad. Unfortunately, this is a bit of an oversimplification.

A primary problem having to do with modes occurs when the user cannot easily move from one mode to another. In our sequence-driven ticketing program, for example, each of the four steps is a mode. But since the program dictates that the user traverse the modes in a strict sequence, the user is prevented from structuring his use of the program to meet the various demands that are made.

Another problem with modes occurs in programs that rely on the user to remember the current mode. Instead, a program should provide visual clues to help the user identify the program's current mode. In Windows, there are many user-interface objects that support this. The shape of the mouse cursor, for example, can indicate when a drawing package is in rectangle drawing mode and when it is in text drawing mode. You will see that modal dialog boxes are a very common way to retrieve input from the user that is required to complete a command.

The modes in a program should be carefully designed to prevent data loss when the user accidentally fumbles into a mode. A story often told about modes involves a text editor called Bravo, which was built at Xerox PARC in the 1970s. In this editor, regular keyboard keys are used for commands. For example, the letter "i" puts the program into insert mode, "d" is used for delete mode, etc. One user wanted to place the word "edit" in a document, but forget to first enter insert mode. The editor interpreted these keystrokes as

E (verything) — select everything in the document.
D (elete)   — delete it.
I (nsert)   — enter insert mode.
T   — type the letter 't'.

Oops. The entire contents of the document were replaced by the letter "T." When designing the user interface of a program, you should be aware of the modes that are created and build in the necessary safeguards to help users avoid such unpleasant surprises.

From a programming point of view, modal programs are easier to implement than modeless programs. The code that supports each mode can be written and debugged in relative isolation from the other parts of the program. And yet, Windows makes it easier to create modeless programs because all interaction with the outside world—all events—are funneled to a program in a modeless manner. All events of interest generate messages.

What is a message? It is information about some change in the user interface, such as a window getting moved, or a keyboard key being pressed. Messages notify a program that a timer has gone off. Messages are used for data-sharing operations.

From a programming point of view, a message is a 16-bit unsigned value that, for ease of reading, is assigned a symbolic constant that starts with the letters "WM_". For example, the WM_LBUTTONDOWN message tells a program that the user has pushed the left mouse button. Another message, which gets sent after the left mouse button has been released, is WM_LBUTTONUP. Throughout this book, we'll introduce messages in the context of the different topics that are covered. But if you're impatient to see all the different types of messages in the system, you may want to skip ahead to Appendix A, which summarizes the various types of Windows messages.

Messages are very important to a Windows programmer. Most of the work that you will do as a Windows programmer involves deciding which messages to process and which messages to ignore. One thing to keep in mind is that messages do not appear in any predefined order. If you are used to a sequentially oriented program, things may seem disorganized and chaotic at first. It may seem that messages fly at you like bullets. To help you understand the flow of messages in the system, Microsoft provides a utility called SPY in the Windows SDK. Figure 1.6 shows SPY listening to the messages of the Windows Program Manager. As you progress in your Windows programming efforts, you will learn which messages to pay attention to and which ones you can safely ignore.

Windows' message orientation is best suited for programs that require a high level of interaction with the user. Therefore language compilers, which tend to have very little interaction with the user, gain little from running as Windows programs. But games and word processing programs are well suited for Windows, since both require a high level of user interaction. Spreadsheets and data entry programs are also good candidates for interactive, event-driven applications.

A message driven operating system like Windows puts a high priority on allowing the user to intervene at any point in a process. A sequence-driven program, on the other hand, puts a high priority on dictating the sequence in which a job must be performed. In a sequence-driven program, it is all too tempting for the programmer

Figure 1.6   *SPY listening to messages belonging to the Program Manager*

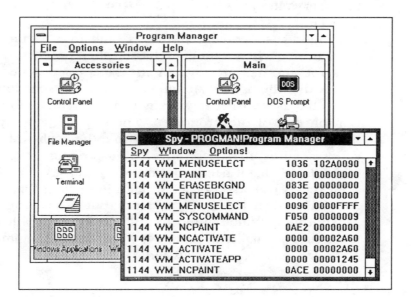

to create arbitrary rules about the order in which steps should be taken. In such cases, the programmer puts artificial and unnecessary limits on what can and cannot be done by the user. While it is possible to create sequence-driven programs in Windows, the extra effort it requires virtually guarantees that such restrictions will only be put in place where they are actually needed.

Messages and Program Scheduling

Windows is a multitasking system. To a user, this means that several programs can run "at the same time." Of course, with a single CPU, programs do not run at the same time. Instead, each is scheduled and each runs one at a time. In traditional operating systems, this scheduling is done by the clock. Each program is allotted a "time-slice" during which it can run. When its time is up, one program is interrupted, and another program is allowed to run. This is called preemptive scheduling. In preemptive scheduling, programs are interrupted by the operating system.

Windows does not schedule programs preemptively. Instead, Windows has a nonpreemptive scheduling system. Windows programs are not interrupted by the operating system; instead, each program voluntarily interrupts its own operation to let other programs run.

Windows' scheduling system is built into its message delivery mechanism. When a program has finished processing a message, it asks for another message. A message-based scheduling system means that the user is the ultimate source of scheduling decisions. When the user wishes to work with a program, he focuses his attention on one of the program's windows, perhaps by clicking the mouse, or by selecting a window from the keyboard. Each of these actions causes messages to flow to a program, which gives it the "time-slices" that it needs to run.

Messages provide a program with input, but that's only half the story. The other half involves the output that a program produces. And output in Windows means just one thing: graphical output. This is the second challenge that new Windows programmers must face, and our next topic of discussion.

Challenge 2: Graphical Output

All output created by Windows programs is graphical. Figure 1.7 shows a sample of some of the lines, filled figures, and text that GDI can draw. Programmers who are used to working in a character-oriented environment will find that graphical output requires a new way of thinking. As you might expect, graphical output means that geometric figures can be drawn—lines, circles, boxes, etc. In addition, text itself is treated as a graphical object. This makes it easier, for example, to freely mix text and geometric figures. Paradoxically, while graphical output systems make the output of geometric shapes easier, they also tend to make the output of text harder.

Geometric shapes are easier because your program does not have to calculate each pixel. By simply calling the **Rectangle** routine, for example, GDI draws a filled rectangle for you. Text output is harder, because GDI's graphical orientation requires that you deal with text as a graphical object. Text is positioned using pixel coordinates rather than by character cell position.

Device-Independent Graphics

GDI provides device-independent graphics. This means a Windows program can draw on any device using the same set of calls. For example, the Rectangle routine is called to draw rectangles on

Figure 1.7   *A sample of GDI's lines, filled figures, and text*

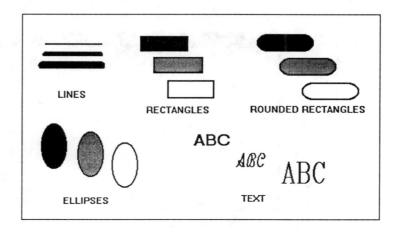

the display screen as well as on printers. GDI works hard so that, from the point of view of a program, all devices look similar. This includes devices that only know how to turn pixels on and off—like the CGA display card—as well as very smart devices that know how to do complex graphics, like Postscript printers. Each device has a device driver that is responsible for doing the actual drawing. For devices that require assistance, GDI provides ***software simulations*** that use the low-level capabilities of a device to provide high-level functionality.

GDI knows about four types of devices: the display screen, hard-copy devices (like printers and plotters), bitmaps, and metafiles. Two of these are physical devices: the display screen and hard-copy devices. The other two, bitmaps and metafiles, are pseudo devices. A pseudo device provides a means to store a picture in RAM or on disk, as well as a standard way to share graphical images between applications.

When displaying information on the display screen, GDI provides window-oriented graphics. Window-oriented graphics means several things. Each window is treated like a separate drawing surface. When a program draws in a window, the default drawing coordinates are set up so that the origin (0,0) is in the upper-left corner of the window's client area (see Figure 1.8).

Window-oriented graphics also means that drawings are automatically clipped to a window. Clipping means that the drawing done

Figure 1.8   *Default origin in client-area coordinates*

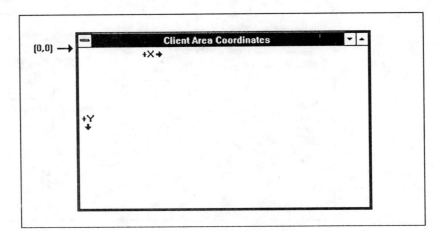

for each window is limited to the window's border. Even if a window tried to draw beyond its own border, it would not be able to. A window is automatically protected from the wayward pixels that other windows might send its way. This protection mechanism works both ways, so that when you draw, you don't have to worry about accidentally overwriting another program's window.

Challenge 3: User-Interface Objects

Windows has built-in support for a number of user-interface objects: windows, icons, menus, dialog boxes, etc. Built-in support means that the amount of effort required to create and maintain these objects is fairly minimal. In particular, if you were to write your own code to support these objects, it would require a vast amount of effort on your part. And the results would probably not be as flexible nor as robust as the user-interface objects that Windows provides.

Taking advantage of what these user-interface objects can provide requires you to understand how each is implemented. As we look at the different types of user-interface objects, we'll provide some insights into the design and implementation of each. In many cases, this will mean a discussion of the messages that are associated with a given user-interface object. In other cases, this means delving into the various Windows library routines that control each type of object. For now, we're going to introduce you to the user-interface objects and describe the role of each in the user interface.

Among user-interface objects, the most important is the window. Any program that wishes to interact with the user must have a window, since a window receives mouse and keyboard input and displays a program's output. All other user-interface objects, like menus, scroll bars, and cursors, play supporting roles for the leading character: the window.

The Window

The window is the most important part of the user interface. From the perspective of a user, a window provides a view of some data object inside the computer. But it is more than that, since to a user, a window *is* an application. When the user starts to run an application, a window is expected to appear. A user closes a window to shut down an application. To decide the specific application to be worked with, a user selects the application's window. Figure 1.9 shows the standard parts of a typical program's main window.

To programmers, a window represents several things. It serves to organize the other user-interface objects together and directs the flow of messages in the system. A window provides a display area that can be used to communicate with the user. Input is channeled

Figure 1.9   *The standard parts of a window*

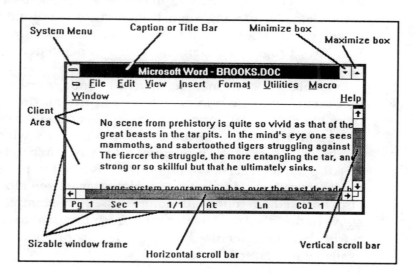

to a window and thereby directed to the program. Applications also use windows to subdivide other windows. For example, dialog boxes are implemented as a collection of small windows inside a larger window.

Every window is created from a **window class**. A window class provides a template from which to create windows. Associated with every window class—and therefore with every window—is a special type of subroutine called a **window procedure**. The job of a window procedure is to process messages. In a message-oriented operating system like Windows, you can imagine that this is an important task. In fact, most of the work that you will do as a Windows programmer will involve deciding how to handle one message or another that is received in a window procedure. It receives the mouse and keyboard input that is directed to a window, which arrives in the form of messages. It receives notifications about other events of interest, such as changes in the size and location of a window. One of the first areas that we're going to explore, starting with the next few chapters, is the way that messages arrive at and are processed by window procedures.

Icons

An icon is a symbol that serves as a reminder to the user. GUI systems are built on the principle that what is concrete and visible is more easily understood than what is abstract and invisible. Icons provide a concrete, visible symbol of a command, a program, or some data. By making such things visible, a Windows program makes them accessible. By making all of a user's choices visible, Windows programs lessen the user's dependence on memorized information.

Examples of icons include standard window ornaments: the system menu box, the minimize box, and the maximize box. As depicted in Figure 1.10, one of the most common uses of an icon is to represent a program. In the Program Manager's window, an icon reminds the user of the programs that are available to be run. On the desktop, an icon serves to remind the user of the programs that are currently running, but whose windows have been closed. Icons can also be used to represent commands. For example, Figure 1.11 shows icons displayed by the Paintbrush program to show users the set of drawing operations available in this program, as well as the available fill patterns.

Figure 1.10   *Icons in the Program Manager and on the desktop*

Menus

A menu is a list of commands and program options. Windows has five types of menus: system menus, menu-bar menus, pull-down menus, nested menus, and tear-off menus. The system menu, shown

Figure 1.11   *Icons as commands in the Paintbrush program*

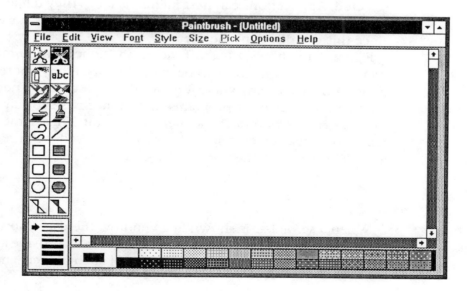

Figure 1.12   *The system menu*

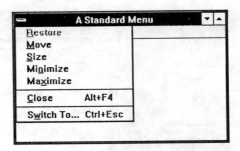

in Figure 1.12, provides a standard set of operations that can be performed on a window. These operations are referred to as "system commands." Users expect to find a system menu on the top-level window of every program they run. System commands require very little work on the part of a program, since Windows itself does everything to make system commands operational and uniform throughout the system.

Figure 1.13 shows the three types of menus that are connected together: the menu-bar menu connects to the top of a window, popup menus appear when a menu bar item is selected, and nested menus are displayed when a popup menu item that has an arrow is selected. Applications can nest menus as far as they'd like, although in general programmers should avoid nestings that go too deep, since this can disorient the user.

Figure 1.14 shows a tear-off menu positioned in the middle of a window. Tear-off menus can be made to appear anywhere in a window, and in fact anywhere on the display screen. They provide another alternative for programs that do not wish to rely solely on menus that descend from the menu-bar menu. Thus, a menu can be made to appear when a specific object is clicked, or in response to a hot-key struck by the user on the keyboard.

Scroll Bars

When a scroll bar is shown in a window, the user knows that the data object is larger than the window. Scroll bars provide a means by which the user can control the display of such objects and also can

Figure 1.13 *Three types of menus*

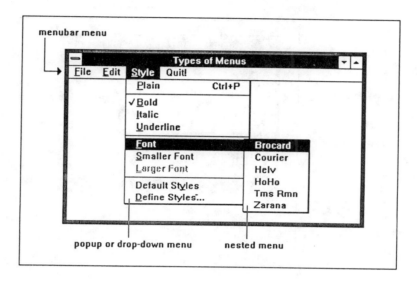

see at a glance the relative location of an object that is being viewed. Scrolling, and the use of scroll bars, is described in detail in Chapter 20. Figure 1.15 shows the two types of scroll bars: vertical and horizontal.

Figure 1.14 *A tear-off menu*

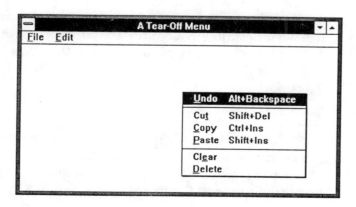

Figure 1.15   *Vertical and horizontal scroll bars*

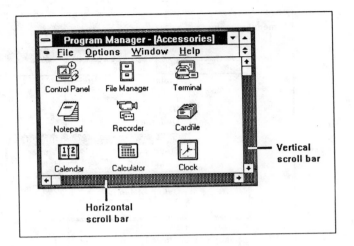

Cursors

A cursor is a bitmap that floats on the display screen in response to the movement of a mouse or other pointing device. Programs can change the shape of the cursor to indicate a change in the system. For example, programs often display an hourglass cursor to let the user know that some lengthy operation is taking place. Programs can also change the cursor to let the user know that a program has entered a specific mode. For example, drawing programs often change the cursor to reflect the type of object that can be drawn.

Using the SDKEDIT utility, which Microsoft includes with the Windows software development kit, programmers can create custom cursors. Cursors can also be created "on the fly," a process that we'll describe in Chapter 16. Of course, you may not need to create your own cursors, if the ones that Windows provides will serve your needs. All of Windows' built-in cursors are shown in Figure 1.16.

Carets

A caret is a tiny bitmap that blinks and serves as a pointer for keyboard control. The window that has control of the keyboard (also known as the focus) may wish to create a caret to notify the user of this fact. Carets are quirky in two ways: the name and the

Figure 1.16 *Windows' predefined cursors*

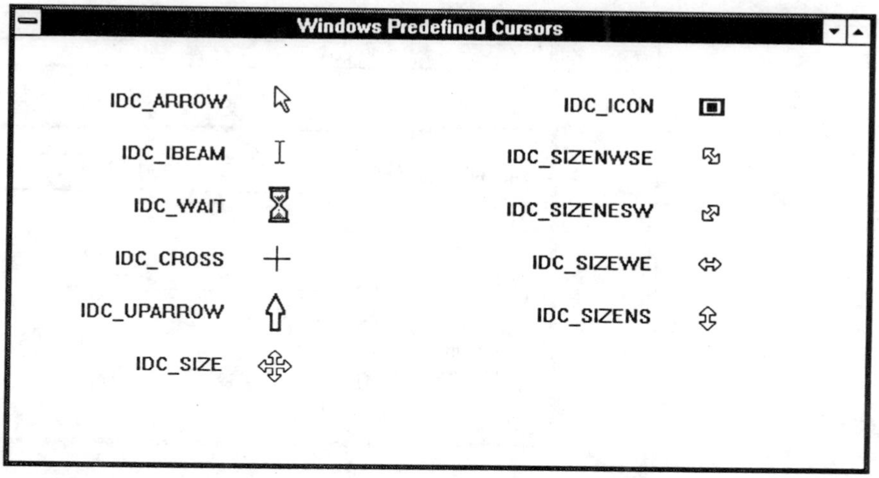

control. The name is quirky because most other environments use the term "cursor" for the keyboard pointer. But in Windows, "cursor" is already used for the mouse pointer.

The second way that carets are quirky is in the way that programs must maintain them. The Windows user interface only supports a single caret at a time. Therefore, programs that wish to use a caret must create one upon receiving the keyboard focus and must destroy it on losing the keyboard focus. In Chapter 15, when we describe keyboard input, we'll look at what a program must do to properly maintain a caret.

Dialog Boxes

Dialog boxes, also known as dialogs, provide a standard way to receive input from users. In particular, when a user has entered a command for which additional information is required, dialog boxes are the standard way to retrieve that input. While browsing through a Windows program, you often see an ellipsis (...) as part of a menu name. This indicates that a dialog box will appear when the menu item is selected.

One dialog box that is quite common is displayed whenever the user asks for a file to be opened. It is the file-open dialog box, shown

Figure 1.17 *A file-open dialog box*

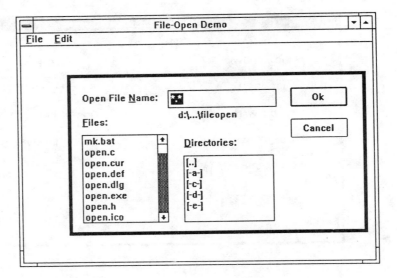

in Figure 1.17. This dialog box provides the user with the opportunity of typing in a filename. It also shows two lists: one of file names and the other of directory names and disk drives. If the user is unable to remember a specific filename, she can browse the directories until she finds the desired file.

Notice that this dialog box has two pushbuttons: one marked "Ok" and the other marked "Cancel." In general, pushbuttons in dialog boxes are used to request an action. For this dialog box, there are two possible actions. The Ok pushbutton tells the program to accept the values that the user has entered. The Cancel pushbutton tells the program to ignore the results that have been entered in the dialog box. In general, wherever possible, programs should allow a user to withdraw a request without incurring any damage to files or data.

Dialog Box Controls

Like all dialog boxes, the file-open dialog is a window that holds individual windows that either display information or accept input from the user. Each of these tiny windows is called a dialog box control. For example, the file-open dialog contains nine dialog box controls: two pushbuttons (Ok and Cancel), two listboxes, an edit control, and four static text controls. Windows has six predefined window classes from which dialog box controls are created: button, combo-box, edit, listbox, scrollbar, and static.

In Chapter 14, we're going to investigate the creation of dialog boxes. You will see that dialog box controls do a lot of the work of interacting with the user. Edit controls, for example, handle all of the keyboard input without your having to intercede. And, once a listbox has received its list of items, it will happily display and scroll the items in a list without your having to intervene to assist it. You will see that, like many other parts of Windows, dialog boxes and dialog box controls are primarily message driven.

The first step to take in learning to program in Windows involves learning about the structure of a Windows program. Windows programs are structured around Windows' event-driven nature. As events occur, they cause messages to be generated. Certain messages are stored in system buffers until your program is ready to receive them. Other messages force their way into your program in a manner that is similar to the way that hardware interrupts force interrupt-handling code to respond.

In the next few chapters, we introduce a minimum Windows program. You may be surprised at the size of this program, but it represents the *minimum* required to respond both to messages that are buffered and to messages that don't wait to be invited in. The minimum Windows program creates a single window and demonstrates how message traffic must be handled in a Windows program. As we look at each piece in the program, we'll describe how it fits in to the overall architecture of Windows itself.

Part 2

A Minimum Windows Program

2
A Minimum Windows Program

This chapter introduces a minimum Windows program. Figure 2.1 shows the window that our program creates. The window can be moved, resized, closed, **minimized** (made into an icon), or **maximized** (enlarged to fill the screen). In other words, to an experienced Windows user, the window created by this program does all of the "right" things.

Figure 2.1   *The window created by our minimum Windows program*

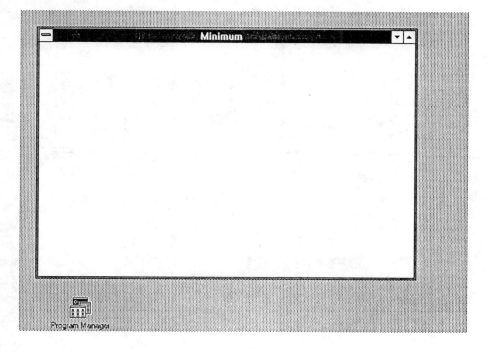

Table 2.1 *Files that make up the minimum Windows program*

min.c	C source code.
min.def	Module definition file, used by linker.
min.mak	Make file, automates program build process.
min.rc	Resource file, for user-interface data objects.
min.ico	Icon file, a resource.
min.cur	Cursor file, another resource.

The six files that make up our minimum Windows program are listed in Table 2.1. Four are text files (min.c, min.def, min.mak, and min.rc) and appear in listings 1, 2, 3, and 4. The other two files contain graphic images (min.cur and min.ico), as depicted in

Figure 2.2 *The icon and cursor for our minimum Windows program*

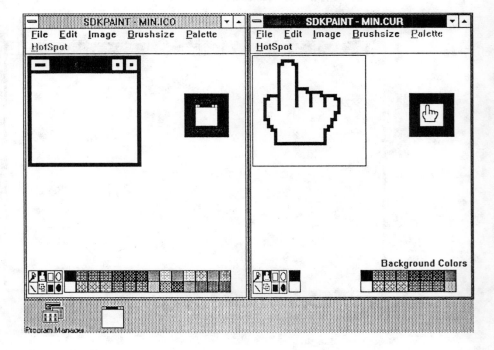

Figure 2.2. Min.cur is a mouse cursor in the shape of a hand. Min.ico is the icon displayed when our program is minimized.

MIN.C: A Minimum Windows Program

```
/*-------------------------------------------------------------*\
|   MIN.C    A Minimum Windows Program that displays a window. |
|            The window can be moved, sized, minimized and     |
|            maximized.                                         |
\*-------------------------------------------------------------*/
#include <Windows.H>


/*-------------------------------------------------------------*\
|                   Function Prototypes.                        |
\*-------------------------------------------------------------*/
long FAR  PASCAL MinWndProc (HWND, WORD, WORD, LONG);
/*-------------------------------------------------------------*\
|                Main Function:  WinMain.                       |
\*-------------------------------------------------------------*/
int PASCAL WinMain (HANDLE hInstance,
                    HANDLE hPrevInstance,
                    LPSTR  lpszCmdLine,
                    int    cmdShow)
    {
    HWND     hwnd;
    MSG      msg;
    WNDCLASS wndclass;

    if (!hPrevInstance)
        {
        wndclass.lpszClassName = "MIN:MAIN";
        wndclass.hInstance     = hInstance;
        wndclass.lpfnWndProc   = MinWndProc;
        wndclass.hCursor       = LoadCursor (hInstance, "hand");
        wndclass.hIcon         = LoadIcon (hInstance,"snapshot");
        wndclass.lpszMenuName  = NULL;
        wndclass.hbrBackground = COLOR_WINDOW+1;
        wndclass.style         = NULL;
        wndclass.cbClsExtra    = 0;
        wndclass.cbWndExtra    = 0;
```

```
        RegisterClass( &wndclass);

    }

    hwnd = CreateWindow("MIN:MAIN",        /* Class name.   */
                        "Minimum",          /* Title.        */
                        WS_OVERLAPPEDWINDOW, /* Style bits.   */
                        CW_USEDEFAULT,       /* x - default.  */
                        0,                   /* y - default.  */
                        CW_USEDEFAULT,       /* cx - default. */
                        0,                   /* cy - default. */
                        NULL,                /* No parent.    */
                        NULL,                /* Class menu.   */
                        hInstance,           /* Creator       */
                        NULL                 /* Params.       */
                        ) ;
    ShowWindow (hwnd, cmdShow);
    while (GetMessage(&msg, 0, 0, 0))
        {
        TranslateMessage(&msg);            /*  Keyboard input.     */
        DispatchMessage(&msg);
        }
    return 0;
    }


/*------------------------------------------------------------------*\
|                 Window Procedure:  MinWndProc.                     |
\*------------------------------------------------------------------*/
long FAR PASCAL MinWndProc (HWND       hWnd,
                            WORD       msg,
                            WORD       wParam,
                            LONG       lParam)
    {
    switch (msg)
        {
        case WM_DESTROY:
            PostQuitMessage(0);
            break;

        default:
            return(DefWindowProc(hWnd,msg,wParam,lParam));
```

```
                    break;
                }
        return 0L;
        }
```

MIN.DEF: Module Definition File

```
NAME      MIN

EXETYPE WINDOWS

DESCRIPTION 'Min -- Minimum Windows Program.'

CODE      MOVEABLE DISCARDABLE
DATA      MOVEABLE MULTIPLE

HEAPSIZE      512
STACKSIZE   5000

EXPORTS
    MinWndProc
```

MIN.MAK: The MAKE File for MAKE

```
min.res: min.rc min.cur min.ico
    rc -r min.rc

min.obj: min.c
    cl -AM -c -d -Gsw -Od -W2 -Zpi min.c

min.exe: min.obj min.def
    link min,min/align:16,min/map, mlibcew libw/NOD/NOE/CO,
min.def
    rc min.res

min.exe: min.res
    rc min.res
```

MIN: The MAKE File for NMAKE

```
all: min.exe

min.res: min.rc min.cur min.ico
    rc -r min.rc

min.obj: min.c
    cl -AM -c -d -Gsw -Od -W2 -Zpi min.c

min.exe: min.obj min.def min.res
    link min,min/align:16,min/map, mlibcew libw/NOD/NOE/CO,
min.def
    rc min.res
```

MIN.RC: The Resource File.

```
snapshot icon min.ico

hand   cursor min.cur
```

You may be surprised at the size of our minimum program. With about 80 lines of source code, MIN.C may be the longest *minimum* program you have ever encountered. The size reflects the amount of work that a program must do to tap into the Windows' user interface. But, once a program has made the necessary connections, Windows does a substantial amount of work for you.

For example, Windows provides default support for the different parts of our window. Consider the system menu, with its seven commands: *Restore*, *Move*, *Size*, *Minimize*, *Maximize*, *Close*, and *Switch To*. Windows does all the right things to make these commands operational, with only a minimum of effort required of our program.

Let's consider just one of the system menu commands. In response to the *Move* command Windows directly interacts with the user to find a new home for our window. Windows makes the other parts of our window work also: the sizing border, the title bar, minimize icon, maximize icon, etc.

All of the *parts* of this minimum program are required to allow Windows to do this work for us. The *structure* of this program supports the flow of information from the user, through the user interface, into our program. The structure of this program is important because it embodies the structure of every Windows program.

Because you may be eager to compile and run this program, we'll start by talking about the tools that you'll need to build Windows programs. Some tools will already be familiar to you, such as the Microsoft C Compiler and the Linker. You'll need to pay special attention to the compiler switches in order to generate Windows-compatible code. As for the linker, it needs a special input file: the **module definition file**. Other tools that we'll describe are specific to that Windows development environment, such as the Resource Compiler and SDKPaint.

After we describe the development tools, we're going to take a minor detour in the next chapter to talk about some of the conventions that have been adopted for Windows programming. This includes the **Hungarian Naming Convention**, which is used to name data structures and variables. And, we'll introduce the Windows include file, **Windows.h**, that contains symbolic constants and data structures needed in Windows programming.

Subsequent chapters will look at the code from our minimum Windows program. We'll start with the WinMain function, which is the name of the entry point for every Windows program. WinMain typically creates one or more windows and then enters an (almost) endless loop to retrieve hardware-related **messages**. A message is a unit of input to a Windows program, as well as the "time-slice" that makes Windows' nonpreemptive multitasking system work.

In Chapter 5, we're going to review the second function in our program, the window procedure. Our tiny window procedure seems to do very little, and yet it plays an important role in every Windows program. We'll use our minimum window procedure to learn about the structure of a typical window procedure, including the function declaration and use of the **default window procedure**. The default window procedure is often overlooked in most discussions of Windows programming. And yet, it provides the minimum heartbeat required to bring this user interface to life. In brief, it processes messages that make most of the standard parts of a window work: the system menu, sizing border, etc.

We'll conclude this section of the book with an in-depth look at the different types of messages that you'll encounter in your Windows programming career. As you'll see, about 250 different messages are defined in Windows.h. We'll divided these messages into eight categories to provide a framework to begin to understand all of the different types.

Let's begin with a look at the development tools that are used to build our minimum Windows program.

The Mechanics of Compiling and Linking MIN.EXE

When you write Windows programs, you'll use some development tools that you may already be pretty familiar with: a language compiler and a linker. If you don't use the Microsoft C Compiler, you should double-check to make sure that the compiler you do use generates Windows-compatible code. Table 2.2 provides a list of compilers and linkers that, as of this writing, provide the necessary support. We use the Microsoft C Compiler, version 6.0.

Some tools are specific to the Windows environment, like the **Resource Compiler**. This tool merges user interface objects into a program's executable file. Almost every Windows program that you write will require you to use the resource compiler. In Chapters 11 and 14, you'll use the resource compiler to attach menu and dialog box definitions to executable program files. For now, we'll use the resource compiler to connect our two graphic objects, the cursor and the icon, to MIN.EXE.

Table 2.2 *Compilers that generate Windows-compatible code*

Manufacturer	Compiler	Comments
Jensen & Partners, International	C, C++	
MetaWare	C	High-C Compiler
Microsoft	C	Version 4.0 and later
Zortech, Inc.	C, C++	

Note to Apple Macintosh programmers: Windows resources are similar to Macintosh resources. Unlike a Macintosh program, however, a Windows program cannot alter the disk-image of its resources. In other words, Windows resources contain read-only data.

To coordinate the use of the development tools, programmers often use a utility called **MAKE**, or an enhanced version called **NMAKE**, which stands for "New Make."

The MAKE and NMAKE Utilities

MAKE and **NMAKE** are utilities provided with many language compilers, including Microsoft's C Compiler. These utilities manage the program creation process to eliminate redundant processing: you only have to compile or link the program files that have changed. To be this smart, these utilities use an input file (called a **make file**) that describes the relationship of each program file to the output file. If you use MAKE, you'll want to use our first make file, MIN.MAK:

```
min.res: min.rc min.cur min.ico
    rc -r min.rc

min.obj: min.c
    cl -AM -c -d -Gsw -Ows -W2 -Zp min.c

min.exe: min.obj min.def min.res
    link min/align:16/map, mlibw mlibcaw /NOD/NOE/CO, min.def
    rc min.res

min.exe: min.res
    rc min.res
```

Notice that four command groups make up our make file, with a blank line separating each group. The easiest way to understand the operation of MAKE is to look at how a command group is handled. Here is the second command group from our make file:

```
min.obj: min.c
    cl -AM -c -d -Gsw -Ow -W2 min.c
```

There are three parts to this (and every) command group: a **target file**, one or more **input files**, and one or more **commands** to be executed. The target file is min.obj. The date and time stamps on the target file are compared with the date and time stamps on all input file(s). In this case, there is only one input file: min.c. If min.obj is *older* than min.c, the command line is run. In the example, the command line runs the C Compiler. If min.obj is *younger* than min.c, the command line is ignored. Command lines are any program names (or DOS commands) that can be run from the DOS command prompt.

The normal use of MAKE is to run it whenever we wish to rebuild our program file. For example, when we make a change to MIN.C, we can recreate MIN.EXE by running MAKE with the following command line:

```
C> MAKE MIN.MAK
```

If you prefer to use the New Make utility, NMAKE, you'll use a slightly different make file and a different command line:

```
all: min.exe

min.res: min.rc min.cur min.ico
    rc -r min.rc

min.obj: min.c
    cl -AM -c -d -Gsw -Od -W2 -Zpi min.c

min.exe: min.obj min.def min.res
    link min/align:16/map, mlibcew libw/NOD/NOE/CO, min.def
    rc min.res
```

In this book, you'll notice that we don't use this form of a make file. But converting from our make files to support NMAKE involves adding a line at the beginning of the make file:

```
all: min.exe
```

Then you run NMAKE with the following syntax:

```
NMAKE /f <makefile> <target>
```

To use the make file we just showed you, MIN., the command line is

```
C> NMAKE /f MIN all
```

C Compiler Switches

Here is Table 2.3, showing our favorite compiler switches for use with Microsoft C. Four sets are shown; your choice depends on whether you wish to create a Windows program or a Windows dynamic link library, and whether you wish to create an optimized production version or an un-optimized version for debugging.

The name of the compiler program is "cl." Each switch or set of switches is preceded by a hyphen (-), although a slash (/) can also be used.

The **-A** switch is for *addressing*. The letters after -A set the compiler defaults for accessing both code and data. The most generally useful type of addressing for Windows programs is often referred to as the **medium memory model**. A memory model refers to the default settings that a compiler uses to address memory. The medium memory model means that *far* code pointers are used, to allow multiple code segments to be created. It also means that *near* data pointers are used, with the result that our program is limited to a single data segment. Both AM and AMw switch settings request the medium memory. Dynamic link libraries require the "w" option to

Table 2.3 *C Compiler Switches*

Type of Module	Switches
Program—production	cl -AM -c -d -Gsw -Ows -W2 -Zp <filename.c>
Program—debugging	cl -AM -c -d -Gsw -Od -W2 -Zip <filename.c>
DLL—production	cl -AMw -c -d -Gsw -Ows -W2 -Zp <filename.c>
DLL—debugging	cl -AMw -c -d -Gsw -Od -W2 -Zip <filename.c>

let the compiler know that some of the assumptions made for the medium memory model do not apply. To use a term that is familiar to many experienced Windows programmers, dynamic link libraries run with "SS != DS."

The **-c** switch tells the C Compiler to compile but not to link. You'll want to use this switch to override the C Compiler's default behavior, which is to call to the linker when compilation is done.

The **-d** switch isn't required for Windows programs, but we find it useful. It asks the C compiler to tell you when a compiler pass is beginning. The Microsoft C compiler is a three-pass compiler. It is often helpful to know if an error happens during the first, second, or third pass. For example, a first-pass error indicates a preprocessor problem. This often means a problem with a #include or #define statement.

The **-Gs** switch tells the C compiler not to call a tiny subroutine that checks for stack overflows. We recommend that you disable stack checking because it requires a special version of Windows to be installed on your computer: the **debug version**. It is a good idea to test your programs against the debug version of Windows, to locate stack overflows and other hidden bugs inside a Windows program. For more information on creating a debug version of Windows, see the Windows SDK.

The **-Gw** switch tells the C compiler to generate special support for Windows programs. This support consists of adding a tiny prolog and epilog to every far function. While this causes some additional overhead to be incurred, it is necessary for the magic of dynamic linking to occur. A complete discussion of the Windows dynamic link mechanism is provided in Chapter 21.

The **-O** switches control optimization. **-Ow** instructs the compiler to optimize in a way that is compatible with Windows programs. **-Os** tells the compiler to favor smaller code size over speed of execution. **-Od** disables optimization. We use this last switch to prepare for the use of a debugger with a Windows program. Since optimization can change the relationship between source code and machine code, the -Od switch helps the debugger to correctly connect source code and machine code.

The **-W2** switch sets the compiler warning level. Some people call this the "whine-level." While this switch is not required to create correct code, it lets the compiler help you find **type-mismatch errors**, among others. Given the complexity of Windows programming, it makes sense to get as much help as the compiler is willing to offer.

The **-Zi** switch tells the compiler to generate symbol information. This is required if you wish to use Microsoft's Codeview debugger with your program.

The **-Zp** switch sets data structure packing level. By default, the C Compiler packs data structures to word (even-byte) boundaries. This generates code that runs a little faster on the Intel family of CPUs, which can take twice as long to access data on odd-byte boundaries. Since, however, memory is the most severely constrained resource in Windows, Microsoft packs all data structures to the byte boundary to save memory even though it does require a little more processing time.

The Resource File

MIN.RC lists the resources that are to be merged into MIN.EXE. To the Windows memory manager, a resource is a read-only data object. By separating a program's read-only data from its read-write data, a Windows program helps the Windows memory manager optimize the way memory is used. Since almost all of the definitions for user interface objects are stored as resources, every Windows program (knowingly or not) is built to help make the best use of memory. Table 2.4 lists the nine types of predefined resources. By "predefined," we mean that there are Windows library routines for

Table 2.4   *Windows' predefined resources*

Resource Type	Covered In Depth
Accelerator table	Chapter 11
Bitmaps	
Cursors	Chapter 16
Dialog box template	Chapter 14
Fonts	Chapter 10
Icons	
Menu template	Chapter 11
String table	Chapter 18

the creation and control of these objects. If your program requires you to use a large block of read-only data, you can create your own custom resource types to further optimize your program's use of memory.

Resources are normally read into memory as they are needed, although you can mark a resource as PRELOAD to make it resident when your program starts running. When read into memory, a resource usually resides in a memory block that is marked as DISCARDABLE. This means that it can be purged from memory if the Windows memory manager needs to reuse the memory for some other data object (perhaps another resource). When the resource is needed again, it is reloaded into memory from the program's executable file.

Our minimum Windows program has two types of resources: an icon and a cursor. To create your own icons and cursors, you'll need a tool called SDKPaint. Microsoft supplies this graphic editor as a part of the Windows Software Development Kit. One very useful feature of this program is that it can read the Windows Clipboard. This means you can use other, more sophisticated drawing tools to create pictures, and then use the Clipboard to move these pictures to SDKPaint.

Cursors are bitmaps that respond to the movement of the mouse. Cursors allow the user to "point to" different objects on the display screen. For our minimum Windows program, we created a pointer in the image of the human hand. We used **PaintBrush** (bundled with Windows) to create the picture. Figure 2.3 shows the PaintBrush drawing next to the SDKPaint image of our picture. Once we transferred the image into SDKPaint, we had to do a little bit of cleanup, which accounts for the difference between the original drawing and the final cursor image. This cleanup is necessary because, at 32 by 32 pixels, the cursor bitmap is quite a bit smaller than the original drawing.

In creating MIN's icon, we took a slightly different approach. Since an icon reminds the user that a program exists, we created our icon from a snapshot taken of MIN while it was running. We created the snapshot using a built-in capability of Windows. When you strike the [PrtSc] (print screen) key, Windows puts a snapshot of the *entire screen* onto the Clipboard. When you strike [Alt] + [PrtSc], Windows limits the snapshot to the currently active window.

We used the [Alt] + [PrtSc] combination to capture a snapshot of MIN.EXE. We then pasted this into **SDKPaint**. After a little bit of cleanup, we had an icon that was ready to use. After we saved the icon and cursor into their own files, we made entries into our resource file, MIN.RC, indicating our name for the resource, the resource type, and the file where the resource data was to be found:

```
snapshot icon min.ico

hand cursor min.cur
```

When our program was built, a copy of each resource was merged into our program's executable file. This means that every Windows program can be built as a stand-alone file, with a minimum requirement for external files.

Figure 2.3   *Paintbrush and SDKPaint used together to create a cursor*

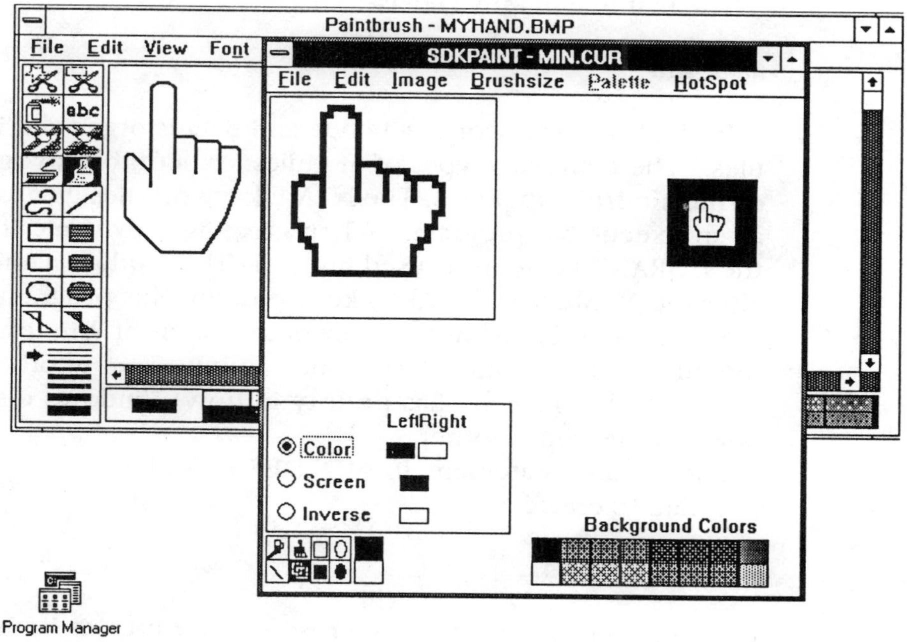

> **Hint**
> ....
>
> The Windows screen-capture capability will be very useful in creating documentation for your Windows programs. In fact, we used this method to create all of the screen shots for this book. We used a monochrome VGA display driver and an HP Laserjet II printer. We then pasted the screen shots into Microsoft Word for Windows, which allowed us to print the final results.

Linking and the Module Definition File

The job of the linker is to build an executable (.EXE) program file from the object (.OBJ) and library (.LIB) files. In addition to these files, the Microsoft linker gets input from a **module definition file** (.DEF) when creating Windows and OS/2 programs. The role of a module definition file is to describe the structure and organization of a program. You can think of the .DEF file as a set of switches to control the operation of the linker. Let's review each statement in our module definition file, MIN.DEF.

The first line in MIN.DEF is

```
NAME MIN
```

In the Windows world, all code and data is organized into "modules." There are two types of modules: **executable programs** and **dynamic link libraries**. The NAME keyword designates a module as an executable program. (When creating a dynamic link library, the LIBRARY keyword is used instead.) The module name is placed after the NAME (or LIBRARY) keyword. For this program, the module name is "MIN." Although previous versions of Windows used the module name to differentiate one module from another, in Windows 3.0 the filename has priority in how Windows distinguishes one module from another.

The second statement in MIN.DEF tells the linker the type of program to create:

```
EXETYPE WINDOWS
```

This is necessary since the Microsoft linker creates both Windows and OS/2 program files.

The DESCRIPTION statement inserts text into our executable file:

```
DESCRIPTION 'Min-Minimum Windows Program.'
```

Usually, this is used for copyright information or version information about a program. To see the description of a Windows program (or dynamic link library), run the EXEHDR utility.

The CODE statement sets the default memory disposition for the code segments in a Windows program:

```
CODE MOVEABLE DISCARDABLE
```

As we will discuss in Chapter 18, the use of the **SEGMENTS** statement allows you to specify the memory disposition for individual code segments. For now, however, the CODE statement by itself will work fine. MOVEABLE (versus FIXED) allows the segment to be relocated. The DISCARDABLE declaration means that, when memory is low, the code segment can be purged from system memory. The dynamic link mechanism allows code to be moved around in memory, as well as removed from memory, in a manner that is completely transparent to your program.

The DATA statement is similar to the CODE statement, except that it sets the memory disposition of a program's data segment:

```
DATA MOVEABLE MULTIPLE
```

MOVEABLE allows the data segment to move in memory. (When a message is delivered to a program, the data segment is "locked" in

Figure 2.4 *The layout of a program's data segment*

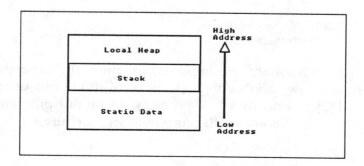

place to avoid unexpected results.) The MULTIPLE declaration is the standard for Windows programs. It allows several copies of a single program to run at the same time.

STACKSIZE sets the size of a program's stack:

```
STACKSIZE 4900
```

The stack has three uses: storing of local variables, passing parameters to called functions, and saving return addresses to allow "anonymous calling." Windows programs must have a minimum stack size of 5K. (If a smaller amount is specified, the Windows loader automatically allocates a 5K stack.) Of this, 2K is meant for your program's use. The other 3K is for Windows' use. This is so because when a program calls a Windows library routine, the arguments to the routine are passed on the program's stack. Use a higher value for programs with a lot of local variables or for recursive operations.

The HEAPSIZE statement sets the initial size of a program's local heap. Our minimum programs uses the following value:

```
HEAPSIZE 512
```

The local heap is one of two places from which dynamic memory allocation can occur. (The other place is the system's global heap.) The local heap is private to a program, and resides in the program's data segment. Figure 2.4 shows the layout of a program's data segment. The HEAPSIZE statement sets the initial size of the local heap. A heap can grow beyond its initial size, limited only by the restriction that a segment cannot be larger than 64 kilobytes.

The EXPORTS statement lists all the functions in MIN that are accessible from outside MIN, sometimes referred to as "exported entry points":

```
EXPORTS
    MinWndProc
```

MIN has only one exported function: the procedure for the main window, MinWndProc(). As we'll discuss in Chapter 19, the EXPORT is necessary to properly set up our program's data segment when Windows calls our window procedure.

A common programming error involves forgetting to export a window procedure or dialog box procedure. Part of the problem is simply that neither the compiler nor the linker is able to detect a missing export declaration. The problem is compounded since a program will run without the required EXPORT declarations. Things seem normal, except that the program develops a "minor" case of amnesia: It forgets all its global variables!

At this point, you have enough information to type in and create the minimum Windows program. We suggest you pause now and do this. It will give you a good opportunity to test that your development environment has been properly set up. It will also give you the chance to become familiar with this program before we delve into its inner workings.

Before we look at the source code to MIN, we are going to address some of the coding conventions of the Windows programming world. Understanding these will help you understand some of the subtleties of MIN, and other Windows programs that you encounter.

3
Windows Programming Conventions

Of all the things for a programmer to be concerned with, you'd probably put the creation of variable names near the bottom of the list. And yet, creating variable names is a task that every programmer must perform. We're going to introduce you to **Hungarian Naming**, a practice that permeates Windows programs. If you're like us, you may be puzzled by your first encounter with Hungarian. But over time, we have become so convinced of its value that we're going to talk about it first.

After we've covered the issues relating to Hungarian Naming, we'll talk about the Windows include file. You may have already noticed that one of the first lines in our Windows program is

```
#include <Windows.h>
```

We'll describe the contents of this file to help you appreciate its importance. Incidentally, all of the symbol names and data structures in this file were created using Hungarian Naming.

We'll discuss **handles**, which are a data type you will encounter quite often in your Windows programming career. Handles are often referred to as "magic-numbers," "magic cookies," and "claim check numbers." Whichever term you prefer, handles identify objects created by one part of the system or another. A handle is a number, but the meaning of the number is only known to the part of the system that created the object and issued the handle.

Finally, we'll touch on an issue that will concern you when you look at older Windows code: **casting**. While it used to be required in the earliest days of Windows programming, developments in language compilers have made this an obsolete practice. In fact, as we'll explain, the use of casts can be downright dangerous and can introduce hard-to-find errors into your code.

Let's get started with a look at Hungarian Naming.

Hungarian Naming

Hungarian Naming is a convention for creating names of variables and functions. It is widely used by Windows programmers because it makes code easier to read and easier to maintain. Hungarian Naming, or Hungarian for short, gets its name from the nationality of the original developer, Charles Simonyi. The name is also a tongue-in-cheek description for the convention because programmers often find Hungarian to be initially confusing. For years, new programmers at Microsoft were given documentation for Hungarian that had a picture of Simonyi next to the words "Blame This Guy!" In spite of this ribbing, Hungarian is both highly regarded and widely used inside Microsoft for application programs as well as for operating system software.

Creating *useful* variable names can be a real challenge. Should they be short and sweet? Short variable names are easy to type, but they can make your code hard to understand. You know what we mean if you've tried reading BASIC programs with very short variable names. What can you tell about the variables "A" and "B" in these lines of BASIC code?

```
20    LET B=10
30    FOR A=1 to 10
40    LET B=B+A
50    NEXT A
```

If short names are cryptic, perhaps we can create useful variable names by making them long and descriptive. Is there any doubt about how a variable called loopindex is used? And yet, this approach can lead to variable names that are long and unwieldy. Consider the names in this list:

```
countofcharacters
numberoffiles
temporaryfilename
windowhandle
pointertoarrayofcharacters
```

While such names may make code more readable, they put a burden on the programmer who has to type them. The use of long names also increases the chance that one will be mistyped.

Hungarian takes a middle road between these two extremes. In Hungarian, variable names are created by putting a short prefix in front of a longer, more descriptive name. The prefix describes the *type of data* referenced by the variable. In some cases, a prefix also describes the *way a variable is used*. For convenience, a prefix can be used alone as a variable name.

Here are some examples of Hungarian:

```
char       ch;
char       achFile[128];
char far * lpszName;
int        cbName;
```

Note that prefixes are lower case, and long names combine upper and lower case. The first variable, ch, is the prefix for character data. It is an example of a prefix used as a variable name. The prefix for achFile has two parts: "a" means this is an array, and "ch" tells us the type of data in the array, characters. The prefix for lpszFirstName also has two parts: "lp" means long-pointer, and "sz" describes the data pointed to, a NULL-terminated string. The variable cbName, contains the prefix "cb" to tell us that the variable contains a count of bytes.

Understanding Hungarian helps us read and understand these otherwise convoluted lines of code:

```
LPSTR      lpszName;
LPSTR      lpsz;
int        cbName;

for (lpsz = lpszName, cbName=0;
     lpsz != NULL;
     lpsz++, cbName++);
```

The prefix "cb" tells us that the variable cbName *must* contain a count of bytes. Since that's the case, it is pretty clear that the purpose of this code is to calculate the number of characters in the null-terminated string referenced by the pointer lpszName. Incidentally, the use of a Hungarian prefix by itself is quite common for "temporary" variables, which is what lpsz is used for.

In addition to helping you read code, Hungarian helps you avoid silly (but very common) programming errors. As you become familiar with Hungarian, you will come to recognize that

```
lpszName = achFile;
```

is a valid statement, while the following is not:

```
lpszName = cbName;
```

After all, it makes sense to assign the address of an array to a pointer. But, it does not make sense to assign a count of bytes to a pointer.

The trick to learning Hungarian is to learn the prefixes. Here is a list of the more common prefixes used in Windows programming:

Prefix	Data Type
a	Array (compound type)
ch	Character
cb	Count of bytes
dw	Unsigned long, (Windows.h typedef: DWORD)
h	Handle—16 bit identifier
hdc	Handle to a device context
hwnd	Handle to a window
i	Index (compound)
l	Long integer, (Windows.h typedef: LONG)
lp	Long (or far) pointer (compound type)
n	Integer
np	Near (or short) pointer (compound type)
pt	An x,y point (Windows.h typedef: POINT)
r	A Rectangle structure (Windows.h typedef: RECT)
sz	Null terminated string
w	Unsigned integer, (Windows.h typedef: WORD)

Notice that some of these prefixes are "compound types." This means they are used as prefixes to other prefixes. The following code fragment shows how two compound prefixes, "a" and "i," define variables that can be used together.

```
char      ch;
int       ich;          /* Index a character array. */
char      achName[64];  /*  Character array. */
.
.
ch = achName[ich];
```

It is worth noting that there is no "official" list of prefixes. Since any given programming project is bound to have its own unique data types, prefixes will have to be created to reflect those types. In general, however, the usefulness of Hungarian comes from a relatively small number of types and from agreement by all members of a project on the definition of each type.

Hungarian naming is also used for function names. There are several "dialects" that we have encountered. One common use combines a verb and a noun to describe the action of a function. For example, three Windows library routines are CreateWindow, DrawText, and LoadIcon. Within the Windows' libraries, you can see other dialects: Some library routines consist of a noun by itself, such as DialogBox. For routines that convert from one type to another, the form XtoY is common. For example, the Windows library routine DPtoLP converts device points into logical points. Two special types of routines, window procedures and dialog box procedures, seem to have their own rules for names: You'll often see the letters "WndProc" embedded into a window procedure, and "DlgProc" embedded into the name of a dialog box procedure.

This book, with a few exceptions, uses the noun-verb convention. To help you distinguish our code from Windows library routines, we have adopted the OS/2 practice of using a three-letter prefix for function names to describe the function's origin. For example, the window procedure in our minimum program is called MinWndProc.

If you choose to adopt Hungarian naming, it will help you write code that is easier to read and easier to maintain. Even if you don't adopt this convention, a familiarity with Hungarian will help you read sample code from this book and from the Windows Software Development Kit. It will also help you read and make sense of definitions that you encounter in the Windows include file, Windows.h. Let's take a look at some of the definitions from Windows.h.

Handles

A handle is an identifier. Handles are 16-bit unsigned integers. In the same way that MS-DOS issues file handles when a file is opened, Windows issues handles to identify objects. Keep in mind that the only use of a handle is as an identifier. It is just a number that has no meaning outside the context for which it was issued. You cannot, for example, cast a handle to a pointer and do any useful work with it. Quite a few Windows library routines return handles. When such routines fail, they return a "null handle" (that is, handle = NULL).

Warning! Be careful—while a NULL value indicates an invalid handle from Windows, an invalid *file* handle has a value of -1. This is because file handles are issued by MS-DOS and not by Windows.

The two most important types of handles to a Windows programmer are *window handles* and *device context handles*.

A window handle identifies a window. Each window in the system has a unique handle. All window manipulation routines use a window handle as a parameter. Once you have a window's handle, you can move it, size it, make it invisible, and in general do anything you want with it.

Device context handles are used for controlling graphics output. All GDI drawing routines take a handle to a device context as the first parameter. When you wish to use the GDI graphics library to draw in a window, you must first get a handle to a device context. The handle to a device context is required to draw on devices other than the screen, such as printers and plotters.

Handles are used to identify other objects as well. User interface objects have handles: menus, strings, icons, and cursors. Drawing objects are identified by handles: pens, brushes, fonts, regions, and bitmaps. Even memory that is dynamically allocated is identified using handles. Windows uses handles to identify just about everything.

The Windows Include File

While C-language libraries are provided with many small include files (stdio.h, string.h, etc.), Windows libraries come with a single, large (110K) include file: `Windows.h`. You need to reference this file in every Windows source file you write because of the definitions it contains. There are three basic types of definitions in Windows.h:

symbolic constants, data types, and library function prototypes. Let's take a moment to look at each of these in some detail.

Symbolic Constants. In general, it's a bad practice to place "magic numbers" like 15 and 400 into a program. It makes your code hard to read. You should use symbolic constants instead. By convention, symbolic constants are written in upper case to distinguish them from variable names. In C, the #define preprocessor statement creates symbolic constants:

```
#define MAXOPENFILES 15
```

In addition to improving the readability of a program, the use of symbolic constants makes program maintenance easier. Instead of hunting through a mountain of source code when a numeric value changes, you only have to find the single line of code that defines the value.

There are about 1500 symbolic constants in Windows.h. To help you sort them out, Hungarian naming is used. For example, the symbols for window messages start with the prefix WM_ (as in WM_CREATE and WM_DESTROY). If a constant is only used with a single library function, the Hungarian prefix is derived from the function name. For example, you can only use the CW_USEDEFAULT constant with the CreateWindow function.

Table 3.1 lists the symbolic constants that are used in MIN.C.

Table 3.1 *Symbolic constants used in MIN.C*

Symbolic Constant	Value	Description
CW_USEDEFAULT	0x8000	CreateWindow constant for default location and/or size of a window being created.
COLOR_WINDOW	5	Identifies a user defined system color, specifically, the default window color. The user defined system colors with the Control Panel.
NULL	0	Value of zero.
WM_DESTROY	0x0002	This window message is sent to a program to tell it that a window has been destroyed.

Data Type Definitions. Quite a few data types are defined in Windows.h. Some of them are little more than a convenient way to refer to commonly used C types. For example, the following statement appears in Windows.h:

```
typedef char far * LPSTR;
```

This definition makes it easy to define a far pointer to a character string, since

```
LPSTR lpszName;
```

is equivalent to

```
char far * lpszName;
```

Here is a list of commonly used data types:

Windows.H Name	C Definition
BOOL	int
BYTE	unsigned char
DWORD	unsigned long
HANDLE	unsigned int
HDC	unsigned int
HWND	unsigned int
LONG	long
LPSTR	char far *
NPSTR	char near *
WORD	unsigned int

Three types are defined *unsigned int*: HANDLE, HDC, and HWND. Each defines a **handle**. Earlier in this chapter, we introduced handles as the method for identifying objects in Windows. The use of handles allows the complexity of an object to be hidden from your program. Objects and object handles are very important to Windows programmers. When your program creates a window, for example, a handle is issued to identify the window: the HWND data type. When you wish to draw on the system display, you do so by referencing a handle to a *device context*, or HDC. Before we are done, you will encounter many more types of handles.

In addition to simple data types, Windows.h holds a number of structure definitions. You might imagine that a rectangle structure would be useful in an environment that creates rectangular windows. You'd be right. Here is the rectangle data structure from Windows.h:

```
typedef struct tagRECT
  {
    int     left;
    int     top;
    int     right;
    int     bottom;
  } RECT;
```

Since Windows allows the user to select objects with a mouse pointer, you might expect to find a data structure to record the location of the mouse pointer. Again, you'd be right on target. Here's the POINT data structure:

```
typedef struct tagPOINT
  {
    int     x;
    int     y;
  } POINT;
```

Function Prototypes. An important feature of the Microsoft C Compiler (and part of ANSI-Standard C) is the ability to create **function prototypes**. Prototypes provide a means by which the C Compiler can perform some critical error checking for you. A function prototype tells the C Compiler how a routine should be called. Consider this protype from Windows.h:

```
BOOL  FAR PASCAL TextOut(HDC, int, int, LPSTR, int);
```

This declaration tells the C Compiler that the routine *must* be called with five parameters. A compiler error is generated if the function is called with too few (or too many) parameters. If you think about it, this capability alone makes the use of prototypes a recommended practice. How many times have you written a function, later added a parameter to the function definition, and then forgotten to change a line of code that calls the function? By doing so, you introduced a bug into your program. (Of course, this type of bug waits to appear until you demo your work to your boss . . .) A prototype lets the C Compiler complain about this type of problem so that you can find and correct it early.

A prototype tells the C Compiler about the expected *type* of each argument. When a type mismatch is encountered, a compiler error is generated. Consider this call to TextOut. It is clear that the fourth parameter is incorrect.

```
TextOut (hDC, 10, 20, 30, 2);
```

Based on the prototype from Windows.h, the fourth parameter should be a far pointer to a character string (char far *). When the C Compiler encounters the value of 30, it complains because the type is incorrect. Correcting this particular problem might require us to place quotes around the number, as in

```
TextOut (hDC, 10, 20, "30", 2);
```

The C Compiler will also check for the correct use of a function's return value. That is, it checks for type-mismatch errors. The prototype for TextOut, for example, defines the return value as BOOL (int in Windows.h). This code causes the C Compiler to complain:

```
char far * lpch;
lpch = TextOut (hDC, 10, 10, "Hello", 5);
```

Every Windows function has a prototype in Windows.h, so that the C Compiler can check your calls. Prototyping is useful for Windows library functions, and we recommend that you create a prototype for every function you write. There is a little known switch in the Microsoft C Compiler that you can use to automatically generate prototype declarations for existing C program files: -Zg.

Be sure to prototype all routines in your Windows code. Prototypes let the C compiler check for errors resulting from calling a routine with the wrong *number* of parameters, the wrong *type* of parameters, or incorrect use of return values.

The availability of function prototypes has made one practice obsolete: casting. And yet, a lot of code was written before function prototypes were available. For this reason, you need to be on the lookout for older Windows programs that may reflect an overuse of explicit casting.

An Outdated Practice: Casting

One of the best ways to learn any new programming environment is to look at someone else's code. You need to be careful, though, not to be mislead by an outdated practice that you might come across in some older Windows programming: *casting of pointers*. This is outdated because newer compilers support function prototypes, which allow the compiler to automatically generate the correct code.

A moment ago, we looked at the function prototype for the Text-Out function:

```
BOOL  FAR PASCAL TextOut(HDC, int, int, LPSTR, int);
```

The earliest Windows programmers had to write code like the following:

```
TextOut (hDC, 10, 10, (LPSTR)"Hello World", 12);
```

Notice the cast to LPSTR. This forces the creation of a *far pointer*. It used to be that, in a small-model or medium-model program, the expression "Hello World" would cause a near pointer to be generated. But the function requires a far pointer, so a cast was required.

At first glance, this casting seems harmless enough. The only problem seems to be that a lot of extra keystrokes are wasted. However, there is a real danger to casting. If you were to follow the old-fashioned practice of casting every pointer, you might hide certain problems that the compiler would otherwise detect for you. Consider the following line of code:

```
TextOut (hDC, 10, 10, (LPSTR)30, 2);
```

Perhaps the programmer had meant to use the string "30" as the fourth parameter. Without the cast, the compiler notifies us of the type-mismatch error. But a cast forces the value to the correct type, hiding the error from the compiler. The cast tells the compiler, in effect, "I know what I'm doing. Please don't ask any questions."

The message is clear: Avoid casting. It negates the compiler's automatic checking, and can hide problems from you.

This is not to say that casts are never needed. For example, they are often needed when working with Windows' dynamic memory allocation routines. These routines are prototyped to return character pointers. If you assign the return value to any other type, the compiler complains. The GlobalLock routine, for example, is defined as returning a LPSTR (char far *):

```
LPSTR  FAR PASCAL GlobalLock(HANDLE);
```

The following lines of code cause the compiler to complain:

```
int far * lpint;  /* Define an integer pointer. */
lpint = GlobalLock(hMem);  /* Compiler whines.  */
```

The second line of code would be required if we had stored an array of integers in the block of memory referenced by the handle hMem. Even though the compiler complains, this line of code creates a correct result. However, it's a good practice to reserve compiler complaints for things that really matter. The cast in the following line of code produces the same result, except that the compiler is now happy that there is no type-mismatch error:

```
lpint = (int far *)GlobalLock(hMem);
```

So you see, there are times when casting is necessary. In general, however, the compiler will let you know when the time is right. The rule still stands: Avoid casting. Then, when the compiler complains, you can look at the offending code and determine whether or not a cast will fix your problem.

Messages

Most programmers are used to writing code that runs in a sequential, procedure-driven manner. In Windows, programmers work with a nonsequential, message-driven programming model. In Windows, programs are structured around messages and not around a program-defined sequence.

What is a message? It is information about some change in the user interface, such as a window getting moved or the user striking a key on the keyboard. Messages are used to notify a program that a timer has gone off. Messages are also used for data sharing operations, which means the clipboard and the Dynamic Data Exchange (DDE).

From a programming point of view, a message is simply a 16-bit unsigned value that, for ease of reading, is given a parameter name that starts with a 'WM_', like WM_LBUTTONDOWN. The WM_LBUTTONDOWN message means that the left button on the mouse has been pushed down. Another message will get sent when the left mouse button is released: WM_LBUTTONUP.

Messages are very important to a Windows programmer. Most of the work that you do as a Windows programmer will involve deciding which messages to process and which messages to ignore. One thing to keep in mind is that there is no predefined order to messages. For this reason, if you are used to a procedural orientation, things may seem disorganized and chaotic at first. Messages will seem to fly at you like bullets. To help you understand the flow of

Figure 3.1 *SPY listening to the Program Manager's messages*

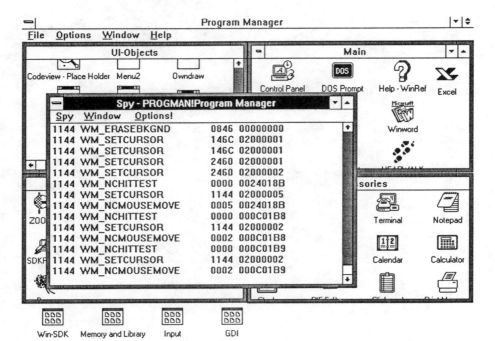

messages in the system, Microsoft includes a utility called SPY with the Windows SDK. Figure 3.1 shows SPY listening to the messages created by the Program Manager. As you progress in your Windows programming efforts, you will learn which messages you should pay attention to. To help you get started, all of the different types of messages that occur in Windows are organized at the end of Chapter 5. For your covenience, this is also included in Appendix A.

Now that we've reviewed some of the basic conventions of Windows programming, it's time to look at the source code for our sample program. We'll take it from the top with a look at WinMain, our program's main entry point.

4
Understanding the WINMAIN Function

One of the first things you might have noticed about our minimum Windows program is that there are two functions: WinMain and MinWndProc. Every Windows program must have a WinMain function. It is the entry point. The other routine, MinWndProc, is a "window procedure," although the name "message processing procedure" is probably a more accurate description. We'll look at our window procedure in the next chapter. For now, we're going to examine the WinMain function to find out what it can tell us about Windows programming.

WinMain is divided into three parts: procedure declaration, program initialization, and a message loop. Most of the complexity of WinMain lies in its initialization. The message loop is an (almost) endless loop that continually reads a message queue and sends messages to the right place for processing.

Procedure Declaration

Let's start our look at WinMain by considering the procedure declaration. WinMain takes four parameters, as follows:

```
int PASCAL WinMain (HANDLE hInstance,
                    HANDLE hPrevInstance,
                    LPSTR  lpszCmdLine,
                    int    cmdShow)
```

When a program starts running, Windows gives it some information about who it is and who it is related to. The hInstance parameter says who a program is. Think of it, if you'd like, as a program's name. Windows gives each program in the system a unique name. Of course, the name is not "Joe" or "Fred," but a 16-bit unsigned integer (the type for which HANDLE is defined in Windows.h).

Windows tells a program its name because certain Windows library routines require this as a parameter. This allows Windows to know "who is calling." Our program calls two routines that take hInstance as a parameter: RegisterClass and CreateWindow.

The second parameter, hPrevInstance, tells a program who it is related to. If it isn't related to any currently running program, the value of hPrevInstance is NULL. How does Windows decide if two programs are related? By name. In the same way that two people with the same last name are (often) related, two programs with the same **module name** are related. Recall that the following entry in our module definition file defines our module's name:

```
NAME MIN
```

When a user selects a program to run, Windows looks at the module name hidden in the executable file (and readable with the help of the EXEHDR utility). If it finds the name of a module that is already running, it starts up a second instance. It lets the program know that it has a relative already present by passing the name of the relative in the hPrevInstance parameter.

Figure 4.1 shows four instances of MIN, three instances of CLOCK, two instances of REVERSI, and a single instance of PAINT-BRUSH with a drawing of a partridge in a pear tree. When each subsequent instance of each program starts running, hPrevInstance has the name of the previous family member.

Why does a program want to know if it has relatives in town? One thing you should know about instances is that, like real-life relations, they share a lot of things. For example, to conserve memory, all instances of a program share code and resources. The only thing that is not shared, in fact, is the instance's data. The reason a Windows program is notified about its relatives is so that it can call them (that is, send them messages) to share even more things! Of course, you don't have to share. But if you want to share with your cousin Jim, you've got his number.

The third parameter to WinMain, lpszCmdLine, gives us the command line arguments for our program. There are a number of ways

Figure 4.1 *Four instances of MIN, three of CLOCK, two of REVERSI and one of Paintbrush*

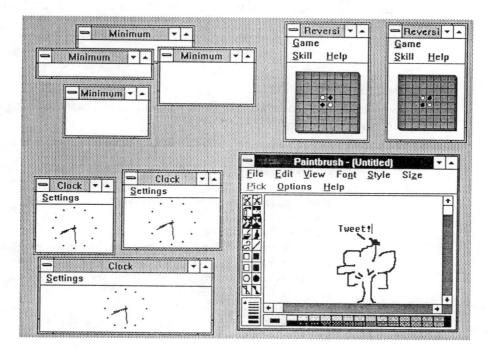

that command line arguments get created. The simplest involves putting the arguments after the program name in the Properties dialog box of the Program Manager. Like the `argv` parameter in the usual C program entry point:

```
main (int argc, char **argv)
```

the `lpszCmdLine` parameter can be used to pass values to our program like filenames, option switches, etc. Unlike `argv`, however, `lpszCmdLine` points to a single character string and not to an array of character pointers.

The final parameter, `cmdShow`, tells a program what to do with its main window when it first starts. Should it be minimized? Should it be displayed full screen? Notice that we later pass this value as the second parameter to the `ShowWindow` routine.

With an understanding of the four WinMain parameters under our belt, we're ready to look at the initialization of our minimum Windows program. This involves creating a window for our program to use.

Program Initialization

Here is the code to the part of WinMain that we consider the program initialization:

```
if (!hPrevInstance)
    {
    wndclass.lpszClassName = "MIN:MAIN";
    wndclass.hInstance     = hInstance;
    wndclass.lpfnWndProc   = MinWndProc;
    wndclass.hCursor       = LoadCursor (hInstance, "hand");
    wndclass.hIcon         = LoadIcon (hInstance,"snapshot");
    wndclass.lpszMenuName  = NULL;
    wndclass.hbrBackground = COLOR_WINDOW+1;
    wndclass.style         = NULL;
    wndclass.cbClsExtra    = 0;
    wndclass.cbWndExtra    = 0;

    RegisterClass( &wndclass);
    }

hwnd = CreateWindow("MIN:MAIN",        /* Class name.  */
                    "Minimum",          /* Title.       */
                    WS_OVERLAPPEDWINDOW, /* Style bits. */
                    CW_USEDEFAULT,      /* x - default. */
                    0,                  /* y - default. */
                    CW_USEDEFAULT,      /* cx - default. */
                    0,                  /* cy - default. */
                    NULL,               /* No parent.   */
                    NULL,               /* Class menu.  */
                    hInstance,          /* Creator      */
                    NULL                /* Params.      */
                    ) ;
ShowWindow (hwnd, cmdShow);
```

Our program initialization consists of calls to three Windows library routines: RegisterClass, CreateWindow, and ShowWindow.

Recall that earlier we said `hPrevInstance` would be NULL when the first copy of a program is run. For all subsequent copies, it contains the instance handle for the previously started program. This means that RegisterClass is called only for the first instance of a program. Whatever RegisterClass does (we'll see in a moment), the results can be shared by every other instance of our program. In addition to sharing code and resources, then, instances share the results of the `RegisterClass` call.

Window Class Registration

It looks as though `RegisterClass` takes a single parameter: a pointer to a structure of type `WNDCLASS`. But this structure contains 10 values, so it would be safer to say that 10 parameters are passed.

RegisterClass defines a window class. Windows simply makes a copy of all of the elements in the data structure and stores this copy in a place that might be called the "Class Database." When a program wants to create a window, it references an entry in the **Class Database**, and uses that information to create the window. One class definition can support multiple windows.

What are the advantages of a class definition? A moment ago, we mentioned that every instance of a program shares the results of the call to RegisterClass. Since RegisterClass creates a class definition, it follows that every instance of a program shares the class definition. One of the benefits this brings is better memory use. Let's look at each of the elements in the WNDCLASS data structure to better understand what an entry in the class database does for us.

Every class has a name. You create the name, place it in a character string, and put a pointer to the string in the `lpszClasssName` element of the WNDCLASS structure. This is the key, or lookup value, that identifies a class database entry.

The `hInstance` value tells Windows who created the class definition. This is needed for Windows internal housekeeping. When the last instance of a program terminates, Windows removes all class definitions created by that family.

The `lpfnWndProc` value gives Windows the address of a function to associate with a window class. This function is usually called a **window procedure**. The role of a window procedure can be simply stated: A window procedure processes messages. This sounds rather bland; but in a moment, when we describe our window procedure, you will see that almost all of the pizazz and sparkle in a

Windows program comes from the way messages are handled by its window procedure(s).

The hCursor value identifies the default mouse cursor for our window class. Every time the cursor moves across our window, its shape will change to the one we define here. As we mentioned earlier, MIN has its own cursor that was defined using the SDKPaint utility. The file that contains the cursor definition, MIN.CUR, is referenced in our resource file, MIN.RC, with the line:

```
hand cursor min.cur
```

To get this cursor definition loaded into memory, we must ask for it. When we do, with the Windows function LoadCursor, we are told Windows' internal "name" (or handle) for the cursor:

```
wndclass.hCursor = LoadCursor (hInstance, "hand");
```

The handle is assigned to the hCursor element in the WNDCLASS structure. Notice that the second parameter to LoadCursor is the name of the resource in MIN.RC, "hand."

The hIcon element of WNDCLASS is handled in a similar manner. We create an icon using SDKPaint and store it in the file MIN.ICO. We make the following entry into our resource file, MIN.RC:

```
snapshot icon min.ico
```

which causes the icon to be bound into MIN.EXE at program creation time. As with cursors (and other resources), we load the resource into memory by making a call to a special routine:

```
wndclass.hIcon = LoadIcon (hInstance,"snapshot");
```

The class definition provides a place to define a menu for our window. But MIN doesn't have a menu, and so we assign NULL to inform Windows of this fact:

```
wndclass.lpszMenuName = NULL;
```

The hbrBackground field of WNDCLASS asks us for one thing, and we give it something else! This requires a little explanation. This field defines the background color for a window. If we were to define a background color for this printed page, we would select white (since the book is printed black text on white paper). Before any drawing is done in a window, we often paint a window with the background color. This gives us a clean surface on which to draw.

The Hungarian prefix "hbr" tells us that this element is a "handle to a brush." In the next chapter, when we introduce the Graphics Device Interface (GDI), we'll talk about brushes. In brief, a brush is the way a Windows program defines a color for filling areas. But we don't use a brush to define our background color (although we could).

Instead, we give Windows a magic number that lets it know we want to use the system's default background color. The user selects a background color using the Control Panel program. To make the default background color a part of our window class definition, we use the special COLOR_WINDOW+1 value:

```
wndclass.hbrBackground = COLOR_WINDOW+1;
```

The definition that appears in Windows.h is

```
#define COLOR_WINDOW        5
```

which is one of 19 system color constants that are defined. You might be wondering why we add one to this constant. It turns out that the first value in this group has the value zero. But zero is an invalid value for a brush handle (or any other handle, for that matter). So, to use these constants in place of a handle, we add one to make the entire range of system colors valid.

The next WNDCLASS structure member that we'll look at is the style field. In the world of Windows programming, the term **style** refers to a collection of options that are each controlled by one or two bits. To conserve space, style fields combine these options into a two-byte (or four-byte) field. We'll delve into the meaning of each style bit in Chapter 13, where we'll cover all the aspects of creating windows. For now, MIN doesn't use any style bits:

```
wndclass.style        = NULL;
```

The last two fields in WNDCLASS, cbClsExtra and cbWndExtra, are used to request that extra space be allocated in the class database (cbClsExtra) and in a related database, the **window database** (cbWndExtra), which contains an entry for every window in the system. This allows you to attach your own, private data to a class or a window. Right now, this may seem like a strange thing to want to do.

After the first instance of our program calls RegisterClass, an entry is made into Window's class database. With an entry in the database, every instance of MIN can create its own private window. We could even modify MIN to create multiple copies of a MIN:MAIN window, if we wanted to. But RegisterClass doesn't do the window creating for us. That job falls to the next Windows routine we're going to discuss: `CreateWindow`.

Window Creation

Once a window class has been registered, we can begin creating windows. Here is the call we make to CreateWindow. As you might expect, the first parameter to CreateWindow specifies the class of window that we wish to create.

```
hwnd = CreateWindow("MIN:MAIN",          /* Class name.   */
                    "Minimum",           /* Title.        */
                    WS_OVERLAPPEDWINDOW, /* Style bits.   */
                    CW_USEDEFAULT,       /* x - default.  */
                    0,                   /* y - default.  */
                    CW_USEDEFAULT,       /* cx - default. */
                    0,                   /* cy - default. */
                    NULL,                /* No parent.    */
                    NULL,                /* Class menu.   */
                    hInstance,           /* Creator       */
                    NULL                 /* Params.       */
                   ) ;
```

The second parameter is the window title. The window title appears in the titlebar when a window is opened, and next to the window's icon when a window is minimized. This is a good place to put the name of our program. After a window has been created, your program can change the title by calling the **SetWindowText** routine.

The third parameter is for style bits. As we mentioned in our discussion of class-style bits, style fields combine several one- and two-bit wide fields into a single two- or four-byte value. For your convenience, top-level windows can use the WS_OVER-LAPPEDWINDOW definition. This combines together six simpler style bits. Here is the definition from Windows.h:

```
#define WS_OVERLAPPEDWINDOW (WS_OVERLAPPED |
        WS_CAPTION | WS_SYSMENU | WS_THICKFRAME |
        WS_MINIMIZEBOX | WS_MAXIMIZEBOX)
```

The C-language bitwise OR operator, |, packs together these simpler bit-definitions:

```
#define WS_OVERLAPPED     0x00000000L
#define WS_CAPTION        0x00C00000L
#define WS_SYSMENU        0x00080000L
#define WS_THICKFRAME     0x00040000L
#define WS_MINIMIZEBOX    0x00020000L
#define WS_MAXIMIZEBOX    0x00010000L
```

The definition of WS_OVERLAPPED has no bits turned on. This field has no effect when ORed with the other bit-values. This style flag is available, however, to help distinguish the three types of windows that can be created. The other two types are created using the following style-flags:

```
#define WS_POPUP          0x80000000L
#define WS_CHILD          0x40000000L
```

WS_OVERLAPPED is simply a place holder so that at a glance you can tell what type of window is being created.

The other style bits that are part of the WS_OVER-LAPPEDWINDOW definition serve to create the different parts of the window. Figure 4.2 shows the relationship of window-style bits to window parts. A complete discussion of all the different window-style bits is in Chapter 13.

The fourth, fifth, sixth, and seventh parameters are used to determine the starting size and location of our window. The X and Y values describe the location of the upper-left corner of our window relative to the upper-left corner of the display screen. The units for all four parameters are pixels. MIN takes the easy way out by asking Windows to create an appropriate size and location for our window with the CW_USEDEFAULT flag. This flag must be set in the X and

Figure 4.2   *Style bits and the parts of a window*

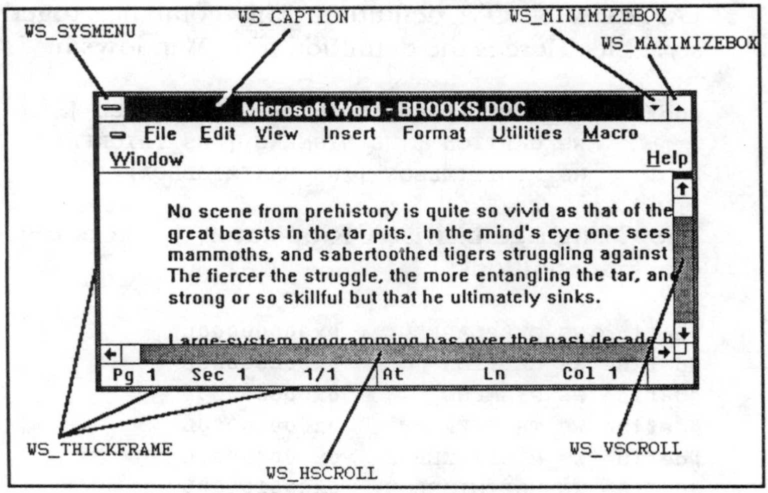

CX fields of CreateWindow. When it is used, the Y and CY values are ignored.

The eighth parameter defines a window's parent. While the term "parent" has lots of connotations, both in the real world and in the world of object-oriented programming, the meaning here is much simpler. It describes where a window lives. In real life, children live in the homes of their parents. For us, a window resides in the pixels of its parent. Like the main window in most programs, the main window in MIN has no parent. We declare this with a value of NULL in this parameter.

The ninth parameter allows us to attach a menu to a window. This is the second chance we have to specify a menu—the first was in the class definition. The WNDCLASS data structure lets us define a menu to be shared by every member of a class. If our class definition had a menu name, we would automatically get the class menu by specifying NULL in this parameter. If a window has a private menu, it can use this field to establish that fact. Our window has no menu, because we set the class menu name to NULL, and set the ninth parameter to `CreateWindow` to NULL as well.

The tenth parameter, an instance handle, identifies the window owner. This lets Windows know which instance of our program has created the window. The reason for this parameter is subtle, but essentially it allows Windows to set up the data segment register correctly when it calls our window procedure. See the box on page 80 for more details on this mechanism, and Chapter 19 for an in-depth discussion of the data-segment side of dynamic linking.

The eleventh parameter lets us pass a data pointer to our window procedure. The pointer is passed to our window procedure with the very first message, WM_CREATE. This is used for providing window initialization data. Since MIN doesn't have any initialization data to pass, we set this parameter to NULL.

Once we return from this call to CreateWindow, Windows has created all the internal information needed to support a window. That is, it has created an entry in the window database. But our window hasn't appeared on the screen yet. For this, we must call the ShowWindow function. It is possible to make a window appear with the CreateWindow call, by specifying the WS_VISIBLE style bit as part of the third parameter. But we don't ordinarily do this for a program's main window, since the ShowWindow routine opens our window in a way that the user has requested.

Our program receives the user's request in WinMain's cmdShow parameter, which we use in the call to ShowWindow:

```
ShowWindow (hwnd, cmdShow);
```

Depending on the value of cmdShow, our program might start out minimized as an icon, as a regular open window, or it might even start maximized.

With the call to ShowWindow, the initialization of our program is complete, and our window is visible on the screen. This initialization sequence is typical for a Windows program. The first instance of a program registers the window class, then it and all subsequent instances create and display their own copy of a window of this class.

But there is more to Windows programming than simply making a window appear. Once a window has been created, it generates messages that communicate its needs to our program. A Windows program needs a mechanism to allow it to receive these messages to maintain the user interface. As you will see, Windows has not one but two message delivery mechanisms.

As we start to investigate the delivery of messages to our program, we're going to introduce a topic that may seem at first to be strangely out of place: Windows' multitasking capability. Because this capability is tightly interwoven into the fabric of the message delivery mechanism, we need to address both topics simultaneously. Let's begin our study of messages, then, starting with the relationship between messages and multitasking.

Messages: Input Mechanism and Multitasking Time Slice

In Chapter 1, we introduced the idea that Windows is a multitasking operating system. Unlike other multitasking systems, however, it does not interrupt one program to allow another to run. An interrupt-based approach to multitasking is sometimes called **preemptive multitasking**, since the operating system preempts one program to allow another to run. Windows, on the other hand, is a **nonpreemptive** system. This means that programs are not interrupted by the operating system, but interrupt themselves to allow other programs to run. How can such a cooperative system be made to work?

Windows' multitasking switcher is embedded into Windows' message delivery system. Windows programs rely on messages to receive input from the user and from user interface objects. Some messages are hardware related, and tell a program that the user has pointed with the mouse or typed a keystroke. Other messages come from user interface objects like windows, menus, and scroll bars. To access the flow of messages, a program calls the message delivery system. It gets one message per call. If a program has no more messages, the message delivery system will start delivering messages to a program that *does* have messages to be delivered.

From this discussion, it is clear that a message serves a larger purpose than its namesake in the real world, that is, it does more than just communicate something. To a Windows program, messages are the unit of processing. They have the effect of creating time-slices during which a program runs. To get a clearer understanding about the dual role that messages play, let's take a closer look at the message delivery system.

A Windows program receives messages in two ways. The first way is by reading message buffers. Windows doesn't allow us direct access to its internal buffers, but rather reads a buffer for us when our program calls a Windows library routine: GetMessage.

There are two system buffers that GetMessage reads. One is called the **hardware event queue**, which holds system-wide mouse and keyboard events. The other buffer is called an **application mes-**

sage queue, used to hold a few other types of messages. Every program has its own message queue. In fact, every *instance* of every program has its own message queue. If it finds a message for a program, GetMessage pulls the message into the program.

If GetMessage doesn't find messages for a program, it puts the program to sleep. At such times, the Window switcher takes over and transfers control to another program that does, in fact, have messages waiting for it. The GetMessage routine, then, serves to make Windows' message-driven multitasking system work.

The second way that our program can receive messages is by a direct call to one of our window procedures. Our window procedure is called, as if it were a subroutine that was a part of Windows. In fact, you can think of a window procedure as an installable extension to Windows. Messages delivered by this mechanism don't wait in a message queue, but are processed immediately when a call is received.

Let's pause a moment and consider the implications of these two approaches. The first method, in which GetMessage reads message buffers for us, is called **pull-model processing**. The name describes the active role our program plays in pulling a message from one of the system buffers. The second method is called **push-model processing**. The name describes the passive role our program plays in waiting to be called and letting Windows *push* a message into our window procedure.

It may strike you as odd that Windows has *two* mechanisms for delivering messages. After all, other systems have been written that are strictly pull-model (the Apple Macintosh) or push-model (like the Xerox Star). Why two mechanisms? A little bit of history may make this clear.

Before Microsoft started shipping Windows in November 1985, it spent two years building the system. The earliest internal versions of Windows (1983–1984) were entirely push-model. In those days, a Windows program was just a subroutine package. For each window class, 10 subroutines were defined, with a subroutine for each of 10 different types of user-interface events. For example, one routine was called when a window was created, another to deliver mouse and keyboard input, and still another when it was time to draw in a window, etc.

Things worked fairly well, with the exception of mouse and keyboard input. The Microsoft engineers had trouble incorporating interrupt-driven hardware into push-model processing. If you think about it, this is a *hard* problem. Push-model processing does its work in a very orderly, synchronized manner. Interrupt-driven hardware, on the other hand, is quite chaotic. Depending on whether the user is typing at 60 words per minute, punching the function keys, or torturing the mouse, input arrives in a random order and at unpredictable times. The solution? Windows uses both push-model processing and pull-model processing.

The advantage of push-model processing is that it allows user interface objects that are part of the operating system to directly interact with application programs. Can you think of a more direct way to be connected to an operating system than to be a *subroutine* to the operating system?

Pull-model processing, on the other hand, lets us buffer unpredictable hardware input. It also allows the creation of *modal loops*, during which time a program filters out all messages except for a specified few. A simple example of a modal loop occurs in non-Windows programs when a message like the following is displayed:

```
Strike Any Key When Ready...
```

and suspends all processing until the user has typed a key on the keyboard.

Used together, pull-model and push-model processing create a unique, hybrid system in Windows. Let's get back to the source code from MIN.C, to understand the implementation details of this hybrid approach.

The Message Loop

Every Windows program has a message loop to allow it to continuously poll for messages. In this way, every Windows program is able to stay in touch with the supply of messages that are so vital to the proper operation of a Windows program. Here is the message loop from MIN.C:

```
while (GetMessage(&msg, 0, 0, 0))
    {
    TranslateMessage(&msg);        /*  Keyboard input.     */
    DispatchMessage(&msg);
    }
```

This loop runs continuously for as long as a Windows program is running. Each iteration through the loop represents the receipt of a single message from the system event queue or from a message queue. With the exception of the WM_QUIT message, every message causes GetMessage to return a value of TRUE. On receipt of the WM_QUIT message, a program drops out of its message queue and terminates. When we discuss the window procedure in Chapter 5, you'll see that it's the job of a top level window to send the WM_QUIT message when it is destroyed. Otherwise, a program will not terminate properly and will remain in memory, taking up space that could be used by other programs.

Let's look at each routine in this tiny message loop. A moment ago, we introduced the idea that GetMessage pulls messages into our program from system buffers—the hardware event queue and an application message queue. We can request GetMessage to filter messages by providing filter information in the second, third, and fourth parameters. Since we're interested in *all* messages, however, filtering is disabled by setting these to zero.

The most interesting parameter to us is the first parameter, which is a pointer to a structure that GetMessage fills with message data. Notice that a pointer to this structure is the sole parameter to the other routines in our message loop.

Our program defines this structure as

```
MSG msg;
```

For the definition of MSG, we can look in Windows.h; and we find the following:

```
typedef struct tagMSG
  {
    HWND   hwnd;
    WORD   message;
    WORD   wParam;
    LONG   lParam;
    DWORD  time;
    POINT  pt;
  } MSG;
```

Let's look at each of the six elements in this structure.

- hwnd, an unsigned integer, contains a window handle. Every window in the system is given a unique handle. Like the in-

stance handle we describe earlier, the window handle is simply
a name given a window. The reason a window handle is associated with a message is that every message is directed at one
window or another.

- `message`, another unsigned integer, contains the *type* of message, encoded as a 16-bit value. Starting on page 93, we'll take a
  look at all the different types of messages in Windows.
- `wParam` and `lParam` contain message data. The meaning depends on the type of message. For example, the menu command message uses `wParam` to identify the menu item that has
  been selected. Mouse messages pack the location of the mouse
  pointer into `lParam`. As far as the way these values are defined,
  `wParam` is an unsigned integer and `lParam` is an unsigned long.
  This gives us six bytes of data for each message.
- The last two items, `time` and `pt`, are rarely used by Windows
  programs. Both describe the state of the system when the message was put into the message queue: `time` holds the time, and
  `pt` holds the location of the mouse pointer.

The second routine in our message loop is a call to `Translate-`
`Message`. This routine calls the Windows keyboard device driver to
convert raw keystroke messages (WM_KEYDOWN) into cooked
ASCII values, which are placed in the messages queue as WM_CHAR
messages. This makes it easy for our program to tell the difference
between "A" and "a" without having to get involved with the state of
the shift key.

`TranslateMessage` also provides support for international keyboards. A British shopkeeper, for example, would probably use the
£ symbol to quote you the special price of 35 £. If the shopkeeper
used a Windows word processor to send you a note with this information, the word processor would call `TranslateMessage` to convert the keystroke to the proper symbol. As part of this translation
process, `TranslateMessage` makes diacritic marks available; it allows Windows programs to display French words like "**Voilà**,"
Spanish phrases like "**¿Hablo Español?**" and German city names
like **München**.

The final routine in this loop, DispatchMessage, takes message
data from the MSG structure and uses it to call the correct window
procedure. It *pushes* the message into the window procedure for
processing.

You might wonder whether you could speed things up by calling a window procedure directly rather than by calling DispatchMessage. The answer is "no." Windows must make all calls to our window procedure.

The reason has to do with the way data is addressed. A windows program usually has its own data segment. The dynamic link library that controls the Windows user interface, USER, also has its own data segment. When USER calls a window procedure, it places the window procedure's data segment identifier into a special place: the AX register of the CPU.

The Compiler generates the following code at the beginning of our window procedures:

```
PUSH DS          ; Save USER's data segment value
MOV  DS, AX      ; Install our data segment value
```

At the very end of the window procedure, right before we return, we restore the USER module's data segment by saying:

```
POP  DS          ; Restore USER's data segment
```

For a Windows program to directly call into a window procedure, it would have to set up the AX register with the proper data segment value. Otherwise, the window procedure would not be able to access its data.

At this point, our walk through WinMain is complete. Along the way, we have explored some of the fundamentals of the Windows architecture. But our journey is not over yet. We still have one more routine to explore: our program's window procedure. This is the subject of our next chapter.

5
Understanding Window Procedures

Until now, the only thing that we have said about window procedures is that they process messages. But what does it mean to *process* a message? We have already explored how messages serve as the time-slice for Windows' multitasking. As we discuss the window procedure, we'll emphasize the other role of messages: communication.

When a window is created, moved, sized, minimized, or closed, messages are generated. When the user types at the keyboard, clicks with the mouse, selects a menu item, or cancels a dialog box, one or more messages are generated to communicate these events. Messages are the lifeblood of this operating system, as well as the time-slice that allocates processor use.

The centerpiece of every Windows program is one (or more) functions that receive and process messages. These functions are called **window procedures**. The user creates a flood of messages to a window procedure when interacting with a Windows program. From this flood, the window procedure scoops up the messages that it needs to do its work. Exactly what this means depends on the message. A window procedure might respond to a message by drawing a pie chart, closing a window, or turning the mouse into a pumpkin. The personality of a Windows program comes from the way it handles the messages it decides to use. In other words, a spreadsheet program, a game, and a word processor each get their unique qualities by the response each makes to the stream of messages that ultimately starts with the user.

From a coding point of view, the structure of a window procedure usually is a `switch` statement, with a different case for each message. Our minimum window procedure processes only one message, but you can see how the switch structure can easily be expanded to include other messages we might want to process:

```
long FAR PASCAL MinWndProc (HWND      hWnd,
                            WORD      msg,
                            WORD      wParam,
                            LONG      lParam)
    {
    switch (msg)
        {
        case WM_DESTROY:
            PostQuitMessage(0);
            break;

        default:
            return(DefWindowProc(hWnd,msg,wParam,lParam));
            break;
        }
    return 0L;
    }
```

Our window procedure is small, but it has a big brother that helps it quite a bit—the default window procedure: DefWindowProc. Notice that every message we don't want is routed to this procedure. This routine takes on the burden of performing all of the default actions required to make each window work. The default window procedure is provided by Microsoft in the Windows software development kit. For your convenience, we have listed it in Appendix B.

Let's dissect our window procedure, starting with the procedure definition. We'll take a look at the single message we process, WM_DESTROY, and a closer look at the workhorse for our program, the default window procedure. And finally, since messages are such an important part of a Windows programmer's life, we're going to examine each type of message that occurs in this system.

The Window Procedure Declaration

Every window procedure must be defined in this way:

```
long FAR PASCAL MinWndProc (HWND  hwnd,
                            WORD  msg,
                            WORD  wParam,
                            LONG  lParam)
```

The procedure name as well as the name of each parameter is, of course, up to you. But the number and type of parameters as well as the procedure declaration must appear as shown here. This is important because you don't write the code that calls this routine. As the push-model part of our program, this routine is always called directly by Windows.

The return value for all window procedures is a `long` value. The meaning of the return value depends on the message. For example, the WM_QUERYENDSESSION message expects a TRUE (nonzero) or FALSE (zero) value. This particular message lets programs vote on whether Windows should honor the user's request to shut down the system (Windows can be very democratic). The WM_GETTEXT message, on the other hand, expects to receive a far pointer to a string (char far *) as a return value.

The name of the window procedure, `MinWndProc`, must be specified in the module definition file, `MIN.DEF`, under the EXPORTS statement. As we'll cover in Chapter 19, this is important to make dynamic linking work properly (and, more specifically, to give your program access to the correct data segment).

Every window procedure has exactly four parameters: a window handle (hWnd), a message identifier (msg), and two parameter values (wParam and lParam).

The window handle, hWnd, identifies the window associated with a message. This is a necessary parameter because a single window procedure can support several different windows on the display screen at the same time. The window handle identifies the window that is "calling" our window procedure. This is very convenient, because most of the Windows library routines that act on a window take this handle as a parameter.

The second parameter, msg, is the window message. If the window handle tells us "who is calling," then the message value tells us "what they want." Perhaps it is to announce that a window has been born (WM_CREATE), lives in a new location (WM_MOVE), has grown up (or shrunk) (WM_SIZE), needs a facelift (WM_PAINT), or has passed away (WM_DESTROY).

The wParam and lParam parameters give some more information about a given message. wParam is defined as a WORD value, which in Windows.h is defined as a 16-bit unsigned integer. lParam is defined as a LONG value, which is a 32-bit unsigned value. The meaning of wParam and lParam depend on the message type. For example, the WM_COMMAND message, which is sent when a menu item is selected, uses wParam to identify the specific menu item that was selected. Mouse messages, like WM_LBUTTONDOWN and WM_MOUSEMOVE, use the lParam to store the location of the mouse cursor in the window's client area.

We have delayed discussing two parts of the window procedure declaration because a longer, more in depth discussion is required. Let's roll up our sleeves and dig into the reasons for the FAR and PASCAL keywords.

The PASCAL Calling Convention

The PASCAL keyword causes a function to use the Pascal Calling Convention. This keyword is not part of ANSI Standard C, but an extension that Microsoft made to their C language compiler. This keyword takes advantage of a quirk in the Intel architecture to generate code that is smaller and faster than the C Compiler's default calling convention. Several years ago, Microsoft converted Windows itself from the C Convention to the Pascal Convention. Afterwards, the code to Windows itself was 9 percent smaller.

If the Pascal Convention generates better code, you might wonder why anyone would want to use the C Convention. The C Convention allows functions to accept a variable number of parameters. C library functions like sprintf() and scanf() *must* be written with the C convention. For a function with a fixed number of parameters, though, the PASCAL Convention can be used. This is the reason it is a part of every window procedure declaration.

Windows takes advantage of the PASCAL calling convention in every possible way. For example, all of the Windows library functions (except one) are declared with this keyword. In this book, we use the PASCAL Convention for all of our functions. Because it results in better code, we recommend that you do the same for all of your functions that use a fixed number of parameters.

The other keyword that we need to explore is the FAR keyword. We'll take this opportunity to explore a related keyword: NEAR.

The NEAR and FAR Keywords

To understand the NEAR and FAR keywords, you need to know something about the architecture of the processors that run Windows. Windows runs on the Intel family of CPUs, which includes the 8088, 8086, 80186, 80286, 80386, and 80486. One characteristic of this family is a segmented memory addressing scheme. The NEAR and FAR keywords give you the ability to control the way a program interacts with the memory architecture.

The key to understanding segmented addressing is to realize that every memory reference is made up of two parts: a **segment identifier** and an **offset** into the segment. A two part address is somewhat unusual in computer architecture. And yet in everyday life addresses with two (or more) parts are quite common. If you write a letter to the President of the United States, you address it to 1600 Pennsylvania Avenue. If you wanted to drop a note to Bill Gates, the CEO of Microsoft Corporation, you send it to One Microsoft Way. In Intel addressing, the segment identifier corresponds to the street name, and the offset to the building number.

The origin of this addressing scheme goes back to the first member of this family, the 8086. When Intel was designing this chip in the mid-1970s, the goal was to create a CPU that would allow compatibility with Intel's earlier CPUs, the 16-bit 8080 and 8085. Both chips had 16-bit address registers. The 8086-family has 16-bit address registers as well; but to overcome the 64K boundary, two registers instead of one are used to reference memory.

This approach has proven to be quite flexible. In the *real mode* of the Intel processors, the two registers are combined to create a 20-bit address. This allows a one-megabyte address space. In the *protect modes* of the higher end processors (80286, 80386 and 80486), the segment identifier references into special tables, called the local and global descriptor tables (LDT and GDT). These tables allow even more memory to be addressable: on the 80286, 16 megabytes of physical memory can be addressed. On the other high-end chips, up to four gigabytes (four billion bytes) of physical memory can be addressed. And since Windows can run in protect mode (if you have enough RAM), Windows programs can take advantage of gobs and gobs of memory. This segmented addressing scheme has allowed Intel to create a compatibility path for their CPUs that has lasted three decades!

Of course, this flexibility has not come without a price. The primary disadvantage of this segmented scheme is that programmers

Figure 5.1   *The Intel-86 family registers and flags*

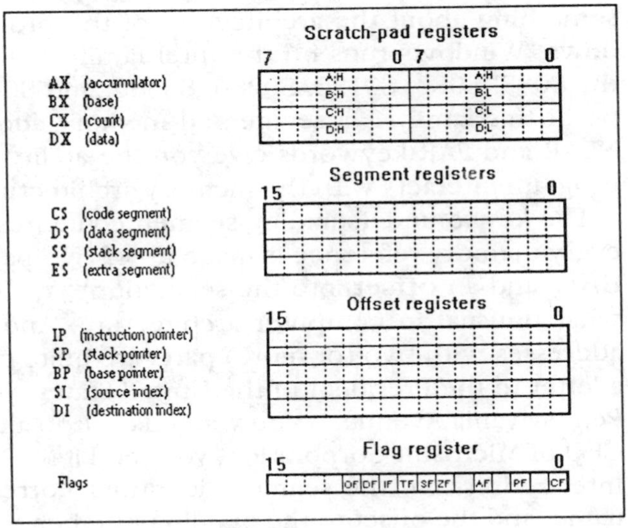

must pay attention to segmented addressing when writing software. If you are not used to working with the segmented addressing, it takes some time to get used to.

Figure 5.1 shows the 14 registers shared by every member of this family. To reference a memory location, we use a segment register for our street name and an offset or scratch register to hold the house number. In real life, if we're going to visit the houses of several friends, it is easier to visit houses on the same street than to visit houses that are all on different streets. The same holds true for addressing memory. In other words, it is more efficient to address several memory locations in the same segment than to address the same number of memory locations if they are all in different segments.

As an example, consider Figure 5.2. There are two segments, which we label 1000 and 2000. To reference a specific location in either segment, we need to specify a segment register and an offset value. If we start at offset 6 in segment 1000, as pointed to by the DS:BX register pair, we only need to change the BX register in order to access offset 2 in the same segment. At least times the work is required if we wish to access offset 4 in segment 2000, since we need to change the DS register to 2000 and the BX register to 4. And

Figure 5.2 *FAR references require twice the work of a NEAR reference*

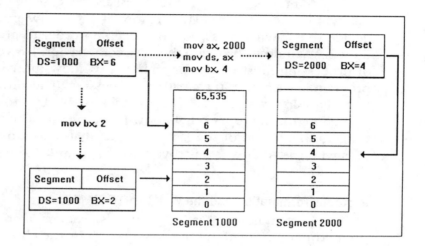

it is even more costly in protect mode, since loading a segment register requires the segment protection information to be loaded by the CPU as well.

To get the best performance from this architecture, you need to pay attention to the way your programs use memory. The NEAR keyword specifies a reference in the same segment. The FAR keyword specifies an intersegment reference.

If NEAR addressing provides better performance, why use FAR addressing? FAR addressing is required in certain situations. The first involves calls to Windows library routines. Since Windows routines reside in their own code segments, programs must use FAR calls to access them. Also, when we pass data pointers as parameters to Windows routines, they must be FAR data pointers.

FAR references are also needed because the maximum size of a segment is 64K. This size limitation comes from the fact that, with the exception of the 80386 and 80486, offsets are 16 bits in the Intel 86 family of processors. A 16-bit offset means we can address no more than two to the sixteenth power, 64 kilobytes (65535).

Programs with more than 64K of code require multiple code segments. Programs with more than 64K of data require multiple data segments. And as we'll discuss in Chapter 18, even if a program has less than 64K of code, there are still good reasons to use multiple code segments.

After this in-depth look at our window procedure's declaration, it's time to move on to look at the message processing performed by our window procedure. The creator of a window procedure will decide the specific messages to process in order to give each window in a Windows program the desired behavior. However, one bit of processing must be performed by a window in every Windows program: that is, the termination processing. The proper termination of a Windows program is a task that usually falls to the window procedure for the top-level window in a program. The message that triggers this is one of the last messages that a window procedure sees when a window is destroyed: WM_DESTROY.

Program Termination and the WM_DESTROY Message

An important issue for every Windows program is proper termination. Proper termination is necessary to allow the cleanup and reclamation of memory and other resources used by your program. In our discussion of WinMain, we introduced the WM_QUIT message. When the GetMessage routine reads this message from our message queue, it returns FALSE, which causes our "infinite message loop" (and our program) to terminate. Let's see how the WM_QUIT message gets into our message queue.

Program termination usually occurs when the program's main window is closed. A user can close a window in any number of ways. Two of the more common ways are by selecting the Close item on the system menu and by striking the [Alt] + [F4] key combination. Each of these user actions cause a stream of messages to be sent to our window procedure. Here is a list of messages that are sent to our window procedure when MIN's window is closed using the [Alt] + [F4] key combination:

Message	Comment
WM_SYSKEYDOWN	[F4] key was struck
WM_SYSCOMMAND	System Command generated
WM_CLOSE	Window is told to close
WM_NCACTIVATE	Turn off titlebar (non-client area) highlight
WM_ACTIVATE	Window is becoming inactive
WM_ACTIVATEAPP	Application is becoming inactive
WM_KILLFOCUS	Window is losing the keyboard
WM_DESTROY	Window has been destroyed
WM_NCDESTROY	Time to clean up non-client area data

The first thing to be said about this stream of messages is that the default window procedure handles the bulk of the work to make the "right things" happen. For example, it takes the first two messages, which are raw keystroke messages, and translates them into the third message: a system command. The system command message is handled by the default window procedure to implement system level commands.

A system command is a generic request for some action to occur (move a window, size a window, etc.). Our window procedures usually do not process these messages. Instead, we'll look for a more specific message to respond to. In this case, that message is WM_CLOSE, a request to close our window.

A typical response to WM_CLOSE message is to check whether there are any unsaved files in our window. If there are, we display a message box like that shown in Figure 5.3 to warn the user of the possible loss of data.

When we are sure it is safe to close a window, our window procedure destroys our window with a call to the DestroyWindow function. This, in fact, is what the default window procedure will do for us. For this reason, our minimum window procedure does not respond to WM_CLOSE, but lets the default window procedure handle it.

When a window is destroyed, a long stream of messages is usually generated. Even though the window is going away, Windows continues to communicate with our window procedure until the win-

Figure 5.3 *Protecting the user from loss of data*

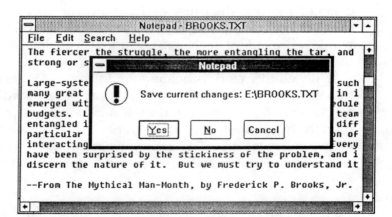

dow destruction process is complete. Each of the remaining messages, after the WM_CLOSE, notifies us about a change in the state of our window.

The message that is of interest to us in terminating our program is WM_DESTROY. This is a notification that belongs to our program, that the default window procedure never touches. In response to WM_DESTROY, our program generates a WM_QUIT message to cause our `GetMessage` loop to exit. This is done by making a call to `PostQuitMessage`.

Of all the work that is required for a minimum Windows program, program termination is the only task that falls to our window procedure. Every other task is taken up by the Windows library routine that translates all the important messages into the proper actions for the maintenance of the Windows user interface. That library routine is the default window procedure, `DefWindowProc`. Let's focus our attention on this workhorse.

Default Message Handling

As we discussed in Chapter 1, the chief reason for the attractiveness of Windows comes from the consistent "look and feel" of the Windows user interface. Even the most casual Windows user notices the remarkable uniformity between programs. For example, menus work the same between two otherwise unrelated programs, and windows in different programs respond in the same way to the same actions.

Deep in the bowels of Windows, it is the work of the default window handler that accounts for this high degree of uniformity. The flood of messages that our window procedure diverts to the default handler is the cause of the similarities between programs. A moment ago, for example, we described the role of the default window procedure in closing a window. The default window procedure performs the same services for all Windows programs.

While all this work is being done for use, there is still something that we must do. Our window procedure plays the role of traffic cop for messages. After all, the default message handler is never called directly by Windows. Instead, our window procedure always receives messages first. To keep the user interface working properly, our program must pass messages on to the default window procedure.

There may, in fact, be times when we wish to vary the behavior of a window away from the default behavior. For example, we might wish to prevent the user from picking up a window by the titlebar. (This is a typical way for a user to move a window.) It is a simple matter to trap the messages associated with this action, and prevent them from arriving at the default window handler. For the most part, however, we'll allow the default window procedure to do its work for us, so that our program can participate in the consistency that makes Windows so usable.

In looking at the different parts of our minimum Windows program, we have talked a lot about the flow of messages through the system. We have also identified a few messages that are important. In order for you to fully understand how the message pipeline can work to your advantage, it will help you to know the types of messages that flow through these pipes. For this reason, we're going to conclude this chapter with an in-depth look at the types of messages in Windows.

A Taxonomy of Messages

There are about 250 predefined messages in Windows. Fortunately, you do not have to be familiar with every single one of them, because most have very specialized uses. For example, a large number of messages are specific to one type of window. Other messages are used for very special purposes, like sharing data or implementing the **multiple-document interface** (MDI) standard. Still other messages float through our message pipeline but are never documented for our use. These are internal messages that Windows creates for its own purposes.

To help you come to terms with messages, we'll divide the messages into eight categories. These categories are intended as a framework in which to begin understanding messages. But this won't be the last you hear about messages. Almost every chapter in this book will provide details on the messages that apply to the different parts of Windows. So let's get started on our look at Windows messages.

Messages have names. Message names are defined in Windows.h like this:

```
#define WM_COMMAND   0X0111
```

The "WM" Hungarian prefix tells us that a symbol is a "window message." In spoken language, the prefix is ignored, so that programmers often refer to WM_COMMAND as a "command message." These symbolic names stand in for the raw numeric value of a message: a 16-bit unsigned integer. Besides the WM prefix, there are other Hungarian prefixes for messages: EM_, BM_, DM_, LB_ and CB_ (like EM_GETSEL, BM_GETCHECK, etc.). These are private messages, which don't concern us at this moment, except that they show that you can create your *own* private messages as you need them.

A useful tool for learning about messages is the SPY program, which Microsoft provides with the Windows Software Development Kit. We like SPY because it lets you eavesdrop on the message traffic for a window—even if you didn't write the program! When you use SPY, you will probably be surprised at the number of messages encountered. For example, Figure 5.4 shows the messages

Figure 5.4   *SPY showing messages generated by making a menu selection*

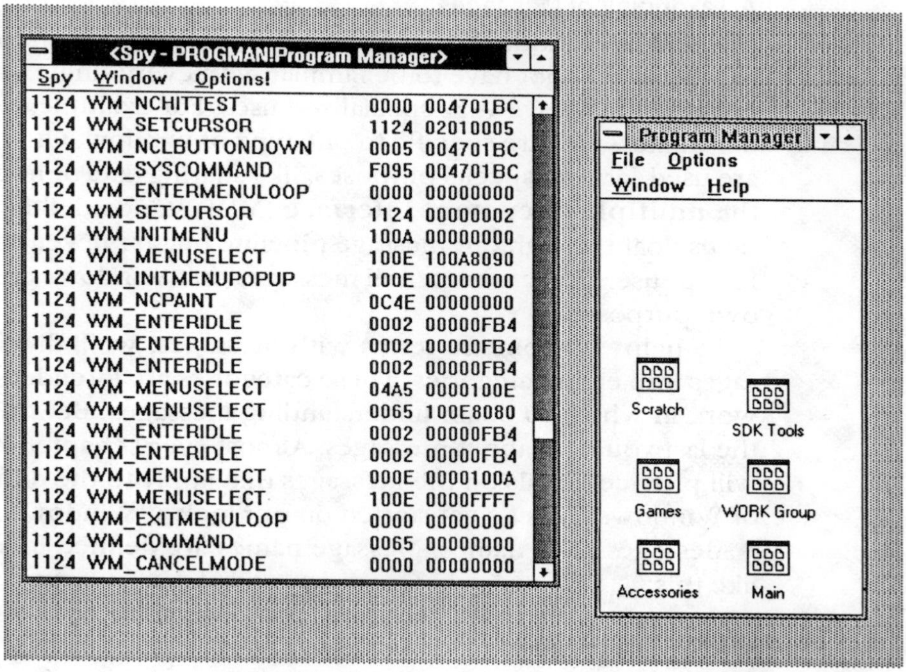

Table 5.1 *The eight types of messages*

Type	Description
Hardware	Mouse and keyboard input
Window Maintenance	Notification, request for action, query
User-Interface Maintenance	Menu, mouse pointer, scroll bar, dialog boxes, MDI
Termination	Application or system shutdown
Private	Dialog box controls: edit, button, list box, combobox
System Resource Notification	Color changes, fonts, spooler, device modes
Data Sharing	Clipboard and Dynamic Data Exchange (DDE)
Internal System	Undocumented messages

generated by the simple action of making a menu selection. Even without knowing what specific messages do, you can tell that this is a lot of messages. A little experimentation with SPY will demonstrate that this is typical for other user actions as well

Why so many messages? Some messages are for Windows' internal use, to synchronize events in different parts of the system. These messages are passed along to the default window procedure, which we introduced a short time ago. Other messages notify the window procedure of actions taken by the user. Messages guarantee that a window procedure will always have the latest information about what the user is doing. Once you understand the type of messages that are generated, messages ultimately mean less work on your part to keep in touch with a lot of information. It's like having a daily paper delivered to your door: "All the Messages Fit to Print."

Table 5.1 shows the eight categories of messages. As we review each category, we'll list the specific messages that are in the category. Since some of the categories are quite specialized, we'll limit our discussion to a brief introduction and omit a list of specific messages. All messages from all categories are listed in Appendix A, in case you're curious about what it is that we're omitting. Let's start with our first message category: hardware messages.

Hardware Messages

A window procedure receives messages generated by three different pieces of hardware: the keyboard, the mouse, and the system timer. Each of these generates hardware interrupts. Since Windows' scheduling is not interrupt-oriented, hardware events have to be buffered. This insures that hardware events are processed in the order in which they occur.

For example, when you strike the "H" key, an interrupt notifies the system that keyboard input is ready. The Windows keyboard device driver retrieves this input and creates an entry into the **hardware event queue**. When its turn comes, messages bearing "H" key information are delivered to the proper window procedure. The mouse and timer messages are handled in a similar fashion. Table 5.2 shows the 29 messages that are generated in response to hardware activity.

Caution: Like mouse and keyboard messages, timer messages are queued. This means that Windows timers are not exact. This is necessary since an interrupt-driven timer message would conflict with the nonpreemptive nature of Windows. The usefulness of a timer is that it lets you know that a minimum amount of time has passed.

With mouse messages, a distinction is made between the mouse messages generated in a window's client area and those generated in the non-client area. (Remember: The non-client area of a window includes its border, system menu, title bar, menu, etc.) In general, an application only pays attention to client-area mouse messages and lets the default window procedure process non-client area mouse messages.

While we're on the subject of mouse messages, the WM_MOUSEMOVE message deserves some special attention. The WM_MOUSEMOVE message is handled in a special way to keep the hardware event queue from overflowing. After all, if you move the mouse quickly, you can easily create hundreds of mouse interrupts. To minimize the disruption this might cause, Windows keeps only *one* mouse move message at a time. When a new mouse move

Table 5.2 *Hardware messages*

Mouse Messages: In a window's client area

WM_LBUTTONDBLCLK	Left button double-click
WM_LBUTTONDOWN	Left button down
WM_LBUTTONUP	Left button up
WM_MBUTTONDBLCLK	Middle button double-click
WM_MBUTTONDOWN	Middle button down
WM_MBUTTONUP	Middle button up
WM_MOUSEMOVE	Mouse move
WM_RBUTTONDBLCLK	Right button double-click
WM_RBUTTONDOWN	Right button down
WM_RBUTTONUP	Right button up

Mouse Messages: In a window's non-client area

WM_NCLBUTTONDBLCLK	Left button double-click
WM_NCLBUTTONDOWN	Left button down
WM_NCLBUTTONUP	Left button up
WM_NCMBUTTONDBLCLK	Middle button double-click
WM_NCMBUTTONDOWN	Middle button down
WM_NCMBUTTONUP	Middle button up
WM_NCMOUSEMOVE	Mouse move
WM_NCRBUTTONDBLCLK	Right button double-click
WM_NCRBUTTONDOWN	Right button down
WM_NCRBUTTONUP	Right button up

Keyboard Messages

WM_CHAR	Character input
WM_DEADCHAR	Dead-character (umlaut, accent, etc.)
WM_KEYDOWN	Key has been depressed
WM_KEYUP	Key has been released
WM_SYSCHAR	System character input
WM_SYSDEADCHAR	System dead-character
WM_SYSKEYDOWN	System key has been depressed
WM_SYSKEYUP	System key has been released

Timer Message

WM_TIMER	Timer has gone off.

message arrives, Windows checks if one already exists. If so, the old message is updated with the new location information. A new entry is made only if a mouse move message isn't already present.

There are two basic types of keyboard messages: regular and system. In general, you can ignore system keyboard messages, which have names like WM_SYSCHAR and WM_SYSKEYDOWN. The default window procedure turns these into the proper system command. The regular keyboard messages are intended for application use. We'll discuss the details of all keyboard messages in Chapter 15, when we talk about getting input from the user.

Window Maintenance Messages

This group has 27 messages. It seems that this is the trickiest group of messages, mostly because it takes a long time to learn the subtle nuances of each. Unfortunately, the names of the messages do not help very much. When we fully explore windowing in Chapter 13, we'll provide more details on these messages.

To begin with, there are three types of window maintenance messages: notification, request for action, and queries. Table 5.3 lists all the window maintenance messages, sorted into these three types.

A notification message tells a window procedure that the state of a window has changed. Nothing is required from the window procedure to perform the action implied by the message name. The WM_MOVE message, for example, is *not* a request for your program to move anything. Instead, it is an after-the-fact message to tell you that your window has already been moved. It is worth noting that nothing in the message tells us how our window was moved. Maybe the user moved a window with the mouse. Or perhaps another program moved our window. Whichever the case, notification messages are one-way communication to a window procedure.

A request for action message requires that some action take place. Without the action, a hole is created in the user interface. For example, the WM_PAINT message is sent to a window procedure when a window has been damaged and needs to be redrawn. If the window procedure doesn't repair the window, it stays broken. For the most part, the default window procedure provides the needed minimum action. There are times, however, when you must intercept and process one of these messages yourself—as is the case with the WM_PAINT message we brought up a moment ago. When you do,

Table 5.3 *Window maintenance messages*

Window Messages: Notification

WM_ACTIVATE	Window is active.
WM_ACTIVATEAPP	Application is active.
WM_CREATE	Window has been created.
WM_DESTROY	Window has been destroyed.
WM_ENABLE	Input to the window has been enabled.
WM_KILLFOCUS	Window has lost keyboard control.
WM_MOUSEACTIVATE	Notifies a window that it is going to become active because of a mouse click.
WM_MOVE	Window has been moved.
WM_SETFOCUS	Window has gained keyboard control.
WM_SIZE	Window has changed size.

Window Messages: Request for action

WM_CLOSE	Close (destroy) window
WM_ERASEBKGND	Erase background
WM_ICONERASEBKGND	Erase background of iconic window
WM_NCACTIVATE	Change title bar to show active state
WM_NCCREATE	Create non-client area data
WM_NCDESTROY	Destroy non-client area data
WM_NCPAINT	Redraw non-client area
WM_PAINT	Redraw client area
WM_PAINTICON	Redraw iconic window client area
WM_SETREDRAW	Inhibit redrawing of window
WM_SETTEXT	Change window text
WM_SHOWWINDOW	Change window visibility

Window Messages: Query

WM_GETMINMAXINFO	What are min/max sizes for window?
WM_GETTEXT	What is the window text?
WM_GETTEXTLENGTH	What is the length of the window text?
WM_NCCALCSIZE	How big should the client area be?
WM_QUERYNEWPALETTE	Do you have a new palette?
WM_QUERYOPEN	Can iconic window be opened?

be sure that you mimic the actions of the default handler. Finding out what this means is simpler than you might think: just look at the source code to **DefWindowProc**.

Because this is an important piece of code, Microsoft provides the source to the default window procedure in the Windows Software Development Kit. For your convenience, we have duplicated a listing in Appendix B of this book for version 3.0 of the Software Development Kit. Check with your software dealer for the latest version of the software development kit, since the listing we provide in the appendix of this book is subject to revision.

A query message requires an answer. This is used for two-way communication between Windows and your program. Like the Request for Action messages, you can rely on the default window procedure to give a reasonable answer for most cases. You may decide to intercept one if you want to change the default answer. For example, you will get a WM_QUERYOPEN message when the user tries to open a minimized window. If you want a program to run only in an iconic state, you simply answer FALSE instead of the default answer of TRUE.

User-Interface Messages

This group contains messages for the other user-interface objects, including the application menu, mouse pointer, scroll bar, dialog boxes, and dialog box controls. It also includes a group of messages used to support the Multiple Document Interface (MDI). See Table 5.4. This is a user interface convention that was first seen in Microsoft's EXCEL spreadsheet program. Since then, it has become something of a standard, so that Windows now includes built-in support for MDI. The use of MDI is beyond the scope of this book, but we'll cover the other types of messages elsewhere: menu messages in Chapter 11, mouse pointer messages in Chapter 16, scroll bar messages in Chapter 20, and dialog box messages in Chapter 14.

Termination Messages

This is the smallest group of messages. See Table 5.5. But these messages are very important, since they are used to control the termination of a Windows program (WM_QUIT), as well as the termination processing for the system (WM_QUERYENDSESSION and WM_ENDSESSION). We covered the WM_QUIT message earlier.

Table 5.4   *User Interface Messages*

Menu Messages

WM_COMMAND	Menu item has been selected.
WM_INITMENU	Initialize menu bar menu.
WM_INITMENUPOPUP	Initialize popup menu.
WM_MENUCHAR	Mnemonic key used to select menu.
WM_MENUSELECT	User is browsing through menus.

System Commands: System Menu, Min/Max Buttons, Titlebar, etc.

WM_SYSCOMMAND	A system command has been selected.

Mouse Pointer Messages

WM_NCHITTEST	Query: Where is mouse on the window?
WM_SETCURSOR	Request: Change pointer to correct shape.

Scroll Bar Messages

WM_HSCROLL	Horizontal scrollbar has been clicked.
WM_VSCROLL	Vertical scrollbar has been clicked.

Dialog Box and Dialog Box Control Messages

WM_COMMAND	Control communicating with Dialog Box.
WM_COMPAREITEM	Sent to the parent of an owner-draw dialog box control, asking to compare two items for the purpose of sorting.
WM_CTLCOLOR	Control asking for colors to be set.
WM_DELETEITEM	Notification to an owner-draw listbox or an owner-draw combobox that an item has been deleted.
WM_DRAWITEM	Request to the parent of an owner-draw control, or owner-draw menu, to draw.
WM_GETDLGCODE	Query control: Want keyboard input?
WM_GETFONT	Query control: What font are you using?
WM_INITDIALOG	Initialize dialog.
WM_MEASUREITEM	Request to the parent of an owner-draw control or an owner-draw item to provide the dimensions of the item that is going to be drawn.
WM_SETFONT	Request to control: Use this font.

(Continued)

Table 5.4 *Continued*

Multiple Document Interface Messages

WM_CHILDACTIVATE	Notifies a parent window that a child is active.
WM_MDIACTIVATE	Notifies an MDI child window that it is either gaining or losing activation.
WM_MDICASCADE	Request to arrange the open MDI child windows in a cascading, stair-step fashion.
WM_MDICREATE	Requests an MDI client window to create an MDI child window.
WM_MDIDESTROY	Request to an MDI client window to destroy an MDI child window.
WM_MDIGETACTIVE	Query an MDI client window for the currently active MDI child window.
WM_MDIICONARRANGE	Request to arrange the iconic MDI child windows in an orderly fashion.
WM_MDIMAXIMIZE	Request to maximize, or zoom, an MDI child window so that it occupies all of its parent's client area.
WM_MDINEXT	Request to activate the next MDI child window.
WM_MDIRESTORE	Request to restore an MDI child window to its previous state—iconic, normal, or zoomed.
WM_MDISETMENU	Adjusts the menu on an MDI frame window.
WM_MDITILE	Request to arrange the open MDI child windows in a tiled fashion in the MDI parent's client window.

Table 5.5 *Termination Messages*

Application and System Termination

WM_QUIT	Request that a program should terminate.
WM_QUERYENDSESSION	A Query: Ready for system shutdown?
WM_ENDSESSION	Notification of results of shutdown query.

Private Messages

Private window messages are for use with a specific window class. The predefined private messages in Windows.h are used with the following window classes: edit, button, listbox, and combobox.

The use of private messages by predefined window types is a pretty good clue that we can use this technique for our own windows. Why would you want to do this? You might find that existing messages do not provide the required functionality. It is a simple matter to define your own private message types and use them for communicating between different windows that you create. Even though 250 message types have already been defined, message variables are unsigned integers, which means that there is room for 65535 different message types. When you define a private message, you should use the range starting at WM_USER, which is defined in Windows.h as follows:

```
#define WM_USER      0x0400
```

If we wrote a window procedure for windows that displays numbers, we might control how numbers appear with the following private messages (PM is Hungarian for "Private message"):

```
#define PM_DECIMAL     WM_USER + 0
#define PM_BINARY      WM_USER + 1
#define PM_HEX         WM_USER + 2
#define PM_OCTAL       WM_USER + 3
#define PM_NODECIMAL   WM_USER + 4
#define PM_DOLLARS     WM_USER + 5
#define PM_WITHCOMMAS  WM_USER + 6
```

Other parts of our program (or other programs that we write) can control the number display window simply by sending messages.

System Resource Notification

There are eight system resource notification messages. See Table 5.6. These are sent to the top-level window of every program when a change has been made to a system resource. For example, when fonts are added or removed from the system, a WM_FONTCHANGE message is distributed. When the user changes the system colors or the system time from the Control

Table 5.6   *System resource notification messages*

System Resources Notification Messages

WM_COMPACTING	Notification that system memory is low, and that the Memory Manager is trying to free up some memory.
WM_DEVMODECHANGE	Printer setup has changed.
WM_FONTCHANGE	Installed fonts in the system have changed.
WM_PALETTECHANGED	Hardware color palette has changed.
WM_SPOOLERSTATUS	Job has been removed from spooler queue.
WM_SYSCOLORCHANGE	One or more system colors has changed.
WM_TIMECHANGE	System time has changed.
WM_WININICHANGE	Initialization file, WIN.INI, changed.

Panel program, the WM_SYSCOLORCHANGE or WM_TIME-CHANGE messages are sent out. The typical response to a notification is to record the change.

Of course, not every change is of interest to every program. For example, a clock program would probably check the new time when it receives a WM_TIMECHANGE message. But if it didn't use different fonts, it would probably ignore the WM_FONTCHANGE message.

Because most programs use the system colors, just about every program will respond to the WM_SYSCOLORCHANGE message. This is a notification that one or more system colors have changed. Ordinarily, system colors are changed by the Control Panel program under the direction of the user. When a change has been made, the Control Panel sends WM_SYSCOLORCHANGE. On receipt of this message, programs that use system colors respond by redrawing with the new colors.

Data Sharing Messages

Data sharing plays an important role in Windows. So it's not surprising that there are messages that are used in data sharing. Both data sharing mechanisms, the Clipboard and Dynamic Data Exchange (DDE), make extensive use of messages. A full discussion of data sharing is beyond the scope of this book; however, Windows' data sharing messages are listed in Table 5.7.

Table 5.7   *Data sharing messages*

Clipboard Messages

WM_ASKCBFORMATNAME	Asks for the name of a Clipboard format.
WM_CHANGECBCHAIN	Notification of a change in the viewing chain.
WM_DESTROYCLIPBOARD	Clipboard contents are being destroyed.
WM_DRAWCLIPBOARD	Clipboard contents have changed.
WM_HSCROLLCLIPBOARD	Horizonal scrolling of owner draw clipboard item.
WM_PAINTCLIPBOARD	Requests drawing of an owner draw clipboard item.
WM_RENDERALLFORMATS	Request to provide the data for all clipboard formats that have been promised.
WM_RENDERFORMAT	Request to provide data for a single clipboard format that has been promised.
WM_SIZECLIPBOARD	Notification to the owner of owner draw clipboard data that the size of the Clipboard viewer window has changed.
WM_VSCROLLCLIPBOARD	Vertical scrolling of an owner draw clipboard item.

Dynamic Data Exchange(DDE) Messages

WM_DDE_ACK	Acknowledgment.
WM_DDE_ADVISE	Request from a DDE client to establish a permanent data link.
WM_DDE_DATA	Send a data item from a DDE server to a DDE client.
WM_DDE_EXECUTE	Request a DDE server to execute a series of commands.
WM_DDE_INITIATE	Logon to a DDE server.
WM_DDE_POKE	Request by a client for a server to update a specific data item.
WM_DDE_REQUEST	One-time request by a DDE client for a piece of information.
WM_DDE_TERMINATE	Logoff from a DDE server.
WM_DDE_UNADVISE	Terminate a permanent data link that was initiated with the WM_DDE_ADVISE message.

Internal System Messages

A large group of messages are defined in Windows.h but not described in any documentation. These are internal system messages, the last group of messages we are going to discuss. Windows uses these messages for its own purposes. This is the same idea as private messages, with the exception that private messages are meant for only one class of window. Internal messages are encountered in the context of every window class.

If Microsoft hasn't told us the reason for these messages, why are they sent to a window procedure? Like other message types, if a window procedure does not process it, the message is passed on to the default message handler. The default message handler does the right thing with this group of messages.

Since you have the source code to the default message handler, you might think that you could reverse-engineer some of these messages and use them for your own purpose. You can do this, but be careful. In a future version of Windows, Microsoft may decide to change the way an internal message is used, or eliminate it altogether! It has been our experience that "undocumented goodies" are interesting to look at, but dangerous to include in software that is intended for general distribution.

Part 3

Introduction to the Graphics Device Interface

6
Overview of GDI

For the next few chapters, we're going to focus on issues relating to the creation of graphical output. We're going to be discussing various types of drawing that can be done using Windows' **Graphic Device Interface (GDI)**. In this chapter, we're going to start by looking at some of the basic concepts and capabilities of GDI. The next few chapters will build on this beginning, by looking at pixels, lines, filled areas, and text. But GDI is much too big a topic to digest at one time, so we're going to postpone a discussion of certain topics to the last section of the book. Let's roll up our sleeves, then, and take a look at Windows' pixel-powered graphic output engine.

An Overview of the Graphics Device Interface

GDI is Windows' graphic output library. GDI handles graphic output for the display screen as well as hardcopy devices like printers and plotters. GDI creates every line, letter, and mark displayed by a Windows program. Windows itself uses GDI to assemble the pieces that make up the user interface: windows, icons, menus, dialog boxes, etc.

GDI Capabilities

Figure 6.1 shows some of the types of graphic objects that GDI can draw: lines, filled figures, and text of different shapes and sizes. This chapter and the chapters that follow introduce the basic concepts and programming techniques needed to take advantage of the capabilities that GDI has to offer.

GDI Devices

GDI can draw on many different types of devices: display screens, laser printers, dot-matrix printers, plotters, etc. For GDI to work

Figure 6.1 *A sample of GDI lines, filled figures, and text*

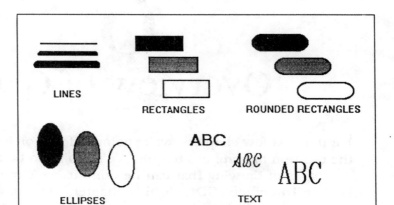

with a specific device, it depends on a special piece of software: a **device driver**. A GDI device driver converts drawing requests into the specific actions needed to draw on a specific device. For example, when a Windows program draws a picture of the space shuttle on an EGA display, GDI calls the EGA device driver to turn on the correct pixels. And when a program generates output on an HP Laserjet printer, GDI calls another device driver for help: the HP printer driver.

In addition to performing this work, a device driver provides GDI with a set of **device capability bits**. These are flags that let GDI know about a device's built-in drawing ability. There are five such flags: one each for curves, lines, polygons, bitmaps, and text. These flags tell GDI when to give a high-level drawing request directly to a device and when it must convert such requests into an equivalent set of low-level drawing requests.

At a minimum, a GDI device must be able to do two things: turn on pixels and draw solid lines. For a device with these minimum capabilities, GDI (with the help of a device driver) is able to do the rest. GDI has a set of built-in software simulations that take a high-level drawing request, like "draw a filled polygon," and convert it into a series of line and pixel operations. The software simulations are one reason that GDI is referred to as a **device-independent** graphics library. For devices with capabilities beyond the minimum, such as a Postscript printer, GDI uses the capability bits to determine when to send a high-level drawing request directly to the device driver.

In addition to physical devices like video screens and printers, GDI supports logical or **pseudo-devices**. Pseudo-devices are used for picture storage. Unlike physical devices, which display pictures using dedicated hardware, pseudo-devices capture a picture in RAM or on disk. GDI supports two types of pseudo devices: **bitmaps** and **metafiles**.

In Windows, bitmaps are always rectangular. A bitmap stores a picture in memory in the same way that a display adapter uses memory to hold graphic images. For this reason, bitmaps provide a fast way to make a copy of a picture. Bitmaps are also used to store images that must be drawn quickly onto the screen. For example, Windows itself uses bitmaps to store icons and cursors, as well as the tiny symbols used to draw system menus, minimize/maximize icons, and the parts of a scroll bar.

Another use of bitmaps is to store scanned images, such as company logos. A scanned image is created by running a paper copy of a logo through a device called a **scanner**. A scanner digitizes an image, making it suitable for storage in a bitmap. Figure 6.2 shows a bitmap that was created using a hand-held scanner, and placed into a PageMaker document.

Figure 6.2   *A scanned image in a PageMaker document*

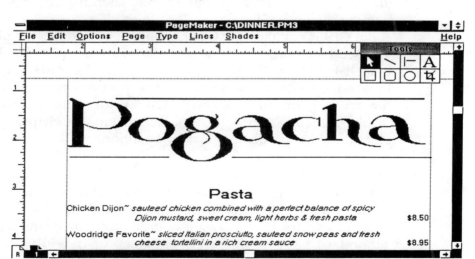

Metafiles are created by GDI's record-and-playback facility. A metafile is cheaper than a bitmap, in terms of memory use, but is slower in terms of drawing time.

A metafile is like a cassette tape. To create a metafile, you place the tape into GDI's cassette deck and push the "Record" button. GDI calls are recorded onto the metafile until you press the "Stop" button. Once a metafile has been created, it can be stored on disk, or passed to another program. For example, the Clipboard is often used to pass GDI metafiles between programs. To recreate the drawing, GDI is given the metafile "tape" and told to replay its contents.

As you get started with GDI programming, you'll probably concentrate most of your efforts on learning to draw on physical devices. After all, there are a number of subtle issues that you need to learn about before you can make effective use of display screens and printers. When you are comfortable drawing on these devices, you will then be ready to begin exploring the ways that the pseudo-devices can be used to enhance your program's graphic output.

The Programming Interface

With the variety of devices and pseudo-devices that GDI supports, you might be concerned that this somehow translates into a complicated and hard to use graphics library. After all, some graphic libraries provide two sets of routines: one for display screens and one for printers. If GDI were like that, you might have *four* different sets of drawing routines to worry about: one each for displays, printers, bitmaps, and metafiles.

But GDI is not like that: GDI has one set of routines for all devices. The SetPixel routine, for example, draws a single pixel on all devices that GDI supports. The Polyline routine draws a series of connected lines on any GDI-supported device or pseudo-device. In this chapter, we're going to focus our attention on writing output to the display screen. Nevertheless, the material in this chapter applies to all of the different devices that GDI supports.

Drawing Coordinates

Before you can use GDI to create any output, you need to understand how GDI interprets drawing coordinates. GDI gives you quite a bit of control over drawing coordinates. For example, you can request GDI to use inches, millimeters, or hybrid units that you specify. For the most control over your drawing, GDI lets you specify units that correspond to a device's native pixels. GDI uses the term **mapping mode** to refer to the different coordinate systems that it supports. Table 6.1 shows the eight mapping modes available in GDI.

In this chapter, we're going to limit ourselves to GDI's default mapping mode: MM_TEXT. In this mapping mode, a unit refers to a pixel—that is, to the smallest "picture element" that a device can draw. This mapping mode gives us the greatest control over graphic output and avoids rounding errors that other mapping modes can create. It is often used for programs that require absolute precision. For example, Aldus PageMaker, a page layout program, uses the MM_TEXT mapping mode to insure that objects aligned on the display screen match the alignment on the printer.

One drawback to MM_TEXT, however, is that it requires additional effort to avoid writing device-specific programs. That's the key advantage to the other mapping modes: they provide a way to draw in a device-independent manner. In Chapter 20, we'll discuss the other mapping modes when we address the theory underlying coordinate systems and coordinate transformations.

An advantage of MM_TEXT coordinates is that they are identical to the coordinates that are used for mouse input. This coordinate system is called **client area coordinates**. In client area coordinates, the origin (0,0) is located at the upper-left corner of the client area.

Table 6.1 *GDI Mapping Modes*

Mapping Mode Name	1 Logical Unit	Inches	Millimeters
MM_TEXT	1 pixel	-	-
MM_HIMETRIC	0.01 mm	0.000394	0.01
MM_TWIPS	1/1440 inches	0.000694	0.0176
MM_HIENGLISH	0.001 inches	0.001	0.0254
MM_LOMETRIC	0.1 mm	0.00394	0.1
MM_LOENGLISH	0.01 inches	0.01	0.254
MM_ISOTROPIC	} Scaling based on ratio between two DC		
MM_ANISOTROPIC	} attribute values: window and viewport extents.		

Figure 6.3 *GDI's default coordinate system*

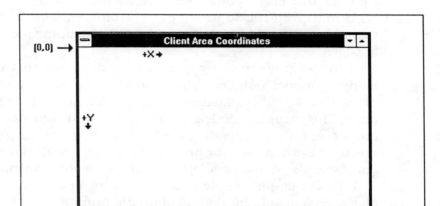

Unlike the Cartesian coordinate system that you may remember from your high school days, the value of Y increases as we move downward. Figure 6.3 shows the location of the origin and the directions in which X and Y values increase.

Logical Drawing Objects

One of the means that GDI uses to achieve device independence is through the use of logical drawing objects. A logical drawing object describes how output should appear: it is a high-level, device-independent request. GDI supports the following logical drawing objects: pens (to draw lines), brushes (to fill areas), fonts (to display text), and logical colors (to describe color).

When a logical drawing object is created, it can be used on any device. But the results may differ from one device to another, since devices have different capabilities. For example, a red pen might draw a red line on a 16-color EGA display but draw a black line on a monochrome dot matrix printer. It's the device driver's job to interpret a logical drawing object in a way that makes sense given a specific device's capabilities.

As we introduce each type of GDI drawing primitive, we'll describe the use of different logical drawing objects, and provide sample code to show how to use them.

The Device Context

To get an idea of how GDI works with different types of devices, let's take a look at a GDI drawing routine: TextOut. This routine displays a single line of text on any GDI-supported device. This line of code writes the word "Hello":

```
TextOut (hdc, 10, 10, "Hello", 5);
```

Notice the first parameter: hdc. This is a commonly used Hungarian prefix for an important GDI data type: a *handle to a device context*. Recall what we have already said about handles: They are 16-bit unsigned integers used to identify objects. The object identified by this handle plays a key role whenever a Windows program wishes to draw on any device: It is a **device context** (or DC, for short).

A device context is a combination of several things rolled into one. It is a toolbox full of drawing tools, a connection to a specific device, and a permission slip to help GDI control the use of different devices by different programs. GDI never gives a program direct access to a device context. Instead, it provides a handle to identify a specific DC. Like the TextOut routine, every GDI drawing routine takes a DC handle as its first parameter.

As a toolbox, the DC is a set of **drawing attibutes** that include one pen to draw lines, one brush to fill areas, and one font to display text. At any time while drawing, you can change the tools in a DC to give you, for example, red lines, green areas, and bold text. Put together, drawing attributes give you total control over the appearance and location of your program's output.

Every DC is a toolbox with 20 drawing attributes. By storing these in the DC, GDI hides complexity from you. There is a slight drawback to this approach, but we think you'll agree in the long run that it makes GDI easier to work with.

The drawback is that, until you become familiar with what they do for you, hidden attributes can be confusing. For example, consider the TextOut routine. We'll add some comments to explain the parameters:

```
TextOut (hdc,      /*  Handle to DC.          */
         10,       /*  X-location of text.    */
         10,       /*  Y-location of text.    */
         "Hello",  /*  Text to display.       */
         5);       /*  Text length.           */
```

From this code, can you tell what color the letters will be—will they be red, blue, or black? And what type of font will be used—will it be 14-point bold Times Roman, or 24-point italicized Helvetica? Because this information is part of the DC, you can't answer these questions by simply reading this line of code.

When the TextOut routine draws, it plucks the drawing attributes it needs from the DC. These attributes determine the appearance and location of the displayed text (including text color and font). As we introduce the different GDI drawing routines, we'll describe the DC attributes that each set of routines depends upon.

By hiding drawing attributes in a DC, Microsoft was able to define library routines with a minimum number of parameters. In practical terms, this means less typing for you when you write code that calls GDI. After all, drawing attributes tend to stay the same from one call to the next. To get an idea of the work that might be required in a world without a DC, consider what the TextOut function might look like:

```
/* Mythical TextOut in a world without a DC. */

TextOut (10,          /*  X-location of text.      */
         10,          /*  Y-location of text.      */
         "Hello",     /*  Text to display.         */
         5,           /*  Length of text.          */
         coFore,      /*  Foreground text color.   */
         coBack,      /*  Background text color.   */
         hClip,       /*  Clipping Region.         */
         hPalette,    /*  Color Palette.           */
         hFont,       /*  Text Font.               */
         iSpace,      /*  Intercharacter spacing.  */
         mmMapMode,   /*  Mapping mode.            */
         xyViewExt,   /*  Viewport extent.         */
         xyViewOrg,   /*  Viewport origin.         */
         xyWinExt,    /*  Window extent.           */
         xyWinOrg);   /*  Window origin.           */
```

Even without knowing the meaning of each drawing attribute, you can tell that 15 is a lot more than the five parameters that TextOut actually needs. In a world without DCs, you'd have a lot of work to do just to say "Hello."

What's in a DC? Here is a list of all the drawing attributes in a DC. For your convenience, we have indicated the type of primitives that use each attribute.

Drawing Attribute	Default Value	Lines	Filled Areas	Text	Raster	Comments
Background Color	White	x	x	x		Styled pen, hatch brush
Background Mode	OPAQUE	x	x	x		On/Off switch
Brush Handle	White Brush		x		x	Filled areas
Brush Origin	(0, 0)		x		x	hatch and dithered brushes
Clipping Region Handle	Entire Surface	x	x	x	x	
Color Palette Handle	Default Palette	x	x	x		
Current Pen Position	(0 , 0)	x				For LineTo routine
Drawing Mode	R2_COPYPEN	x	x			Boolean mixing
Font Handle	System Font			x		
Intercharacter Spacing	0			x		
Mapping Mode	MM_TEXT	x	x	x	x	One unit = 1 pixel
Pen Handle	Black Pen	x	x			
Polygon-Filling Mode	Alternate		x			For polygon routine
Stretching Mode	Black on White				x	For StretchBlt routine
Text Alignment	Left & Top			x		
Text Color	Black			x		
Viewport Extent	(1 , 1)	x	x	x	x	Coordinate mapping
Viewport Origin	(0 , 0)	x	x	x		Coordinate mapping
Window Extent	(1 , 1)	x	x	x	x	Coordinate mapping
Window Origin	(0 , 0)	x	x	x	x	Coordinate mapping

Not every drawing attribute in the DC is used by every drawing routine. For example, the text color is never used to draw lines.

Instead, each drawing routine takes the attributes it needs from the DC. Let's look at the other roles played by the DC.

The second role of a DC is that it connects a program to a specific drawing surface. For example, a program that wants to draw on the system display must gain access to a DC for the system display (we'll describe how this is done in a moment). To draw on a printer, or on a pseudo-device like a bitmap, a program obtains a DC to connect to each of these drawing surfaces.

The connection that the DC provides is a logical connection and not a physical one. Windows, after all, is a multitasking system. If programs had direct access to the physical device, it would cause confusion both for the user and for the Windows programs. As each program fought to maintain control of a given device, the result would be mixed up graphical nonsense.

To understand what we mean by a physical connection, consider the way an MS-DOS program like LOTUS 1-2-3 works. When it draws on the display, it writes directly to the memory buffers on the video adapter board. It directly manipulates the hardware registers to cause the hardware to perform the necessary tricks to display the desired spreadsheet or graph. To support this capability, it requires a private device driver so that it can tell the difference between the CGA, VGA, and 8514/a display cards. LOTUS 1-2-3 is able to do this because MS-DOS is a single-tasking operating system. There isn't any danger that other programs might be disrupted.

But Windows is multitasking, so programs cannot access a physical output device without disrupting other programs. Instead, a Windows program must use the logical connection represented by the DC. All Windows programs use this approach, so that GDI can resolve the conflicts that might otherwise disrupt the system when two programs access the same device. This introduces the third role of a DC: its role as a permission slip.

To avoid conflicts on shared devices, a DC is a permission slip that a program must have before it can draw on any device. The permission system works in one of two ways, depending on the type of device. On hardcopy devices, the process is known as **spooling**. On video display devices, the permission system is called **clipping**.

On printers and plotters, GDI borrows a technique from mainframe computers: Output is spooled to disk. The Windows Spooler, also known as the Print Manager, plays the role of a traffic cop to direct the flow of output to hardcopy devices. Otherwise, the output of one program might get mixed in with the pages of another. For spooled output, the DC helps GDI keep different print jobs separate.

On the display screen, Windows takes a different approach to separate the output from different programs. The method is called **clipping**. Clipping involves the creation of imaginary fences around a program's drawing area. To paraphrase an old saying: "Fences make good Windows programs."

My next-door neighbor has a fence around his yard that prevents his dog from running away. The dog can go where he wants inside the yard, but cannot stray into my yard. The fences that GDI creates provide the same type of boundary enforcement. When a program wants to draw in a window, it gets a DC from the Window Manager that has a built-in fence around the window's client area. Inside the fence, a program is free to draw what it wants. But the fence prevents the program from letting its drawing stray.

An example might clarify exactly what we mean by clipping. Figure 6.4 shows two programs sharing the display screen: SPY and CLOCK. Before either program draws, a fence is built to prevent the program from drawing outside its client area.

The SPY program's fence forms a rectangle. Notice that the fence prevents SPY from drawing on the face of the CLOCK. It also prevents SPY from drawing on the non-client area of its own window. After all, like most Windows programs, SPY doesn't maintain the non-client area of its window; it leaves that work to Windows.

The clipping for CLOCK is a little more complex. But we know that the clipping works because CLOCK's sweeping second hand doesn't brush SPY away. Instead, the clock hands appear to go "behind" the SPY window. Figure 6.5 shows the shape of the fence that prevents SPY from drawing outside its client area.

You might imagine that CLOCK has its work cut out for it to avoid drawing on SPY. In fact, CLOCK doesn't even know that SPY is present. The DC that CLOCK gets from the Window Manager is the key to this magic. When CLOCK calls different GDI drawing routines, the DC handle lets GDI check the location of the fence to make sure that no drawing is done out of bounds. Hence, there is very little work that CLOCK must do; GDI does it all.

How does GDI perform boundary checking? Let's look at the simpler case: the way GDI clips SPY's output to the rectangle that makes up SPY's client area. GDI works with the device driver to

Figure 6.4   *Output from Clock and Spy are kept separate through clipping*

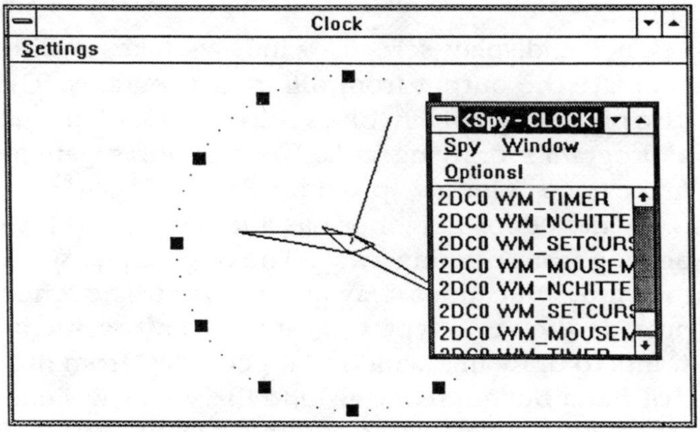

establish a rectangular fence, which is defined in terms of four coordinates: top side, left side, bottom side, and right side. The boundaries of this fence are part of a drawing attribute in the DC: the **clipping region**. Every GDI drawing routine checks these boundaries when it draws. As you can tell by looking at the SPY window, this means that letters might be chopped in half. But this is necessary to make windowing a reality.

Figure 6.5   *The shape of the fence around Spy*

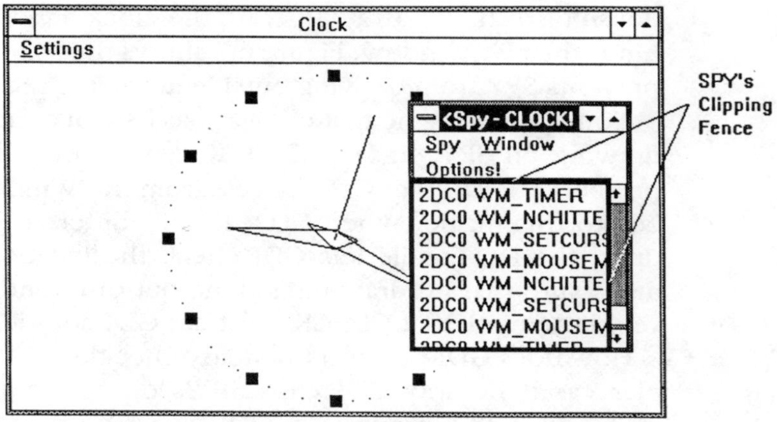

The more complex clipping we observe in CLOCK can be understood in terms of this simpler case. Namely, GDI defines clipping for CLOCK in terms of the four rectangles shown in Figure 6.6. Now instead of the four boundaries for one rectangle, GDI works with 16 boundaries for four rectangles. The principle is the same, even though GDI does four times as much work. To handle clipping like this, GDI treats each drawing operation like four separate drawing operations, with one for each clipping rectangle.

This complex clipping gives us a clue to how GDI stores clipping information. A set of one or more rectangles is combined into a data structure called a clipping region. As we mentioned earlier, a clipping region is an attribute that is part of the DC. This means that clipping can be performed on any GDI device. A clipping region might contain the entire drawing surface. Or, as we have seen, it might contain a set of one or more rectangles.

While clipping can be done on any device, clipping on the display screen is special. The reason is that Windows provides the clipping information to keep one program from accidentally overwriting another program's output. The part of Windows that takes care of display screen clipping is the part of Windows responsible for creating windows: the Window Manager.

Figure 6.6   *The four clip rectangles for Clock*

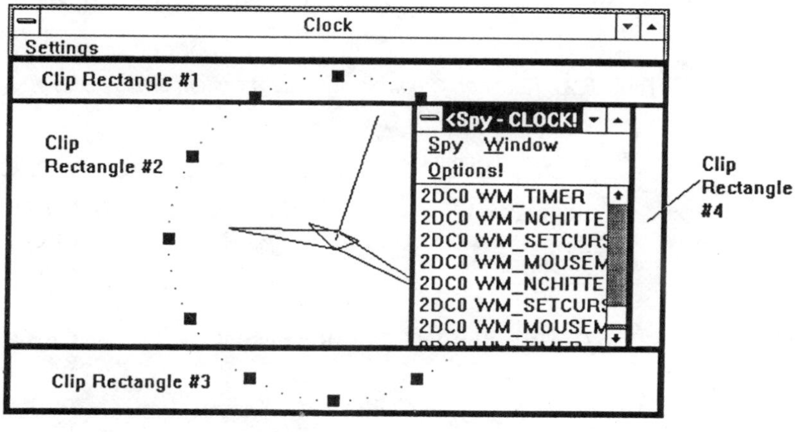

Clipping and the Window Manager

From our discussion of the interaction between SPY and CLOCK, it is clear that GDI's ability to perform clipping is what makes windowing possible. It lets programs share the display screen without requiring programs to worry about stepping on each other's toes.

Although GDI routines provide the clipping service, GDI itself does not set window boundaries. That job belongs to the Window Manager. When we introduced the Window Manager in Chapter 1, we said it was responsible for the user interface. Since the user interface resides on the display screen, the Window Manager builds and maintains all the display screen "fences."

The Window Manager owns a set of DCs for drawing on the system display. When a program wants to draw in a window, it borrows one of these DCs. Before it lends a DC to a program, the Window Manager installs a clipping region. There are three different Window Manager routines that a program can use to borrow a DC. For each of them, a different clipping region is installed in the DC. These routines are shown in Table 6.2, along with the routine that is used to return the DC to the Window Manager. When a program borrows a DC from the Window Manager, it must be careful to return the DC when it is finished. As you'll see shortly, this is the role of the "Sandwich" code construction.

Figure 6.7 gives an example of how clipping is set for each of these three routines.

The first routine, BeginPaint, allows a program to respond to requests by the Window Manager to draw in a window or repair

Table 6.2   *Routines to borrow and return system display DCs*

Borrowing Routine	Returning Routine	Description
BeginPaint	EndPaint	Clip to invalid part of client area
GetDC	ReleaseDC	Clip to entire client area
GetWindowDC	ReleaseDC	Clip to entire window (client and non-client areas)

Figure 6.7 *Three ways that the Window Manager sets clipping*

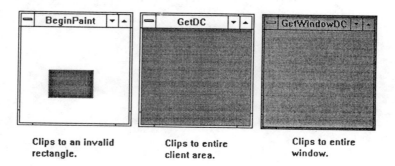

Clips to an invalid rectangle.   Clips to entire client area.   Clips to entire window.

damage that has been done to part of a window. The Window Manager sends the **WM_PAINT** message to let a program know that a window needs to be repaired. As you'll see, this message plays a central role in the maintenance of a window's client area.

The second routine, GetDC, allows a program to draw in the client area of a window. The clipping fence keeps output in the client area, even if another program's window is lying on top of the client area, as we saw in the CLOCK-SPY example. This routine is used for most drawing *outside* the WM_PAINT message. For example, in response to a WM_CHAR message, we might wish to echo the character typed.

The third routine, GetWindowDC, sets clipping to allow drawing anywhere in a window, including the non-client area. This routine is called by the Window Manager itself to draw the non-client parts of a window. After all, a Windows program typically does not do this work itself, but lets the default window procedure take care of it.

This introduction to GDI may have left you hungering for some sample code to provide a framework for understanding all of the concepts that we've introduced. In our next chapter, we're going to look at a program that illuminates a single pixel, but it will also introduce you to one of the most important messages that Windows programs work with: WM_PAINT. We'll also discuss how Windows handles color, and we'll enhance GDI's drawing primitives by creating one of our own to draw markers.

7
Pixels and Markers

The first program that we're going to look at lights up a single pixel. In doing so, it introduces you to the most important message for any program that draws on the display: WM_PAINT. Figure 7.1 shows three instances of PIXEL running. As you can see, the program illuminates a pixel in the very center of the client area.

Like other programs in this book, MIN serves as a starting point for this program. Here is the source listing for the files that make up PIXEL.

Figure 7.1 *Three instances of PIXEL*

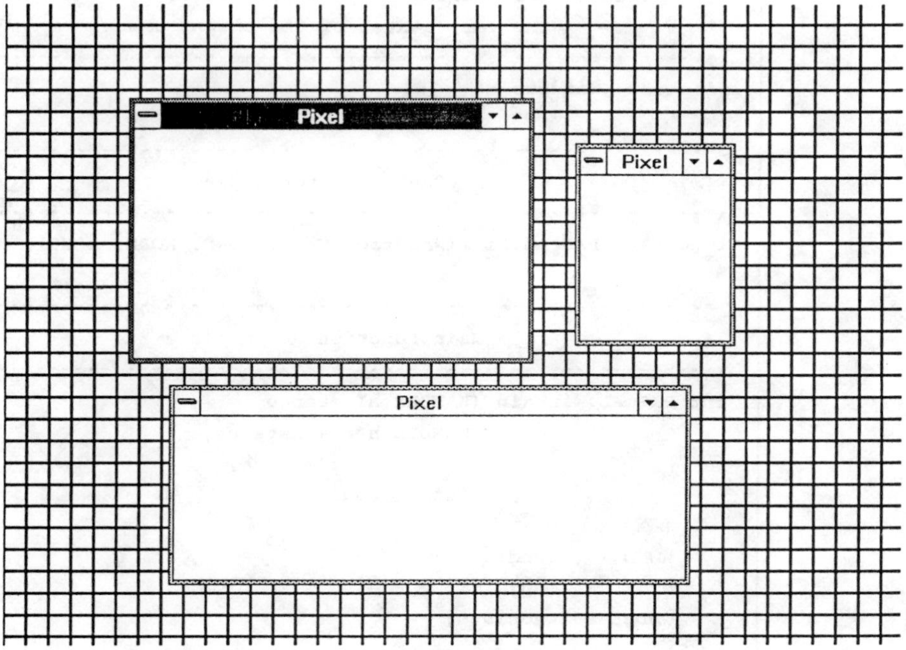

PIXEL.MAK

```
pixel.res: pixel.rc pixel.cur pixel.ico
    rc -r pixel.rc

pixel.obj: pixel.c
    cl -AM -c -d -Gsw -Od -W2 -Zpi pixel.c

pixel.exe: pixel.obj pixel.def
    link pixel,/align:16,/map, mlibcew libw/NOD/NOE/CO,\
        pixel.def
    rc pixel.res pixel.exe


pixel.exe: pixel.res
    rc pixel.res pixel.exe
```

PIXEL.C

```
/*-------------------------------------------------------------*\
|    PIXEL.C  GDI Drawing Program #1.   Illuminates a pixel in  |
|                the very center of the client area.           |
\*-------------------------------------------------------------*/
#include <Windows.H>


/*-------------------------------------------------------------*\
|                      Function Prototypes.                    |
\*-------------------------------------------------------------*/
long FAR  PASCAL PixelWndProc (HWND, WORD, WORD, LONG);


/*-------------------------------------------------------------*\
|                   Main Function:  WinMain.                   |
\*-------------------------------------------------------------*/
int PASCAL WinMain (HANDLE hInstance,
                    HANDLE hPrevInstance,
                    LPSTR  lpszCmdLine,
                    int    cmdShow)
    {
    HWND     hwnd;
    MSG      msg;
    WNDCLASS wndclass;
```

```
if (!hPrevInstance)
    {
    wndclass.lpszClassName = "PIXEL:MAIN";
    wndclass.hInstance     = hInstance;
    wndclass.lpfnWndProc   = PixelWndProc;
    wndclass.hCursor       = LoadCursor (hInstance, "hand");
    wndclass.hIcon         = LoadIcon (hInstance,"snapshot");
    wndclass.lpszMenuName  = NULL;
    wndclass.hbrBackground = COLOR_WINDOW+1;
    wndclass.style         = CS_HREDRAW | CS_VREDRAW;
    wndclass.cbClsExtra    = 0;
    wndclass.cbWndExtra    = 0;

    RegisterClass( &wndclass );
    }


hwnd = CreateWindow("PIXEL:MAIN",      /* Class name.  */
                    "Pixel",           /* Title.       */
                    WS_OVERLAPPEDWINDOW, /* Style bits. */
                    CW_USEDEFAULT,     /* x - default. */
                    0,                 /* y - default. */
                    CW_USEDEFAULT,     /* cx - default. */
                    0,                 /* cy - default. */
                    NULL,              /* No parent.   */
                    NULL,              /* Class menu.  */
                    hInstance,         /* Creator      */
                    NULL               /* Params.      */
                    ) ;

ShowWindow (hwnd, cmdShow);


while (GetMessage(&msg, 0, 0, 0))
    {
    TranslateMessage(&msg);         /*  Keyboard input.    */
    DispatchMessage(&msg);
    }
return 0;
}
```

```
/*----------------------------------------------------------------*\
 |               Window Procedure:  PixelWndProc.                  |
\*----------------------------------------------------------------*/
long FAR PASCAL PixelWndProc (HWND hWnd,    WORD msg,
                                 WORD wParam, LONG lParam)
    {
    switch (msg)
        {
        case WM_DESTROY:
            PostQuitMessage(0);
            break;

        case WM_PAINT:
            {
            int x, y;
            PAINTSTRUCT ps;
            RECT r;

            BeginPaint (hWnd, &ps);
            GetClientRect (hWnd, &r);
            x = r.right/2;
            y = r.bottom/2;
            SetPixel (ps.hdc, x, y, RGB (0, 0, 0));
            EndPaint (hWnd, &ps);
            }
            break;

        default:
            return(DefWindowProc(hWnd,msg,wParam,lParam));
            break;
        }
    return 0L;
    }
```

PIXEL.RC

```
snapshot icon pixel.ico

hand   cursor pixel.cur
```

PIXEL.DEF

```
NAME      PIXEL

EXETYPE WINDOWS

DESCRIPTION 'Demo SetPixel'

CODE      MOVEABLE DISCARDABLE
DATA      MOVEABLE MULTIPLE


HEAPSIZE     512
STACKSIZE    5000


EXPORTS
    PixelWndProc
```

Although PIXEL's WinMain function is essentially the same as MIN's, there is one change worth mentioning. We have added two new style bits to the window class definition:

```
wndclass.style        = CS_HREDRAW | CS_VREDRAW;
```

These style bits direct the Window Manager to generate a WM_PAINT message when the size of the window changes, in either the vertical direction (CS_VREDRAW) or in the horizontal direction (CS_HREDRAW). These style bits cause the entire window to be redrawn (via the WM_PAINT message) whenever the window size changes to insure that the pixel is always at the center of our window.

The WM_PAINT message is the most important message for any program that draws in a window. Like a bull in a china shop, the user can cause quite a bit of damage as he tromps across the display screen: windows are moved, resized, opened, and closed. Dialog boxes are brought up and dismissed, and data is scrolled inside various windows.

Each of these actions can cause holes to appear in the user interface. Windows does its best to patch these holes, but in many cases Windows can't do it alone. In particular, when the client area of a window has been overwritten, Windows has a limited ability to repair the damage.

There are occasions when Windows is able to anticipate that an object (like a dialog box or a menu) will overwrite a window for a very short period of time. In these cases, Windows takes a snapshot of the area that is about to be overwritten. When the short-term guest disappears, Windows restores the screen without any outside help.

But such snapshots are quite memory intensive, and so Windows only does this when it is critical to the performance of the user interface. For example, Windows takes a snapshot of the area that a menu is going to overwrite. This allows a menu to appear and disappear very quickly. Otherwise, if this critical part of the user interface ran slowly, it would make the entire system seem sluggish.

Most of the time, Windows calls on your program to help repair a hole in the user interface. The request arrives as a WM_PAINT message. In response to WM_PAINT, a window procedure repairs the damaged window by redrawing its contents. This requires the window procedure to obtain a DC, which gives it the drawing tools, device access, and permission slip it needs to draw in a window.

The BeginPaint Routine

As shown in our PIXEL program, the `BeginPaint` routine provides a DC handle that a program uses in responding to the WM_PAINT message. BeginPaint borrows a DC from the supply that the Window Manager maintains. This routine is specially designed to work with the WM_PAINT message, because it installs a clipping region in the DC that corresponds to the damaged part of our window. This area is sometimes referred to as a window's **invalid region**, or **invalid rectangle** if the region is defined in terms of a simple rectangle.

The invalid region might consist of the entire client area of our window, but in many cases it includes only a portion of the client area. For example, Figure 7.2 shows CLOCK and PIXEL sharing the display screen, with one corner of CLOCK covering part of PIXEL's client area. When we click on PIXEL to activate its window, the covered part of the PIXEL's client area must be redrawn. That's the job of the WM_PAINT message. The dotted lines in the figure show the shape of the clipping region that is installed in the DC that BeginPaint returns. By making the invalid region a subset of the total client area, the Window Manager helps minimize the amount of effort that is required to repair a damaged window.

Figure 7.2   *CLOCK covering part of PIXEL's client area*

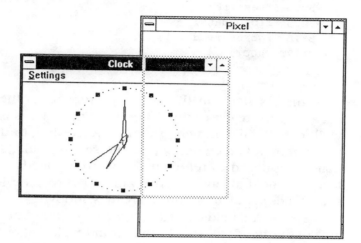

From our earlier discussion on clipping, you may recall that the clipping rectangle shown in Figure 7.2 only allows drawing inside the boundaries of the clipping fence. Outside the fence, no drawing is allowed. Why is clipping set in this manner?

Recall that the purpose of a WM_PAINT message is to repair damage to a window. As shown in the example, the clipping fence surrounds the exact part of the window that has been damaged. On the one hand, this is the only area in which our program will be allowed to draw. But on the other hand, this is the only part into which we need to draw. After all, by definition we don't need to draw into the undamaged part of our window in response to a WM_PAINT message.

Let's take a closer look at the code involved with handling the WM_PAINT message, to get a better idea of what is involved.

BeginPaint takes two parameters: a window handle and a pointer to a PAINTSTRUCT data structure. The window handle identifies the window whose client area is to be repaired.

The PAINTSTRUCT data structure is defined in Windows.h as follows:

```
typedef struct tagPAINTSTRUCT
    {
    HDC    hdc;
    BOOL   fErase;
```

```
    RECT    rcPaint;
    BOOL    fRestore;
    BOOL    fIncUpdate;
    BYTE    rgbReserved[16];
} PAINTSTRUCT;
```

Of the six fields in this data structure, only the first and third, rcPaint, are really useful. The first field, hdc, is a DC handle that we'll pass to GDI drawing routines. According to the Windows Development Kit documentation, the second field, fErase, is a flag that is supposed to tell us if our window needs erasing or not. In fact, this field always has the value of zero. The fourth, fifth, and sixth fields are all used internally by Windows.

The rcPaint field describes a rectangle that bounds the damaged area of our window—that is, the invalid region of our window. While most programs ignore this field, it serves as a hint that a program can use to minimize the amount of work it forces GDI to do. For example, if a program did a lot of drawing in a window, it might use this rectangle to decide exactly what needed to be repaired inside the window. By pre-clipping to this rectangle, drawing intensive programs can get a substantial performance improvement.

BeginPaint gives us a handle to a DC , which is all we need to draw our pixel. Let's look at the other routines that our window procedure calls in response to the WM_PAINT message.

GetClientRect Routine

Earlier, we compared a window to a canvas on which an artist draws. Unlike an artist's canvas, however, a window can change size. To help you cope with that change, the GetClientRect routine allows you to determine the size of a window's client area (saving this information from the WM_SIZE message also does the trick). GetClientRect takes two parameters:

- A Window Handle. We use the window handle that was passed to our window procedure.
- A Pointer to a Rectangle (RECT) Data Structure. The size of the client area, in pixels, is returned in this structure.

The RECT structure is defined in Windows.h as shown here:

```
typedef struct tagRECT
  {
    int  left;
    int  top;
    int  right;
    int  bottom;
  } RECT;
```

One aspect of this routine is that it always returns zero in two of these fields: `left` and `top`, so they can be safely ignored. To determine the width and height of a client area, the `right` and `bottom` fields are used. We position the pixel in the middle of the client area using the values r.right/2 and r.bottom/2 as X and Y coordinates.

SetPixel Routine

The SetPixel routine takes four parameters:

```
SetPixel (hDC, X, Y, crColor);
```

- Handle to a Device Context. We use the handle provided by BeginPaint.
- X and Y Coordinates. We positioned the pixel in the middle of the client area by dividing the values returned in GetClientRect by two.
- Color. GDI provides three ways to specify color: an RGB triplet, a palette index, and a palette relative RGB triplet.

An RGB triplet gets its name from its three parts: a red value, a green value, and a blue value. An RGB triplet is always an unsigned long integer, that is, a four-byte-wide, 32-bit value. Three of the bytes are used to store the red, green, and blue intensity of the color you are looking for. With one byte per color, that means there are 256 intensities for each color, and over 16 million unique combinations.

The RGB macro in Windows.H provides the easiest means for creating an RGB triplet. The syntax for this macro is

```
rgbColor = RGB (bRed, bGreen, bBlue)
```

where bRed, bGreen, and bBlue are integers between 0 and 255. The RGB macro packs the intensity of all three colors into a single unsigned long integer.

Although you can specify over 16 million different RGB combinations, the actual color that is produced will depend on the device. For example, the 16-color EGA adapter will map the RGB values to the nearest available physical color. When we talk about pens, we'll talk about how GDI **dithers** to simulate many more colors on a device. But for pixels, the only colors that are available are the physical, or "pure," colors. Two RGB triplets have guaranteed results: RGB (0, 0, 0) is always black, and RGB (255, 255, 255) is always white.

A second way to specify color is with a palette index. A Palette is a table of RBG triplets. Therefore, at first glance, a palette index is another way to specify an RGB triplet.

But unlike RGB triplets, palettes allow a program to specify the exact physical color that should be represented. For example, the VGA and 8514/a display adapters have hardware that supports 262,144 different colors. But only 256 of these colors are available at any one moment. The device driver selects a palette that is distributed evenly across the color range. But this isn't good enough for some uses. Palettes allow a program to select the exact colors to be used in the 256 available slots.

On devices that support GDI palettes, a program can actually change the hardware registers of a device to represent the exact set of colors that are required. For example, if a program wants to display a color bitmap of a woodland scene, it might need 150 shades of green to show all the subtle nuances in the grasses, trees, and shrubs. Or a color bitmap of skiers on a snow-covered mountain might require 100 shades of white, 50 shades of hot-pink and orange, and 10 shades of blue. Palettes allow a program to show images like these on a display screen with near picture-perfect representation.

Like RGB triplets, palette indices are unsigned long integers. The only difference is that a flag is set in the fourth, unused byte to indicate that the value is a palette index and not an actual RGB triplet. The PALETTEINDEX macro selects a palette index value. For example, to select color number 137, you would use the following:

```
PALETTEINDEX (137);
```

The third and final way to specify color is with a palette-relative RGB index. Like an RGB triplet, this allows you to specify a red, green, and blue portion of a color. But a PALETTEINDEX color is never dithered. Instead, GDI finds the nearest pure color in the existing palette, and uses it. The PALETTERGB macro creates this type of color reference:

```
PALETTERGB (0, 128, 255);
```

EndPaint Routine

After all the drawing for the WM_PAINT message is done, a program calls the EndPaint routine to return the display DC to the Window Manager. When the Window Manager receives the DC, it restores all the drawing attributes to the default state so that the DC is ready to be loaned to the next program that needs to draw in a window.

The EndPaint routine also notifies the Window Manager that the damaged window has been repaired. In Windows' terms, the *invalid* part of a window has been made *valid*. Later in this chapter, you'll see that a program can call the InvalidateRect routine to declare a client area damaged, which causes a WM_PAINT message to be generated. The EndPaint routine calls another Windows library routine, ValidateRect, which tells the Window Manager to recognize that the window has been repaired.

If a program does not call EndPaint in response to a WM_PAINT message, the Window Manager will send a constant stream of WM_PAINT messages. Until the Window Manager is told that a window has been repaired, it will continue to ask you to repair it—which it does via the WM_PAINT message.

The use of the BeginPaint/EndPaint pair is the standard way that programs respond to WM_PAINT. As you'll see, the use of a pair of routines like this is common in other parts of Windows programming: for locking memory, reading files, and accessing the Clipboard. We call this construction the **windows sandwich**. Let's take a moment to describe this construction in more detail.

The Windows Sandwich

A construction that you will encounter often in your Windows programming career is what we call the windows sandwich. While

Figure 7.3   *The Windows programming sandwich*

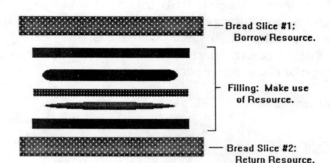

Bread Slice #1: Borrow Resource.

Filling: Make use of Resource.

Bread Slice #2: Return Resource.

this term is not something you will read about in any book on structured programming, it is important in Windows programming.

Like its culinary counterpart, the Windows sandwich has three parts: two outside pieces (the bread) which serve to hold the third part: the filling. When I was a child, my mother made sandwiches with two pieces of wheat bread and a filling of peanut butter and jelly. All three ingredients were important to the proper creation of my lunchtime meal. When making a sandwich for lunch, it's important to remember all three ingredients. It is also important to arrange the three ingredients in the proper order.

Figure 7.3 shows the three parts of the Windows programming sandwich. The first piece of bread represents a line of code that grabs a resource. The second piece of bread is the final line of code that returns the resource. In between, the filling is made up of one or more lines of code.

This construction is important because there are certain resources that you must share with every other program that's running. Windows is a multitasking system, after all. Programs must cooperate with each other to share the scarce resources of the system. The sandwich represents the most common way that this is done.

The resource we borrow might be a connection to a graphics output device, a disk file, or the Windows clipboard. In general, a sandwich holds the resource for the duration of a single message, like the DC that we borrow in response to the WM_PAINT message.

```
case WM_PAINT:
     BeginPaint(hWnd, &ps);      /* Top slice.    */
          .
          .                      /* Filling.      */
          .
     EndPaint (hWnd, &ps);       /* Bottom slice. */
```

The BeginPaint call borrows the DC from the Window Manager. A handle to that resource is stored in the variable hdc. From that line until the EndPaint line, the program has complete use of the DC. The filling of this sandwich in our PIXEL program drew a single pixel on the display. Once the EndPaint routine returns the DC, we no longer have access to it. Our program should not try to draw in the window after the second slice of bread.

You don't have to be a chef at a four-star restaurant to tell that these sandwiches have been made incorrectly. The problem with this first sandwich is that the filling is outside the bread. You have jelly on your fingers:

```
/*  Don't do this: jelly on your fingers.  */
case WM_PAINT:
     BeginPaint(hwnd, &ps);// Top Slice
     EndPaint (hwnd, &ps);      //  Bottom Slice
     SetPixel (ps.hdc, x, y, RGB (0, 0, 0)); // Filling
     break;
```

This sandwich is only made from a single slice of bread: the bottom slice of bread is missing. Again, you have jelly on your fingers:

```
/*  Don't do this: only one slice of bread.  */
case WM_PAINT:
     BeginPaint(hwnd, &ps);// Top Slice
     SetPixel (ps.hdc, x, y, RGB (0, 0, 0)); // Filling
     break;
```

This sandwich is made without any bread at all. Peanut butter and jelly everywhere. Yuk.

```
/*  Don't do this: No bread at all.  */
case WM_PAINT:
    SetPixel (ps.hdc, x, y, RGB (0, 0, 0)); // Filling
    break;
```

A few sandwich constructions span multiple messages. You might call this a double-decker sandwich, or a Dagwood Sandwich (named for the cartoon character who liked to make huge sandwiches). An example involves the capture of the mouse pointer. Sometimes, it is advantageous for a program to request exclusive use of the mouse pointer. Here is the code structure for such a sandwich:

```
case WM_LBUTTONDOWN:
    SetCapture(hWnd);   /* Top slice.          */
    .
    .
    break;
case WM_MOUSEMOVE:
    .                   /* Filling.            */
    .
    break;
case WM_LBUTTONUP:
    ReleaseCapture();   /* Bottom slice.       */
    break;
```

We'll take a closer look at this double-decker sandwich in Chapter 17, when we discuss mouse input. Let's move on to our next drawing primitive. This is not actually a GDI primitive, but one that we're going to build on top of the SetPixel routine.

Creating Markers

Our second GDI program introduces a type of drawing primitive that is not native to GDI: **markers**. The most obvious use of a marker is on a graph, like the one in Figure 7.4. Each "+" symbol is a marker. In this example, each marker represents a population value for a given year.

Figure 7.4 *Markers highlight points on a graph*

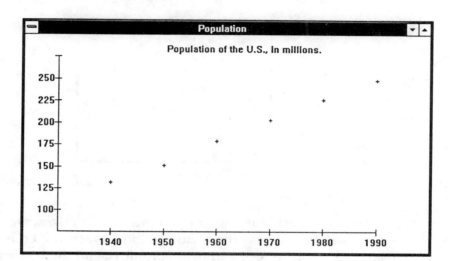

At first glance, you might wonder why markers are special. After all, from the chart it is clear that GDI can display text. What's the difference between a marker and a text character?

As you'll see in Chapter 10, GDI text routines make it easy to work with different sizes and styles of text on a variety of devices. This very flexibility makes it difficult to guarantee that a specific letter will be centered on a specific location.

For example, if you used GDI letters to mark the location of buried treasure on a map, you introduce a margin of error. The location of the cross-hairs on the letter X, for example, will move depending on the font you are using.

Markers overcome this limitation since a marker is guaranteed to be centered over an exact location. That's the reason that markers are used for graphs. In the chapters that follow, you'll see that we use markers to help explain all of the GDI drawing routines.

One way to mark a location is with the SetPixel routine that we introduced in the preceding section. But a single pixel is often hard to see. For this reason, we create our "+" marker by grouping several pixels together.

From this, it should be clear that a marker primitive is a useful part of any graphics library, even if Microsoft left it out of GDI. In fact, other graphic libraries have marker routines, including Microsoft's OS/2 Presentation Manager.

Figure 7.5 *Sample output of MARKER*

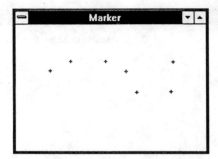

When we introduce other GDI drawing primitives, we're going to use markers to show the relationship between the coordinates we specify when we call a drawing primitive and the resulting output. This will help clarify GDI's "inclusive-exclusive" drawing approach, and help you see how GDI creates lines, filled areas, and text output.

Figure 7.5 shows a sample of the output produced by our marker program, MARKER.C. This program uses mouse input to place markers.

Here are the source files to MARKER:

MARKER.MAK

```
Marker.res: Marker.rc Marker.cur Marker.ico
    rc -r Marker.rc

Marker.obj: Marker.c
    cl -AM -c -d -Gsw -Od -W2 -Zpi Marker.c

marker.exe: Marker.obj Marker.def
    link Marker,/align:16,/map, mlibcew libw/NOD/NOE/CO,\
        Marker.def
    rc Marker.res marker.exe

marker.exe: Marker.res
    rc Marker.res marker.exe
```

MARKER.C

```
/*----------------------------------------------------------------*\
|    MARKER.C  -  Draws a marker in response to a mouse click. |
\*----------------------------------------------------------------*/
#include <Windows.H>


/*----------------------------------------------------------------*\
|                  Function Prototypes.                           |
\*----------------------------------------------------------------*/
long FAR  PASCAL MarkerWndProc (HWND, WORD, WORD, LONG);
VOID NEAR PASCAL MarkerDrawMarker (HDC hdc, int x, int y);


/*----------------------------------------------------------------*\
|                  Main Function:  WinMain.                        |
\*----------------------------------------------------------------*/
int PASCAL WinMain (HANDLE hInstance,   HANDLE hPrevInstance,
                    LPSTR  lpszCmdLine, int    cmdShow)
    {
    HWND      hwnd;
    MSG       msg;
    WNDCLASS  wndclass;

    if (!hPrevInstance)
        {
        wndclass.lpszClassName = "MARKER:MAIN";
        wndclass.hInstance     = hInstance;
        wndclass.lpfnWndProc   = MarkerWndProc;
        wndclass.hCursor       = LoadCursor (hInstance, "hand");
        wndclass.hIcon         = LoadIcon (hInstance,"snapshot");
        wndclass.lpszMenuName  = NULL;
        wndclass.hbrBackground = COLOR_WINDOW+1;
        wndclass.style         = CS_HREDRAW | CS_VREDRAW;
        wndclass.cbClsExtra    = 0;
        wndclass.cbWndExtra    = 0;

        RegisterClass( &wndclass);
        }

    hwnd = CreateWindow("MARKER:MAIN",          /* Class name.  */
                        "Markers",              /* Title.       */
```

```
                              WS_OVERLAPPEDWINDOW,   /* Style bits.   */
                              CW_USEDEFAULT,         /* x - default.  */
                              0,                     /* y - default.  */
                              CW_USEDEFAULT,         /* cx - default. */
                              0,                     /* cy - default. */
                              NULL,                  /* No parent.    */
                              NULL,                  /* Class menu.   */
                              hInstance,             /* Creator       */
                              NULL                   /* Params.       */
                          ) ;

    ShowWindow (hwnd, cmdShow);

    while (GetMessage(&msg, 0, 0, 0)) /*  Get queued input.    */
        {
        TranslateMessage(&msg);        /*  Keyboard input.      */
        DispatchMessage(&msg);         /*  Call window proc.    */
        }
    return 0;
    }


/*-------------------------------------------------------------------*\
|              Window Procedure:  MarkerWndProc.                      |
\*-------------------------------------------------------------------*/
long FAR PASCAL MarkerWndProc (HWND hwnd,  WORD msg,
                               WORD wParam,LONG lParam)

    {
    static POINT   pt[32];
    static int     cpt = 0;

    switch (msg)
        {
        case WM_DESTROY:
            PostQuitMessage(0);
            break;

        case WM_LBUTTONDOWN:
            if (cpt < 32)
                {
                pt[cpt] = MAKEPOINT (lParam);
                cpt++;
```

```
                    InvalidateRect (hwnd, NULL, TRUE);
                    }
            break;

        case WM_PAINT:
            {
            PAINTSTRUCT ps;
            int i;

            BeginPaint (hwnd, &ps);
            for (i=0; i< cpt; i++)
                MarkerDrawMarker (ps.hdc, pt[i].x, pt[i].y);
            EndPaint (hwnd, &ps);
            }
            break;

        default:
            return(DefWindowProc(hwnd,msg,wParam,lParam));
            break;
        }
    return 0L;
    }

#define MARKERSIZE 3
VOID NEAR PASCAL MarkerDrawMarker (HDC hdc, int x, int y)
    {
    DWORD dwColor;
    int i;

    dwColor = GetPixel (hdc, x, y);
    dwColor = ~dwColor;
    SetPixel (hdc, x, y, dwColor);

    for (i=1;i<=MARKERSIZE; i++)
        {
        dwColor = GetPixel (hdc, x+i, y);
        dwColor = ~dwColor;
        SetPixel (hdc, x+i, y, dwColor);

        dwColor = GetPixel (hdc, x-i, y);
        dwColor = ~dwColor;
```

```
        SetPixel (hdc, x-i, y, dwColor);

        dwColor = GetPixel (hdc, x, y+i);
        dwColor = ~dwColor;
        SetPixel (hdc, x, y+i, dwColor);

        dwColor = GetPixel (hdc, x, y-i);
        dwColor = ~dwColor;
        SetPixel (hdc, x, y-i, dwColor);
        }


    }
```

MARKER.RC

```
snapshot icon Marker.ico

hand   cursor Marker.cur
```

MARKER.DEF

```
NAME    MARKER

EXETYPE WINDOWS

DESCRIPTION 'Marker Demo'

CODE    MOVEABLE DISCARDABLE
DATA    MOVEABLE MULTIPLE

HEAPSIZE    512
STACKSIZE   5000

EXPORTS
    MarkerWndProc
```

The window procedure in our program, MrkWndProc, processes three messages: WM_DESTROY, WM_LBUTTONDOWN, and WM_PAINT. We respond to WM_DESTROY in the same way that all top-level window procedures do: We post a WM_QUIT message to cause our GetMessage loop to terminate.

The WM_LBUTTONDOWN is a mouse message. Our window procedure receives a WM_LBUTTONDOWN message when two things happen at the same time: the mouse cursor is in our client area, and the user pushes the left mouse button.

Every time the window procedure receives this mouse message, it records the X and Y location of the mouse cursor. For all mouse messages, the cursor location is provided in the lParam parameter, in client area coordinates. As you may recall, this coordinate system has its origin (0,0) at the upper left corner of the client area.

In response to the WM_LBUTTONDOWN message, we store the X and Y location of the mouse cursor in an array of POINT structures. The POINT data type is defined in Windows.h as

```
typedef struct tagPOINT
   {
   int   x;
   int   y;
   } POINT;
```

The line:

```
pt[cpt] = MAKEPOINT (lParam);
```

uses the MAKEPOINT macro to moves the four-byte lParam value into the four-byte point structure.

Once a new point has been added to the array, our program forces the window to be redrawn:

```
InvalidateRect (hwnd, NULL, TRUE);
```

This routine causes a WM_PAINT message to be generating by telling Windows that "the window is completely damaged."

InvalidateRect takes three parameters:

- Handle of the window to be redrawn.
- A far pointer to a rectangle that is being declared damaged. NULL means that the entire window is to be redrawn.
- An "erase first" flag. TRUE means erase the background before redrawing; FALSE means do not erase first.

In response to the WM_PAINT message, our MARKER program uses the BeginPaint/ EndPaint sandwich to borrow a DC from the Window Manager. The filling of the sandwich is a loop that calls our marker routine, MrkDrawMarker, giving the X and Y location of every point in the array pt.

The marker routine, MrkDrawMarker, is built using two GDI routines: GetPixel and SetPixel. In general, if you don't find a GDI drawing routine that creates the exact output that you need, it is often a simple matter to write a routine that builds on top of existing GDI routines, as we've done here.

One word of caution. GetPixel and SetPixel are not supported on all devices (like some printers and plotters), so you may wish to rewrite this routine using a line drawing primitive from the next chapter.

Our last program, PIXEL, wrote a single black pixel with the following call:

```
SetPixel (hdc, r.right/2, r.bottom/2, RGB (0,0,0));
```

We could draw a black marker by simply making several calls like this. But what happens when we try to draw a marker on an area that is already black? The marker disappears.

Our marker routine solves this problem with Boolean algebra. Before we write a pixel, we read a pixel with the GetPixel routine. GetPixel returns an RGB triplet that lets us know the color of the pixel. We perform a bit-wise negation of the RGB value to invert the color, and write a pixel with a call to SetPixel. Here is a code fragment to show what we mean:

```
dwColor = GetPixel (hdc, x, y);
dwColor = ~dwColor;
SetPixel (hdc, x, y, dwColor);
```

By making a series of calls like this, we draw a marker that will show up on just about any surface, regardless of its original color.

The ˜ operator performs a one's complement on the operand, which in this case is an RGB triplet value. All of the zeros are turned into ones, and all of the ones into zeros. While this might seem strange, in fact this type of Boolean arithmetic is very useful in the world of graphics. Later on, we'll describe how **drawing modes** let us perform logical operation when we draw lines, fill areas, or copy bitmaps.

For now, though, you can rest assured that this approach will be effective in making a mark on a display surface. This approach has one shortcoming: two markers placed at the same location have the effect of negating each other. The markers disappear! Can you think of a way to solve this problem?

One way around this problem would require your program to walk the list of points every time it draws. If it finds a duplicate point, it simply ignores it instead of drawing it. Another way to avoid this problem might involve walking the list of points every time the user clicks the mouse. If a point has already been highlighted, a program could beep at the user to announce that the point is invalid.

We introduced the marker routine to help describe how native GDI routines work. Let's put our markers to work helping us understand the way that GDI draws lines. This is the subject of the next chapter.

8
Drawing Lines

Before we begin to draw lines with GDI routines, let's stop to consider: *What exactly is a line, anyway* ? A line is a geometric figure created by joining a set of points. Lines are considered **open figures**, meaning that our interest is in the line itself, and not on the area around the line. In the next chapter, we're going to look at **closed figures**, in which a line plus the area it surrounds make up a single geometric figure.

A GDI line is a geometric figure drawn by a GDI line drawing routine. Every GDI line has a starting point and an ending point. GDI draws lines using what graphics programmers refer to as an **inclusive/exclusive algorithm**. That is, the starting point is *included* in the line, but the ending point is *excluded*.

Let's use the ZoomIn tool from the Software Development Kit to convince ourselves that this is the case. ZoomIn lets you magnify the pixels on any part of the display screen. Figure 8.1 shows a GDI line with markers to highlight the end points and the ZoomIn utility to show the inclusive/exclusive drawing.

The white pixel in the center of the marker at the starting point shows that starting point is *included* in the line. The marker, after all, is drawn by inverting the existing pixels: The inverse of black gives us white. The center of the marker at the ending point, however, is black, indicating that the ending point has been *excluded* from the line.

Although inclusive/exclusive drawing may seem odd at first, it lets you draw complex figures by making many simple line drawing calls. Each new figure picks up where the other left off. And as we'll see in Chapter 16, when we create dragable objects for the mouse pointer, this is especially important when using different drawing modes.

As you'll see, inclusive/exclusive drawing is used by all of GDI's line drawing routines. Let's take a brief tour through the available

Figure 8.1   *ZoomIn shows GDI's inclusive/exclusive line drawing*

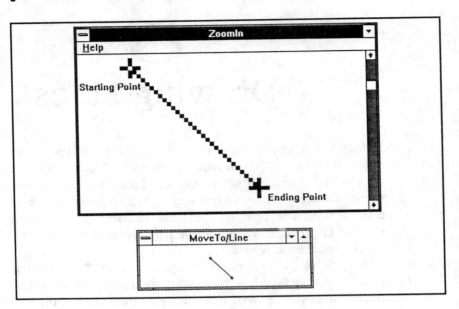

routines, to see what GDI can do for us. After that, we'll review the DC attributes that affect line drawing, concentrating our attention on the most important line drawing attribute: pens.

Line Drawing Primitives

GDI has four line drawing routines: MoveTo, LineTo, Polyline, and Arc. We'll consider each in turn. Let's start with the first two routines, which are always used together, MoveTo and LineTo.

MoveTo and LineTo

Our first routine, MoveTo, doesn't actually draw lines. Instead, it stores a pair of X and Y values in a DC attribute called the **current position**. The second routine, LineTo, uses this value as a starting point for a line. The LineTo function itself provides the ending point as a parameter. Here is how you use these routines to draw a line from point X1,Y1 to point X2, Y2:

```
MoveTo (hdc, X1, Y1);
LineTo (hdc, X2, Y2);
```

After the LineTo function has drawn a line, it updates the value of the current position in the DC to reflect the end point of the line. You can connect a series of points by making calls like the following:

```
MoveTo (hdc, X1, Y1);
LineTo (hdc, X2, Y2);
LineTo (hdc, X3, Y3);
LineTo (hdc, X4, Y4);
```

When these routines are called in this way, they produce the same result as our next routine, the Polyline function. You might wonder why GDI has this kind of redundancy.

It is partly a question of convenience. You will find that MoveTo/LineTo requires less work, since each takes an X,Y value as a parameter. The Polyline function, on the other hand, requires the X,Y values to be stored in an array of POINTS.

Although it requires its parameters in a special format, the Polyline routine is the obvious choice when performance is important. The speed advantage is a direct result of the overhead incurred when a function is called. One Polyline call will draw many lines. Using MoveTo/LineTo, many calls would be required to draw the same lines.

Like the MoveTo/LineTo pair, Polyline draws straight lines. Unlike this pair, however, Polyline does not use the current position value in the DC. Instead, it relies solely on an array of POINTS that are passed as a parameter. If we store the points (x1, y1), (x2, y2), (x3, y3), and (x4, y4) in an array like this:

```
POINTS pt[] = {x1, y1, x2, y2, x3, y3, x4, y4};
```

the following call to Polyline connects the points:

```
Polyline (hdc, pt, 4);
```

The Arc function draws a curved line. The parameters to Arc define three boundaries: a bounding box, a starting point, and an ending point (see Figure 8.2). If the starting point and the ending point are the same, the Arc function draws a complete ellipse (or a circle, if the bounding box is a square). Otherwise, Arc draws a portion of an ellipse.

With the other line-drawing functions, the relationship of starting point to ending point was important, since GDI uses inclusive/ex-

Figure 8.2 *The ARC function*

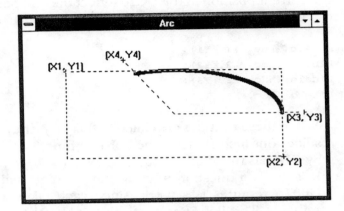

clusive drawing. This is also true for arcs. In addition, arcs are always drawn in a counterclockwise direction. Figure 8.3 shows how two different curves are drawn if the starting and ending points are swapped.

Our line drawing program is really three programs in one, with one version for each line-drawing primitive. Each version records mouse clicks in an array of POINTS, and uses the points to demonstrate one of the line primitives. The creation of a version is controlled by conditional preprocessor statements. In our listing, the following #define statement controls the version that is created:

```
#define ARC
```

Figure 8.3 *Arcs are drawn counterclockwise*

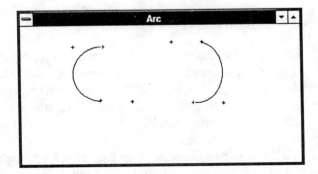

Figure 8.4 *The three primitives that LINES can draw*

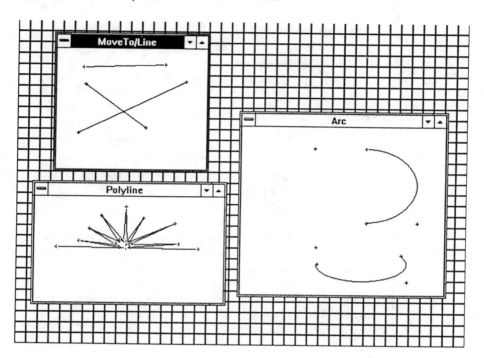

Figure 8.4 shows the output created by each versions of our program. A complete listing of all the files that make up LINES is shown below.

LINES.MAK

```
Lines.res: Lines.rc Lines.cur Lines.ico
    rc -r Lines.rc

Lines.obj: Lines.c
    cl -AM -c -d -Gsw -Od -W2 -Zpi Lines.c

lines.exe: Lines.obj Lines.def
    link Lines,/align:16,/map, mlibcew libw/NOD/NOE/CO,\
        Lines.def
    rc Lines.res lines.exe
```

```
lines.exe: Lines.res
    rc Lines.res lines.exe
```

LINES.C

```
/*----------------------------------------------------------------*\
|    LINES.C  GDI Program #3 - Line Drawing Primitives.  To        |
|             draw lines with LineTo, define value of LINETEO      |
|             as in:                                               |
|                     #define LINETO                               |
|             To create an Arc drawing program, use:               |
|                     #define ARC                                  |
|             and for a Polyline program:                          |
|                     #define POLYLINE                             |
\*----------------------------------------------------------------*/
#define LINETO


#include <Windows.H>
/*----------------------------------------------------------------*\
|                      Function Prototypes.                        |
\*----------------------------------------------------------------*/
long FAR  PASCAL LinWndProc (HWND, WORD, WORD, LONG);
VOID NEAR PASCAL MrkDrawMarker (HDC hdc, int x, int y);


#ifdef LINETO
char szWindowTitle[] = "MoveTo/Line";
#endif
#ifdef ARC
char szWindowTitle[] = "Arc";
#endif
#ifdef POLYLINE
char szWindowTitle[] = "Polyline";
#endif


/*----------------------------------------------------------------*\
|                   Main Function:  WinMain.                       |
\*----------------------------------------------------------------*/
```

```
int PASCAL WinMain (HANDLE hInstance,
                    HANDLE hPrevInstance,
                    LPSTR  lpszCmdLine,
                    int    cmdShow)
    {
    HWND      hwnd;
    MSG       msg;
    WNDCLASS wndclass;

    if (!hPrevInstance)
        {
        wndclass.lpszClassName = "LINES:MAIN";
        wndclass.hInstance     = hInstance;
        wndclass.lpfnWndProc   = LinWndProc;
        wndclass.hCursor       = LoadCursor (hInstance, "hand");
        wndclass.hIcon         = LoadIcon (hInstance,"snapshot");
        wndclass.lpszMenuName  = NULL;
        wndclass.hbrBackground = COLOR_WINDOW+1;
        wndclass.style         = CS_HREDRAW | CS_VREDRAW;
        wndclass.cbClsExtra    = 0;
        wndclass.cbWndExtra    = 0;

        RegisterClass( &wndclass);
        }

    hwnd = CreateWindow("LINES:MAIN",       /* Class name.   */
                        szWindowTitle,      /* Title.        */
                        WS_OVERLAPPEDWINDOW, /* Style bits.  */
                        CW_USEDEFAULT,      /* x - default.  */
                        0,                  /* y - default.  */
                        CW_USEDEFAULT,      /* cx - default. */
                        0,                  /* cy - default. */
                        NULL,               /* No parent.    */
                        NULL,               /* Class menu.   */
                        hInstance,          /* Creator       */
                        NULL                /* Params.       */
                        ) ;

    ShowWindow (hwnd, cmdShow);

    while (GetMessage(&msg, 0, 0, 0))
```

```
        {
        TranslateMessage(&msg);          /* Keyboard input.      */
        DispatchMessage(&msg);
        }
    return 0;
    }

/*------------------------------------------------------------*\
|                Window Procedure:  LinWndProc.                |
\*------------------------------------------------------------*/
long FAR PASCAL LinWndProc (HWND      hwnd,
                            WORD      msg,
                            WORD      wParam,
                            LONG      lParam)
    {
    static POINT    pt[32];
    static int      cpt = 0;
    static int      fDrawRectangle = 0;

    switch (msg)
        {
        case WM_CREATE:
            pt[0].x = 100; pt[0].y = 20;
            pt[1].x = 130; pt[1].y = 50;
            cpt = 2;
            break;

        case WM_DESTROY:
            PostQuitMessage(0);
            break;

        case WM_LBUTTONDOWN:
            if (cpt < 32)
                {
                pt[cpt] = MAKEPOINT (lParam);
                cpt++;
                InvalidateRect (hwnd, NULL, TRUE);
                }
            break;

        case WM_RBUTTONDOWN:
```

```
                    /* Xor operator to toggle drawing switch.  */
                    fDrawRectangle= fDrawRectangle ^ 1;
                    InvalidateRect (hwnd, NULL, TRUE);
                    break;

            case WM_PAINT:
                {
                PAINTSTRUCT ps;
                int i;

                    BeginPaint (hwnd, &ps);

#ifdef LINETO
                    for (i=0;i<cpt;i+=2)
                        {
                        MoveTo (ps.hdc, pt[i].x, pt[i].y);
                        LineTo (ps.hdc, pt[i+1].x, pt[i+1].y);
                        }
#endif

#ifdef ARC
                    SelectObject (ps.hdc, GetStockObject (NULL_BRUSH));
                    for (i=0;i<cpt;i+=4)
                        {
                        Arc (ps.hdc, pt[i].x, pt[i].y,
                                     pt[i+1].x, pt[i+1].y,
                                     pt[i+2].x, pt[i+2].y,
                                     pt[i+3].x, pt[i+3].y);
                        if (fDrawRectangle)
                            Rectangle (ps.hdc, pt[i].x, pt[i].y,
                                               pt[i+1].x, pt[i+1].y);
                        }
#endif

#ifdef POLYLINE
                    Polyline (ps.hdc, pt, cpt);
#endif
                    for (i=0; i< cpt; i++)
                        MrkDrawMarker (ps.hdc, pt[i].x, pt[i].y);
                    EndPaint (hwnd, &ps);
                }
                break;
```

```
        default:
            return(DefWindowProc(hwnd,msg,wParam,lParam));
            break;
        }
    return 0L;
    }


#define MARKERSIZE 2
VOID NEAR PASCAL MrkDrawMarker (HDC hdc, int x, int y)
    {
    DWORD dwColor;
    int i;

    dwColor = GetPixel (hdc, x, y);
    dwColor = ~dwColor;
    SetPixel (hdc, x, y, dwColor);

    for (i=1;i<=MARKERSIZE; i++)
        {
        dwColor = GetPixel (hdc, x+i, y);
        dwColor = ~dwColor;
        SetPixel (hdc, x+i, y, dwColor);

        dwColor = GetPixel (hdc, x-i, y);
        dwColor = ~dwColor;
        SetPixel (hdc, x-i, y, dwColor);

        dwColor = GetPixel (hdc, x, y+i);
        dwColor = ~dwColor;
        SetPixel (hdc, x, y+i, dwColor);

        dwColor = GetPixel (hdc, x, y-i);
        dwColor = ~dwColor;
        SetPixel (hdc, x, y-i, dwColor);
        }


    }
```

LINES.RC

```
snapshot icon Lines.ico

hand   cursor Lines.cur
```

LINES.DEF

```
NAME    LINES

EXETYPE WINDOWS

DESCRIPTION 'GDI Line drawing demo'

CODE    MOVEABLE DISCARDABLE
DATA    MOVEABLE MULTIPLE

HEAPSIZE    512
STACKSIZE   5000

EXPORTS
    LinWndProc
```

To help you get a better idea of the relationship between the Arc parameters and the actual Arc that is drawn, the program can draw the bounding rectangle that is specified by Arc's first two parameters. Figure 8.5 shows two copies of the program: one with the bounding rectangles, and one without. From the program listing, can you tell the user action that controls the display of a rectangle around the arc? It's the WM_RBUTTONDOWN message, of course. This message—which is generated when the user clicks with the right mouse button inside the client area of our window—toggles the value of fDrawRectangle between TRUE and FALSE. When it is TRUE, a bounding rectangle is drawn.

Now that we've looked at GDI's line drawing routines, let's examine the DC drawing attributes that affect lines.

Figure 8.5 *Two copies of ARC: One with and one without the bounding rectangle*

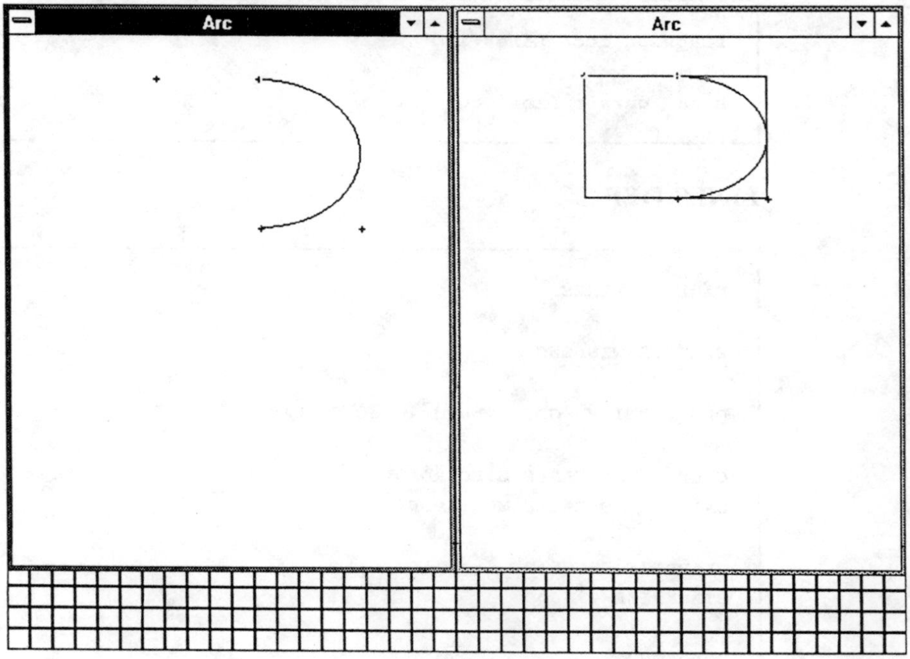

DC Attributes

Five DC attributes are used by the GDI to draw lines:

Drawing attribute	Comments
Background Color	second color for non-solid pens
Background Mode	turns on/off background color
Current Position	(x,y) position for LineTo routine
Drawing Mode	Boolean drawing operation
Pen	line color, width, and style

Without a doubt, the most important attribute is the pen, which determines the appearance of the line in terms of color, width, and style (or pattern, such as solid or dotted). The term **styled lines** is often used for lines with a non-solid style: dotted, dashed, etc.

The second most important attribute is the drawing mode, which lets us specify a Boolean operator to use in a drawing operation. More on that later.

Of the other three attributes, two affect *styled* lines, but not solid lines: background color and background mode. GDI uses the background color for the spaces between the lines—that is, between the foreground dashes or dots. The background mode toggles whether the background part of a styled line should be filled in or left alone. Keep in mind while using these two attributes that they also affect filled areas—when a hatched brush is used—and text.

The background color is set using the SetBkColor routine, defined as follows:

```
SetBkColor (hDC, crColor)
```

- hDC is a handle to a DC.
- crColor is a color reference value, using (a) RGB triplet, (b) palette index, or (c) palette relative RGB value.

The following line of code sets the background color to blue:

```
SetBkColor (hDC, RGB(0, 0, 0xFF)
```

To set the background mode, you call the SetBkMode routine, whose syntax is

```
SetBkMode (hDC, nBkMode)
```

- hDC is a handle to a DC.
- nBkMode is the on/off switch: Set to OPAQUE to enable background color, and to TRANSPARENT to disable background color.

The final attribute, the current position, is a DC attribute that we discussed in relation to the MoveTo/LineTo routines. It is an X,Y value that is used by these routines as part of their drawing: MoveTo sets the current position, LineTo uses it as the starting point for the line to draw. LineTo updates the current position to the end point of the line it draws.

Let's take a close look at pens, and the way they are created and manipulated.

About Pens

A pen is a DC drawing attribute that describes how lines are drawn. Pens have three qualities: color, width, and style. If you'd like, you can think of each of these qualities as a drawing attribute in its own right. In the world of graphics programming, when drawing attributes are grouped in this way, the group is called an **attribute bundle**. Attribute bundles are convenient because they let you refer to several drawing attributes at the same time.

GDI is very flexible in the way it lets you share pens: Pens can be shared between programs and between devices. GDI has a set of stock pens that any program can use, or a program can create a set of custom pens and let different devices share them. The net effect of this sharing is that GDI minimizes the amount of memory needed to store drawing attributes. GDI is thrifty with memory because earlier versions of Windows had to run in only 640K of RAM.

Pens and Device Independence

How can pens be used for different devices? The term **logical pen** describes how this is possible. A pen is a request to a device to create lines with a particular appearance. When GDI is ready to draw on a specific device, it makes a request to the device to **realize** a pen. Only at this time does the device driver create the data structures needed to draw lines with the desired qualities. This aspect is hidden in the GDI device-driver interface, but it allows a program to share pens between devices.

Creating and Using Pens

When Windows starts up, GDI creates a set of pens that can be shared by all programs. These are known as **stock pens**. GDI has three stock pens: one black, one white, and one null (invisible ink) pen. The null pen is a placeholder, since every DC must contain a valid pen. The other two pens draw solid lines with a width of one pixel.

Pens are identified by a handle. To get the handle of a stock pen, you call the GetStockObject routine, as shown here:

```
HPEN hpen;

hpen = GetStockObject (BLACK_PEN);   /* or */
hpen = GetStockObject (WHITE_PEN);   /* or */
hpen = GetStockObject (NULL_PEN);
```

Once you have a pen handle, you call another GDI routine to install the pen into the DC:

```
SelectObject (hdc, hpen);
```

After a pen has been selected into a DC, it is used for all subsequently drawn lines. This includes lines drawn with MoveTo/LineTo, Polyline, and Arc.

One thing about a DC is that it only has room for a single pen at any point in time. Therefore, by selecting one pen into a DC, you automatically remove the old pen. For your convenience, the Select-Object routine returns the handle of the pen being removed. For example, the following leaves the DC unchanged:

```
/* No Change to DC.  */
hpenOld = SelectObject (hdc, hpenNew);
SelectObject (hdc, hpenOld);
```

If the three stock pens do not provide you with all the line drawing capability that you need, GDI has two routines for creating pens: CreatePen and CreatePenIndirect. The only difference between these two routines is in the way parameters are specified. The syntax for CreatePen is

```
hpen = CreatePen (nPenStyle, nWidth, crColor);
```

- nPenStyle selects a pen style from the flags shown in Figure 8.6.
- nWidth sets the width in the X direction. Since we're limiting ourselves to pixels, the units are in pixels. But when we discuss coordinate transformations, you'll see that the width value reflects the coordinate system installed in the DC into which the pen is installed.
- crColor is a color reference; as before, it is (a) an RGB triplet, (b) a color palette index, or (c) a palette relative RGB value.

So to create a 1 pixel wide black solid pen, you say:

```
hpen = CreatePen (PS_SOLID, 1, RGB (0, 0, 0));
```

The syntax for CreatePenIndirect, on the other hand, is

```
LOGPEN logpen;
hpen = CreatePenIndirect (&logpen)
```

LOGPEN is defined in Windows.h as

```
typedef struct tagLOGPEN
  {
    WORD  lopnStyle;
    POINT lopnWidth;
    DWORD lopnColor;
  } LOGPEN;
```

One difference between CreatePen and CreatePenIndirect is that the LOGPEN structure uses a POINT structure to hold the pen width. As you may recall, the POINT structure has two members, one for an X value and one for a Y value. To create the same black pen as above, you say:

```
LOGPEN logpen;
logpen.lopnStyle = PS_SOLID;
logpen.lopnWidth.x = 1;
logpen.lopnColor = RGB (0, 0, 0));
hpen = CreatePenIndirect (&logpen)
```

GDI supports seven pen styles, as illustrated in Figure 8.6. The last style, PS_INSIDEFRAME, provides the same results as the PS_SOLID style with two important differences: color, and use in filled figures. This is the only line style that uses dithered colors. All other pens are only available in solid colors.

In the context of filled figures, the PS_INSIDEFRAME style has some unique features. As you'll see when we discuss filled figures, a pen with the style PS_INSIDEFRAME draws on the inside of the boundaries. Other pens are centered on the boundary so that half is

Figure 8.6 *GDI's seven pen styles*

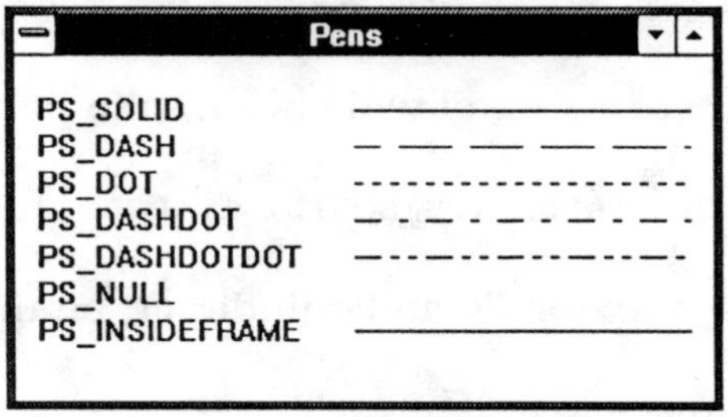

inside the border and half is outside. If this seems confusing, it will be made clear when we talk about filled figures.

You specify the width of a pen in logical units. This corresponds to the units of the current mapping mode in the x-axis. Since we have limited ourselves to the MM_TEXT mapping mode, this means that our units are pixels. When we discuss mapping modes in Chapter 25, we'll describe the effect of the mapping mode on pens. If you specify a pen width of zero, then regardless of the mapping mode, you will get a pen that is exactly 1 pixel wide.

Most GDI devices currently do not support *wide* styled lines—that is, styled lines that have a width greater than 1. For this reason, if you ask for a six-unit wide *dotted* pen, you will most likely get a six-unit wide *solid* pen. As hardware gets smarter, however, you'll see wide-styled lines on more devices. Until then, you should assume that if you want a non-solid pen, you'll have to settle for those that are 1 pixel wide.

Like pixel colors, pen colors are defined using one of three methods: an RGB triplet, a palette index value, or a palette relative RGB triplet. Whichever you choose, pens are ordinarily created from solid colors. The exception is pens with the PS_INSIDEFRAME style. The color of such a pen can include dithered colors.

Dithered colors are created by combining two or more colors. In the real-world, color mixing is nothing new. If you go to buy paint, for example, the store clerk might mix a little bit of black into a can of white paint to give it a shade of gray.

GDI creates dithered colors by combining two (or more) colors in a regular pattern to create the illusion of hundreds of colors on 16-color devices, like EGA and VGA display adapters. On monochrome devices, like the Hercules and CGA display adapters, dozens of shades of gray can be created using this technique. Dithering works so well that, without the aid of a special program like ZoomIn, it is often hard to tell a dithered color from a pure color.

Because dithered colors require a little more work for a device driver, only one pen style supports dithering: PS_INSIDEFRAME. Usually, dithering is reserved for brushes—a subject we'll cover when we discuss the creation of filled figures.

Figure 8.7 shows the output of our PENS program. Ten lines are drawn using all the pen styles. Each line has a marker to highlight the end points. Notice for the wide lines that the markers appear in the middle of each line. In addition, notice that the end of each line is rounded. To GDI, a pen is a round drawing object.

Figure 8.7   *Lines drawn using GDI pens*

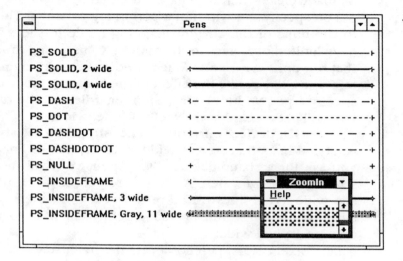

Another thing worth noting is the fact that, with the exception of PS_INSIDEFRAME pens, pens are limited to solid (nondithered) colors. With the help of ZoomIn, you can see that the line in our figure that was drawn with the PS_INSIDEFRAME pen is, in fact, dithered. Here is the listing of our PENS program:

PENS.MAK

```
Pens.res: Pens.rc Pens.cur Pens.ico
    rc -r Pens.rc

Pens.obj: Pens.c
    cl -AM -c -d -Gsw -Od -W2 -Zpi Pens.c

pens.exe: Pens.obj Pens.def
    link Pens,/align:16,/map, mlibcew libw/NOD/NOE/CO, Pens.def
    rc Pens.res pens.exe

pens.exe: Pens.res
    rc Pens.res pens.exe
```

PENS.C

```
/*------------------------------------------------------------*\
 |     PENS.C - Shows different types of pens.               |
\*------------------------------------------------------------*/
#include <Windows.H>

typedef struct tagPENDATA {
    WORD     wStyle;
    int      iWidth;
    COLORREF crColor;
    char *   pchName;
    } PENDATA;


/*------------------------------------------------------------*\
 |                   Function Prototypes.                    |
\*------------------------------------------------------------*/
long FAR  PASCAL PensWndProc (HWND, WORD, WORD, LONG);
VOID NEAR PASCAL MarkerDrawMarker (HDC hdc, int x, int y);


/*------------------------------------------------------------*\
 |                   Main Function:  WinMain.                |
\*------------------------------------------------------------*/
int PASCAL WinMain (HANDLE hInstance,
                    HANDLE hPrevInstance,
                    LPSTR  lpszCmdLine,
                    int    cmdShow)
    {
    HWND     hwnd;
    MSG      msg;
    WNDCLASS wndclass;

    if (!hPrevInstance)
        {
        wndclass.lpszClassName = "PENS:MAIN";
        wndclass.hInstance     = hInstance;
        wndclass.lpfnWndProc   = PensWndProc;
        wndclass.hCursor       = LoadCursor (hInstance, "hand");
        wndclass.hIcon         = LoadIcon (hInstance, "snapshot");
        wndclass.lpszMenuName  = NULL;
        wndclass.hbrBackground = COLOR_WINDOW+1;
```

```
        wndclass.style          = CS_HREDRAW | CS_VREDRAW;
        wndclass.cbClsExtra     = 0;
        wndclass.cbWndExtra     = 0;

        RegisterClass( &wndclass);
        }

    hwnd = CreateWindow("PENS:MAIN",            /* Class name.  */
                        "Pens",                 /* Title.       */
                        WS_OVERLAPPEDWINDOW,    /* Style bits.  */
                        CW_USEDEFAULT,          /* x - default. */
                        0,                      /* y - default. */
                        CW_USEDEFAULT,          /* cx - default. */
                        0,                      /* cy - default. */
                        NULL,                   /* No parent.   */
                        NULL,                   /* Class menu.  */
                        hInstance,              /* Creator      */
                        NULL                    /* Params.      */
                        ) ;

    ShowWindow (hwnd, cmdShow);

    while (GetMessage(&msg, 0, 0, 0))
        {
        TranslateMessage(&msg);                 /*  Keyboard input.   */
        DispatchMessage(&msg);
        }
    return 0;
    }


/*----------------------------------------------------------------*\
|                 Window Procedure:  PensWndProc.                  |
\*----------------------------------------------------------------*/
long FAR PASCAL PensWndProc (HWND hwnd,    WORD msg,
                            WORD wParam, LONG lParam)
    {
#define PENCOUNT 11
    static PENDATA pens[PENCOUNT] = {
            PS_SOLID, 1, RGB (0,0,0), "PS_SOLID",
            PS_SOLID, 2, RGB (0,0,0), "PS_SOLID, 2 wide",
            PS_SOLID, 4, RGB (0,0,0), "PS_SOLID, 4 wide",
```

```
           PS_DASH, 1, RGB (0,0,0), "PS_DASH",
           PS_DOT, 1, RGB (0,0,0), "PS_DOT",
           PS_DASHDOT, 1, RGB (0,0,0), "PS_DASHDOT",
           PS_DASHDOTDOT, 1, RGB (0,0,0), "PS_DASHDOTDOT",
           PS_NULL, 1, RGB (0,0,0), "PS_NULL",
           PS_INSIDEFRAME, 1, RGB (0,0,0), "PS_INSIDEFRAME",
           PS_INSIDEFRAME, 3, RGB (0,0,0),
                         "PS_INSIDEFRAME, 3 wide",
           PS_INSIDEFRAME, 11, RGB (180,180,180),
                         "PS_INSIDEFRAME, Gray, 11 wide   "};

static HPEN hpen[PENCOUNT];

switch (msg)
    {
    case WM_CREATE:
        {
        int i;
        for (i=0;i<PENCOUNT; i++)
            hpen[i] = CreatePen (pens[i].wStyle,
                                 pens[i].iWidth,
                                 pens[i].crColor);
        }
        break;

    case WM_DESTROY:
        {
        int i;
        for (i=0;i<PENCOUNT; i++)
            DeleteObject (hpen[i]);
        PostQuitMessage(0);
        }
        break;

    case WM_PAINT:
        {
        DWORD dw;
        int i;
        int xEnd, xStart, xText;
        int yIncr, yLine, yText;
        PAINTSTRUCT ps;
```

```
            RECT r;

            BeginPaint (hwnd, &ps);

            GetClientRect (hwnd, &r);
            yIncr = r.bottom/ (PENCOUNT+2);
            yText = yIncr;
            xText = 10;
            dw = GetTextExtent (ps.hdc, pens[10].pchName,
                                lstrlen(pens[10].pchName));

            for (i=0;i<PENCOUNT; i++)
                {
                TextOut (ps.hdc, xText, yText,
                        pens[i].pchName,
                        lstrlen(pens[i].pchName));

                xStart = xText + LOWORD(dw);
                xEnd   = r.right - 10;
                yLine  = yText + HIWORD(dw)/2;
                SelectObject (ps.hdc, hpen[i]);
                MoveTo (ps.hdc, xStart, yLine);
                LineTo (ps.hdc, xEnd, yLine);

                /* Draw Markers.  */
                MarkerDrawMarker (ps.hdc, xStart, yLine);
                MarkerDrawMarker (ps.hdc, xEnd, yLine);
                yText += yIncr;
                }

            EndPaint (hwnd, &ps);
            }
            break;

    default:
            return(DefWindowProc(hwnd,msg,wParam,lParam));
            break;
        }
    return 0L;
    }
```

```
#define MARKERSIZE 3
VOID NEAR PASCAL MarkerDrawMarker (HDC hdc, int x, int y)
    {
    DWORD dwColor;
    int i;

    dwColor = GetPixel (hdc, x, y);
    dwColor = ~dwColor;
    SetPixel (hdc, x, y, dwColor);

    for (i=1;i<=MARKERSIZE; i++)
        {
        dwColor = GetPixel (hdc, x+i, y);
        dwColor = ~dwColor;
        SetPixel (hdc, x+i, y, dwColor);

        dwColor = GetPixel (hdc, x-i, y);
        dwColor = ~dwColor;
        SetPixel (hdc, x-i, y, dwColor);

        dwColor = GetPixel (hdc, x, y+i);
        dwColor = ~dwColor;
        SetPixel (hdc, x, y+i, dwColor);

        dwColor = GetPixel (hdc, x, y-i);
        dwColor = ~dwColor;
        SetPixel (hdc, x, y-i, dwColor);
        }
    }
```

PENS.RC

```
snapshot icon Pens.ico

hand   cursor Pens.cur
```

PENS.DEF

```
NAME       PENS

EXETYPE WINDOWS

DESCRIPTION 'GDI Pen Demo'

CODE       MOVEABLE DISCARDABLE
DATA       MOVEABLE MULTIPLE

HEAPSIZE     512
STACKSIZE    5000

EXPORTS
    PensWndProc
```

This program creates 10 pens in response to the WM_CREATE message and destroys them in response to WM_DESTROY. This is important. Every Windows program must take care to dispose of its pens (and other drawing objects) properly. The problem actually results from one of the nice features of pens: They can be shared.

To allow GDI objects to be shared, Windows doesn't clean up leftover objects. If a program terminates without cleaning up its pens, that memory is lost forever (at least until the computer is turned off). So take care to always destroy your pens when you no longer need them.

We're now going to investigate the last DC drawing attribute that affects lines: the drawing mode. In the process, we'll give you a preview of our mouse input program from Chapter 16.

Drawing Modes and Lines

A **drawing mode** is a Boolean operation that directs GDI how to draws pixels, lines, and filled figures. The drawing mode, sometimes called a raster operation or 'ROP' for short, determines how the source and destination interact.

In the context of lines, the drawing mode describes how a pen interacts with the pixels that are already on the display surface. In the physical world, pens ordinarily overwrite what is already on the drawing surface. But you'll get a better idea about drawing modes if you imagine drawing with a fountain pen onto a wet colored surface: Some mixing takes place.

In an earlier chapter, the MARKER program used the NOT operator to insure that a marker is visible. A drawing mode provides a faster, convenient means to get the same effect. It is faster since the logic is part of the device driver.

Another use of drawing modes lets us draw shapes that seem to "float" on the display screen. This is the technique used for the mouse cursor, which wanders everywhere without leaving a trail of dirty pixels. In Chapter 16, we'll write a program that uses drawing modes to drag objects across the display. Figure 8.8 previews this object-dragging program.

It may seem strange that we want to perform Boolean algebra on graphic output. And yet, in a digital computer, every piece of data is encoded as a number. RGB triplets, for example, are numbers that describe colors. In the depths of graphic devices like the EGA display, numbers make up the pixels of a graphic image.

Drawing modes take advantage of this to allow the application of Boolean operations. And since a computer's CPU uses Boolean alge-

Figure 8.8   *One use of drawing modes: dragable objects*

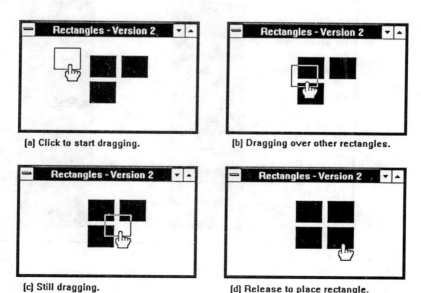

[a] Click to start dragging.

[b] Dragging over other rectangles.

[c] Still dragging.

[d] Release to place rectangle.

bra as part of its day-to-day operation, it is a simple matter to apply Boolean operations to graphic images.

Figure 8.9 shows the 16 raster operations that GDI supports, along with the lines that are created with a white and with a black pen. Notice how every drawing mode is different. If you'd like, you can inhibit output with the R2_NOP mode, or guarantee that something will be drawn using the R2_NOT mode. Notice that two of the modes, R2_BLACK and R2_WHITE, ignore the pen color.

One thing to keep in mind about drawing attributes is that they affect more than just lines: They affect the output of pixels (SetPixel routine) and filled geometric figures (which we'll discuss in the next chapter). GDI doesn't use drawing modes when drawing text, however. The reason primarily has to do with performance. Even though raster operations are implemented at the level of the device driver and are quite fast, nevertheless they slow down the output of text and so are not used by GDI's text drawing routines.

Figure 8.9 *GDI's sixteen drawing modes*

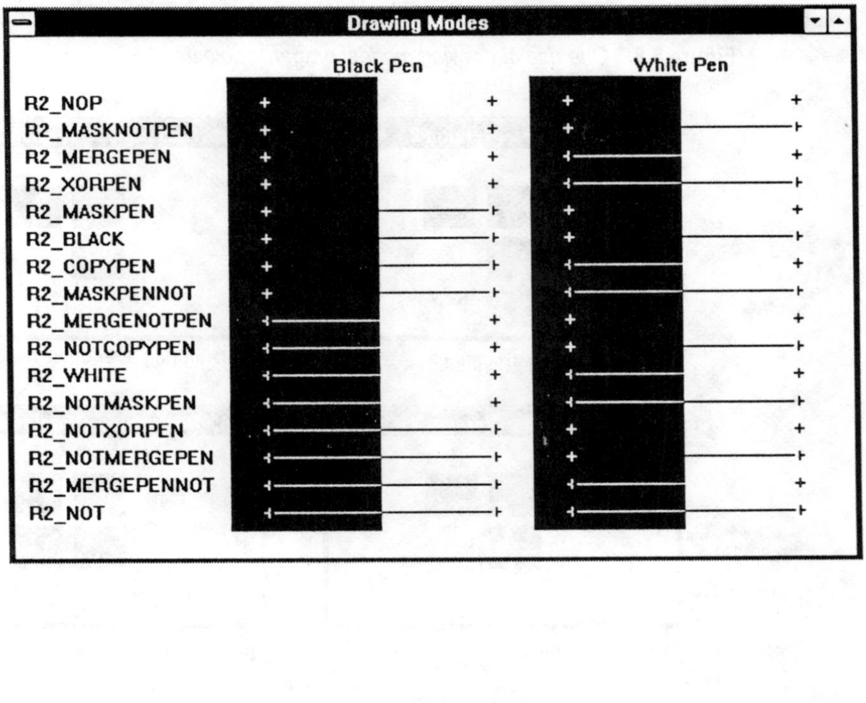

To find out the current setting of the drawing mode, you call the GetROP2 routine. To set a new drawing mode value in the DC, you call the SetROP2 routine, as in

```
SetROP2 (hdc, R2_XORPEN);
```

Here is a newer, faster version of our marker routine, done using ROP codes:

```
#define MARKERSIZE 3
VOID NEAR PASCAL MrkDrawMarker (HDC hdc, int x, int y)
    {
    int i;
    int rop;

    rop = SetROP2 (hdc, R2_NOT);
    SetPixel (hdc, x, y, RGB(0, 0, 0));

    for (i=1;i<=MARKERSIZE; i++)
        {
        SetPixel (hdc, x+i, y, RGB(0, 0, 0));
        SetPixel (hdc, x-i, y, RGB(0, 0, 0));
        SetPixel (hdc, x, y+i, RGB(0, 0, 0));
        SetPixel (hdc, x, y-i, RGB(0, 0, 0));
        }

    SetROP2 (hdc, rop);
    }
```

As you recall, the SetPixel routine illuminates a pixel with the color specified by the last parameter. In this routine, RGB(0, 0, 0) selects black. But since we're using the R2_NOT drawing mode, GDI ignores the color we specify and inverts the destination pixel.

In our next chapter, we're going to discuss filled figures. Every filled figure has a border, which is simply a GDI line drawn to outline the filled area. As you will see, everything that we have discussed dealing with line drawing applies equally well to the creation of GDI filled figures.

9
Drawing Filled Figures

The next set of GDI drawing routines that we're going to look at are those that create filled figures. A filled figure has two parts: an area and a border around the area. Filled figures are sometimes referred to as **closed figures** because the border closes in on itself. In line drawing terms, the starting and ending points are the same.

Figure 9.1 shows some examples of the types of filled figures that GDI can draw. Notice the variation in the thickness and style of different borders. These are the result of different pens. After all, a border is simply a line, and GDI uses pens to draw lines.

Notice also the variation in the interior area of the figures in the illustration. This is the result of another GDI drawing object: a **brush**. In the same way that you use different pens to draw different types of lines, you use different brushes for different filled areas.

To understand the way that GDI draws filled figures, it is important to understand how coordinates are interpreted. Filled figure coordinates are slightly different from those used in line drawing. If

Figure 9.1 *Examples of GDI filled figures*

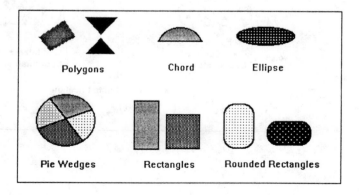

you draw both types of figures, you will need to make adjustments to insure that objects line up the way you expect them to.

In the world of graphics programming, there are two primary ways to interpret a coordinate. Put simply, the issue is: Do coordinates lie in the center of pixels or at the intersections of a grid surrounding the pixels? Figure 9.2 illustrates pixel-centered and grid-intersection coordinates.

All of GDI's line-drawing primitives use pixel-centered coordinates. Of GDI's seven area-filling primitives, two use pixel-centered coordinates and five use grid-intersection coordinates. While this may seem odd, each type of coordinate has its own uses that makes sense in its own right. Table 9.1 shows GDI's seven area filling primitives, and the type of coordinates that each uses:

Notice that two of the filled-figure routines use pixel-centered coordinates: Polygon and PolyPolygon. You can think of these routines as extensions to Polyline, one of GDI's line primitives. It's easy to use these routines with line-drawing routines, since both sets use pixel-centered coordinates.

The other five routines use grid-intersection coordinates. These are the coordinates that GDI uses to define clipping regions. This makes it easy to use these routines with GDI's clipping routines.

Figure 9.2 *Pixel-centered and grid-intersection coordinates*

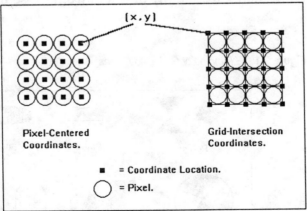

Table 9.1   *GDI's area filling routines*

Routine	Coordinates	Description
Polygon	pixel-centered	A filled Polyline
PolyPolygon	pixel-centered	Multiple Polygons
Chord	grid-intersection	Partial arc joined by a straight line
Ellipse	grid-intersection	Full arc
Pie	grid-intersection	Pie wedge
Rectangle	grid-intersection	Rectangle
RoundRect	grid-intersection	Rectangle with rounded corners

GDI uses pixel-centered coordinates when the emphasis of a routine is line-drawing, and grid-intersection coordinates when the emphasis is a two-dimensional area. However, if you wish to use both types of routines, it's usually a simple matter to modify the coordinates of one type of routine to fit in with the other type of routine.

The visible effect of grid-intersection coordinates is that filled figures seem to be one pixel smaller than expected. With the help of ZoomIn, you can see this in Figure 9.3.

The program that created this output is RECT. The source code to RECT is in the accompanying listing. This program uses two mouse messages to draw a rectangle: WM_LBUTTONDOWN and WM_LBUTTONUP. Each message provides one of the two pairs of points that are required by the Rectangle routine. Rectangle takes five parameters:

```
Rectangle (hdc, X1, Y1, X2, Y2);
```

The points (X1, Y1) and (X2, Y2) are opposite corners of the rectangle that is drawn.

Figure 9.3   *Grid-intersection coordinates seem to be one pixel off*

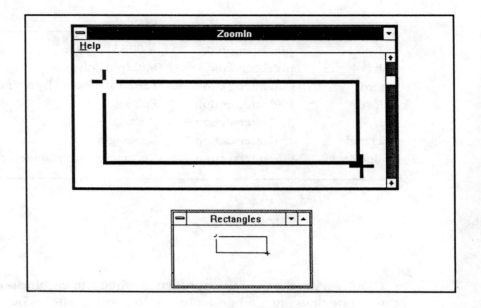

RECT.MAK

```
Rect.res: Rect.rc Rect.cur Rect.ico
    rc -r Rect.rc

Rect.obj: Rect.c
    cl -AM -c -d -Gsw -Od -W2 -Zpi Rect.c

rect.exe: Rect.obj Rect.def
    link Rect,/align:16,/map, mlibcew libw/NOD/NOE/CO, Rect.def
    rc Rect.res rect.exe

rect.exe: Rect.res
    rc Rect.res rect.exe
```

RECT.C

```
/*-------------------------------------------------------------*\
 |    RECT.C - Draws a set of rectangles in response to mouse  |
 |            messages generated by the left mouse button.     |
 \*-------------------------------------------------------------*/
#include <Windows.H>


/*-------------------------------------------------------------*\
 |                    Function Prototypes.                     |
 \*-------------------------------------------------------------*/
long FAR  PASCAL RecWndProc (HWND, WORD, WORD, LONG);
VOID NEAR PASCAL MrkDrawMarker (HDC hdc, int x, int y);


/*-------------------------------------------------------------*\
 |                  Main Function: WinMain.                    |
 \*-------------------------------------------------------------*/
int PASCAL WinMain (HANDLE hInstance,
                    HANDLE hPrevInstance,
                    LPSTR  lpszCmdLine,
                    int    cmdShow)
    {
    HWND     hwnd;
    MSG      msg;
    WNDCLASS wndclass;

    if (!hPrevInstance)
        {
        wndclass.lpszClassName = "RECT:MAIN";
        wndclass.hInstance     = hInstance;
        wndclass.lpfnWndProc   = RecWndProc;
        wndclass.hCursor       = LoadCursor (hInstance, "hand");
        wndclass.hIcon         = LoadIcon (hInstance,"snapshot");
        wndclass.lpszMenuName  = NULL;
        wndclass.hbrBackground = COLOR_WINDOW+1;
        wndclass.style         = CS_HREDRAW | CS_VREDRAW;
        wndclass.cbClsExtra    = 0;
        wndclass.cbWndExtra    = 0;

        RegisterClass( &wndclass);
        }
```

```
        hwnd = CreateWindow("RECT:MAIN",           /* Class name.  */
                            "Rectangles",          /* Title.       */
                            WS_OVERLAPPEDWINDOW,    /* Style bits.  */
                            CW_USEDEFAULT,          /* x - default. */
                            0,                      /* y - default. */
                            CW_USEDEFAULT,          /* cx - default. */
                            0,                      /* cy - default. */
                            NULL,                   /* No parent.   */
                            NULL,                   /* Class menu.  */
                            hInstance,              /* Creator.     */
                            NULL                    /* Params.      */
                            );

    ShowWindow (hwnd, cmdShow);

    while (GetMessage (&msg, 0, 0, 0))
        {
        TranslateMessage (&msg);        /* Keyboard input.    */
        DispatchMessage (&msg);
        }
    return 0;
    }

/*------------------------------------------------------------------*\
|                 Window Procedure: RecWndProc.                      |
\*------------------------------------------------------------------*/
long FAR PASCAL RecWndProc (HWND hWnd,   WORD msg,
                            WORD wParam, LONG lParam)
    {
    static RECT   arRectangles[50]; /* array of rectangles.  */
    static int    cRects = 0;       /* count of rectangles.  */

    switch (msg)
        {
        case WM_DESTROY:
            PostQuitMessage(0);
            break;

        case WM_LBUTTONDOWN:
            {
            POINT pt;
```

```
        pt = MAKEPOINT (lParam);
        arRectangles[cRects].left = pt.x;
        arRectangles[cRects].top  = pt.y;
        }
        break;

case WM_LBUTTONUP:
    {
    POINT pt;

    pt = MAKEPOINT (lParam);
    arRectangles[cRects].right  = pt.x;
    arRectangles[cRects].bottom = pt.y;
    cRects++;
    if (cRects == 50) cRects = 0;
    InvalidateRect (hWnd, NULL, TRUE);
    }
    break;

case WM_PAINT:
    {
    PAINTSTRUCT ps;
    int i;

    BeginPaint (hWnd, &ps);

    for (i = 0; i < cRects ; i++ )
        {
        Rectangle (ps.hdc, arRectangles[i].left,
                           arRectangles[i].top,
                           arRectangles[i].right,
                           arRectangles[i].bottom);

        MrkDrawMarker (ps.hdc, arRectangles[i].left,
                               arRectangles[i].top);
        MrkDrawMarker (ps.hdc, arRectangles[i].right,
                               arRectangles[i].bottom);
        }

    EndPaint (hWnd, &ps);
    }
```

```
                break;

          default:
                return(DefWindowProc(hWnd,msg,wParam,lParam));
                break;
          }
     return 0L;
     }

#define MARKERSIZE 3
VOID NEAR PASCAL MrkDrawMarker (HDC hdc, int x, int y)
     {
     int i;
     int rop;

     rop = SetROP2 (hdc, R2_NOT);
     SetPixel (hdc, x, y, RGB(0, 0, 0));

     for (i=1;i<=MARKERSIZE; i++)
          {
          SetPixel (hdc, x+i, y, RGB(0, 0, 0));
          SetPixel (hdc, x-i, y, RGB(0, 0, 0));
          SetPixel (hdc, x, y+i, RGB(0, 0, 0));
          SetPixel (hdc, x, y-i, RGB(0, 0, 0));
          }

     SetROP2 (hdc, rop);
     }
```

RECT.RC

```
snapshot icon Rect.ico

hand   cursor Rect.cur
```

RECT.DEF

```
NAME     RECT

EXETYPE WINDOWS

DESCRIPTION 'Sample Rectangle Drawing'

CODE     MOVEABLE DISCARDABLE
DATA     MOVEABLE MULTIPLE

HEAPSIZE     512
STACKSIZE    5000

EXPORTS
    RecWndProc
```

To store the points that describe each rectangle, we allocate an array of type RECT:

```
static RECT     arRectangles[50];
```

The RECT type is defined in Windows.h as

```
typedef struct tagRECT
  {
    int  left;
    int  top;
    int  right;
    int  bottom;
  } RECT;
```

The elements of this array are named in a somewhat odd fashion, reflecting the use of this structure for clipping rectangles. In general, you can assume that left and right are X values, and that top and bottom are Y values.

We use the MAKEPOINT macro to copy the mouse location from the lParam parameter of a mouse message to a POINT variable. For the WM_BUTTONDOWN message, we store the mouse location in the left and top portions of arRectangles. We get an X,Y pair from the WM_LBUTTONUP routine and store the values in the right and bottom parts of arRectangles.

The last thing that we do in response to WM_LBUTTONUP is to declare the entire window to be damaged with the InvalidateRect routine. As you recall, this causes a WM_PAINT message to be generated. This allows us to put all our rectangle drawing code in one place.

In response to the WM_PAINT message, we run through the entire array of rectangles. We conclude by placing a marker at the two points that we passed to `Rectangle` to draw the routine.

This brief introduction to the Rectangle routine, and GDI's two different types of coordinates, has gotten us ready to look at the rest of GDI's filled-figure routines.

GDI Filled-Figure Routines

Let's take a close look at each of GDI's filled-figure routines. GDI has seven such routines: Polygon, PolyPolygon, Chord, Ellipse, Pie, Rectangle, and RoundRect.

Let's start with the two routines that use pixel-centered coordinates.

Polygon and PolyPolygon

The Polygon routine is defined:

```
Polygon (hDC, lpPoints, nCount)
```

- hDC is a handle to a device context.
- lpPoints is a pointer to an array of type POINT. It is the points to connect.
- nCount is the number of points to connect.

Like the Polyline routine that we encountered in the last chapter, this routine connects a series of points using the pen that is currently installed in the DC. In addition, if the first and last points are not the same, a line is drawn to close the figure, and the area inside the figure is filled using the brush that is currently installed in the DC.

Polygon is GDI's most flexible filled area routine, since you can use it to draw any figure of the other filled area routines. For example, Figure 9.4 shows rectangles drawn using Polygon. Notice that,

Figure 9.4   *Rectangles drawn with the Polygon routine*

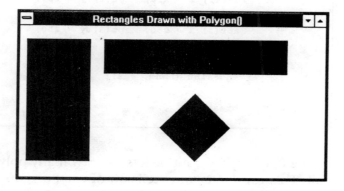

unlike the normal Rectangle routine, we can even draw rotated rectangles.

Here is the code fragment that created this illustration:

```
case WM_PAINT:
    {
    PAINTSTRUCT ps;
    POINT apt[4];

    BeginPaint (hWnd, &ps);
    SelectObject (ps.hdc, GetStockObject (BLACK_BRUSH));

    apt[0].x =  10;  apt[0].y =  20;
    apt[1].x = 100;  apt[1].y =  20;
    apt[2].x = 100;  apt[2].y = 200;
    apt[3].x =  10;  apt[3].y = 200;
    Polygon (ps.hdc, apt, 4);

    apt[0].x = 120;  apt[0].y = 20;
    apt[1].x = 380;  apt[1].y = 20;
    apt[2].x = 380;  apt[2].y = 70;
    apt[3].x = 120;  apt[3].y = 70;
    Polygon (ps.hdc, apt, 4);

    apt[0].x = 200;  apt[0].y = 150;
```

```
        apt[1].x = 250;   apt[1].y = 100;
        apt[2].x = 300;   apt[2].y = 150;
        apt[3].x = 250;   apt[3].y = 200;
        Polygon (ps.hdc, apt, 4);

        EndPaint (hWnd, &ps);
        }
        break;
```

The PolyPolygon routine lets us draw many polygons with a single call. This routine is an extension of the Polygon routine. Programs that draw many polygons will run faster if they call PolyPolygon than if they make many separate calls to Polygon. The speed advantage is a direct result of the overhead involved with making a function call.

PolyPolygon is defined as follows:

```
PolyPolygon (hDC, lpPoints, lpPolyCount, nCount);
```

- hDC is a handle to a device context.
- lpPoints is a pointer to an array of type POINT. It is the points to connect to create the various polygons.
- lpPolyCount is a pointer to an array of type INT. The elements of this array indicate the number of points in each polygon.
- nCount is an integer for the number of points in the lpPolyCount array. In other words, it is the number of polygons to draw.

Here is the code that draws the previous figure using a single call to PolyPolygon:

```
case WM_PAINT:
    {
    PAINTSTRUCT ps;
    POINT apt[15];
    int   ai[3];

    BeginPaint (hWnd, &ps);
```

```
SelectObject (ps.hdc, GetStockObject (BLACK_BRUSH));

/*  First Rectangle.  */
apt[0].x =  10;   apt[0].y =   20;
apt[1].x = 100;   apt[1].y =   20;
apt[2].x = 100;   apt[2].y =  200;
apt[3].x =  10;   apt[3].y =  200;
apt[4].x =  10;   apt[4].y =   20;
ai[0] = 5;

/*  Second Rectangle.  */
apt[5].x = 120;   apt[5].y =  20;
apt[6].x = 380;   apt[6].y =  20;
apt[7].x = 380;   apt[7].y =  70;
apt[8].x = 120;   apt[8].y =  70;
apt[9].x = 120;   apt[9].y =  20;
ai[1] = 5;

/*  Third Rectangle.  */
apt[10].x = 200;   apt[10].y = 150;
apt[11].x = 250;   apt[11].y = 100;
apt[12].x = 300;   apt[12].y = 150;
apt[13].x = 250;   apt[13].y = 200;
apt[14].x = 200;   apt[14].y = 150;
ai[2] = 5;

PolyPolygon (ps.hdc, apt, ai, 3);

EndPaint (hWnd, &ps);
}
break;
```

When we talk about Polygons, we normally think of figures with flat sides—like the rectangles we drew in our sample code. But we can also use the Polygon routines to draw curves—as long as we provide enough points. In fact, that's how GDI simulates curves— with a series of short lines. Of course, if we want to draw curves in this way, we have our work cut out for us. We'd have to calculate all of the points along the curve.

GDI has a set of routines that do this work for us and make it easy to draw filled figures with curved sides. Let's take a look at those routines.

Ellipse, Chord, and Pie

GDI has three routines that create filled figures with curved sides. As you'll see in a moment, you can think of these routines as extensions of the Arc routine that we covered in the last chapter. Each routine uses a bounding rectangle to draw a curve.

Here is the definition of the Ellipse function:

```
Ellipse (hDC, X1, Y1, X2, Y2)
```

- hDC is a handle to a device context.
- (X1, Y1) is a corner of the bounding rectangle.
- (X2, Y2) is the opposite corner of the bounding rectangle.

The Ellipse function creates an ellipse whose perimeter is tangent to the sides of the bounding rectangle, as illustrated in Figure 9.5.

The Chord function also makes use of a bounding rectangle to draw a partial arc connected with a line segment. This function is defined as follows:

```
Chord (hDC, X1, Y1, X2, Y2, X3, Y3, X4, Y4)
```

- hDC is a handle to a device context.
- (X1, Y1) and (X2, Y2) define the bounding rectangle.
- (X3, Y3) is the starting point of the line segment.
- (X4, Y4) is the ending point of the line segment.

Figure 9.5   *A figure drawn with the Ellipse function*

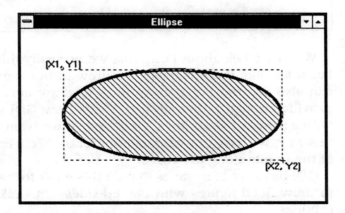

Figure 9.6   *A figure drawn with the Chord function*

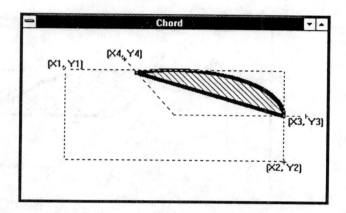

Figure 9.6 shows a chord drawn with this function, with notation to show the bounding box and the line segment coordinates.

The Pie function takes the same parameters as the Chord function. This function draws a wedge of a pie instead of a chord. The function is defined as follows:

```
Pie (hDC, X1, Y1, X2, Y2, X3, Y3, X4, Y4)
```

- hDC is a handle to a device context.
- (X1, Y1) and (X2, Y2) define the bounding rectangle.
- (X3, Y3) is the starting point of the wedge.
- (X4, Y4) is the ending point of the wedge.

Figure 9.7 shows a pie wedge, with the bounding box, starting point, and ending point shown.

Rectangle and RoundRect

We have seen the Rectangle function before, but for completeness sake, here is the function definition:

```
Rectangle (hDC, X1, Y1, X2, Y2)
```

- hDC is a device context handle.
- (X1, Y1) is one corner of the rectangle.
- (X2, Y2) is the opposite corner of the rectangle.

Figure 9.7   *Figure drawn with the Pie function*

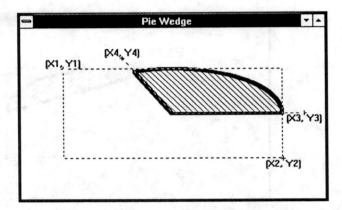

Like other GDI filled-figure routines, Rectangle uses the pen from the DC to draw the rectangle border and the brush to fill the interior. This routine only draws rectangles with sides that are parallel with the X and Y axes. For rotated rectangles, you must use either the Polygon function or the PolyPolygon function. Figure 9.8 illustrates the relationship of the two control points to the rectangle that is drawn.

The RoundRect routine draws a rectangle with rounded corners. It is defined as follows:

```
RoundRect (hDC, X1, Y1, X2, Y2, X3, Y3)
```

Figure 9.8   *Figure drawn with the Rectangle function*

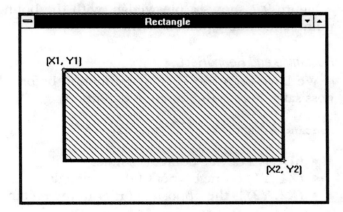

Figure 9.9 *Sample of RoundRect output*

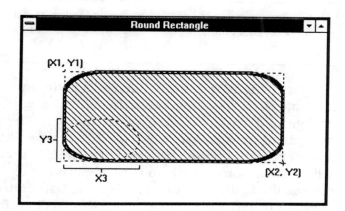

- hDC is a device context handle.
- (X1, Y1) is one corner of the rectangle.
- (X2, Y2) is the opposite corner of the rectangle.
- (X3, Y3) define a bounding box for an ellipse that is used to draw the rounded corners.

Figure 9.9 shows an example of the type of output that RoundRect can be used to create.

DC Attributes

As with other GDI drawing primitives, we must visit the device context to fully understand how much control GDI gives us over filled figures. The attributes that affect filled figures are shown in this table:

Drawing Attribute	Comments
Background Color	Second color for hatched brushes and non-solid pens
Background Mode	Turns on/off background color
Brush	Color for filling interior
Brush Origin	Alignment of hatched brushes
Drawing Mode	Boolean drawing operation

(Continued)

Drawing Attribute	Comments
Pen	Border color, width, and style
Polygon Filling Mode	For Polygon and PolyPolygon routines

Since the border of every filled area is simply a line, all of the DC attributes that affect lines also affect filled areas: background color, background mode, drawing mode, and pen. An important point to note about pens is that, when used to draw a filled figure, a pen is always centered on the border. For example, a nine-pixel-wide pen will draw a border with four pixels inside the figure, four pixels outside the figure, and one pixel on the border itself.

Pens created with a style of PS_INSIDEFRAME, however, never draw borders that extend beyond the border of the figure. A nine-pixel-wide PS_INSIDEFRAME pen, for example, will draw a border that has one pixel on the exact border and eight pixels inside the figure.

Three attributes are specific to filled areas: brush, brush origin, and Polygon-filling mode. Before we discuss GDI brushes, we're going to briefly discuss two of these: Polygon-filling mode, and drawing mode.

The names of drawing modes seem to imply that they only affect lines. For example, the default drawing mode, R2_COPYPEN, includes the word "pen," which is associated with line drawing. In spite of this unfortunate choice of names, drawing modes affect the inside as well as the border of filled figures. To put it briefly, drawing modes affect pens and brushes equally.

The Polygon filling mode determines how to fill complex figures created by two routines: Polygon and PolyPolygon. For simple figures, like squares and rectangles, the Polygon-filling mode has no effect. For complex figures, like the star in Figure 9.10, the Polygon-filling mode determines which areas to fill.

The WINDING mode fills all areas inside the border. The ALTERNATE mode, on the other hand, fills only the odd areas. That is, if you were to draw a line segment through a figure, filling is turned *on* after odd boundary crossings (1, 3, 5, etc.), and turned *off* after even boundary crossings (2, 4, 6).

The SetPolyFillMode routine, which sets this drawing attribute, is defined as follows:

```
SetPolyFillMode (hDC, nPolyFillMode)
```

Figure 9.10 *Polygon filling modes only affect complex Polygons*

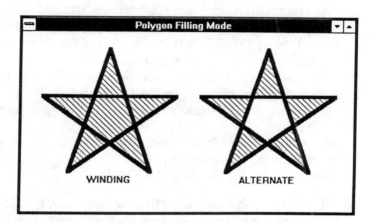

- hDC is a handle to a device context.
- nPolyFillMode is either ALTERNATE or WINDING.

Now let's turn our attention to the attribute that has the most effect on the appearance of filled figures: GDI brushes.

About Brushes

A brush is a DC drawing attribute for filling areas. Three qualities make up a brush: a style, a color, and a pattern. The size of a brush is 8 pixels by 8 pixels. When we discussed GDI pens, we mentioned that attribute bundles allow a convenient way for a program to refer to several attributes at the same time. The convenience factor is certainly one of the reasons for brushes.

We mentioned earlier that pens can be shared between programs and between devices. The same is true of brushes. Just as there are stock pens, there are stock brushes. That is, GDI creates a set of brushes for use by any program. If stock brushes don't provide what you need, it is a simple matter to create your own brushes. And finally, like pens, you must be sure to clean up all of the brushes that you create. Otherwise, the memory is lost from the system. Let's look at some of the details surrounding the creation and use of brushes.

Creating and Using Brushes

At system start-up time, GDI creates the following stock brushes: black, dark gray, gray, light gray, white, and null (or hollow). Like the null pen, a null brush is a place holder. You can think of a null brush as one having a transparent color.

The GetStockObject routine provides a handle to stock brushes. To use a brush, install it into a DC with the `SelectObject` routine. Here is one way to draw a rectangle with a gray interior:

```
hpen = GetStockObject (GRAY_BRUSH);
SelectObject (hdc, hpen);
Rectangle (hdc, X1, Y1, X2, Y2);
```

To supplement the stock brushes, you can create custom brushes. There are three types of custom brushes: solid, hatched, and pattern. Figure 9.11 shows examples of each type. GDI provides five routines to create brushes: CreateBrushIndirect, CreateDIBPatternBrush, CreateHatchBrush, CreatePatternBrush, and CreateSolidBrush.

We're going to take a close look at the last three routines in this list. The first, CreateBrushIndirect, is able to do the job of any of the other routines. It is unique in that it takes as a parameter a pointer to a data structure that can describe any brush: a LOGBRUSH (logical brush).

The second routine in this list, CreateDIBPatternBrush, creates a brush from a device-independent bitmap, also known as a 'DIB.' DIBs are bitmaps whose color information is stored in a standard format. The colors in a DIB can be correctly interpreted on any GDI device.

Let's now turn our attention to the three types of bitmaps: solid, hatched, and pattern. As we examine each, we'll look at the three routines that we use in our sample program to create these types of brushes: CreateSolidBrush, CreateHatchBrush, and CreatePatternBrush.

A **solid brush** is a brush that is created from either a pure or a dithered color. We introduced dithered colors in the last chapter in our discussion of dithered pens. Dithered colors are created by mixing pure colors.

For example, the device that created Figure 9.11 has just two colors: black and white. By dithering, we can create many different shades of gray, like the one that was used to draw the rectangle labeled 'Solid Gray Brush' in our figure.

The CreateSolidBrush routine lets you create these brushes. It is defined as

```
HBRUSH CreateSolidBrush (crColor)
```

- crColor is a color reference. This can be an RGB triplet, a palette index, or a palette relative RGB value.

For example, here's how to create a white brush:

```
hbr = CreateSolidBrush (RGB (255, 255, 255));
```

A **hatch brush** fills areas with a pattern created with hatch marks. GDI provides six built-in hatch patterns, as shown in Figure 9.11. The CreateHatchBrush routine is the easiest way to create a hatch brush (although the CreateBrushIndirect routine can be used as well).

The syntax of CreateHatchBrush is as follows:

```
HBRUSH CreateSolidBrush (nIndex, crColor)
```

Figure 9.11 *Eleven different brushes*

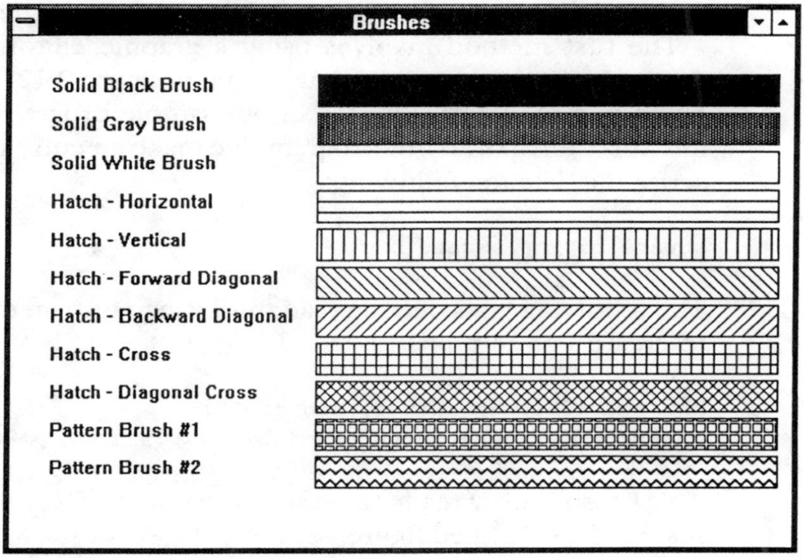

- nIndex can be any one of six values:

```
HS_BDIAGONAL
HS_CROSS
HS_DIAGCROSS
HS_FDIAGONAL
HS_HORIZONTAL
HS_VERTICAL
```

- crColor is a color reference. This can be an RGB triplet, a palette index, or a palette relative RGB value.

A **pattern brush** is a brush created from a bitmap pattern. If the six styles of hatch brushes aren't enough for you, a pattern brush can be created with just about any hatch pattern you'd like to use. A pattern brush can also be made to resemble a solid brush, although this is usually more work than it's worth.

To create a pattern brush, you use the CreatePatternBrush routine. It's syntax is as follows:

```
HBRUSH CreatePatternBrush (hBitmap)
```

- hBitmap is a handle to a bitmap.

To create a pattern brush, you first need a bitmap. There are many ways to create a bitmap; as we'll cover in Chapter 21. For now, let's look at the two methods we use in our sample program.

The first method involves using a graphic editor, SDKPaint, to draw a bitmap pattern like that shown in figure 9.12. This pattern is saved to a file (SQUARE.BMP in our sample program). To incorporate this bitmap into our program, we make an entry in the resource script file, like the following:

```
square bitmap square.bmp
```

The following lines of code read this bitmap into memory, and use it to create a pattern brush:

```
hbm = LoadBitmap (hInst, "square");
hbr[9] = CreatePatternBrush (hbm);
```

This brush is now ready to be selected into a DC for use in filling the inside of a GDI filled figure.

Figure 9.12 *SDKPaint used to create a bitmap*

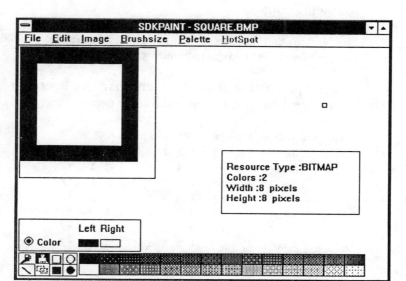

The second method that can be used to create a bitmap is to call the CreateBitmap routine with a pointer to the bits to include in the bitmap. The CreateBitmap routine is defined:

```
HBITMAP CreateBitmap (nWidth, nHeight, nPlanes,
                      nBitCount, lpBits)
```

- nWidth and nHeight are the width and height of the bitmap in pixels. Since all GDI brushes are 8 pixels wide by 8 pixels high, the value of both fields must be set to 8.
- nPlanes is the number of planes in the bitmap. Planes provide one means to store color information (for example, the EGA display adapter uses this method). We're going to create a monochrome bitmap, so we'll use the value 1 here.
- nBitCount is the number of bits per color. Packed pixels provide a second way to store color information (some modes of the CGA display adapter use this method). Since we are creating a monochrome bitmap, we set this to 1.
- lpBits is a pointer to the bits to use to initialize the bitmap.

Our program creates its second pattern bitmap by making the following calls:

```
hbm = CreateBitmap (8, 8, 1, 1, acPattern);
hbr[10] = CreatePatternBrush (hbm);
```

The last parameter of the CreateBitmap call is a pointer to an array of character values. It is defined in our program as

```
static unsigned char acPattern[] =
        {0xFF, 0,   /*  1 1 1 1 1 1 1 1  */
         0xE7, 0,   /*  1 1 1 0 0 1 1 1  */
         0xC3, 0,   /*  1 1 0 0 0 0 1 1  */
         0x99, 0,   /*  1 0 0 1 1 0 0 1  */
         0x3C, 0,   /*  0 0 1 1 1 1 0 0  */
         0x7E, 0,   /*  0 1 1 1 1 1 1 0  */
         0xFF, 0,   /*  1 1 1 1 1 1 1 1  */
         0xFF, 0};  /*  1 1 1 1 1 1 1 1  */
```

Our array is defined with hexadecimal values, but for your convenience the comment shows the values in binary. The 1's represent white pixels and the 0's represent black pixels. Since bitmap data is expected to be aligned on 16-bit boundaries, we have an additional zero byte between each of our bitmap byte values.

Each of these routines creates a **logical brush**. Like logical pens, logical brushes are requests that can be passed to any device. When asked to use a brush, the device driver *realizes* the brush—that is, it converts the logical request to a form that matches the capabilities of the specific device.

All the source code to our brush creation program, BRUSH, are shown here:

BRUSH.MAK

```
Brushes.res: Brushes.rc Brushes.cur Brushes.ico
    rc -r Brushes.rc

Brushes.obj: Brushes.c
    cl -AM -c -d -Gsw -Od -W2 -Zpi Brushes.c
```

```
brushes.exe: Brushes.obj Brushes.def
    link Brushes,/align:16,/map, mlibcew libw/NOD/NOE/CO,\
        Brushes.def
    rc Brushes.res brushes.exe

brushes.exe: Brushes.res
    rc Brushes.res brushes.exe
```

BRUSH.C

```c
/*--------------------------------------------------------------*\
 |    BRUSHES.C - Shows different types of GDI brushes.         |
\*--------------------------------------------------------------*/
#include <Windows.H>

HANDLE hInst;
/*--------------------------------------------------------------*\
 |                    Function Prototypes.                      |
\*--------------------------------------------------------------*/
long FAR  PASCAL BruWndProc (HWND, WORD, WORD, LONG);


/*--------------------------------------------------------------*\
 |                  Main Function: WinMain.                     |
\*--------------------------------------------------------------*/
int PASCAL WinMain (HANDLE hInstance,
                    HANDLE hPrevInstance,
                    LPSTR  lpszCmdLine,
                    int    cmdShow)
    {
    HWND     hwnd;
    MSG      msg;
    WNDCLASS wndclass;

    if (!hPrevInstance)
        {
        wndclass.lpszClassName = "BRUSHES:MAIN";
        wndclass.hInstance     = hInstance;
        wndclass.lpfnWndProc   = BruWndProc;
```

```
        wndclass.hCursor       = LoadCursor (hInstance, "hand");
        wndclass.hIcon         = LoadIcon (hInstance,"snapshot");
        wndclass.lpszMenuName  = NULL;
        wndclass.hbrBackground = COLOR_WINDOW+1;
        wndclass.style         = CS_HREDRAW | CS_VREDRAW;
        wndclass.cbClsExtra    = 0;
        wndclass.cbWndExtra    = 0;


        RegisterClass( &wndclass);
        }

    hInst = hInstance;

    hwnd = CreateWindow("BRUSHES:MAIN",      /* Class name.  */
                        "Brushes",           /* Title.       */
                        WS_OVERLAPPEDWINDOW, /* Style bits.  */
                        CW_USEDEFAULT,       /* x - default. */
                        0,                   /* y - default. */
                        CW_USEDEFAULT,       /* cx - default. */
                        0,                   /* cy - default. */
                        NULL,                /* No parent.   */
                        NULL,                /* Class menu.  */
                        hInstance,           /* Creator      */
                        NULL                 /* Params.      */
                       ) ;


    ShowWindow (hwnd, cmdShow);

    while (GetMessage(&msg, 0, 0, 0))
        {
        TranslateMessage(&msg);        /*  Keyboard input.    */
        DispatchMessage(&msg);
        }
    return 0;
    }

#define BRUSHCOUNT 11
/*-------------------------------------------------------------------*\
 |              Window Procedure:  BruWndProc.                        |
 \*-------------------------------------------------------------------*/
long FAR PASCAL BruWndProc (HWND     hwnd,
```

```
                              WORD msg,
                              WORD      wParam,
                              LONG      lParam)
    {
static HBRUSH hbr[BRUSHCOUNT];
static char * apszDesc[BRUSHCOUNT];
static unsigned char acPattern[] =
        {0xFF, 0,  /*  1 1 1 1 1 1 1 1  */
         0xE7, 0,  /*  1 1 1 0 0 1 1 1  */
         0xC3, 0,  /*  1 1 0 0 0 0 1 1  */
         0x99, 0,  /*  1 0 0 1 1 0 0 1  */
         0x3C, 0,  /*  0 0 1 1 1 1 0 0  */
         0x7E, 0,  /*  0 1 1 1 1 1 1 0  */
         0xFF, 0,  /*  1 1 1 1 1 1 1 1  */
         0xFF, 0}; /*  1 1 1 1 1 1 1 1  */

switch (msg)
    {
    case WM_CREATE:
        {
        HBITMAP hbm;

        apszDesc[0] = "Solid Black Brush";
        hbr[0] = CreateSolidBrush (RGB (0, 0, 0));

        apszDesc[1] = "Solid Gray Brush";
        hbr[1] = CreateSolidBrush (RGB (64, 64, 64));

        apszDesc[2] = "Solid White Brush";
        hbr[2] = CreateSolidBrush (RGB (255, 255, 255));

        apszDesc[3] = "Hatch - Horizontal";
        hbr[3] = CreateHatchBrush (HS_HORIZONTAL , RGB(0, 0, 0));

        apszDesc[4] = "Hatch - Vertical";
        hbr[4] = CreateHatchBrush (HS_VERTICAL , RGB(0, 0, 0));

        apszDesc[5] = "Hatch - Forward Diagonal";
        hbr[5] = CreateHatchBrush (HS_FDIAGONAL , RGB(0, 0, 0));

        apszDesc[6] = "Hatch - Backward Diagonal   ";
        hbr[6] = CreateHatchBrush (HS_BDIAGONAL, RGB(0, 0, 0));
```

```
        apszDesc[7] = "Hatch - Cross";
        hbr[7]  = CreateHatchBrush (HS_CROSS , RGB(0, 0, 0));

        apszDesc[8] = "Hatch - Diagonal Cross";
        hbr[8]  = CreateHatchBrush (HS_DIAGCROSS , RGB(0, 0, 0));

        apszDesc[9] = "Pattern Brush #1";
        hbm = LoadBitmap (hInst, "square");
        hbr[9]  = CreatePatternBrush (hbm);
        DeleteObject (hbm);

        apszDesc[10] = "Pattern Brush #2";
        hbm = CreateBitmap (8, 8, 1, 1, acPattern);
        hbr[10] = CreatePatternBrush (hbm);
        DeleteObject (hbm);
        }
        break;

case WM_DESTROY:
    {
    int i;
    for (i=0;i<BRUSHCOUNT; i++)  DeleteObject (hbr[i]);
    PostQuitMessage(0);
    }
    break;

case WM_PAINT:
    {
    DWORD dw;
    HDC hdc;
    int i;
    int xStart, xEnd, xText;
    int yIncr, yLine, yText;
    int cxWidth, cyHeight;
    PAINTSTRUCT ps;
    RECT r;
    TEXTMETRIC tm;

    hdc = BeginPaint (hwnd, &ps);

    /*  Divide available client area.  */
```

```
            GetClientRect (hwnd, &r);
            yIncr = r.bottom/ (BRUSHCOUNT+2);
            yText = yIncr;

            /*  Get measurements to indent text 4 spaces.  */
            GetTextMetrics (hdc, &tm);
            xText = tm.tmAveCharWidth * 4;

            /*  Get measurements of longest text string.  */
            dw = GetTextExtent (hdc, apszDesc[6],
                            lstrlen(apszDesc[6]));
            cxWidth = LOWORD(dw);
            cyHeight = HIWORD (dw);

            /*  Calculate width of rectangles.  */
            xStart = xText + cxWidth;
            xEnd  = r.right - 10;

            /*  Loop through all brushes.  */
            for (i=0;i<BRUSHCOUNT; i++, yText += yIncr)
                {
                TextOut (hdc, xText, yText,apszDesc[i],
                        lstrlen(apszDesc[i]));

                SelectObject (hdc, hbr[i]);
                yLine = yText + yIncr - tm.tmHeight/4;
                Rectangle (hdc, xStart, yText, xEnd, yLine);
                }

            EndPaint (hwnd, &ps);
            }
            break;

        default:
            return(DefWindowProc(hwnd,msg,wParam,lParam));
            break;
        }
    return 0L;
    }
```

BRUSH.RC

```
snapshot icon Brushes.ico

hand   cursor Brushes.cur

square bitmap square.bmp
```

BRUSH.DEF

```
NAME      BRUSHES

EXETYPE WINDOWS

DESCRIPTION 'GDI Brushes'

CODE      MOVEABLE DISCARDABLE
DATA      MOVEABLE MULTIPLE

HEAPSIZE    512
STACKSIZE   5000

EXPORTS
    BruWndProc
```

Our window procedure is interested in three messages: WM_CREATE, WM_DESTROY, and WM_PAINT.

The WM_CREATE message is received when the window is created. It is a very useful time to perform whatever initialization our window requires. In this case, we create all the GDI brushes that our program uses and the GDI bitmaps needed to create these brushes.

When our window procedure receives the WM_DESTROY message, it knows that a window has been closed. That's the time to destroy all GDI objects, to avoid losing valuable pieces of system memory.

In response to the WM_PAINT message, our program divides up the available client area to display 11 rectangles using the 11 brushes that we've created. For easy identification, each of these rectangles is labeled with the brush type.

In the course of this program, we call three GDI text routines: GetTextMetrics, GetTextExtent, and TextOut. GetTextMetrics provides measurement information for the current font, or text pattern table. GetTextExtent is used to determine the width and height of a specific line of text. And TextOut displays a line of text.

In the next chapter, we're going to take a closer look at these routines and all of the other facilities that GDI provides for the creation of text output.

10
Drawing Text

In most programs, text serves as the primary output media. And yet, we have postponed a discussion of text until now because text output in GDI is quite different from text output in traditional programming environments. GDI treats text as a type of graphic object.

You may have written programs with **line-oriented output**. This method was first used on the earliest interactive computer systems, which used typewriters to display output and receive input. With today's display screens, this type of output causes lines of text to roll off the top of a screen into an imaginary "bit-bucket." Interaction is simple: the computer displays a request, the user responds. Beginning C programmers always start with this type of output, because it is part of the standard C library. Here is an example:

```
printf ("Enter first number:");
scanf ("%i", &iValue);
```

The next step up is **screen-oriented output**, which treats the display screen as a grid of character cells. Programs like word processors and full screen editors typically use this method. One popular MS-DOS database language, dBASE, uses commands like these to write text and receive input on the display screen:

```
@ 10, 25 SAY "Please Enter Your Name:"
@ 10, 49 GET NAME
```

GDI's approach to text can be described as **pixel-oriented**, since GDI has no built-in idea of the size of a character cell. Instead, GDI lets you position text using the same pixel grid that you use for lines, rectangles, and other geometric shapes. This gives you a great deal of control over text placement and makes it easy to mix text with geometric figures. You can even mix different sizes and styles of text with a minimum of effort.

Unlike other graphic objects, text is not drawn using simple geometric equations. Instead, **fonts** are required to create text output. A font is a database of patterns that describe the shape and size of every letter, number, and punctuation mark. Each GDI device supports one or more fonts. Figure 10.1 shows some of the VGA display adapter's base fonts. The accompanying box discusses GDI's base fonts.

GDI Base Fonts

Every GDI display driver is equipped with a set of base fonts, like those shown in Figure 10.1. A common set of base fonts insures a minimum level of support will be available on all video displays.

Microsoft carefully chose the following fonts as part of the base set.

Courier—*provides fixed-pitch fonts for typewriter-like output.*

Tms Rmn—*are a set of proportional, serif fonts available in a fairly wide range of sizes. This set can be used as a "stand-in" for other serif fonts for programs that wish to mimic a printer's output on a display screen.*

Helv—*are a set of proportional, sans-serif Helvetica-like fonts, also available in a wide range of sizes. Like Tms Rmn, they are meant for use in programs that mimic a printer's output on a display screen.*

Symbol—*shows that an alternative character set can be used in a font; this font uses Greek letters.*

Roman, Modern and Script—*are vector fonts, which means the letter patterns are represented as sequences of vectors, or line segments.*

Figure 10.1 *A sampling of VGA base fonts*

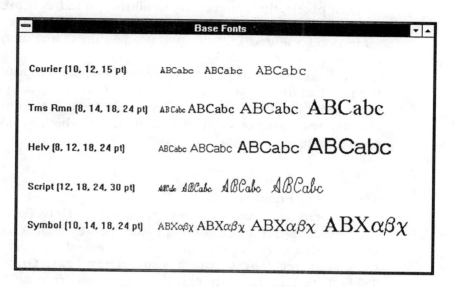

The available fonts can be extended beyond this base set. An end-user can purchase fonts and install them using the Windows Control Panel. Programmers can create custom fonts and incorporate them into Windows programs. Microsoft plans to incorporate a whole new set of fonts in a future version of Windows, using the *TrueType* "font engine." As of this writing, this technology is still being built in the development labs of Microsoft and Apple Computer.

Placing text often involves determining the **font metrics**, which is a table of values that tells you height and width information for a specific font.

If you wish to think in terms of a 25-line, 80-column output area, GDI gives you the tools to do so. You will find, however, that there are a few more things that you have to keep in mind—like the size of your output area (windows can shrink or grow), and the size of your text (every display has over 20 sizes and styles to choose from). And you'll want to do all of this in a way that allows your program to run on any display or printer—you'll want to do this in a device-independent manner.

Although it may seem strange at first to position text in a framework of pixels, this is necessary to allow you to freely mix text with other types of graphic objects. In GDI, text is positioned using the same pixel-oriented grid that we used to draw markers, lines, and rectangles.

We're going to start by reviewing the available text routines. We'll then look at the DC attributes that affect text and give special attention to the most important attribute: the font. We'll conclude this chapter with a discussion of text metrics, which is important to create device-independent text output.

Text Drawing Primitives

There are five routines for outputting text: DrawText, ExtTextOut, GrayString, TabbedTextOut, and TextOut. Strictly speaking, three of these are not part of GDI, but instead are part of the Window Manager. These routines are: DrawText, GrayString, and TabbedTextOut. Even though these routines are not GDI routines, they provide some useful enhancements to GDI and so are worth considering in our discussion.

Let's begin by looking at TextOut, probably the most widely used GDI text routine.

TextOut

TextOut is GDI's simplest text routine: it draws a single line of text. We used this routine to write labels in some of our earlier programs, but now it's time to give it a closer look. TextOut is defined as

```
TextOut (hDC, x, y, lpString, nCount)
```

- hDC is a DC handle. It tells GDI the device to draw on, and the drawing attributes to use.
- x and y are integers that specify a **control point** used to position the text. The control point is a location in the coordinate system as defined in the DC. Since we're limiting ourselves to the MM_TEXT coordinate system, our units are pixels.
- lpString is a far pointer to a character string. This does not have to be a null-terminated string, since TextOut gets the string size from the nCount parameter.
- nCount is the number of characters in the text string.

Figure 10.2   *Default relationship of control point to text*

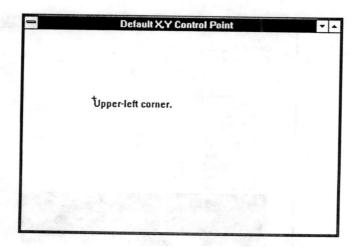

By default, GDI positions a line of text with the upper-left corner at the control point. Figure 10.2 demonstrates this with a marker. Later in this chapter, when we talk about DC attributes, we'll describe how other text alignment choices can be selected.

It is often convenient to call TextOut like this:

```
static char ac[] = "Display This Text.";

BeginPaint (hwnd, &ps);
TextOut (ps.hdc, X, Y, ac, lstrlen(ac));
EndPaint (hwnd, &ps);
```

This code calculates string length "on the fly" using `lstrlen`, a Windows routine that mimics the standard `strlen` function.

Some programmers prefer to split length calculation from drawing, as in

```
static char ac[] = "Display This Text.";
static int  cb = sizeof(ac) - 1;

BeginPaint (hwnd, &ps);
TextOut (ps.hdc, X, Y, ac, cb);
EndPaint (hwnd, &ps);
```

so that text length is calculated at compile time and not at run time. The result is faster drawing. In many cases, the time saved is hardly noticed. But when performance is critical, every little bit helps.

Figure 10.3 *ExtTextOut*

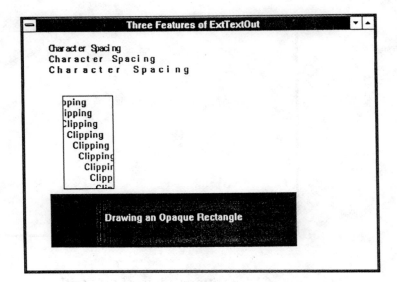

The next text routine is similar to TextOut, but provides some extra features.

ExtTextOut

Like TextOut, ExtTextOut draws a single line of text, but adds three options: character width control, clipping, and an opaque rectangle. You can mix and match these options as your needs require. Figure 10.3 shows text drawn with each of these options.

ExtTextOut is defined as follows:

```
ExtTextOut (hDC, X, Y, wOptions, lpRect, lpString,
     nCount, lpDx);
```

- hDC is a DC handle. It tells GDI the device to draw on and the drawing attributes to use.
- x and y are integers that specify a **control point** used to position the text. The control point is a location in the coordinate system as defined in the DC. Since we're limiting ourselves to the MM_TEXT coordinate system, our units are pixels.
- wOptions is a flag for two of the three extras that this routine provides. It can be 0, ETO_CLIPPED, ETO_OPAQUE, or a combination: ETO_CLIPPED | ETO_OPAQUE. We'll explain these options in a moment.

- lpRect is a pointer to a rectangle. Depending on the value of wOptions, lpRect points to a clip rectangle, an opaque rectangle, or both.
- lpString is a far pointer to a character string. This does not have to be a null-terminated string, since TextOut gets the string size from the nCount parameter.
- nCount is the number of characters in the text string.
- lpDx points to an array of character width values.

The first option that we're going to discuss is character spacing, which gives you total control over the amount of space between characters. Unlike TextOut, which uses the default spacing defined in a font, ExtTextOut lets you specify your own width values for each character. You specify width values by passing an array of integers. The last parameter, lpDx, points to this array.

Here is source code to our sample program, **EXTTXT**:

EXTTEXT.MAK

```
Exttxt.res: Exttxt.rc Exttxt.cur Exttxt.ico
    rc -r Exttxt.rc

Exttxt.obj: Exttxt.c
    cl -AM -c -d -Gsw -Od -W2 -Zpi Exttxt.c

exttxt.exe: Exttxt.obj Exttxt.def
    link Exttxt,/align:16,/map, mlibcew libw/NOD/NOE/CO,\
        Exttxt.def
    rc Exttxt.res exttext.exe

exttxt.exe: Exttxt.res
    rc Exttxt.res exttxt.exe
```

EXTTEXT.C

```
/*-------------------------------------------------------------*\
|    EXTTXT.C - Program to show capabilities of ExtTextOut.     |
\*-------------------------------------------------------------*/
#include <Windows.H>
```

```
/*--------------------------------------------------------------*\
|                    Function Prototypes.                        |
\*--------------------------------------------------------------*/
long FAR  PASCAL ExtTxtWndProc (HWND, WORD, WORD, LONG);
void NEAR PASCAL ExtTxtClipping(HDC hdc, HWND hwnd);
void NEAR PASCAL ExtTxtOpaqueRect(HDC hdc, HWND hwnd);
void NEAR PASCAL ExtTxtSpacing(HDC hdc, HWND hwnd);


/*--------------------------------------------------------------*\
|                   Main Function:  WinMain.                     |
\*--------------------------------------------------------------*/
int PASCAL WinMain (HANDLE hInstance,    HANDLE hPrevInstance,
                    LPSTR  lpszCmdLine, int    cmdShow)
    {
    HWND     hwnd;
    MSG      msg;
    WNDCLASS wndclass;

    if (!hPrevInstance)
        {
        wndclass.lpszClassName = "MIN:MAIN";
        wndclass.hInstance     = hInstance;
        wndclass.lpfnWndProc   = ExtTxtWndProc;
        wndclass.hCursor       = LoadCursor (hInstance, "hand");
        wndclass.hIcon         = LoadIcon (hInstance,"snapshot");
        wndclass.lpszMenuName  = NULL;
        wndclass.hbrBackground = COLOR_WINDOW+1;
        wndclass.style         = CS_HREDRAW | CS_VREDRAW;
        wndclass.cbClsExtra    = 0;
        wndclass.cbWndExtra    = 0;

        RegisterClass( &wndclass);
        }

    hwnd = CreateWindow("MIN:MAIN",             /* Class name.  */
                                                /* Title.       */
                        "Three Features of ExtTextOut",
                        WS_OVERLAPPEDWINDOW,    /* Style bits.  */
                        CW_USEDEFAULT,          /* x - default. */
                        0,                      /* y - default. */
                        CW_USEDEFAULT,          /* cx - default. */
                        0,                      /* cy - default. */
```

```
                         NULL,                /* No parent.   */
                         NULL,                /* Class menu.  */
                         hInstance,           /* Creator      */
                         NULL                 /* Params.      */
                         ) ;

    ShowWindow (hwnd, cmdShow);

    while (GetMessage(&msg, 0, 0, 0))
        {
        TranslateMessage(&msg);          /* Keyboard input.     */
        DispatchMessage(&msg);
        }
    return 0;
    }


/*-----------------------------------------------------------*\
 |            Window Procedure:   ExtTxtWndProc.              |
\*-----------------------------------------------------------*/
long FAR PASCAL ExtTxtWndProc (HWND hwnd,   WORD wMsg,
                               WORD wParam, LONG lParam)
    {
    switch (wMsg)
        {
        case WM_DESTROY:
            PostQuitMessage(0);
            break;

        case WM_PAINT:
            {
            PAINTSTRUCT ps;

            BeginPaint (hwnd, &ps);

            ExtTxtSpacing(ps.hdc, hwnd);
            ExtTxtClipping(ps.hdc, hwnd);
            ExtTxtOpaqueRect(ps.hdc, hwnd);

            EndPaint (hwnd, &ps);
            }
            break;
```

```
        default:
            return(DefWindowProc(hwnd,wMsg,wParam,lParam));
            break;
        }
    return 0L;
    }


/*--------------------------------------------------------------*\
 | ExtTxtSpacing: Demonstrate ExtTextOut character              |
 |                spacing.                                       |
\*--------------------------------------------------------------*/
void NEAR PASCAL ExtTxtSpacing(HDC hdc, HWND hwnd)
    {
    static char ac1[] = "Character Spacing";
    static int  cb1  = sizeof (ac1) - 1;
    static int  ai1[] = {6, 6, 6, 6, 6, 6, 6, 6,
                             6, 6, 6, 6, 6, 6, 6, 6};
    static int  ai2[] = {9, 9, 9, 9, 9, 9, 9, 9,
                             9, 9, 9, 9, 9, 9, 9, 9};
    static int  ai3[] = {12, 12, 12, 12, 12, 12, 12, 12,
                             12, 12, 12, 12, 12, 12, 12, 12};
    int x;
    int y;
    int yHeight;
    RECT r;
    TEXTMETRIC tm;

    GetTextMetrics (hdc, &tm);
    yHeight = tm.tmHeight + tm.tmExternalLeading;
    x = tm.tmAveCharWidth * 5;
    y = yHeight;

    ExtTextOut (hdc, x, y, 0, NULL, ac1, cb1, ai1);
    y += yHeight;
    ExtTextOut (hdc, x, y, 0, NULL, ac1, cb1, ai2);
    y += yHeight;
    ExtTextOut (hdc, x, y, 0, NULL, ac1, cb1, ai3);
    y += yHeight;
    }

/*--------------------------------------------------------------*\
 |     ExtTxtClipping: Demonstrate ExtTextOut Clipping.         |
\*--------------------------------------------------------------*/
```

```
void NEAR PASCAL ExtTxtClipping(HDC hdc, HWND hwnd)
    {
    static char ach[] = "Clipping";
    static int  cch  = sizeof (ach) - 1;
    int x;
    int y;
    int yHeight;
    RECT r;
    TEXTMETRIC tm;

    GetTextMetrics (hdc, &tm);
    yHeight = tm.tmHeight + tm.tmExternalLeading;
    x = tm.tmAveCharWidth * 5;
    y = yHeight * 6;

    r.top = y;
    r.left  = x + 20;
    r.right = x + 90;
    r.bottom = y + tm.tmHeight * 8 + tm.tmHeight/2;
    Rectangle (hdc, r.left-1, r.top-1,
               r.right+1, r.bottom+1);
    while (y< r.bottom)
        {
        ExtTextOut (hdc, x, y, ETO_CLIPPED, &r, ach, cch, NULL);
        y += yHeight;
        x += 8;
        }
    }


/*-----------------------------------------------------------*\
 |  ExtTxtOpaqueRect: Demonstrate ExtTextOut opaque          |
 |                    rectangle.                             |
\*-----------------------------------------------------------*/
void NEAR PASCAL ExtTxtOpaqueRect(HDC hdc, HWND hwnd)
    {
    static char ach[] = "Drawing an Opaque Rectangle";
    static int  cch  = sizeof (ach) - 1;
    int x;
    int y;
    int yHeight;
    RECT r;
```

```
    TEXTMETRIC tm;

    GetTextMetrics (hdc, &tm);
    yHeight = tm.tmHeight + tm.tmExternalLeading;
    x = tm.tmAveCharWidth * 5;
    y = yHeight * 15;

    GetClientRect (hwnd, &r);
    r.top = y;
    r.bottom = r.top + (5 * tm.tmHeight);
    r.left = x;
    r.right = x + tm.tmAveCharWidth * 50;
    SetBkColor (hdc, RGB (0, 0, 0));
    SetTextColor (hdc, RGB (255, 255, 255));
    SetTextAlign (hdc, TA_CENTER | TA_BASELINE);
    x = (r.left + r.right) / 2;
    y = (r.top  + r.bottom) / 2;
    ExtTextOut (hdc, x, y, ETO_OPAQUE, &r, ach, cch, NULL);
    }
```

EXTTEXT.RC

```
snapshot icon Exttxt.ico

hand  cursor Exttxt.cur
```

EXTTEXT.DEF

```
NAME    EXTTXT

EXETYPE WINDOWS

DESCRIPTION 'ExtTextOut Demo'

CODE    MOVEABLE DISCARDABLE
DATA    MOVEABLE MULTIPLE
```

```
HEAPSIZE      512
STACKSIZE     5000


EXPORTS
    ExtTxtWndProc
```

Each of the subroutines, ExtTxtSpacing, ExtTxtClipping and Ext-TxtOpaqueRect, demonstrates a different feature of ExtTextOut.

In our example, we display "Character Spacing" using arrays with three different widths: 6, 9, and 12 pixels. Notice that the third line is twice as wide as the first line. This option is used to justify text. Text justification lets us expand lines of text to the left and right margins. For example, the text on this page is justified text. Depending on how we fill the character width array, we could fit a line of text into just about any margin. Here is the code for the text in our example:

```
/*-------------------------------------------------------------*\
| ExtTxtSpacing: Demonstrate ExtTextOut character              |
|                   spacing.                                   |
\*-------------------------------------------------------------*/
void NEAR PASCAL ExtTxtSpacing(HDC hdc, HWND hwnd)
    {
    static char ac1[] = "Character Spacing";
    static int  cb1   = sizeof (ac1) - 1;
    static int  ai1[] = {6, 6, 6, 6, 6, 6, 6, 6,
                         6, 6, 6, 6, 6, 6, 6, 6};
    static int  ai2[] = {9, 9, 9, 9, 9, 9, 9, 9,
                         9, 9, 9, 9, 9, 9, 9, 9};
    static int  ai3[] = {12, 12, 12, 12, 12, 12, 12, 12,
                         12, 12, 12, 12, 12, 12, 12, 12};
    int x;
    int y;
    int yHeight;
    RECT r;
    TEXTMETRIC tm;

    GetTextMetrics (hdc, &tm);
    yHeight = tm.tmHeight + tm.tmExternalLeading;
    x = tm.tmAveCharWidth * 5;
```

```
   y = yHeight;

   ExtTextOut (hdc, x, y, 0, NULL, ac1, cb1, ai1);
   y += yHeight;
   ExtTextOut (hdc, x, y, 0, NULL, ac1, cb1, ai2);
   y += yHeight;
   ExtTextOut (hdc, x, y, 0, NULL, ac1, cb1, ai3);
   y += yHeight;
   }
```

Our character array has 17 characters, which means there are 16 spaces between letters. For this reason, our character width array has 16 values. Each value defines the width of one character cell. While it requires some extra work to maintain a character width array, it also means that you have a tremendous amount of control over the placement of each letter in a line of text.

Notice the call to GetTextMetrics. This provides measurement information for the current font. We use the values returned by this routine to position our first line of text one line from the top of the window, and five spaces from the left side of the window. We'll explore this routine more fully later in this chapter.

The second option available with ExtTextOut lets you specify a clip rectangle for text. When we introduced the DC, we said that every DC comes equipped with a clipping region. With the ETO_CLIPPED option, ExtTextOut lets you specify an additional clipping rectangle. This option provides a way to create a window of text without incurring the overhead of creating an actual window. Here is the code for the clipped text in our example:

```
/*-----------------------------------------------------------*\
|      ExtTxtClipping: Demonstrate ExtTextOut Clipping.       |
\*-----------------------------------------------------------*/
void NEAR PASCAL ExtTxtClipping(HDC hdc, HWND hwnd)
    {
    static char ach[] = "Clipping";
    static int  cch   = sizeof (ach) - 1;
    int x;
    int y;     int yHeight;
    RECT r;
    TEXTMETRIC tm;
```

```
GetTextMetrics (hdc, &tm);
yHeight = tm.tmHeight + tm.tmExternalLeading;
x = tm.tmAveCharWidth * 5;
y = yHeight * 6;

r.top = y;
r.left  = x + 20;
r.right = x + 90;
r.bottom = y + tm.tmHeight * 8 + tm.tmHeight/2;
Rectangle (hdc, r.left-1, r.top-1,
            r.right+1, r.bottom+1);
while (y< r.bottom)
    {
    ExtTextOut (hdc, x, y, ETO_CLIPPED, &r,
                ach, cch, NULL);
    y += yHeight;
    x += 8;
    }
}
```

Once again, we rely on the GetTextMetrics routine to help us decide where to draw lines of text. In this case, we start six lines from the top of the window and five spaces from the left side of the window.

We have arbitrarily made our clip rectangle 70 pixels wide and eight and one-half lines high. The coordinates used in a clip rectangle are *grid-intersection coordinates*, which we first encountered in the context of drawing filled areas in Chapter 9. To make the clip rectangle more readily apparent, we draw a rectangle just outside its border.

ExtTextOut's third option creates an opaque rectangle; it is like having a free call to the Rectangle routine. It's useful for drawing many lines of unequal length to insure that the background is the correct color. Incidentally, as indicated in our sample code, the background color is selected by making a call to the SetBkColor routine, which sets a DC attribute value that is used by all text-drawing routines. We'll explore this and other DC attributes later in this chapter.

Here is the code that created the opaque rectangle:

```
/*-------------------------------------------------------------*\
|   ExtTxtOpaqueRect: Demonstrate ExtTextOut opaque            |
|                     rectangle.                               |
\*-------------------------------------------------------------*/
void NEAR PASCAL ExtTxtOpaqueRect(HDC hdc, HWND hwnd)
    {
    static char ach[] = "Drawing an Opaque Rectangle";
    static int  cch   = sizeof (ach) - 1;
    int x;
    int y;
    int yHeight;
    RECT r;
    TEXTMETRIC tm;

    GetTextMetrics (hdc, &tm);
    yHeight = tm.tmHeight + tm.tmExternalLeading;
    x = tm.tmAveCharWidth * 5;
    y = yHeight * 15;

    r.top = y;
    r.bottom = r.top + (5 * tm.tmHeight);
    r.left = x;
    r.right = x + tm.tmAveCharWidth * 50;

    SetBkColor (hdc, RGB (0, 0, 0));
    SetTextColor (hdc, RGB (255, 255, 255));
    SetTextAlign (hdc, TA_CENTER | TA_BASELINE);

    x = (r.left + r.right) / 2;
    y = (r.top  + r.bottom) / 2;
    ExtTextOut (hdc, x, y, ETO_OPAQUE, &r, ach, cch, NULL);
    }
```

Once again, we rely on the GetTextMetrics routine to help us place the text and its black opaque background. In this case, the top of the rectangle is situated 15 lines from the top of the window and five spaces from the left side.

We set the size of our rectangle to be five character cells high and 50 character cells wide. To make the opaque rectangle visible, we

Figure 10.4 *TabbedTextOut*

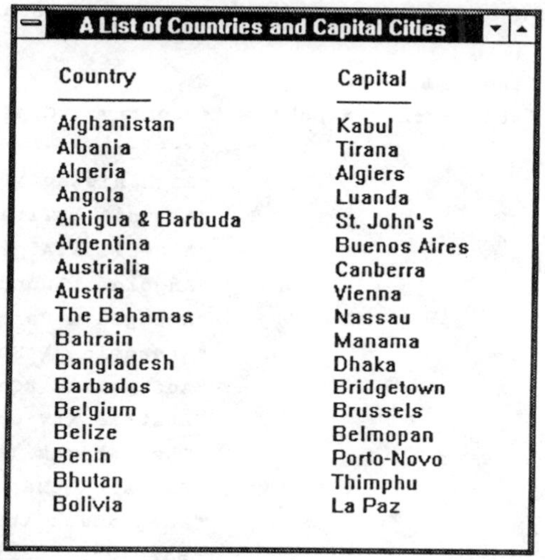

changed two DC attributes: the text color (set to white) and the background color (set to black). We used a third DC attribute, text alignment, to center the text inside the rectangle.

TabbedTextOut

Our third text-drawing primitive draws a single line of text, but expands tabs to tab stops. This provides a convenient way to align columns of data. Microsoft included this routine in the Windows library for listboxes to make it easy to create lists of column-oriented data. But it's a simple matter to use this routine in your programs to achieve the same benefit.

Figure 10.4 shows an example of text drawn with this routine. Here is the window procedure to the code that created the sample output:

```
/*-------------------------------------------------------------*\
|                 Window Procedure:  TxtTabWndProc.            |
\*-------------------------------------------------------------*/
long FAR PASCAL TxtTabWndProc (HWND hwnd,
                              WORD wMsg,
```

```
                                WORD wParam,
                                LONG lParam)
    {
#define COUNT 19
    static char *apch[]= {"Country \tCapital",
                          "--------------- \t------------",
                          "Afghanistan \tKabul",
                          "Albania \tTirana",
                          "Algeria \tAlgiers",
                          "Angola \tLuanda",
                          "Antigua & Barbuda \tSt. John's",
                          "Argentina \tBuenos Aires",
                          "Australia \tCanberra",
                          "Austria \tVienna",
                          "The Bahamas \tNassau",
                          "Bahrain \tManama",
                          "Bangladesh \tDhaka",
                          "Barbados \tBridgetown",
                          "Belgium \tBrussels",
                          "Belize \tBelmopan",
                          "Benin \tPorto-Novo",
                          "Bhutan \tThimphu",
                          "Bolivia \tLa Paz"};

    switch (wMsg)
        {
        case WM_DESTROY:
            PostQuitMessage(0);
            break;

        case WM_PAINT:
            {
            DWORD dwSize;
            int i;
            int xTab;
            int xText;
            int yText;
            int yHeight;
            PAINTSTRUCT ps;

            BeginPaint (hwnd, &ps);
```

```
                dwSize = GetTextExtent (ps.hdc, "X", 1);
                yHeight = yText = HIWORD(dwSize);
                xText = 3 * LOWORD (dwSize);
                xTab  = 20 * LOWORD (dwSize);

                for (i=0;i<COUNT;i++, yText += yHeight)
                    {
                    TabbedTextOut (ps.hdc, xText, yText,
                                   apch[i], lstrlen(apch[i]),
                                   1, &xTab, xText);
                    }
                EndPaint (hwnd, &ps);
                }

            break;

        default:
            return(DefWindowProc(hwnd,wMsg,wParam,lParam));
            break;
        }
    return 0L;
    }
```

This code calls GetTextExtent to determine the width and height of the letter X in the current (system) font. In previous examples, we've used the GetTextMetrics routine to determine this information, but for the sake of variety we have chosen this alternative method. Notice the use of the HIWORD and LOWORD macros, which filter out the desired part of this routine's return value.

We use the results to calculate three values: the X and Y starting position of the text (one line from the top and three characters from the left), and the location of the tab-stop. In this case, we have placed the tab-stop at approximately 20 spaces from the X and Y starting point. If there had been more than a single tab-stop, we would have had to allocate an array to hold them. As it is, we get by with allocating a single integer value and then passing this value to our routine.

DrawText

Like TabbedTextOut, DrawText provides some formatting capability. In our opinion, the most useful option is the ability to perform

Figure 10.5 *DrawText*

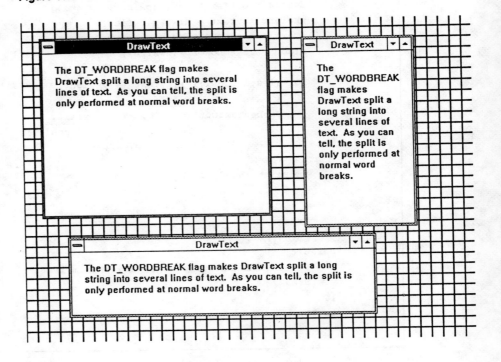

word wrapping for multiple lines of text (although this is just one of several things that DrawText will do for you).

Figure 10.5 shows three instances of a sample program that uses DrawText to display a long line of text in an area of different sizes and shapes. Here is the code to our sample program:

```
/*-------------------------------------------------------------*\
|              Window Procedure:  DrwTxtWndProc.              |
\*-------------------------------------------------------------*/
long FAR PASCAL DrwTxtWndProc (HWND hwnd,
                               WORD wMsg,
                               WORD wParam,
                               LONG lParam)

    {
```

```
        static char *apchDesc = "The DT_WORDBREAK flag makes "
                                "DrawText split a long string "
                                "into several lines of text.  "
                                "As you can tell, the split is "
                                "only performed at normal word "
                                "breaks.";
    switch (wMsg)
        {
        case WM_DESTROY:
            PostQuitMessage(0);
            break;

        case WM_PAINT:
            {
            DWORD dwSize;
            PAINTSTRUCT ps;
            RECT r;

            BeginPaint (hwnd, &ps);
            dwSize = GetTextExtent(ps.hdc, "X", 1);

            GetClientRect (hwnd, &r);
            r.top    += HIWORD (dwSize);
            r.bottom -= HIWORD (dwSize);
            r.left   += LOWORD (dwSize) * 2;
            r.right  -= LOWORD (dwSize) * 2;

            DrawText (ps.hdc, apchDesc, lstrlen (apchDesc),
                    &r, DT_WORDBREAK);

            EndPaint (hwnd, &ps);
            }
            break;

        default:
            return(DefWindowProc(hwnd,wMsg,wParam,lParam));
            break;
        }
    return 0L;
    }
```

Figure 10.6   *GrayString*

Once more, we use GetTextExtent to determine the width and height of the letter X. We use these values to offset the dimensions of our client area so that there is a margin around our text.

The GetClientRect routine gets the dimensions of the client area into a RECT variable. We then modify the values in this structure to create margins on all four sides of the text.

The resulting rectangle is passed to DrawText, which uses the values to determine where to position the text.

GrayString

The text produced by this routine is best described as checkered. But the name of the routine describes the primary reason that Microsoft created this routine: to create text with a gray appearance.

The Window Manager uses this routine for disabled menu items and disabled dialog box controls. If you write your own custom dialog box controls (discussed in Chapter 14), or create owner-drawn menu items (discussed in Chapter 12), then this routine may be quite useful to you. Figure 10.6 shows an example of a gray string.

Here is the code that created this output:

```
/*----------------------------------------------------------*\
|              Window Procedure:  TxtGryWndProc.             |
\*----------------------------------------------------------*/
long FAR PASCAL TxtGryWndProc (HWND hwnd,
                               WORD wMsg,
                               WORD wParam,
                               LONG lParam)
    {
    static char acString[] = "This is a Gray String";
```

```
        static int  cb = sizeof (acString) - 1;

    switch (wMsg)
        {
        case WM_DESTROY:
            PostQuitMessage(0);
            break;

        case WM_PAINT:
            {
            DWORD dwSize;
            int xText, yText;
            PAINTSTRUCT ps;
            TEXTMETRIC tm;

            BeginPaint (hwnd, &ps);
            GetTextMetrics (ps.hdc, &tm);
            xText = tm.tmAveCharWidth * 3;
            yText = tm.tmHeight * 2;

            GrayString (ps.hdc, GetStockObject (BLACK_BRUSH),
                        NULL, (DWORD)(LPSTR)acString, cb,
                        xText, yText, 0, 0);

            EndPaint (hwnd, &ps);
            }
            break;

        default:
            return(DefWindowProc(hwnd,wMsg,wParam,lParam));
            break;
        }
    return 0L;
    }
```

As in earlier examples, we depend on the results of GetTextMetrics to give us some size information to help us position lines of text. Here, we place the gray string two lines from the top of the window and three character widths from the left margin.

This is the only text-drawing routine that uses a brush. The color of the brush determines the foreground color of the checkered text:

In this case we use a black brush, which gives the text a grayed appearance. If we had chosen a red brush, it would give the appearance of red and white checkered text.

This concludes our tour of the different GDI text-drawing routines. As you can see, there are quite a few different effects that you can achieve by making a single call to one of these routines. But the library routines are only one-half of the story. To get the complete picture of the amount of control that GDI allows you over text drawing, we need to address the issue of DC attributes that affect text appearance.

DC Attributes for Text Drawing

Six attributes affect the appearance and positioning of text:

Attribute	Description
Background Color	Color of "empty space" in text
Background Mode	Turns on/off background color
Font	Text style and size
Intercharacter Spacing	Extra pixels between characters for text justification
Text Alignment	Relationship of text to control point
Text Color	Color of letters themselves

The most important of these attributes is the font, which determines the shape and size of the individual characters. Before we delve into the way GDI handles fonts, let's explore some of the other text attributes, starting with those that control color.

Color

Three different DC attributes deal with the color of text: text color, background color, and background mode. Text can only be drawn with *pure* colors, and not dithered colors like those available for filled areas. Like pixel, pen, and brush colors, you can use any of three methods to define colors: an RGB triplet, a palette index, or an RGB palette relative value.

The text color attribute determines the actual color of the letters. If GDI had been used to create the letters on this page, it would have been with text color set to black. To set the text color, you must call the SetTextColor routine. Its parameters are

```
SetTextColor (hDC, crColor);
```

where crColor is a color reference value, using one of the three methods. Here is how to set text color to blue, using an RGB triplet:

```
SetTextColor (hDC, RGB (0, 0, 0xFF));
```

The background color attribute determines the color of the areas inside character cells not touched by the text color. From GDI's point of view, the text on this page has a white background, since that's the color of the space between letters and the area inside hollow letters like O and Q.

As you may have noticed, the background color attribute is also used for hatched brushes and styled lines to set, respectively, the color *between* the hatches and the blank area *inside* the pattern of a style line.

To set the background color, call the SetBkColor routine, which takes the same two parameters as SetTextColor:

```
SetBkColor (hDC, crColor);
```

For example, here is how to request a green background:

```
SetBkColor (hDC, RGB (0, 0xFF, 0));
```

Our third color attribute, background mode, is a toggle switch for the background color. The routine that controls this attribute, Set-BkMode, takes two parameters:

```
SetBkMode (hDC, nBkMode);
```

When nBkMode is OPAQUE, the background color is turned *on*. When set to TRANSPARENT, the background color is turned *off*.

Figure 10.7 draws three lines of text, using different foreground and background colors. Notice that the second line of text is unreadable, because we set both foreground and background colors to black. Here is the windows procedure that created this figure:

Figure 10.7 *Three lines showing different foreground/background colors*

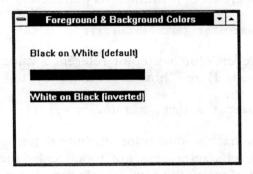

```
/*------------------------------------------------------------*\
|             Window Procedure:  TxtClrWndProc.               |
\*------------------------------------------------------------*/
long FAR PASCAL TxtClrWndProc (HWND hwnd,
                               WORD wMsg,
                               WORD wParam,
                               LONG lParam)
    {
    static char acFirst[]  = "Black on White (default)";
    static char acSecond[] = "Black on Black (invisible)";
    static char acThird[]  = "White on Black (inverted)";

    switch (wMsg)
        {
        case WM_DESTROY:
            PostQuitMessage(0);
            break;

        case WM_PAINT:
            {
            int X;
            int Y;
            PAINTSTRUCT ps;
            TEXTMETRIC tm;

            BeginPaint (hwnd, &ps);
```

```
                GetTextMetrics (ps.hdc, &tm);
                X = tm.tmAveCharWidth * 3;
                Y = tm.tmHeight * 2;

                TextOut (ps.hdc, X, Y, acFirst, lstrlen (acFirst));
                Y += tm.tmHeight * 2;

                SetBkColor (ps.hdc, RGB (0, 0, 0));
                TextOut (ps.hdc, X, Y, acSecond,
                        lstrlen (acSecond));
                Y += tm.tmHeight * 2;

                SetTextColor (ps.hdc, RGB (255, 255, 255));
                TextOut (ps.hdc, X, Y, acThird, lstrlen (acThird));

                EndPaint (hwnd, &ps);
                }
                break;

        default:
                return(DefWindowProc(hwnd,wMsg,wParam,lParam));
                break;
        }
    return 0L;
    }
```

Although our example is in black and white, it is a simple matter to create red or green text on devices that support color: supply the appropriate color reference, and GDI does the rest.

Text Alignment

The text alignment attribute lets you change the relationship between the control point, which is the (X,Y) pair that is passed to each routine, and the text to be displayed. Figure 10.8 shows the nine possible ways to align text, with a marker at each control point to emphasize the alignment.

To set text alignment, you call the SetTextAlign routine, which has the following syntax:

```
SetTextAlign (hDC, wFlags);
```

Figure 10.8   *Nine different text alignments*

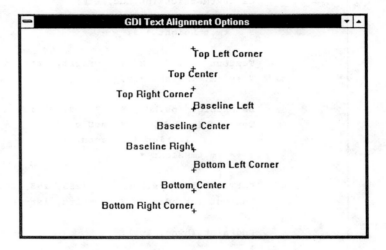

As indicated in the example, there are nine possible alignments. Select an alignment by combining two flags from the following table, with one flag taken from each of the two categories.

Horizontal Flag	Vertical Flag
TA_LEFT	TA_TOP
TA_CENTER	TA_BASELINE
TA_RIGHT	TA_BOTTOM

The default alignment is TA_LEFT | TA_TOP. To set alignment to the bottom right, you say

```
SetTextAlign (hDC, TA_BOTTOM | TA_RIGHT);
```

Here is the code for our example:

```
/*-------------------------------------------------------------*\
|                Window Procedure:  TxtAlnWndProc.              |
\*-------------------------------------------------------------*/
long FAR PASCAL TxtAlnWndProc (HWND hwnd,
```

```
                                    WORD wMsg,
                                    WORD wParam,
                                    LONG lParam)
        {
#define LINECOUNT 9
    static char * apchDesc[LINECOUNT] =
            { "Top Left Corner",
              "Top Center",
              "Top Right Corner",
              "Baseline Left",
              "Baseline Center",
              "Baseline Right",
              "Bottom Left Corner",
              "Bottom Center",
              "Bottom Right Corner"};
    static int  fAlign [LINECOUNT] =
            {
            TA_LEFT | TA_TOP ,
            TA_CENTER | TA_TOP ,
            TA_RIGHT | TA_TOP ,
            TA_LEFT | TA_BASELINE ,
            TA_CENTER | TA_BASELINE,
            TA_RIGHT | TA_BASELINE ,
            TA_LEFT | TA_BOTTOM ,
            TA_CENTER | TA_BOTTOM ,
            TA_RIGHT | TA_BOTTOM };

    switch (wMsg)
        {
        case WM_DESTROY:
            PostQuitMessage(0);
            break;

        case WM_PAINT:
            {
            int i;
            int xText;
            int yText;
            int yLineHeight;
            PAINTSTRUCT ps;
            RECT r;
```

```
        BeginPaint (hwnd, &ps);
        GetClientRect (hwnd, &r);
        xText = r.right/2;
        yLineHeight = r.bottom/ (LINECOUNT+1);
        yText = yLineHeight;

        for (i = 0; i < LINECOUNT; i++)
            {
            SetTextAlign (ps.hdc, fAlign[i]);

            TextOut (ps.hdc, xText, yText, apchDesc[i],
                        lstrlen(apchDesc[i]));
            MrkDrawMarker (ps.hdc, xText, yText);
            yText += yLineHeight;


            }
        EndPaint (hwnd, &ps);
        }
        break;

    default:
        return(DefWindowProc(hwnd,wMsg,wParam,lParam));
        break;
    }
    return 0L;
    }
```

In this code, we have departed from our usual practice of spacing lines. Instead of using the GetTextMetrics or GetTextExtent routines, we have split the available space in the window into ten areas, with one line per area. Since GDI treats text as a graphic object, there is nothing to stop you from devising interesting and useful methods like this to take advantage of available screen real estate when you draw text.

Intercharacter Spacing

This attribute allows you to insert extra pixels between characters. It provides another option (besides the ExtTextOut routine) to expand a line of text to fit an arbitrary margin. Figure 10.9 shows six

Figure 10.9 *Intercharacter spacing (also known as character extra spacing)*

lines of text, with extra spacing varying from zero to five pixels. It is difficult to detect the difference from one line to the next, but between the top and bottom lines the difference is quite apparent.

Here is the code we used to generate the example:

```
/*-----------------------------------------------------*\
|               Window Procedure:  ExtWndProc.          |
\*-----------------------------------------------------*/
long FAR PASCAL ExtWndProc (HWND hwnd,
                            WORD wMsg,
                            WORD wParam,
                            LONG lParam)
    {
#define COUNT 6
    static char acLine[] = "AaBbCcDdEeFfGgHhIiJjKkLlMm"
                           "NnOoPpQqRrSsTtUuVvWwXxYyZz";
    static char *apch[] = {"0", "1", "2", "3", "4", "5"};
    static int  cbLine = sizeof (acLine) - 1;

    switch (wMsg)
        {
        case WM_DESTROY:
            PostQuitMessage(0);
            break;
```

```
        case WM_PAINT:
            {
            int i;
            int xText;
            int xText2;
            int yText;
            PAINTSTRUCT ps;
            TEXTMETRIC tm;

            BeginPaint (hwnd, &ps);
            GetTextMetrics (ps.hdc, &tm);
            xText  = tm.tmAveCharWidth * 3;
            xText2 = tm.tmAveCharWidth * 6;
            yText = tm.tmHeight * 2;
            for (i=0;i<COUNT;i++)
                {
                SetTextCharacterExtra (ps.hdc, i);
                TextOut (ps.hdc, xText, yText,
                        apch[i], lstrlen (apch[i]));
                TextOut (ps.hdc, xText2, yText,
                        acLine, cbLine);
                yText += tm.tmHeight;
                }

            EndPaint (hwnd, &ps);
            }
            break;

        default:
            return(DefWindowProc(hwnd,wMsg,wParam,lParam));
            break;
        }
    return 0L;
    }
```

We have one more DC attribute to describe, which plays the most
important role in determining the shape and size of letters that GDI
draws: the font.

About Fonts

A font is a collection of patterns used to create text output. Fonts come in all shapes, sizes, and styles. Fonts have a lot in common with other GDI drawing objects, like pens and brushes. For one thing, fonts can be shared between programs. And like these other GDI objects, fonts are referenced using a handle. When a program is ready to use a specific font, it selects the font handle into a DC using the SelectObject routine:

```
SelectObject (hDC, hFont);
```

Internally, GDI recognizes two types of fonts: **logical fonts** and **physical fonts**. A logical font describes text in a standard, device-independent manner. As we'll see in a moment, a logical font consists of the set of values in the data structure LOGFONT. By itself, a logical font isn't enough information to draw text on a device. Instead, like other logical drawing objects, a logical font is a *request* for text with a specific appearance.

The GDI **font mapper** selects a physical font from the description contained in a logical font. The mapping is done when a logical font handle is selected into a DC. A physical font is a device-*dependent* set of patterns. These patterns are used to create the letters, numbers, and punctuation marks that we normally associate with text. A physical font might live in the device hardware, which is typical for printer fonts. Or, it may be kept in memory by GDI.

Physical fonts are device-dependent, because every font is created with a specific type of device in mind. Two measurements are used to match fonts to devices: resolution (pixels per inch) and aspect ratio (the *squareness* of the pixels). By default, the GDI mapper only selects physical fonts that match the metrics of a given device. Otherwise, the results might be very odd.

For example, a VGA display has approximately 72 pixels per inch. Today's typical laser printer has 300 pixels per inch. If you tried to mix fonts between these two devices, the results would be strange: VGA fonts on a laser printer would create text that is too small to be readable. Going the other way, if you used laser printer fonts to create text on a VGA, the resulting text would be too large.

If a program needs precise control over its text selection, it can ask for a list of available physical fonts that a device can support. This process is called **font enumeration**. When a device driver enumerates fonts, it provides a logical font description for each physical font. When a program wishes to use a specific font, it turns the process around: It gives the logical font description to GDI, which in turn makes the connection to the physical font.

Many programs don't need a lot of control over the appearance of text. Such programs can use the default fonts. Every device has a default font. And not surprisingly, the default font is the default selection in the DC.

On a video display, the default font is also called the **system font**. Windows 1.x and 2.x used a fixed-pitch system font—that is, a font in which every character is the same width. Starting with Windows 3.0, the system font is proportionally spaced—some characters are wider than others. W, for example, is given more room than i. Microsoft made this change because proportionally spaced text is easier to read than fixed-pitch text and gives a better overall appearance.

Windows uses the system font for menus, title bars, dialog box controls, and, of course, as the default font in any DC that a program gets its hands on. Microsoft has decreed that every Windows display driver must provide a system font that allows a minimum of 25 lines and 80 columns of text to be displayed. This guarantees that Windows programs will be able to display at least as much text as their MS-DOS counterparts.

To maintain compatibility with programs written for earlier versions of Windows (versions 1.x and 2.x), every display driver also maintains a fixed-pitch system font. When GDI detects that a program was written for an older version of Windows, it provides a system font that these programs expect.

Here is a list showing the characteristics of the default font on four popular displays and four popular printers:

Device	Size of Drawing Surface	Default Font Height	Default Font Width (avg)
CGA Display	640 x 200	8	7
EGA Display	640 x 350	12	7
VGA Display	640 x 480	16	7
8514/a Display	1024 x 768	20	9
Apple Imagewriter II Printer	2550 x 3300	42	25
Epson LQ-1050 (24 pin) Printer	3060 x 1980	25	36

(Continued)

Device	Size of Drawing Surface	Default Font Height	Width (avg)
HP Laserjet II Printer	2550 x 3300	50	30
Okidata ML 320 (9 pin) Printer	1020 x 792	10	12

As you can see, the size of the default font can vary quite widely from one device to another. To make sure the text created by your program looks good on every device, it's important to ask GDI about the size of a font before you start drawing. GDI provides two routines for this purpose: `GetTextExtent` and `GetTextMetrics`.

GetTextExtent

The `GetTextExtent` routine calculates the size of a line of text using the font currently selected in a DC. Here is how to calculate the width and height of the phrase "Device Independent":

```
DWORD dwSize;
WORD  yHeight, xWidth;

dwSize = GetTextExtent (hDC, "Device Independent", 18);
yHeight = HIWORD (dwSize);
xWidth  = LOWORD (dwSize);
```

This routine takes three parameters: a DC handle, a long pointer to a string, and the count of characters. The return value is a single DWORD (unsigned long) value, in which are packed the height and width of the text. The HIWORD and LOWORD macros separate these two values.

GetTextMetrics

A more complete set of font measurements are provided by the GetTextMetrics routine. Every physical font has a header record that includes font metric information. There are 20 fields, defined by the data structure TEXTMETRIC. Here is a call that retrieves the metrics of the font currently selected in a DC:

```
TEXTMETRIC tm;

GetTextMetrics (hDC, &tm);
```

Figure 10.10 *Key TextMetric fields visually defined*

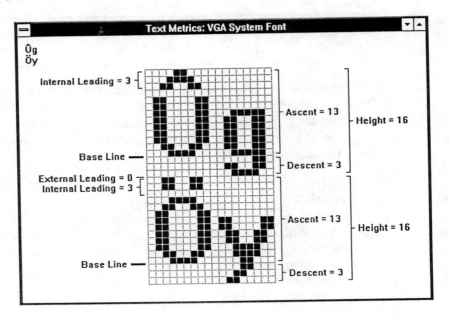

Figure 10.10 shows five of the key fields in this data structure.

The tmHeight field defines the size of the characters in the font in pixels (since we're using the MM_TEXT mapping mode) or in the units of the currently selected mapping mode. Notice that this field has two components: tmAscent, which is the height above the baseline, and tmDescent, which is the height below the baseline for characters like "g" and "y."

The tmInternalLeading field describes the size of the area for diacritic marks, such as accents, umlauts, etc. Notice that, with two lines of text, the top of the diacritic marks can touch the bottom of descenders. This is normal for many fonts.

If, however, a font designer wants to avoid this situation, he does so with the tmExternalLeading field. The value in this field is the suggested width to place between lines of text. Notice that in our example, this field is zero. The term "leading" comes from the days when type was cast in lead and set by hand. To separate lines of text, typesetters would add a thin bar of lead between rows of type.

You may have noticed that many of our sample programs combine tmHeight and tmExternalLeading for the height of a line, as in

```
int yLineHeight;
TEXTMETRIC tm;

GetTextMetrics (hDC, &tm);
yLineHeight = tm.tmHeight + tm.tmExternalLeading;
```

This is a very common method for spacing lines of text.

All this theory about fonts is well and good, but now it's time to do something practical. We're going to explore the use of different fonts and the display of multiple lines of text.

Creating and Using Logical Fonts

As we discussed earlier, a logical font is a request. It provides a way for a program to describe the physical font it wants to use. Two routines create logical fonts: CreateFont and CreateFontIndirect. The results of both are the same: The difference is in the way parameters are passed. CreateFont takes 14 parameters, CreateFontIndirect takes a single parameter: a pointer to a structure filled with the same 14 values. We're going to limit our discussion to CreateFontIndirect, since it is somewhat easier to use.

CreateFontIndirect takes one parameter: a pointer to a LOGFONT structure. LOGFONT is defined in Windows.H as

```
typedef struct tagLOGFONT
  {
  int    lfHeight;        /* Character Height */
  int    lfWidth;         /* Average width  */
  int    lfEscapement;    /* Text angle */
  int    lfOrientation;   /* Individual character angle */
  int    lfWeight;        /* Average pixels/1000 */
  BYTE   lfItalic;        /* Flag != 0 if italic */
  BYTE   lfUnderline;     /* Flag != 0 if underlined */
  BYTE   lfStrikeOut;     /* Flag != 0 if strikeout */
  BYTE   lfCharSet;       /* Character set: ANSI, OEM */
  BYTE   lfOutPrecision;  /* Mapping precision-unused */
```

```
BYTE    lfClipPrecision; /* Clip precision - unused  */
BYTE    lfQuality;       /* Draft or proof quality  */
BYTE    lfPitchAndFamily; /* Flags for font style   */
BYTE    lfFaceName[LF_FACESIZE]; /* Typeface name   */
} LOGFONT;
```

We're going to postpone a complete discussion of these fields until Chapter 26. For now, let's look at the fields that we're going to use in our sample program: lfFaceName, lfHeight, lfWidth, lfItalic, and lfUnderline.

lfFaceName is a 32-character-wide field for the font name. A program can use font names to tell users about available fonts. In this way, a user can select fonts by name. Here is a list of the face names for the Windows base fonts:

Courier	Helv	Modern	Roman
Script	Symbol	System	Terminal
Tms Rmn			

Each font is available in different sizes and styles.

The **lfHeight** field is identical to the tmHeight field in the TEXTMETRIC data structure. Since we're dealing with the MM_TEXT mapping mode, the units are pixels. When another coordinate system is used, GDI converts the values to the mapping mode currently selected in the DC.

The **lfWidth** field is the average width of characters in the font. There is also a field in the TEXTMETRIC data structure that contains the identical information, tmAveCharWidth.

· The **lfItalic** field is a flag: A nonzero value requests an italic font.

The **lfUnderline** field is also a flag: A nonzero value requests an underlined font.

Our next program displays text using three different fonts. The first font is the system font, which is already installed in the DC for us. The other two are fonts that we request by defining a logical font: a Times Roman (Tms Rmn) and a Helvetica font (Helv).

The program displays the first eight TEXTMETRIC fields for each of the fonts, as shown in Figure 10.11. The name of each font is also included, for ease of reference.

Figure 10.11   *Three fonts*

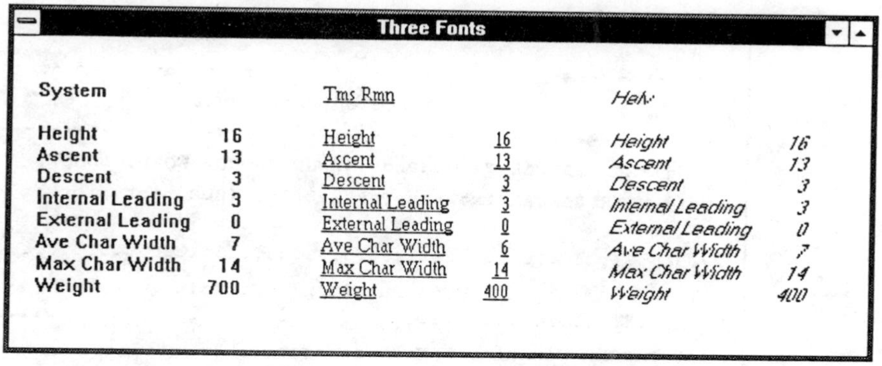

Here is the code to our program:

TXTLINES.MAK

```
TxtLines.res: TxtLines.rc TxtLines.cur TxtLines.ico
    rc -r TxtLines.rc

TxtLines.obj: TxtLines.c
    cl -AM -c -d -Gsw -Od -W2 -Zpi TxtLines.c

txtlines.exe: TxtLines.obj TxtLines.def
    link TxtLines,/align:16,/map, mlibcew libw/NOD/NOE/CO,\
        TxtLines.def
    rc TxtLines.res txtlines.exe

txtlines.exe: TxtLines.res
    rc TxtLines.res txtlines.exe
```

TXTLINES.C

```
/*------------------------------------------------------------*\
|    TXTLINES.C  - Text output sample of three fonts.          |
\*------------------------------------------------------------*/
```

```
#include <Windows.H>
#include "memory.h"

/*------------------------------------------------------------*\
|                    Function Prototypes.                      |
\*------------------------------------------------------------*/
long FAR  PASCAL TxtWndProc (HWND, WORD, WORD, LONG);
void NEAR PASCAL TxtWriteTextMetrics (HDC, int, int);


/*------------------------------------------------------------*\
|                   Main Function:  WinMain.                   |
\*------------------------------------------------------------*/
int PASCAL WinMain (HANDLE hInstance,
                    HANDLE hPrevInstance,
                    LPSTR  lpszCmdLine,
                    int    cmdShow)
    {
    HWND     hwnd;
    MSG      msg;
    WNDCLASS wndclass;

    if (!hPrevInstance)
        {
        wndclass.lpszClassName = "MIN:MAIN";
        wndclass.hInstance     = hInstance;
        wndclass.lpfnWndProc   = TxtWndProc;
        wndclass.hCursor       = LoadCursor (hInstance, "hand");
        wndclass.hIcon         = LoadIcon (hInstance,"snapshot");
        wndclass.lpszMenuName  = NULL;
        wndclass.hbrBackground = COLOR_WINDOW+1;
        wndclass.style         = CS_HREDRAW | CS_VREDRAW;
        wndclass.cbClsExtra    = 0;
        wndclass.cbWndExtra    = 0;

        RegisterClass( &wndclass);
        }

    hwnd = CreateWindow("MIN:MAIN",             /* Class name.  */
                                                /* Title.       */
                        "Three Fonts",
                        WS_OVERLAPPEDWINDOW,    /* Style bits.  */
```

```
                        CW_USEDEFAULT,          /* x - default.  */
                        0,                      /* y - default.  */
                        CW_USEDEFAULT,          /* cx - default. */
                        0,                      /* cy - default. */
                        NULL,                   /* No parent.    */
                        NULL,                   /* Class menu.   */
                        hInstance,              /* Creator       */
                        NULL                    /* Params.       */
                        ) ;

    ShowWindow (hwnd, cmdShow);

    while (GetMessage(&msg, 0, 0, 0))
        {
        TranslateMessage(&msg);         /*  Keyboard input.      */
        DispatchMessage(&msg);
        }
    return 0;
    }


/*-----------------------------------------------------------------*\
|                 Window Procedure:  TxtWndProc.                    |
\*-----------------------------------------------------------------*/
long FAR PASCAL TxtWndProc (HWND hwnd,
                            WORD wMsg,
                            WORD wParam,
                            LONG lParam)
    {
    static HANDLE hfontTmsRmn;
    static HANDLE hfontHelv;

    switch (wMsg)
        {
        case WM_CREATE:
            {
            LOGFONT lf;

            memset (&lf, 0, sizeof (LOGFONT));
            lf.lfHeight = 16;
            lf.lfWidth = 6;
            lf.lfUnderline = 1;
```

```
        lstrcpy (lf.lfFaceName, "Tms Rmn");
        hfontTmsRmn = CreateFontIndirect (&lf);

        memset (&lf, 0, sizeof (LOGFONT));
        lf.lfHeight = 16;
        lf.lfWidth = 7;
        lf.lfItalic = 1;
        lstrcpy (lf.lfFaceName, "Helv");
        hfontHelv   = CreateFontIndirect (&lf);
        }
        break;

case WM_DESTROY:
    DeleteObject (hfontTmsRmn);
    DeleteObject (hfontHelv);
    PostQuitMessage(0);
    break;

case WM_PAINT:
    {
    DWORD dwSize;
    HDC hdc;
    int xText;
    int yText;
    PAINTSTRUCT ps;
    RECT r;

    hdc = BeginPaint (hwnd, &ps);
    GetClientRect (hwnd, &r);

    dwSize = GetTextExtent (hdc, "X", 1);
    yText = HIWORD (dwSize) * 2;
    xText = LOWORD (dwSize) * 2;
    TxtWriteTextMetrics (hdc, xText, yText);

    SelectObject (hdc, hfontTmsRmn);
    xText += r.right/3;
    TxtWriteTextMetrics (hdc, xText, yText);

    SelectObject (hdc, hfontHelv);
    xText += r.right/3;
```

```
                TxtWriteTextMetrics (hdc, xText, yText);

                EndPaint (hwnd, &ps);
                }
            break;

        default:
            return(DefWindowProc(hwnd,wMsg,wParam,lParam));
            break;
        }
    return 0L;
    }


/*------------------------------------------------------------------*\
 |  TxtWriteTextMetrics - Writes metrics of currently selected |
 |                          font.                               |
\*------------------------------------------------------------------*/
void NEAR PASCAL TxtWriteTextMetrics (HDC hdc,
                                      int xText,
                                      int yText)

    {

    char buffer[80];
    DWORD dwSize;
    int  nLength;
    int  yLineHeight;
    int  xIndent;
    TEXTMETRIC tm;
    static char *apchLabel[] =
                { "Height",                /* [0] */
                  "Ascent",                /* [1] */
                  "Descent",               /* [2] */
                  "Internal Leading",      /* [3] */
                  "External Leading",      /* [4] */
                  "Ave Char Width",        /* [5] */
                  "Max Char Width",        /* [6] */
                  "Weight"};               /* [7] */

    GetTextMetrics (hdc, &tm);
    yLineHeight = tm.tmHeight + tm.tmExternalLeading;
```

```
nLength = GetTextFace (hdc, sizeof(buffer) - 1, buffer);
TextOut (hdc, xText, yText, buffer, nLength);
yText += yLineHeight * 2;

dwSize = GetTextExtent (hdc, apchLabel[4],
                            lstrlen (apchLabel[4]));
xIndent = LOWORD (dwSize);
dwSize = GetTextExtent (hdc, "XXXX", 4);
xIndent += LOWORD (dwSize);

/*  Height.  */
TextOut (hdc, xText, yText, apchLabel[0],
        lstrlen (apchLabel[0]));
nLength = wsprintf (buffer, "%d", tm.tmHeight);
SetTextAlign (hdc, TA_RIGHT);
TextOut (hdc, xText + xIndent, yText, buffer, nLength);
SetTextAlign (hdc, TA_LEFT);
yText += yLineHeight;

/*  Ascent.  */
TextOut (hdc, xText, yText, apchLabel[1],
        lstrlen (apchLabel[1]));
nLength = wsprintf (buffer, "%d", tm.tmAscent);
SetTextAlign (hdc, TA_RIGHT);
TextOut (hdc, xText + xIndent, yText, buffer, nLength);
SetTextAlign (hdc, TA_LEFT);
yText += yLineHeight;

/*  Descent.  */
TextOut (hdc, xText, yText, apchLabel[2],
        lstrlen (apchLabel[2]));
nLength = wsprintf (buffer, "%d", tm.tmDescent);
SetTextAlign (hdc, TA_RIGHT);
TextOut (hdc, xText + xIndent, yText, buffer, nLength);
SetTextAlign (hdc, TA_LEFT);
yText += yLineHeight;

/*  Internal Leading.  */
TextOut (hdc, xText, yText, apchLabel[3],
         lstrlen (apchLabel[3]));
nLength = wsprintf (buffer, "%d", tm.tmInternalLeading);
```

```
          SetTextAlign (hdc, TA_RIGHT);
          TextOut (hdc, xText + xIndent, yText, buffer, nLength);
          SetTextAlign (hdc, TA_LEFT);
          yText += yLineHeight;

          /*  External Leading.  */
          TextOut (hdc, xText, yText, apchLabel[4],
                   lstrlen (apchLabel[4]));
          nLength = wsprintf (buffer, "%d", tm.tmExternalLeading);
          SetTextAlign (hdc, TA_RIGHT);
          TextOut (hdc, xText + xIndent, yText, buffer, nLength);
          SetTextAlign (hdc, TA_LEFT);
          yText += yLineHeight;

          /*  Average Character Width.  */
          TextOut (hdc, xText, yText, apchLabel[5],
                   lstrlen (apchLabel[5]));
          nLength = wsprintf (buffer, "%d", tm.tmAveCharWidth);
          SetTextAlign (hdc, TA_RIGHT);
          TextOut (hdc, xText + xIndent, yText, buffer, nLength);
          SetTextAlign (hdc, TA_LEFT);
          yText += yLineHeight;

          /*  Max Character Width.  */
          TextOut (hdc, xText, yText, apchLabel[6],
                   lstrlen (apchLabel[6]));
          nLength = wsprintf (buffer, "%d", tm.tmMaxCharWidth);
          SetTextAlign (hdc, TA_RIGHT);
          TextOut (hdc, xText + xIndent, yText, buffer, nLength);
          SetTextAlign (hdc, TA_LEFT);
          yText += yLineHeight;

          /*  Weight.  */
          TextOut (hdc, xText, yText, apchLabel[7],
                   lstrlen (apchLabel[7]));
          nLength = wsprintf (buffer, "%d", tm.tmWeight);
          SetTextAlign (hdc, TA_RIGHT);
          TextOut (hdc, xText + xIndent, yText, buffer, nLength);
          SetTextAlign (hdc, TA_LEFT);

     }
```

TXTLINES.RC

```
snapshot icon TxtLines.ico

hand   cursor TxtLines.cur
```

TXTLINES.DEF

```
NAME      TXTLINES

EXETYPE WINDOWS

DESCRIPTION 'Text output sample'

CODE      MOVEABLE DISCARDABLE
DATA      MOVEABLE MULTIPLE


HEAPSIZE     512
STACKSIZE    5000


EXPORTS
    TxtWndProc
```

To create a logical font, this program sets the desired fields in a
LOGFONT structure and calls CreateFontIndirect. This routine ignores zero values and creates a font request using the fields we have
explicitly set. That is the reason we call the C-library routine,
memset, to initialize all fields to zero.

Like other GDI objects, logical fonts take up memory, which must
be explicitly freed to avoid depleting system memory from other
uses. In response to the WM_DESTROY message, the program removes the logical fonts with calls to DeleteObject.

Most of the work in our program is done in response to the
WM_PAINT message. It starts by getting the width of the window,
using GetClientRect, and splitting the window into three columns.
We first display the metric information for the system font before
proceeding to the Times Roman and Helvetica fonts. It is worth
noting that, although the logical font has already been created, the

physical font is not determined until the logical font handle is selected into the DC, as in

```
SelectObject (hDC, hfontTmsRmn);
```

Our routine, TxtWriteTextMetrics, displays the first eight fields in
the TEXTMETRIC data structure for each of the fonts. To obtain the
name of each font face, we call the GetTextFace routine, which is
defined as

```
GetTextFace (hDC, nCount, lpFaceName);
```

in which hDC is a handle to a device context, nCount is the size of
the buffer to receive the font face name, and lpFaceName is a long
pointer to a character buffer.

We call GetTextExtent twice, to determine the width of the wid-
est field name, "External Leading," and then again to determine the
width of "XXXX." The variable xIndex holds the sum of these two
widths and is used as a margin between the field names and the
value.

Notice that for each TEXTMETRIC field, we display the field name
and then call on the `wsprintf` routine to convert the numeric value
into a text string suitable for display with the TextOut routine.
wsprintf behaves in the same way as the C library `sprintf` routine,
except that it overcomes some of the incompatibilities of that routine in the Windows environment.

Notice also that we use the text alignment attribute (via SetTextA-
lign) to create a table with neatly left-justified text, and right-justified
numeric values.

As you can see, GDI treats text as a graphic object. This means that
you get a great deal of control over the placement, sizing, and color
of text. You can freely mix text and geometric shapes, and combine
text of different sizes and styles onto the same page. We think you'll
find that the extra effort required is well worth the device-independent punch that GDI packs in text creation.

For programmers who don't need a lot of variety in text, GDI
guarantees that you will find a default font for every GDI device. This
will provide reasonable-looking text output with a minimum of effort on your part.

Part 4

User Interface Objects

11

Commands: Menu and Accelerator Basics

Windows has built-in support for two user-interface objects that retrieve command input from users: menus and accelerators. Menus allow a program to show users available actions and options, and encourage users to explore the capabilities of a program. Menus help beginners by eliminating the need to memorize commands. More advanced users can take advantage of accelerators, which translate keystrokes into program commands. To bridge the gap between menus and accelerators, programs often list accelerator keys inside menus. Figure 11.1 shows a menu with a description of the accelerator keys that correspond to each menu item. In this example, a user can press the Shift and Delete keys instead of selecting the *Cut* menu item.

Programs that adhere to the Windows standards for accelerators and menus are easier for users to learn than programs that do not. Therefore, it's important for programmers who plan to design menus to first learn these standards. There are two things you can do that will help you become familiar with these standards: you can use Windows, and you can read the style guidelines that Microsoft includes with the software development kit. Learning the standards is time well spent, since it will minimize the time required for a user to become comfortable with your program. Users who are familiar with the "look and feel" that pervades Windows programs will be put off by programs that ignore widely accepted standards.

Let's start with a quick look at some of the things that users expect to find in menus.

Figure 11.1   *A menu with accelerator key entries*

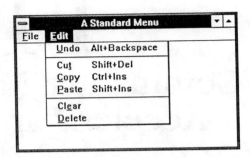

User Interface Standards

Users expect to find two types of items in a menu: **actions** and **options**. A menu action is usually expressed as a verb, or as a noun-verb combination. For example, many programs have an "Open" menu item inside a "File" menu. Menu actions usually act on a specific object that the user has selected. But menu actions can also cause a change that will affect an entire program. The *Close* item in a system menu, for example, can cause a program to terminate when the window being closed is the program's main, top-level window.

Options are toggle switches. Unlike menu actions, which create a short-lived response, options have a more long-lasting effect that is usually reversible. Programs often display checkmarks in menus to indicate whether an option is active or not. For example, the **Program Manager** has an *Options* menu that lets the user enable and disable two features: "Auto Arrange" and "Minimize on Use." While certain important options are set inside menus, most large programs make use of dialog boxes to allow the user to control a program's settable options. In other words, you don't need to put every available option inside menus. The less frequently required options can be placed into dialog boxes, which we'll discuss in more detail in Chapter 14.

Users expect to see **visual clues** in menus. Visual clues can be subtle, like the ellipses (...) that appear when the selection of a menu item causes a dialog box to appear. Or, it can be as obvious as the way menu items are grouped. Here is a list of some of the different visual clues that can be incorporated into menus to indicate special handling of menu items:

- *Accelerator keystrokes* tell the user the accelerator key that matches the menu selection.
- An *arrow* indicates that a menu item is a doorway to a nested menu. The nested menu appears when the user touches the menu item, either by dragging the mouse or moving the menu selection using keyboard cursor keys.
- A *separator* divides longer menus into smaller groups of menu items.
- A *check-mark* next to a menu item indicates that that option has been turned on.
- An *ellipsis* (...) after a menu item tells the user to expect a dialog box when the menu item is selected.
- An *exclamation-point* at the end of a menu item in a top-level menu indicates that the menu item causes an action and will not cause a popup menu to appear.
- A *grayed* menu item is unavailable. In the system menu, for example, several menu items are grayed when a window is maximized.
- An *underlined letter* in the menu item text indicates the letter can be used to select the menu item. Such a letter is called a **mnemonic**. To make a popup menu appear, the Alt key is pressed with the mnemonic of the popup menu. Once a popup has appeared, menu items can be selected by pressing the mnemonic corresponding to the desired menu item.

Figure 11.2 shows a menu with an example of each of these different visual clues.

Users expect every program to have a **system menu**. From a programming point of view, this is easily accomplished, since Windows creates and maintains the system menu for you. In general, programs should not alter the contents of the system menu without a very good reason. A program may *add* certain items to the system menu. In particular, programs which only run in a minimized (or iconic) state can add private menu items to the system menu. The system menu, after all, is the only menu to appear when a program is iconic. Tiny utility and toy applications can add items to the sys-

Figure 11.2   *Menu showing various visual clues*

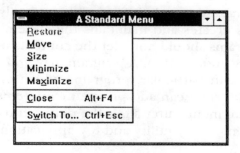

tem menu as well, to avoid the fuss of creating private menus. It's not something you'll do often, but under certain conditions it makes sense to. Figure 11.3 shows a standard system menu.

In programs that work with data files, users expect to find a **File** popup menu. This menu provides access to the commands involved with opening, closing, and printing files. Notice, as shown in Figure 11.4, the *Exit* menu item is a standard part of the File menu. When selected, this item causes the program to terminate. While this duplicates the *Close* menu item in the system menu of a top-level window, it is a standard that users have come to expect. If you write

Figure 11.3   *The standard system menu*

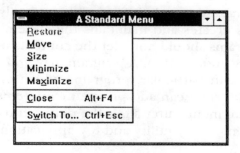

Figure 11.4 *A typical file menu*

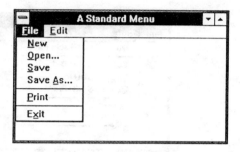

a program that does *not* have a File menu, you'll still want to put an *Exit* menu item at the bottom of your first popup menu.

Another standard menu that users expect is the **Edit** popup menu. This menu lists general purpose editing actions, including clipboard control, search and replace, undo previous actions, and repeat previous actions. A program can add other items to the standard Edit menu to allow an application-specific object to be manipulated. For example, a word processing program might list an action in its Edit menu to allow a user to edit the header or footer of a document. Figure 11.5 shows a typical Edit menu, which is part of the first program we're going to write.

Menus can be accessed using any combination of mouse and keyboard input. For example, after a mouse click makes a popup menu appear, users can browse through menu items by pressing arrow keys and can select a menu item by pressing the return key. As an alternative, users can activate a popup menu from the keyboard by pressing the Alt or the F10 key. Menu browsing and selection can then be done with the mouse.

This ability to choose between the mouse and the keyboard for menu operations is part of a larger plan to allow these devices to be used interchangeably in other actions as well. Of course, there are limits—entering characters with the mouse is difficult. But aside from these extremes this ability to choose is important for program designers to keep in mind. Some users will rely solely on the keyboard—either because they don't have a mouse or because they prefer the keyboard. Others may switch between the two input methods, depending on the operation and their personal preference. In Chapters 15 and 16, when we discuss mouse and keyboard

Figure 11.5 *A Typical Edit Menu*

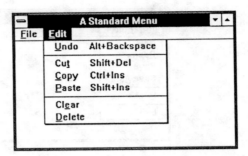

input in more detail, we'll reiterate this choice as an important part of the overall design for Windows programs. For now, let's get into the programming details of creating menus.

Menu Programming Issues

Windows has a very robust, flexible menuing system that is, at the same time, quite easy to work with. While menus are easy to create for Windows programmers, the creation of the menuing system proved one of the most challenging tasks in the creation of Windows. The code that supports menuing has been reworked, tuned, and rewritten more than any other part of the system. One of the reasons has to do with performance: From the beginning, menus had to be snappy. Otherwise, the system itself would risk appearing sluggish. To help menus disappear quickly with minimum performance impact, a bitmap "snapshot" is taken of the screen where a menu is going to be drawn. When a user has finished using a menu, the snapshot is used to restore the area where the menu had been.

After all of Microsoft's efforts to make menus work quickly and efficiently, you'll be happy to know that menu creation is easy. As we'll see shortly, the quickest way to create a menu involves writing a short menu description in a program's resource file. When a window class is registered, a WNDCLASS parameter accepts a menu name. When a window of that class is created, a menu is created as well. The only other thing that a programmer must do is to process the WM_COMMAND messages that the menu sends to the window procedure.

Since we're working with a message-driven system, it probably won't surprise you to learn that menus created in Windows use messages to communicate with your program. Or, more precisely, messages are used to communicate with your *window procedure*. The most important menu message is the WM_COMMAND message, which is sent to noftify you that a menu item has been selected.

Table 11.1 shows the different steps in the operation of a menu, the mouse and keyboard actions that lead to each step, and the associated messages. Notice that identical message traffic occurs whether the mouse or the keyboard is used. The details of the interaction between the user and your menus are hidden in the menu system, so that your program can simply respond to the messages with complete trust that the menuing system is taking care of the rest.

While the WM_COMMAND message is the most useful, you'll want to understand the role of the other messages since there are times that they can be useful as well. For example, if a program wishes to initialize a top-level menu before the user makes a selection, it would respond to the WM_INITMENU message. To initialize a popup menu before it appears, a program would respond to WM_INITMENUPOPUP. Programs that use the clipboard often respond to one of these initialization messages to let the user know, for example, whether or not there is data on the clipboard that can be pasted. If there is, the Paste item in the Edit menu is enabled. Otherwise, it is grayed.

Table 11.1 *Menu operation and menu messages*

Menu Operation	Mouse Action	Keyboard Action	Message
Initiate menu use	n/a	F10 or Alt key	WM_INITMENU
Display a popup	n/a	arrow or mnemonic keys	WM_INITMENUPOPUP
Initiate and display popup	<Click>	Alt + mnemonic key	WM_INITMENU and WM_INITMENUPOPUP
Browse a menu item	<Drag>	arrow keys	WM_MENUSELECT
Select a menu item	<Release>	Enter key or mnemonic key	WM_COMMAND

As the user browses through the items in a menu, the WM_MENUSELECT message tells a program the specific menu item that the user is highlighting at every moment in time. This information can be used to support an "information area" to display hints about the meaning of each menu item. This might be another window on the screen where information is displayed for the user to see. Quite a few commercial Windows programs provide this feature to assist in the selection of menu items. In Chapter 13, where we discuss issues relating to windowing, we'll show you a program that creates a window and processes WM_MENUSELECT messages in this way.

Menu Template

The simplest menus start with a menu template. A menu template defines the popup menus and menu items that make up a menu. A menu template is a hierarchical data structure, like the DOS file system with its root directory and subdirectories. At the top of the hierarchy—the root directory—are the items for the menu bar, also known as the **action bar**. At this top level, items can be either menu items, which send command messages when selected, or the tops of popup menus. As a side note, it's something of a curiosity that another term used to refer to a popup menu is **pull-down menu**.

Popup menus are like subdirectories that are one level below the root directory in the DOS file hierarchy. And in the same way that subdirectories can themselves contain *other* subdirectories, a popup menu can contain other popup menus. There isn't any limit to the number of nested menu levels that the menu subsystem will provide. But common sense would indicate that three levels of menus—the main menu bar and two levels of popup menus—is the deepest you will most likely want to go. Otherwise, you risk losing your user in a sea of menus.

A resource file menu template has the following form:

```
menuID MENU [load option] [memory option]
BEGIN
    MENUITEM or POPUP statement
    MENUITEM or POPUP statement
    .
    .
    .
END
```

The [load option] can be either PRELOAD or LOADONCALL, and the [memory option] can be either FIXED, MOVEABLE or DISCARD-ABLE. These describe how the menu data itself is handled as a memory object. PRELOAD causes a menu resource to be loaded into memory before a program starts running. LOADONCALL causes the menu item to be loaded only when it is needed. The other three options, FIXED, MOVEABLE, and DISCARDABLE, describe how the memory object should behave once it has been loaded into memory. In Chapter 17, we'll describe in detail the meaning of these three options. Since the default behavior of LOADONCALL and the memory option of DISCARDABLE are good enough for now, we won't bother specifying these options in our menu examples.

Each MENUITEM statement defines a menu item that, when selected, causes a WM_COMMAND message to be sent. Each POPUP statement starts the definition of a popup menu, with a BEGIN and an END statement to bracket other MENUITEM or POPUP statements. Incidentally, if you want to save yourself some typing, you can use the C language squiggly brackets, "{" and "}", in place of the BEGIN and END statements. Here is the menu definition for the File and Edit menus that we discussed earlier in this chapter:

```
7 MENU
    {
    POPUP "&File"
        {
        MENUITEM "&New",                    1
        MENUITEM "&Open...",                2
        MENUITEM "&Save",                   3
        MENUITEM "Save &As...",             4
        MENUITEM SEPARATOR
        MENUITEM "&Print",                  5
        MENUITEM SEPARATOR
        MENUITEM "E&xit",                   6
        }
    POPUP "&Edit"
        {
        MENUITEM "&Undo\tAlt+Backspace",    7
        MENUITEM SEPARATOR
        MENUITEM "Cu&t\tShift+Del",         8
        MENUITEM "&Copy\tCtrl+Ins",         9
        MENUITEM "&Paste\tShift+Ins",      10
        MENUITEM SEPARATOR
```

```
        MENUITEM "Cl&ear",           11
        MENUITEM "&Delete",          12
    }
}
```

The menu identifier is the number 7. Although we could have specified an ASCII text string, using a number is more efficient. This identifier is our name for the menu; it is how we'll identify this menu definition to Windows. Each ampersand (&) defines a mnemonic, which is a letter used in the keyboard interface to menus. The \t causes a tab character to be generated, to separate an accelerator keystroke name from a menu item name.

Perhaps the most important value in the definition of each menu item is the command result code. This is the number at the end of each of these MENUITEM statements that distinguishes one menu item from another. The menu system uses the result code to identify menu items for the WM_COMMAND and WM_MENUSELECT messages.

The general syntax of the POPUP statement is

```
POPUP text [,optionlist]
```

and the MENUITEM statement has the following syntax:

```
MENUITEM text, result-code [,optionlist]
```

The big difference between the two statements is that a MENUITEM statement has a result code and the POPUP statement does not. As far as the [optionlist] goes, there are five options that can be selected. The first three select the initial state of the menu item:

CHECKED   Places a checkmark next to the popup or menu item name. This only affects items inside a popup menu, and not items in the top level menu.

GRAYED   Item is initially grayed and inactive.

INACTIVE   Item appears normally, but cannot be selected. The GRAYED option is better, since it provides the user with visual feedback that a menu item isn't available.

The other two options change the physical layout of the menu itself:

MENUBREAK   Causes a menu break. For horizontal (top-level) menus, this means a break in the vertical direction. For vertical (popup) menus, this means a break in the horizontal direction. If used with wild abandon, you could have vertical top-level and horizontal popup menus.

MENUBARBREAK   Causes a menu break. In popup menus, the break is accompanied by a vertical bar.

In a top-level menu, these last two options have the same effect, which is to cause a menu item to start on a new line. For example, consider the following menu definition:

```
7 MENU
    {
    MENUITEM "Item-1", 1
    MENUITEM "Item-2", 2, MENUBREAK
    MENUITEM "Item-3", 3
    MENUITEM "Item-4", 4
    MENUITEM "Item-5", 5, MENUBARBREAK
    MENUITEM "Item-6", 6
    }
```

As depicted in Figure 11.6, the two break statements, MENUBREAK and MENUBARBREAK, cause the menu to wrap on the second and the fifth menu items. Windows itself will break top-level menus when the window is too narrow. But if you want to control when and how this occurs, these options are what you'll need.

To see the effect of these two options in a popup menu, consider the following menu template:

```
7 MENU
    {
    POPUP "Popup"
        {
        MENUITEM "Item-1", 1
        MENUITEM "Item-2", 2, MENUBREAK
        MENUITEM "Item-3", 3
        MENUITEM "Item-4", 4
        MENUITEM "Item-5", 5, MENUBARBREAK
        MENUITEM "Item-6", 6
        }
    }
```

Figure 11.7 shows the resulting popup menu. Notice that both options cause the menus to begin a new column, but that the

Figure 11.6 *Results of a MENUBREAK and MENUBARBREAK option on a top-level menu*

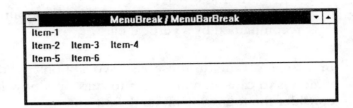

MENUBARBREAK option adds a vertical bar to separate the different columns of menu items that are created.

An additional option is listed in the Microsoft documentation, HELP, but it no longer applies to the current standard for menus and so it has no effect. The old standard put the Help menu on the far right side of the top-level menu, with a vertical bar separating it from the other menu items. The current standard simply calls for making the Help menu the last item on the top-level menu. If you experiment with this option, you'll see that the menu system simply ignores it.

Let's take a look at a full-blown program that incorporates a menu. The menus we'll use are the standard File and Edit menus that we looked at earlier.

A Sample Program: STANMENU

This program shows all of the pieces that must be put together to get a working menu. The menu itself is defined in the resource file, STANMENU.RC. But a resource by itself is just a data definition. To

Figure 11.7 *Results of a MENUBREAK and MENUBARBREAK option in a popup menu*

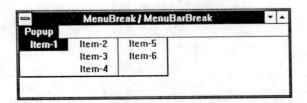

bring it into a program and make it work requires some code. There is room in the window class data structure, WNDCLASS, for a menu name. And so, we add one as follows:

```
wndclass.lpszMenuName = "#7";
```

The number sign indicates that we've used a numeric value in our menu definition. This is one of the easiest and most efficient ways to reference a menu. A regular ASCII name could have been used, but this would waste memory and take more time to use.

   If we did not want to associate this menu with our window class, we could have placed a reference to our menu in the call to Create-Window as the ninth parameter. In this way, a single window class can be associated with several different menus. Here is an example of how we might have called CreateWindow for the same menu:

```
hmenu = LoadMenu (hInstance, "#7");
hwnd = CreateWindow("Stanmenu:MAIN",/* Class name.   */
            "A Standard Menu",    /* Title.        */
            WS_OVERLAPPEDWINDOW,  /* Style bits.   */
            CW_USEDEFAULT,        /* x - default.  */
            0,                    /* y - default.  */
            CW_USEDEFAULT,        /* cx - default. */
            0,                    /* cy - default. */
            NULL,                 /* No parent.    */
            hmenu,                /* Private menu. */
            hInstance,            /* Creator       */
            NULL                  /* Params.       */
            ) ;
```

   The call to LoadMenu retrieves a menu handle, which is what the CreateWindow routine expects to find. A third alternative to creating this menu would involve making a call to the SetMenu routine after our window was created. Like CreateWindow, SetMenu takes a handle to a menu as a parameter. Here is another way we could have created the same menu:

```
hmenu = LoadMenu (hInstance, "#7");
SetMenu (hwnd, hmenu);
```

   Here is the code to our first sample menu creation program.

STANMENU.MAK

```
stanmenu.res: stanmenu.rc stanmenu.cur stanmenu.ico
    rc -r stanmenu.rc

stanmenu.obj: stanmenu.c
    cl -AM -c -d -Gsw -Ow -W2 -Zpi stanmenu.c

stanmenu.exe: stanmenu.obj stanmenu.def
    link stanmenu,/align:16,/map, mlibcew libw/NOD/NOE/CO,\
        stanmenu.def
    rc stanmenu.res

stanmenu.exe: stanmenu.res
    rc stanmenu.res
```

STANMENU.C

```c
/*------------------------------------------------------------*\
|   STANMENU.C  -  Program showing a standard File and Edit   |
|                  menu.                                       |
\*------------------------------------------------------------*/
#include <Windows.H>


/*------------------------------------------------------------*\
|                    Function Prototypes.                      |
\*------------------------------------------------------------*/
long FAR  PASCAL StanmenuWndProc (HWND, WORD, WORD, LONG);


/*------------------------------------------------------------*\
|                  Main Function:  WinMain.                    |
\*------------------------------------------------------------*/
int PASCAL WinMain (HANDLE hInstance,
                    HANDLE hPrevInstance,
                    LPSTR  lpszCmdLine,
                    int    cmdShow)

    {
    HWND     hwnd;
    MSG      msg;
    WNDCLASS wndclass;
```

```
    if (!hPrevInstance)
        {
        wndclass.lpszClassName = "Stanmenu:MAIN";
        wndclass.hInstance     = hInstance;
        wndclass.lpfnWndProc   = StanmenuWndProc;
        wndclass.hCursor       = LoadCursor (hInstance, "hand");
        wndclass.hIcon         = LoadIcon (hInstance,"snapshot");
        wndclass.lpszMenuName  = "#1";
        wndclass.hbrBackground = COLOR_WINDOW+1;
        wndclass.style         = NULL;
        wndclass.cbClsExtra    = 0;
        wndclass.cbWndExtra    = 0;

        RegisterClass( &wndclass );
        }


    hwnd = CreateWindow("Stanmenu:MAIN",      /* Class name.  */
                        "A Standard Menu",    /* Title.       */
                        WS_OVERLAPPEDWINDOW,  /* Style bits.  */
                        CW_USEDEFAULT,        /* x - default. */
                        0,                    /* y - default. */
                        CW_USEDEFAULT,        /* cx - default. */
                        0,                    /* cy - default. */
                        NULL,                 /* No parent.   */
                        NULL,                 /* Class menu.  */
                        hInstance,            /* Creator      */
                        NULL                  /* Params.      */
                       ) ;
    ShowWindow (hwnd, cmdShow);
    while (GetMessage(&msg, 0, 0, 0))
        {
        TranslateMessage(&msg);        /*  Keyboard input.    */
        DispatchMessage(&msg);
        }
    return 0;
    }


/*-----------------------------------------------------------------*\
 |            Window Procedure:  StanmenuWndProc.                  |
 \*-----------------------------------------------------------------*/
long FAR PASCAL StanmenuWndProc (HWND hwnd,   WORD wMsg,
                                 WORD wParam, LONG lParam)
    {
```

```
switch (wMsg)
    {
    case WM_COMMAND:
        {
        char buffer[80];

        if (wParam == 6)
            DestroyWindow (hwnd);
        else
            {
            wsprintf (buffer, "Command = %d", wParam);
            MessageBox (hwnd, buffer, "WM_COMMAND", MB_OK);
            }
        }
        break;

    case WM_DESTROY:
        PostQuitMessage(0);
        break;

    default:
        return(DefWindowProc(hwnd,wMsg,wParam,lParam));
        break;
    }
    return 0L;
    }
```

STANMENU.RC

```
#include <Windows.h>

snapshot icon stanmenu.ico

hand  cursor stanmenu.cur

7 MENU    {
    POPUP "&File"
        {
        MENUITEM "&New",        1
        MENUITEM "&Open...",    2
```

```
      MENUITEM "&Save",          3
      MENUITEM "Save &As...", 4
      MENUITEM SEPARATOR
      MENUITEM "&Print",         5
      MENUITEM SEPARATOR
      MENUITEM "E&xit",          6
      }
   POPUP "&Edit"
      {
      MENUITEM "&Undo\tAlt+Backspace", 7
      MENUITEM SEPARATOR
      MENUITEM "Cu&t\tShift+Del",      8
      MENUITEM "&Copy\tCtrl+Ins",      9
      MENUITEM "&Paste\tShift+Ins",   10
      MENUITEM SEPARATOR
      MENUITEM "Cl&ear",          11
      MENUITEM "&Delete",         12
      }
   }
```

STANMENU.DEF

```
NAME    STANMENU

EXETYPE WINDOWS

DESCRIPTION 'Sample Menu'

CODE    MOVEABLE DISCARDABLE
DATA    MOVEABLE MULTIPLE

HEAPSIZE    512
STACKSIZE   5000

EXPORTS
    StanmenuWndProc
```

As menu items are selected, a WM_COMMAND message is sent to our program to let us know. When a WM_COMMAND message arrives, the wParam parameter contains a result code that lets us know exactly which menu item has been selected. As you might expect, you'll want to make each value different so that you can tell the difference between different menu items. In STANMENU, we don't do very much when a WM_COMMAND message arrives:

```
case WM_COMMAND:
    {
    char buffer[80];

    if (wParam == 6)
        DestroyWindow (hwnd);
    else
        {
        wsprintf (buffer, "Command = %d", wParam);
        MessageBox (hwnd, buffer, "WM_COMMAND", MB_OK);
        }
    }
    break;
```

If the menu result code is 6, which is the value of the Exit item in the File menu, we terminate our program by destroying the main window. Otherwise, we display a message box that displays the menu item result code. Typically, the code to process a WM_COMMAND in programs with a lot of menu items is a switch statement, with a different case for each of the different command result codes.

Most programs get along quite nicely using the methods shown in STANMENU. They allow menus to be created and attached to a window, with the result that the WM_COMMAND message arrives to tell us what the user wants to do. For programs (and programmers) that demand more, Windows has 26 menu support routines that you can use. To help you get a grasp of them, we're going to divide these routines into six main types and discuss each type in turn.

Menu Support Routines

Windows has 26 menu support routines, which can be divided into six categories. Each category describes a different type of activity that can be performed on a menu. The categories are creation, place in a window, destruction, modification, query, and tracking. When you need more than just the simplest menu operations, you'll find that you can go to each group of routines and find one or more that will help you with whatever problem you have. Table 11.2 summarizes the various categories of menu functions.

Let's look at each type of menu routine, starting with the menu creation routines.

Table 11.2 *A summary of menu functions*

Category	Routine	Description
Creation (4)	CreateMenu	Creates an empty menu in memory.
	CreatePopupMenu	Creates an empty popup menu in memory.
	LoadMenu	Creates a menu from a disk-based (.EXE or .DLL file) menu resource.
	LoadMenuIndirect	Creates a menu from a memory-based menu resource.
Connect to a Window (1)	SetMenu	Attaches a top-level menu to a window.
Destruction (2)	DeleteMenu	Removes a menu item from a top-level or popup menu, and destroys any associated popup menus.
	DestroyMenu	Destroys a specific top-level or popup menu and all the menus below it.
Modification (10)	AppendMenu	Adds items to the end of a top-level or popup menu.
	ChangeMenu	Old Windows 1.x and 2.x menu modification function.
	CheckMenuItem	Toggles a checkmark inside a popup menu.
	DrawMenuBar	Forces the top-level menu to be redrawn after it has been changed.
	EnableMenuItem	Enables, disables, and grays menu items.

(Continued)

Table 11.2   *Continued*

Category	Routine	Description
	HiliteMenuItem	Toggles highlighting of an item in a top-level menu.
	InsertMenu	Puts a new item into a menu.
	ModifyMenu	Changes an item in a menu.
	RemoveMenu	Removes a menu item or a popup menu. After a popup menu is removed, it is not destroyed, which means it can be reused.
	SetMenuItemBitmaps	Defines two bitmaps to be used in place of the default checked and unchecked display.
Query (8)	GetMenu	Retrieves the menu handle for a window's top-level menu.
	GetMenuCheckMarkDimensions	Gets the size of the default menu check mark, as set by the display driver.
	GetMenuItemCount	Returns the number of items in a top-level or popup menu.
	GetMenuItemID	Finds the menu ID for a given menu item.
	GetMenuState	Returns the flags that are set for a given menu item.
	GetMenuString	Returns the label of a menu item.
	GetSubMenu	Retrieves the menu handle of a popup menu.
	GetSystemMenu	Retrieves a handle to a system menu.
Tracking (1)	TrackPopupMenu	Creates a floating popup menu to appear anywhere on the display screen.

Menu Creation

To the user, menus are user-interface objects that sit inside windows. All of the work that Windows does to support a menu remains hidden behind the scenes. It's the programmer's job, however, to understand what goes on behind the scenes, to make sure that things operate smoothly and efficiently. From a programmer's point of view, menu support requires that certain data structures be created that define the shape and behavior of a menu. Most programs take the easy route to menu creation by attaching a menu resource to a window class. As the window is created, the menu is automatically created as well.

But a program can become more intimately involved in a menu's internal data structures. We have already seen that a program can call **LoadMenu** to request that a menu resource be loaded. Let's see what other possibilities are available.

Using the **CreateMenu** and **CreatePopup** routines, a program can build empty menus, which can then be filled with menu command items and connected to other popup menus. Adding a menu item can involve any of several of the menu modification routines. In the following example, we've decided to use **AppendMenu**. This code fragment creates from scratch a menu like the one that STANMENU built using a menu resource:

```
{
HMENU hSub;
HMENU hTop;

hTop = CreateMenu ();

hSub = CreatePopupMenu ();
AppendMenu (hSub, MF_STRING, 1, "&New");
AppendMenu (hSub, MF_STRING, 2, "&Open...");
AppendMenu (hSub, MF_STRING, 3, "&Save");
AppendMenu (hSub, MF_STRING, 4, "Save &As...");
AppendMenu (hSub, MF_SEPARATOR, 0, 0);
AppendMenu (hSub, MF_STRING, 5, "&Print");
AppendMenu (hSub, MF_SEPARATOR, 0, 0);
AppendMenu (hSub, MF_STRING, 6, "E&xit");

AppendMenu (hTop, MF_POPUP, hSub, "&File");

hSub = CreatePopupMenu ();
AppendMenu (hSub, MF_STRING, 7, "&Undo\tAlt+Backspace");
AppendMenu (hSub, MF_SEPARATOR, 0, 0);
AppendMenu (hSub, MF_STRING, 8, "Cu&t\tShift+Del");
AppendMenu (hSub, MF_STRING, 9, "&Copy\tCtrl+Ins");
AppendMenu (hSub, MF_STRING,10, "&Paste\tShift+Ins");
```

```
AppendMenu (hSub, MF_SEPARATOR, 0, 0);
AppendMenu (hSub, MF_STRING,11, "Cl&ear");
AppendMenu (hSub, MF_STRING,12, "&Delete");

AppendMenu (hTop, MF_POPUP, hSub, "&Edit");
SetMenu (hwnd, hTop);
}
```

The **AppendMenu** routine provides the glue to put the different menu pieces together. It attaches menu items to menus and connects popup menus to top level menus. AppendMenu is defined as

```
BOOL AppendMenu (hMenu, wFlags, wIDNewItem, lpNewItem)
```

- hMenu is a handle to a menu, either a popup or a top-level menu.
- wFlags is a combination of one or more of the MF_ flags, as described below.
- wIDNewItem is the result code delivered with the WM_COMMAND message, or a handle to a popup menu when a popup menu is being appended.
- lpNewItem is a long value that can contain three different types of values. When inserting a string, it is a long pointer to a text string. When inserting a bitmap, it is a bitmap handle. Otherwise, if you are creating an "owner-draw" menu item, it identifies the specific item that you wish to draw.

AppendMenu has several different uses, depending on whether you are attaching a regular menu item or a popup menu, and whether the new item will display a string, a bitmap, or an owner-draw menu item. To put a new string item in a menu for a regular command item, you can call AppendMenu like this:

```
AppendMenu (hMenu, MF_STRING, wID, "Open...");
```

The value of wID is the command result code that will be sent with the WM_COMMAND message when the user selects the menu item, which will be identified by the label "Open..."

Alternatively, AppendMenu can be used to attach a popup menu to a top-level menu (or a popup menu to another popup menu). In such cases, it could be called like this:

```
AppendMenu (hMenuTop, MF_POPUP, hMenuPopup,"File");
```

In this case, the value of the third parameter, hMunePopup, is not a command result code, but it is a handle to a popup menu that is to be appended to the end of the menu identified by the hMenuTop menu handle. When the popup is added, it will be identified with the string "File".

AppendMenu can also be used to install a bitmap in place of a string as the label that is displayed for a menu item. When a bitmap is used, the last parameter is used to hold the bitmap handle, instead of a long pointer to a string. In the following example, the variable hbm is a bitmap handle, and it is packed into the last parameter using the MAKELONG macro:

```
AppendMenu (hMenu, MF_BITMAP, wID, MAKELONG(hbm, 0));
```

Of the 12 flags for the wFlags field, 10 duplicate features that can be requested from a resource file entry. The other two are only available for dynamically generated menus: MF_BITMAP and MF_OWNERDRAW. In Chapter 12, you'll find sample programs that show how to use these two types of menu items. Table 11.3 lists and describes each menu flag. To put these flags into a slightly different perspective, there are four general categories of flags: type of object, checked or not, enabled or not, and menu break or not. Table 11.4 lists each of the categories and the flags that are in each. The top item in each list is the default value.

The only menu creation routine we have not investigated is **LoadMenuIndirect**. This routine builds a menu from a memory-resident menu template. This routine is just like **LoadMenu**, except that **LoadMenu** creates a menu from a disk-based menu template. **LoadMenuIndirect** creates a menu using data that is memory-resident. Thus, you can create a menu template "on-the-fly" and give it to the menu system for use in creating a menu. Doing this requires that you duplicate what the resource compiler does in creating a memory object that describes a menu. The data structures in Windows.h that have been defined for this purpose include the MENUITEMTEMPLATEHEADER and MENUITEMTEMPLATE.

The next routine that we're going to cover is **SetMenu**. This routine provides the one and only way to attach a menu to a window.

Connect to a Window

A single Windows function supports the placement of a menu in a window: **SetMenu**. This single function gets its own category be-

Table 11.3 *The MF_ Menu creation flags*

Menu Flag	Available in a Resource	Description
MF_BITMAP	No	Displays a GDI bitmap instead a text string for a menu item. It provides one way that graphic images can be displayed in a menu. The other way involves an MF_OWNERDRAW menu item.
MF_CHECKED	Yes	Puts a checkmark next to a menu item.
MF_DISABLED	Yes	Disables a menu item. Use the MF_GRAYED flag instead, since it provides the user with visual feedback.
MF_ENABLED	Yes	Enables a menu item.
MF_GRAYED	Yes	Disables and grays a menu item.
MF_MENUBARBREAK	Yes	Creates a menu break, and a vertical bar for items inside a popup menu.
MF_MENUBREAK	Yes	Creates a menu break.
MF_OWNERDRAW	No	The creator of the menu is sent a message, WM_DRAWITEM, which includes a handle to a device context to be used for drawing custom menu labels using GDI drawing calls. Cannot be used for top-level menu items.
MF_POPUP	Yes	A popup menu is being attached to a top-level menu, or to another popup.
MF_SEPARATOR	Yes	A horizontal separator should be created in a menu item.
MF_STRING	Yes	A text string is being supplied for a menu item label.
MF_UNCHECKED	Yes	Menu item should be drawn without a check mark.

cause it provides the only way to replace a top-level menu. In addition, there are some system memory cleanup issues that this routine raises, which we'll describe in a moment. The syntax of this routine is

```
BOOL SetMenu (hWnd, hMenu)
```

Table 11.4 *Four categories of menu flags*

Type of Object	Checked	Enabled	Menu Break
MF_STRING	MF_UNCHECKED	MF_ENABLED	\<none\>
MF_POPUP	MF_CHECKED	MF_GRAYED	MF_MENUBARBREAK
MF_BITMAP		MF_DISABLED	MF_MENUBREAK
MF_SEPARATOR			
MF_OWNERDRAW			

- hWnd is a window handle to a WS_OVERLAPPED or WS_POPUP window. A menu cannot be attached to a WS_CHILD window.
- hMenu is the handle of a top-level menu to be attached to a window.

A program can create several menus and make a different menu available to the user at different times during the operation of a program. There are several reasons why a program might want to do this. One has to do with supporting different levels of users. A beginner might only want to see short menus, with a program's most basic commands. More advanced users can set a program option to allow them to view a program's longer, more complete menus.

Another reason for a program to have multiple menus involves program security. Different menus can be used to enforce privilege levels in a program. For example, a program might ask for a password at program startup time. The menu that is installed will depend on which password is used. A regular user might get an abbreviated set of menus, while more privileged users get a more complete set of menus giving them the ability to do more privileged operations.

Yet another reason for a program to have different menus is to support the multiple-document interface (MDI) standard. This user-interface standard opens a new document window for each new document that a user asks to work with. Different types of documents may need different menus. For example, Microsoft's Excel spreadsheet has two types of documents: worksheets and charts. There are two menus, one for each type of document. Excel switches between the two menus, depending on the type of document with which the user is working.

Whatever your reason for having different menus, SetMenu lets you quickly switch from one menu to another. If you do this, however, a word of caution is in order. When you remove a menu from a window, Windows forgets about the menu. If your program terminates without explicitly destroying this menu, the memory taken up by the menu is lost forever (or, until the user exits Windows). Therefore, be sure to destroy menus that have been detached from a window. Otherwise, your program will inadvertently waste system memory (in the USER module's data segment) every time it runs. The next section discusses how to destroy menus.

If you replace an menu by calling **SetMenu**, be sure to hold onto the handle of the old menu. Then, when your program exits, destroy the menu since menus that aren't attached to windows are not cleaned up automatically.

Menu Destruction

Windows has two routines that destroy menus and free the memory associated with them: **DestroyMenu** and **DeleteMenu**.

The **DestroyMenu** routine destroys menus that are *not* connected to any window. If you pass it the menu handle for a menu connected to a window, your program will crash. **DestroyMenu** is defined as follows:

```
BOOL DestroyMenu (hmenu)
```

- hmenu is the handle of a top-level or popup menu that is to be destroyed. The menu specified, and all associated popup menus, are destroyed.

Here is code that will determine the currently installed menu, remove it from the window, and destroy it:

```
HMENU hmenu;

hmenu = GetMenu(hwnd);   /* Find out menu handle. */
SetMenu (hwnd, NULL);    /* Remove menu.          */
DestroyMenu (hmenu);     /* Destroy the menu.     */
```

You don't have to do this for every menu you create, though, because a menu that is attached to a window is automatically destroyed when the window is destroyed.

The second menu destruction routine, **DeleteMenu**, actually does two things: It removes a menu item from a menu and destroys whatever popup menus are associated with the menu item. This routine frees the memory used by the menu in the same way that **DestroyMenu** does.

DeleteMenu is defined as

```
BOOL DeleteMenu (hMenu, nPosition, wFlags)
```

- hMenu is a handle to either a top-level or a popup menu.
- nPosition identifies the menu item of interest. The meaning of this field depends on the value of the last parameter, wFlags.
- wFlags is either MF_BYPOSITION or MF_BYCOMMAND.

If wFlags is MF_BYPOSITION, then the menu item is selected by its relative position in the menu: The first item in a menu has an offset of zero, the next has an offset of one, and so forth. This is necessary to reference popup menus, which don't have an associated result code. Here is one way to remove the Edit popup menu from the top-level menu in the STANMENU program:

```
HMENU hmenu;

hmenu = GetMenu (hwnd);
DeleteMenu (hmenu, 1, MF_BYPOSITION);
DrawMenuBar (hwnd);
```

As we'll discuss in the next section, the call to **DrawMenuBar** is necessary whenever the top-level menu changes, to request that it be completely redrawn.

The MF_BYPOSITION flag also can be used to remove an item in a popup menu. But you must first get a handle to the popup menu that contains the item by calling **GetSubMenu**. For example, here is how to delete the *Copy* command, which is the fourth item in our standard menu:

```
HMENU hmenu;
HMENU hmenuEdit;
```

```
hmenu = GetMenu (hwnd);
hmenuEdit = GetSubMenu (hMenu, 1);
DeleteMenu (hmenuEdit, 3, MF_BYPOSITION);
```

Menu items can also be deleted by using the command result code, by using the MF_BYCOMMAND flag in **DeleteMenu**'s last parameter. For deleting items in popup menus, using the command result code is faster than using the relative position, since the command result code lets you reference any item in the menu hierarchy by referencing the handle to the top-level menu. For example, here is another way to remove the *Copy* command from the Edit menu in STANMENU:

```
HMENU hmenu;

hmenu = GetMenu (hwnd);
DeleteMenu (hmenu, 9, MF_BYCOMMAND);
```

Our discussion of **DeleteMenu** has introduced two more menu flags: MF_BYCOMMAND and MF_BYPOSITION. These two plus the 12 flags that were introduced in the discussion of the **AppendMenu** routine brings to 14 the total number of menu flags that we have encountered. These 14 form the core set that you will use in just about all of the work you do with menus.

The next set of routines that we're going to look at are used to modify a menu once it has been created.

Menu Modification

Once a program has created a menu and attached it to a window, there is no reason for the menu to remain unchanged. In fact, Windows provides 10 routines that let you fiddle with menus as much as you need to. We've looked at one of them already, **AppendMenu**. Four other routines change the structure of an existing menu: **ChangeMenu**, **InsertMenu**, **ModifyMenu**, and **RemoveMenu**. In general, the **ChangeMenu** routine should be avoided since it was created for an earlier version of Windows and is somewhat clumsy and complicated to use. More to the point, its capabilities are replaced by the other three menu modification routines.

InsertMenu installs a new menu item or popup menu into an existing menu. Unlike **AppendMenu**, which can only create new items at the *end* of a menu, **InsertMenu** creates new items anywhere. The **ModifyMenu** routine *changes* an existing menu item. For example, it can be used to change the menu string, the command result code, to enable a grayed menu item, or to gray and disable a menu item. The **RemoveMenu** routine detaches a popup menu from a top-level or other popup menus. This routine leaves the internal menu structure intact, so that a menu can be reused later. Of course, if you remove a menu item from a menu, you must remember to destroy the menu item before your program exits, since otherwise the memory will be lost to the system.

Our first routine, **InsertMenu**, is defined as follows:

```
BOOL InsertMenu( hMenu, nPosition, wFlags, wID, lpNew)
```

- hMenu is a handle to a popup or top-level menu.
- nPosition indicates the menu item before which the new item is to be created. This value can be either the relative position of a menu item or the result code of a menu item, depending on whether the MF_BYPOSITION or MF_BYCOMMAND flag is selected.
- wFlags is a combination of the 12 menu flags that were described earlier with the AppendMenu routine. Two other flags indicate how the new item location is selected: MF_BYPOSITION and MF_BYCOMMAND.
- wID is the result code for a new menu item and is the value delivered with the WM_COMMAND message. Or, when a popup menu is being inserted, it is a popup menu handle.
- lpNew is a long value that can contain three different types of values. When inserting a string, it is a long pointer to a text string. When inserting a bitmap, it is a bitmap handle. Otherwise, if you are creating an "owner-draw" menu item, it identifies the specific item that you wish to draw.

Here is one way to add a *Close* command to the File menu, underneath the *Open...* menu item:

```
HMENU hmenu;
HMENU hmenuFile;

hmenu = GetMenu (hwnd);
hmenuFile = GetSubMenu (hmenu, 0);
InsertMenu (hmenuFile, 2, MF_BYPOSITION, 13, "&Close");
```

This code fragment uses the MF_BYPOSITION method to specify the location of the new menu item. Since we're inserting a menu item in a popup menu, this approach requires us to get a handle to the popup menu. The GetMenu routine gets a handle to the top-level menu. The GetSubMenu routine gets a handle to the File menu, since it's the first (zeroth) item in the top-level menu. Once we have a handle to the correct popup menu, the InsertMenu routine inserts a new menu command that will produce a result code of 13. The second parameter, 2, specifies that the menu item is to be inserted *before* menu item 2. In zero-based counting, that means before the *third* item. Figure 11.8 shows the File menu with the newly added *Close* menu item.

Another, slightly simpler way to add this menu item involves using the MF_BYCOMMAND option to specify the position for the new menu item. This approach is simpler, since it can be done using a handle to the top-level menu instead of requiring a handle to the specific popup where we're going to insert our new item.

```
HMENU hmenu;

hmenu = GetMenu (hwnd);
InsertMenu (hmenu, 3, MF_BYCOMMAND, 13, "&Close");
```

This code fragment also creates a Close menu item in the File menu. This time, however, the MF_BYCOMMAND parameter lets us specify the location using a command result code. In this case, the value of 3 is chosen since this is the result code for the Save menu item, before which we wish to have a menu item inserted.

The **ModifyMenu** routine, which can change any aspect of a menu item, takes the same parameters and flags as **InsertMenu**. This routine uses the same two methods for specifying a specific menu item: MF_BYPOSITION and MF_BYCOMMAND. Of course, since this routine modifies existing menu items instead of inserting new menu items, the way an item is specified is a little different. With **InsertMenu**, we point to the item that will follow the new menu item. **ModifyMenu**, on the other hand, requires us to point to the item itself.

ModifyMenu can put a new label on a menu item, gray a regular menu item, or enable a grayed menu item. It can be used to change a regular menu item into a bitmap or into an owner-draw menu item. In brief, anything that can be added to a menu with **InsertMenu** or

Figure 11.8 *File menu with newly added Close menu item*

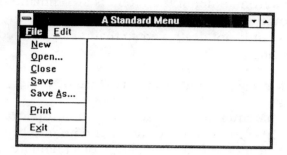

AppendMenu can be changed using **ModifyMenu**. For example, here is how **ModifyMenu** can be used to change the labels on a menu item. We're going to change the Edit menu's Cut, Copy, and Paste menu items so that each menu item displays the equivalent French phrase instead. Using the MF_BYPOSITION option, we would say:

```
HMENU hmenu;
HMENU hmenuEdit;

hmenu = GetMenu (hwnd);
hmenuEdit = GetSubMenu (hmenu, 1);
ModifyMenu (hmenuEdit, 2, MF_BYPOSITION, 8,  "Couper");
ModifyMenu (hmenuEdit, 3, MF_BYPOSITION, 9,  "Copier");
ModifyMenu (hmenuEdit, 4, MF_BYPOSITION, 10, "Coller");
```

As we saw in earlier examples, the MF_BYPOSITION option requires us to get the handle of the specific menu or submenu that contains the item of interest. A simpler approach involves using the MF_BYCOMMAND option. Here is how to use the MF_BY-COMMAND option to achieve the same results as in our previous example, except it requires no call to **GetSubMenu**:

```
HMENU hmenu;

hmenu = GetMenu (hwnd);
ModifyMenu (hmenu,  8, MF_BYCOMMAND,  8, "Couper");
ModifyMenu (hmenu,  9, MF_BYCOMMAND,  9, "Copier");
ModifyMenu (hmenu, 10, MF_BYCOMMAND, 10, "Coller");
```

Our next menu modification function, **RemoveMenu**, removes items from a menu. If an item is a command, it is removed and the memory associated with it is freed. However, if an item is a popup menu, it is not destroyed so that it can be used again. RemoveMenu is defined as

```
BOOL RemoveMenu (hMenu, nPosition, wFlags)
```

- hMenu is a handle to a popup or top-level menu.
- nPosition indicates the menu item to be removed. This value is either the relative position of a menu item, or the result code of a menu item, depending on whether the MF_BYPOSITION or MF_BYCOMMAND flag is selected.
- wFlags is either MF_BYPOSITION or MF_BYCOMMAND.

Using the MF_BYCOMMAND flag, we could delete the *Clear* menu item with

```
HMENU hmenu;

hmenu = GetMenu (hwnd);
RemoveMenu (hmenu, 11, MF_BYCOMMAND);
```

If we wanted to remove the entire Edit menu, we would have to use the MF_BYPOSITION flag as shown here:

```
HMENU hmenu;

hmenu = GetMenu (hwnd);
hmenuEdit = GetSubMenu (hmenu, 1);
RemoveMenu (hmenu, 1, MF_BYPOSITION);
DrawMenuBar (hwnd);
```

Since we are removing a popup menu from the menu hierarchy, unless we attach it later on we're going to have to be sure to destroy the menu before our program terminates:

```
DestroyMenu (hmenuEdit);
```

so that the memory associated with the Edit menu is freed.

You may have noticed the call to **DrawMenuBar** after the popup menu is removed. Whenever a change is made to a top-level menu,

DrawMenuBar should be called. The reason is that the menu modification routines *only* change the internal data structures that support a menu. For the user to see the change, **DrawMenuBar** must be called to redraw the newly modified menu. Otherwise, the change does not appear to the user, which is sure to result in some confusion.

All of the remaining routines in this group are used to change the state of existing menu items. **CheckMenuItem**, for example, is used to place a checkmark next to a menu item, or to remove a checkmark. Incidentally, if you don't like the shape of the default checkmark, you can create a bitmap that has an image that you do like and associate it with a menu item by calling **SetMenuItem-Bitmaps**. This routine also lets you select the bitmap to be displayed when a menu it is not checked. In Chapter 12, when we discuss how to enhance menu items using graphics, we'll show you exactly how this is done.

The **EnableMenuItem** routine lets you pick one of three enable states for a menu item: enabled, disabled, and grayed. As we mentioned earlier, because the disabled state provides no visual feedback to the user, it is probably best to avoid using it. For the other two, *enabled* is the default state of a menu in which it can be selected and manipulated in a normal manner. A *grayed* menu item, on the other hand, is displayed in a grayed text and cannot be selected by the user.

A final routine, **HiliteMenuItem**, lights up items in the top-level menu. This routine is used by the keyboard accelerator support code when a keyboard accelerator is pressed. The top-level menu item that is associated with the selected menu item is highlighted for a moment. Unless you plan to simulate this functionality yourself, you'll probably not find occasion to use this routine.

Our next set of routines perform a query—that is, they ask the menu system for some information.

Query

The Query routines let you ask for information about menus. There are two types of routines: one set returns a handle to a menu, the other provides menu attribute information. In general, if you can set a value or a flag, there is a query routine to let you know the currently selected value or flag associated with a menu item.

Three query routines give you menu handle information: **Get-Menu**, **GetSubMenu**, and **GetSystemMenu**. Figure 11.9 gives a graphic depiction of the menu handles returned by these three routines. **GetMenu** gives you a handle to the top-level menu that is attached to a window. Here is how it is called:

```
hmenuTop = GetMenu (hwnd);
```

Once you have the handle to a top-level menu, you get a handle to one of its popups by calling:

```
hmenu = GetSubMenu (hmenuTop, nPosition);
```

where nPosition is the zero-based index of the popup in the top-level menu, or the index of a popup within another popup menu. Once you have a popup menu handle, it can be used with any of the menu modification routines to add, remove, or modify any item in the menu.

The **GetSystemMenu** routine has two uses, to handle the special nature of the system menu. Most programs will use the default system menu, and so Windows only maintains a single copy. However, a copy is automatically created for a window if it calls GetSystemMenu like this:

```
hmenuSys = GetSystemMenu (hwnd, 0);
```

Figure 11.9 *Three query routines return menu handles*

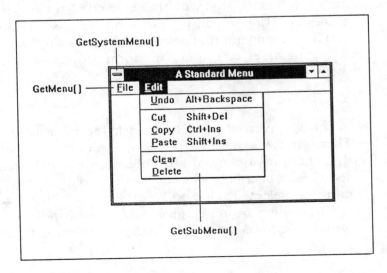

The zero in the second parameter tells the menu system to give you a handle to a private system menu that you can modify. If, after changing the system menu, you decide that you want to return to the original system menu, you make a call like this:

```
hmenuSys = GetSystemMenu (hwnd, 1);
```

A nonzero value in the second parameter attaches the default system menu to your window, which cannot be modified by you.

The other five query routines return menu attribute information. Figure 11.10 shows the specific attribute for four of the routines. To find out the number of items in a menu, you call:

```
w = GetMenuItemCount (hMenu);
```

where hMenu is either a top-level menu handle or a popup menu handle. The number of items includes the vertical separators that appear in the menu. If you need to find out the result code for a menu item command, you can call:

```
w = GetMenuItemID (hMenu, nPosition);
```

This routine can't tell you about a popup menu item, since they don't have result codes. If you ask for the result code for a popup menu, you get a -1. To find out the handle of a popup menu, you need to call GetSubMenu.

Another menu query routine is **GetMenuState**, which tells you the current settings for various menu flags. If you want to test for a specific menu flag, you use the logical AND function. For example, this code fragment gets the flags for the menu command item that has a result code of 38, then checks to see if the menu item is grayed or not:

```
WORD wFlags;

wFlags = GetMenuState (hmenu, 38, MF_BYCOMMAND);
if (wFlags & MF_GRAYED)
    {
    .
    .
    .
```

Figure 11.10 *Menu attributes that a program can query*

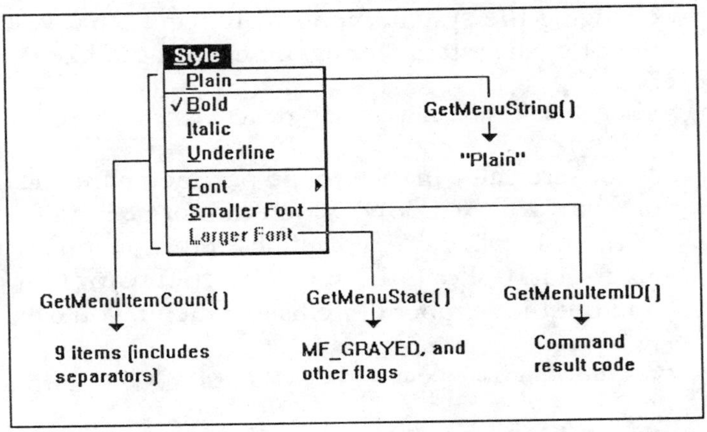

Be careful when using this routine, however. All of the default flags (MF_STRING, MF_UNHILITE, MF_ENABLED, and MF_UN-CHECKED) have a value of zero. You really can't test for them with the logical AND, since ANDing with zero always gives a result of zero. Instead, to test for any of the default flags, you need to check whether the flags that represent the opposite are present. For example, here is how to check whether or not a menu is enabled:

```
WORD wFlags

wFlags = GetMenuState (hmenu, 38, MF_BYCOMMAND);
if (!(wFlags & (MF_DISABLED | MF_GRAYED))
    {
    .
    .
    .
```

If the disabled and grayed flags are not set, this conditional statement returns a value of true. While it may seem like an odd way to test for the presence of a flag, it is necessary because of the way that the default flag information is stored. Notice that the GetMenuState routine lets you choose between the MF_BYCOMMAND and MF_BYPOSITION flags for picking a specific menu item.

Figure 11.11 *Check-mark dimensions returned by GetMenuCheckMark*

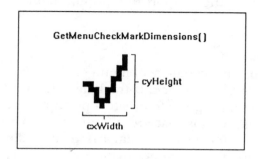

If you have a menu item that displays a string (as opposed to a separator, a bitmap, or an owner-draw item), you can retrieve a copy of the string by calling:

```
cbSize = GetMenuString (hmenu, wID, lpBuff, bufsize, wFlag);
```

where hmenu is a menu handle, wID is either a command result code or the relative position of an item, lpBuff is a long pointer to a character buffer, bufsize is the buffer size, and wFlag is either MF_BYCOMMAND or MF_BYPOSITION. The return value, cbSize, is the number of bytes that were copied.

Our last menu query routine has perhaps the longest routine name in Windows: **GetMenuCheckMarkDimensions**. As indicated in Figure 11.11, this routine returns the width and height of a default menu check mark. This is useful for programs that wish to install custom check marks to replace the default check mark. In addition, a program can install a mark that is displayed when the menu item is *not* checked. This routine returns a four-byte value that must be split apart to yield the two size values:

```
DWORD dwCheck;
int cxWidth;
int cyHeight;
dwCheck  = GetMenuCheckMarkDimensions();
cxWidth  = LOWORD (dwCheck);
cyHeight = HIWORD (dwCheck);
```

As indicated in the code example, this routine takes no parameters.

298 Peter Norton's Windows 3 Power Programming Techniques

There is one more category to look at that deals with tracking, which is the support of a popup menu outside a window's regular menu.

Tracking

Our final category of menu routines is made up of a single routine that is used for menu tracking. This routine, **TrackPopupMenu**, allows a program to create a popup menu anywhere on the display screen. Menus that are not attached to a top-level menu are sometimes referred to as **tear-off** menus, since they look like regular popup menus, except that they can appear anywhere. TrackPopup-Menu is defined as

```
BOOL TrackPopupMenu (hMenu, 0, x, y, 0, hWnd, 0L)
```

- hMenu is a handle to a popup menu.
- x is the X value of the upper-left corner of the menu, in screen coordinates.
- y is the Y value of the upper-left corner of the menu, in screen coordinates.
- hWnd is a handle of the window to which the WM_COMMAND and other menu messages are sent.
- The second, fifth, and seventh parameters are reserved values and must be zero, as shown here.

An important point to keep in mind with this routine is that the popup menu is *not* positioned in client area coordinates but in **screen coordinates**. Like client area coordinates, screen coordinates are a pixel-based coordinate system. However, the origin (0,0) in screen coordinates is always the upper-left corner of the display screen. If you wish to put a popup menu in your client area, you must convert client area coordinates to screen coordinates. The **ClientToScreen** routine does this for you quite nicely. Here is how a left-button up mouse message can be used to trigger a tear-off menu at the point where the user clicks the mouse:

```
case WM_LBUTTONUP:
    {
    HMENU hmenu;
    HMENU hmenuEdit;
    POINT pt;
```

```
hmenu = GetMenu (hwnd);
hmenuEdit = GetSubMenu (hmenu, 1);
pt = MAKEPOINT (lParam);
ClientToScreen(hwnd, &pt);
TrackPopupMenu (hmenuEdit, /* Popup menu handle. */
                0,         /* Reserved.          */
                pt.x,      /* X-coordinate.      */
                pt.y,      /* Y-coordinate.      */
                0,         /* Reserved.          */
                hwnd,      /* Hwnd to send msgs. */
                0L);       /* Reserved.          */
}
break;
```

This code fragment makes the Edit menu from STANMENU appear anywhere in the client area.

The popup menu created by the **TrackPopupMenu** routine is just like a regular popup menu. An important difference, however, is that a WM_INITMENUPOPUP message is *not* sent before this menu is displayed. Instead, the only menu initialization message that you receive is the WM_INITMENU message.

The reason is that a tear-off menu created by **TrackPopupMenu** is treated as a top menu in a menu hierarchy. From the point of view of the menu system, then, it has equal status with the menu-bar menu displayed under a window's caption bar. The WM_INITMENU message is reserved for the initialization of all top-level menus, including the popup menu displayed by **TrackPopupMenu**. But if a tear-off menu created by **TrackPopupMenu** were to have any nested popup menus, a WM_INITMENUPOPUP message is sent to tell you to perform whatever initialization is required for these lower level, nested menus.

Although menus allow a program to show the user the commands that are available, some users prefer to enter keyboard commands. To help you give these users what they want, Windows supports the creation of keyboard accelerators. Keyboard accelerators provide a virtually seamless connection between keyboard input and menu commands. The connection is so good that accelerator commands even cause a menu item to be briefly illuminated to let the user know that a command has been selected. Let's take a look at the capabilities that are available with keyboard accelerators and see how they can be incorporated into a Windows program.

Keyboard Accelerators

Keyboard accelerator support was one of the last pieces to be put in place when Microsoft was getting ready to ship the first version of Windows in 1985. Windows' original design called for a user interface that relied primarily on the mouse for command input. But after taking a second look at the existing base of computers—most of which didn't have a mouse—Microsoft had second thoughts. Another factor that strongly influenced their decision to put accelerator support into Windows was feedback from software developers who were considering the use of Windows for their applications. Some of the software developers had successful DOS programs that relied heavily on a keyboard interface, and they were concerned about the suitability of Windows for their products. Microsoft's response was to provide keyboard accelerators.

Keyboard accelerators tie together keyboard input and menu command selection. For users who don't have a mouse, or who prefer to use the keyboard to enter commands, accelerators link keystrokes with the creation of messages that match the menu messages we described earlier in this chapter. For programmers, this means that a minimum amount of effort is required to incorporate accelerator support in a Windows program.

Microsoft did such a good job of creating accelerator support that programmers usually think of accelerators as little more than an extension to the menu system. In fact, it is a separate part of Windows that can support commands that have no menu equivalent. Carried to an extreme, you could even write programs that rely *solely* on accelerator keystrokes for command input, and which make no use of menus. Of course, you probably won't want to do this since the presence of *both* menus and accelerators makes for a very flexible user interface.

In Chapter 15, when we discuss keyboard input, you'll see that keyboard input goes through a *two-step* translation process. Keyboard hardware generates **scan codes** to report keyboard activity. In fact, every key on the keyboard has *two* scan codes: one that says the key is being pressed and another that says the key is being released. A scan code lets the keyboard hardware report that a change has taken place. In general, scan codes are not interesting to most programs since they are too low-level to work with, and because Windows' keyboard driver translates scan codes into more useful information.

The first translation process converts scan codes into **virtual key codes**. Virtual key codes get us one step closer to character information, but they don't distinguish, for example, between a capital "A" and a lower-case "a". This is because virtual key codes don't represent characters, but keyboard keys. From the point of view of accelerators, virtual key codes are the most useful way to think about keyboard input. After all, when a user enters a keyboard command such as Ctrl+A, it should have the same effect whether or not the Caps Lock key is active. In other words, there shouldn't be a difference between Ctrl+A (capital A) and Ctrl+a (lower-case a).

The second translation process converts virtual key codes into the extended **ASCII** character set that Windows supports. Programs that wish to receive character input—such as a word processor—are most interested in ASCII characters and ignore scan codes and virtual key codes. From the point of view of accelerators, a program *can* incorporate ASCII characters as accelerators. But this could be very limiting, for example, to a word processing program if certain letters were command keys and not interpreted as data. Of course, if you're writing a program that uses keyboard input *only* for command input, there is no reason not to use ASCII characters.

Windows lets you define accelerator keys using either virtual key code information or ASCII characters. Virtual keys are the more common type of accelerator, because they do not rely on the state of shift keys, such as the Caps Lock key. But if you wish to create a case-sensitive command key, then ASCII character accelerators are what you need.

For a program to get access to accelerators, an accelerator table must be created. Programs can have more than one accelerator table, but only one can be active at any moment. Acclerator tables are created by making an entry in a program's resource file using the ACCELERATORS keyword. This template shows the two basic types of accelerator table entries. Each line in the table represents a different keyboard accelerator:

```
table-name ACCELERATORS
    {
    <key>,<cmd>,VIRTKEY,  [,NOINVERT] [,ALT] [,SHIFT] [,CONTROL]
    <key>,<cmd>,ASCII     [,NOINVERT] [,ALT] [,SHIFT] [,CONTROL]
    }
```

- <key> is the key, either text in quotes, "A", or a virtual key constant from Windows.H, like VK_F1. It can also be a numeric value, like 58 or 0x6C.
- <cmd> is the command result code to be included with the WM_COMMAND message to notify a program that an accelerator key combination has been pressed.
- VIRTKEY specifies that the value of <key> represents a virtual key code.
- ASCII specifies that <key> is an ASCII key code.
- NOINVERT inhibits the automatic highlighting of the related menu command.
- ALT indicates that an accelerator uses the Alt key.
- SHIFT indicates that an accelerator uses the Shift key.
- CONTROL indicates that an accelerator uses the Ctrl key.

Here is an example of an accelerator table containing only ASCII values:

```
AscKeys ACCELERATORS
    {
    "A", 25, ASCII
    "a", 26, ASCII
    "1", 27, ASCII
    }
```

The command result code is the value sent to the window procedure in the wParam parameter as part of the WM_COMMAND message. For example, here is code that would trap and process the keystrokes for the AscKeys accelerator table:

```
long FAR PASCAL WindowProc (...)
    {
    switch (msg)
        {
        case WM_COMMAND:
            switch (wParam)
                {
                case "A":
                    .
                    .
                case "a":
                    .
                    .
```

```
          case "1":
                .
                .
          }
       }
    }
```

This approach would allow you to write a program that uses regular character values as commands. Notice, though, that the use of ASCII makes your commands case-sensitive. The capital-A command is created when either the Shift key is pressed *or* Caps-Lock is on. As you're probably aware, when both keys are active, they cancel each other out, to create lower-case letters.

Instead of using ASCII accelerators, most programs use virtual key code accelerators. Virtual key codes let you define accelerators in a case-insensitive fashion. It also allows you to combine keys with any combination of the Alt, Shift, and Control keys. Here is another accelerator table showing how virtual key accelerators can be defined:

```
VirtKeys ACCELERATORS
    {
    "A",    35, VIRTKEY, CONTROL
    VK_F1, 36, VIRTKEY
    VK_F8, 37, VIRTKEY, ALT, CONTROL, SHIFT
    }
```

This table defines three virtual key accelerators: Control+A, F1, and Alt+Control+Shift F8. Because virtual key codes are tied to keyboard *keys* and not ASCII code values, the Control+A accelerator ignores the state of the Caps-Lock key. For this reason, virtual key accelerators are less confusing to the user. The second accelerator in this table causes the F1 function key to send a WM_COMMAND message with a value of 36 in the wParam parameter. The last accelerator in this table shows that an accelerator can be defined using all three shift keys: Alt, Control, and Shift. Of course, it's probably *not* a good idea to use all three shift keys in a single accelerator, since you'd be asking your user to press four keys simultaneously just to make a command selection. Of course, if you *do* need this capability, you will sleep better at night knowing that it's available.

Certain key combinations should not be used as accelerator keys. Some of them are shown in this accelerator table:

```
AvoidThese ACCELERATORS
  {
  VK_TAB,       99, VIRTKEY, ALT        ; switch programs
  VK_SPACE,    100, VIRTKEY, ALT        ; system menu
  VK_F10,      101, VIRTKEY             ; menu hot key
  VK_F4,       102, VIRTKEY, ALT        ; close window
  VK_ESCAPE,   103, VIRTKEY, CONTROL ; get task list
  VK_ESCAPE,   104, VIRTKEY, ALT        ; switch programs

  VK_MENU,     105, VIRTKEY             ; Alt key
  VK_SHIFT,    106, VIRTKEY             ; Shift key
  VK_CONTROL,107, VIRTKEY              ; Control key

  VK_DELETE,   108, VIRTKEY, CONTROL, ALT   ; Reboot!
  }
```

The first set of accelerator definitions are key combinations that are reserved for Windows' use. If you create an accelerator key for one of them, you will prevent that key combination from playing its standard role in the user interface. The second set of accelerator keys involves the use of the Alt, Shift, and Control keys alone. The keyboard accelerator system ignores these keys when used alone, since they are reserved for use with other keys. The very last accelerator key in this table needs no further explanation other than to say that you will never use it as an accelerator key command.

You'll want to avoid another set of accelerator key combinations, except when you need them for the actions for which they are reserved. Shift+Del, for example, is reserved for the Edit / Cut menu item, a standard menu item for programs that use the Clipboard. Table 11.5 summarizes these reserved accelerator keys and describes the use of each. From this set, you can see that the number of reserved accelerator keys is small and that you are left with a very wide range of keyboard combinations to choose from.

If you are creating a Windows program that may someday be translated for use in a different language, you will probably want to avoid creating any accelerators that combine Alt with a letter key, for example Alt + A. Such accelerators create the possibility of a conflict with mnemonic keystrokes. As we discussed earlier, a mnemonic keystroke lets the user strike Alt + letter to call up a popup menu. If an accelerator is defined for such a keystroke, like Alt + A, and a popup menu uses the letter as a mnemonic, the mnemonic is disabled because accelerator key combinations have a higher priority.

Table 11.5 *Reserved accelerator key combinations*

Key Combination	Description
Alt + Backspace	Edit / Undo menu item.
Shift + Del	Edit / Cut menu item to remove an item to the clipboard.
Ctrl + Ins	Edit / Copy to place a copy of an item on the clipboard.
Shift + Ins	Edit / Paste to copy the contents of the clipboard into a document.
Del	Edit / Clear or Edit / Delete to remove data without affecting the contents of the clipboard.
F1	Help.
F6	Switch to a different panel in a split window.
Ctrl + F6	Switch to a different window under the multiple document interface.

At first glance, you might think that the solution would be simply to avoid creating accelerators that conflict with mnemonic letters. Consider a program with two popups: File and Edit. If Alt-F and Alt-E are the only two mnemonic keystrokes that the program uses, you might think that you can use Alt-T without any problem. But when the time comes for you to convert your product to be used in Finland, where the word for file is "Tiedosto," you will find that your accelerator, Alt-T, has collided with the most obvious mnemonic for this menu. See Figure 11.12 for an example of how a Finnish program might appear.

As you can see from looking at this program, either an Alt+T or Alt+M accelerator would collide with the mnemonics in the Finnish version of our program for the File (Tiedosto) or Edit (Muokkaus) menus. The easiest way to avoid this problem is simply to avoid creating accelerator keys that consist of Alt and a letter key alone.

Once an accelerator table has been defined in the resource file, bringing it into a program requires a call to the **LoadAccelerators** routine. This is defined as

```
HANDLE LoadAccelerators (hInstance, lpTableName)
```

- hInstance is an instance handle passed to a program as a parameter to WinMain.
- lpTableName is a long pointer to a character string containing the name of an accelerator table in the program's resource file.

The return value is a handle to an accelerator table, which identifies the specific set of accelerator keystrokes to be used. You would load an accelerator table named VIRTKEYS as shown here:

```
HANDLE hAccel;

hAccel = LoadAccelerators (hInstance, "VIRTKEYS");
```

Just like other resources (such as the menus described earlier), a numeric value can be used to identify an accelerator table, as in

```
23 ACCELERATORS
    {
    "A",   35, VIRTKEY, CONTROL
    .
    .
    }
```

To load this accelerator table into memory, you would make a call like this:

```
hAccel = LoadAccelerators (hInstance, "#23");
```

Figure 11.12 *A sample Finnish program*

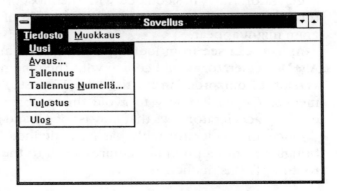

Or, the MAKEINTRESOURCE macro can be used to package the value in another way so that it is recognized as a numeric identifier:

```
hAccel=LoadAccelerators(hInstance,MAKEINTRESOURCE(23));
```

Once an accelerator table has been loaded, using it requires calling **TranslateAccelerator**. This routine is defined as

```
int TranslateAccelerator (hWnd, haccTable, lpMsg)
```

- hWnd is a handle of the window that is to receive the command and menu control messages created by keyboard accelerators. This window will normally have a menu attached, so that menu and accelerator support can be seamlessly integrated.
- haccTable is a handle to an accelerator table loaded with the **LoadAccelerators** routine.
- lpMsg is a long pointer to an MSG data structure.

The most common way to use accelerators is to modify the standard GetMessage loop in your WinMain function. Here is the standard GetMessage loop:

```
while (GetMessage(&msg, 0, 0, 0))
    {
    TranslateMessage(&msg);  /* Keyboard input. */
    DispatchMessage(&msg);
    }
```

TranslateAccelerator can check the message traffic received by GetMessage and convert it to the appropriate menu messages. If it performs a translation, it provides a return code of TRUE. Otherwise, the return code is FALSE. Here is the most common way to incorporate this routine into a standard message loop:

```
while (GetMessage(&msg, 0, 0, 0))
    {
    if (!TranslateAccelerator (hwnd, hAccel, &msg))
        {
        TranslateMessage(&msg);  /* Keyboard input. */
        DispatchMessage(&msg);
        }
    }
```

If **TranslateAccelerator** does not find an accelerator, it returns a value of FALSE. This causes the message to be handled normally by **TranslateMessage** and **DispatchMessage**. Otherwise, if an accelerator was found, then no other steps are required by the GetMessage loop, since it is handled entirely by **TranslateAccelerator**.

Here is a complete program that shows how an accelerator table can be implemented. This program is built on the standard menu program we introduced at the beginning of this chapter, STANMENU. We have added the four standard accelerators that support the standard clipboard operations: undo, cut, copy, and paste.

ACCEL.MAK

```
Accel.res: Accel.rc Accel.cur Accel.ico
    rc -r Accel.rc

Accel.obj: Accel.c
    cl -AM -c -d -Gsw -Ow -W2 -Zpi Accel.c

Accel.exe: Accel.obj Accel.def
    link Accel,/align:16,/map, mlibcew libw/NOD/NOE/CO, Accel.def
    rc Accel.res

Accel.exe: Accel.res
    rc Accel.res
```

ACCEL.C

```
/*------------------------------------------------------------*\
 |  Accel.C - Demo showing creation of keyboard accelerators.  |
\*------------------------------------------------------------*/
#include <Windows.H>


/*------------------------------------------------------------*\
 |                   Function Prototypes.                      |
\*------------------------------------------------------------*/
long FAR  PASCAL AccelWndProc (HWND, WORD, WORD, LONG);


/*------------------------------------------------------------*\
 |                 Main Function:  WinMain.                    |
\*------------------------------------------------------------*/
```

```
int PASCAL WinMain (HANDLE hInstance,

                    HANDLE hPrevInstance,
                    LPSTR  lpszCmdLine,
                    int    cmdShow)
    {
    HANDLE    hAccel;
    HWND      hwnd;
    MSG       msg;
    WNDCLASS  wndclass;

    if (!hPrevInstance)
        {
        wndclass.lpszClassName = "Accel:MAIN";
        wndclass.hInstance     = hInstance;
        wndclass.lpfnWndProc   = AccelWndProc;
        wndclass.hCursor       = LoadCursor (hInstance, "hand");
        wndclass.hIcon         = LoadIcon (hInstance,"snapshot");
        wndclass.lpszMenuName  = "#1";
        wndclass.hbrBackground = COLOR_WINDOW+1;
        wndclass.style         = NULL;
        wndclass.cbClsExtra    = 0;
        wndclass.cbWndExtra    = 0;

        RegisterClass( &wndclass);
        }

    hwnd = CreateWindow("Accel:MAIN",          /* Class name.  */
                        "Accelerators",        /* Title.       */
                        WS_OVERLAPPEDWINDOW,   /* Style bits.  */
                        CW_USEDEFAULT,         /* x - default. */
                        0,                     /* y - default. */
                        CW_USEDEFAULT,         /* cx - default. */
                        0,                     /* cy - default. */
                        NULL,                  /* No parent.   */
                        NULL,                  /* Class menu.  */
                        hInstance,             /* Creator      */
                        NULL                   /* Params.      */
                        ) ;
    ShowWindow (hwnd, cmdShow);

    hAccel = LoadAccelerators (hInstance, "#1");
```

```
    while (GetMessage(&msg, 0, 0, 0))
        {
        if (!TranslateAccelerator (hwnd, hAccel, &msg))
            {
            TranslateMessage(&msg);    /* Keyboard input.    */
            DispatchMessage(&msg);
            }
        }
    return 0;
    }


/*-----------------------------------------------------------------*\
|                Window Procedure:  AccelWndProc.                   |
\*-----------------------------------------------------------------*/
long FAR PASCAL AccelWndProc (HWND hwnd,   WORD wMsg,
                             WORD wParam, LONG lParam)
    {
    switch (wMsg)
        {
        case WM_COMMAND:
            {
            char buffer[80];

            if (wParam == IDM_EXIT)
                DestroyWindow (hwnd);
            else
                {
                wsprintf (buffer, "Command = %d", wParam);
                MessageBox (hwnd, buffer, "WM_COMMAND", MB_OK);
                }
            }
            break;

        case WM_DESTROY:
            PostQuitMessage(0);
            break;

        default:
            return(DefWindowProc(hwnd,wMsg,wParam,lParam));
            break;
        }
```

```
    return 0L;
    }
```

ACCEL.H

```
/*-----------------------------------------------------------------*\
 |   Accel.h  - Include file for Accel.c.                          |
 \*-----------------------------------------------------------------*/

#define IDM_NEW        1
#define IDM_OPEN       2
#define IDM_SAVE       3
#define IDM_SAVEAS     4
#define IDM_PRINT      5
#define IDM_EXIT       6

#define IDM_UNDO       7
#define IDM_CUT        8
#define IDM_COPY       9
#define IDM_PASTE     10
#define IDM_CLEAR     11
#define IDM_DELETE    12
```

ACCEL.RC

```
#include <Windows.h>
#include "Accel.h"

snapshot icon Accel.ico

hand   cursor Accel.cur

1 MENU
    {
    POPUP "&File"
        {
```

```
            MENUITEM "&New",           IDM_NEW
            MENUITEM "&Open...",       IDM_OPEN
            MENUITEM "&Save",          IDM_SAVE
            MENUITEM "Save &As...",  IDM_SAVEAS
            MENUITEM SEPARATOR
            MENUITEM "&Print",         IDM_PRINT
            MENUITEM SEPARATOR
            MENUITEM "E&xit",          IDM_EXIT
            }
      POPUP "&Edit"
          {
          MENUITEM "&Undo\tAlt+Backspace", IDM_UNDO
          MENUITEM SEPARATOR
          MENUITEM "Cu&t\tShift+Del",       IDM_CUT
          MENUITEM "&Copy\tCtrl+Ins",       IDM_COPY
          MENUITEM "&Paste\tShift+Ins",     IDM_PASTE
          MENUITEM SEPARATOR
          MENUITEM "Cl&ear",                IDM_CLEAR
          MENUITEM "&Delete",               IDM_DELETE
          }
      }


1 ACCELERATORS
    {
    VK_BACK,    IDM_UNDO,    VIRTKEY, ALT
    VK_DELETE,  IDM_CUT,     VIRTKEY, SHIFT
    VK_INSERT,  IDM_COPY,    VIRTKEY, CONTROL
    VK_INSERT,  IDM_PASTE,   VIRTKEY, SHIFT
    }
```

ACCEL.DEF

```
NAME      Accel

EXETYPE WINDOWS

DESCRIPTION 'Accelerators'
```

```
CODE       MOVEABLE DISCARDABLE
DATA       MOVEABLE MULTIPLE


HEAPSIZE      512
STACKSIZE     5000


EXPORTS
   AccelWndProc
```

All of the accelerator processing in our code is done in the WinMain function, which loads the accelerator table into memory. It contains a modified message loop that scans for accelerator key combinations and diverts the flow of messages as appropriate.

You may have also noticed that, instead of using numeric constants in our resource file, we have defined a set of symbolic constants in an include file, ACCEL.H. This allows you to use a more meaningful value, like IDM_NEW, instead of "magic numbers" that can't explain what they are used for. With the set of values defined in the include file, both the resource file and our C source files can access this file with the familiar include statement:

```
#include "Accel.H"
```

Windows gives you a comprehensive set of menu creation and management routines and lets you create accelerator keystrokes to define keyboard commands. It communicates via messages each action taken by the user with menus. The menu system is robust, fast, and flexible. You can create static menu templates, build menus on the fly, or change any part of an existing menu.

In the next chapter, we're going to see how we can get a little more sparkle out of our menus by adding graphics. We're going to explore three techniques to allow us to use GDI drawing routines to change the appearance of menu items: owner draw menu items, bitmaps in menus, and custom check marks.

12

Enhancing Menus with Graphics

Windows uses the System Font, a bold, Helvetica-like proportionally-spaced font, to draw the text inside menus. This default font was chosen because it is easy to read and has a slick, modern look. However, there may be times when you want to use another font inside a menu. Or, you might want to create a menu that contains geometric figures or graphic images. When you want to do this, Windows lets you hook into its menu creation mechanism so that you can enhance the look of your menus with graphical objects. In this chapter, we're going to look at three methods that are available to you: owner-draw menu items, bitmaps in menus, and custom check marks.

Owner-Draw Menu Items

All of the menus that we've created up to now have used a text label drawn with the system font. For most applications, this is a reasonable approach to take. But there may be times when you wish to replace the text with a graphic object. Or, you may wish to change the font that is used. Owner-draw menu items give you the ability to create graphical menu images using GDI drawing calls. Thus, instead of just *telling* a user what a menu item will produce, you can *show* them. A drawing program might use this capability to show the user the different lines, shapes, and fonts that are available. A flowchart program might put different flowchart elements into menus to provide instant feedback on which flowchart elements are available.

Because the resource compiler does not provide any support for owner-draw menu items, you have to dynamically create the menu items by calling one of the menu modification routines we discussed in the last chapter. If you want an owner-draw menu item to appear in your menu the first time your window appears, you'll probably want to add the menu item in response to the WM_CREATE message.

After an owner-draw menu item has been inserted into a menu, two messages will be sent to the window procedure to measure and draw the menu item: WM_MEASUREITEM and WM_DRAWITEM. The WM_MEASUREITEM message arrives before the menu item is ever drawn. Your program must respond to this message by filling in a data structure that describes the width and height of your menu item in pixels. The second message, WM_DRAWITEM, is sent whenever drawing is needed for the menu item. Drawing is needed when a menu is displayed and when the menu item is highlighted to provide the user with visual feedback while menu items are browsed.

Before we look at the handling of these two messages in detail, it's worth mentioning that these two messages are also sent for the other types of owner-draw objects: buttons, comboboxes, and listboxes. As you'll see, there are elements of the owner-draw mechanism, intended for use with the other owner-draw objects, that can be safely ignored when dealing with owner-draw menu items. As we look at each part of this mechanism, we'll be sure to identify these elements for you.

The WM_MEASUREITEM Message

An owner-draw item can be as small or as large as you would like to make it. The WM_MEASUREITEM message provides a way for you to let the menu system know the exact size that you need to draw the menu item. The units are in pixels, but since you're going to use GDI routines to draw, you can use GDI's coordinate mapping system, described in more detail in Chapter 20.

When calculating the size of the area that you'll need in an owner-draw menu item, you need to take into account space for a margin around the menu item. For one thing, you'll want to allow enough space between your menu item and other menu items. It's also a good idea to reserve space for a check mark on the left side of your menu. You can call the **GetMenuCheckMarkDimensions** routine for information about the default width and height of a check mark. Even if you don't use a check mark for your owner-draw menu item, you'll still want to do this. The width of a check mark is the standard left margin of a menu item; using this value will help give your owner-draw menu items a consistent look with normal menu items.

To accommodate the higher resolution of devices that we may see some day, it's a good idea to avoid hard-coding any specific sizes for owner-draw menu items. Instead, you should make your drawing relative to the size of system objects, because they are automatically scaled for different device resolutions. Icons are a type of system object that can serve as a good reference point for owner-draw menu items. Icon dimensions are determined by the system display device driver. To determine the dimensions of an icon, you call **GetSystemMetrics**. If you wanted to make your menu items the same size as an icon, here's how you could do it:

```
DWORD dwCheckMark;
int cxWidth, cyHeight;

cxWidth  = GetSystemMetrics (SM_CXICON); /* Width.  */
cyHeight = GetSystemMetrics (SM_CYICON); /* Height. */

/* Adjust for check mark.  */
dwCheckMark = GetMenuCheckMarkDimensions();
cxWidth +=       LOWORD(dwCheckMark);
cyHeight = max (HIWORD(dwCheckMark), cyHeight);
```

We add a value for the width of the check mark, and we also update cyHeight to make sure that it can accommodate the height of a check mark.

As an alternative, you can base the size of your owner-draw items on the metrics of the system font. When we discuss dialog boxes in Chapter 14, you'll see that the dialog box manager uses this approach to provide device-independent **dialog box coordinates**. To calculate the dimensions of an owner-draw menu item that is twice as tall as the system font, and which has a width equal to that of 15 characters, you can say:

```
DWORD dwCheckMark;
HDC hdc
int cxWidth, cyHeight;
TEXTMETRIC tm;

hdc = GetDC (hwnd);
GetTextMetrics (hdc, &tm);
ReleaseDC (hwnd, hdc);

cxWidth  = tm.tmMaxCharWidth * 15;
```

```
cyHeight = tm.tmHeight * 2;

/*  Adjust for check mark. */
dwCheckMark = GetMenuCheckMarkDimensions();
cxWidth +=      LOWORD(dwCheckMark);
cyHeight = max (HIWORD(dwCheckMark), cyHeight);
```

The **GetTextMetrics** routine, which we first discussed in Chapter 10, gets the metrics of the font that is currently installed in a DC. In the absence of special window class styles (discussed in Chapter 13), **GetDC** returns a DC with the a system font installed. As in the earlier example, this code includes the dimensions of a menu check mark in the overall dimensions of the owner-draw item.

Whichever method you choose, one WM_MEASUREITEM message is sent for each owner-draw menu item. When it arrives, the lParam parameter contains a long pointer to a structure of type MEASUREITEMSTRUCT. This structure is defined in Windows.h as

```
typedef struct tagMEASUREITEMSTRUCT
  {
    WORD    CtlType;     /*  ODT_MENU            */
    WORD    CtlID;       /*  Ignore for menus.   */
    WORD    itemID;
    WORD    itemWidth;   /*  Return width.       */
    WORD    itemHeight;  /*  Return height.      */
    DWORD   itemData;
  } MEASUREITEMSTRUCT;
```

When you get a WM_MEASUREITEM message, the two fields that you use to return the width and height of your owner-draw item are `itemWidth` and `itemHeight`. The other fields in this data structure help you identify a specific owner-draw item, since you will have one WM_MEASUREITEM message for each owner-draw menu item that you have. When working with owner-draw menu items, one of these fields can be ignored since it's only used for owner-draw dialog box controls: `CtlID`.

The `CtlType` field describes the type of owner-draw item. It is set to ODT_MENU for menus. The presence of this field means a single body of code can support owner-draw objects in menus, listboxes or comboboxes.

`itemID` is the command result code for a menu item. It is the value that gets sent in the wParam parameter of a WM_COMMAND message. As we'll see in a moment, this value is set when a menu item is created.

The `itemData` field provides another way to identify an owner-draw menu item. It is a 32-bit field that you create and provide when you create an owner-draw menu item. When you create an owner-draw popup menu (as opposed to a regular command menu item), this field provides the only way to distinguish one owner-draw popup menu from another, since popup menu items do not have a command result code.

If you create an owner-draw menu item by calling **AppendMenu** like this:

```
AppendMenu (hmenu, MF_OWNERDRAW, 38, (LPSTR)200);
```

it creates a menu item with an `itemID` of 38 and an `itemData` value of 200. The last parameter is cast as an LPSTR because that is how this routine is prototyped. Otherwise, the compiler issues an unnecessary warning message. If the variables **cxWidth** and **cyHeight** contained the desired dimensions of this menu item, we could respond to the WM_MEASUREITEM message like this:

```
case WM_MEASUREITEM:
    {
    LPMEASUREITEMSTRUCT lpmi;

    lpmi = (LPMEASUREITEMSTRUCT)lParam;

    if (lpmi->itemID == 38)
        {
        lpmi->itemWidth  = cxWidth;
        lpmi->itemHeight = cyHeight;
        }
    }
```

Another approach involves checking `itemData` for the specific owner-draw menu item:

```
case WM_MEASUREITEM:
    {
    LPMEASUREITEMSTRUCT lpmi;

    lpmi = (LPMEASUREITEMSTRUCT)lParam;
```

```
if (lpmi->itemData == 200)
    {
    lpmi->itemWidth  = cxWidth;
    lpmi->itemHeight = cyHeight;
    }
}
```

A program only receives a single WM_MEASUREITEM message for each owner-draw item. After that, the menu system remembers the dimensions of the menu item and sends a WM_DRAWITEM message whenever it needs a menu item to be drawn.

The WM_DRAWITEM Message

A WM_DRAWITEM message is sent to your window procedure when a popup menu is opened that contains an owner-draw menu item. Then, as the user browses through a menu, this message is sent to toggle menu highlighting. As you'll see in a moment, the WM_DRAWITEM message provides flags that let you know the effect that the menu system requires.

When the WM_DRAWITEM message is sent, the window procedure's lParam parameter contains a long pointer to a structure of type DRAWITEMSTRUCT, defined in Windows.h as follows:

```
typedef struct tagDRAWITEMSTRUCT
    {
    WORD    CtlType;     /* ODT_MENU.                 */
    WORD    CtlID;       /* Ignore for menus.         */
    WORD    itemID;
    WORD    itemAction;  /* Ignore for menus.         */
    WORD    itemState;   /* Selected,grayed,checked.  */
    HWND    hwndItem;    /* Handle to popup menu.      */
    HDC     hDC;
    RECT    rcItem;      /* Bounding rectangle.        */
    DWORD   itemData;
    } DRAWITEMSTRUCT;
```

Four of the items in this data structure are identical to items in the data structure that is sent with the WM_MEASUREITEM message: **CtlType, CtlID, itemID,** and **itemData.**

The `CtlType` field describes the type of owner-draw item. It is set to ODT_MENU for menus.

The **CtlID** field can be ignored for owner-draw menu items, since it is only used for owner-draw dialog box controls.

itemID is the command result code for a menu item, which is the value sent to a window procedure in the wParam parameter of a WM_COMMAND message.

The **itemData** field provides another way to identify an owner-draw menu item and is the only way to distinguish one owner-draw popup menu from another.

The **itemAction** field describes the action the menu system wants you to perform. However, since menu items are drawn to reflect the menu item state, you can usually ignore this field and determine the menu state from the next field.

The **itemState** field defines the current state of the menu item, as shown here:

Value	Menu Item State
ODS_CHECKED	Check mark is to appear in the menu.
ODS_DISABLED	Menu to be drawn disabled.
ODS_FOCUS	Ignore—not used for menus.
ODS_GRAYED	Menu to be drawn grayed.
ODS_SELECTED	Menu to be drawn selected.

The most important flag is ODS_SELECTED. When this bit is set, it indicates that the menu item needs to be highlighted. A highlighted menu item is drawn in a different color from a regular menu item to provide visual feedback while the user is browsing a menu. You should draw highlighted menu items using two system colors that are defined for this purpose. To obtain the RGB values of the required system colors, call the **GetSysColor** routine. Here are the color indices that you should use for menu highlights:

Value	Description
COLOR_HIGHLIGHT	Background color of the highlighted object.
COLOR_HIGHLIGHTTEXT	Foreground color of the highlighted object.

If you plan to set the state of an owner-draw menu item to checked, or if you plan to gray the menu item, your reponse to the WM_DRAWITEM message must provide for this. You will need to test the value in the **itemState** field and change the way you draw your menu item according to the desired effect. For example, you might use a shade of gray in your drawing to indicate a grayed menu item. You can draw a check mark using a bitmap that is built into the display driver. Here is one way to obtain a handle to that bitmap, and draw with it:

```
hbm = LoadBitmap (NULL,MAKEINTRESOURCE(OBM_CHECK));
hdcBitmap = CreateCompatibleDC (hDC);
hbmOld = SelectObject (hdcBitmap, hbm);

dwDimensions = GetMenuCheckMarkDimensions();
cxWidth  = LOWORD(dwDimensions);
cyHeight = HIWORD(dwDimensions);

BitBlt (ps.hdc, 0, 0, cxWidth, cyHeight,
        hdcBitmap, 0, 0, SRCCOPY);

SelectObject (hdcBitmap, hbmOld);
DeleteDC (hdcBitmap);
```

In spite of its name, the **hwndItem** field is not a window handle but instead is a popup menu handle for the menu that contains the owner-draw item. Its name comes from its use with owner-draw dialog box controls, when it does contain a window handle. When a program receives a WM_DRAWITEM message, it might wish to use the popup menu handle to call a menu query routine to find out, for example, the number of items that are in the current menu, or the state of other menu items.

The **hDC** field is a handle to a device context for drawing in the menu. Be sure to restore the DC to its initial state when you are done, otherwise you risk causing problems for the menu system when it draws other parts of your menu.

The **rcItem** field defines a rectangle within which you can draw your menu item. You should not go beyond this rectangle, since doing so risks overwriting other menu items.

The owner-draw items supported by these messages and data structures give a program a remarkable amount of flexibility in deciding how a menu item should appear. Let's look at a sample pro-

Figure 12.1 *An owner-draw menu showing three fonts*

gram that shows how to put these messages and data structures to work for you.

A Sample Program: OWNDRAW

Our sample program, **OWNDRAW**, shows how owner-draw menu items can be used to display different fonts in a menu. The menu from OWNDRAW is shown in Figure 12.1. Not only is the user provided with the *name* of the font, but also with the *image* of the font itself. This would be a useful technique in any program that lets the user select a font. If you do this, you should keep in mind the fact that only display fonts can be used to draw in menus. Therefore, if you wish to show a user the printer fonts that are available, you would be limited in some cases to the name of the font. Of course, with the coming of TrueType font technology in a future version of Windows, the differences between display and printer fonts is going to be substantially reduced.

Here is the source listing of OWNDRAW. To write this program, we used the STANMENU program as a base and added the items needed for our owner-draw items.

OWNDRAW.MAK

```
owndraw.res: owndraw.rc owndraw.cur owndraw.ico
    rc -r owndraw.rc

owndraw.obj: owndraw.c
    cl -AM -c -d -Gsw -Ow -W2 -Zpi owndraw.c
```

```
owndraw.exe: owndraw.obj owndraw.def
    link owndraw,/align:16,/map, mlibcew libw/NOD/NOE/CO,\
        owndraw.def
    rc owndraw.res

owndraw.exe: owndraw.res
    rc owndraw.res
```

OWNDRAW.C

```
/*------------------------------------------------------------*\
 | Owndraw.C  -  A sample owner-draw menu.                     |
\*------------------------------------------------------------*/
#include <Windows.H>
#include <memory.h>
#include "owndraw.h"


/*------------------------------------------------------------*\
 |                  Function Prototypes.                       |
\*------------------------------------------------------------*/
long FAR PASCAL OwndrawWndProc (HWND, WORD, WORD, LONG);


/*------------------------------------------------------------*\
 |                    Static Data.                            |
\*------------------------------------------------------------*/
HFONT hfontTmsRmn;
HFONT hfontHelv;
HFONT hfontCour;


/*------------------------------------------------------------*\
 |                  Main Function:  WinMain.                   |
\*------------------------------------------------------------*/
int PASCAL WinMain (HANDLE hInstance,
                    HANDLE hPrevInstance,
                    LPSTR  lpszCmdLine,
                    int    cmdShow)

    {
    HWND     hwnd;
    MSG      msg;
    WNDCLASS wndclass;
```

```
      if (!hPrevInstance)
          {
          wndclass.lpszClassName = "Owndraw:MAIN";
          wndclass.hInstance     = hInstance;
          wndclass.lpfnWndProc   = OwndrawWndProc;
          wndclass.hCursor       = LoadCursor (hInstance, "hand");
          wndclass.hIcon         = LoadIcon (hInstance,"snapshot");
          wndclass.lpszMenuName  = "#1";
          wndclass.hbrBackground = COLOR_WINDOW+1;
          wndclass.style         = NULL;
          wndclass.cbClsExtra    = 0;
          wndclass.cbWndExtra    = 0;

          RegisterClass( &wndclass);
          }

      hwnd = CreateWindow("Owndraw:MAIN",      /* Class name.  */
                          "Owner-Draw Menu",   /* Title.       */
                          WS_OVERLAPPEDWINDOW, /* Style bits.  */
                          CW_USEDEFAULT,       /* x - default. */
                          0,                   /* y - default. */
                          CW_USEDEFAULT,       /* cx - default. */
                          0,                   /* cy - default. */
                          NULL,                /* No parent.   */
                          NULL,                /* Class menu.  */
                          hInstance,           /* Creator.     */
                          NULL);               /* Params.      */

      ShowWindow (hwnd, cmdShow);

      while (GetMessage(&msg, 0, 0, 0))
          {
          TranslateMessage(&msg);           /*  Keyboard input.      */
          DispatchMessage(&msg);
          }
      return 0;
      }
/*------------------------------------------------------------*\
|            Window Procedure:  OwndrawWndProc.              |
\*------------------------------------------------------------*/
long FAR PASCAL OwndrawWndProc (HWND hwnd,   WORD wMsg,
```

```
                                     WORD wParam, LONG lParam)
{
static COLORREF crHighlight;
static COLORREF crHighlightText;

switch (wMsg)
    {
    case WM_CREATE:
        {
        HDC    hdc;
        HMENU  hmenu;
        HMENU  hmenuPopup;
        LOGFONT lf;
        TEXTMETRIC tm;

        /*  Create a menu with three owner-draw items    */
        /*  for the three fonts we're going to create.    */

        hmenu = GetMenu (hwnd);
        hmenuPopup = CreatePopupMenu();
        AppendMenu (hmenu, MF_POPUP, hmenuPopup, "Fo&nt");

        AppendMenu (hmenuPopup,
                    MF_OWNERDRAW,
                    IDM_COURIER,
                    MAKEINTRESOURCE(IDM_COURIER));
        AppendMenu (hmenuPopup,
                    MF_OWNERDRAW,
                    IDM_TMSRMN,
                    MAKEINTRESOURCE(IDM_TMSRMN));
        AppendMenu (hmenuPopup,
                    MF_OWNERDRAW,
                    IDM_HELV,
                    MAKEINTRESOURCE(IDM_HELV));

        /*  Create three logical fonts, with different    */
        /*  sizes and styles.                             */

        memset (&lf, 0, sizeof (LOGFONT));

        hdc = GetDC (hwnd);
```

```
        GetTextMetrics (hdc, &tm);
        ReleaseDC (hwnd, hdc);

        lf.lfWeight = 700;                    /*  Bold.            */

        lstrcpy (lf.lfFaceName, "Courier");
        lf.lfHeight = tm.tmHeight;         /*  Sysfont height. */
        hfontCour = CreateFontIndirect (&lf);

        lstrcpy (lf.lfFaceName, "Tms Rmn");
        lf.lfHeight = tm.tmHeight + tm.tmHeight/4; /* 125%.*/
        hfontTmsRmn = CreateFontIndirect (&lf);

        lstrcpy (lf.lfFaceName, "Helv");
        lf.lfHeight = tm.tmHeight + tm.tmHeight/2; /* 150%.*/
        hfontHelv = CreateFontIndirect (&lf);

        /*  Get system colors for our owner-draw items.   */
        crHighlight = GetSysColor (COLOR_HIGHLIGHT);
        crHighlightText = GetSysColor (COLOR_HIGHLIGHTTEXT);
        }
        break;

    case WM_DESTROY:
        DeleteObject (hfontTmsRmn);
        DeleteObject (hfontHelv);
        DeleteObject (hfontCour);
        PostQuitMessage(0);
        break;

    case WM_DRAWITEM:
        {
        char buff[80];
        COLORREF crFore;
        COLORREF crBack;
        DWORD dwCheckMark;
        DWORD dwSize;
        HFONT hfontOld;
        HFONT hfont;
        int fSwapColors;
        int xText,yText;
```

```
                   int cxCheck;
                   LPDRAWITEMSTRUCT lpdi;

                   lpdi = (LPDRAWITEMSTRUCT)lParam;

                   switch (lpdi->itemID)
                       {
                       case IDM_COURIER:
                           lstrcpy (buff, "Courier");
                           hfont = hfontCour;
                           break;
                       case IDM_TMSRMN:
                           lstrcpy (buff, "Times Roman");
                           hfont = hfontTmsRmn;
                           break;
                       case IDM_HELV:
                           lstrcpy (buff, "Helvetica");
                           hfont = hfontHelv;
                           break;
                       }
                   hfontOld = SelectObject (lpdi->hDC, hfont);

                   /*   If current menu item should be highlighted,   */
                   /*   install the correct system colors.            */

                   if (lpdi->itemState & ODS_SELECTED)
                       {
                       crFore = SetTextColor (lpdi->hDC,
                                               crHighlightText);
                       crBack = SetBkColor (lpdi->hDC,
                                               crHighlight);
                       fSwapColors= TRUE;
                       }
                   else
                       fSwapColors= FALSE;

                   /* Get width of checkmark.                         */
                   dwCheckMark = GetMenuCheckMarkDimensions();
                   cxCheck = LOWORD (dwCheckMark);

                   xText = lpdi->rcItem.left + cxCheck;
```

```
        yText = lpdi->rcItem.top;



        /*  Display line of text.                              */
        ExtTextOut (lpdi->hDC, xText, yText,
                    ETO_OPAQUE,
                    &lpdi->rcItem,
                    buff,
                    lstrlen(buff),
                    NULL);


        /*  Restore DC before we send it home.                 */

        SelectObject (lpdi->hDC, hfontOld);     /*  Font.  */
        if (fSwapColors)
            {
            SetTextColor (lpdi->hDC, crFore); /*  Colors. */
            SetBkColor (lpdi->hDC, crBack);
            }
        }
        break;

    case WM_MEASUREITEM:
        {
        char buff[80];
        DWORD dwSize;
        DWORD dwCheckMark;
        HDC hdc;
        HFONT hfont;
        int cxWidth, cyHeight;
        int cxCheck, cyCheck;
        LPMEASUREITEMSTRUCT lpmi;

        lpmi = (LPMEASUREITEMSTRUCT)lParam;
        switch (lpmi->itemID)
            {
            case IDM_COURIER:
                lstrcpy (buff, "Courier");
                hfont = hfontCour;
                break;
            case IDM_TMSRMN:
```

```
                              lstrcpy (buff, "Times Roman");
                              hfont = hfontTmsRmn;
                              break;
                        case IDM_HELV:
                              lstrcpy (buff, "Helvetica");
                              hfont = hfontHelv;
                              break;
                  }

            /*  Find size of string.                           */
            hdc = GetDC (hwnd);
            SelectObject (hdc, hfont);
            dwSize = GetTextExtent (hdc, buff, lstrlen(buff));
            ReleaseDC (hwnd, hdc);

            /*  Start with string size information.            */
            cxWidth  = LOWORD(dwSize);
            cyHeight = HIWORD(dwSize);

            /*  Add in check mark size information.            */
            dwCheckMark = GetMenuCheckMarkDimensions();
            cxCheck = LOWORD (dwCheckMark);
            cyCheck = HIWORD (dwCheckMark);

            lpmi->itemWidth  = cxWidth + cxCheck;
            lpmi->itemHeight = max (cyHeight, cyCheck);
            }
            break;

      default:
            return(DefWindowProc(hwnd,wMsg,wParam,lParam));
            break;
      }
   return 0L;
   }
```

OWNDRAW.H

```
/*------------------------------------------------------------*\
|  Owndraw.H - Include file for Owndraw.c                      |
\*------------------------------------------------------------*/
```

```
#define IDM_NEW        1
#define IDM_OPEN       2
#define IDM_SAVE       3
#define IDM_SAVEAS     4
#define IDM_PRINT      5
#define IDM_EXIT       6

#define IDM_UNDO       7
#define IDM_CUT        8
#define IDM_COPY       9
#define IDM_PASTE     10
#define IDM_CLEAR     11
#define IDM_DELETE    12

#define IDM_TMSRMN    13
#define IDM_HELV      14
#define IDM_COURIER   15
```

OWNDRAW.RC

```
#include <Windows.h>
#include "owndraw.h"

snapshot icon owndraw.ico

hand   cursor owndraw.cur

1 MENU
    {
    POPUP "&File"
        {
        MENUITEM "&New",         IDM_NEW
        MENUITEM "&Open...",     IDM_OPEN
        MENUITEM "&Save",        IDM_SAVE
        MENUITEM "Save &As...",  IDM_SAVEAS
        MENUITEM SEPARATOR
        MENUITEM "&Print",       IDM_PRINT
        MENUITEM SEPARATOR
        MENUITEM "E&xit",        IDM_EXIT
        }
```

```
    POPUP "&Edit"
        {
        MENUITEM "&Undo\tAlt+Backspace",  IDM_UNDO
        MENUITEM SEPARATOR
        MENUITEM "Cu&t\tShift+Del",        IDM_CUT
        MENUITEM "&Copy\tCtrl+Ins",        IDM_COPY
        MENUITEM "&Paste\tShift+Ins",      IDM_PASTE
        MENUITEM SEPARATOR
        MENUITEM "Cl&ear",   IDM_CLEAR
        MENUITEM "&Delete",  IDM_DELETE
        }
    }
```

OWNDRAW.DEF

```
NAME     OwnDraw

EXETYPE WINDOWS

DESCRIPTION 'Owner-Draw Menus'

CODE     MOVEABLE DISCARDABLE
DATA     MOVEABLE MULTIPLE

HEAPSIZE    512
STACKSIZE   5000

EXPORTS
    OwndrawWndProc
```

In response to the WM_CREATE message, OWNDRAW creates three owner-draw menu items and three logical fonts. It also calls GetSysColor to determine the foreground and background colors to use in our menu. In response to the WM_MEASUREITEM message, calls are made to GDI to calculate the dimensions of each string that will appear in the menu. The size of each item is adjusted to make sure there is room for a check mark, so that our menu items have a reasonable left margin.

Once the measurement information has been provided, our window procedure starts to receive WM_DRAWITEM messages. Since we're not interested in grayed or disabled items, OWNDRAW doesn't check for these flags. We also don't check whether or not the item should display a check mark. If we wanted a check mark, we would have to draw it ourselves in response to the WM_DRAWITEM message. That is to say, if we are going to draw *part* of a menu item, we must draw the *entire* menu item.

Keyboard mnemonics are not supported in owner-draw menu items. In general, this makes sense, since a graphic image can hardly be expected to have an associated keyboard keystroke. However, the presence of text inside these owner-draw menu items creates the paradox that, even though our owner-draw items could certainly use a mnemonic keystroke as graphic objects, Windows does not provide mnemonic keystroke support for owner-draw items. If this is important to you, there is a way for an owner-draw menu item to simulate a mnemonic. You start by underlining the mnemonic letter in each of the font names. Then, in response to the WM_MENUCHAR message, you would check for the mnemonic letters and indicate either an error or a menu selection in the return value. The WM_MENUCHAR message is sent when the user strikes a keystroke that doesn't correspond to any mnemonic or accelerator key. When the default window procedure receives this message, it provides a return value that tells the menu system to beep at the user. But processing this message yourself would allow you to provide the necessary return value so that the menu system would handle the keystroke as a regular mnemonic.

The fonts that were created in response to the WM_CREATE message are, of course, GDI drawing objects that take up memory in GDI's local heap. Before OWNDRAW can exit, it must destroy these objects; otherwise the memory occupied by them will be lost and unavailable for other programs to use. OWNDRAW makes several calls to DestroyObject in response to the WM_DESTROY message:

```
case WM_DESTROY:
    DeleteObject (hfontTmsRmn);
    DeleteObject (hfontHelv);
    DeleteObject (hfontCour);
    PostQuitMessage(0);
    break;
```

The use of owner-draw items gives a program the greatest control and flexibility in the appearance of menu items. From one moment to the next, a menu item may change in response to some outside event. But you may not need this much flexibility in the graphic images you put in a menu. You have a second choice, which in some respects is easier to implement than owner-draw menu items. It involves the creation of a GDI bitmap. Such a bitmap can be associated with a menu item and automatically displayed by the menu system without any intervention required on your part. Let's take a look at what is involved in putting bitmaps into menu items.

Bitmaps In Menus

In Chapter 6, in our introduction to GDI, we discussed how bitmaps are useful for storing graphic images. Once a graphic image has been created in a bitmap, it can be incorporated into a menu as an alternative to the text that is normally displayed in menus. Bitmaps in menus provide a somewhat easier method than owner-draw menu items for getting graphic images into menus.

To take advantage of this capability, we need to start by describing how a Windows program goes about creating and using GDI bitmaps. The clearest way to understand what GDI expects is to examine a code fragment that shows how all the pieces are brought together. Here is one way to create a GDI bitmap that can be displayed in a menu:

```
HDC     hdcScreen;
HDC     hdcBitmap;
HBITMAP hbm;
HBITMAP hbmOld;

hdcScreen = GetDC (hwnd);
hdcBitmap = CreateCompatibleDC (hdcScreen);
hbm = CreateCompatibleBitmap (hdc, cxWidth, cyHeight);
ReleaseDC (hwnd, hdcScreen);

hbmOld = SelectObject (hdcBitmap, hbm);
```

Using a bitmap requires that two objects be created and connected together: a bitmap and a device context. Creating a bitmap requires us to specify the size of the rectangular display image that we wish to store. GDI responds by allocating the required memory. We need a device context because, as you're aware, every GDI drawing routine takes a handle to a DC as its first parameter. Without this special "membership card," the bitmap won't be admitted to the private club that all GDI devices belong to. But *with* the DC, a bitmap becomes a full participant in all the drawing capabilities that GDI has to offer.

The quickest and easiest way to create a DC involves asking GDI to clone an existing DC, by calling **CreateCompatibleDC**. This routine takes a single parameter, a handle to an existing DC. Since our bitmap is going to be copied to the display screen, we pass a display DC that we obtained by calling GetDC. To create a bitmap that is compatible with the display screen, we call a related routine, **CreateCompatibleBitmap**. This routine also takes a DC handle as a parameter, along with a width and a height value for the size of the drawing surface to create.

The only thing missing is a way to connect the bitmap and the DC. The routine we use is a familiar one:

```
hbmOld = SelectObject (hdcBitmap, hbm);
```

You probably remember that we use this routine to install pens, brushes, and fonts into DCs. Here you see it has another use: connecting a bitmap to a device context. Once this connection has been made, we can use any GDI drawing routines to draw in our bitmap. For example, we could draw an ellipse in the bitmap with the following call:

```
Ellipse (hdcBitmap, x1, y1, x2, y2);
```

Or we could make any other call to a GDI drawing routine.

When you have finished drawing into the bitmap, you place the bitmap into a menu by calling one of these routines: **AppendMenu**, **InsertMenu**, or **ModifyMenu**. Here is a call to AppendMenu that inserts the bitmap at the end of a popup menu, and gives the new menu item a command result code of 23:

```
HMENU hmenu;
HMENU hmenuPopup;

hmenu = GetMenu (hwnd);
hmenuPopup = GetSubMenu (hmenu, 1);

AppendMenu (hmenuPopup, MF_BITMAP, 23,
            MAKEINTRESOURCE(hbm));
```

Figure 12.2 *Menu containing bitmaps with GDI brush images*

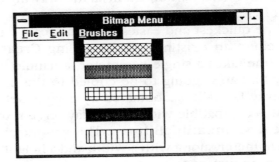

Once the bitmap has been installed into the menu, our DC isn't needed anymore, so we destroy it. But first, we must remove the bitmap handle from the DC. When we installed the bitmap handle into our DC, SelectObject returned a value that we stored in `hbm-old`. This value represents a place-holder for a bitmap. Before we can destroy the DC, we must first break the connection between the DC and the bitmap. This is accomplished by another call to **Select-Object**:

```
SelectObject (hdcBitmap, hbmOld);
```

after which, we can destroy the DC with this call:

```
DeleteDC (hdcBitmap);
```

Figure 12.2 shows a menu that was created by attaching five bitmaps to five different menu items. Each menu item represents a different brush that the user can select to draw with. This menu was created by our next sample program, BITMENU.

BITMENU.MAK

```
bitmenu.res: bitmenu.rc bitmenu.cur bitmenu.ico
    rc -r bitmenu.rc

bitmenu.obj: bitmenu.c
    cl -AM -c -d -Gsw -Ow -W2 -Zpi bitmenu.c
```

```
bitmenu.exe: bitmenu.obj bitmenu.def
    link bitmenu,/align:16,/map, mlibcew libw/NOD/NOE/CO,\
        bitmenu.def
    rc bitmenu.res


bitmenu.exe: bitmenu.res
    rc bitmenu.res
```

BITMENU.C

```c
/*-----------------------------------------------------------*\
|   Bitmenu.C  -  Demo showing the creation of bitmaps in a  |
|                 menu.                                       |
\*-----------------------------------------------------------*/
#include <Windows.H>
#include "Bitmenu.H"


/*-----------------------------------------------------------*\
|                   Function Prototypes.                     |
\*-----------------------------------------------------------*/
long FAR  PASCAL BitmenuWndProc (HWND, WORD, WORD, LONG);
VOID NEAR PASCAL BitmenuCreate(HWND hwnd);


/*-----------------------------------------------------------*\
|                      Static Data.                          |
\*-----------------------------------------------------------*/
HBITMAP hbm[COUNT];
HBRUSH  hbr[COUNT];


/*-----------------------------------------------------------*\
|                   Main Function:  WinMain.                 |
\*-----------------------------------------------------------*/
int PASCAL WinMain (HANDLE hInstance,
                    HANDLE hPrevInstance,
                    LPSTR  lpszCmdLine,
                    int    cmdShow)
    {
    HWND    hwnd;
    MSG     msg;
```

```
        WNDCLASS wndclass;

    if (!hPrevInstance)
        {
        wndclass.lpszClassName = "Bitmenu:MAIN";
        wndclass.hInstance     = hInstance;
        wndclass.lpfnWndProc   = BitmenuWndProc;
        wndclass.hCursor       = LoadCursor (hInstance, "hand");
        wndclass.hIcon         = LoadIcon (hInstance,"snapshot");
        wndclass.lpszMenuName  = "#1";
        wndclass.hbrBackground = COLOR_WINDOW+1;
        wndclass.style         = NULL;
        wndclass.cbClsExtra    = 0;
        wndclass.cbWndExtra    = 0;

        RegisterClass( &wndclass);
        }

    hwnd = CreateWindow("Bitmenu:MAIN",         /* Class name.    */
                        "Bitmap Menu",          /* Title.         */
                        WS_OVERLAPPEDWINDOW,    /* Style bits.    */
                        CW_USEDEFAULT,          /* x - default.   */
                        0,                      /* y - default.   */
                        CW_USEDEFAULT,          /* cx - default.  */
                        0,                      /* cy - default.  */
                        NULL,                   /* No parent.     */
                        NULL,                   /* Class menu.    */
                        hInstance,              /* Creator.       */
                        NULL);                  /* Params.        */

    ShowWindow (hwnd, cmdShow);
    while (GetMessage(&msg, 0, 0, 0))
        {
        TranslateMessage(&msg);         /*  Keyboard input.      */
        DispatchMessage(&msg);
        }
    return 0;
    }

/*------------------------------------------------------------------*\
    |             Window Procedure:  BitmenuWndProc.               |
\*------------------------------------------------------------------*/
```

```
long FAR PASCAL BitmenuWndProc (HWND hwnd,    WORD wMsg,
                                WORD wParam, LONG lParam)
    {
    switch (wMsg)
        {
        case WM_COMMAND:
            {
            char buffer[80];

            if (wParam == 6)
                DestroyWindow (hwnd);
            else
                {
                wsprintf (buffer, "Command = %d", wParam);
                MessageBox (hwnd, buffer, "WM_COMMAND", MB_OK);
                }
            }
            break;

        case WM_CREATE:
            BitmenuCreate(hwnd);
            break;

        case WM_DESTROY:
            {
            int i;

            for (i=0;i<COUNT;i++)
                {
                DeleteObject (hbr[i]);
                DeleteObject (hbm[i]);
                }
            }
            PostQuitMessage(0);
            break;

        default:
            return(DefWindowProc(hwnd,wMsg,wParam,lParam));
            break;
        }
    return 0L;
    }
```

```
/*------------------------------------------------------------*\
|            BitmenuCreate:  Process WM_CREATE Messages.       |
\*------------------------------------------------------------*/

VOID NEAR PASCAL BitmenuCreate(HWND hwnd)
    {
    COLORREF crBackground;
    HBITMAP  hbmOld;
    HBRUSH   hbrBackground;
    HBRUSH   hbrOld;
    HDC      hdcScreen;
    HDC      hdcBitmap;
    HMENU    hmenu;
    HMENU    hmenuPopup;
    int      i;
    int      cxWidth;
    int      cyHeight;
    int      cyOffset;

    /*  Calculate bitmap size information.                      */
    cxWidth  = GetSystemMetrics (SM_CXICON) * 3;
    cyHeight = GetSystemMetrics (SM_CYICON);
    cyOffset = cyHeight - cyHeight/5;

    /*  Create the background brush to initialize bitmaps.      */
    crBackground = GetSysColor (COLOR_MENU);
    hbrBackground = CreateSolidBrush (crBackground);

    /*  Create the needed GDI objects: DCs and bitmaps.         */
    hdcScreen = GetDC (hwnd);
    hdcBitmap = CreateCompatibleDC (hdcScreen);
    SelectObject (hdcBitmap, hbrBackground);

    for (i=0;i<COUNT;i++)
        {
        hbm[i] = CreateCompatibleBitmap (hdcScreen,
                                         cxWidth, cyHeight);
        if (i==0)
            hbmOld = SelectObject (hdcBitmap, hbm[0]);
        else
            SelectObject (hdcBitmap, hbm[i]);
```

```
        PatBlt (hdcBitmap, 0, 0, cxWidth, cyHeight, PATCOPY);
        }
ReleaseDC (hwnd, hdcScreen);

/*  Create an empty popup menu, and attach it to menu-bar. */
hmenuPopup = CreatePopupMenu ();
hmenu = GetMenu (hwnd);
AppendMenu (hmenu, MF_POPUP, hmenuPopup, "&Brushes");

/*  Create the brushes we're going to use.                  */
hbr[0] = CreateHatchBrush (HS_DIAGCROSS , RGB(0, 0, 0));
hbr[1] = CreateSolidBrush (RGB (64, 64, 64));
hbr[2] = CreateHatchBrush (HS_CROSS , RGB(0, 0, 0));
hbr[3] = CreateSolidBrush (RGB (0, 0, 0));
hbr[4] = CreateHatchBrush (HS_VERTICAL , RGB(0, 0, 0));

/*  Put a brush into the DC, attach the DC to a bitmap,     */
/*  and then draw a rectangle into the bitmap.  Finally,    */
/*  create a new menu item using the bitmap.                */
for (i=0;i<COUNT;i++)
    {
    SelectObject (hdcBitmap, hbr[i]);
    SelectObject (hdcBitmap, hbm[i]);
    Rectangle (hdcBitmap,
               0,
               cyOffset,
               cxWidth,
               cyHeight-cyOffset);
    AppendMenu (hmenuPopup, MF_BITMAP, IDM_FIRST+i,
               MAKEINTRESOURCE(hbm[i]));
    }

/*  Clean up all GDI objects we've created.                 */
SelectObject (hdcBitmap, GetStockObject(BLACK_BRUSH));
DeleteObject (hbrBackground);

SelectObject (hdcBitmap, hbmOld);
DeleteDC (hdcBitmap);
}
```

BITMENU.H

```
/*-----------------------------------------------------------*\
|  Bitmenu.H  -  Include file for Bitmenu sample program.   |
\*-----------------------------------------------------------*/

#define IDM_NEW        1
#define IDM_OPEN       2
#define IDM_SAVE       3
#define IDM_SAVEAS     4
#define IDM_PRINT      5
#define IDM_EXIT       6

#define IDM_UNDO       7
#define IDM_CUT        8
#define IDM_COPY       9
#define IDM_PASTE      10
#define IDM_CLEAR      11
#define IDM_DELETE     12

#define IDM_FIRST      13
#define COUNT 5
```

BITMENU.RC

```
#include <Windows.h>
#include "Bitmenu.h"

snapshot icon Bitmenu.ico

hand   cursor Bitmenu.cur

1 MENU
    {
    POPUP "&File"
        {
        MENUITEM "&New",        IDM_NEW
        MENUITEM "&Open...",    IDM_OPEN
        MENUITEM "&Save",       IDM_SAVE
```

```
        MENUITEM "Save &As...",  IDM_SAVEAS
        MENUITEM SEPARATOR
        MENUITEM "&Print",         IDM_PRINT
        MENUITEM SEPARATOR
        MENUITEM "E&xit",          IDM_EXIT
        }
    POPUP "&Edit"
        {
        MENUITEM "&Undo\tAlt+Backspace", IDM_UNDO
        MENUITEM SEPARATOR
        MENUITEM "Cu&t\tShift+Del",     IDM_CUT
        MENUITEM "&Copy\tCtrl+Ins",     IDM_COPY
        MENUITEM "&Paste\tShift+Ins",   IDM_PASTE
        MENUITEM SEPARATOR
        MENUITEM "Cl&ear",   IDM_CLEAR
        MENUITEM "&Delete",  IDM_DELETE
        }
    }
```

BITMENU.DEF

```
NAME    BITMENU

EXETYPE WINDOWS

DESCRIPTION 'Bitmap Menu Demo'

CODE    MOVEABLE DISCARDABLE
DATA    MOVEABLE MULTIPLE

HEAPSIZE    512
STACKSIZE   5000

EXPORTS
    BitmenuWndProc
```

BITMENU does most of its work in response to the WM_CREATE message, when it creates the five bitmaps and places them in the menu. It starts by calling **GetSystemMetrics** to determine the dimensions that the display device driver has set for icons. It uses these dimensions to calculate the size of the bitmap to create. As we mentioned earlier, this avoids the use of hard-coded sizes, which might produce unexpected results on display devices with very high resolutions. BITMENU sets the dimensions of the menu bitmaps in the following way:

```
cxWidth  = GetSystemMetrics (SM_CXICON) * 3;
cyHeight = GetSystemMetrics (SM_CYICON);
```

That is, the bitmaps are three times as wide as the display's standard icon and have the same height.

When a memory bitmap is created, GDI does not initialize the drawing surface to any particular color. Before we can draw on the bitmap, we need to erase the surface to avoid the appearance of random colors. In the same way that the OWNDRAW program called GetSysColors to find the correct menu colors to use, BITMENU makes the same call and uses the resulting color to create a solid brush to erase the background of the bitmaps:

```
crBackground = GetSysColor (COLOR_MENU);
hbrBackground = CreateSolidBrush (crBackground);
```

As you may recall from our discussion of the OWNDRAW program, GDI can be called to draw on a bitmap only when a DC has been created and connected to the bitmap. We call **Create-CompatibleDC** to ask GDI to clone a display DC for us, and then install the background brush into the DC so it is ready to help us initialize each of the bitmaps:

```
hdcBitmap = CreateCompatibleDC (hdcScreen);
SelectObject (hdcBitmap, hbrBackground);
```

The next step for BITMENU is to create the bitmaps and initialize them to the menu background color. As each bitmap is created, BITMENU calls the PatBlt routine to fill each newly created bitmap with the color of the brush that is currently installed in the DC, that is, with the color of our background brush:

```
for (i=0;i<COUNT;i++)
    {
    hbm[i]= CreateCompatibleBitmap (hdcScreen,
                            cxWidth, cyHeight);
```

```
if (i==0)
    hbmOld = SelectObject (hdcBitmap, hbm[0]);
else
    SelectObject (hdcBitmap, hbm[i]);
PatBlt (hdcBitmap,0,0, cxWidth, cyHeight, PATCOPY);
}
```

BITMENU then creates an empty popup menu and attaches it to the top-level menu:

```
hmenuPopup = CreatePopupMenu();
hmenu = GetMenu (hwnd);
AppendMenu (hmenu, MF_POPUP, hmenuPopup, "&Brushes");
```

It then creates a set of brushes to be used to create the bitmaps that are going to be installed in the menu:

```
hbr[0] = CreateHatchBrush (HS_DIAGCROSS, RGB(0,0,0));
hbr[1] = CreateSolidBrush (RGB(64, 64, 64));
hbr[2] = CreateHatchBrush (HS_CROSS, RGB(0, 0, 0));
hbr[3] = CreateSolidBrush (RGB(0, 0, 0));
hbr[4] = CreateHatchBrush (HS_VERTICAL, RGB(0, 0, 0));
```

Next, BITMENU enters a loop that calls SelectObject to connect each bitmap in turn to the bitmap DC. **SelectObject** is called a second time to install one of our brushes into the DC. With that done, we are ready to draw an image of the brush in the bitmap. We do this by calling the **Rectangle** routine, which, as you may recall, draws a rectangle using the currently installed pen for the border and the currently installed brush for the inside area. Once this is done, the bitmap is ready to be added to the menu, which is accomplished by calling **AppendMenu**:

```
for (i=0;i<COUNT;i++)
    {
    SelectObject (hdcBitmap, hbr[i]);
    SelectObject (hdcBitmap, hbm[i]);
    Rectangle (hdcBitmap,
               0,
               cyOffset,
```

```
                    cxWidth,
                    cyHeight-cyOffset);
     AppendMenu (hmenuPopup, MF_BITMAP, IDM_FIRST+i,
                    MAKEINTRESOURCE(hbm[i]));

     }
```

Once all the bitmaps have been created and attached to a menu, the last thing we have to deal with is cleanup of the GDI objects that were created. But before a GDI object can be destroyed, it must be free of connection to any other object. Before we destroy our background brush, we select one of the stock brushes into the DC, which causes the background brush to be de-selected:

```
SelectObject (hdcBitmap, GetStockObject(BLACK_BRUSH));
DeleteObject (hbrBackground);
```

And then we detach the last menu bitmap from the bitmap DC by calling **SelectObject**. When we do this, we install the bitmap handle that was returned when we installed our first bitmap handle. Pushing this handle into our DC causes the last of our bitmaps to pop out:

```
SelectObject (hdcBitmap, hbmOld);
DeleteDC (hdcBitmap);
```

This leaves two sets of GDI objects that still need to be cleaned up. However, we can't destroy the bitmaps until the menu that uses them is destroyed. In addition, we aren't going to destroy the brushes that we created, since our program may want to use them to draw the objects that the user has selected from our bitmap menu items. For both sets of GDI objects, BITMENU waits until our window is destroyed; which is to say that we wait for the WM_DESTROY message to do the rest of our cleanup:

```
case WM_DESTROY:
    {
    int i;

    for (i=0;i<COUNT;i++)
        {
        DeleteObject (hbr[i]);
```

```
            DeleteObject (hbm[i]);
            }
        }
    PostQuitMessage(0);
    break;
```

Bitmaps in menus and owner-draw menu items are just two ways that you can incorporate graphical objects in your menus. We're going to look at the third type now: custom check marks.

Creating Custom Menu Check Marks

In the last chapter, we mentioned that check marks provide one type of visual clue in menus. Although the standard check mark is useful in many situations, you may want to use a different symbol in your menus. You can call GDI routines to create your own custom check marks and install them into menus. When you do this, the menu system lets you attach *two* different bitmaps to every menu item. One bitmap is displayed when the menu item is in a *checked* state, the other is for the *unchecked* state.

Creating a check mark bitmap starts with the creation of a regular GDI bitmap. We discussed how to do this in the context of the BITMENU program earlier in this chapter. You must create a bitmap, create a DC, and then connect the two. From there, you use GDI routines to draw whatever figure you wish to use to reflect the checked and unchecked states. You have to be careful, though, because your drawing has to be small enough to fit in the space that the menu system has set aside for check marks.

To determine the proper size to use, you call **GetMenuCheck-MarkDimensions**. This routine takes no parameters, but returns a DWORD (unsigned long) value into which is packed the required dimensions of a check mark bitmap. Here is how to extract the dimension information from the return value:

```
DWORD dwCheck;
int cxWidth, cyHeight;

dwCheck  = GetMenuCheckMarkDimension();
cxWidth  = LOWORD (dwCheck);
cyHeight = HIWORD (dwCheck);
```

Using the size information provided by this routine, you can create a pair of bitmaps, draw checked and unchecked images that you wish to use, and attach the bitmap to the specific menu items that you wish to have use the check marks. Since bitmaps are shared GDI objects, you can create a single pair of checkmark bitmaps and use them in many different menu items. To attach a bitmap to a menu item, you call the **SetMenuItemBitmaps** routine, which is defined:

```
BOOL SetMenuItemBitmaps (hMenu, nPosition, wFlags,
                         hbmUnchecked, hbmChecked)
```

- hMenu is a menu handle.
- nPosition identifies the menu item to which the pair of bitmaps are to be attached. If the next parameter, wFlags, is MF_BY-COMMAND, then nPosition is a command result code. If it is MF_BYPOSITION, nPosition is the relative position of the menu item in the menu identified by hMenu.
- wFlags is either MF_BYCOMMAND or MF_BYPOSITION.
- hbmUnchecked is a handle of a GDI bitmap to be displayed when the menu is not checked.
- hbmChecked is a handle of a GDI bitmap to be displayed when the menu item is checked.

Once the checkmark bitmaps are attached to a menu item, they are used automatically without requiring any additional effort from your program. All you need to do at this point is call **CheckMenu-Item** to set the checked state to either MF_CHECKED or MF_UN-CHECKED.

If, at any time, you wish to remove a custom check mark, you call **SetMenuItemBitmaps** with a NULL value in the bitmap handle parameter corresponding to the bitmap that you wish to have removed. Figure 12.3 shows two sets of custom check marks created by **CHEKMENU**, our sample program.

CHEKMENU creates two pairs of custom menu check marks. One pair uses a square box, with an X in the box for the checked state and an empty box for the unchecked state. The second pair is a circle check mark, with a filled interior for the checked state and an empty interior for the unchecked state. Having created these two pairs of checkmark bitmaps, we could then use them for any or all of the menu items in our menu. As you can tell by looking at Figure 12.3, CHEKMENU uses the standard menu that we created in the last chapter.

Figure 12.3 *Two pairs of custom menu check marks*

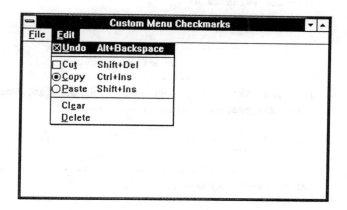

CHEKMENU.MAK

```
Chekmenu.res: Chekmenu.rc Chekmenu.cur Chekmenu.ico
    rc -r Chekmenu.rc

Chekmenu.obj: Chekmenu.c
    cl -AM -c -d -Gsw -Ow -W2 -Zpi Chekmenu.c

Chekmenu.exe: Chekmenu.obj Chekmenu.def
    link Chekmenu,/align:16,/map, mlibcew libw/NOD/NOE/CO,\
        Chekmenu.def
    rc Chekmenu.res

Chekmenu.exe: Chekmenu.res
    rc Chekmenu.res
```

CHEKMENU.C

```
/*-----------------------------------------------------------------*\
 |  Chekmenu.C  -  Program showing a standard File and Edit        |
 |                 menu.                                           |
 \*-----------------------------------------------------------------*/
```

```
#include <Windows.H>
#include "Chekmenu.h"

/*-------------------------------------------------------------------*\
|                     Function Prototypes.                          |
\*-------------------------------------------------------------------*/
long FAR  PASCAL ChekmenuWndProc (HWND, WORD, WORD, LONG);
VOID NEAR PASCAL ChekmenuCreate (HWND);

/*-------------------------------------------------------------------*\
|                         Static Data.                              |
\*-------------------------------------------------------------------*/
HANDLE hbmCheck[COUNT];

/*-------------------------------------------------------------------*\
|                    Main Function:  WinMain.                       |
\*-------------------------------------------------------------------*/
int PASCAL WinMain (HANDLE hInstance,
                    HANDLE hPrevInstance,
                    LPSTR  lpszCmdLine,
                    int    cmdShow)
    {
    HWND     hwnd;
    MSG      msg;
    WNDCLASS wndclass;

    if (!hPrevInstance)
        {
        wndclass.lpszClassName = "Chekmenu:MAIN";
        wndclass.hInstance     = hInstance;
        wndclass.lpfnWndProc   = ChekmenuWndProc;
        wndclass.hCursor       = LoadCursor (hInstance, "hand");
        wndclass.hIcon         = LoadIcon (hInstance,"snapshot");
        wndclass.lpszMenuName  = "#1";
        wndclass.hbrBackground = COLOR_WINDOW+1;
        wndclass.style         = NULL;
        wndclass.cbClsExtra    = 0;
        wndclass.cbWndExtra    = 0;

        RegisterClass( &wndclass);
        }
```

```
        hwnd = CreateWindow("Chekmenu:MAIN",        /* Class name.  */
                                                    /* Title.       */
                            "Custom Menu Checkmarks",
                            WS_OVERLAPPEDWINDOW,    /* Style bits.  */
                            CW_USEDEFAULT,          /* x - default. */
                            0,                      /* y - default. */
                            CW_USEDEFAULT,          /* cx - default. */
                            0,                      /* cy - default. */
                            NULL,                   /* No parent.   */
                            NULL,                   /* Class menu.  */
                            hInstance,              /* Creator.     */
                            NULL                    /* Params.      */
                            ) ;
        ShowWindow (hwnd, cmdShow);

        while (GetMessage(&msg, 0, 0, 0))
            {
            TranslateMessage(&msg);        /*  Keyboard input.      */
            DispatchMessage(&msg);
            }
        return 0;
        }

/*-----------------------------------------------------------*\
|            Window Procedure:  ChekmenuWndProc.              |
\*-----------------------------------------------------------*/
long FAR PASCAL ChekmenuWndProc (HWND hwnd,   WORD wMsg,
                                 WORD wParam, LONG lParam)
    {
    switch (wMsg)
        {
        case WM_COMMAND:
            {
            char buffer[80];

            if (wParam == 6)
                DestroyWindow (hwnd);
            else
                {
                wsprintf (buffer, "Command = %d", wParam);
```

```
                      MessageBox (hwnd, buffer, "WM_COMMAND", MB_OK);
                    }
             }
          break;


      case WM_CREATE:
          ChekmenuCreate(hwnd);
          break;

      case WM_DESTROY:
          {
          int i;

          for (i=0;i<COUNT;i++)
              DeleteObject (hbmCheck[i]);
          }
          PostQuitMessage(0);
          break;

      default:
          return(DefWindowProc(hwnd,wMsg,wParam,lParam));
          break;
      }
   return 0L;
   }


/*-------------------------------------------------------------*\
|           ChekmenuCreate:  Process WM_CREATE Messages.        |
\*-------------------------------------------------------------*/

VOID NEAR PASCAL ChekmenuCreate (HWND hwnd)
    {
    COLORREF  crBackground;
    DWORD     dwCheck;
    HBITMAP   hbmOld;
    HBRUSH    hbrBackground;
    HDC       hdcScreen;
    HDC       hdcBitmap;
    HMENU     hmenu;
```

```
int      cxWidth;
int      cyHeight;
int      xMin, xMax;
int      yMin, yMax;
int      cxFourth;
int      cyFourth;
int      cxMargin;
int      i;

/*  Get checkmark dimension information.                    */
dwCheck  = GetMenuCheckMarkDimensions();
cyHeight = HIWORD (dwCheck);
cxWidth  = LOWORD (dwCheck);

/*  Calculate a margin based on border widths.             */
cxMargin = GetSystemMetrics (SM_CXBORDER);
xMin = cxMargin;
xMax = cxWidth - cxMargin;
yMin = cxMargin;
yMax = cyHeight - cxMargin;
cxFourth = cxWidth/4;
cyFourth = cyHeight/4;

/*  Create the background brush to initialize bitmaps.     */
crBackground = GetSysColor (COLOR_MENU);
hbrBackground = CreateSolidBrush (crBackground);

/*  Create a DC and a set of bitmaps.                      */
hdcScreen = GetDC (hwnd);
hdcBitmap = CreateCompatibleDC (hdcScreen);
SelectObject (hdcBitmap, hbrBackground);

for (i=0;i<COUNT;i++)
    {
    hbmCheck[i] = CreateCompatibleBitmap (hdcScreen,
                                    cxWidth, cyHeight);
    if (i==0)
        hbmOld = SelectObject (hdcBitmap, hbmCheck[0]);
    else
        SelectObject (hdcBitmap, hbmCheck[i]);
    PatBlt (hdcBitmap, 0, 0, cxWidth, cyHeight, PATCOPY);
```

```
        }
     ReleaseDC (hwnd, hdcScreen);


     /*  Draw first unchecked menu item.                        */
     SelectObject (hdcBitmap, hbmCheck[0]);
     Rectangle (hdcBitmap, xMin, yMin,
                           xMax, yMax);

     /*  Draw first checked menu item.                          */
     SelectObject (hdcBitmap, hbmCheck[1]);
     Rectangle (hdcBitmap, xMin, yMin,
                           xMax, yMax);

     MoveTo (hdcBitmap, xMin, yMin);
     LineTo (hdcBitmap, xMax, yMax);
     MoveTo (hdcBitmap, xMin, yMax-1);
     LineTo (hdcBitmap, xMax-1, yMin);

     /*  Draw second unchecked menu item.                       */
     SelectObject (hdcBitmap, hbmCheck[2]);
     Ellipse (hdcBitmap, xMin, yMin,
                         xMax, yMax);

     /*  Draw second checked menu item.                         */
     SelectObject (hdcBitmap, hbmCheck[3]);
     Ellipse (hdcBitmap, xMin, yMin,
                         xMax, yMax);
     SelectObject (hdcBitmap, GetStockObject (BLACK_BRUSH));

     Ellipse (hdcBitmap, xMin+cxFourth, yMin+cyFourth,
                         xMax-cxFourth, yMax-cyFourth);

     /*  Get handle to top-level menu.                          */
     hmenu = GetMenu (hwnd);

     /*  Attach check marks to four menu items.                 */

     /*  (1) Edit-Undo, and set it to checked.                  */
     SetMenuItemBitmaps (hmenu, IDM_UNDO, MF_BYCOMMAND,
                         hbmCheck[0], hbmCheck[1]);
```

```
            CheckMenuItem (hmenu, IDM_UNDO, MF_BYCOMMAND | MF_CHECKED);

            /*  (2) Edit-Cut, and leave it unchecked.              */
            SetMenuItemBitmaps (hmenu, IDM_CUT, MF_BYCOMMAND,
                            hbmCheck[0], hbmCheck[1]);

            /*  (3) Edit-Copy, and set it to checked.              */
            SetMenuItemBitmaps (hmenu, IDM_COPY, MF_BYCOMMAND,
                            hbmCheck[2], hbmCheck[3]);
            CheckMenuItem (hmenu, IDM_COPY, MF_BYCOMMAND | MF_CHECKED);

            /*  (4) Edit-Paste, and leave it unchecked.            */
            SetMenuItemBitmaps (hmenu, IDM_PASTE, MF_BYCOMMAND,
                            hbmCheck[2], hbmCheck[3]);

            /*  Clean up the GDI objects we've created.            */
            SelectObject (hdcBitmap, GetStockObject(BLACK_BRUSH));
            DeleteObject (hbrBackground);

            SelectObject (hdcBitmap, hbmOld);
            DeleteDC (hdcBitmap);
            }
```

CHEKMENU.H

```
/*------------------------------------------------------------------*\
 |  Chekmenu.H  -  Include file for Chekmenu.c                       |
 \*------------------------------------------------------------------*/

#define IDM_NEW       1
#define IDM_OPEN      2
#define IDM_SAVE      3
#define IDM_SAVEAS    4
#define IDM_PRINT     5
#define IDM_EXIT      6

#define IDM_UNDO      7
#define IDM_CUT       8
```

```
#define IDM_COPY      9
#define IDM_PASTE     10
#define IDM_CLEAR     11
#define IDM_DELETE    12

#define COUNT 4
```

CHEKMENU.RC

```
#include <Windows.h>
#include "Chekmenu.h"

snapshot icon Chekmenu.ico

hand   cursor Chekmenu.cur

1 MENU
    {
    POPUP "&File"
        {
        MENUITEM "&New",          IDM_NEW
        MENUITEM "&Open...",      IDM_OPEN
        MENUITEM "&Save",         IDM_SAVE
        MENUITEM "Save &As...",   IDM_SAVEAS
        MENUITEM SEPARATOR
        MENUITEM "&Print",        IDM_PRINT
        MENUITEM SEPARATOR
        MENUITEM "E&xit",         IDM_EXIT
        }
    POPUP "&Edit"
        {
        MENUITEM "&Undo\tAlt+Backspace", IDM_UNDO
        MENUITEM SEPARATOR
        MENUITEM "Cu&t\tShift+Del",      IDM_CUT
        MENUITEM "&Copy\tCtrl+Ins",      IDM_COPY
        MENUITEM "&Paste\tShift+Ins",    IDM_PASTE
        MENUITEM SEPARATOR
        MENUITEM "Cl&ear",   IDM_CLEAR
        MENUITEM "&Delete", IDM_DELETE
        }
    }
```

CHEKMENU.DEF

```
NAME      Chekmenu

EXETYPE WINDOWS

DESCRIPTION 'Custom Menu Checkmarks'

CODE      MOVEABLE DISCARDABLE
DATA      MOVEABLE MULTIPLE


HEAPSIZE      512
STACKSIZE    5000


EXPORTS
    ChekmenuWndProc
```

The creation of custom check marks starts by asking the menu system for the expected size of a check mark:

```
/*  Get checkmark dimension information.              */
dwCheck  = GetMenuCheckMarkDimensions();
cyHeight = HIWORD (dwCheck);
cxWidth  = LOWORD (dwCheck);
```

With this information in hand, CHEKMENU calculates a border around the edges of our check mark. This is necessary because the area that we are given actually touches the left border of a menu. The creation of a margin avoids the crowded appearance this might cause. We calculate our border by calling **GetSystemMetrics** with the SM_CXBORDER parameter, to get the width of a thin window border to use as a checkmark margin:

```
/*  Calculate a margin based on border widths.        */
cxMargin = GetSystemMetrics (SM_CXBORDER);
xMin = cxMargin;
xMax = cxWidth - cxMargin;
yMin = cxMargin;
yMax = cyHeight - cxMargin;
cxFourth = cxWidth/4;
cyFourth = cyHeight/4;
```

Since we're going to create a bitmap, we're going to want to initialize the background of the bitmap. We call GetSysColor to determine the menu background color and create a brush to use to fill our checkmark background before we draw into it:

```
/* Create the background brush to initialize bitmaps.*/
crBackground = GetSysColor (COLOR_MENU);
hbrBackground = CreateSolidBrush (crBackground);
```

As we saw in the BITMENU program, to draw in a bitmap you must have a DC. Here is how CHEKMENU creates a DC, creates a set of bitmaps, and uses the background brush to initialize our bitmaps to the menu background color:

```
/*  Create a DC and a set of bitmaps.              */
hdcScreen = GetDC (hwnd);
hdcBitmap = CreateCompatibleDC (hdcScreen);
SelectObject (hdcBitmap, hbrBackground);

for (i=0;i<COUNT;i++)
    {
    hbmCheck[i] = CreateCompatibleBitmap (hdcScreen,
                                   cxWidth, cyHeight);
    if (i==0)
        hbmOld = SelectObject (hdcBitmap, hbmCheck[0]);
    else
        SelectObject (hdcBitmap, hbmCheck[i]);
    PatBlt (hdcBitmap, 0, 0, cxWidth, cyHeight, PATCOPY);
    }
ReleaseDC (hwnd, hdcScreen);
```

Drawing the four check-mark images is as simple as calling a few GDI routines. Of course, since our four bitmaps are sharing a DC, we use the **SelectObject** routine to create the connection that allows us to draw in each bitmap in turn:

```
/*  Draw first unchecked menu item.                */
SelectObject (hdcBitmap, hbmCheck[0]);
Rectangle (hdcBitmap, xMin, yMin,
                      xMax, yMax);

/*  Draw first checked menu item.                  */
```

```
SelectObject (hdcBitmap, hbmCheck[1]);
Rectangle (hdcBitmap, xMin, yMin,
                    xMax, yMax);

MoveTo (hdcBitmap, xMin, yMin);
LineTo (hdcBitmap, xMax, yMax);
MoveTo (hdcBitmap, xMin, yMax-1);
LineTo (hdcBitmap, xMax-1, yMin);

/*  Draw second unchecked menu item.              */
SelectObject (hdcBitmap, hbmCheck[2]);
Ellipse (hdcBitmap, xMin, yMin,
                    xMax, yMax);

/*  Draw second checked menu item.                */
SelectObject (hdcBitmap, hbmCheck[3]);
Ellipse (hdcBitmap, xMin, yMin,
                    xMax, yMax);
SelectObject (hdcBitmap, GetStockObject (BLACK_BRUSH));

Ellipse (hdcBitmap, xMin+cxFourth, yMin+cyFourth,
                    xMax-cxFourth, yMax-cyFourth);
```

Attaching the four check marks to our four menu items involves first getting a handle to our window's top-level menu, then making four calls to **SetMenuItemBitmaps**:

```
/*  Get handle to top-level menu.                  */
hmenu = GetMenu (hwnd);

/*  Attach check marks to four menu items.         */

/*  (1) Edit-Undo, and set it to checked.          */
SetMenuItemBitmaps (hmenu, IDM_UNDO, MF_BYCOMMAND,
                    hbmCheck[0], hbmCheck[1]);
CheckMenuItem (hmenu, IDM_UNDO, MF_BYCOMMAND |
                    MF_CHECKED);

/*  (2) Edit-Cut, and leave it unchecked.          */
SetMenuItemBitmaps (hmenu, IDM_CUT, MF_BYCOMMAND,
                    hbmCheck[0], hbmCheck[1]);

/*  (3) Edit-Copy, and set it to checked.          */
```

```
SetMenuItemBitmaps (hmenu, IDM_COPY, MF_BYCOMMAND,
                    hbmCheck[2], hbmCheck[3]);
CheckMenuItem (hmenu, IDM_COPY, MF_BYCOMMAND |
                    MF_CHECKED);

/*  (4) Edit-Paste, and leave it unchecked.         */
SetMenuItemBitmaps (hmenu, IDM_PASTE, MF_BYCOMMAND,
                    hbmCheck[2], hbmCheck[3]);
```

And, of course, whenever GDI objects are created, they must be destroyed before your program terminates. CHEKMENU takes care of some of these right after the menu check marks have been set:

```
/*  Clean up the GDI objects we've created.         */
SelectObject (hdcBitmap, GetStockObject(BLACK_BRUSH));
DeleteObject (hbrBackground);

SelectObject (hdcBitmap, hbmOld);
DeleteDC (hdcBitmap);
```

But the final cleanup of the check-mark bitmaps must wait until the menu itself has been destroyed. Since this is part of the window destruction process, we just have to wait for the WM_DESTROY message:

```
case WM_DESTROY:
    {
    int i;

    for (i=0;i<COUNT;i++)
        DeleteObject (hbmCheck[i]);
    }
    PostQuitMessage(0);
    break;
```

The creation of custom check marks is straightforward, although it requires an understanding of how to create and manipulate GDI bitmaps. Once a bitmap has been created and attached to a DC, drawing in the bitmap only requires you to call the various GDI drawing routines: **PatBlt** is first called to erase the bitmap background. Then **Rectangle**, **Ellipse**, **MoveTo**, and **LineTo** draw the actual check mark images. And, as we have shown in our other sample programs, it is important to clean up whatever GDI drawing objects you have created or used.

Our next chapter returns to a subject that we first touched on in Chapter 2 when we introduced our minimum Windows program. The issue is that of window creation. While a program doesn't have to create more than a single window to be useful, there are times when it is indispensable for providing a good user interface. And even if you never create more than one window in your windows programs, some of Windows' special capabilities are hidden in the window creation process. Let's roll up our sleeves and take a look at what those capabilities are.

13
Windowing

Up to now, all the programs that we have written in this book have had a single top-level window. While you could use this approach for all of your Windows programs, there are times when it makes sense for a program to have more than a single window. For example, programs that use the **multiple document interface** (MDI) standard create a new window for every new document. Programs that use dialog boxes also use multiple windows, since dialog boxes themselves are windows, as are the pushbuttons, listboxes, and other controls that live inside dialog boxes. We'll describe dialog boxes further in Chapter 14.

A program might create multiple windows to divide a single window into smaller work areas. For example, programs often place scroll bars, which are windows, inside other windows so the user can control which portion of the data is visible. Consider a terminal emulation program, which might use a tiny text window to display communication status information. Another type of application, such as a word processing program, might show a document's margin and tab settings inside a small window resting next to a larger document window. There are as many possibilities as there are different kinds of applications.

To help you understand how to use multiple windows effectively, we're going to discuss the implementation details that make Windows' windows unique. We're going to start by looking at the two-step process for creating a window: window class registration and window creation. We'll then discuss the issue of how big to make an application's top-level window. And finally, we'll discuss the creation of a child window to output menu information to help users browse through a program's menu. And, in keeping with the spirit of this book, we'll provide working samples to help you with your own programming projects.

The Window Creation Process

In Chapter 2, we introduced the minimum Windows program. At the time, we said that window creation was a two-step process. We introduced you to the two routines that control the operation of each of those steps, **RegisterClass** and **CreateWindow**; but we refrained from going into more detail until now. As you'll see, the window creation process is quite involved and gives you quite a few choices over the shape, size, style, and behavior of a window. When we first described the window creation process, you probably suspected that we were holding out on you. In particular, the sheer number of fields in the WNDCLASS data structure and the number of parameters that are passed to CreateWindow hint at more possibilities than we told you.

Ok. It's time for us to come clean with you. Let's start by looking at the first part of the window creation process, which revolves around a single data structure: the window class.

Window Classes

Over the next few years, we're going to be hearing a lot about **object oriented programming**. One of the aspects of this technology involves the creation and use of **object classes**. An object class is a template for the creation of objects. In the world of Windows programming, a window class plays the same role as the object class: Window classes are templates for the creation of windows.

Associated with every object class is a body of code; in Windows, we call this a window procedure. In the world of object oriented programming, the code is a collection of **methods**. You act on an object by sending a **message**, which is both the term we use in Windows and the term that is used in object-oriented programming.

The more you compare Windows to object-oriented programming, the more you realize that the developers of Windows were influenced by some of the early work that was done in the field of object-oriented programming. But at the time that Windows was being first developed, object-oriented programming was little more than a collection of theories for the research lab and hadn't developed into full-scale, commercially available development tools. Nonetheless, Windows' early connection to object-oriented programming will help make Windows a primary environment for object-oriented development tools. In fact, there are a number of such tools available today, including several C++ compilers and Whitewater's Actor programming language, to name just a few.

One reason for creating an object class is that you can make many copies of the object with a minimum of overhead. You already know, for example, that only the first instance of a program has to register its window classes. In all our sample programs, we register a window class using code like this:

```
WNDCLASS wndclass;

if (!hPrevInstance)
    {
    wndclass.lpszClassName = "MIN:MAIN";
    wndclass.hInstance     = hInstance;
    wndclass.lpfnWndProc   = MinWndProc;
    wndclass.hCursor       = LoadCursor(hInstance, "hand");
    wndclass.hIcon         = LoadIcon(hInstance,"snapshot");
    wndclass.lpszMenuName  = NULL;
    wndclass.hbrBackground = COLOR_WINDOW+1;
    wndclass.style         = NULL;
    wndclass.cbClsExtra    = 0;
    wndclass.cbWndExtra    = 0;

    RegisterClass( &wndclass);
    }
```

Since it's the WNDCLASS data structure that defines a window class, let's take a closer look at each element of this data structure.

The **lpszClassName** field defines an ASCII text string for the class name. Although in earlier versions of Windows there was a problem creating names that were identical with existing class names, in Windows 3.0 and later all window classes are **private classes** by default. A private window class is only accessible from a single program. This means that you can use any name you'd like and know that it won't interfere with the class names of other programs. Of course, you'll probably want to avoid the predefined dialog box classes to avoid interfering with dialog boxes. The names of these classes are: **button**, **combobox**, **edit**, **listbox**, **scrollbar**, and **static**. And, to avoid getting into the way of the built-in support that Windows provides for the multiple document interface (MDI), you'll want to avoid creating a class with the name **mdiclient**.

The **hInstance** field tells Windows which program created the window class. The primary reason has to do with internal housekeeping. After every instance of a program has terminated, then Windows de-registers the classes that the program created.

The **lpfnWndProc** field identifies the function that will process messages for the windows in the class. You might wonder how a single function can support multiple different windows. This ability to clone windows is an important part of the capability of Windows. Cloning reduces the amount of memory required for window support code.

A single window procedure can support several windows because each window has a unique window handle. A window handle is a signature that uniquely identifies each window in the system. When a message is delivered to a window procedure, the window handle tells the window procedure exactly *which* window is sending the message. If you want to treat different windows in a different manner, you only need to look at the window handle to know which one is calling.

The **hCursor** field is a handle to a cursor shared by all members of a window class. The default window procedure uses this to install the correct cursor whenever it receives a WM_SETCURSOR message. If you want a window to have its own *private* cursor, different from the class cursor, you can find out how in Chapter 16, which covers issues relating to the mouse, mouse message traffic, and custom cursors.

The **hIcon** field is a handle to an icon that is displayed when a window in the class is minimized. Not every kind of window will use its icon. Icons are only displayed for top-level windows (windows that have no parents) and document windows in programs that use the multiple document interface (MDI). The typical way for a program to define the icon handle involves making a call to load the icon, as shown here:

```
wndclass.hIcon          = LoadIcon(hInstance,"snapshot");
```

A program can also draw an icon "on-the-fly" by defining a NULL icon:

```
wndclass.hIcon = NULL;
```

When the window is iconized, it appears as a tiny, empty window. Creating a drawing for the icon is surprisingly simple: You handle the WM_PAINT message just as you would when the window is *not* iconized. The only difference is that you need to be prepared to draw into a very tiny area. Here is a sample code fragment that draws an icon when the window is minimized:

```
                case WM_PAINT:
                    {
                    char ach[40];
                    HBRUSH hbr;
                    PAINTSTRUCT ps;
                    POINT apt[4];
                    RECT r;
                    TEXTMETRIC tm;

                    BeginPaint(hwnd, &ps);

                    if (IsIconic (hwnd))
                        {
                        GetTextMetrics (ps.hdc, &tm);
                        GetClientRect (hwnd, &r);
                        r.bottom -= tm.tmHeight/2;

                        /*  Draw a rectangle.                 */
                        Rectangle (ps.hdc, 0, 0, r.right, r.bottom);

                        /*  Draw an ellipse.                  */
                        hbr = GetStockObject (GRAY_BRUSH);
                        SelectObject (ps.hdc, hbr);
                        Ellipse (ps.hdc, 0, 0, r.right, r.bottom);

                        /*  Draw a triangle.                  */
                        hbr = GetStockObject (BLACK_BRUSH);
                        SelectObject (ps.hdc, hbr);
                        apt[0].x = r.right/2;  apt[0].y = 0;
                        apt[1].x = 0;          apt[1].y = r.bottom;
                        apt[2].x = r.right;    apt[2].y = r.bottom;
                        apt[3].x = r.right/2;  apt[3].y = 0;

                        Polygon (ps.hdc, apt, 4);
                        }

                    EndPaint (hwnd, &ps);
                    }
                break;
```

The icon created by this code fragment is shown in Figure 13.1. It creates our "on-the-fly" icon by drawing a rectangle, an ellipse, and a triangle.

A window created from a window class with a NULL icon has one more issue to deal with. That issue involves the choice of icons to display when the user drags the iconic program. When the user drags a program that does have an icon, the mouse cursor changes to the shape of that icon. But when a program's window doesn't have an icon, it has two choices: It can let the system display a default icon, or it can provide one in response to the WM_QUERYDRAGICON message. Here, for example, is what a program without an icon might do when sent this message:

```
long FAR PASCAL WndProc (...)
    {
    switch (msg)
        {
        case WM_QUERYDRAGICON:
            {
            HANDLE hIcon;

            hIcon = LoadIcon (hInstance, "DRAGICON");
            return (MAKELONG(hIcon, 0));
            }
            .
            .
```

A top-level window without an icon will see other message traffic that is different from that which is sent to windows that *do* have an icon. As our earlier code fragment indicates, a top-level window without an icon will receive a WM_PAINT message when it's time to draw its iconicized image. Top-level windows *with* icons receive a WM_PAINTICON message instead. The default window procedure responds to this message by displaying the icon for the window

Figure 13.1   *Drawing in a NULL icon*

class. A program that had a class icon that wanted to draw a custom icon could respond to the WM_PAINTICON message and create an "on-the-fly" icon if it wanted to.

The **lpszMenuName** field identifies the class menu by name. As we discussed in Chapter 11 when we introduced menus, this value can take one of three forms. For a menu resource defined like this:

```
15 MENU
    {
    POPUP "File"
        {
        MENUITEM "New", IDM_NEW
        .
        .
        .
```

the menu name can be a character string preceded by a # sign:

```
wndclass.lpszMenuName   = "#15";
```

Alternatively, the MAKEINTRESOURCE macro can be used to sneak an integer value in place of a long pointer to a string. Here is an example showing how the MAKEINTRESOURCE macro can be used:

```
wndclass.lpszMenuName   = MAKEINTRESOURCE(15);
```

A third choice, but a less attractive one because it consumes more memory and is slower, involves using a regular character string:

```
MyMenu MENU
    {
    POPUP "File"
        {
        MENUITEM "New", IDM_NEW
        .
        .
        .
```

To load this menu into memory, you provide the name of the menu in the WNDCLASS data structure, as shown here:

```
wndclass.lpszMenuName   = "MyMenu";
```

The disadvantage to this approach is that a string takes up more space than an integer. This means that this approach takes more memory. When the time comes to load the menu, an integer identifier allows faster loading than a string identifier since an integer compare is faster than a string compare. From the point of view of performance and memory use, integer values are better.

The **hbrBackground** field is a handle to a brush that is used to fill the background before any drawing is done. The default window procedure fills in the background in response to the WM_ERASEBACKGROUND message. This seems like a funny name for the messages, since in fact the background is really *painted* and not erased. However, it *does* suggest the idea that whatever was in the window before is removed to provide a clean surface on which to draw. There are two types of values that can be placed in this field: a brush handle and an index to a system color. Here is how to use a stock black brush for the background:

```
wndclass.hbrBackground = GetStockObject (BLACK_BRUSH);
```

A better alternative, however, involves using a "magic number" for the background color, like this:

```
wndclass.hbrBackground = COLOR_WINDOW+1;
```

When the default window procedure sees this value, it uses the default window background color that the user has defined from the Control Panel.

The **cbClsExtra** field defines the number of bytes that are added at the end of the class definition as a reserved data area. These bytes are known as **class extra bytes**. This data area can be used by a program for any purpose, but Windows does not provide a pointer to the data area itself. Instead, you must set these values using the **SetClassWord** and **SetClassLong** routines, and retrieve them using the **GetClassWord** and **GetClassLong** routines. If you don't plan to use class extra bytes, be sure to initialize **cbClsExtra** to zero. If you don't explicitly initialize this field to zero, it is possible that some random, large value will be passed as the number of bytes to be allocated. Initializing to zero avoids an accidental waste of memory.

The **cbWndExtra** field, like the **cbClsExtra** field, defines a reserved data area for the private use of your application. These bytes are referred to as **window extra bytes**. Unlike class extra bytes,

Figure 13.2   *The thirteen WNDCLASS style bits*

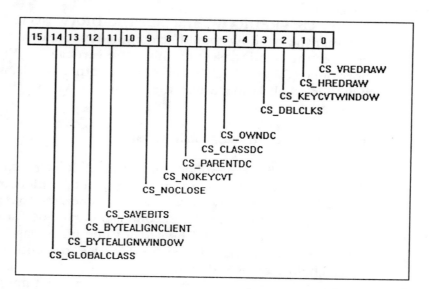

which are shared by every window in a class, window extra bytes are reserved for the private use of each individual window. It provides a way for a window to have its own "bank account" for bytes that it wishes to use—like having a Swiss bank account. To read the value of the window extra bytes, a program calls either **GetWindowWord** or **GetWindowLong**. These routines take a window handle as a parameter to identify exactly whose bytes are to be accessed. To write values into the window extra bytes, a program must call the **SetWindowWord** or **SetWindowLong** routines. These routines also take a window handle, which lets the Window Manager know into whose bank account you wish to make a deposit.

The **style** field is a 16-bit field that contains a set of flags that describes various features of the window class. There are 13-style flags, as shown in Figure 13.2. Let's look at each of the window class style bits in detail.

Window Class Style Bits

A lot of the subtlety in creating windows actually comes from certain class style bits that you can select. Let's take a look at all of them, to try to understand where they can be useful in a Windows program.

The **CS_VREDRAW** and **CS_HREDRAW** styles determine whether the window should be completely redrawn when the user changes the window size in either the vertical (CS_VREDRAW) or horizontal (CS_HREDRAW) direction. In other words, it determines whether a call is made like the following when a window's size changes:

```
InvalidateRect (hwnd, NULL, TRUE);
```

As you probably remember, the InvalidateRect routine is used to mark a portion of a window as damaged, which means that a WM_PAINT message will eventually be generated to repair the window. A NULL value in the second parameter declares the *entire* window to be damaged. The TRUE value in the last parameter requests that the damaged area (in this case, the entire window) be erased before being redrawn.

Two style bits are referenced in Windows.h but not mentioned in the Microsoft documentation: **CS_KEYCVTWINDOW** and **CS_NOKEYCVT**. They seem to be remnants of support for a Kanji conversion window for Japanese Windows. However, Microsoft has created a separate version of Windows for the Japanese market, which also requires its own special version of the Windows software development kit. Therefore, even though these style bits promise built-in Kanji support, you must obtain the special SDK to develop Windows programs for the Japanese-speaking market.

If you want a window to receive double-click mouse messages (WM_LBUTTONDBLCLK, WM_MBUTTONDBLCLK or WM_RBUTTONDBLCLK), then you must use the **CS_DBLCLKS** style bit. As we'll describe in Chapter 16, when we discuss mouse input, this special style bit causes a timer to be set when an initial mouse click is received. A double-click message is generated only when a second click is received before the timer runs out. The presence of this style bit helps the Window Manager to decide when to start the timer in response to a mouse click message.

Two style bits allow a window to have a private device context (DC): **CS_OWNDC** and **CS_CLASSDC**. When we introduced the device context in Chapter 6, we mentioned that most programs borrow a DC from the system DC cache. But because of the overhead associated with checking out and returning a DC, some programs prefer to have their own. In the same way that library books require more effort than books that you own, borrowed DCs require more effort. Of course, like private book collections, private DCs cost more in terms of memory required.

How much *does* a private DC cost? Although there has been talk among Windows programmers for some years that a DC is 800 bytes, in fact the actual size is about 200 bytes, all of which is allocated from GDI's local heap. While this doesn't seem like a lot, the allocation of a private DC has to be weighed against the fact that, as we'll discuss in Chapter 18, GDI's local heap space is a shared resource that all programs compete for. Therefore, avoid allocating a private DC unless you really need it.

So when is the cost of a private DC justified? In general, programs that do a lot of drawing, and programs that interact with the user *while* drawing, may run faster with a private DC. A word processor program, for example, that displays text as the user types may get a performance boost by getting its own, private DC. Or a drawing package that interacts with the user to interactively draw pictures may get a slight performance benefit from a private DC. In general, in a program that uses keystrokes or mouse clicks to draw, you might find that a private DC is faster to work with than a shared, system DC.

The **CS_OWNDC** style bit gives a private DC to *every window* in a class. This type of DC is the most expensive, in terms of memory used, but gives the fastest response. It is the most expensive because one is allocated for each window in a class. It is fastest because you don't incur the overhead of borrowing and returning the DC every time you draw. As illustrated in the following code fragment, a window created from a class with the **CS_OWNDC** style bit can get a DC handle during the WM_CREATE message and use it when it needs to draw for any other message:

```
long FAR PASCAL WndProc (...)
    {
    static HDC hdc;
    switch(msg)
        {
        case WM_CREATE:
            hdc = GetDC (hwnd);
            break;

        case WM_CHAR:
            TextOut (hdc, ...);
            break;
```

```
        case WM_LBUTTONUP:
            Rectangle (hdc, ...);
            break;

        case WM_PAINT:
            BeginPaint (hwnd, &ps);
                .
                .
            EndPaint (hwnd, &ps);

        default:
            DefWindowProc (...);
        }
    }
```

Besides the WM_CREATE message, the only other time this window procedure asks for a DC is in response to a WM_PAINT message, when a regular BeginPaint/EndPaint sandwich is used. This contrasts sharply with the approach that programs must take when they use a system DC. As shown in this code fragment, such programs must borrow and return a DC for each message:

```
long FAR PASCAL WndProc (...)
    {
    HDC hdc;
    switch(msg)
        {
        case WM_CHAR:
            hdc = GetDC (hwnd);
            TextOut (hdc, ...);
            ReleaseDC (hwnd, hdc);
            break;

        case WM_LBUTTONUP:
            hdc = GetDC (hwnd);
            Rectangle (hdc, ...);
            ReleaseDC (hwnd, hdc);
            break;

        case WM_PAINT:
            BeginPaint (hwnd, &ps);
                .
                .
            EndPaint (hwnd, &ps);
```

```
        default:
            DefWindowProc (...);
        }
    }
```

From this, you can see that one advantage of a private DC is that programs don't have to borrow a DC every time they wish to draw. A second advantage is that a program can set up the DC's drawing attributes and then not have to worry about them again. In contrast with this is the way programs must work with system DCs. Every time a system DC is borrowed, its drawing attributes are reset to their initial, default state. Programs that use a system DC have to set up the DC drawing attributes every time they wish to draw.

Programs with a private DC must still use a BeginPaint / EndPaint sandwich in response to a WM_PAINT message. This is because the WM_PAINT message can only be turned off by the use of these two routines. BeginPaint is smart enough to recognize when a window has a private DC, and it returns the correct DC handle inside the PAINTSTRUCT structure. The only difference is that the DC will have a clipping region installed to limit drawing to the damaged part of the window.

The **CS_CLASSDC** style provides a DC that is similar to a private DC except that it is shared by an entire class of Windows and not owned by a single window. Like a private DC, the drawing attributes in a class DC are not reset every time the DC is returned. This gives us a slight performance improvement over a regular system DC, in which drawing attributes *are* reset. Therefore, a class DC has some of the benefits of a private DC except that it is shared between several windows of the same class. Because it is shared between windows, a class DC must be handled like a system DC. In other words, it must be borrowed when needed—using either GetDC or BeginPaint—and returned when it is not needed—using either ReleaseDC or EndPaint.

The **CS_PARENTDC** style can also help improve performance when drawing in a window. Unlike the private DC and the class DC, however, a parent DC does not cause a new DC to be allocated in the system. Instead, a window with this style bit will receive a regular DC from the system's DC cache.

The difference lies in the way that clipping is set in the DC. Unlike a regular DC, in which clipping is either set to the visible part of the client area (by GetDC) or to the damaged part of a window (by BeginPaint), clipping in a parent DC is set to the boundaries of the parent window. Figure 13.3 compares the clipping that is set up in a regular system DC and in a parent DC. With the parent DC, the child window can draw anywhere in the client area of its parent's window. If you have children, this may sound like a familiar state of affairs. Even if your children have their own rooms, they certainly are not shy about wandering into other rooms in your home.

You might be wondering why on earth anyone would give a child window the ability to draw into its parent's client area. This is a performance optimization to help in situations when the child is drawing in a very small space and may accidentally draw outside its own border (kids will be kids). We give the child windows a little leeway so that they are not clipped in an unexpected way—this would slow them down and also clip their drawing in a way that may not be expected.

The parent DC style bit is set for the predefined classes that create Windows' dialog box controls. As you will see when we discuss dialog boxes in Chapter 14, dialog box controls are given a size and a position using a special set of coordinates called **dialog box coordinates**. Since there can be some degree of imprecision with these coordinates, the parent DC style bit gives the dialog box controls room to maneuver. If you create your own custom dialog box controls, you may wish to use the CS_PARENTDC style bit for them as well.

The CS_PARENTDC style bit is not compatible with the WS_CLIPCHILDREN style that we'll discuss when we look at **CreateWindow** style bits. If the parent window has this window

Figure 13.3 *Comparison of clipping in a system cache DC and in a parent DC*

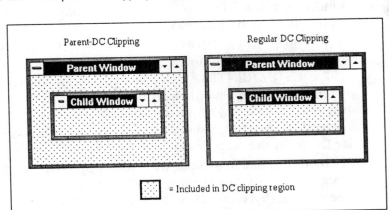

style bit set, then its child windows cannot draw in the parent's window. You might call this the "Aunt Edna" style bit, since the kids don't run around as much (or at all) when your Aunt Edna comes over (she has a way with kids).

The **CS_NOCLOSE** class style removes the Close item from the system menu. You use this with windows that have a system menu, which shouldn't be closed by the user. Of course, as we discussed in Chapter 11, another way to achieve the same result involves modifying the system menu using the various menu modification routines. This style bit provides a simpler way to achieve the same end, providing that you need this behavior for every window in the window class.

The **CS_SAVEBITS** class style is a performance bit that you set for windows that visit the display screen for very short periods of time. The save-bits style asks the Window Manager to take a snapshot of the bits that the window overwrites when it appears. You may recall that this is how menus are able to make a graceful exit when they leave. After a menu disappears, a window never gets a WM_PAINT message to redraw the area that the menu had occupied. Menus are very polite: They don't damage any window on the display screen.

The save-bits style asks every window in a class to provide the same courtesy. The class of windows that are used to create dialog boxes are set up this way. For the most part, when a dialog box visits your window, it can disappear quickly and easily without requiring your window to be sent a WM_PAINT message to redraw. But sometimes things happen that thwart the save-bits style. For example, if the dialog box moves, the bitmap snapshot of the area behind the dialog box can no longer be used to restore the area after the dialog box is removed. Or, if any drawing is done underneath the dialog box, then the bitmap snapshot will also be unusable to restore the area covered by the dialog box. In both cases, a WM_PAINT message is generated to repair the damage caused by the exit of the dialog box (or the other window).

Two class style bits are used to specify how a window should be positioned on the display screen: **CS_BYTEALIGNWINDOW** and **CS_BYTEALIGNCLIENT**. These style bits never affect the height of a window or its placement in the Y-axis. However, they *do* affect the width of a window and its placement in the X-axis. As the names suggest, these style bits force either a window or its client area to be aligned on a byte boundary. This allows a performance improvement for certain types of operations: moving the window, drawing menu items, and drawing into the window.

Byte-aligned drawing is faster on certain types of devices: monochrome displays and color displays that use multiple planes to represent color. In fact, the only kind of device that doesn't really benefit from byte-aligned drawing is a color display that uses a packed pixel approach to storing data. Since all of the most popular display devices are either monochrome or color with multiple planes (including EGA, VGA, and 8514), the byte-aligned style can give a program a slight performance improvement.

The **CS_GLOBALCLASS** class style is used for window classes that are going to be shared among different programs. For example, if you are going to create a custom dialog box control, you'll want to register the window class of your dialog box control as a global class. This allows a single window class to be shared among several programs. For example, you could use your custom dialog box control to create your spreadsheet program, your word processing program, and even for your database program.

Once a window class has been registered, you can create as many copies of the window as you like. There are two Windows library routines that do this for you, which is what we're going to look at next.

Creating a Window

There are two Windows library routines that directly create a window: **CreateWindow** and **CreateWindowEx**. The "Ex" at the end of the second routine's name stands for "extended." It does all of the things that the first routine can do, plus a little more. The CreateWindowEx routine was created because Microsoft ran out of style bits in the CreateWindow routine. This being the case, we're going to start by looking at the parameters to these routines and then consider all of the available style bits—both regular and extended.

CreateWindow is defined as follows:

```
CreateWindow (lpClassName, lpWindowName,
              dwStyle, X, Y, nWidth, nHeight,
              hWndParent, hMenu, hInstance, lpParam.
```

The extended style bits parameter is the first one in CreateWindowEx, which is defined as:

```
CreateWindowEx (dwExStyle, lpClassName, lpWindowName,
                dwStyle, X, Y, nWidth, nHeight,
                hWndParent, hMenu, hInstance, lpParam.
```

The value of **dwExStyle** is an unsigned long (DWORD) value of the extended style bits for use with the CreateWindowEx routine. We'll discuss the regular and extended style bits in a moment.

The **lpClassName** parameter is a long pointer to a character string for the class name. This is either the class name that you defined using the RegisterClass routine or it can be the name of a public window class that was created by someone else. For example, Windows makes available the following public window classes: **button, combobox, edit, listbox, scrollbar,** and **static.** We'll take a closer look at each of these classes when we discuss dialog boxes in Chapter 14.

The **lpWindowName** parameter is a long pointer to a character string for the window text. The window text is displayed in the title bar (also known as a caption bar) for windows that have a title bar. When a window is minimized—is put into an iconic state—the window text is displayed as a label for the icon. Certain types of windows that don't have a title bar, like push buttons, use the window text as a window label.

The **dwStyle** parameter is an unsigned long (DWORD) value that contains a set of flags to define the shape, size, and behavior of the window you wish to create. We'll discuss style bits, along with the extended style bits, in a moment.

The **X** and **Y** parameters identify the X and Y coordinates of the upper-left corner of the window. For top-level windows—that is, windows that don't have parents—this location is relative to the upper-left corner of the display screen, also known as **screen coordinates.** For child windows, this is relative to the upper-left corner of the parent window's client area, also known as client area coordinates.

The Window Manager calculates the location of a top-level window when the value of the X coordinate is set to CW_USEDEFAULT. When this option is used, each subsequent top-level window is given an initial position that cascades from the previous window. This option arranges top-level windows in an orderly fashion, like soldiers in a row. Figure 13.4 shows the cascading effect created by this flag.

Figure 13.4   *Cascading effect of the CW_USEDEFAULT flag*

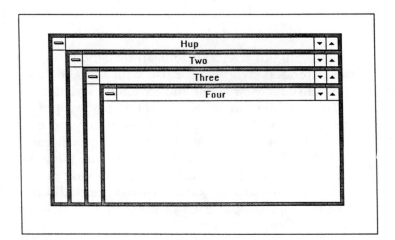

The **nWidth** and **nHeight** fields allow you to define the width and height of a window. For top-level windows, you can set nWidth to CW_USEDEFAULT. This tells the Window Manager to set the size of your window for you. But this feature is not available for child windows, so you will have to calculate their size yourself.

When you calculate the size of a window—whether it is a child window or a top-level window—you'll need to keep in mind that **CreateWindow** and **CreateWindowEx** expect the size of the *entire* window and not just the client area. Many programmers make the mistake of calculating the size of the client area and using those dimensions. But an additional step is required: You must add in the size of the various nonclient area objects. When we discuss the issue of window metrics later in this chapter, we'll describe two different ways to calculate the size of the actual window to get a client area of the desired size.

The **hwndParent** parameter identifies the window that is to be the parent of the newborn window. Windows that don't have a parent can pass a NULL value in this field, which effectively makes the window a child of the desktop window. Children of the desktop are considered top-level windows and are shown in the Task List window that appears with the Ctrl + Esc key combination.

When we discuss window style bits, you'll see that there are three different kinds of windows: overlapped, popup, and child. When you create a child window, it *must* have a parent window. This agrees with the way we think of human parents and children: Children depend on their parents for their well-being. The other two types of windows do not require a parent.

The **hMenu** parameter identifies the menu that is to be associated with a window. We have already seen that a menu name can be supplied in the lpszMenuName field when we register a window class. But, to use a menu that is different from the default class menu, we can specify a menu handle in this field. As we discussed in Chapter 11 when we introduced menus, the LoadMenu routine provides one way to obtain a menu handle when a menu has been defined in a program's resource file:

```
HANDLE hMenu;
hMenu = LoadMenu (hInstance, "MENUNAME");
```

The **hInstance** parameter is a handle to an instance. Earlier, we said that this identifies the instance currently running. When we discuss dynamic linking in Chapter 19, you'll see that the instance handle is actually a memory handle that identifies a program's default data segment. The presence of this value in the parameter list plays a part in making sure that the window procedure is able to access its data segment correctly.

While this may seem like an odd issue when you are creating a window, keep in mind that a window procedure is a call-back function that is, in effect, a subroutine used exclusively by Windows. The part of Windows that calls this subroutine—Windows' USER module—has its own data segment. When a call is made into the window procedure, it goes through a gateway that uses the value of hInstance to store the value of our data segment into the CPU's AX register. As we'll discuss in more detail in Chapter 19, the compiler, linker, and the Windows' loader work together so that this value ends up in the CPU's DS or data segment register.

Fortunately, this mechanism is transparent to you. Your window procedure is able to access your program's static data without having to do anything special—it only requires that you use the right compiler switches and that you list your window procedure in the EXPORTS section of the module definition (.DEF) file. All the rest is taken care of for you through the magic of dynamic linking.

The **lpParam** parameter is an optional, four-byte long value that you can use to pass private data to your window procedure along with the WM_CREATE message. If you translate this Hungarian notation into English, this field is intended to hold a long pointer, presumably to a private parameter block. But if you only have, say, two bytes of private data to pass, then you don't need to use it as a long pointer but can simply pass the two bytes inside the pointer field.

If you do wish it to pass a parameter block, here is an example to show you how to go about doing it. We start by allocating a data block and passing a pointer to the block in the last parameter of **CreateWindow**:

```
LPSTR  lp;
RECT   rPrivate;

rPrivate.left = 10;    rPrivate.top    = 20;
rPrivate.right = 200;  rPrivate.bottom = 100;

lp = (LPSTR)&rPrivate;

hwnd = CreateWindow("MIN:MAIN",    /* Class name.   */
          "Minimum",               /* Title.        */
          WS_OVERLAPPEDWINDOW,     /* Style bits.   */
          CW_USEDEFAULT,           /* x - default.  */
          0,                       /* y - default.  */
          CW_USEDEFAULT,           /* cx - default. */
          0,                       /* cy - default. */
          NULL,                    /* No parent.    */
          NULL,                    /* Class menu.   */
          hInstance,               /* Creator.      */
          lp);                     /* Params.       */
```

In this example, our data block is simply a RECT structure containing two (x,y) pairs that presumably are of interest to our window procedure. A pointer to this structure is placed in the lpParam parameter, which is the last parameter of **CreateWindow**.

The time to get a pointer to our data block is during the processing for the WM_CREATE message. The lParam parameter of our window procedure will contain a pointer to a data structure defined in Windows.h as **CREATESTRUCT**. It is defined in Windows.h as

```
typedef struct tagCREATESTRUCT
    {
    LPSTR   lpCreateParams;
    HANDLE  hInstance;
    HANDLE  hMenu;
```

```
HWND    hwndParent;
int     cy;
int     cx;
int     y;
int     x;
LONG    style;
LPSTR   lpszName;
LPSTR   lpszClass;
DWORD   dwExStyle;
} CREATESTRUCT;
```

The first item in this structure, lpCreateParams, is the value that we passed as our last parameter to CreateWindow. Here is one way to create a pointer to our rectangle data:

```
long FAR PASCAL WndProc (...)
    {
    int xTop;
    LPCREATESTRUCT lpcs;
    LPRECT lpr;

    switch (msg)
        {
        case WM_CREATE:
            lpcs = (LPCREATESTRUCT)lParam;
            lpr  = (LPRECT)lpcs->lpCreateParams;

            xTop = lpr -> top; /* =20    */
            break;
            .
            .
```

If you pass a pointer to a data block, you'll want to make a local copy of the data block for your window procedure, since the pointer may not be valid after the conclusion of the WM_CREATE message. As we'll discuss in Chapter 17 when we discuss memory issues, when Windows is operating in Real Mode, pointers can become invalid since the address of data objects can move. The pointer may also become invalid if the caller decides to free the memory that had been allocated to hold the data object.

At this point, we have discussed all of the parameters to **Create-Window** and **CreateWindowEx**. To get a complete picture of what these routines have to offer, we need to dig a little deeper and investigate the different style bits that can be passed in the dwEx-Style and dwStyle parameters.

Window Creation Style Bits

There are five categories of style bits to control window creation for **CreateWindow** and **CreateWindowEx**: type of window, window border, nonclient area components, the window's initial state, and performance bits. These are summarized in Table 13.1.

Type of Window

The best way to explain the three types of windows is to describe the intended use of each. The WS_OVERLAPPED window, for example, is meant to serve as a program's main, top-level window. A window created with the WS_POPUP style has some things in common with overlapped windows, and this style is intended for dialog boxes and other secondary "free-floating" windows outside a program's main window. WS_CHILD windows are used to organize the use of overlapped, popup, and other child windows into functional areas. An example of child window use is as a dialog box control (pushbutton, listbox, etc.) in a dialog box.

When you create a window with the WS_OVERLAPPED style, the Window Manager gives you some help in making sure that the window meets the minimum standards required of a top-level window. For one thing, it makes sure that your window has a caption bar and a border. (But you'll still need to specify the WS_CAPTION style if you wish to create a system menu or other caption bar elements.) Since overlapped windows are expected to serve as the top-level windows, the Window Manager will automatically size and position an overlapped window using the CW_USEDEFAULT flag. And finally, an overlapped window is always positioned in screen coordinates. This means that, even if an overlapped window has a parent, it is positioned independent of its parent.

A window created with the WS_POPUP style is a popup window. In many respects, a popup window behaves like an overlapped window: It can reside anywhere on the display screen and is positioned in screen coordinates. So why have two different styles? It's mostly an accident of history.

Version 1.x of Windows used *tiled windows* as main program windows. Popup windows were the only kind of overlapping

Table 13.1 *Summary of CreateWindow and CreateWindowEx style bits*

Category	Style Bit	Description
Type of Window (3)	WS_OVERLAPPED	Create an overlapped window, suitable for use as a top-level window. Overlapped windows always have a caption whether or not you specify the WS_CAPTION style. And they always have a border. A border of type WS_BORDER is used if no other type has been requested.
	WS_POPUP	Create a popup window, suitable for use as a dialog box or secondary window.
	WS_CHILD	Create a child window, suitable for dividing up the area of overlapped, popup, and other child windows into smaller functional areas.
Window Border (4)	WS_BORDER	Window is to have a thin border. This is the default when a caption bar has been requested (with the WS_CAPTION style).
	WS_DLGFRAME	Window is to have a thick, solid border. In previous versions of Windows, this was the standard for dialog boxes. The WS_EX_DLGMODALFRAME style bit is used in Windows 3.0 instead.
	WS_THICKFRAME	Window is to have a thick frame. The presence of this border indicates that a window can be resized. The WS_CAPTION style must accompany this selection.

(Continued)

Table 13.1 *Continued*

	WS_EX_DLGMODALFRAME	Window is to have an extended dialog frame, to include a system menu and caption bar, if requested. This is the standard style for dialog boxes.
Non-Client Components (6)	WS_CAPTION	Window has a caption, also known as a title bar. A caption is always accompanied by a border, with the WS_BORDER selected by default.
	WS_HSCROLL	Specifies to create the window with a horizontal scroll bar. Scroll bars created using this style bit are always on the bottom edge of the window. To place a scroll bar in another part of a window, you must create a scroll bar control.
	WS_MAXIMIZEBOX	Window is to have a maximize box. The WS_CAPTION style must accompany this selection.
	WS_MINIMIZEBOX	Window is to have a minimize box. The WS_CAPTION style must accompany this selection.
	WS_SYSMENU	Window is to have a system menu. The WS_CAPTION style must accompany this selection.
	WS_VSCROLL	Window is to have a vertical scroll bar. Scroll bars created using this style bit are always placed on the right edge of the window. To locate a scroll bar at another location, you must create a scroll bar control.
Initial State (5)	WS_DISABLED	Window is initially disabled, which means that mouse and keyboard input is not delivered to the window. If the user tries to click on a disabled window, a warning beep is generated.

(Continued)

Table 13.1 *Continued*

	WS_ICONIC	Window is initially iconic or minimized, which means that window is closed, and only its icon is displayed.
	WS_MAXIMIZE	Window is initially maximized. For top-level windows, this means it occupies the complete display screen. For child windows, it means it occupies its parent's entire client area.
	WS_MINIMIZE	Window is initially iconic. This style bit is the same as the WS_ICONIC style bit.
	WS_VISIBLE	Window is initially visible. This is a very important style bit, since without it a window will not appear.
Performance Bits (3)	WS_CLIPCHILDREN	Clipping in software is expensive; therefore, a parent window usually does not clip, to avoid drawing in its children. However, if you wish a parent window to avoid overwriting its children, the parent must have this style set.
	WS_CLIPSIBLINGS	Clipping in software is expensive; therefore, sibling windows—that is, windows that have the same parent—do not make any extra effort to avoid drawing over each other. This style bit ensures that siblings do not overwrite each other. It prevents what some Windows programmers refer to as "sibling rivalry."

(Continued)

Table 13.1   *Continued*

`WS_EX_NOPARENTNOTIFY`	By default, a child window sends quite a few notification messages to its parent, in the form of the WM_PARENTNOTIFY message. Notification messages are sent when the child is created, when it receives mouse click messages, and when it is destroyed. This style bit prevents a child from writing so many letters home. This decreased message traffic helps improve performance. Dialog box controls, for example, are always created with this style.

window that could be created, and these were used for dialog boxes. Starting with version 2.x of Windows, overlapping windows replaced tiled windows as the style used for main program windows. Since then, the differences between overlapped and popup windows have been mostly cosmetic, since they behave in exactly the same way.

With Windows 3.x, the differences between the two types have been reduced even further. For one thing, starting with Windows 3.x, dialog boxes have title bars. So then, what's the difference between the two? It is mostly an issue of conventional usage. As we said earlier, overlapped windows are intended for a program's main window. Popup windows are intended for dialog boxes. Presumably, if a difference should appear between these two uses in a future version of Windows, programs that follow this convention will have no problem running with whatever convention is adopted.

A window created with the WS_CHILD style is a child window. Child windows are used to divide other windows—overlapped, popup, and other child windows—into smaller functional areas. Since this is the case, a child window *must* have a parent. At window creation time, the parent is the window whose handle is passed as the **hwndParent** parameter of the **CreateWindow** and **CreateWindowEx** routines. Like human children, **child windows** require a parent because the parent provides a place to live. A child window is only visible when positioned inside the client area of its parent. If it is moved outside the client area by either a program or by a user action, any portion that lies outside of the parent's client area will not be visible.

Window Border

Figure 13.5 shows the four types of borders that are available. Notice that, among the different window border styles, only the WS_DLGFRAME cannot be used with a caption. This is an older style that has been replaced by the WS_EX_DLGMODALFRAME border for dialog boxes but is still present to maintain compatibility with programs created for older versions of Windows.

As we mentioned earlier, a WS_OVERLAPPED window must have a border. If a border is not specified, the thin WS_BORDER is automatically created for the window. The other types of windows do not require a border, which is convenient when you wish to use a child window to invisibly divide up a larger window. However, it doesn't make sense to create a popup window without a border. Without a border, a popup can easily be lost as windows are shuffled around the screen.

Figure 13.5 *The four types of borders, shown in both inactive and active states*

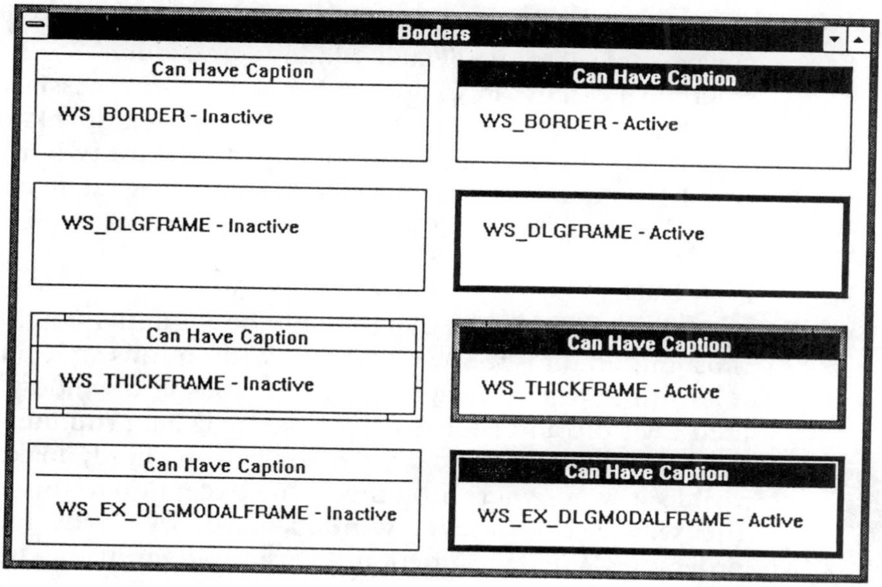

The border of a window and the caption bar change colors to let the user see a difference between active windows and inactive windows, as shown in Figure 13.5. The borders of top-level windows are changed automatically by the system, which sends a WM_NCACTIVATE message to inform a window to redraw its nonclient area to reflect either an active or an inactive state. However, this message is not sent for child windows. If you wish to change a child window's border and caption to reflect an active state, you can use the following line of code to transmit your message:

```
SendMessage (hwndChild, WM_NCACTIVATE, TRUE, 0L);
```

Changing the border and caption to reflect an inactive state involves the same message, with a zero or FALSE value for the wParam:

```
SendMessage (hwndChild, WM_NCACTIVATE, FALSE, 0L);
```

Non-Client Area Components

Figure 13.6 shows a window with all of the nonclient area components with a style flag labeling the corresponding part. With the exception of the two scroll bars, each nonclient area component is managed by the default window procedure. This means, of course, that a window procedure must forward the various nonclient area messages on to the window procedure for these components to work properly. But this is hardly a new requirement, since you are used to the idea that the messages you don't process yourself are always sent on to the default window procedure.

As we'll discuss in Chapter 22 when we cover issues relating to scrolling, scroll bars send messages that let a window know how the user is interacting with the scroll bar. There are two messages that scroll bars send: A WM_HSCROLL message is sent by horizontal scroll bars, and WM_VSCROLL is sent by vertical scroll bars.

Initial State

Of the four style bits that set a window's initial state, perhaps the most important is the WS_VISIBLE. Without this style bit, a window does not appear at creation time. Of course, a window can be created invisible and later made visible by calling routines like **Show-Window**, but it is often easier for you to simply make a window visible at window creation time. One exception to this, of course, is the way that top-level windows are ordinarily handled in a program's WinMain function. Every program in this book, in fact,

Figure 13.6   *The non-client area components of a window*

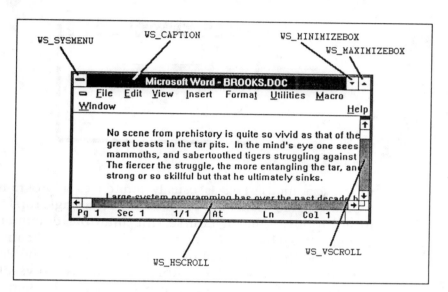

creates an invisible top-level window and then calls **ShowWindow** to make it appear. Here is how this is typically done:

```
hwnd = CreateWindow("MIN:MAIN",     /* Class name.   */
            "Minimum",              /* Title.        */
            WS_OVERLAPPEDWINDOW,    /* Style bits.   */
            CW_USEDEFAULT,          /* x - default.  */
            0,                      /* y - default.  */
            CW_USEDEFAULT,          /* cx - default. */
            0,                      /* cy - default. */
            NULL,                   /* No parent.    */
            NULL,                   /* Class menu.   */
            hInstance,              /* Creator.      */
            NULL                    /* Params.       */
            ) ;

ShowWindow (hwnd, cmdShow);
```

As we discussed earlier, the cmdShow parameter is the value passed as the last parameter in the WinMain function, which tells a program how its top-level window should first appear.

The WS_MINIMIZE and WS_MAXIMIZE style bits describe whether a window should be initially minimized (iconic) or maxi-

Figure 13.7   *A disabled push button displays its label in grayed text*

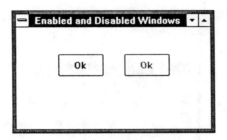

mized (zoomed). This is usually limited to a program's top-level window, since users have come to expect a single top-level window in an application. Of course, the multiple document interface changes this a bit, since a document window can be minimized and rest inside the client area of its parent window. The Program Manager provides a good example of how windows other than a program's top-level window can be managed when either minimized or maximized. In older Windows programs, you may see the WS_ICONIC style used instead of WS_MINIMIZE. If you check Windows.H, you'll notice that these two flags have identical values, and therefore can be used interchangeably.

The WS_DISABLED style bit lets you create a window that may be visible but is not available for user interaction. This is like having a door that is locked from the outside and that displays a "Closed" sign. All of the predefined dialog box controls take on a grayed appearance when they are disabled. In this way, not only is the user locked out from using the window, but the window provides visual feedback to make this aspect clear. You may wish to use this same approach if you plan to have windows that are visible, but not accessible. The two pushbuttons in Figure 13.7 show one way to let the user know that a window is not available.

Performance Bits

When we discussed the various style bits that are available for window classes, we looked at several style flags that we referred to as performance bits. In those cases, each of those performance bits provided a way to give a bit of a boost in speed for certain types of operations.

Of the three flags that we call performance bits, only one of them actually improves the performance of the system. The other two actually cause things to slow down a bit, although from your viewpoint they mean that less effort is required by your program to make things work right. For this reason, we feel justified in calling them performance bits, although perhaps a better term would be "performance *related*" style bits.

The first two styles, WS_CLIPCHILDREN and WS_CLIPSIBLINGS, control the amount of clipping that is set up in the DC when drawing in a window. In Chapter 6, when we first discussed the role of clipping we mentioned that clipping allows windowing. Without clipping, one program might accidentally overwrite another program's window. Between two windows that don't belong to the same program, clipping is automatically provided.

But between windows that belong to the same program, clipping is not so strictly enforced. In particular, there is no automatic mechanism to prevent a parent window from overwriting a child (WS_CHILD) window. And between child windows, there is no automatic clipping to prevent one child window from overwriting another. The primary reason that clipping is turned *off* in these situations is performance. If a program has put a window in a particular spot, the Window Manager assumes that the program will not allow other windows to interfere with the operation of that window. This works well and eliminates the overhead that would otherwise occur when a window has more than a few child windows.

However, things begin to break down when the user is able to move windows. In this case, a program has less control over the placement of child windows. When there is the risk that the user will cause two windows to interfere with each other, the WS_CLIPSIBLINGS style bit should be used to avoid "sibling rivalry," which is a tongue-in-cheek term for what happens when two child windows don't respect each other's boundaries.

The other clipping style bit, WS_CLIPCHILDREN, is used to prevent a parent window from overwriting its children. This is required when (a) a user can pick up a child window and move it around and (b) the window's parent draws in its own client area. The fix involves using this style bit to force the Window Manager to do a little more work in setting up the clipping that will cause the parent window to respect the boundaries of its children.

The last performance bit is WS_EX_NOPARENTNOTIFY. This performance bit reduces the number of messages that a child window sends to its parent. By default, a child window sends its parent a message when it is created, when it receives mouse click messages, and when it is destroyed. This message prevents the

WM_PARENTNOTIFY message from being sent when child windows are created and destroyed (but still sends notify messages for mouse clicks). While it seems like a lot of effort to eliminate two messages, when there are a lot of windows being created or destroyed at one time, it slows things down a bit. This is why, for example, dialog box controls use this style.

Compound Window Styles

The last three styles that we're going to look at are values that have been defined in Windows.h for the sake of convenience: WS_OVERLAPPEDWINDOW, WS_POPUPWINDOW, and WS_CHILDWINDOW. These compound styles are defined as follows:

```
#define WS_OVERLAPPEDWINDOW
                (WS_OVERLAPPED | WS_CAPTION |
                 WS_SYSMENU | WS_THICKFRAME |
                 WS_MINIMIZEBOX | WS_MAXIMIZEBOX)
#define WS_POPUPWINDOW
                (WS_POPUP | WS_BORDER | WS_SYSMENU)
#define WS_CHILDWINDOW
                (WS_CHILD)
```

These values are available for the sake of convenience, to make it easier to select the most commonly selected style bits.

Top-Level Window Considerations

A program's top-level window is the main doorway through which users access your program. When it first opens, it creates an initial impression of what a user can expect from your program. For this reason, it would seem that programmers would wish to make that initial impression a favorable one. And yet, that doesn't seem to be the case in many of today's programs. We're not interested in flashy graphics, spiffy logos, or sexy animation. What we're concerned with is much simpler than any special effects: A program will give a distinct impression based on the initial position and size of its main window.

On the one hand, quite a few programs use the CW_USEDEFAULT flag and let the Window Manager control the size and positioning of a program's main window. But, if you spend very much time using Windows, you soon find that this behavior can be annoying. Even though Windows creates this effect by keeping careful track of the location of each new top-level window that it positions, to the user the effect is one of chaos. The process of starting a program can seem to a user to be out of control, since programs seem to start up at seemingly random positions. The cascading effect creates more work for the user, since the first thing a user does is reposition the window of a newly started program to a convenient location.

If you agree that this is a problem, there are several possible solutions. One involves always creating your program's top-level window at a fixed location and with a fixed size. For example, a program might create its top-level window with a location of (10, 10) and make its window 320 pixels wide and 240 pixels high. The problem with hard-coding values like this is that the effect you produce is dependent on the type of display the user happens to be using. For example, a window of this size would occupy about one-half of a CGA screen, which is 640x200 pixels. But on an 8514, which has a resolution of 1024x768, this window would only occupy one-twelfth of the screen.

As an alternative, a program can call **GetSystemMetrics** to determine the size of the display screen and then set the size of the top-level window accordingly. Our next sample program, OWNSIZE, does just that. It creates a top-level window that is equal to the width of the display screen. It makes the window almost as tall as the display screen but leaves enough room at the bottom of the display screen so that program icons that are resting there are visible. Figure 13.8 shows our program's top-level window when it is first created.

Here is the source code to OWNSIZE:

OWNSIZE.MAK

```
OwnSize.res: OwnSize.rc OwnSize.cur OwnSize.ico
    rc -r OwnSize.rc

OwnSize.obj: OwnSize.c
    cl -AM -c -d -Gsw -Ow -W2 -Zpi OwnSize.c

OwnSize.exe: OwnSize.obj OwnSize.def
    link OwnSize,/align:16,/map, mlibcew libw/NOD/NOE/CO,\
        OwnSize.def
    rc OwnSize.res

OwnSize.exe: OwnSize.res
    rc OwnSize.res
```

Figure 13.8   *A top-level window that defines its own size*

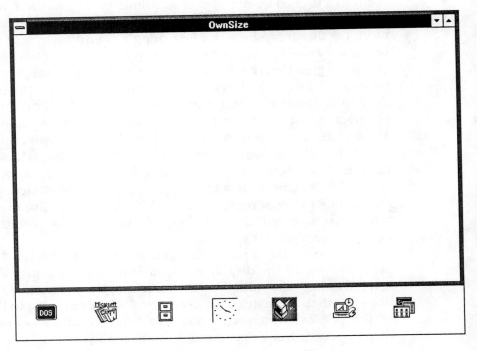

OWNSIZE.C

```
/*--------------------------------------------------------------*\
|  OwnSize.C  -  Demonstrate window creation using system        |
|                metric values and use of profile file.          |
\*--------------------------------------------------------------*/
#include <Windows.H>
#define REOPEN_NORMAL  0
#define REOPEN_ZOOM    1
#define REOPEN_DEFAULT 2


/*--------------------------------------------------------------*\
|                     Function Prototypes.                       |
\*--------------------------------------------------------------*/
long FAR  PASCAL OwnSizeWndProc (HWND, WORD, WORD, LONG);
```

```
/*------------------------------------------------------------*\
 |                       Static Data.                          |
\*------------------------------------------------------------*/
char achPr[]   = "OWNSIZE";     /* Profile file key name. */
char achFile[] = "OWNSIZE.INI"; /* Profile file name.  */


/*------------------------------------------------------------*\
 |                  Main Function:  WinMain.                   |
\*------------------------------------------------------------*/
int PASCAL WinMain (HANDLE hInstance,
                    HANDLE hPrevInstance,
                    LPSTR  lpszCmdLine,
                    int    cmdShow)
    {
    HWND      hwnd;
    int       x, y, cx, cy;
    int       iReopen;
    MSG       msg;
    WNDCLASS  wndclass;

    if (!hPrevInstance)
        {
        wndclass.lpszClassName = "OwnSize:MAIN";
        wndclass.hInstance     = hInstance;
        wndclass.lpfnWndProc   = OwnSizeWndProc;
        wndclass.hCursor       = LoadCursor (hInstance, "hand");
        wndclass.hIcon         = LoadIcon (hInstance,"snapshot");
        wndclass.lpszMenuName  = NULL;
        wndclass.hbrBackground = COLOR_WINDOW+1;
        wndclass.style         = NULL;
        wndclass.cbClsExtra    = 0;
        wndclass.cbWndExtra    = 0;

        RegisterClass( &wndclass);

        /* For first instance, set position & size to that  */
        /* of window when we last ran.                       */
        cy = GetSystemMetrics (SM_CYSCREEN) -
             GetSystemMetrics (SM_CYICON)   -
            (GetSystemMetrics (SM_CYCAPTION) * 2);
```

```
        x = GetPrivateProfileInt (achPr, "x", 0, achFile);
        y = GetPrivateProfileInt (achPr, "y", 0, achFile);


        cx = GetSystemMetrics (SM_CXSCREEN);
        cx = GetPrivateProfileInt (achPr, "cx", cx, achFile);
        cy = GetPrivateProfileInt (achPr, "cy", cy, achFile);


        iReopen = GetPrivateProfileInt (achPr, "Reopen", 0,
                                        achFile);


        if (iReopen == REOPEN_ZOOM)
            cmdShow = SW_SHOWMAXIMIZED;
        if (iReopen == REOPEN_DEFAULT)
            {
            x  = CW_USEDEFAULT;
            cx = CW_USEDEFAULT;
            }
        }
    else
        {
        /*  Other instances, use default position & size.      */
        x = cx = CW_USEDEFAULT;
        y = cy = 0;
        }

    hwnd = CreateWindow("OwnSize:MAIN",       /* Class name.   */
                        "OwnSize",            /* Title.        */
                        WS_OVERLAPPEDWINDOW,  /* Style bits.   */
                        x,                    /* x.            */
                        y,                    /* y.            */
                        cx,                   /* cx.           */
                        cy,                   /* cy.           */
                        NULL,                 /* No parent.    */
                        NULL,                 /* Class menu.   */
                        hInstance,            /* Creator.      */
                        NULL                  /* Params.       */
                        ) ;
    ShowWindow (hwnd, cmdShow);

    while (GetMessage(&msg, 0, 0, 0))
```

```
            {
        TranslateMessage(&msg);           /*  Keyboard input.        */
        DispatchMessage(&msg);
        }
    return 0;
    }


/*------------------------------------------------------------------*\
|               Window Procedure:  OwnSizeWndProc.                   |
\*------------------------------------------------------------------*/
long FAR PASCAL OwnSizeWndProc (HWND hwnd,    WORD wMsg,
                                WORD wParam, LONG lParam)
    {
    static int xLeft;
    static int yTop;
    static int cxWidth;
    static int cyHeight;

    switch (wMsg)
        {
        case WM_DESTROY:
            {
            char ach[80];
            int  iReopen;

            /*  Update private OwnSize entry.                    */

            wsprintf (ach, "%d",xLeft);
            WritePrivateProfileString (achPr, "x",   /*  X.  */
                ach, achFile);

            wsprintf (ach, "%d",yTop);
            WritePrivateProfileString (achPr, "y",   /*  Y.  */
                ach, achFile);

            if (cxWidth==0) cxWidth=CW_USEDEFAULT;
            wsprintf (ach, "%u",cxWidth);
            WritePrivateProfileString (achPr, "cx",  /*  CX.  */
                ach, achFile);

            wsprintf (ach, "%d",cyHeight);
```

```
            WritePrivateProfileString (achPr, "cy",  /*  CY.    */
                ach, achFile);

            /*  Write reopen flags for iconic/zoomed windows.  */
            iReopen = REOPEN_NORMAL;
            if (IsZoomed (hwnd))  iReopen = REOPEN_ZOOM;
            if (IsIconic (hwnd))  iReopen = REOPEN_DEFAULT;

            wsprintf (ach, "%d", iReopen);
            WritePrivateProfileString (achPr, "Reopen",
                ach, achFile);

            PostQuitMessage(0);
            }
            break;

    case WM_MOVE:
        if (IsZoomed(hwnd))  /* Save last non-zoomed size. */
            break;

        xLeft  = LOWORD (lParam);
        xLeft -= GetSystemMetrics (SM_CXFRAME);

        yTop  = HIWORD (lParam);
        yTop -= (GetSystemMetrics (SM_CYFRAME) +
                    GetSystemMetrics (SM_CYCAPTION) - 1);
        break;

    case WM_SIZE:
        if (IsZoomed(hwnd))  /* Save last non-zoomed size. */
            break;

        cxWidth  = LOWORD (lParam);
        cxWidth += 2 * GetSystemMetrics (SM_CXFRAME);

        cyHeight  = HIWORD (lParam);
        cyHeight += (2 * GetSystemMetrics (SM_CYFRAME)) +
                        GetSystemMetrics (SM_CYCAPTION) - 1;
        break;

    default:
```

```
            return(DefWindowProc(hwnd,wMsg,wParam,lParam));
            break;
        }
    return 0L;
    }
```

OWNSIZE.RC

```
snapshot icon OwnSize.ico

hand   cursor OwnSize.cur
```

OWNSIZE.DEF

```
NAME     OwnSize

EXETYPE WINDOWS

DESCRIPTION 'Own size and profile file'

CODE     MOVEABLE DISCARDABLE
DATA     MOVEABLE MULTIPLE

HEAPSIZE     512
STACKSIZE    5000

EXPORTS
    OwnSizeWndProc
```

OWNSIZE demonstrates two programming techniques that may
be interesting to you. First, it uses the **GetSystemMetrics** routine to
determine the size of its top-level window when it is first run. When
OWNSIZE is about to exit, it writes the size of its window to a
private **profile file**. A profile file is an ASCII text file that a program
can use to store values that it wants to remember. OWNSIZE uses a
profile file to save the location and dimensions of its window, so the

next time it is run it can start up with the same size. Also, the profile sets a flag if the window was zoomed, so that the next time the program is started it can make its window zoomed as well. The profile file provides a sense of continuity for a program.

The initial width of the window in OWNSIZE is set to the width of the display screen. To determine the width of the display screen, a call is made to GetSystemMetrics with the SM_CXSCREEN parameter, as shown here:

```
cx = GetSystemMetrics (SM_CXSCREEN);
```

The initial height of the window in OWNSIZE is set so that when the window is open, the row of icons at the bottom of the display screen is visible. To calculate the required value, we make three calls to GetSystemMetrics. The first determines the screen height; the second determines the height of an icon; and the third call determines the height of a caption, since each icon is accompanied by a caption. Here is the line of code that does this calculation:

```
cy = GetSystemMetrics (SM_CYSCREEN) -
     GetSystemMetrics (SM_CYICON)    -
     (GetSystemMetrics (SM_CYCAPTION) * 2);
```

The caption height is multiplied by two just to make sure there is enough room.

GetSystemMetrics provides measurement information for quite a few objects that make up the Windows user interface. Included are the size of cursors, icons, menus, captions, as well as the widths of the different types of borders. Let's take a moment to look at some of the different measurement values that this routine can provide.

System Metrics

Table 13.2 lists all of the system metrics that are defined for Windows, along with the symbolic value for the index. To get a better idea of what each value represents, Figures 13.9 through 13.11 provide the same information in a visual form.

Table 13.2   *Windows system metrics*

Type	Index	Description
Screen Metrics (4)	SM_CXSCREEN	Screen width in pixels.
	SM_CYSCREEN	Screen height in pixels.
	SM_CXFULLSCREEN	Screen width in pixels.
	SM_CYFULLSCREEN	Screen height in pixels minus the height of a window caption.
Border Sizes (6)	SM_CXBORDER	Width of a border created with the WS_BORDER style.
	SM_CYBORDER	Height of a border created with the WS_BORDER style.
	SM_CXFRAME	Width of a border on a window created with the WS_THICKFRAME style bit.
	SM_CYFRAME	Height of a border on a window created with the WS_THICKFRAME style bit.
	SM_CXDLGFRAME	Width of a border on a window with either a WS_EX_DLGMODALFRAME or WS_DLGFRAME style border.
	SM_CYDLGFRAME	Height of a border on a window with either a WS_EX_DLGMODALFRAME or WS_DLGFRAME style border.
Scroll Bar Metrics (6)	SM_CXVSCROLL	Width of the arrow bitmap in a vertical scroll bar.
	SM_CYHSCROLL	Height of the arrow bitmap in a horizontal scroll bar.
	SM_CYVSCROLL	Height of the arrow bitmap in a vertical scroll bar.

(Continued)

Table 13.2 *Continued*

	SM_CXHSCROLL	Width of the arrow bitmap in a horizontal scroll bar.
	SM_CYVTHUMB	Height of the thumb in a vertical scroll bar.
	SM_CXHTHUMB	Width of the thumb in a horizontal scroll bar.
Window Components (8)	SM_CYCAPTION	Height of a caption bar.
	SM_CYMENU	Height of a single-line menu item.
	SM_CXICON	Width of an icon.
	SM_CYICON	Height of an icon.
	SM_CXCURSOR	Width of a cursor.
	SM_CYCURSOR	Height of a cursor.
	SM_CXSIZE	Width of the system menu, minimize and maximize icons.
	SM_CYSIZE	Height of the system menu, minimize and maximize icons.
Window Tracking (4)	SM_CXMIN	Minimum width of a window.
	SM_CYMIN	Minimum height of a window.
	SM_CXMINTRACK	Minimum tracking width of a window.
	SM_CYMINTRACK	Minimum tracking height of a window.
Miscellaneous Flags (4)	SM_DEBUG	Nonzero if the debug version of Windows is installed.
	SM_SWAPBUTTON	Nonzero if the left and right mouse buttons are swapped.
	SM_MOUSEPRESENT	Nonzero if a mouse is present.
	SM_CMETRICS	Count of the number of system metric values.

Figure 13.9 *Border size system metrics*

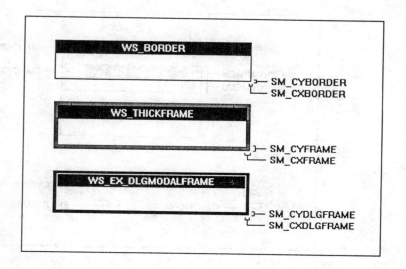

Figure 13.10 *Scroll bar system metrics*

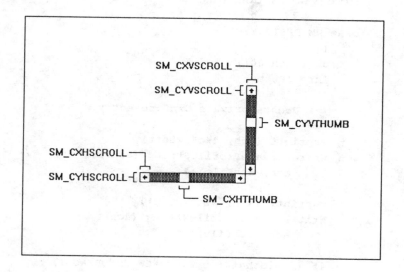

Figure 13.11 *Window component system metrics*

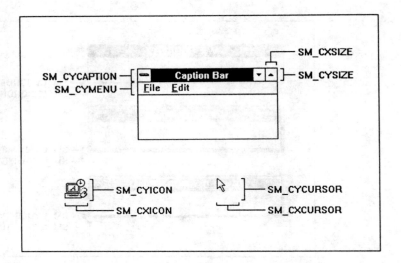

By using the values from **GetSystemMetrics**, OWNSIZE initially creates its top-level window with a reasonable size and avoids the cascading effect that seems to serve only to confuse the user. When OWNSIZE terminates, it records its last size and position onto disk. Here is how it does this:

```
case WM_DESTROY:
    {
    char ach[80];
    int iReopen;

    /* Update private OwnSize entry.              */

    wsprintf (ach, "%d",xLeft);
    WritePrivateProfileString (achPr, "x",    /*  X. */
        ach, achFile);

    wsprintf (ach, "%d",yTop);
    WritePrivateProfileString (achPr, "y",    /*  Y. */
        ach, achFile);

    if (cxWidth==0) cxWidth=CW_USEDEFAULT;
    wsprintf (ach, "%u",cxWidth);
```

```
WritePrivateProfileString (achPr, "cx",  /*  CX. */
     ach, achFile);

wsprintf (ach, "%d",cyHeight);
WritePrivateProfileString (achPr, "cy",  /*  CY. */
     ach, achFile);

/*  Write reopen flags for iconic/zoomed windows.*/
iReopen = REOPEN_NORMAL;
if (IsZoomed (hwnd))  iReopen = REOPEN_ZOOM;
if (IsIconic (hwnd))  iReopen = REOPEN_DEFAULT;

wsprintf (ach, "%d", iReopen);
WritePrivateProfileString (achPr, "Reopen",
     ach, achFile);

PostQuitMessage(0);
}
break;
```

It uses a set of routines that are part of the support Windows provides for private profile files.

Private Profile Files

One way that a program can improve its rapport with a user is to remember the preferences that the user has expressed. This might mean remembering the menu options that were selected, the preferred color to use for negative numbers, or something as simple as the position of the program's top-level window. To help make this easy for you to do, Windows includes a set of routines that support the creation of private profile files, also known as private initialization files. Of course, you might prefer to keep user preference data in your own format, but the profile file support provides an easy way to read and write user preference information.

A profile file is an ASCII text file, which means that users can modify the file using a text editor. Here is the profile file that our program, OWNSIZE, created:

```
[OWNSIZE]
x=0
y=0
cx=640
```

```
cy=408
Reopen=0
```

As you can tell from this example, profile files have the following format:

```
[application name]
keyname1 = value1
keyname2 = value2
keyname3 = value3
```

OWNSIZE keeps four numeric values that correspond to the location and the dimensions of the window when OWNSIZE was last run. These are associated with the keynames x, y, cx, and cy. A fifth numeric value, associated with the keyname "Reopen," is used when the window was either zoomed or iconic (maximized or minimized), in which case the program provides special handling.

Windows provides six routines that can be used to read and write profile files. Three of them are for reading and writing WIN.INI, which is the profile file used by Windows and older Windows programs: **GetProfileInt**, **GetProfileString**, and **WriteProfileString**. The other three provide support for private initialization files: **GetPrivateProfileInt**, **GetPrivateProfileString**, and **WritePrivateProfileString**.

OWNDRAW writes into its private profile file, OWNDRAW.INI, by calling **WritePrivateProfileString**, which is defined as

```
WritePrivateProfileString (lpApplication, lpKey,
                           lpString, lpFile)
```

- lpApplication is a long pointer to the application name. This is the name placed in square brackets in the profile file to identify a group of keyname/value pairs.
- lpKey is the long pointer to the name of the data identifier. That is, it is the string on the left of the equal sign in a keyname/value pair.
- lpString is a long pointer to the string to be placed on the right side of the equal sign in a keyname/value pair.
- lpFile is a long pointer to a character string for the filename to be used as a profile file. If no directory is given, the profile file is written into Windows' directory.

Here, for example, is how OWNSIZE writes the x location of the window:

```
wsprintf (ach, "%d",xLeft);
WritePrivateProfileString (achPr, "x",    /*   X. */
     ach, achFile);
```

When OWNDRAW starts up, it calls **GetPrivateProfileInt** to retrieve the various numeric values that it uses for the initial size and position of its window. This routine allows a program to establish a default value in case the requested integer value is not available. **GetPrivateProfileInt** is defined as follows:

```
WORD GetPrivateProfileInt (lpApp, lpKey, nDefault,
                           lpFile)
```

- lpApplication is a long pointer to the application name. This is the name placed in square brackets in the profile file to identify a group of keyname/value pairs.
- lpKey is the long pointer to the name of the data identifier. That is, it is the string on the left of the equal sign in a keyname/value pair.
- nDefault is the value to be used if the keyname is not available in the initialization file, or if the initialization file does not exist.
- lpFile is a long pointer to a character string for the file name to be used as a profile file. If no directory is given, the profile file is written into Windows' directory.

The return value is an unsigned integer value that is the value in the private profile file, or the default value if the profile entry could not be found. Here is how OWNDRAW retrieves the (x,y) location from the private profile file:

```
x = GetPrivateProfileInt (achPr, "x", 0, achFile);
y = GetPrivateProfileInt (achPr, "y", 0, achFile);
```

The next topic we're going to discuss is the use of child windows in a program's top-level window.

Creating a Child Window

In our discussion of the **CreateWindow** and **CreateWindowEx** routines, we mentioned that there are three types of windows: overlapped, popup, and child. All of the windows that we have created up until now have been overlapped windows. In the next chapter, we'll create quite a few popup and child windows when we create dialog boxes. Right now, though, let's look at what is involved in creating a child window inside the client area of our program's main window.

Creating a child window involves the same two-step process that we have been using for creating overlapped windows: first, a window class is registered by calling **RegisterClass**, and second, we create a window by calling either **CreateWindow** or **CreateWindowEx**. There are a few things that you'll need to keep in mind, however, to ensure success in the creation of a child window.

When you register a class of windows that you plan to use as child windows, you'll need to define a window procedure to handle the messages that are sent to your child windows. The window procedure must be declared FAR and PASCAL and must take the four parameters with which you have become familiar from our other window procedures:

```
long FAR PASCAL ChildWndProc (HWND hwnd, WORD wMsg,
                             WORD wParam, LONG lParam)
```

When you create a new window procedure, be sure to list the procedure name in the EXPORTS section of your program's module definition file:

```
EXPORTS
    MinWndProc
    ChildWndProc
```

If you forget, your child window won't be able to access your program's static data area. To find out why, you'll need to read about dynamic linking and the module data segment in Chapter 19. One of the problems with forgetting to export a window procedure is that neither the compiler nor the linker are able to detect this problem.

The next sample program that we're going to look at is STATLINE, which creates a child window to display status information about menu items as the user browses the menus.

Figure 13.12 *STATLINE uses a child window to display menu selection information*

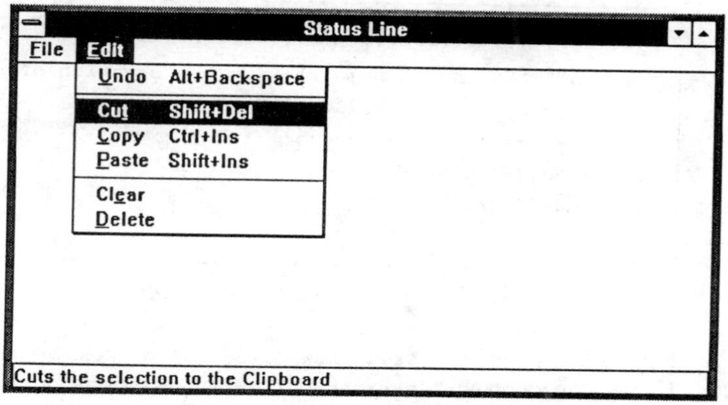

STATLINE: Menu Status Information

In Chapter 11, when we discussed the message traffic associated with menu, we mentioned that the WM_MENUSELECT message gets sent when the user browses through a menu. STATLINE responds to this message by displaying additional information about each menu item in a child window that resides at the bottom of the top-level window. Figure 13.12 shows STATLINE and the child window that displays menu status information.

Here is the source code to STATLINE:

STATLINE.MAK

```
StatLine.res: StatLine.rc StatLine.cur StatLine.ico
    rc -r StatLine.rc

StatLine.obj: StatLine.c
    cl -AM -c -d -Gsw -Ow -W2 -Zpi StatLine.c

StatLine.exe: StatLine.obj StatLine.def
    link StatLine,/align:16,/map, mlibcew libw/NOD/NOE/CO,\
        StatLine.def
    rc StatLine.res

StatLine.exe: StatLine.res
    rc StatLine.res
```

STATLINE.C

```c
/*--------------------------------------------------------------*\
|    STATLINE.C  -  Demo showing the creation of a status line |
|                        child window.                         |
\*--------------------------------------------------------------*/
#include <Windows.H>
#include "statline.h"


/*--------------------------------------------------------------*\
|                    Function Prototypes.                       |
\*--------------------------------------------------------------*/
long FAR  PASCAL StatLineWndProc (HWND, WORD, WORD, LONG);
long FAR  PASCAL StatLineChildWndProc (HWND, WORD, WORD, LONG);


/*--------------------------------------------------------------*\
|                      Static Data.                            |
\*--------------------------------------------------------------*/
HWND hwndChild;
int  cyChildHeight;


/*--------------------------------------------------------------*\
|                 Main Function:  WinMain.                     |
\*--------------------------------------------------------------*/
int PASCAL WinMain (HANDLE hInstance,   HANDLE hPrevInstance,
                    LPSTR lpszCmdLine, int    cmdShow)

    {
    HWND      hwnd;
    MSG       msg;
    WNDCLASS wndclass;

    if (!hPrevInstance)
        {
        wndclass.lpszClassName = "StatLine:MAIN";
        wndclass.hInstance     = hInstance;
        wndclass.lpfnWndProc   = StatLineWndProc;
        wndclass.hCursor       = LoadCursor (hInstance, "hand");
        wndclass.hIcon         = LoadIcon (hInstance,"snapshot");
        wndclass.lpszMenuName  = "#1";
        wndclass.hbrBackground = COLOR_WINDOW+1;
        wndclass.style         = NULL;
```

```
        wndclass.cbClsExtra    = 0;
        wndclass.cbWndExtra    = 0;

        RegisterClass( &wndclass);

        wndclass.lpszClassName = "StatLine:CHILD";
        wndclass.hInstance     = hInstance;
        wndclass.lpfnWndProc   = StatLineChildWndProc;
        wndclass.hCursor       = LoadCursor (hInstance, "hand");
        wndclass.hIcon         = NULL;
        wndclass.lpszMenuName  = NULL;
        wndclass.hbrBackground = COLOR_WINDOW+1;
        wndclass.style         = NULL;
        wndclass.cbClsExtra    = 0;
        wndclass.cbWndExtra    = 0;

        RegisterClass( &wndclass);
        }

    hwnd = CreateWindow("StatLine:MAIN",      /* Class name.   */
                    "Status Line",            /* Title.        */
                    WS_OVERLAPPEDWINDOW |     /* Style bits.   */
                    WS_CLIPCHILDREN,
                    CW_USEDEFAULT,            /* x - default.  */
                    0,                        /* y - default.  */
                    CW_USEDEFAULT,            /* cx - default. */
                    0,                        /* cy - default. */
                    NULL,                     /* No parent.    */
                    NULL,                     /* Class menu.   */
                    hInstance,                /* Creator.      */
                    NULL);                    /* Params.       */

    hwndChild = CreateWindow("StatLine:CHILD",/* Class name.   */
                    NULL,                     /* Title.        */
                    WS_CHILD    |             /* Style bits.   */
                    WS_BORDER   |
                    WS_VISIBLE,
                    0, 0, 0, 0,               /* Size/Location.*/
                    hwnd,                     /* Parent.       */
                    NULL,                     /* Class menu.   */
                    hInstance,                /* Creator.      */
```

```
                              NULL);                    /* Params.          */

    ShowWindow (hwnd, cmdShow);

    while (GetMessage(&msg, 0, 0, 0))
        {
        TranslateMessage(&msg);          /* Keyboard input.         */
        DispatchMessage(&msg);
        }
    return 0;
    }

/*--------------------------------------------------------------------*\
|           Window Procedure: StatLineWndProc.                        |
\*--------------------------------------------------------------------*/
long FAR PASCAL StatLineWndProc (HWND hwnd,     WORD wMsg,
                                 WORD wParam, LONG lParam)
    {
    switch (wMsg)
        {
        case WM_CREATE:
            {
            HDC hdc;
            int cyBorder;
            TEXTMETRIC tm;

            hdc = GetDC (hwnd);
            GetTextMetrics (hdc, &tm);
            ReleaseDC (hwnd, hdc);

            cyBorder = GetSystemMetrics (SM_CYBORDER);

            cyChildHeight = tm.tmHeight + cyBorder * 2;
            }
            break;

        case WM_DESTROY:
            PostQuitMessage(0);
            break;

        case WM_MENUSELECT:
```

```
                    SendMessage (hwndChild, wMsg, wParam, lParam);
                    break;

            case WM_SIZE:
                {
                int cxWidth;
                int cyHeight;
                int xChild;
                int yChild;

                cxWidth  = LOWORD (lParam);
                cyHeight = HIWORD (lParam);

                xChild = 0;
                yChild = cyHeight - cyChildHeight + 1;

                MoveWindow (hwndChild,
                            xChild,
                            yChild,
                            cxWidth,
                            cyChildHeight,
                            TRUE);
                }
                break;

            default:
                return(DefWindowProc(hwnd,wMsg,wParam,lParam));
                break;
            }
        return 0L;
        }


/*------------------------------------------------------------*\
|         Window Procedure:  StatLineChildWndProc.             |
\*------------------------------------------------------------*/
long FAR  PASCAL StatLineChildWndProc (HWND hwnd,    WORD wMsg,
                                    WORD wParam, LONG lParam)
    {
    static STATUSDATA sd[COUNT] =
        { 0xffff, "",
```

```
            IDM_SYS,   "Move, size or close application window",
            IDM_FILE,  "Create, open, save, print, or quit",
            IDM_EDIT,  "Undo, cut, copy, paste and delete",

            IDM_NEW,   "Creates a new item",
            IDM_OPEN,  "Open an existing item",
            IDM_SAVE,  "Save existing item",
            IDM_SAVEAS, "Save the current item with a new name",
            IDM_PRINT, "Prints the current item",
            IDM_EXIT,  "Quits Statline",

            IDM_UNDO,  "Reverse the last action",
            IDM_CUT,   "Cuts the selection to the Clipboard",
            IDM_COPY, "Copies the selection to the Clipboard",
            IDM_PASTE, "Copies the selection from the Clipboard",
            IDM_CLEAR, "Erases the currently selected item",
            IDM_DELETE, "Erases the currently selected item",

            SC_SIZE,   "Changes window size",
            SC_MOVE,   "Changes window position",
            SC_MINIMIZE,"Reduces window to an icon",
            SC_MAXIMIZE,"Enlarges the active window to full size",
            SC_CLOSE,  "Quits Statline",
            SC_RESTORE, "Restores window to normal size",
            SC_TASKLIST, "Switches to the task list"
        };

    static HMENU hmenuEdit;
    static HMENU hmenuFile;
    static HMENU hmenuSys;

    switch (wMsg)
        {
        case WM_CREATE:
            {
            HMENU hmenu;
            HWND  hwndParent;

            hwndParent = GetParent (hwnd);
            hmenu = GetMenu (hwndParent);
```

```
        hmenuFile = GetSubMenu (hmenu, 0);
        hmenuEdit = GetSubMenu (hmenu, 1);
        hmenuSys  = GetSystemMenu (hwndParent, 0);
        PostMessage (hwndParent, WM_CHAR, hmenuSys, 0L);
        }
        break;

    case WM_MENUSELECT:
        {
        char ach[50];
        HDC hdc;
        int isd;
        int i;
        RECT rClient;
        WORD wFlag;

        wFlag = LOWORD (lParam);

        isd=0;
        if (wFlag == 0xffff)
            isd=0;
        else if (wFlag & MF_POPUP)
            {
            if (hmenuSys == wParam)
                isd = 1;
            if (hmenuFile == wParam)
                isd = 2;
            if (hmenuEdit == wParam)
                isd = 3;
            }
        else
            {
            for (i=0;i<COUNT;i++)
                {
                if (wParam == sd[i].wCode)
                    {
                    isd = i;
                    break;
                    }
                }
            }
```

```
            GetClientRect (hwnd, &rClient);

            hdc = GetDC (hwnd);
            ExtTextOut (hdc,
                    0,                      /*  X.                */
                    0,                      /*  Y.                */
                    ETO_OPAQUE,             /*  Opaque rectangle. */
                    &rClient,               /*  Rectangle.        */
                    sd[isd].achMsg,         /*  String.           */
                    lstrlen(sd[isd].achMsg), /*  Length.          */
                    NULL);
            ReleaseDC (hwnd, hdc);
            }
            break;

        default:
            return(DefWindowProc(hwnd,wMsg,wParam,lParam));
            break;
        }
    return 0L;
    }
```

STATLINE.H

```
/*------------------------------------------------------------*\
|    Statline.h  -- include file for Statline.C.               |
\*------------------------------------------------------------*/

#define IDM_NEW        1
#define IDM_OPEN       2
#define IDM_SAVE       3
#define IDM_SAVEAS     4
#define IDM_PRINT      5
#define IDM_EXIT       6

#define IDM_UNDO       7
#define IDM_CUT        8
#define IDM_COPY       9
```

```
#define IDM_PASTE    10
#define IDM_CLEAR    11
#define IDM_DELETE   12

#define IDM_SYS      13
#define IDM_FILE     14
#define IDM_EDIT     15

#define COUNT 23

typedef struct tagSTATUSDATA
    {
    WORD wCode;
    char achMsg[80];
    } STATUSDATA;
```

STATLINE.RC

```
#include <Windows.h>
#include "statline.h"

snapshot icon StatLine.ico

hand   cursor StatLine.cur

1 MENU
    {
    POPUP "&File"
        {
        MENUITEM "&New",          IDM_NEW
        MENUITEM "&Open...",      IDM_OPEN
        MENUITEM "&Save",         IDM_SAVE
        MENUITEM "Save &As...",   IDM_SAVEAS
        MENUITEM SEPARATOR
        MENUITEM "&Print",        IDM_PRINT
        MENUITEM SEPARATOR
        MENUITEM "E&xit",         IDM_EXIT
        }
    POPUP "&Edit"
```

```
        {
        MENUITEM "&Undo\tAlt+Backspace", IDM_UNDO
        MENUITEM SEPARATOR
        MENUITEM "Cu&t\tShift+Del",      IDM_CUT
        MENUITEM "&Copy\tCtrl+Ins",      IDM_COPY
        MENUITEM "&Paste\tShift+Ins",    IDM_PASTE
        MENUITEM SEPARATOR
        MENUITEM "Cl&ear",  IDM_CLEAR
        MENUITEM "&Delete", IDM_DELETE
        }
    }
```

STATLINE.DEF

```
NAME     StatLine

EXETYPE WINDOWS

DESCRIPTION 'Window status line'

CODE     MOVEABLE DISCARDABLE
DATA     MOVEABLE MULTIPLE

HEAPSIZE      512
STACKSIZE     5000

EXPORTS
    StatLineWndProc
    StatLineChildWndProc
```

Creating the child window in STATLINE starts by registering the child window class, which is accomplished by calling **Register-Class**:

```
wndclass.lpszClassName = "StatLine:CHILD";
wndclass.hInstance     = hInstance;
wndclass.lpfnWndProc   = StatLineChildWndProc;
```

```
wndclass.hCursor        = LoadCursor (hInstance,"hand");
wndclass.hIcon          = NULL;
wndclass.lpszMenuName   = NULL;
wndclass.hbrBackground  = COLOR_WINDOW+1;
wndclass.style          = NULL;
wndclass.cbClsExtra     = 0;
wndclass.cbWndExtra     = 0;

RegisterClass( &wndclass);
```

Once registered, the creation of a child window involves making a call to **CreateWindow** or **CreateWindowEx**. Since we don't need the extra style bits that **CreateWindowEx** provides, we're happy to construct our child window using **CreateWindow**:

```
hwndChild = CreateWindow("StatLine:CHILD",/* Class Name.  */
                NULL,                      /* Title.       */
                WS_CHILD   |               /* Style bits.  */
                WS_BORDER  |
                WS_VISIBLE,
                0, 0, 0, 0,                /* Size/Location. */
                hwnd,                      /* Parent.      */
                NULL,                      /* Class menu.  */
                hInstance,                 /* Creator.     */
                NULL);                     /* Params.      */
```

The first thing to be said about creating a child window is that it must have a parent. We define the parent of our status line window by using the handle of our program's top-level window as the eighth parameter in our call to **CreateWindow**. A child window needs a parent because it has to live in the pixels of another window. One thing that may seem odd to you is the initial size and location of our window. We have used all zeros for the four parameters that define a window size: x, y, cx, and cy. We select a window with no size or location because we want to postpone calculating the size and location of our child window until we know the size of the parent window. We do this to make sure that the child window occupies the very bottom of the parent window.

To make sure that our child window always sits on the bottom of its parent, we need to put code in the window procedure of the parent window to modify the size and location of the child window whenever the size of the parent window changes. To do this, the window procedure for our parent window responds to the WM_SIZE message as shown here:

```
case WM_SIZE:
    {
    int cxWidth;
    int cyHeight;
    int xChild;
    int yChild;

    cxWidth  = LOWORD (lParam);
    cyHeight = HIWORD (lParam);

    xChild = 0;
    yChild = cyHeight - cyChildHeight + 1;

    MoveWindow (hwndChild,
                xChild,
                yChild,
                cxWidth,
                cyChildHeight,
                TRUE);
    }
```

The MoveWindow routine changes the location of the child window to reflect the new size of the parent window. The Move-Window routine is defined as

```
MoveWindow (hWnd, X, Y, cxWidth, cyHeight, bRepaint)
```

- hWnd identifies the window to be moved.
- X and Y are the new location of the window.
- cxWidth and cyHeight are the new width and height of the window.
- bRepaint is a Boolean flag. When set to TRUE, it causes the window to be completely redrawn in its new location. When set to FALSE, it prevents redrawing.

When the size of a window's client area changes, the window is sent a WM_SIZE message to notify it of the change.

When the user browses through a program's menus, menu messages are sent to the window procedure of the window that owns the menu. In the case of STATLINE, that means the top-level window. When the top-level window procedure receives the WM_MENUSELECT message, which is a notification that the user is browsing through a menu, it passes the message on to the window procedure of the child window by calling the **SendMessage** routine:

```
case WM_MENUSELECT:
    SendMessage (hwndChild, wMsg, wParam, lParam);
    break;
```

SendMessage delivers a message to a window procedure just as if it were directly calling the child window's window procedure. However, **SendMessage** should be used in place of a direct call, since Windows' dynamic link mechanism won't allow a direct call to a window procedure or to any other exported procedure.

In response to the WM_MENUSELECT message, the child window procedure checks to see what kind of menu selection is being made:

```
case WM_MENUSELECT:
    {
    char ach[50];
    HDC hdc;
    int isd;
    int i;
    RECT rClient;
    WORD wFlag;

    wFlag = LOWORD (lParam);

    isd=0;
    if (wFlag == 0xffff)
        isd=0;
    else if (wFlag & MF_POPUP)
        {
        if (hmenuSys == wParam)
            isd = 1;
        if (hmenuFile == wParam)
            isd = 2;
        if (hmenuEdit == wParam)
            isd = 3;
        }
```

```
    else
        {
        for (i=0;i<COUNT;i++)
            {
            if (wParam == sd[i].wCode)
                {
                isd = i;
                break;
                }
            }
        }

    GetClientRect (hwnd, &rClient);

    hdc = GetDC (hwnd);
    ExtTextOut (hdc,
                0,                       /* X.                */
                0,                       /* Y.                */
                ETO_OPAQUE,              /* Opaque rectangle.*/
                &rClient,                /* Rectangle.        */
                sd[isd].achMsg,          /* String.           */
                lstrlen(sd[isd].achMsg), /* Length.   */
                NULL);
    ReleaseDC (hwnd, hdc);
    }
    break;
```

The WM_MENUSELECT message lets you know about three types of events: browsing a regular menu item, browsing the top of a popup menu, and terminating a menu browsing. To tell the difference between these three events, you must look in the low-order word of the lParam. When it is equal to 0xFFFF, that means the browsing has terminated. When the MF_POPUP bit is set, then the value in the wParam parameter is the window handle of the popup menu. Otherwise, the wParam is the command result code for the menu item that the user is currently viewing.

When STATLINE figures out exactly which menu is being browsed, it calls the **ExtTextOut** routine to display the description of the menu item. One of the nice features of this routine is the availability of the ETO_OPAQUE flag, which causes ExtTextOut to paint an opaque rectangle to erase whatever was drawn previously in the background.

The two sample programs in this chapter, OWNSIZE and STATLINE, provide a template that you can use to fine-tune the handling of windows in your own programming projects. But this is only the beginning of how you can take advantage of Windows' windows. In the next two chapters, we're going to be looking at a part of the user interface that is built on top of windowing. What we are referring to, of course, is the topic of dialog boxes.

14
Dialog Boxes

Dialog boxes are windows that provide a standard way for a program to ask a user for additional information that may be required to complete a command. For example, a user may select the "Open..." menu item from a program's File popup menu. The ellipsis (...) at the end of the menu text indicates that a dialog box will appear. For the program to determine *which* file to open, it displays a dialog box. The user can either type the name of the file to be opened or select a file from a list. Figure 14.1 shows a standard file-open dialog box.

A dialog box itself is a window that contains child windows. In the context of dialog boxes, these child windows are called **dialog box controls**. Windows provides six window classes to support a wide range of dialog box controls. Dialog box controls can be created using the button, combobox, edit, listbox, scrollbar, and static window classes. And, if these predefined window classes don't provide the exact type of control that is needed, creating a custom dialog box control is as easy as creating a new window class.

Figure 14.1 *A standard file-open dialog box*

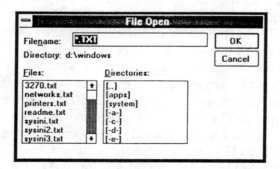

Dialog boxes come in two flavors: modal and modeless. **A modal dialog box** prevents the user from interacting with other windows in a program. **System modal dialog boxes** are a special type of modal dialog boxes that prevent the user from interacting with any window in the *system*. A **modeless dialog box**, on the other hand, doesn't interfere with a user's interaction with other windows, but instead lets the user choose the window to work with.

Internally, the difference between the two has to do with the way the flow of messages is controlled. A modal dialog box cuts off the flow of mouse and keyboard messages to its parent and sibling windows by making its parent window **disabled**. If the user tries to interact with the disabled parent window by clicking the mouse in its client area, in its menu, or in any other part of its nonclient area, the system responds with a warning beep. A second way that modal dialog boxes control message flow is that each has its own message processing loop. Instead of using your **GetMessage** loop, a modal dialog box establishes its own. This means that if you have any keyboard accelerators that depend on the call to **Translate-Accelerator** in your message loop, you will find that these are disabled as well. A modal dialog box alters the flow of messages by disabling its parent window and disabling keyboard accelerators.

A modeless dialog box, on the other hand, does not alter the flow of messages to any part of your program. Once a modeless dialog box has been opened, the user is free to work with other windows in your program or to access keyboard accelerators. Modeless dialog boxes act like a set of windows that your program creates itself by calling **CreateWindow**. In fact, this is how both modeless *and* modal dialog boxes are created. The routines that create them simply make a sequence of calls to **CreateWindow** for you.

At first glance, modeless dialog boxes may seem more attractive than modal dialog boxes, since they give the user more choices over the structure of an interaction. In spite of this initial impression, you will find that most of the dialog boxes you create are modal dialog boxes. A modal dialog box provides an ideal way to focus the user's attention on the command they have selected. Once you have their attention, they must make a decision whether to provide the information that is required to complete the command, or to cancel the request. The ability of the user to cancel a modal dialog box is part of the reason that modal dialogs can get away with being so strict in the way they structure interactions with the user.

Dialog boxes are an important part of the Windows user interface, and there are a standard set of dialog box controls that users quickly learn how to manipulate. The success of your dialog box programming depends to a large degree on how well you understand these conventions. For this reason, we're going to start by looking at some of the conventions that have been developed for dialog boxes and dialog box controls.

Dialog Box User Interface Standards

Perhaps the first thing to be said about interacting with a dialog box is that the user should be able to cancel a dialog box at any time without any ill effects. For this reason, every dialog box will have a **push button** marked "Cancel." The user can click on this button with the mouse or use the equivalent Esc key stroke to dismiss an unwanted dialog box.

A dialog box will have other push buttons as well, to allow the user to request different types of actions. A push button marked "Ok" provides a standard way for the user to indicate that all data has been entered into the dialog box, and that the program should perform whatever action had been requested that first caused the dialog to be created. In the same way that a dialog box can be canceled by either mouse or keyboard action, the user can click with the mouse on the Ok button, or use the Tab key to position the keyboard focus indicator and strike Enter to push the Ok button. At a minimum, users expect to see at least two push buttons: one to accept the changes and one to reject them.

There are other types of push buttons that a user can create, including a push button that displays a text label followed by an ellipsis (...). Like its counterpart in menus, this push button causes a dialog box to be displayed. A variation on this theme is a push button with a chevron (> >) after the button label. When such a button is pushed, it causes the dialog box to grow and reveal hidden dialog box controls. Figure 14.2 shows four types of push buttons: Ok, Cancel, ellipsis (...), and chevron (> >).

Push buttons indicate the set of actions that users can request from a dialog box. When a dialog box opens, one push button will be the default, which means it is selected when the user strikes the Enter key. The default push button has a thicker border than normal, so that the user knows it at a glance. When the user strikes the Tab key to move between dialog box controls, the push button that has the keyboard focus will always be the default push button.

Two other types of buttons are **radio buttons** and **check boxes**. Radio buttons always come in groups. A group of radio buttons is

Figure 14.2 *Four push button types, from the Paintbrush program's Save As dialog box*

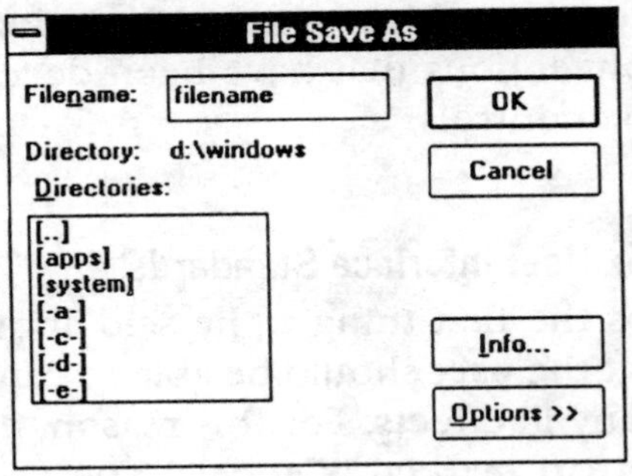

```
+---------------------------------------------------+
| [=]              File Save As                     |
|                                                   |
|  Filename:    filename            +-----------+   |
|                                   |    OK     |   |
|  Directory:   d:\windows          +-----------+   |
|  Directories:                                     |
|                                   +-----------+   |
|  +------------------+             |  Cancel   |   |
|  | [..]             |             +-----------+   |
|  | [apps]           |                             |
|  | [system]         |                             |
|  | [-a-]            |             +-----------+   |
|  | [-c-]            |             |  Info...   |   |
|  | [-d-]            |             +-----------+   |
|  | [-e-]            |             +-----------+   |
|  +------------------+             | Options >> |   |
|                                   +-----------+   |
+---------------------------------------------------+
```

like a question in a multiple-choice test: at least one of the answers must be correct. A check box is like an on/off switch: when it is checked, it is turned on and when it is not checked, it is turned off. Figure 14.3 shows a dialog box containing radio buttons and check boxes.

An **edit control** lets the user enter and edit text. There are several different styles of edit controls, including single line and multi-line, automatic conversion to either upper or lower case, and character masking to hide text when entering passwords. Like most of the other standard parts of the Windows user interface, edit controls

Figure 14.3 *Radio buttons and check boxes*

```
+-----------------------------------------------------------+
| [=]                  Communications                       |
|                                                           |
|  +-Baud Rate-------------------------+  +-----------+      |
|  | O 110  O 300  O 600  (*) 1200     |  |    OK     |      |
|  | O 2400 O 4800 O 9600 O 19200      |  +-----------+      |
|  +-----------------------------------+  +-----------+      |
|                                         |  Cancel   |      |
|  +-Data Bits----------------+  +-Stop Bits---------+       |
|  | O 5 O 6 O 7 (*) 8        |  | (*) 1 O 1.5 O 2   |       |
|  +-------------------------+   +------------------+        |
|                                                           |
|  +-Parity--+ +-Flow Control-+  +-Connector---------+      |
|  | (*) None| | (*) Xon/Xoff |  | None          [^] |      |
|  | O Odd   | | O Hardware   |  | COM1:             |      |
|  | O Even  | | O None       |  | COM2:         [v] |      |
|  | O Mark  | +--------------+  +-------------------+      |
|  | O Space |   [ ] Parity Check   [X] Carrier Detect      |
|  +---------+                                               |
+-----------------------------------------------------------+
```

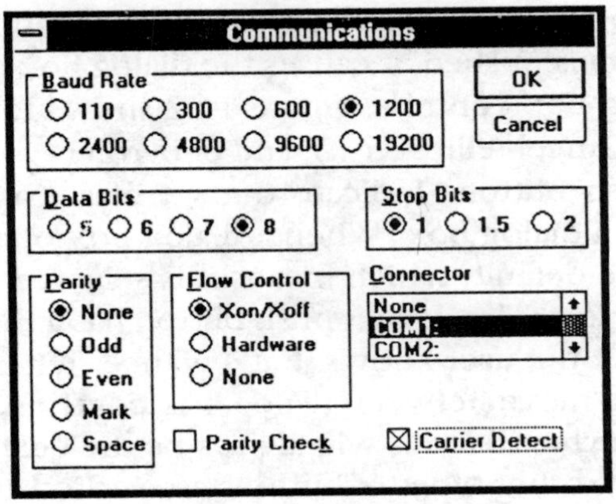

Figure 14.4   *An edit control from the File Manager*

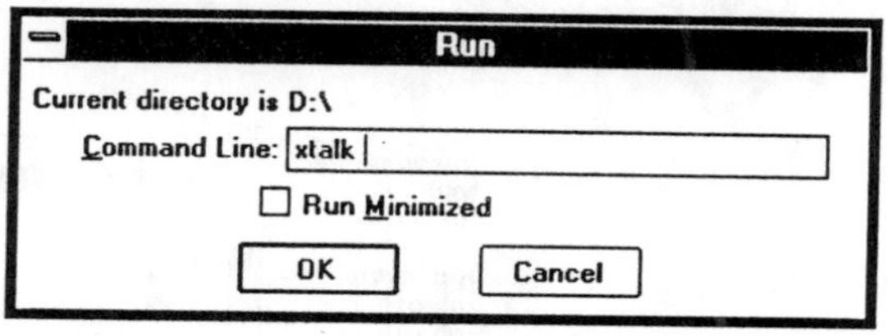

Run

Current directory is D:\

Command Line: xtalk

☐ Run Minimized

OK   Cancel

can be manipulated with the mouse or the keyboard. Either device can be used to select a character or a range of characters, or move the insertion point. A multi-line edit control can be equipped with a scroll bar for when the text might not be able to fit into the area available in an edit control. Figure 14.4 shows a typical edit control.

The **static** window class creates controls that are used to display icons, text labels, empty and filled rectangles. Figure 14.5 shows a group of static controls in a dialog box.

A **listbox** shows the user a set of choices that are available. The most common type of listbox contains text, but graphic images can also be drawn into a listbox when the set of choices is best represented by a picture instead of by words. Listboxes can have scroll bars, which are necessary when the items in a list cannot all be displayed simultaneously. Figure 14.6 shows a listbox.

A **combobox** combines a listbox with an edit control or a listbox with a static text control. A combobox can hide its listbox until the

Figure 14.5   *A group of static controls in a dialog box*

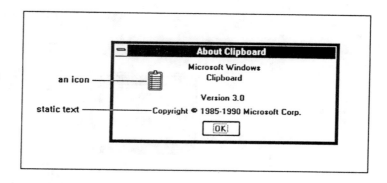

Figure 14.6   *A pair of listboxes: one with and one without a scroll bar*

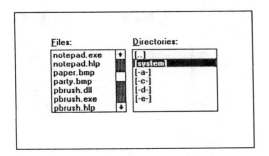

user clicks on an arrow icon to call up the listbox. Like regular listboxes, a combobox can have a scroll bar and can display either text or graphic images. From a user's point of view, a combobox looks and acts exactly like a listbox paired with a static or edit control. From a programming point of view, however, a combobox is much easier to support. Figure 14.7 shows an example of a combobox.

A **scroll bar** is a graphical representation of three related numbers: a minimum, a maximum, and a current value that lies between the two. You may recall that a scroll bar is installed in a regular window that was created with either the WS_HSCROLL or WS_VSCROLL style bits. Also, as we mentioned earlier, listboxes and edit controls can be created with a built-in scroll bar. However, you can request a stand-alone scroll bar as a dialog box control. Figure 14.8 shows a vertical and a horizontal scroll bar in the Program Manager application.

Figure 14.7   *A pair of comboboxes: one showing and one hiding a listbox*

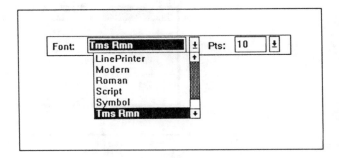

Figure 14.8   *Vertical and horizontal scroll bars*

Programs that have special input requirements that cannot be met by Windows' predefined dialog box controls can provide their own. Custom dialog box controls can be incorporated into a dialog box alongside Windows' own dialog box controls.

Now that we've reviewed Windows' predefined dialog box controls, we're ready to look at what's involved in writing code to support a dialog box. What you'll find is that the predefined controls do most of the work for you. All the while, they issue notification messages that help your program keep track of the user's progress in entering data. We're going to start by looking at the creation of modal dialog boxes, because they are the more common. Then, we'll take a look at modeless dialog boxes.

Modal Dialog Boxes

Creating a dialog box—whether modal or modeless—requires a combination of three ingredients: a dialog box template, code to create the dialog box, and code to maintain the dialog box. Each of these elements puts a different twist on the dialog box creation process, so we're going to look at them one at a time.

Dialog Box Template

A dialog box template is a data object that defines the size of the dialog box, the type of controls in the dialog box, as well as the size and positioning of each dialog box control. The most common type of dialog box template is one built with a graphic editor called the **Dialog Box Editor**, which creates an ASCII text script that defines each element of the dialog box. Here is an example of a dialog box template created by the dialog box editor:

```
IDD_ABOUT DIALOG LOADONCALL MOVEABLE DISCARDABLE
                20, 24, 180, 84
STYLE WS_DLGFRAME | WS_POPUP
BEGIN
    CONTROL "A Sample About Box", IDD_TEXT1, "static",
            SS_CENTER | WS_CHILD, 47, 13, 84, 8
    CONTROL "Windows 3.0 Power Programming Techniques",
            IDD_TEXT2, "static", SS_CENTER | WS_CHILD,
            0, 30, 180, 8
    CONTROL "By Peter Norton and Paul Yao", IDD_TEXT3,
            "static", SS_CENTER | WS_CHILD,
            0, 42, 180, 8
    CONTROL "Ok", IDD_OK, "button",
            BS_DEFPUSHBUTTON | WS_TABSTOP | WS_CHILD,
            70, 64, 40, 16
    CONTROL "snapshot", IDD_ICON, "static",
            SS_ICON | WS_CHILD, 18, 8, 16, 16
END
```

The DIALOG statement is a lot like the MENU statement, which is the resource key word for defining a menu. The syntax of the DIALOG statement is

```
dialogID DIALOG [load option] [memory option] x, y, cx, cy
```

- dialogID identifies the dialog box resource.
- [load option] is either PRELOAD or LOADONCALL. PRELOAD causes a dialog to be loaded into memory before a program starts running. LOADONCALL causes the dialog to be loaded only when it is needed.
- [memory option] is either FIXED, MOVEABLE, or DISCARDABLE, and describes the behavior of the object once it has been loaded. For more details on these options, refer to the discussion in Chapter 18.
- x and y is the position of the dialog box window, in dialog box coordinates, relative to the client area of the dialog box's parent window.
- cx and cy is the width and height of the control, in dialog box coordinates.

Each CONTROL statement in the dialog box definition defines a different dialog box control. The general syntax of the CONTROL statement is

```
CONTROL <text>, nID, <class>, <styles>, x, y, cx, cy
```

- <text> is a character string in double quotes that later becomes the window text of the window that is created.
- nID is an integer value that uniquely identifies the dialog control window.
- <class> is the character string name of the window class from which a dialog control is to be created.
- <styles> are a set of generic window class styles and control-specific styles that are ORed together.
- x and y is the position of the control in the dialog box window, in dialog box coordinates.
- cx and cy is the width and height of the control, in dialog box coordinates.

You may have noticed that the position and size of the dialog box itself, and of each control in the dialog box, is specified in a coordinate system called **dialog box coordinates**. This coordinate system helps a dialog box definition be somewhat device-independent, since the units are defined relative to the size of the system font. In dialog box coordinates, units in the X direction are approximately 1/4 of the average width of the system font. In the Y direction, they are 1/8 of the height of the system font. **GetDialogBoxUnits** provides the necessary base units, which can be used to convert between dialog box units and pixels using code like the following:

```
int   xBase,  yBase;
int   xDlg,   yDlg;
int   xPixel, yPixel;
LONG  lBase;

lBase = GetDialogBoxUnits();
xBase = LOWORD (lBase);
yBase = HIWORD (lBase);

xPixel = (xDlg * xBase)/4;
yPixel = (yDlg * yBase)/8;
```

The STYLE statement in the DIALOG statement lists the window styles that are part of the dialog box window when it is created. From this, you may have already guessed that the dialog box template is little more than a convenient way to list the parameters of the **CreateWindow** routine. But, as you will see shortly, creating a dialog box does not require you to call **CreateWindow**. But, you should keep in mind that the dialog box creation code actually calls **CreateWindow** for you: once for the dialog box frame and once for each control in the dialog box.

If you find that you're a bit overwhelmed by all the details that are involved in the definition of the dialog box template, you'll be glad to know there is an easier way. Rather than messing with the creation of a dialog box template by hand, there is a tool that is provided in the Windows software development kit for this purpose: the dialog box editor.

The Dialog Box Editor

The very first Windows programmers, back at the beginning of (Windows) time, had to create dialog box templates from scratch. This involved taking pencil to graph paper to create dialogs that looked somewhat reasonable. Getting a dialog box to look good required many hours of work. Fortunately, those days are long gone, and Windows programmers can take advantage of a graphic tool that allows them to draw a dialog box and create a dialog box template from the image they draw.

Figure 14.9 shows the dialog box editor with an image of the dialog box definition that we looked at earlier. The dialog box editor allows you to draw and manipulate a dialog box definition until you feel you have gotten it looking just right. It supports all of the pre-defined type of dialog box controls, as well as custom controls as long as they are in a dynamic link library that has been set up correctly. The dialog box editor is fairly simple to use, although it has a few quirks that you will want to work around.

For one thing, although the dialog box editor is able to edit include (.H) files, you'll probably want to set up a separate include file for each dialog box that you define. The dialog box editor does not know how to interpret the syntax of normal C include files, and can only understand the symbolic constants that you create with a #define statement. One include file for each dialog box definition is a good idea, since the editor insists that each symbolic constant have

Figure 14.9   *The dialog box editor*

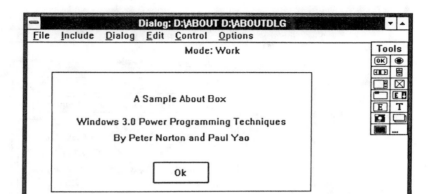

a unique value. This requirement is actually a fairly small price to pay considering the convenience provided by this tool.

To fine-tune a specific dialog box control, you can select the Edit-Styles menu item or double-click on the control. This causes a customizing dialog box to appear, which allows you to change a control's text, its ID value, and the specific style bits that will control the appearance and behavior of the control. There is a different customizing dialog box for each class of dialog box control, since each class has its own, private style bits. Figure 14.10 shows the customizing dialog box that allows you to select the different styles available for static class dialog box controls.

Creating the dialog box template involves creating a resource object that describes the shape, size, and position of the dialog box itself and that of each control in a dialog box. This object is placed into your program's resource file, along with the icon, resource, and menu definitions that are part of your application program. With the resource defined, the next ingredient that you'll need to create a dialog box is the actual code that triggers the dialog box creation.

Figure 14.10   *Customizing a static class dialog box control*

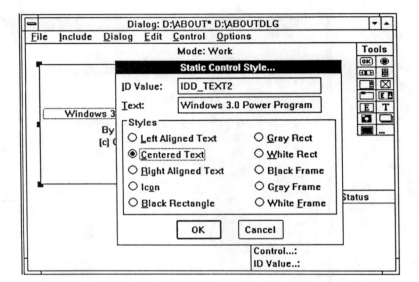

Creating a Modal Dialog Box

Windows provides four routines for creating a modal dialog box: **DialogBox**, **DialogBoxIndirect**, **DialogBoxIndirectParam**, and **DialogBoxParam**. The most basic of these routines is the first one. The others simply provide some slight variations for added flexibility in the dialog box creation process. **DialogBox** is defined

```
int DialogBox (hInstance, lpszTemplate, hwndParent,
               lpDialogProc);
```

- hInstance is the instance handle of the program or dynamic link library that owns the dialog box definition.
- lpszTemplate is a far pointer to a character string for the name of the dialog box definition, as defined in the dialog box template. Alternatively, it can be an integer value wrapped inside the MAKEINTRESOURCE macro, when an integer is used in place of a character string to identify the dialog box template.

- hwndParent is a handle to the parent window of the dialog box. The parent window of a modal dialog box is disabled when the dialog box is displayed.
- lpDialogProc is a far pointer to a piece of code that maintains the dialog box while it is being displayed. This is a function that is referred to as a dialog box procedure. The address passed in this parameter is not the actual address of the routine itself, but the instance thunk created by the **MakeProcInstance** routine for the dialog box procedure.

The first and third parameters are relatively straightforward, since we have encountered instance handles and window handles before. Let's take a closer look at the second and fourth parameters.

The second parameter to DialogBox is defined as an LPSTR value, which means it can hold a far pointer to a character string. The second parameter identifies the dialog box template from the resource file definition. This can be a regular character string for dialog box templates that are defined that way:

```
DialogBox (hInst, "MYDIALOG", hwndParent, lpproc);
```

As an alternative, an integer value can be used to define a dialog box template. When this is the case, a program can use the MAKEINTRESOURCE macro to disguise an integer value in a character string position:

```
DialogBox (hInst, MAKEINTRESOURCE(15), hwndParent, lpproc);
```

Or, instead of the MAKEINTRESOURCE macro, a pound sign can be placed in a character string to identify a dialog box template with a numeric identifier:

```
DialogBox (hInst, "#15", hwndParent, lpproc);
```

The fourth parameter to DialogBox identifies the code that will maintain the dialog box while it is opened—it will process the messages that are sent from the dialog box controls as notifications of the user's activity. The code is a call-back procedure called a **dialog box procedure**. In Chapter 2, when we introduced the minimum Windows program, we encountered another call-back procedure known as a window procedure.

A dialog box is similar to a window procedure in a number of ways, but there are differences in structure and in the messages that are received. A dialog box procedure also is never addressed directly, but instead is always addressed using a small piece of code called an instance thunk. In Chapter 21, we're going to go into more detail about what an instance thunk does. Briefly, an instance thunk is an outgrowth of Windows' dynamic link mechanism, which connects a program's code to the code of a dynamic link library. An instance thunk ensures that dynamically linked code has access to the proper *data segment*. Creating an instance thunk involves making a call to **MakeProcInstance**. This routine is defined as

```
FARPROC MakeProcInstance (lpProc, hInstance)
```

- lpProc is the address of a call-back procedure for which an instance thunk is to be created.
- hInstance is an instance handle.

Therefore, the creation of a dialog box involves making *two* calls: one to **MakeProcInstance** and one to **DialogBox**. Consider a dialog box procedure named **AboutDlgProc**, with a dialog box template defined with the symbolic constant

```
#define IDD_ABOUT 15
```

Here is the code to create a modal dialog box:

```
{
FARPROC lpitAbout;

lpitAbout = MakeProcInstance (AboutDlgProc, hInstance);
DialogBox (hInstance,
          MAKEPROCINSTANCE(IDD_ABOUT),
          hwnd,
          lpitAbout);
FreeProcInstance (lpitAbout);
}
```

The **MakeProcInstance** routine returns a far pointer to our instance thunk, which is stored in the lpitAbout variable (the "lpit"

Hungarian stands for "long pointer to an instance thunk"). This value is passed as the fourth parameter to **DialogBox**, which causes the modal dialog box to appear. As we mentioned earlier, modal dialog boxes have their own, private message loop. This means that control is not returned from the **DialogBox** routine until the dialog box has been dismissed.

Once we are finished with the dialog box, the instance thunk can be destroyed by calling **FreeProcInstance**. This routine forms the second slice of a sandwich, with the call to **MakeProcInstance** as the top slice. The sandwich construction is needed to ensure that the memory used by the **MakeProcInstance** routine is available for other uses. This is not the only way that an instance thunk can be used, however, and we'll see an alternative approach in our first sample program.

This covers the first two ingredients needed to create a dialog box: the dialog box template and the code needed to create the dialog box. There is one more ingredient that is important to the creation of both modal and modeless dialog boxes: the code that maintains the dialog box.

Maintaining the Dialog Box

The code that maintains a dialog box is referred to as a dialog box procedure. A dialog box procedure has a lot in common with a window procedure. This is the case because a dialog box procedure has a role similar to that of a window procedure: It processes messages. In addition, as with a window procedure, you must list the names of every dialog box procedure in the EXPORTS section of your program's module definition file:

```
EXPORTS
    AboutDlgProc
```

Otherwise, you risk disconnecting the code in your dialog box procedure from your static data in your program's default data segment (a topic that is more fully explored in Chapter 19, when the topic of dynamic linking is discussed).

But a dialog box procedure is *not* itself a window procedure, but rather is called by the standard, default dialog box window procedure to customize the behavior of a specific dialog box. Figure 14.11

Figure 14.11   *Message flow to a normal window procedure*

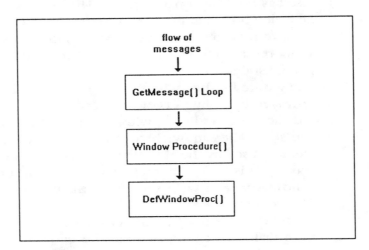

shows the typical message flow of a regular window procedure. By contrast, Figure 14.12 shows how this message flow is diverted from the default dialog box window procedure to a custom dialog box procedure.

A dialog box procedure returns one of two values: TRUE and FALSE. As the figure suggests, a return value of TRUE means that the dialog box procedure has processed the message, and no further processing is required. A return value of FALSE means that the dialog box procedure has not processed the message. It is up to the default dialog box procedure, **DefDlgProc**, to process the message if it sees fit, or to pass the message on the default window procedure, **DefWindowProc**.

Since a dialog box procedure processes messages just like a regular window procedure, it takes the same four parameters as a window procedure. But, because it returns a TRUE and FALSE value, dialog box procedures are defined with a Boolean (BOOL) return value instead of the normal long value that window procedures return. Here is a typical procedure declaration for a dialog box procedure:

```
BOOL FAR PASCAL DlgProc (HWND hdlg,   WORD wMsg,
                         WORD wParam, LONG lParam);
```

Figure 14.12   *Message flow to a dialog box procedure*

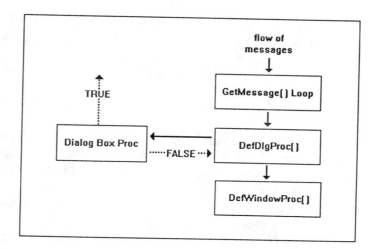

What types of messages is a dialog box procedure interested in? Since a dialog box procedure has a window procedure to take care of the nitty gritty issues of supporting the window, dialog box procedures mainly focus on two messages: WM_INITDIALOG and WM_COMMAND.

The WM_INITDIALOG message is sent to the dialog box procedure after all of the dialog box control windows have been created, but before they have been made visible. In response to this message, a dialog box procedure will initialize each of the dialog box controls to the correct initial state. For example, it might fill a listbox with the items to be viewed by the user. Or, it might set the state of radio buttons or check box buttons to a state that reflects the current settings. If there is an edit control in the dialog box, the dialog box procedure might insert a string at initialization time.

Once the dialog box controls have been given their initial settings, they work on their own to accept user input, modify the current settings, and keep out of each other's way. As they work, they send WM_COMMAND messages to the dialog box procedure to notify it of just about every action that the user takes. In some respects, dialog box controls are like children away at summer camp, who write home to tell their parents about the day's activities:

Dear Mom and Dad Window,

Camp is fun. Today we went hiking, played volleyball, received the input focus from the user, and a mouse click or two.

Your child window control,

Check-Box

The WM_COMMAND notification messages allow the dialog box procedure to respond to the changes that take place in a dialog box control. In some respects, the WM_COMMAND message sent from a dialog box control is just like the WM_COMMAND message sent from a menu item when the user has made a menu selection. The wParam contains the identifier that was defined to the item in the resource file, to allow your program to know the specific item with which the user is interacting. But because a dialog box control has more to say than a menu item, the lParam contains some more information: the high-order word contains a notification code, and the low-order word contains the window handle of the control that is sending the message. Figure 14.13 graphically depicts the contents of the parameters to the WM_COMMAND message.

Since dialog box procedures are primarily interested in two messages, here is a template that you can use for just about every dialog box procedure that you create:

```
BOOL FAR PASCAL DlgProc (HWND hdlg,    WORD wMsg,
                         WORD wParam, LONG lParam);

    {
    switch (wMsg)
        {
        case WM_INITDIALOG:
            /*  Put initialization code here.  */
            return TRUE;

        case WM_COMMAND:
            /*  Receive & process notifications. */
            return TRUE;

        default:
            return FALSE;
        }
    }
```

Figure 14.13   *The parameters in a WM_COMMAND notification message*

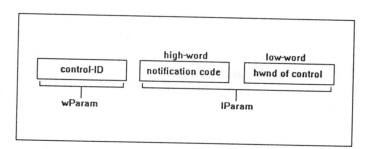

In addition to the messages that a dialog box procedure receives, there are quite a few messages that will get sent from a dialog box procedure to its dependent controls. Sending messages, in fact, provides the primary mechanism by which a dialog box procedure will communicate with its controls. Thus, at initialization time, the dialog box procedure sets the initial state of a dialog box control by sending it messages. And, as the dialog box procedure receives the notification message, it may send more messages to fine-tune the behavior of the dialog box controls based on the type of input that was reported in the notification message.

The one final issue that needs to be addressed is that of terminating a dialog box. In this respect, a modal dialog box is quite different from a modeless dialog box. We'll discuss the required termination of a modeless dialog box, after we present a sample program that shows in detail how to handle a modal dialog box. In general, modal dialog boxes are dismissed after the user has selected a push button that indicates whether to continue with the command that initially caused the dialog box to appear or whether to abandon the command. When such a push button has been clicked, it causes a WM_COMMAND notification message to be sent to the dialog box procedure. In either case, a call to **EndDialog** is all that is needed to dismiss the modal dialog box and return control to the calling program. **EndDialog** is defined

```
void EndDialog (hDlg, nResult)
```

- hDlg is a handle to the modal dialog box to be dismissed.
- nResult is a result code that is provided as the return value of the function that created the dialog box (either **DialogBox**,

DialogBoxIndirect, **DialogBoxIndirectParam**, or **Dialog-BoxParam**).

Consider a dialog box with an Ok and a Cancel button. If the Ok button had a control ID equal to the symbolic constant IDD_OK, and the Cancel button had an ID equal to IDD_CANCEL, here is what the code in the dialog box procedure might look like to dismiss the dialog box:

```
BOOL FAR PASCAL DlgProc (HWND hdlg,    WORD wMsg,
                         WORD wParam, LONG lParam);

    {
    switch (wMsg)
        {
        case WM_INITDIALOG:
            /*  Put initialization code here.  */
            return TRUE;

        case WM_COMMAND:
            switch (wParam)
                {
                case IDD_OK:
                    EndDialog (hDlg, TRUE);
                    return TRUE;
                case IDD_CANCEL:
                    EndDialog (hDlg, FALSE);
                    return TRUE;
                }
                break;

        default:
            return FALSE;
        }
    }
```

Although this example uses a result code of either TRUE or FALSE, any unsigned integer value could be used as well. Since the result code is the return value to the dialog box creation routine, here is how that code might be modified to respond:

```
    {
    BOOL    bRetVal;
    FARPROC lpitAbout;
```

```
lpitAbout = MakeProcInstance (AboutDlgProc, hInstance);
bRetVal =   DialogBox (hInstance,
                        MAKEPROCINSTANCE(IDD_ABOUT),
                        hwnd,
                        lpitAbout);
FreeProcInstance (lpitAbout);

if (bRetVal)
    {
    /*  User clicked Ok.       */
    .
    .
    .
    }
else
    {
    /*  User clicked Cancel.  */
    .
    .
    .
    }
}
```

Most of the time and energy required to fine-tune the behavior of a dialog box will be spent working on this third ingredient that is required for a dialog box: the dialog box procedure. Let's look at a sample program that brings these three elements together. Our next sample program creates an About box, which is one of the simplest kind of dialog boxes that a program can create. An About box provides a standard means by which programs can display copyright information, as well as other details about a program. When you see the simple dialog box procedure in this program, don't be fooled into thinking that all dialog box procedures will be as simple. As you'll see in our later programming examples, they can be quite involved.

A Simple Dialog Box: ABOUT

Our first, and simplest, dialog box will be an About box. This dialog box is displayed by programs to tell the user about a program: its creator, version number, and any copyright information. An About box is usually displayed by a program in response to a menu selection made from the standard Help menu, depicted in Figure 14.14. The About dialog box that our program displays is shown in Figure 14.15.

Figure 14.14   *A standard Help menu*

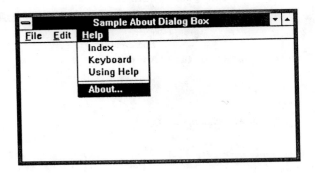

Figure 14.15   *An About dialog box*

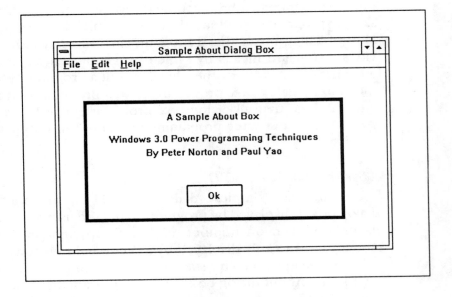

Here is the source code to our program:

ABOUT.MAK

```
About.res: About.rc About.cur About.ico About.dlg
    rc -r About.rc

About.obj: About.c About.h About.dlg Aboutdlg.h
    cl -AM -c -d -Gsw -Ow -W2 -Zpi About.c

About.exe: About.obj About.def
    link About,/align:16,/map, mlibcew libw/NOD/NOE/CO,\
        About.def
    rc About.res

About.exe: About.res
    rc About.res
```

ABOUT.C

```
/*------------------------------------------------------------*\
 |    ABOUT.C   Sample About dialog box sample.               |
\*------------------------------------------------------------*/
#include <Windows.H>
#include "About.h"
#include "Aboutdlg.h"


/*------------------------------------------------------------*\
 |                    Function Prototypes.                    |
\*------------------------------------------------------------*/
long FAR  PASCAL AboutWndProc (HWND, WORD, WORD, LONG);
BOOL FAR  PASCAL AboutDlgProc (HWND, WORD, WORD, LONG);


/*------------------------------------------------------------*\
 |                       Static Data.                         |
\*------------------------------------------------------------*/
FARPROC lpitAbout;
HANDLE  hInst;
```

```
/*-------------------------------------------------------------*\
|                 Main Function:  WinMain.                     |
\*-------------------------------------------------------------*/
int PASCAL WinMain (HANDLE hInstance,
                    HANDLE hPrevInstance,
                    LPSTR  lpszCmdLine,
                    int    cmdShow)

    {
    HWND      hwnd;
    MSG       msg;
    WNDCLASS wndclass;

    if (!hPrevInstance)
        {
        wndclass.lpszClassName = "About:MAIN";
        wndclass.hInstance     = hInstance;
        wndclass.lpfnWndProc   = AboutWndProc;
        wndclass.hCursor       = LoadCursor (hInstance, "hand");
        wndclass.hIcon         = LoadIcon (hInstance,"snapshot");
        wndclass.lpszMenuName  = "#1";
        wndclass.hbrBackground = COLOR_WINDOW+1;
        wndclass.style         = NULL;
        wndclass.cbClsExtra    = 0;
        wndclass.cbWndExtra    = 0;

        RegisterClass( &wndclass);
        }

    hInst = hInstance;

    hwnd = CreateWindow("About:MAIN",        /* Class name.  */
                                             /* Title.       */
                    "Sample About Dialog Box",
                    WS_OVERLAPPEDWINDOW,     /* Style bits.  */
                    CW_USEDEFAULT,           /* x - default. */
                    0,                       /* y - default. */
                    CW_USEDEFAULT,           /* cx - default. */
                    0,                       /* cy - default. */
                    NULL,                    /* No parent.   */
                    NULL,                    /* Class menu.  */
                    hInstance,               /* Creator.     */
```

```
                              NULL);                    /* Params.       */
        ShowWindow (hwnd, cmdShow);


        lpitAbout = MakeProcInstance (AboutDlgProc, hInst);

        while (GetMessage(&msg, 0, 0, 0))
            {
            TranslateMessage(&msg);          /* Keyboard input.      */
            DispatchMessage(&msg);
            }
        return 0;
        }


/*-------------------------------------------------------------------*\
  |               Window Procedure:  AboutWndProc.                    |
\*-------------------------------------------------------------------*/
long FAR PASCAL AboutWndProc (HWND hwnd,    WORD wMsg,
                              WORD wParam, LONG lParam)
        {
       switch (wMsg)
           {
           case WM_COMMAND:
               switch (wParam)
                   {
                   case IDM_EXIT:
                       DestroyWindow (hwnd);
                       break;
                   case IDM_HELP_ABOUT:
                       DialogBox (hInst,
                                  MAKEINTRESOURCE(IDD_ABOUT),
                                  hwnd,
                                  lpitAbout);
                       break;
                   default:
                       MessageBox (hwnd,
                                   "Feature not implemented",
                                   "About",
                                   MB_OK);
                   }
               break;
```

```
        case WM_DESTROY:
            PostQuitMessage(0);
            break;

        default:
            return(DefWindowProc(hwnd,wMsg,wParam,lParam));
            break;
        }
    return 0L;
    }


/*------------------------------------------------------------*\
|              Dialog Box Procedure:  AboutDlgProc             |
\*------------------------------------------------------------*/
BOOL FAR PASCAL AboutDlgProc (HWND hdlg,    WORD wMsg,
                              WORD wParam, LONG lParam)

    {
    switch (wMsg)
        {
        case WM_COMMAND:
            EndDialog (hdlg, TRUE);
            return TRUE;
        default:
            return FALSE;
        }
    }
```

ABOUT.H

```
/*------------------------------------------------------------*\
| About.h  - Include file for About.c.                        |
\*------------------------------------------------------------*/


#define IDM_NEW      1
#define IDM_OPEN     2
#define IDM_SAVE     3
#define IDM_SAVEAS   4
#define IDM_PRINT    5
```

```
#define IDM_EXIT        6

#define IDM_UNDO        7
#define IDM_CUT         8
#define IDM_COPY        9
#define IDM_PASTE       10
#define IDM_CLEAR       11
#define IDM_DELETE      12

#define IDM_HELP_INDEX 13
#define IDM_HELP_KEYS   14
#define IDM_HELP_USING 15
#define IDM_HELP_ABOUT 16
```

ABOUTDLG.H

```
#define IDD_OK          1
#define IDD_TEXT1       100
#define IDD_TEXT2       101
#define IDD_TEXT3       102
#define IDD_TEXT4       103

#define IDD_ABOUT       10
```

ABOUT.RC

```
#include <Windows.h>
#include "About.h"
#include "Aboutdlg.h"

snapshot icon About.ico

hand   cursor About.cur

#include "about.dlg"

1 MENU
```

```
{
POPUP "&File"
    {
    MENUITEM "&New",          IDM_NEW
    MENUITEM "&Open...",      IDM_OPEN
    MENUITEM "&Save",         IDM_SAVE
    MENUITEM "Save &As...",   IDM_SAVEAS
    MENUITEM SEPARATOR
    MENUITEM "&Print",        IDM_PRINT
    MENUITEM SEPARATOR
    MENUITEM "E&xit",         IDM_EXIT
    }
POPUP "&Edit"
    {
    MENUITEM "&Undo\tAlt+Backspace", IDM_UNDO
    MENUITEM SEPARATOR
    MENUITEM "Cu&t\tShift+Del",     IDM_CUT
    MENUITEM "&Copy\tCtrl+Ins",     IDM_COPY
    MENUITEM "&Paste\tShift+Ins",   IDM_PASTE
    MENUITEM SEPARATOR
    MENUITEM "Cl&ear",              IDM_CLEAR
    MENUITEM "&Delete",             IDM_DELETE
    }
POPUP "&Help"
    {
    MENUITEM "Index",               IDM_HELP_INDEX
    MENUITEM "Keyboard",            IDM_HELP_KEYS
    MENUITEM "Using Help",          IDM_HELP_USING
    MENUITEM SEPARATOR
    MENUITEM "About...",            IDM_HELP_ABOUT
    }
}
```

ABOUT.DLG

```
IDD_ABOUT DIALOG LOADONCALL MOVEABLE DISCARDABLE 20, 24, 180, 84
STYLE WS_DLGFRAME | WS_POPUP
BEGIN
    CONTROL "A Sample About Box", IDD_TEXT1, "static",
```

```
              SS_CENTER | WS_CHILD, 0, 6, 180, 8
   CONTROL "Windows 3.0 Power Programming Techniques",
           IDD_TEXT2, "static", SS_CENTER | WS_CHILD,
           0, 22, 180, 8
   CONTROL "By Peter Norton and Paul Yao", IDD_TEXT3,
           "static", SS_CENTER | WS_CHILD, 0, 32, 180, 8
   CONTROL "(c) Copyright 1990 By Paul Yao", IDD_TEXT4,
           "static", SS_CENTER | WS_CHILD, 0, 42, 180, 8
   CONTROL "Ok", IDD_OK, "button",
           BS_DEFPUSHBUTTON | WS_TABSTOP | WS_CHILD,
           70, 60, 40, 16
END
```

ABOUT.DEF

```
NAME     About

EXETYPE WINDOWS

DESCRIPTION 'Sample About Dialog Box'

CODE     MOVEABLE DISCARDABLE
DATA     MOVEABLE MULTIPLE

HEAPSIZE    512
STACKSIZE   5000

EXPORTS
   AboutWndProc
   AboutDlgProc
```

While reviewing the source code to ABOUT, you may notice that
the dialog box template is in a separate file from the resource file.
The resource file has a **#include** statement that causes the dialog
box template to be loaded into the resource file when it is compiled.
ABOUT has a separate include file that contains the symbolic constants used in the About box template definition. The primary reason for having separate files for the dialog box definition is to make
it easier to work with the dialog box editor.

You may also have noticed that instead of a sandwich construction, with a call to **DialogBox** in between calls to **MakeProcInstance** and **FreeProcInstance**, the dialog box seems to be created with a single call to **DialogBox**:

```
case WM_COMMAND:
    switch (wParam)
        {
        case IDM_EXIT:
            DestroyWindow (hwnd);
            break;
        case IDM_HELP_ABOUT:
            DialogBox (hInst,
                       MAKEINTRESOURCE(IDD_ABOUT),
                       hwnd,
                       lpitAboutDlgProc);
            break;
        default:
            MessageBox (hwnd,
                        "Feature not implemented",
                        "About",
                        MB_OK);
        }
    break;
```

But if you look in ABOUT's WinMain function, you'll find that it creates an instance thunk during program initialization time:

```
lpitAbout = MakeProcInstance (AboutDlgProc, hInst);
```

This approach helps dialog boxes to be created a little more quickly because the instance thunk is created only once. Creating and destroying an instance thunk every time it is needed may not slow down the system very much, but it does slow the system down. Every task database has eight instance thunks preallocated for use by your program, therefore you can create up to eight of them without requiring any additional memory. Of course, if you need more than eight, an additional memory block is allocated for your program's use.

The dialog box procedure for the About dialog box is simple, because the dialog box doesn't do anything but wait for the user to push the push button. The dialog box doesn't need to have anything initialized, so the dialog box procedure doesn't process the WM_INITDIALOG message. When the user does push the button—

either with a mouse click or by pressing the return key—a WM_COMMAND message is sent to the dialog box procedure, with a notification code of BN_CLICKED in the high-word of the lParam. But since this is the only notification code that can be sent our dialog box procedure by any control in the dialog box, ABOUT doesn't bother checking for the notification code, but simply terminates on receipt of the WM_COMMAND message by calling **EndDialog**:

```
BOOL FAR PASCAL AboutDlgProc (HWND hdlg,    WORD wMsg,
                              WORD wParam, LONG lParam)
    {
    switch (wMsg)
        {
        case WM_COMMAND:
            EndDialog (hdlg, TRUE);
            return TRUE;
        default:
            return FALSE;
        }
    }
```

Creating the modal dialog box required that three ingredients be brought together: a dialog box template, code to create the dialog box, and code to maintain the dialog box. Next, we're going to look at what is involved in creating a modeless dialog box. You'll see that there are quite a few small differences between modal and modeless dialog boxes.

Modeless Dialog Boxes

The three elements needed to create a modeless dialog box are essentially the same as those needed for a modal dialog box. But the differences are significant enough to warrant a separate discussion of modeless dialog box creation. Let's look at each of the three items required for modeless dialog boxes, starting with the dialog box template.

Dialog Box Template

The dialog box template that you create for modeless dialog boxes is almost identical with the templates you use for modal dialog boxes. But, you'll need to change the dialog box styles to make your modeless dialog box behave properly. The easiest way to do this involves the use of the Dialog Box Editor's "Dialog Box Style..."

Figure 14.16 *Dialog Box Editor's customizing options for a dialog box*

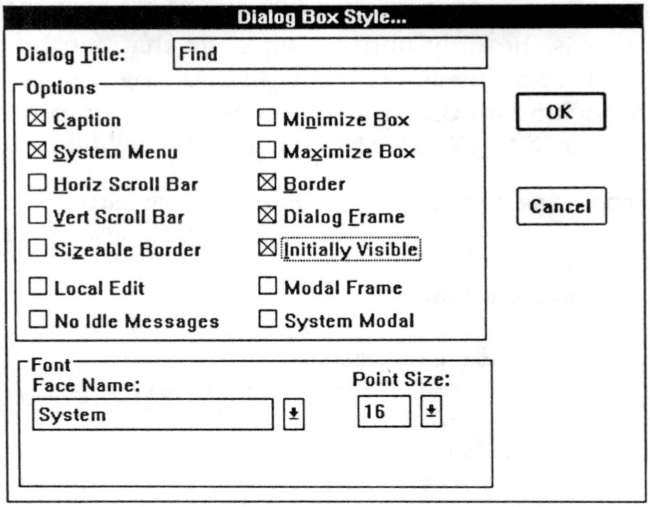

customizing box, shown in Figure 14.16. You'll need some additional options over and above the ones required for modal dialog boxes. Perhaps the most important is the check box marked "Initially Visible." This causes the WS_VISIBLE creation style to be added to the dialog box template's style bits. You aren't required to have this bit set for a modal dialog box, because modal dialogs are automatically made visible. It makes sense: Otherwise, a modal dialog box would disable its parent and then not be visible. Without the visible bit, however, a modeless dialog box would simply not appear.

Another style bit that is useful for modeless dialog boxes is WS_CAPTION, which is produced when you select the check box marked "Caption." This gives the user something to grab when they need to move a modeless dialog box out of the way, using the mouse. To enable the movement of a modeless dialog box from the keyboard, be sure to install the WS_SYSMENU style, which results from checking the check box marked "System Menu."

Although it's not used in our programming example, notice that the "Dialog Box Style..." dialog box in Figure 14.16 also allows you to change the font used in a dialog box. This causes an additional statement to be added to a dialog box template, which selects the indicated font for all of the controls in a given dialog box. Each of the controls is automatically scaled to provide the same relative proportions that are provided for the system font.

For the first element of a dialog box, the dialog box template, the only difference between a modal and a modeless dialog box is the style bits we just discussed. Let's look at the differences that modeless dialog boxes require for the second dialog box element: the code that creates a dialog box.

Creating a Modeless Dialog Box

Four routines create a modeless dialog box: **CreateDialog**, **CreateDialogIndirect**, **CreateDialogIndirectParam**, and **CreateDialogParam**. Just like the routines that create modal dialog boxes, three of these provide slight variations for added flexibility in creating a dialog box, but most programmers can get by with the first routine. For this reason, we're going to focus our attention on the first routine, **CreateDialog**, because it provides all the basic services that we'll need. **CreateDialog** is defined

```
int CreateDialog (hInstance, lpszTemplate, hwndParent,
                  lpDialogProc);
```

- hInstance is the instance handle of the program or dynamic link library that owns the dialog box definition.
- lpszTemplate is a far pointer to a character string for the name of the dialog box definition, as defined in the dialog box template. Alternatively, it can be an integer value wrapped inside the MAKEINTRESOURCE macro, when an integer is used in place of a character string to identify the dialog box template.
- hwndParent is a handle to the parent window of the dialog box. The parent window of a modal dialog box is disabled when the dialog box is displayed.
- lpDialogProc is a far pointer to a piece of code that maintains the dialog box while it is being displayed. This is a function that is referred to as a dialog box procedure. The address passed in this parameter is not the actual address of the routine itself, but the instance thunk created by the **MakeProcInstance** routine for the dialog box procedure.

It's interesting to note that the parameters to **CreateDialog** are identical with those of **DialogBox**. Even though you probably will never create a dialog box that is both modal and modeless, the similarity between these two routines makes it possible. One of the reasons for the similarity is that **DialogBox** itself calls **Create-Dialog** to build the actual dialog box. The difference between the two, of course, is that **DialogBox** disables its parent and has its own message loop, while **CreateDialog** simply returns when the dialog box has been built.

Just like a modal dialog box, the creation of a modeless dialog box requires an instance thunk to make sure the dialog box procedure has access to your program's data segment. This is accomplished with a call to **MakeProcInstance**:

```
lpitFind = MakeProcInstance (FindDlgProc, hInst);
```

The value returned is a far pointer to an instance thunk. This is passed as the fourth parameter to **CreateDialog**:

```
hwndFindDialog = CreateDialog (hInst,
            MAKEINTRESOURCE (IDD_FIND),
            hwnd,
            lpitFind);
```

The value that **CreateDialog** returns is a window handle to the dialog box itself.

A program should always save the return value from the Create-Dialog function, because this handle is going to be needed to support the keyboard interface of the modeless dialog box. But this is getting us into a discussion around the third element that is needed for a dialog box: the code that maintains the dialog box.

Maintaining a Modeless Dialog Box

Maintaining a modeless dialog box requires a dialog box procedure that is similar to the dialog box procedure required for modal dialog boxes. In a moment, we'll examine some of the differences. Outside the dialog box procedure itself, there is need for an additional element that provides the keyboard interface to a modeless dialog box.

The keyboard interface to a *modal* dialog box consists of support for several keys: Tab, Enter, Esc, and the arrow keys. These keys allow the user to move between controls and dismiss the dialog box. They are automatically available for modal dialog boxes because, as you may recall, a modal dialog box has its own message loop. To get these keys to work in a *modeless* dialog box, you must modify your program's message loop to include a call to **IsDialogMessage**. This routine is defined as

```
BOOL IsDialogMessage (hDlg, lpMsg)
```

- hDlg is a handle to a modeless dialog box.
- lpMsg is a far pointer to a structure of type MSG.

IsDialogMessage returns TRUE when the message was for a dialog box or a dialog box control. In this case, **IsDialogMessage** makes the necessary calls to **TranslateMessage** and **DispatchMessage**. **IsDialogMessage** returns FALSE when the message was not for the dialog box or (already done) control in the dialog box. In that case, the message loop can handle the message in the usual way.

Here is an example of a message loop that has been modified to correctly call **IsDialogMessage** to handle the keyboard interface for a modeless dialog box:

```
while (GetMessage(&msg, 0, 0, 0))
    {
    if (hwndFindDialog)
        if (IsDialogMessage (hwndFindDialog, &msg))
            continue;
    TranslateMessage(&msg);  /*  Keyboard input.    */
    DispatchMessage(&msg);
    }
```

Notice that IsDialogMessage is only called if the value of hwndFind-Dialog is nonzero. This is the variable in which is stored either the window handle of a modeless dialog box or a zero when the modeless dialog box is not open.

The dialog box procedure for a modeless dialog box is almost identical to that of a modal dialog box. One difference between a modeless and a modal dialog box procedure is that a modeless dialog box is not dismissed with a call to **EndDialog**. Instead, a dialog box procedure for a modeless dialog box must dismiss the dialog box by calling **DestroyWindow**:

```
DestroyWindow (hdlg);
```

Otherwise, a modeless dialog box has the same declaration as a modal dialog box, with a FAR and PASCAL declaration, and the four parameters that are so familiar to you from working with window procedures:

```
BOOL FAR PASCAL FindDlgProc (HWND hdlg,    WORD wMsg,
                            WORD wParam, LONG lParam)
```

And, like any other call-back procedure, a modeless dialog box procedure must be listed in the EXPORTS section of the module definition file:

```
EXPORTS
    FindDlgProc
```

There are clearly enough differences between modal and modeless dialog boxes that you'll probably want to see a complete program that shows all of these elements put together. The next sample program creates and maintains a modeless dialog box, and also shows a few interesting programming techniques that can be applied to modal as well as modeless dialog boxes.

A Modeless Dialog Box: FIND

The modeless dialog box that we're going to create is modeled after a modeless dialog box that is used by a program that is bundled with Windows: Write. It creates a modeless dialog box when the user selects the Find... menu item in the Search menu that can be opened and left open to support an ongoing string search function. The user can continue working with the word processing document and ignore the FIND dialog box; he can move the dialog box out of the way, or dismiss it entirely. Figure 14.17 shows the dialog box that our program creates.

Figure 14.17 *A modeless dialog box*

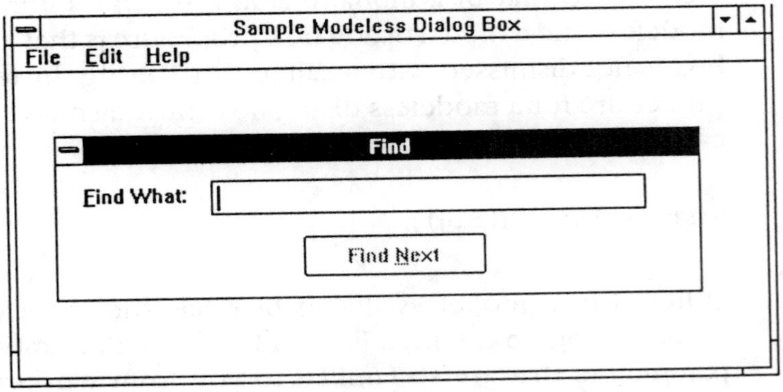

Here is the code to our modeless dialog box program:

FIND.MAK

```
Find.res: Find.rc Find.cur Find.ico Find.dlg
    rc -r Find.rc

Find.obj: Find.c Find.h Find.dlg Finddlg.h
    cl -AM -c -d -Gsw -Ow -W2 -Zpi Find.c

Find.exe: Find.obj Find.def
    link Find,/align:16,/map, mlibcew libw/NOD/NOE/CO,\
        Find.def
    rc Find.res

Find.exe: Find.res
    rc Find.res
```

FIND.C

```c
/*-------------------------------------------------------------*\
|    FIND.C  Sample Modeless dialog box sample.                 |
\*-------------------------------------------------------------*/
#include <Windows.H>
#include "Find.h"
#include "finddlg.h"


/*-------------------------------------------------------------*\
|                     Function Prototypes.                      |
\*-------------------------------------------------------------*/
long FAR  PASCAL FindWndProc  (HWND, WORD, WORD, LONG);
BOOL FAR  PASCAL FindDlgProc (HWND, WORD, WORD, LONG);


/*-------------------------------------------------------------*\
|                       Static Data.                            |
\*-------------------------------------------------------------*/
FARPROC lpitFind;
HANDLE  hInst;
HWND    hwndFindDialog;
char    achFindBuffer [FINDBUFFERSIZE];
```

```
/*-----------------------------------------------------------*\
|                    Main Function: WinMain.                  |
\*-----------------------------------------------------------*/
int PASCAL WinMain (HANDLE hInstance,   HANDLE hPrevInstance,
                    LPSTR lpszCmdLine, int    cmdShow)

    {
    HWND      hwnd;
    MSG       msg;
    WNDCLASS wndclass;

    if (!hPrevInstance)
        {
        wndclass.lpszClassName = "Find:MAIN";
        wndclass.hInstance     = hInstance;
        wndclass.lpfnWndProc   = FindWndProc;
        wndclass.hCursor       = LoadCursor (hInstance, "hand");
        wndclass.hIcon         = LoadIcon (hInstance,"snapshot");
        wndclass.lpszMenuName  = "#1";
        wndclass.hbrBackground = COLOR_WINDOW+1;
        wndclass.style         = NULL;
        wndclass.cbClsExtra    = 0;
        wndclass.cbWndExtra    = 0;

        RegisterClass( &wndclass);
        }

    hInst = hInstance;

    hwnd = CreateWindow("Find:MAIN",              /* Class name.  */
                                                  /* Title.       */
                        "Sample Modeless Dialog Box",
                        WS_OVERLAPPEDWINDOW,      /* Style bits.  */
                        CW_USEDEFAULT,            /* x - default. */
                        0,                        /* y - default. */
                        CW_USEDEFAULT,            /* cx - default. */
                        0,                        /* cy - default. */
                        NULL,                     /* No parent.   */
                        NULL,                     /* Class menu.  */
                        hInstance,                /* Creator.     */
                        NULL);                    /* Params.      */
```

```
        ShowWindow (hwnd, cmdShow);

        lpitFind = MakeProcInstance (FindDlgProc, hInst);

        while (GetMessage(&msg, 0, 0, 0))
            {
            if (hwndFindDialog)
                if (IsDialogMessage (hwndFindDialog, &msg))
                    continue;
            TranslateMessage(&msg);        /*  Keyboard input.    */
            DispatchMessage(&msg);
            }
        return 0;
        }

/*-----------------------------------------------------------------*\
  |               Window Procedure:  FindWndProc.                   |
\*-----------------------------------------------------------------*/
long FAR PASCAL FindWndProc (HWND hwnd,    WORD wMsg,
                             WORD wParam, LONG lParam)
    {
    switch (wMsg)
        {
        case WM_COMMAND:
            switch (wParam)
                {
                case IDM_EXIT:
                    DestroyWindow (hwnd);
                    break;
                case IDM_FIND:
                    if (hwndFindDialog)
                        SetActiveWindow (hwndFindDialog);
                    else
                        hwndFindDialog = CreateDialog (hInst,
                                MAKEINTRESOURCE (IDD_FIND),
                                hwnd,
                                lpitFind);
                    break;
                default:
                    MessageBox (hwnd,
                                "Feature not implemented",
```

```
                                        "Find",
                                        MB_OK);

                        }
                break;

            case WM_DESTROY:
                PostQuitMessage(0);
                break;

            case PM_FIND:
                MessageBox (hwnd,
                            achFindBuffer,
                            "Find Request Received",
                            MB_OK);

                break;

            default:
                return(DefWindowProc(hwnd,wMsg,wParam,lParam));
                break;
        }
    return 0L;
    }


/*------------------------------------------------------------------*\
|                 Dialog Box Procedure:  FindDlgProc                 |
\*------------------------------------------------------------------*/
BOOL FAR PASCAL FindDlgProc (HWND hdlg,    WORD wMsg,
                              WORD wParam, LONG lParam)

    {
    switch (wMsg)
        {
        case WM_INITDIALOG:
            {
            HWND hCtl;

            hCtl = GetDlgItem (hdlg, IDD_BUTTON);
            EnableWindow (hCtl, FALSE);
            return TRUE;
            }
            break;
```

```
case WM_COMMAND:
    switch (wParam)
        {
        case IDD_CANCEL:
            DestroyWindow (hdlg);
            hwndFindDialog = 0;
            break;

        case IDD_BUTTON:
            {
            HWND hwndParent;

            GetDlgItemText (hdlg,
                            IDD_EDIT,
                            achFindBuffer,
                            FINDBUFFERSIZE);

            hwndParent = GetParent (hdlg);
            SendMessage (hwndParent, PM_FIND, 0, 0L);
            }
            break;

        case IDD_EDIT:
            {
            HWND hCtl;
            int  cc;
            WORD wNotifyCode;

            wNotifyCode = HIWORD (lParam);
            hCtl = LOWORD (lParam);
            if (wNotifyCode == EN_CHANGE)
                {
                cc = (int)SendMessage (hCtl,
                                       WM_GETTEXTLENGTH,
                                       0, 0L);

                hCtl = GetDlgItem (hdlg, IDD_BUTTON);
                EnableWindow (hCtl, cc);
                }
            }
            break;
```

```
                }
            return TRUE;
            break;

        default:
            return FALSE;
        }
    }
```

FIND.H

```
/*------------------------------------------------------------------*\
|   About.h  - Include file for About.c.                             |
\*------------------------------------------------------------------*/

#define IDM_NEW        1
#define IDM_OPEN       2
#define IDM_SAVE       3
#define IDM_SAVEAS     4
#define IDM_PRINT      5
#define IDM_EXIT       6


#define IDM_UNDO       7
#define IDM_CUT        8
#define IDM_COPY       9
#define IDM_PASTE     10
#define IDM_CLEAR     11
#define IDM_DELETE    12


#define IDM_HELP_INDEX 13
#define IDM_HELP_KEYS  14
#define IDM_HELP_USING 15
#define IDM_HELP_ABOUT 16


#define IDM_FIND       17


#define FINDBUFFERSIZE 80
```

```
#define PM_FIND        WM_USER

#define IDD_CANCEL     2
```

FINDDLG.H

```
#define IDD_FIND     11
#define IDD_EDIT     100
#define IDD_BUTTON   101
#define IDD_TEXT5    102
```

FIND.RC

```
#include <Windows.h>
#include "Find.h"
#include "Finddlg.h"

snapshot icon Find.ico

hand   cursor Find.cur


#include "find.dlg"

1 MENU
    {
    POPUP "&File"
        {
        MENUITEM "&New",        IDM_NEW
        MENUITEM "&Open...",    IDM_OPEN
        MENUITEM "&Save",       IDM_SAVE
        MENUITEM "Save &As...", IDM_SAVEAS
        MENUITEM SEPARATOR
```

```
        MENUITEM "&Print",        IDM_PRINT
        MENUITEM SEPARATOR
        MENUITEM "E&xit",         IDM_EXIT
        }
    POPUP "&Edit"
        {
        MENUITEM "&Undo\tAlt+Backspace", IDM_UNDO
        MENUITEM SEPARATOR
        MENUITEM "Cu&t\tShift+Del",    IDM_CUT
        MENUITEM "&Copy\tCtrl+Ins",    IDM_COPY
        MENUITEM "&Paste\tShift+Ins",  IDM_PASTE
        MENUITEM SEPARATOR
        MENUITEM "Cl&ear",             IDM_CLEAR
        MENUITEM "&Delete",            IDM_DELETE
        MENUITEM SEPARATOR
        MENUITEM "Find...",            IDM_FIND
        }
    POPUP "&Help"
        {
        MENUITEM "Index",              IDM_HELP_INDEX
        MENUITEM "Keyboard",           IDM_HELP_KEYS
        MENUITEM "Using Help",         IDM_HELP_USING
        MENUITEM SEPARATOR
        MENUITEM "About...",           IDM_HELP_ABOUT
        }
    }
```

FIND.DLG

```
IDD_FIND DIALOG LOADONCALL MOVEABLE DISCARDABLE
              9, 27, 216, 47
CAPTION "Find"
STYLE WS_BORDER | WS_CAPTION | WS_DLGFRAME | WS_SYSMENU |
    WS_VISIBLE | WS_POPUP
BEGIN
    CONTROL "&Find What:", IDD_TEXT5, "static",
            SS_LEFT | WS_CHILD, 9, 7, 39, 10
    CONTROL "", IDD_EDIT, "edit",
            ES_LEFT | WS_BORDER | WS_TABSTOP | WS_CHILD,
```

```
                    52, 6, 146, 12
        CONTROL "Find &Next", IDD_BUTTON, "button",
                BS_DEFPUSHBUTTON | WS_TABSTOP | WS_CHILD,
                83, 26, 61, 14
    END
```

FIND.DEF

```
    NAME    Find

    EXETYPE WINDOWS

    DESCRIPTION 'Sample Modeless Dialog Box'

    CODE    MOVEABLE DISCARDABLE
    DATA    MOVEABLE MULTIPLE

    HEAPSIZE    512
    STACKSIZE   5000

    EXPORTS
        FindWndProc
        FindDlgProc
```

The modeless dialog box procedure in FIND must be accessed through an instance thunk. This is created by a call to **MakeProc-Instance**, inside our WinMain function:

```
lpitFind = MakeProcInstance (FindDlgProc, hInst);
```

After this call, the value of lpitFind is a long pointer to an instance thunk, which provides the necessary connection between the dialog box procedure, FindDlgProc, and our program's data segment. We'll pass the value of lpitFind to CreateDialog as the required address of the dialog box procedure.

The modeless dialog box itself is displayed after the user selects a menu item that we added to the Edit menu, depicted in Figure 14.18. When this menu item is selected, a WM_COMMAND message

Figure 14.18 *The "Find" menu item triggers the creation of the modeless dialog box*

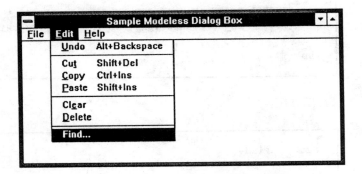

is sent to the window procedure of FIND's main window, with a value of IDM_FIND in the wParam. This causes the following code to create our dialog box:

```
hwndFindDialog =
    CreateDialog (hInst,
                MAKEINTRESOURCE (IDD_FIND),
                hwnd,
                lpitFind);
```

CreateDialog returns a window handle, which we store away for use in the call to **IsDialogMessage**, embedded in our message loop, to enable the modeless dialog box's keyboard interface.

The "Find" push button in the modeless dialog box is initially grayed, to notify the user that it cannot be selected. Actually, our dialog box doesn't gray the dialog box control. Instead, it disables it with a call to **EnableWindow**. This causes a WM_ENABLE message to be delivered to the dialog box control, in response to which it grays itself. **EnableWindow** is defined:

```
BOOL EnableWindow (hwnd, bEnable)
```

- hwnd is a handle of the window to be enabled or disabled.
- bEnable is TRUE (nonzero) to enable a window and FALSE (zero) to disable it.

The dialog box procedure does not enable the push button unless there are characters in the edit control.

The easiest way for a dialog box procedure to detect the presence of characters in an edit control is to wait for the edit control to send an EN_CHANGE notification. All notifications come as WM_COMMAND messages, with the notification code embedded in the high word of the lParam parameter. The EN_CHANGE notification is sent whenever characters are added or deleted from the edit control. Determining whether an edit control has characters or not involves sending a query message to the edit control: WM_GETTEXTLENGTH. The return value is the count of characters in the edit control. We can use the count of characters as a parameter to the EnableWindow function, since zero will disable the push button and nonzero values will enable it:

```
wNotifyCode = HIWORD (lParam);
hCtl = LOWORD (lParam);
if (wNotifyCode == EN_CHANGE)
    {
    cc = (int)SendMessage (hCtl,
                    WM_GETTEXTLENGTH,
                    0, 0L);

    hCtl = GetDlgItem (hdlg, IDD_BUTTON);
    EnableWindow (hCtl, cc);
    }
```

Only when the Find button is enabled can the user push it (either with a mouse click or, since it's a default push button, by striking the Enter key). This causes the push button to send a notification to the dialog box procedure: a WM_COMMAND message with the push button's ID in the wParam, and a BN_CLICKED notification code in the high-word of the lParam. This allows the following switch statement to detect when the button has been pushed and to notify the main window procedure of this fact:

```
case WM_COMMAND:
    switch (wParam)
        {
        case IDD_CANCEL:
            DestroyWindow (hdlg);
            hwndFindDialog = 0;
```

```
        break;

    case IDD_BUTTON:
        {
        HWND hwndParent;

        GetDlgItemText (hdlg,
                        IDD_EDIT,
                        achFindBuffer,
                        FINDBUFFERSIZE);

        hwndParent = GetParent (hdlg);
        SendMessage (hwndParent, PM_FIND, 0, 0L);
        }
        break;
```

We don't bother checking for the BN_CLICKED notification code, since a push button can only send one other notification code, BN_DOUBLECLICKED, which will always come after a BN_CLICKED notification.

Notifying the part window involves sending a private message, PM_FIND, that has been defined as

```
#define PM_FIND WM_USER
```

This is an example of an application-defined message. Presumably, if this were part of a full-blown program, upon receipt of this message, the parent window would start a search. In this program, a message box is simply displayed to tell us that a search was requested.

You may have noticed that the dialog box procedure tests for a notification sent from a control with an ID value of IDD_CANCEL. And yet, if you look at the dialog box template, you'll see that there is no dialog box control with this identifier. Built into the dialog box handling mechanism is automatic support for sending this notification whenever the user strikes the Esc key. Also, since this dialog box has a system menu, the user can also select the Close item from this menu to cause the same notification to be sent. In response to either of these actions, the modeless dialog box is dismissed with a call to **DestroyWindow**. This routine must be used in place of the counterpart for modal dialog boxes, **EndDialog**, because this latter

Figure 14.19 *A File-Open dialog box*

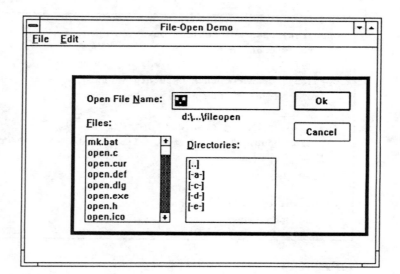

routine performs some special termination processing that only makes sense for a modal dialog box.

This modeless dialog box has shown how two dialog box controls can be interconnected: The push button is grayed when the edit control is empty, and enabled when the edit control has character information. As you build dialog boxes that are more and more complex, you'll see that this is quite typical for dialog boxes. The next programming example that we're going to look at will provide several examples of this type of interconnected dialog box controls.

A File Open Dialog Box

Any program that reads and writes files to disk will need to have a dialog box to allow the user to select the file to be opened. This is such a standard that perhaps someday Microsoft will include a standard file-open dialog box as part of the Windows libraries. Until then, here is a program that shows you how to implement a complete, robust file-open dialog box.

Figure 14.19 shows the standard file-open dialog box that our program creates, and here is the source code:

OPEN.MAK

```
Open.res: Open.rc Open.cur Open.ico Open.dlg
    rc -r Open.rc

Open.obj: Open.c Open.h Open.dlg Opendlg.h
    cl -AM -c -d -Gsw -Ow -W2 -Zpi Open.c

Open.exe: Open.obj Open.def
    link Open,/align:16,/map, mlibcew libw/NOD/NOE/CO,\
        Open.def
    rc Open.res

Open.exe: Open.res
    rc Open.res
```

OPEN.C

```c
/*------------------------------------------------------------*\
|   Open.C  Sample Open-File dialog box.                       |
\*------------------------------------------------------------*/
#include <Windows.H>
#include "Open.h"
#include "Opendlg.h"


/*------------------------------------------------------------*\
|                   Function Prototypes.                       |
\*------------------------------------------------------------*/
long FAR  PASCAL OpenWndProc (HWND, WORD, WORD, LONG);
BOOL FAR  PASCAL OpenDlgProc (HWND, WORD, WORD, LONG);


/*------------------------------------------------------------*\
|                      Static Data.                            |
\*------------------------------------------------------------*/
char    achOpenFile[MAXFILENAMELEN];
char    achInvalid[] = "File name or path is invalid.";


FARPROC lpitOpenDlgProc;
HANDLE  hInst;
```

```
/*-------------------------------------------------------------*\
 |                  Main Function:  WinMain.                    |
 \*-------------------------------------------------------------*/
int PASCAL WinMain (HANDLE hInstance,   HANDLE hPrevInstance,
                    LPSTR lpszCmdLine, int    cmdShow)
    {
    HWND      hwnd;
    MSG       msg;
    WNDCLASS wndclass;

    if (!hPrevInstance)
        {
        wndclass.lpszClassName = "Open:MAIN";
        wndclass.hInstance     = hInstance;
        wndclass.lpfnWndProc   = OpenWndProc;
        wndclass.hCursor       = LoadCursor (hInstance, "hand");
        wndclass.hIcon         = LoadIcon (hInstance,"snapshot");
        wndclass.lpszMenuName  = "#1";
        wndclass.hbrBackground = COLOR_WINDOW+1;
        wndclass.style         = NULL;
        wndclass.cbClsExtra    = 0;
        wndclass.cbWndExtra    = 0;

        RegisterClass( &wndclass);
        }

    hInst = hInstance;

    hwnd = CreateWindow("Open:MAIN",            /* Class name.  */
                        "File-Open Demo",       /* Title.       */
                        WS_OVERLAPPEDWINDOW,    /* Style bits.  */
                        CW_USEDEFAULT,          /* x - default. */
                        0,                      /* y - default. */
                        CW_USEDEFAULT,          /* cx - default. */
                        0,                      /* cy - default. */
                        NULL,                   /* No parent.   */
                        NULL,                   /* Class menu.  */
                        hInstance,              /* Creator.     */
                        NULL);                  /* Params.      */
```

```
        ShowWindow (hwnd, cmdShow);

        lpitOpenDlgProc = MakeProcInstance (OpenDlgProc, hInst);

        while (GetMessage(&msg, 0, 0, 0))
            {
            TranslateMessage(&msg);          /*  Keyboard input.        */
            DispatchMessage(&msg);
            }
        return 0;
        }


/*-------------------------------------------------------------------*\
  |                  Window Procedure:  OpenWndProc.                | 
\*-------------------------------------------------------------------*/
long FAR PASCAL OpenWndProc (HWND hwnd,    WORD wMsg,
                             WORD wParam, LONG lParam)

    {
    switch (wMsg)
        {
        case WM_COMMAND:
            switch (wParam)
                {
                case IDM_EXIT:
                    DestroyWindow (hwnd);
                    break;
                case IDM_OPEN:
                    DialogBox (hInst,
                               MAKEINTRESOURCE(IDD_OPEN),
                               hwnd,
                               lpitOpenDlgProc);

                    break;
                default:
                    MessageBox (hwnd,
                                "Feature not implemented",
                                "Open",
                                MB_OK);
                }
            break;
```

```
        case WM_DESTROY:
            PostQuitMessage(0);
            break;

        default:
            return(DefWindowProc(hwnd,wMsg,wParam,lParam));
            break;
        }
    return 0L;
    }


/*------------------------------------------------------------------*\
|               Dialog Box Procedure:  OpenDlgProc                   |
\*------------------------------------------------------------------*/
BOOL FAR PASCAL OpenDlgProc (HWND hdlg,    WORD wMsg,
                             WORD wParam, LONG lParam)
    {
    static char achWild[MAXFILENAMELEN];

    switch (wMsg)
        {
        case WM_INITDIALOG:
            {
            HWND hCtl;

            /*  Initialize directory listing.              */
            lstrcpy (achWild, "*.*");
            DlgDirList (hdlg,
                        achWild,
                        IDD_DIRLIST,
                        IDD_CURDIR,
                        0xC010);

            /*  Initialize file listing.                   */
            DlgDirList (hdlg,
                        achWild,
                        IDD_FILELIST,
                        IDD_CURDIR,
                        0);
```

```
                        /*  Limit text length in edit control.            */
                        hCtl = GetDlgItem (hdlg, IDD_NAME);
                        SendMessage (hCtl,
                                    EM_LIMITTEXT,
                                    MAXFILENAMELEN,
                                    0);

                        /*  Put wild card into edit control.              */
                        SendMessage (hCtl,
                                    WM_SETTEXT,
                                    0,
                                    (LONG)(LPSTR)achWild);

                        /*  Select text in edit control.                  */
                        SendMessage (hCtl,
                                    EM_SETSEL,
                                    0,
                                    MAKELONG (0, MAXFILENAMELEN));
                        }
                        return TRUE;
                        break;

                case WM_COMMAND:
                    {
                    BOOL      bWild;
                    char      achBuff[MAXFILENAMELEN];
                    HWND      hCtl;
                    int       cc;
                    int       iFile;
                    int       iRet;
                    OFSTRUCT  of;
                    PSTR      p;
                    WORD      wNotify;

                    wNotify = HIWORD (lParam);
                    hCtl    = LOWORD (lParam);

                    switch (wParam)
                        {
                        case IDD_OK:
```

```
                         /*   Read file name from edit control.      */
DoOK:                    hCtl = GetDlgItem (hdlg, IDD_NAME);
                         SendMessage (hCtl,
                                        WM_GETTEXT,
                                        MAXFILENAMELEN,
                                        (LONG)(LPSTR)achBuff);

                         /*  Trim leading blanks from file name.    */
                         p = achBuff;
                         while (*p == ' ')
                             p++;
                         if (p != achBuff)
                             lstrcpy (achBuff, p);

                         /*  Trim trailing blanks from file name.   */
                         cc = lstrlen (achBuff);
                         for (p = achBuff + cc - 1; *p == ' '; p--)
                             *p = 0;

                         /*  Check for wild cards.                   */
                         bWild = FALSE;

                         for (p = achBuff;*p != NULL; p++)
                             {
                             if (*p == '?' || *p == '*')
                                {
                                bWild = TRUE;
                                break;
                                }
                             }

                         /*  If no wild cards, try to open it.       */
                         if (!bWild)
                             {
                             /* Is it a valid file name?             */
                             iFile = OpenFile (achBuff,
                                               &of,
                                               OF_EXIST);

                             /*  If so, then we are done.            */
                             if (iFile != -1)
```

```
                    {
                    lstrcpy (achOpenFile, achBuff);
                    EndDialog (hdlg, TRUE);
                    break;
                    }
             else   /*  If not, add wild card        */
                    /*  and continue.                */
                    {
                    p--;
                    if (*p != '\\' && *p != '/')
                        lstrcat (achBuff, "\\");
                    lstrcat (achBuff, achWild);
                    }
             }


    /*  Rebuild list boxes.                          */
    iRet = DlgDirList (hdlg,
                       achBuff,
                       IDD_DIRLIST,
                       IDD_CURDIR,
                       0xC010);

    /*  Did DlgDirList report an error?              */
    if (!iRet)
       {
       MessageBox (hdlg,
                   achInvalid,
                   "Open-File",
                   MB_OK);
       }
    else
       {
       /*  Initialize file list box.                 */
       DlgDirList (hdlg,
                   achBuff,
                   IDD_FILELIST,
                   IDD_CURDIR,
                   0);

       /*  Make local copy of wild card.             */
```

```
                    lstrcpy (achWild, achBuff);

                    /*  Put wild card into edit control.   */
                    hCtl = GetDlgItem (hdlg, IDD_NAME);
                    SendMessage (hCtl,
                                 WM_SETTEXT,
                                 0,
                                 (LONG)(LPSTR)achWild);
                    }

                /*  Select text in edit control.         */
                SendMessage (hCtl,
                             EM_SETSEL,
                             0,
                             MAKELONG (0, MAXFILENAMELEN));

                /*  Give keyboard to edit control.       */
                SetFocus (hCtl);
                break;

        case IDD_CANCEL:
            EndDialog (hdlg, FALSE);
            break;

        case IDD_NAME:
            if (wNotify == EN_CHANGE)
                {
                /*  Enable or disable push button      */
                /*  based on whether edit control is   */
                /*  empty or not.                      */
                cc = (int)SendMessage (hCtl,
                                       WM_GETTEXTLENGTH,
                                       0, 0L);
                hCtl = GetDlgItem (hdlg, IDD_OK);
                EnableWindow (hCtl, cc);
                }
            break;

        case IDD_FILELIST:
            if (wNotify == LBN_SELCHANGE)
                {
```

```
                    DlgDirSelect (hdlg,
                                  achBuff,
                                  IDD_FILELIST);

                    hCtl = GetDlgItem (hdlg, IDD_NAME);
                    SendMessage (hCtl,
                                 WM_SETTEXT,
                                 0,
                                 (LONG)(LPSTR)achBuff);

                    }

              if (wNotify == LBN_DBLCLK)
                  goto DoOK;
              break;

          case IDD_DIRLIST:
              if (wNotify == LBN_SELCHANGE)
                  {
                  DlgDirSelect (hdlg,
                                achBuff,
                                IDD_DIRLIST);

                  hCtl = GetDlgItem (hdlg, IDD_NAME);
                  lstrcat (achBuff, achWild);
                  SendMessage (hCtl,
                               WM_SETTEXT,
                               0,
                               (LONG)(LPSTR)achBuff);

                  }

              if (wNotify == LBN_DBLCLK)
                  {
                  DlgDirSelect (hdlg,
                                achBuff,
                                IDD_DIRLIST);
                  DlgDirList (hdlg,
                              achBuff,
                              IDD_DIRLIST,
                              IDD_CURDIR,
                              0xC010);
```

```
                              /*  Initialize file listing.          */
                              DlgDirList (hdlg,
                                          achWild,
                                          IDD_FILELIST,
                                          IDD_CURDIR,
                                          0);

                              /*  Put wild card into edit control.   */
                              hCtl = GetDlgItem (hdlg, IDD_NAME);
                              SendMessage (hCtl,
                                          WM_SETTEXT,
                                          0,
                                          (LONG)(LPSTR)achWild);

                              /*  Select all text in edit control.   */
                              SendMessage (hCtl,
                                          EM_SETSEL,
                                          0,
                                          MAKELONG (0, MAXFILENAMELEN));

                              /*  Give keyboard to edit control.     */
                              SetFocus (hCtl);
                              }
                          return TRUE;
                          break;
                  }
              }
          return TRUE;
      default:
          return FALSE;
      }
  }
```

OPEN.H

```
/*-------------------------------------------------------------------*\
|   Open.h  - Include file for Open.c.                                |
\*-------------------------------------------------------------------*/
```

```
#define IDM_NEW       1
#define IDM_OPEN      2
#define IDM_SAVE      3
#define IDM_SAVEAS    4
#define IDM_PRINT     5
#define IDM_EXIT      6

#define IDM_UNDO      7
#define IDM_CUT       8
#define IDM_COPY      9
#define IDM_PASTE     10
#define IDM_CLEAR     11
#define IDM_DELETE    12


#define MAXFILENAMELEN 80
```

OPENDLG.H

```
#define IDD_OK        1
#define IDD_CANCEL    2
#define IDD_OPEN      11
#define IDD_CURDIR    201
#define IDD_DIRLIST   202
#define IDD_FILELIST  200
#define IDD_NAME      203
```

OPEN.RC

```
#include <Windows.h>
#include "Open.h"
#include "opendlg.h"

snapshot icon Open.ico

hand   cursor Open.cur
```

```
#include "open.dlg"

1 MENU
    {
    POPUP "&File"
        {
        MENUITEM "&New",          IDM_NEW
        MENUITEM "&Open...",      IDM_OPEN
        MENUITEM "&Save",         IDM_SAVE
        MENUITEM "Save &As...",   IDM_SAVEAS
        MENUITEM SEPARATOR
        MENUITEM "&Print",        IDM_PRINT
        MENUITEM SEPARATOR
        MENUITEM "E&xit",         IDM_EXIT
        }
    POPUP "&Edit"
        {
        MENUITEM "&Undo\tAlt+Backspace", IDM_UNDO
        MENUITEM SEPARATOR
        MENUITEM "Cu&t\tShift+Del",      IDM_CUT
        MENUITEM "&Copy\tCtrl+Ins",      IDM_COPY
        MENUITEM "&Paste\tShift+Ins",    IDM_PASTE
        MENUITEM SEPARATOR
        MENUITEM "Cl&ear",               IDM_CLEAR
        MENUITEM "&Delete",              IDM_DELETE
        }
    }
```

OPEN.DLG

```
IDD_OPEN DIALOG
        LOADONCALL MOVEABLE DISCARDABLE
        36, 24, 207, 114
STYLE WS_DLGFRAME | WS_POPUP
BEGIN
    CONTROL "Open File &Name:", -1, "static",
            SS_LEFT | WS_CHILD, 8, 11, 60, 8
    CONTROL "&Files:", -1, "static",
```

```
                    SS_LEFT | WS_CHILD, 8, 29, 22, 8
    CONTROL "&Directories:", -1, "static",
            SS_LEFT | WS_CHILD, 80, 45, 41, 8
    CONTROL "", IDD_CURDIR, "static",
            SS_LEFT | WS_CHILD, 76, 24, 76, 8
    CONTROL "", IDD_NAME, "edit", ES_OEMCONVERT |
            ES_LEFT | WS_BORDER | WS_TABSTOP | WS_CHILD,
            69, 10, 77, 13
    CONTROL "", IDD_FILELIST, "listbox",
            LBS_NOTIFY | LBS_SORT | LBS_STANDARD |
            WS_TABSTOP | WS_BORDER | WS_VSCROLL | WS_CHILD,
            8, 43, 60, 65
    CONTROL "", IDD_DIRLIST, "listbox",
            LBS_NOTIFY | LBS_SORT | LBS_STANDARD |
            WS_TABSTOP | WS_BORDER | WS_VSCROLL | WS_CHILD,
            80, 59, 63, 49
    CONTROL "Ok", IDD_OK, "button",
            BS_DEFPUSHBUTTON | WS_TABSTOP | WS_CHILD,
            156, 9, 40, 14
    CONTROL "Cancel", IDD_CANCEL, "button",
            BS_PUSHBUTTON | WS_TABSTOP | WS_CHILD,
            156, 32, 40, 14
END
```

OPEN.DEF

```
NAME    OPEN

EXETYPE WINDOWS

DESCRIPTION 'File-Open Dialog Box Demo'

CODE    MOVEABLE DISCARDABLE
DATA    MOVEABLE MULTIPLE

HEAPSIZE    512
STACKSIZE   5000

EXPORTS
    OpenWndProc
    OpenDlgProc
```

The dialog box editor provides the best way to define a dialog box template since it allows you to visually arrange the layout of dialog box controls. It's often a good idea, however, to inspect the dialog box template that has been created, to make sure that the style flags are what you expect. For example, the dialog box editor includes the LBS_WANTKEYBOARDINPUT style when you create a listbox. However, this prevents the user from using the keyboard interface with a listbox. Therefore, you'll probably want to remove this style bit (or, from inside the dialog box editor, review the style bits in the listbox customizing dialog box and turn off the check box marked "Keyboard Input").

Another style bit that you'll want to pay attention to that is necessary for the keyboard interface to a dialog box is the WS_TABSTOP style bit. When incorporated into the definition of a dialog box control, this style causes the dialog control to serve as a "bus-stop" when the user is striking the Tab key to browse through a dialog box.

The tabbing order of a dialog box is determined by the order in which controls are listed in the dialog box template. This is another reason to review the order that the dialog box editor created. It's a simple matter to cut and paste the dialog box template until you have defined a tabbing order that is right.

The creation of our open file dialog box starts with the creation of an instance thunk:

```
lpitOpenDlgProc = MakeProcInstance (OpenDlgProc, hInst);
```

As with the other dialog box examples in this chapter, this instance thunk is created during OPEN's initialization in the WinMain function. The dialog box itself is created when the user selects the Open... item on the File menu. This triggers the call to **DialogBox** that actually creates the dialog:

```
case IDM_OPEN:
    DialogBox (hInst,
              MAKEINTRESOURCE(IDD_OPEN),
              hwnd,
              lpitOpenDlgProc);
```

This creates a modal dialog box, using the OpenDlgProc routine in our program as the dialog box procedure. The dialog box procedure is a very long one, primarily because we need to handle all the different cases that arise when the user wants to change directories, change the wild card that selects the set of files to display, and perform necessary error checking. Much of the work of the dialog box procedure is performed by the **DlgDirList** routine, which is defined:

```
int DlgDirList (hDlg, lpPath, nIDList, nIDStatic, wType)
```

- hDlg is a handle to the dialog box.
- lpPath is a long pointer to a character string for a directory path. It can consist of any portion of a fully qualified file path, including disk drive, directories, and wild card values.
- nIDList is the identifier of the listbox control that is to be filled with the files that match the file specification.
- nIDStatic is the identifier of a static text control to be used to display the current directory.
- wType holds flags that are used to determine the files to include in the listbox. It can be any combination of values ORed together from the following table:

Attribute Value	Description
0x0000	Read/write files with no other attributes.
0x0001	Files marked "read-only".
0x0002	Hidden files.
0x0004	System files.
0x0010	Subdirectories.
0x0020	Files that have the "archive" bit set.
0x4000	Drive letters.
0x8000	Exclude normal read/write files.

An additional attribute value requests that messages be transmitted as pull-model messages instead of push-model messages. That is, that the **PostMessage** routine be used instead of **SendMessage** to transmit the messages to the list box and the static control. This makes it easier for a program to intercept and manipulate the messages that are sent to these two controls:

Attribute Value	Description
0x2000	Transmit messages using **PostMessage** instead of **SendMessage**.

One of the truly convenient features of this routine is that it parses the path that it receives. This means that, as you can see from our dialog box routine, you only need to do a minimum amount of parsing. **DlgDirList** communicates with DOS to change the current disk drive, change the current directory, and display only the files that match the wild card specification. It even strips the disk and directory information from the path information, so that separating the wild card values from these other parts of the path is quite simple.

Whenever the user clicks in either of the two listboxes, this causes the file or directory name to be copied to the edit control. A filename is copied by itself, although a directory name will always have the wild card specification appended to the end of it. Checking for a mouse click involves watching for a WM_COMMAND message with an LBN_SELCHANGE notification code. Here, for example, is how a click in the file listbox is handled:

```
case IDD_FILELIST:
    if (wNotify == LBN_SELCHANGE)
        {
        DlgDirSelect (hdlg,
                      achBuff,
                      IDD_FILELIST);

        hCtl = GetDlgItem (hdlg, IDD_NAME);
        SendMessage (hCtl,
                     WM_SETTEXT,
                     0,
                     (LONG) (LPSTR) achBuff);
        }
```

DlgDirSelect conveniently reads the contents of a listbox. This code gets a handle to the edit control by calling **GetDlgItem**, and sends a WM_SETTEXT message to put the filename into the edit control.

Placing the filename into the edit control sets the stage for the handling of a double-click message. When the mouse double-clicks in a listbox, the second click has the effect of clicking on the Ok push button. This is why, in response to the LBN_DLBCLK notification from the files listbox, our dialog box procedure does very little except cause a jump to occur to the part of the dialog box procedure that handles a click on the Ok push button:

```
if (wNotify == LBN_DBLCLK)
    goto DoOK;
```

Responding to the Ok push button is the most complex part of the open file dialog box. The reason is not that it is so hard to select a file, but the dialog box procedure must be prepared to handle error checking and also to allow the user to change the current disk, the current directory, and the wild card file specification. The first thing that our dialog box procedure does when the Ok button is pushed is to read the file name from the edit control:

```
case IDD_OK:

        /*  Read file name from edit control.      */
DoOK:               hCtl = GetDlgItem (hdlg, IDD_NAME);
    SendMessage (hCtl,
            WM_GETTEXT,
            MAXFILENAMELEN,
            (LONG) (LPSTR) achBuff);
```

Our dialog box procedure is very forgiving if the user entered leading or trailing blanks, as these are simply trimmed:

```
/*  Trim leading blanks from file name.    */
p = achBuff;
while (*p == ' ')
    p++;
if (p != achBuff)
    lstrcpy (achBuff, p);

/*  Trim trailing blanks from file name.    */
cc = lstrlen (achBuff);
for (p = achBuff + cc - 1; *p == ' '; p--)
    *p = 0;
```

A quick check is done for wild cards, by scanning the string for either the "?" or the "*" character. If one is not found, then we assume that the user has entered a valid filename. If this is the case, we try to open the file to test for its existence. If the file can be opened, then **EndDialog** is called to terminate the dialog box, as our work is over. But if the file cannot be opened, then our dialog box procedure assumes that the user has entered the name of a directory instead of the name of a file.

```
/*  Check for wild cards.                    */
bWild = FALSE;
for (p = achBuff;*p != NULL; p++)
    {
    if (*p == '?' || *p == '*')
        {
        bWild = TRUE;
        break;
        }
    }

/*  If no wild cards, try to open it.        */
if (!bWild)
    {
    /* Is it a valid file name?               */
    iFile = OpenFile (achBuff,
                      &of,
                      OF_EXIST);

    /*  If so, then we are done.              */
    if (iFile != -1)
        {
        lstrcpy (achOpenFile, achBuff);
        EndDialog (hdlg, TRUE);
        break;
        }
    else  /*  If not, add wild card           */
          /*  and continue.                   */
        {
        p--;
        if (*p != '\\' && *p != '/')
            lstrcat (achBuff, "\\");
        lstrcat (achBuff, achWild);
        }
    }
```

Since we assume that the user has entered the name of a directory, we rebuild both dialog boxes by calling **DlgDirList** twice: once for the file listbox and once for the directories listbox. We start by setting up the directories listbox:

```
/*  Rebuild list boxes.                      */
iRet = DlgDirList (hdlg,
```

```
                              achBuff,
                              IDD_DIRLIST,
                              IDD_CURDIR,
                              0xC010);
```

If **DlgDirList** doesn't like what it finds, then we can assume that the user has entered an incorrect file specification. Perhaps a nonexistent disk drive was referenced. Or maybe a nonexistent directory name was entered. It might even be that that the wild card specification was somehow incorrect. Whatever the cause, a message box is displayed if **DlgDirList** didn't like what it saw. Otherwise, the reinitialization of the file listbox and the edit control is identical to what was done in response to the WM_INITIDIALOG message:

```
/*  Did DlgDirList report an error?         */
if (!iRet)
    {
    MessageBox (hdlg,
                achInvalid,
                "Open-File",
                MB_OK);
    }
else
    {
    /*  Initialize file list box.            */
    DlgDirList (hdlg,
                achBuff,
                IDD_FILELIST,
                IDD_CURDIR,
                0);

    /*  Make local copy of wild card.        */
    lstrcpy (achWild, achBuff);

    /*  Put wild card into edit control.     */
    hCtl = GetDlgItem (hdlg, IDD_NAME);
    SendMessage (hCtl,
                WM_SETTEXT,
                0,
                (LONG)(LPSTR)achWild);
    }
```

Whether or not there was an error, our dialog box procedure always leaves the keyboard focus in the edit control and makes sure that the characters in the edit control are selected. This makes it quite simple for the user to overwrite any unwanted values in the list box.

```
/*  Select text in edit control.           */
SendMessage (hCtl,
         EM_SETSEL,
         0,
         MAKELONG (0, MAXFILENAMELEN));

/*  Give keyboard to edit control.          */
SetFocus (hCtl);
break;
```

If you take a close look at our open file dialog box procedure, you'll notice that there is some room for improvement. In particular, we have not put any code into subroutines since this has the effect of making the code a little harder to read. However, if you want to make the code smaller, it should be a simple matter to reorganize the code into two or more smaller subroutines.

Another improvement that could be made to this routine has to do with the way that the **OpenFile** routine works. Our program calls on this routine to check for the existence of a file. However, when this routine is called, it is provided just the name of the file that was entered in the edit control. The problem is that **OpenFile** will search through several directories if the file is not found in the current directory. While this may seem a minor point, it can slow down the check for a file, particularly if there are network directories in your search path. In spite of these two shortcomings, this open file dialog box should be complete enough and robust enough to be used in your applications.

Part 5

Message Driven Input

15
Keyboard Input

In earlier chapters, we looked at the way a Windows program creates graphic output. The facilities available for graphics output can be considered quite high-level: Sophisticated drawing can be accomplished with a minimum of effort. In particular, this is the case if you consider how much code would be required to accomplish the same results without the help of GDI.

In this chapter and the one that follows, we're going to look at the way that Windows handles *input*. In contrast to GDI's high-level output, the form in which input arrives can be regarded as very low-level. That is, keyboard input arrives in the form of individual keystroke messages, with two or three messages generated per key typed. And the actions of the mouse are reported as a stream of messages that give a blow by blow account of the actions of this pointing device.

This chapter discusses keyboard input, leaving the next chapter to describe mouse input.

How a Windows Program Receives Keyboard Input

Figure 15.1 shows all the pieces that play a role in handling keyboard input. The black lines represent data flow.

We'll start our study of keyboard input by tracing the flow of data from the keyboard, through the various software layers into a typical Windows program. Every Windows program has a GetMessage loop which is responsible for pulling all keyboard messages into a program. But as you'll see, that's only half the story; once raw keyboard data arrives in a Windows program, a special Windows library routine must be called to cook the data to create truly useful character input. You've seen this routine before, since it is a standard part of every GetMessage loop: TranslateMessage. While Windows provides an abundant set of messages to describe keyboard activity, you will

Figure 15.1 *The flow of keyboard data*

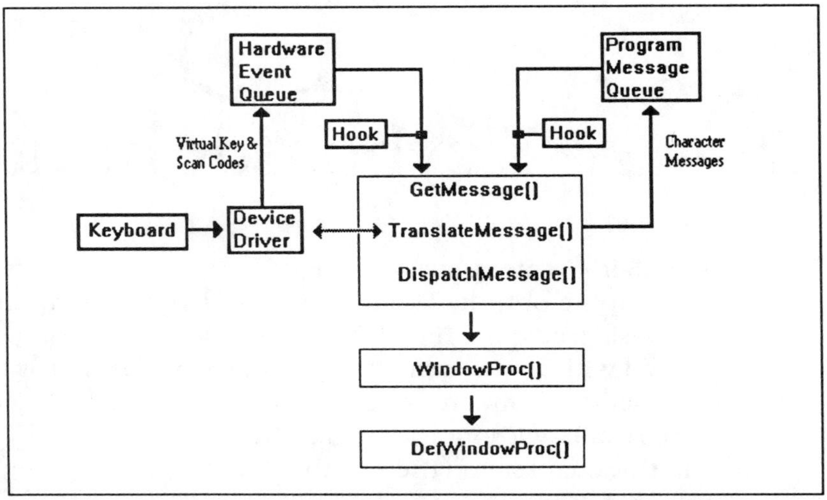

find that you can concentrate your efforts on a subset of these messages, which we'll describe as we follow the path of the wily keyboard messages. Keyboard input starts in the hardware of the keyboard, so that's where we'll begin.

The Keyboard

Windows runs on IBM-compatible personal computers, and so the range of keyboards you're likely to encounter is small. Nonetheless, since IBM introduced its first PC in 1981, the keyboard has changed. The first IBM PC had an 83-key keyboard. IBM introduced a new keyboard with its PC/AT, which moved a few keys around and added the SysReq key, for a total of 84 keys. With its current line of PS/2 computers, IBM has adopted yet another keyboard, the Enhanced 101/102-key keyboard. This keyboard added two function keys, but most of the new keys were simply duplicates of keys already on the keyboard. With some minor variations, makers of IBM compatible computers have adapted the same keyboard layout as IBM machines.

Although successive keyboards have moved a key here and added a key there, the basic operation of all keyboards has stayed the same. Every time you press or release a key, the keyboard hardware generates a one- or two-byte **scan code** that uniquely identifies the key. Every key produces two different scan codes, depending on whether the key is pressed or released. When you press a key, the value of the scan code is between 01H and 58H (for IBM-compatible keyboards). When you release the key, the value of the scan code is 80H higher. For example, when you press the letter Z, the keyboard generates a scan code of 2CH. When it is released, the keyboard generates a scan code of ACH (2CH + 80H).

From the keyboard's point of view, the two scan codes are the only meaningful information associated with a given key. The meaning of the scan code is interpreted by the software that receives the keyboard input. In our case, that means the Windows keyboard device driver. Consider the two scan codes from the previous example: 2CH and ACH. When the keyboard driver is told that a U.S. English keyboard is present, these codes are interpreted as the letter Z. But the same scan codes will be interpreted as the letter W if the keyboard driver is told that a French keyboard is present. From this example, you can see how international support is provided: The keyboard driver simply needs the correct scan-code to virtual key code and virtual key code to ASCII translation tables.

As keys are pressed and released, scan codes are sent via the keyboard cable to control circuitry on the system board of the computer. When the control circuitry senses that keyboard input is available, it generates a hardware interrupt 09H. When DOS is present, this interrupt results in a call to the ROM BIOS keyboard handler. But when Windows is present, another mechanism is put into place which meets the special requirements that Windows has for handling keyboard input. That mechanism is part of the Windows keyboard device driver, which we'll look at next.

The Windows Keyboard Device Driver

During Windows start up, the Windows keyboard driver installs an interrupt handler to receive keyboard scan codes. The interrupt handler is called any time a key is pressed or released. It reads scan values from the keyboard port and maps these onto a set of **virtual key** values that make up the **Windows virtual keyboard**.

The virtual keyboard defines a standard set of keys for all keyboards currently on the market. It also defines keys that don't correspond to any current keyboard, to allow room for growth. Table 15.1 lists all of the keys in the virtual keyboard, along with the symbolic names as defined in Windows.h.

Table 15.1   *The Windows virtual keys*

(hex)	(dec)	Symbolic Name	Key Pressed (US English 101/102 Kbd)
1	1	VK_LBUTTON	
2	2	VK_RBUTTON	
3	3	VK_CANCEL	Ctrl-Break
4	4	VK_MBUTTON	
8	8	VK_BACK	Backspace
9	9	VK_TAB	Tab
C	12	VK_CLEAR	5 on Numeric keypad w/Num Lock OFF
D	13	VK_RETURN	Enter
10	16	VK_SHIFT	Shift
11	17	VK_CONTROL	Ctrl
12	18	VK_MENU	Alt
13	19	VK_PAUSE	Pause (or Ctrl-Num Lock)
14	20	VK_CAPITAL	Caps Lock
1B	27	VK_ESCAPE	Esc
20	32	VK_SPACE	Spacebar
21	33	VK_PRIOR	Page Up
22	34	VK_NEXT	Page Down
23	35	VK_END	End
24	36	VK_HOME	Home
25	37	VK_LEFT	
26	38	VK_UP	Up Arrow
27	39	VK_RIGHT	Right Arrow
28	40	VK_DOWN	Down Arrow
29	41	VK_SELECT	<unused>
2A	42	VK_PRINT	<unused>
2B	43	VK_EXECUTE	<unused>
2C	44	VK_SNAPSHOT	Print Screen
2D	45	VK_INSERT	Ins
2E	46	VK_DELETE	Del
2F	47	VK_HELP	<unused>
30-39	48-57	VK_0 to VK_9	0 to 9 above letter keys
41-5A	65-90	VK_A to VK_Z	A to Z

(Continued)

Table 15.1 *Continued*

(hex)	(dec)	Symbolic Name	Key Pressed (US English 101/102 Kbd)
60	96	VK_NUMPAD0	0 on Numeric keypad w/Num Lock ON
61	97	VK_NUMPAD1	1 on Numeric keypad w/Num Lock ON
62	98	VK_NUMPAD2	2 on Numeric keypad w/Num Lock ON
63	99	VK_NUMPAD3	3 on Numeric keypad w/Num Lock ON
64	100	VK_NUMPAD4	4 on Numeric keypad w/Num Lock ON
65	101	VK_NUMPAD5	5 on Numeric keypad w/Num Lock ON
66	102	VK_NUMPAD6	6 on Numeric keypad w/Num Lock ON
67	103	VK_NUMPAD7	7 on Numeric keypad w/Num Lock ON
68	104	VK_NUMPAD8	8 on Numeric keypad w/Num Lock ON
69	105	VK_NUMPAD9	9 on Numeric keypad w/Num Lock ON
6A	106	VK_MULTIPLY	* on Numeric keypad
6B	107	VK_ADD	+ on Numeric keypad
6C	108	VK_SEPARATOR	<unused>
6D	109	VK_SUBTRACT	- on Numeric keypad
6E	110	VK_DECIMAL	. on Numeric keypad w/Num Lock ON
6F	111	VK_DIVIDE	/ on Numeric keypad
70	112	VK_F1	F1 function key
71	113	VK_F2	F2 function key
72	114	VK_F3	F3 function key
73	115	VK_F4	F4 function key
74	116	VK_F5	F5 function key
75	117	VK_F6	F6 function key
76	118	VK_F7	F7 function key
77	119	VK_F8	F8 function key

(Continued)

Table 15.1   *Continued*

(hex)	(dec)	Symbolic Name	Key Pressed (US English 101/102 Kbd)
78	120	VK_F9	F9 function key
79	121	VK_F10	F10 function key
7A	122	VK_F11	F11 function key
7B	123	VK_F12	F12 function key
7C	124	VK_F13	
7D	125	VK_F14	
7E	126	VK_F15	
7F	127	VK_F16	
90	144	VK_NUMLOCK	Num Lock
91	145		Scroll Lock

The following code apply to US keyboards only

BA	186		colon/semicolon
BB	187		plus/equal
BC	188		less than/comma
BD	189		underscore/hyphen
BE	190		greater than/period
BF	191		question/slash
C0	192		tilde/back accent
DB	219		left squiggle brace/left square brace
DC	220		horizontal bar/backslash
DD	221		right squiggle brace/right square brace
DE	222		double quote/single quote

Once the keyboard driver has translated the scan code information into a virtual key code, it calls Windows. Windows puts both scan code and virtual key data into a special buffer called the **hardware event queue**. We briefly discussed the role of this buffer in Chapter 4, when we talked about the message loop. Let's return to this topic to see how it affects keyboard input.

The Hardware Event Queue

From the point of view of keyboard input, the hardware event queue is simply a type-ahead buffer. It can hold up to 120 hardware events, which means 60 characters worth of data since two events are generated when a keyboard key is pressed and released. Even for the fastest typists, this should be enough to prevent data loss.

A type-ahead buffer is necessary because of the way that a Windows program retrieves keyboard input. As you may recall from an earlier discussion, Windows' multitasking is nonpreemptive. That is, the operating system does not interrupt one program to allow another to run. Instead, programs interrupt themselves. This polite form of multitasking works because it is built into Windows' message delivery mechanism. All input to a program, including keyboard input, is delivered in the form of messages. Since Windows does not interrupt programs to deliver keyboard information, the data has to be stored someplace: That place is the hardware event queue. Otherwise, a fast typist might outpace a program's ability to retrieve keyboard input.

The contents of the hardware event queue are eventually delivered to a windows program in the form of two messages: WM_KEY-DOWN and WM_KEYUP. These correspond to the two types of scan codes: key press and key release. As indicated by the diagram in Figure 15.1, a program gets these two messages from the hardware event queue by calling GetMessage.

But the real meaning of keyboard messages comes from the values stored in one 2-byte integer value and one 4-byte integer value which make up the wParam and lParam parameters of a window procedure. The format of these two fields is the same for both messages.

wParam contains the virtual key code of the key that was pressed or released. The keyboard driver generates this value from the scan code that it received from the keyboard hardware. By far and away this is the most important field that Windows provides with these two messages. After all, the virtual key code represents how the keyboard driver views a keyboard event in the context of Windows taking into account the type of keyboard that is currently attached to the system.

The lParam parameter is divided into six fields, as shown in Figure 15.2. Let's review these one at a time.

Repeat Count. Built into the hardware of the keyboard is the ability to automatically repeat a single character if a key is held down: a

Figure 15.2 *Six Fields of lParam for keystroke messages*

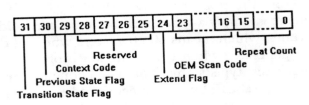

feature that IBM calls **typematic**. To prevent such keys from over-flowing the hardware event queue, Windows increments the repeat count when it finds that a new keyboard event is identical with the previous keyboard event that is still in the queue. In doing so, Windows combines several WM_KEYDOWN messages into a single message.

A repeat count greater than 1 means that keyboard events are occurring faster than your program is able to process them. In such cases, a program can interpret each WM_KEYDOWN message as multiple messages, depending on the repeat value.

OEM Scan Code. This field contains the scan code value as it was sent from the keyboard. For most programs, the virtual key code is more useful, since it represents a device-independent code for a key stroke. Because the scan code represents a hardware-dependent value, in most cases you'll want to avoid using this field. But sometimes it is necessary to use the scan code information to tell the difference, for example, between the left shift key and the right shift key. For certain keys, the keyboard driver uses the hardware scan code to translate the WM_KEYDOWN message into a WM_CHAR message. This is the case, for example, with keys in the numeric keypad.

Extend Flag. This field is actually an extension of the OEM Scan Code. In effect, it tells a program that the key that was pressed was one of the duplicate keys on IBM's extended keyboard. Like the Scan Code, the value of this field is device-dependent, and so great care should be taken when using it.

Context Code. This flag is 1 if the Alt key is down, otherwise it has a value of 0.

Previous Key State. This flag helps to identify messages generated by typematic action. It has a value of 1 if the previous state of the key was down, and a value of 0 if the previous state of the key was up.

Transition State. This flag is 1 if the key is being released and 0 if the key is being pressed. It will always be 1 for WM_KEYUP and 0 for the WM_KEYDOWN message.

From these messages, a program receives both the raw keyboard scan codes and the half-cooked virtual key codes. As you'll see shortly, the most useful keyboard data arrive as fully cooked character messages. But there are some keystrokes that are not available as character messages, since they do not represent characters but rather keyboard commands.

Table 15.2 shows a list of the keystrokes that can only be detected with the WM_KEYDOWN and WM_KEYUP messages. In a moment, we'll discuss the WM_CHAR message, which provides ASCII character information. The keys in this table do not produce ASCII characters, and so they do not generate WM_CHAR messages. Therefore, if you are interested in detecting key strokes generated by these keys, you'll watch for the WM_KEYDOWN message.

To detect one of these keys in a Windows program, you'll test the value of wParam against the virtual key values listed in Table 15.1. For example, here is code that checks for a key-down transition of the F1 function key:

```
WindowProc (HWND hwnd,  WORD msg,
            WORD wParam,LONG lParam)
{
    switch (msg)
        {
        case WM_KEYDOWN:
            if (wParam == VK_F1)
                /*  F1 Keydown. */
                .
                .
                .
        break;
```

For programming the function keys, it is often easier to define an Accelerator.

While it would involve a lot of work, it would be possible to receive all the keyboard input that you might require using WM_KEYDOWN and WM_KEYUP messages. Notice, however, that to tell the difference between a capital letter and a lower-case letter would require you to know the state of the shift key in addition to detecting the keystroke message. There's no reason to go to all that

Table 15.2 *Keystrokes only available with WM_KEYDOWN and WM_KEYUP*

Keystroke	Description
F1-F9, F11-F16	Function Keys. The F10 function key is reserved for Windows use as the Menu Select Hot Key.
Shift, Ctrl, Alt	Shift Keys. The Alt key is a reserved system key and does not generate WM_KEYDOWN or WM_KEYUP unless the Ctrl key is down. Normally, it only generates WM_SYSKEY-DOWN and WM_SYSKEYUP messages.
Caps Lock, Num Lock, and Scroll Lock	Toggle Keys.
Print Screen	Reserved key for copying screen to clipboard (Print Screen alone), or for copying the active window to the clipboard (Alt + Print Screen). Windows eats the WM_KEYDOWN message, leaving WM_KEYUP.
Pause	Pause key.
Insert, Delete, Home, End, Page Up, Page Down	Text editing keys. Although there are two of each of these keys on the 101/102 keyboard, each pair has only one virtual key code. However, they can be distinguished with the Extend flag.
Up, Left, Down, Right	Direction Keys. Although there are eight keys in this set, like the text editing keys the duplicate keys do not have a separate virtual key code. However, they can be distinguished with the Extend flag.

work, since Windows has a built-in facility that will do the work for you. The routine that provides this service is a standard part of every message loop: TranslateMessage.

The GetMessage Loop

The minimum standard message loop is as follows:

```
while (GetMessage (&msg, 0, 0, 0))
    {
    TranslateMessage (&msg);
```

```
DispatchMessage (&msg);
}
```

GetMessage reads messages from two places: the hardware event queue and from a program's private message queue. For every message it retrieves, a call is made to TranslateMessage, which ignores every message except two: WM_KEYDOWN and WM_SYS-KEYDOWN.

WM_SYSKEYDOWN is one of three **system keyboard messages**. The other two are WM_SYSKEYUP and WM_SYSCHAR. The behavior of these messages parallel the behavior of the three regular keyboard messages, but system keyboard messages are used primarily as part of the keyboard interface to menus. We'll look at another use of these messages when we discuss the window procedure in a short while.

The role of TranslateMessage is simple. It takes the virtual key data from the WM_KEYDOWN (or WM_SYSKEYDOWN) message and calls the keyboard device driver to convert the virtual key code into an ASCII code. For keys with no ASCII equivalent, no translation is done. For the rest, a WM_CHAR (or WM_SYSCHAR) message is generated and placed in the private message queue.

The sequence of messages that are created in response to hitting the "w" key, for example, are as follows:

Key	wParam Contains
WM_KEYDOWN	Virtual key W
WM_CHAR	ASCII code w
WM_KEYUP	Virtual key W

And when a capital letter is struck, the sequence of messages is even more involved. Here is the message traffic when the user types "W":

Key	wParam Contains
WM_KEYDOWN	Virtual key VK_SHIFT
WM_KEYDOWN	Virtual key W
WM_CHAR	ASCII code W
WM_KEYUP	Virtual key W
WM_KEYUP	Virtual key VK_SHIFT

On some non-English keyboards (French and German, to name two), special key combinations are used to create diacritical marks over vowels. For example, to type the words château (the French word for "castle" and München (the German name for the city of Munich) on a French keyboard, you need to use special key combinations because there is no dedicated â or ü key.

These special keys are called **dead-keys**, since they are not expected to produce characters, but modify the keystroke that follows. In response to a WM_KEYDOWN (or WM_SYSKEYDOWN) for such keys, TranslateMessage generates a WM_DEADCHAR (or WM_SYSDEADCHAR) message. You can safely ignore these messages, since Windows will create the correct character message from the keystrokes that follow.

If you'd like to experiment with dead-key processing, you can install a different keyboard translation table using the Control Panel. Bring up the International Settings dialog box and select the country whose keyboard layout you want to work with. If you bring up the French keyboard, you'll discover that the A and Q keys have been switched, as have the W and Z keys. The dead-key for the circumflex is located at the key marked "[," and the dead-key for the umlaut is shift-[.

The message sequence that is generated on a French keyboard to produce the letter â is as follows:

Key	wParam Contains
WM_KEYDOWN	Scan code for pressing circumflex key
WM_DEADCHAR	Dead Character message for circumflex key
WM_KEYUP	Scan code for releasing circumflex key
WM_KEYDOWN	Scan code for pressing 'a'
WM_CHAR	Character message for 'â'
WM_KEYUP	Scan code for releasing 'a'

With the exception of the keys listed in Table 15.2, keyboard input will normally come from the WM_CHAR messages that are created by TranslateMessage. The translation that takes place takes into account the state of the various shift keys, to provide upper- and lower-case letters, numbers, and punctuation marks. Since the ASCII character set includes a complete range of accented vowels, this mechanism also supports international keyboards.

After TranslateMessage generates the WM_CHAR (or WM_SYS-CHAR) message, it returns control to the message loop. The DispatchMessage routine then pushes the WM_KEYDOWN or WM_SYSKEYDOWN message to the window procedure for processing.

Since the character message is placed on the program's message queue, it does not become available to the program until Get-Message is called to read a new message. At that time, the WM_CHAR (or WM_SYSCHAR) message is read in, passed to TranslateMessage (which ignores it), and finally sent on to the window procedure by DispatchMessage. Although the key-down message causes the character message to be generated, by the time the window procedure sees the character message, the key-down message has already been processed.

The window procedure parameters for the WM_CHAR message are similar to those for the other keyboard messages we discussed earlier. That is, the lParam field in a character message contains the same six fields as the WM_KEYDOWN and WM_KEYUP messages.

The WM_CHAR message is different, however, in that the wParam parameter contains the ASCII code of the character whose key was pressed. It's the job of the window procedure to trap this message and read whatever character input is required.

To build bullet-proof processing for character input, you'll probably want to filter out some of the WM_CHAR messages which are created for keystrokes that aren't ordinarily printed. This includes the tab, backspace, and return keys. These, along with the others in the list in Table 15.2, will require special processing apart from the regular character messages.

Keystroke	ASCII Value (hex)	(dec)	Description
Ctrl-A to Ctrl-G	1–7	1–7	Nonprintable characters.
Backspace	8	8	Backspace key (VK_BACK).
Ctrl-H	8	8	Surrogate backspace key (VK_BACK).
Tab	9	9	Tab key (VK_TAB).
Ctrl-I	9	9	Surrogate Tab key (VK_TAB).
Ctrl-J	A	10	Linefeed.
Ctrl-K to Ctrl-L	B–C	11–12	Nonprintable characters.

(Continued)

Keystroke	ASCII Value (hex)	(dec)	Description
Return	D	13	Return key (VK_RETURN).
Ctrl-M	D	13	Surrogate return key (VK_RETURN).
Ctrl-N to Ctrl-Z	E–1A	15–26	Nonprintable characters.
Esc	1B	27	Escape key (VK_ESCAPE).

When an accelerator has been defined with a Ctrl + letter key combination, then no WM_CHAR is generated for that keystroke. We explored accelerators in Chapter 11.

The Window Procedure

We've traced the path that keyboard data takes on its way from the hardware to our program. Although some handling of keyboard input is done in the message loop, the bulk of processing is handled in the window procedure.

Table 15.3 summarizes all of the keyboard messages that we have encountered so far. You can safely ignore most of them, however, and concentrate your efforts on two messages: WM_CHAR for all character input, and WM_KEYDOWN for all non-character function key input. In the example program, KEYINPUT, these are the only messages we rely on to create a text-entry and editing window.

In certain situations, you may wish to process system keyboard messages as well. In particular, when the active window in the system is iconic, Windows substitutes the system keyboard messages (WM_SYSKEYDOWN, WM_SYSKEYUP, WM_SYSCHAR) in place of the regular keyboard messages. Since most programs are not interested in keyboard input when they are iconic, this convention helps avoid spurious input. If you *do* want to receive keyboard input in this situation, however, you'll need to pay attention to the system keyboard messages.

In general, however, you'll ignore system keyboard messages, which are primarily used by Windows for its own internal housekeeping purposes. Since some of this housekeeping is done in the default window procedure, you'll want to be sure that—like other unused messages—these messages get passed on.

Table 15.3   *A summary of keyboard messages*

WM_KEYDOWN	Key pressed
WM_CHAR	Character input
WM_DEADCHAR	Dead-character
WM_KEYUP	Key released
WM_SYSKEYDOWN	System key pressed
WM_SYSCHAR	System character input
WM_SYSDEADCHAR	System dead-character
WM_SYSKEYUP	System key released

The Default Window Procedure

All of the messages that a window procedure does not use should be passed on to the default window procedure. The default window procedure ignores all regular keyboard messages, so window procedures that don't use keyboard messages can safely pass them on.

But the default window procedure plays an important role in handling the system keyboard messages. System keyboard messages are usually generated in place of regular keyboard messages when the Alt key is down. In this way, system keyboard messages are used by the default window procedure to provide keyboard access to menus.

For example, when a window has a system menu icon, the system menu will appear when you strike the Alt + spacebar keys. When we discuss menus in Chapters 17 and 18, you'll see that you can define your own menu "hot-key" that will cause a pull-down menu to appear when the hot-key is hit with the Alt key. A menu hot-key is also called a **mnemonic**, since it is always a letter in the name of the menu. These keystrokes are handled as system keyboard messages.

The default window procedure also plays a role in making certain keyboard combinations operate correctly. For example, you can quit an application by typing Alt-F4, go to the Task List by pressing Ctrl-Esc, and switch the active program with Alt-Tab. For these system hot keys to work properly, the default window procedure must get all system keyboard messages.

In our look at the path taken by keyboard events, there is one item that we have overlooked: hooks. The subject of hooks is outside the scope of this book, but it is important for you to be aware of them because they can affect the path of keyboard input.

Hooks

A hook is a subroutine that is installed into Windows' message handling mechanism. Hooks allow you to monitor and trap certain types of messages. Figure 15.1 shows the relationship of hooks to the flow of keyboard data.

Windows has a total of seven different hooks, although we're going to limit our discussion to two of them: keyboard hooks and getmessage hooks. All hooks are installed on a systemwide basis. That is, if a program installs a hook, it affects every program running in the system.

The keyboard hook taps into the flow of keyboard messages coming out of the hardware event queue and provides a means of listening to all keyboard input in the system. Creating a keyboard hook in Windows is comparable to stealing the keyboard interrupt under DOS; it gives you complete control over the flow of keystroke messages (WM_KEYDOWN and WM_KEYUP) in the system.

One use of a keyboard hook is to watch for special "Hot Keys." For example, you might want to give a user the ability to call up your program at any time by simply typing the Alt-F12 key combination. You accomplish this by installing a keyboard hook when your program starts running. The hook lets all keyboard input pass, until it encounters the desired keystroke. At that time, it lets Windows know that it wants the key for itself, which causes the key to be ignored by the rest of the system. The hook then notifies the program (perhaps via a message) that the hot key has been struck. At that time, it is up to the program to respond in a way that makes sense. Perhaps that means opening a window to offer some service to the user.

The second type of hook that affects keyboard input is the getmessage hook. This hook is actually called by the GetMessage routine for every message that it receives before it gives the message to a program. This hook can do anything it wants to the message, including change any of the parameters, or even the value of the message!

Since a getmessage hook has access to every message that is received by the GetMessage routine, it can be used for many different types of applications. A hot-key could be implemented using a getmessage hook, for example. Or, it could be used to detect mouse

Figure 15.3   *Output from KEYINPUT program*

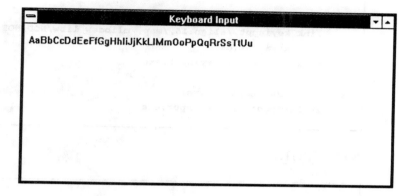

button messages on a given window—perhaps to prevent a user from accessing any other window until a password has been typed correctly. The getmessage hook can be used for any messages that GetMessage retrieves, which means all keyboard and mouse messages as well as the WM_PAINT and WM_TIMER messages.

A Sample Program

To demonstrate the way a program can receive keyboard input, we have written KEYINPUT. This program creates a simple single-line text entry window. Figure 15.3 shows a sample of the output created by this program.

KEYINPUT shows how the WM_CHAR and WM_KEYDOWN messages can be used to receive character input and perform some simple editing. The following cursor movement keys are recognized: Home, End, Left Arrow, and Right Arrow. In addition, the Backspace and Delete keys can be used to erase characters.

KEYINPUT.MAK

```
keyinput.res: keyinput.rc keyinput.cur keyinput.ico
    rc -r keyinput.rc

keyinput.obj: keyinput.c
    cl -AM -c -d -Gsw -Ow -W2 -Zpi keyinput.c
```

```
keyinput.exe: keyinput.obj keyinput.def
    link keyinput,/align:16,/map, mlibcew libw/NOD/NOE/CO, \
        keyinput.def
    rc keyinput.res keyinput.exe


keyinput.exe: keyinput.res
    rc keyinput.res keyinput.exe
```

KEYINPUT.C

```c
/*-------------------------------------------------------------*\
|   KEYINPUT.C -- Sample text input program.                  |
\*-------------------------------------------------------------*/
#include <Windows.H>


/*-------------------------------------------------------------*\
|                   Function Prototypes.                      |
\*-------------------------------------------------------------*/
long FAR  PASCAL MinWndProc (HWND, WORD, WORD, LONG);


/*-------------------------------------------------------------*\
|                   Main Function:  WinMain.                  |
\*-------------------------------------------------------------*/
int PASCAL WinMain (HANDLE hInstance,
                    HANDLE hPrevInstance,
                    LPSTR  lpszCmdLine,
                    int    cmdShow)
    {
    HWND     hwnd;
    MSG      msg;
    WNDCLASS wndclass;

    if (!hPrevInstance)
        {
        wndclass.lpszClassName = "MIN:MAIN";
        wndclass.hInstance     = hInstance;
        wndclass.lpfnWndProc   = MinWndProc;
        wndclass.hCursor       = LoadCursor (hInstance, "hand");
```

```
        wndclass.hIcon          = LoadIcon (hInstance,"snapshot");
        wndclass.lpszMenuName    = NULL;
        wndclass.hbrBackground   = COLOR_WINDOW+1;
        wndclass.style           = CS_HREDRAW | CS_VREDRAW;
        wndclass.cbClsExtra      = 0;
        wndclass.cbWndExtra      = 0;

        RegisterClass( &wndclass);
        }

    hwnd = CreateWindow("MIN:MAIN",          /* Class name.   */
                        "Keyboard Input",     /* Title.        */
                        WS_OVERLAPPEDWINDOW,  /* Style bits.   */
                        CW_USEDEFAULT,        /* x - default.  */
                        0,                    /* y - default.  */
                        CW_USEDEFAULT,        /* cx - default. */
                        0,                    /* cy - default. */
                        NULL,                 /* No parent.    */
                        NULL,                 /* Class menu.   */
                        hInstance,            /* Creator       */
                        NULL );               /* Params.       */

    ShowWindow (hwnd, cmdShow);
    while (GetMessage(&msg, 0, 0, 0))
        {
        TranslateMessage(&msg);          /* Keyboard input.      */
        DispatchMessage(&msg);
        }
    return 0;
    }

/*-------------------------------------------------------------*\
|                Window Procedure:  MinWndProc.                 |
\*-------------------------------------------------------------*/
long FAR PASCAL MinWndProc (HWND hwnd,    WORD wMsg,
                            WORD wParam, LONG lParam)


    {
#define BUFSIZE 40
    static unsigned char acInput[BUFSIZE];/*  Input array.    */
    static int  cc = 0;                   /*  Character count. */
```

```
static int  icc = 0;                        /*  Array index.     */
static int  yLineHeight;
static int  xLeftMargin;

switch (wMsg)
    {
    case WM_CHAR:
        {
        int i;

        /*  Backspace.  */
        if (wParam == VK_BACK)
            {
            if (icc == 0)
                MessageBeep(0);
            else  /*  Remove a character.  */
                {
                icc--;
                for (i=icc;i<cc;i++)
                    acInput[i]=acInput[i+1];
                cc--;
                InvalidateRect (hwnd, NULL, TRUE);
                }
            break;
            }

        /*  Filter out unwanted character codes.  */
        if (wParam <= VK_ESCAPE)
            {
            MessageBeep(0);  /*  Complain.  */
            break;
            }

        /*  Complain if buffer is full.  */
        if (cc >= BUFSIZE)
            {
            MessageBeep (0);
            break;
            }

        /*  Make room for a new character.  */
        for (i=cc;i>icc;i--)
            acInput[i]=acInput[i-1];
```

```
                  /*  Put new character in buffer.  */
                  acInput[icc] = (unsigned char)wParam;
                  icc++;
                  cc++;

                  InvalidateRect (hwnd, NULL, TRUE);
                  }
                  break;

          case WM_CREATE:
               {
               HDC hdc;
               TEXTMETRIC tm;

               hdc = GetDC (hwnd);
               GetTextMetrics (hdc, &tm);
               yLineHeight = tm.tmHeight + tm.tmExternalLeading;
               xLeftMargin = tm.tmAveCharWidth;
               ReleaseDC (hwnd, hdc);
               }
               break;

          case WM_DESTROY:
               PostQuitMessage(0);
               break;

          case WM_KEYDOWN:
               switch (wParam)
                   {
                   case VK_DELETE:
                       /*  If end of buffer, complain.  */
                       if (icc == cc)
                           MessageBeep(0);
                       else  /*  Remove a character.  */
                           {
                           int i;
                           for (i=icc;i<cc;i++)
                               acInput[i]=acInput[i+1];
                           cc--;
                           InvalidateRect (hwnd, NULL, TRUE);
                           }
                       break;
```

```
                    case VK_END:
                        icc = cc;
                        break;
                    case VK_HOME:
                        icc = 0;
                        break;
                    case VK_LEFT:
                        if (icc > 0) icc--;
                        else MessageBeep(0);
                        break;
                    case VK_RIGHT:
                        if (icc < cc) icc++;
                        else MessageBeep(0);
                        break;
                }
            break;

        case WM_PAINT:
            {
            PAINTSTRUCT ps;

            BeginPaint (hwnd, &ps);
            TextOut (ps.hdc, xLeftMargin, yLineHeight,
                    acInput, cc);
            EndPaint (hwnd, &ps);
            }
            break;

        default:
            return(DefWindowProc(hwnd,wMsg,wParam,lParam));
            break;
        }
    return 0L;
    }
```

KEYINPUT.RC

```
snapshot icon keyinput.ico

hand   cursor keyinput.cur
```

KEYINPUT.DEF

```
NAME      KEYINPUT

EXETYPE WINDOWS

DESCRIPTION 'Keyboard Input'

CODE      MOVEABLE DISCARDABLE
DATA      MOVEABLE MULTIPLE

HEAPSIZE      512
STACKSIZE   5000

EXPORTS
    MinWndProc
```

Like the other sample programs in this book, KEYINPUT was built on top of the minimum Windows program that we introduced in Chapter 2. This program handles five different messages: WM_CHAR, WM_CREATE, WM_DESTROY, WM_KEYDOWN, and WM_PAINT. The window procedure is organized alphabetically by message name to help make the code easier to read. If you find this helps, you might wish to adopt this convention in your own programs.

As the WM_CHAR keyboard character messages occur, KEY-INPUT accumulates the characters in a character array defined as

```
static unsigned char acInput[BUFSIZE];
```

The use of the *unsigned* character type is a good practice that will help when working with the extended ASCII character set that Windows supports. It helps avoid the confusion that otherwise can occur with normal signed characters, which use the high-order bit as a sign bit. Since Windows' extended ASCII uses this high-order bit for the characters between 128 and 255 (80h to ffh), this can cause unexpected results. Consider the following lines of code:

```
unsigned char chUnsigned;
char chSigned;
```

```
chUnsigned = 'â';   /*   In Windows' extended ASCII,   */
chSigned   = 'â';   /*        â = e2h.                 */

if (chSigned == 'â')
    {
    /*  This will never be true.  */
    }

if (chUnsigned == 'â')
    {
    /*  This will always be true.  */
    }
```

The problem occurs because of the way various compilers interpret the numeric value of characters. Character values are converted into two-byte word values before a comparison is done. When this happens, the sign bit is extended to provide the correct word value. If you use unsigned char arrays, you will avoid this problem.

Getting back to our sample program, KEYINPUT has two variables that keep track of the contents of acInput: cc and icc. cc is the count of characters in the array, and icc is an index into the array, and functions as the insertion point when new characters are typed. KEYINPUT increments and decrements these two fields as characters are entered and deleted.

Every time a change is made to the values in the character array, KEYINPUT generates a WM_PAINT message by calling Invalidate-Rect:

```
InvalidateRect (hwnd, NULL, TRUE);
```

which tells Windows, in effect, that the entire window is damaged and that it should be completely erased and redrawn. This is a pretty radical step to take. It means that every time the user types a letter key, the entire window is redrawn. And the same happens when a single letter is deleted. But it guarantees that the contents of the window is always correct, since the WM_PAINT message reads the character array with the changes in place.

One way to improve this program involves eliminating this excessive drawing, which means replacing the calls to InvalidateRect with actions that change the display screen in the smallest possible way. This requires a little more work, but avoids the annoying blinking that occurs when characters are typed or erased. For example, here is how we could draw each new character (and the characters that follow in the array) when a new letter is typed:

```
/*  Put new character in buffer.  */
acInput[icc] = (unsigned char)wParam;


{  /*  New Code in Brackets.  */
DWORD dw;
HDC hdc;


cc++;
hdc = GetDC(hwnd);
dw = GetTextExtent (hdc, &acInput[0], icc);
TextOut (hdc,
         xLeftMargin+LOWORD(dw),
         yLineHeight,
         &acInput[icc],
         cc - icc);
ReleaseDC (hwnd, hdc);
}


icc++;
/* cc++;  Comment this line out.  */
```

This code redraws from the current position to the end of the line. As characters are inserted or typed at the end of the line, characters to the left of the insertion point are left alone. Only characters to the right of the insertion point are redrawn.

Quite a few other improvements could be made to this program, but it is enough to give you the basic idea about how keyboard input can be collected and displayed. We'll come back to this program in a minute, to see how a **caret** can be used to highlight the current insertion point. Before that, we need to discuss some issues that are critical in correctly handling character data: character sets and other internationalization issues.

Character Sets and International Support

As keyboard data travels from the keyboard to your program, it undergoes a number of conversions: Keyboard data starts out as scan codes, which are converted by the device driver into virtual key information. And finally, virtual key codes are converted into ASCII character values to provide upper- and lower-case letters,

Figure 15.4 *ANSI Character Set*

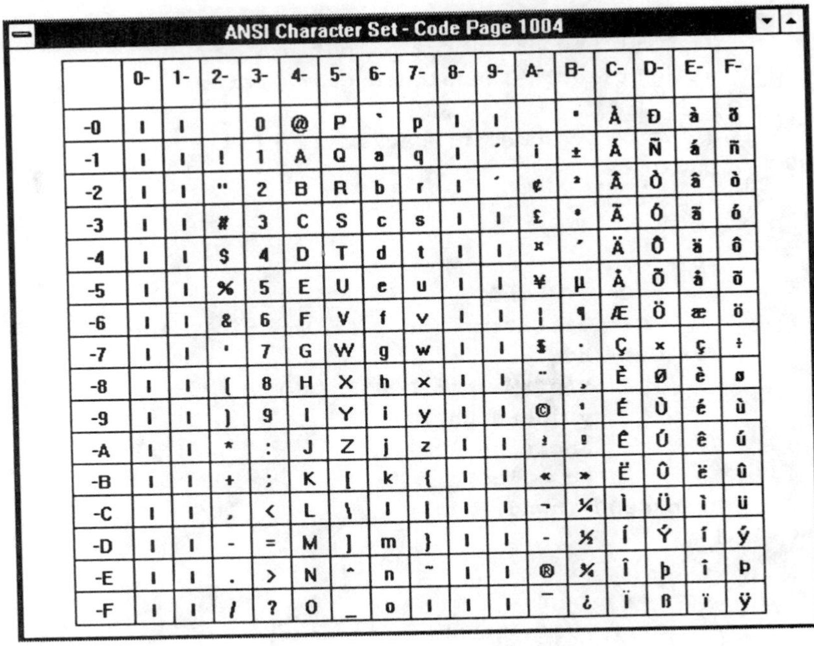

ANSI Character Set - Code Page 1004

	0-	1-	2-	3-	4-	5-	6-	7-	8-	9-	A-	B-	C-	D-	E-	F-
-0	I	I		0	@	P	`	p	I	I		°	À	Ð	à	ð
-1	I	I	!	1	A	Q	a	q	I	´	¡	±	Á	Ñ	á	ñ
-2	I	I	"	2	B	R	b	r	I	´	¢	²	Â	Ò	â	ò
-3	I	I	#	3	C	S	c	s	I	I	£	³	Ã	Ó	ã	ó
-4	I	I	$	4	D	T	d	t	I	I	¤	´	Ä	Ô	ä	ô
-5	I	I	%	5	E	U	e	u	I	I	¥	µ	Å	Õ	å	õ
-6	I	I	&	6	F	V	f	v	I	I	¦	¶	Æ	Ö	æ	ö
-7	I	I	'	7	G	W	g	w	I	I	§	·	Ç	×	ç	÷
-8	I	I	(	8	H	X	h	x	I	I	¨	¸	È	Ø	è	ø
-9	I	I	)	9	I	Y	i	y	I	I	©	¹	É	Ù	é	ù
-A	I	I	*	:	J	Z	j	z	I	I	ª	º	Ê	Ú	ê	ú
-B	I	I	+	;	K	[	k	{	I	I	«	»	Ë	Û	ë	û
-C	I	I	,	<	L	\	l			I	I	¬	¼	Ì	Ü	ì	ü
-D	I	I	-	=	M	]	m	}	I	I		½	Í	Ý	í	ý
-E	I	I	.	>	N	^	n	~	I	I	®	¾	Î	Þ	î	þ
-F	I	I	/	?	O	_	o	I	I	I	¯	¿	Ï	ß	ï	ÿ

numbers, and punctuation marks. Figure 15.4 shows Windows' ANSI Character Set.

What is a character set? It is a convention or a standard that helps avoid confusion. For example, according to the ANSI Character Set, the value 41h (65 decimal) stands for a capital A. Microsoft adopted the ANSI Character Set to allow the data created by a Windows program to be readable by other Windows programs, and interpreted correctly on different brands of computers and different brands of printers, as well as computers and peripherals in different countries.

Windows uses the ANSI character set to interpret how a text character should be displayed, and provides a standard that allows file sharing between different Windows computers. But this isn't the only character set that you'll want to know how to work with. In addition to the ANSI character set, every Windows computer has a second character set that DOS uses. For example, IBM-compatible computers that are manufactured for use in the United States have a character set that IBM calls code page 437. Figure 15.5 shows the

Figure 15.5   *DOS Character Set in the United States: Code Page 437*

OEM Character Set - Code Page 437

	0-	1-	2-	3-	4-	5-	6-	7-	8-	9-	A-	B-	C-	D-	E-	F-
-0		►		0	@	P	`	p	Ç	É	á	░	└	╨	α	≡
-1	☺	◄	!	1	A	Q	a	q	ü	æ	í	▒	┴	╤	ß	±
-2	☻	↕	"	2	B	R	b	r	é	Æ	ó	▓	┬	╥	Γ	≥
-3	♥	‼	#	3	C	S	c	s	â	ô	ú	│	├	╙	π	≤
-4	♦	¶	$	4	D	T	d	t	ä	ö	ñ	┤	─	╘	Σ	⌠
-5	♣	§	%	5	E	U	e	u	à	ò	Ñ	╡	┼	╒	σ	⌡
-6	♠	▬	&	6	F	V	f	v	å	û	ª	╢	╞	╓	µ	÷
-7	•	↨	'	7	G	W	g	w	ç	ù	º	╖	╟	╫	τ	≈
-8	◘	↑	(	8	H	X	h	x	ê	ÿ	¿	╕	╚	╪	Φ	°
-9	○	↓	)	9	I	Y	i	y	ë	Ö	⌐	╣	╔	┘	Θ	∙
-A	◙	→	*	:	J	Z	j	z	è	Ü	¬	║	╩	┌	Ω	·
-B	♂	←	+	;	K	[	k	{	ï	¢	½	╗	╦	█	δ	√
-C	♀	∟	,	<	L	\	l	|	î	£	¼	╝	╠	▄	∞	ⁿ
-D	♪	↔	-	=	M	]	m	}	ì	¥	¡	╜	═	▌	φ	²
-E	♫	▲	.	>	N	^	n	~	Ä	₧	«	╛	╬	▐	ε	■
-F	☼	▼	/	?	O	_	o	⌂	Å	ƒ	»	┐	╧	▀	∩	

characters in code page 437. This is the character set that DOS programs use when they create data files, and is the character set used by DOS for filenames.

For upper- and lower-case letters, numbers, and punctuation marks, this character set is identical to the Windows ANSI character set. Thus, if you are writing a Windows program for use only in the United States, you can mix and match data files between DOS and Windows programs with little chance for confusion. This will be true as long as your Windows and DOS programs use printable characters in the range 20h to 7ef (32 to 126 decimal).

For Windows programs to work on computers outside the United States, some effort is required on your part. In the first place, other code pages besides 437 are used on computers manufactured for different languages. For example, code page 860 substitutes 16 accented characters that are not available in code page 437 that are required for computers sold in Portugal. Code page 863 has 22 new accented and other special characters to meet the requirements of

French Canada. And code page 865 has four characters that change the U.S. code page for use in creating Norwegian data files.

Therefore, every machine that runs Windows will have at least two character sets: Windows' ANSI character set (sometimes known as code page 1004), which has the most complete support for accented characters, and what Microsoft calls an OEM character set, which is the character set that DOS uses to meet the language needs of different countries (code page 437).

When a DOS program is running in a window, Windows uses a font that contains characters that match the OEM character set. In this way, the character set provide backwards compatibility between Windows and DOS. If you are writing a program to display a text file created by a DOS program, there is a stock font available that uses the OEM character set. You can access this font by saying:

```
hfontOEM = GetStockObject (OEM_FIXED_FONT);
SelectObject (hdc, hfontOEM);
```

Converting Between Character Sets

If a Windows program reads files that are written by DOS programs, for the program to work properly on all non-U.S. machines, the files must be converted from the OEM character set to Windows ANSI character set. Conversely, if a Windows program writes to a file that a DOS program may read, the Windows program should convert from the ANSI character set to the native OEM character set that DOS programs expect in order to work outside the United States. Fortunately, some Windows library routines are available to do the conversion for you:

Routine	Description
AnsiToOem	Convert null-terminated ANSI string to DOS characters
AnsiToOemBuff	Convert n ANSI characters to DOS characters
OemToAnsi	Convert null-terminated DOS characters to ANSI
OemToAnsiBuff	Convert n DOS characters to ANSI

In addition to DOS data files, the DOS file system itself uses the OEM character set for filenames. However, if you use the OpenFile Windows library routine, your filenames are automatically converted to the OEM character set before DOS is called.

Upper and Lower Case Conversion

Programmers in the United States who work with characters exclusively in the range 20h to 7ef (32 to 126 decimal) often play tricks to convert text to upper or lower case. In this range, the upper- and lower-case letters are 20h (32) apart, like those shown here:

Upper Case	Ascii (hex)	(dec)	Lower Case	(hex)	(dec)
A	41h	65	a	61h	97
B	42h	66	b	62h	98
C	43h	67	c	63h	99
.					
.					
Z	5ah	90	z	7ah	122

In this range, upper-case conversion is easy; here is code that does this for us:

```
for (i=0;i<cc;i++)
    {
    if (ach[i] >= 'a' && ach[i] <= 'z')
        ach[i] -= 32;
    }
```

But consider the following pairs of upper- and lower-case accented letters:

Upper Case	Ascii (hex)	(dec)	Lower Case	(hex)	(dec)
A	c0h	192	à	e0h	224
Ç	c7h	199	ç	e7h	231
E	c8h	200	è	e8h	232
I	cfh	207	ï	efh	239
O	d5h	213	o	f5h	245
U	dbh	219	û	fbh	251

If the array in our earlier example included any of the lower-case letters in this table, the case conversion would not have worked correctly. If you are writing a program that will be sold outside the

United States, you should use the following Windows library routines for upper- and lower-case conversion instead of writing your own.

Routine	Description
AnsiLower	Converts null-terminated string to lower case
AnsiLowerBuff	Converts *n* characters to lower case
AnsiUpper	Converts null-terminated string to upper case
AnsiUpperBuff	Converts *n* characters to upper case

To convert a null-terminated character string to all upper case, you could pass a long pointer to AnsiUpper, as in

```
AnsiUpper (lpszConvert);
```

or, using AnsiUpperBuff, you could say:

```
i = lstrlen (lpszConvert);
AnsiUpperBuff (lpszConvert, i);
```

Another set of routines tests whether character information is upper or lower case, whether it is an alphabetic character, or whether it is alphanumeric:

Routine	Description
IsCharAlpha	Returns TRUE if character is alphabetic character.
IsCharAlphaNumeric	Returns TRUE if character is either alphabetic or numeric character.
IsCharLower	Returns TRUE if character is lower case.
IsCharUpper	Returns TRUE if character is upper case.

Sorting Character Strings

The existence of accented characters require special handling when converting text strings to upper case or to lower case. The same is true when sorting character strings. Programmers who perform a simple numeric sort of character strings will put words with accents out of order. For example, the following sort order results from a simple numeric sort:

cheese
chocolate
church
château

Of course, the problem is that the numeric value of the character â is e2h (226 decimal), which comes after "e" (65h or 101 decimal), "o" (6fh or 111 decimal), and "u" (75h or 117 decimal). Since this is the way that the C-runtime library routine, strcmp, works, this routine should be avoided if you wish for your product to work correctly outside the United States.

Putting château at the top of the list, where it belongs, requires that we call a Windows library routine to perform string comparison for us during our sort. Actually, there are two such routines: one that compares in a case-insensitive fashion, **lstrcmpi**, and one that compares in a case-sensitive fashion, **lstrcmp**.

String Tables

Windows has a facility that will help in the effort to prepare a product for translation to another language—a process that Microsoft calls **localization**. The facility is the **string table**. A string table allows you to put all the strings from a program in a central place: the resource file. When your programs need to access a string, it makes a call to Windows using a numeric index. In this way, all messages for the user are centralized in one place. The job of a translator is simplified, since there is only one file that must be converted to localize an entire application.

To create a string table, entries are made in the .RC resource file, like the following:

```
#include "myinclude"

STRINGTABLE
    {
    FILENOTFOUND, "File Not Found."
```

```
HELPPROMPT, "For Help, Type F1."
RECALCMESSAGE, "Recalculating."
}
```

The file myinclude would contain definitions like the following:

```
#define FILENOTFOUND  101
#define HELPPROMPT    102
#define RECALCMESSAGE 103
```

which provide a unique, numeric ID for each string. When the time comes to use a string, a Windows library routine, LoadString, is called:

```
char acMessage[BUFSIZE];

LoadString (hInstance,      // instance handle
            FILENOTFOUND,   // string id value
            acMessage,      // character buffer
            BUFSIZE);       // buffer size
```

and the string can be displayed, perhaps using the TextOut routine.

There are other benefits to using string tables besides the international support issue. Objects in a string table are read-only data, and as such Windows loads them when needed and purges them from memory when not needed. In other words, the benefit of string tables is that they are very efficient in terms of the memory that is used.

Entering Characters from the Numeric Keypad

You may be aware that, when running DOS, you can enter ASCII codes directly from the numeric keypad. Windows provides the same mechanism, which is supported by the Windows keyboard driver. You can actually enter characters from either the ANSI or OEM character sets.

To enter characters from the ANSI character set, with Num-Lock toggled on, hold down the Alt key and enter a zero followed by the decimal ASCII character code. To enter the letter À, for example, you hold Alt and type 0192.

You can enter characters from the OEM character set as well, although they will be mapped to the corresponding ANSI character set value. With the Num-Lock toggled on, hold down the Alt key and enter the decimal OEM character code. For example, to enter the letter á, you hold Alt and type 160.

Multitasking Issues

Now that we've covered the basics of handling keyboard input and dealing with different character sets, there are a few more issues that you must be aware of in order to make effective use of the keyboard.

Windows is multitasking, which means there has to be a mechanism for sharing devices like the keyboard. There are two concepts that Windows uses to direct where keyboard input is sent: the **active window** and the **focus**.

When a program creates a window, the program decides whether the window is a **top-level window** or a child of another top-level window. Most programs create a single top-level window. This window serves as the primary means by which the user interacts with the program. One characteristic of top-level windows is that they appear on the Task List that is displayed in response to the Ctrl-Esc key combination. The Task List, shown in Figure 15.6, lets the user select the top-level window that he wishes to make active.

The active window, then, is simply the top-level window that the user has decided to work with. Of course, there are other ways to make a window active besides selecting from the Task List. For example, a user could click with the mouse to make a window active, or hit the Alt-Tab key combination continuously to circulate among the top-level windows. The active window is always on top of every other top-level window in the system. This makes sense, for

Figure 15.6   *The Windows Task List*

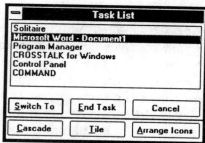

if the user has decided to work with a particular window, it should be completely visible.

When a top-level window becomes active, Windows sends it a WM_ACTIVATE message with a nonzero value in wParam. This tells the window, in effect, that "the boss wants to see you. Now." Windows also sends a WM_NCACTIVATE message, which causes the window's caption bar to change colors so that the user has a visual clue to the active window. Like other non-client area messages, this one is handled by the default window procedure.

In response to a WM_ACTIVATE message, the default window procedure gives the active window the focus. Here is the actual code from DefWindowProc:

```
case WM_ACTIVATE:
    if (wParam)
        SetFocus (hWnd);
```

The focus is simply an indicator within Windows that identifies which window should get keyboard input. In effect, when a window has the focus, it has the keyboard. It alone will receive keyboard messages.

When a window receives the focus, Windows lets it know by sending it a message: WM_SETFOCUS. But before it does that, it sends a WM_KILLFOCUS message to the window that is losing the keyboard. By watching these two messages, a window procedure can keep track of whether it has control of the keyboard or not.

But why should a window care whether it has the keyboard or not? Won't it still get the proper keyboard messages? The answer is: Yes. But sometimes a window procedure will want to know when it has the focus, and will want to take special steps. One such case occurs when we wish to have a keyboard pointer, or **caret**, in a window. That is the next topic that we plan to discuss.

Creating a Keyboard Pointer: Carets

As a program receives keyboard input, it's quite common to display a keyboard pointer to let the user know where the next character will be entered. In most environments, this is called a **cursor**. But Windows uses the term cursor to refer to the mouse pointer, and instead uses the term caret to refer to a keyboard pointer.

A caret is a rectangular blinking bitmap that lets the user know several things. First of all, it lets the user know which window has the keyboard—that is, which window has the focus. Second, as we mentioned a moment ago, it lets the user know the current position—the location where text (or some other object) will appear next.

While the most obvious use of a caret is to highlight a text entry point, that is certainly not the only use. For example, a caret can be used to indicate the "current object" in a drawing program, and is used in listboxes to show the user which item would be affected by keyboard input.

Windows has four routines for creating and maintaining the keyboard caret:

Routine Name	Description
CreateCaret	Creates a caret
SetCaretPos	Positions the caret
ShowCaret	Makes a caret visible
DestroyCaret	Destroys a caret

You might be tempted to create a caret at the beginning of your program and hold onto it until your program exits, but this wouldn't give you the results you expect. The reason is that internally, Windows is only able to recognize one caret for the entire system. Thus, you cannot keep a caret for the life of your program. You can only keep it for as long as you have the focus. For this reason, do not create a caret like this:

```
/*  DO NOT DO THIS!   */
case WM_CREATE:   /* Window Creation Message.*/
   CreateCaret (hwnd, 0, xWidth, yHeight);
   break;

case WM_DESTROY:   /* Window Destruction Message.*/
   DestroyCaret ();
   break;
```

Instead, the proper way to create and destroy a caret is in response to the WM_SETFOCUS and WM_KILLFOCUS messages. Every time your window gains the keyboard focus, it will create a caret, and every time it loses the keyboard focus, it destroys its caret. It might seem that this is a lot of trouble for a tiny, blinking bitmap; but this approach is necessary to properly maintain a caret in a Windows program.

```
/*  Correct Way to Create a Caret.  */
case WM_SETFOCUS:  /* You have the keyboard.*/
    CreateCaret (hwnd, 0, xWidth, yHeight0);
    break;

case WM_KILLFOCUS: /* You've lost the keyboard.*/
    DestroyCaret ();
    break;
```

The CreateCaret routine is defined as follows:

```
void CreateCaret (hWnd, hBitmap, nWidth, nHeight)
```

- hWnd is a handle to the window where the caret is to be located.
- hBitmap is a handle to a bitmap. It can be 0, 1, or a real bitmap handle.
- nWidth is the caret width.
- nHeight is the caret height.

The second field, hBitmap, is the key field that determines the shape and color of the caret. If it is set to zero, then the bitmap will be a black square nWidth by nHeight. If set to one, the bitmap is a gray square nWidth by nHeight. Otherwise, if it is a GDI bitmap, the caret takes on the shape of the bitmap.

When we create a caret, we'll want to make sure it is large enough to be visible. Since we're going to use the caret to highlight a text entry point, it makes sense to make the caret the same height as the text. Here is how to create a black cursor that fits the bill:

```
    .
    .
case WM_CREATE:
    {
    HDC hdc;
    TEXTMETRIC tm;
    hdc = GetDC (hwnd);
    GetTextMetrics (hdc, &tm);
    cyHeight = tm.tmHeight;
    ReleaseDC (hwnd, hdc);
    }

case WM_SETFOCUS:
    CreateCaret (hwnd,
```

```
            0,        // default black caret
            0,        // default width
            cyHeight);
    .
    .
```

Here is how to create a gray caret that is the same size:

```
CreateCaret (hwnd,
             1,        // default gray caret
             0,        // default width
             cyHeight);
```

By selecting a width of zero, we let Windows use the default size. This will be the width of a window border, to make sure that the caret is visible.

We could also create a bitmap, draw onto it using GDI drawing routines, and use it as a caret. We're going to create a monochrome bitmap. The portion of the bitmap that is black will be ignored while the portion that is white will blink. Here is how to make a caret in the shape of an I-Beam. Notice that most of the work involves creating the bitmap and drawing onto it:

```
case WM_CREATE:
    {
    HBITMAP hbmOld;
    HDC hdc;
    HDC hdcBitmap;
    TEXTMETRIC tm;

    hdc = GetDC (hwnd);
    GetTextMetrics (hdc, &tm);
    yLineHeight = tm.tmHeight + tm.tmExternalLeading;
    ReleaseDC (hwnd, hdc);

    hdcBitmap = CreateCompatibleDC (hdc);
    hbm = CreateBitmap (xLeftMargin,
                        yLineHeight,
                        1, 1, NULL);
    hbmOld = SelectObject (hdcBitmap, hbm);

    /*  Blank out bitmap.  */
    SelectObject (hdcBitmap,
```

```
                              GetStockObject (BLACK_BRUSH));
                    Rectangle (hdcBitmap, 0, 0,
                            xLeftMargin, yLineHeight);

                    /*  Do actual drawing in white.  */
                    SelectObject (hdcBitmap,
                              GetStockObject (WHITE_PEN));
                    MoveTo (hdcBitmap, 0, 0);
                    LineTo (hdcBitmap, xLeftMargin+1, 0);
                    MoveTo (hdcBitmap, xLeftMargin/2, 0);
                    LineTo (hdcBitmap, xLeftMargin/2, yLineHeight-1);
                    MoveTo (hdcBitmap, 0, yLineHeight-1);
                    LineTo (hdcBitmap, xLeftMargin+1, yLineHeight-1);
                    SelectObject (hdcBitmap, hbmOld);
                    DeleteDC (hdcBitmap);

                 }
                 break;

         case WM_DESTROY:
                 DeleteObject (hbm);
                 PostQuitMessage(0);
                 break;

         case WM_KILLFOCUS:
                 DestroyCaret();
                 break;

         case WM_SETFOCUS:
                 {
                 CreateCaret(hwnd,
                            hbm,      // hBitmap
                            0,        // xWidth
                            0);       // yWidth
                 SetCaretPos (x, y);
                 ShowCaret(hwnd);
                 }
```

And, of course, this code fragment assumes that a bitmap handle has been allocated as a static object:

```
static HBITMAP hbm;
```

Let's look at an actual program that uses a caret. We've modified the KEYINPUT program so that it uses a caret. In addition to creating and deleting the caret properly, it also moves the caret in response to the cursor-movement keys on the keyboard. Here is our caret-handling program: CARET.

CARET.MAK

```
caret.res: caret.rc caret.cur caret.ico
    rc -r caret.rc

caret.obj: caret.c
    cl -AM -c -d -Gsw -Ow -W2 -Zpi caret.c

caret.exe: caret.obj caret.def
    link caret,/align:16,/map, mlibcew libw/NOD/NOE/CO, caret.def
    rc caret.res caret.exe

caret.exe: caret.res
    rc caret.res caret.exe
```

CARET.C

```
/*-------------------------------------------------------------------*\
 |    CARET.C -- Shows proper handling of a keyboard pointer.        |
\*-------------------------------------------------------------------*/
#include <Windows.H>


/*-------------------------------------------------------------------*\
 |                    Function Prototypes.                           |
\*-------------------------------------------------------------------*/
long FAR  PASCAL MinWndProc (HWND, WORD, WORD, LONG);
void NEAR PASCAL CaretSetCaretPos (HWND, int, char *, int *,
                                   int *, int);


/*-------------------------------------------------------------------*\
 |                    Main Function:  WinMain.                       |
\*-------------------------------------------------------------------*/
int PASCAL WinMain (HANDLE hInstance,
```

```
                        HANDLE hPrevInstance,
                        LPSTR  lpszCmdLine,
                        int    cmdShow)

{
HWND      hwnd;
MSG       msg;
WNDCLASS wndclass;

if (!hPrevInstance)
    {
    wndclass.lpszClassName = "MIN:MAIN";
    wndclass.hInstance     = hInstance;
    wndclass.lpfnWndProc   = MinWndProc;
    wndclass.hCursor       = LoadCursor (hInstance, "hand");
    wndclass.hIcon         = LoadIcon (hInstance,"snapshot");
    wndclass.lpszMenuName  = NULL;
    wndclass.hbrBackground = COLOR_WINDOW+1;
    wndclass.style         = CS_HREDRAW | CS_VREDRAW;
    wndclass.cbClsExtra    = 0;
    wndclass.cbWndExtra    = 0;

    RegisterClass( &wndclass);
    }

hwnd = CreateWindow("MIN:MAIN",            /* Class name.   */
                    "Caret Demo",          /* Title.        */
                    WS_OVERLAPPEDWINDOW,   /* Style bits.   */
                    CW_USEDEFAULT,         /* x - default.  */
                    0,                     /* y - default.  */
                    CW_USEDEFAULT,         /* cx - default. */
                    0,                     /* cy - default. */
                    NULL,                  /* No parent.    */
                    NULL,                  /* Class menu.   */
                    hInstance,             /* Creator       */
                    NULL);                 /* Params.       */

ShowWindow (hwnd, cmdShow);
while (GetMessage(&msg, 0, 0, 0))
    {
    TranslateMessage(&msg);               /* Keyboard input.  */
    DispatchMessage(&msg);
```

```
            }
        return 0;
            }


/*------------------------------------------------------------------*\
|                  Window Procedure:  MinWndProc.                    |
\*------------------------------------------------------------------*/
long FAR PASCAL MinWndProc (HWND hwnd,     WORD wMsg,
                            WORD wParam, LONG lParam)


    {
#define BUFSIZE 40
    static unsigned char acInput[BUFSIZE];/*  Input array.     */
    static int  cc = 0;                    /*  Character count. */
    static int  icc = 0;                   /*  Array index.     */
    static int  yLineHeight;
    static int  xLeftMargin;
    static int  xCaretPos, yCaretPos;

    switch (wMsg)
        {
      case WM_CHAR:
            {
            int i;


            /*  Backspace.  */
            if (wParam == VK_BACK)
                {
                if (icc == 0)
                    MessageBeep(0);
                else  /*  Remove a character.  */
                    {
                    icc--;
                    CaretSetCaretPos (hwnd, icc, acInput,
                        &xCaretPos, &yCaretPos, xLeftMargin);

                    for (i=icc;i<cc;i++)
                        acInput[i]=acInput[i+1];
                    cc--;
                    InvalidateRect (hwnd, NULL, TRUE);
                    }
```

```
            break;
            }

        /*  Filter out unwanted character codes.  */
        if (wParam <= VK_ESCAPE)
            {
            MessageBeep(0);  /* Complain.  */
            break;
            }

        /*  Complain if buffer is full.  */
        if (cc >= BUFSIZE)
            {
            MessageBeep (0);
            break;
            }

        /*  Make room for a new character.  */
        for (i=cc;i>icc;i--)
            acInput[i]=acInput[i-1];

        /*  Put new character in buffer.  */
        acInput[icc] = (unsigned char)wParam;;

        icc++;
        cc++;
        CaretSetCaretPos (hwnd, icc, acInput,
            &xCaretPos, &yCaretPos, xLeftMargin);

        InvalidateRect (hwnd, NULL, TRUE);
        }
        break;

case WM_CREATE:
    {
    HDC hdc;
    TEXTMETRIC tm;

    hdc = GetDC (hwnd);
    GetTextMetrics (hdc, &tm);
    yLineHeight = tm.tmHeight + tm.tmExternalLeading;
```

```
        xLeftMargin = tm.tmAveCharWidth;
        yCaretPos = yLineHeight;
        ReleaseDC (hwnd, hdc);
        }
    break;

case WM_DESTROY:
    PostQuitMessage(0);
    break;

case WM_KEYDOWN:
    {
    int i;

    switch (wParam)
        {
        case VK_DELETE:
            /*  If end of buffer, complain.  */
            if (icc == cc)
                MessageBeep(0);
            else  /*  Remove a character.  */
                {
                for (i=icc;i<cc;i++)
                    acInput[i]=acInput[i+1];
                cc--;
                InvalidateRect (hwnd, NULL, TRUE);
                }
            break;
        case VK_END:
            icc = cc;
            CaretSetCaretPos (hwnd, icc, acInput,
                &xCaretPos, &yCaretPos, xLeftMargin);
            break;
        case VK_HOME:
            icc = 0;
            CaretSetCaretPos (hwnd, icc, acInput,
                &xCaretPos, &yCaretPos, xLeftMargin);
            break;
        case VK_LEFT:
            if (icc > 0)
                {
```

```
                          icc--;
                          CaretSetCaretPos (hwnd, icc, acInput,
                              &xCaretPos, &yCaretPos,
xLeftMargin);

                          }
                      else MessageBeep(0);
                      break;
                case VK_RIGHT:
                    if (icc < cc)
                        {
                        icc++;
                        CaretSetCaretPos (hwnd, icc, acInput,
                              &xCaretPos, &yCaretPos,
xLeftMargin);

                        }
                    else MessageBeep(0);
                    break;
                }
            }
        break;

    case WM_KILLFOCUS:
        DestroyCaret();
        break;

    case WM_PAINT:
        {
        PAINTSTRUCT ps;

        BeginPaint (hwnd, &ps);
        TextOut (ps.hdc, xLeftMargin, yLineHeight,
                acInput, cc);
        EndPaint (hwnd, &ps);
        }
        break;

    case WM_SETFOCUS:
        CreateCaret(hwnd,
                    0,              // hBitmap
                    0,              // xWidth
                  yLineHeight);   // yWidth
```

```
                    CaretSetCaretPos (hwnd, icc, acInput,
                         &xCaretPos, &yCaretPos, xLeftMargin);
                    ShowCaret (hwnd);
                    break;

               default:
                    return(DefWindowProc(hwnd,wMsg,wParam,lParam));
                    break;
          }
     return 0L;
     }



void NEAR PASCAL CaretSetCaretPos (HWND hwnd,
                                   int icc,
                                   char * acInput,
                                   int *pxCaretPos,
                                   int *pyCaretPos,
                                   int xLeftMargin)
     {
     DWORD dw;
     HDC hdc;

     hdc = GetDC (hwnd);
     dw = GetTextExtent (hdc, acInput, icc);
     ReleaseDC (hwnd, hdc);
     *pxCaretPos = LOWORD(dw) + xLeftMargin;
     SetCaretPos (*pxCaretPos, *pyCaretPos);
     }
```

CARET.RC

```
snapshot icon min.ico

hand   cursor min.cur
```

CARET.DEF

```
NAME      CARET

EXETYPE WINDOWS

DESCRIPTION 'Caret'

CODE      MOVEABLE DISCARDABLE
DATA      MOVEABLE MULTIPLE

HEAPSIZE      512
STACKSIZE    5000

EXPORTS
    MinWndProc
```

In this program, one subroutine does most of the work: CaretSet-CaretPos. Any time the current position moves, this routine is called to adjust the location of the caret—in fact, this means any time the variable icc changes, since this points to the current character position in the array of characters.

Not a lot of additional code is required to support a caret. The only requirement is that the caret be created and destroyed at the proper time. Carets must be created in response to the WM_SETFOCUS message, because this message is sent to tell a window procedure that it owns the keyboard. Since the caret is a keyboard pointer, we create a caret in response to this message to let the user know the next input location. And because Windows only supports one caret in the system at a time, we destroy our caret in response to the WM_KILLFOCUS message, which is sent to our window procedure to inform us that we have lost the keyboard. If a program fails to destroy a caret at this time, it will confuse the Window Manager, which may then leave an orphaned caret in your window. Avoiding this problem is easy: Create and destroy a caret in response to the proper messages.

This concludes our look at keyboard input, and at carets. You see now that keyboard input goes through a two-step conversion process: from scan code to virtual key and from virtual key to ASCII character code. This two-step process helps Windows be an international operating environment, and allows Windows programs to run unchanged around the world.

In the next chapter, we're going to look at the other type of input device available to Windows programs: the mouse. Ideally, a Windows program will allow a user to switch between the mouse and the keyboard for all of its operations. Let's see what this involves.

16
Mouse Input

A mouse is a pointing device about the size of a deck of playing cards connected via cable to a computer. The first mouse was developed in the mid-1960s at the Stanford Research Institute (SRI). During the 1970s, the mouse played a key role in the computer research done at Xerox's Palo Alto Research Center (PARC). But the mouse didn't come into widespread use until the 1980s, with the advent and immense popularity of personal computers.

The mouse allows a user to quickly point to different objects and locations on the display screen. Objects can be picked up, moved, and directly manipulated with a versatility that is not possible with the keyboard alone. The advantage of the mouse over the keyboard is that pointing is a very natural, human action that we are capable of from a very young age. Pressing letter combinations on a keyboard is arguably a less natural way to communicate.

The mouse is a very important input device in Windows. Used alone, quite a bit of interaction is possible: programs can be started, windows moved, menu items selected, and, in programs that allow it, data objects can be directly manipulated. As you begin to create Windows programs, you'll want to keep in mind the tremendous possibilities that are possible through the simple act of pointing.

Even though Windows and Windows applications make significant use of the mouse, not every Windows computer will have a mouse. And even on computers that are equipped with a mouse, there may be times when a particular user prefers to avoid the mouse. Early in the development of Windows, this issue was raised by the developers of some popular software packages. In particular, the developers of DOS-based programs that relied primarily on keyboard input were concerned with the suitability of Windows for their programs. In response, Microsoft adopted the position that all available mouse functions should also be available with the keyboard. Ideally, programs should allow users to switch from one to the other at any time.

This approach is built into the way that Windows handles menus. Consider the system menu. When you want to see the system menu, you can click the mouse on the system menu icon or strike the Alt + Spacebar keys. Once the system menu has made its appearance, you can select system menu commands using either the mouse or the keyboard. Using the mouse, you click on the desired menu item. Using the keyboard, there are two choices: You can use the arrow keys followed by the return key, or simply strike a letter key that matches an underlined letter in a menu item name. On the other hand, having seen the system menu, you might decide that you don't want to select any of its commands after all. Again, there is a keyboard approach and a mouse approach to dismissing the system menu. From the keyboard, you hit the Esc key. Using the mouse, simply click anywhere outside the system menu.

This flexibility allows the user to alternate between the two devices based on personal preference. We suggest that you take a similar approach while designing the user interface to your Windows programs. It will require some thought on your part to create a robust, flexible interface—but the increased *usability* of your program will most likely cause an increase in the *use* of your program.

If you have never used a mouse before, you might be skeptical about its usefulness as an input device. There's a story about a researcher at Xerox PARC, Larry Tesler, who used to think that way. He set up an experiment to prove that the mouse wasn't a very useful input device. He took people off the streets, and taught them to use a full-screen editor with cursor keys. After an hour or so, he would introduce the mouse as an alternative to the cursor keys. After playing with the mouse a little, most people ended up ignoring the cursor keys in favor of the mouse. The experiment backfired: Although he was trying to demonstrate that the mouse was an unsuitable input device, Tesler found that most users were more comfortable using the mouse instead of the keyboard to select input locations on a display screen.

Perhaps, like many programmers, you are primarily oriented toward keyboard input. If so, it might be worth your time to practice using the mouse. This will help you become a better Windows programmer, since it will help you to better understand the benefits that the mouse can provide to your users. To get you started, the next section discusses some of the common uses of the mouse in Windows.

The Uses of a Mouse

We're going to start our discussion of the mouse from the point of view of the user. That is, we're going to answer the question: What is a mouse used for? If you're an experienced mouse user, you might wish to skip ahead a few pages to where our discussion of programming issues begins.

In use, the mouse rests on a flat surface like a desk top. It controls the movement of a tiny symbol on the display screen called a **cursor**. The cursor sometimes changes shape to let you know that a particular location on the screen has significance. For example, some windows have a thick border for use in resizing the window. When positioned on top of such a border, the cursor changes into a two-headed arrow to let you know that resizing can take place.

A mouse may have one or more buttons. While the cursor location is important, it's actually the use of the buttons that triggers an action. There are several different uses of the mouse buttons that are common in the world of Windows, including clicking, double-clicking, clicking with a shift key, and dragging. We're going to discuss each of these briefly, to introduce the basic mouse actions, and to discuss some of the techniques that you'll see mentioned in this chapter. A more complete discussion of mouse interaction techniques can be found in the IBM publication *Systems Application Architecture, Common User Access: Advanced Interface Design Guide* (SC26-4582-0). This document describes a set of user-interface standards that have been adopted for Windows and OS/2 Presentation Manager programs. Microsoft considers this guide important enough to include as part of the Windows Software Development Kit (SDK).

The first mouse action that we're going to describe is **Clicking**. Clicking involves pressing and releasing a mouse button without moving the mouse. A click is used to select objects and actions. For example, clicking causes menus to appear and is used to make scrollbars operate.

Double-clicking involves two clicking operations at the same location in a very short time interval. The default time interval is one-half second, but this can be changed using the Control Panel. While a single click makes a selection, a double-click means "do the default action." For example, a double-click on the system menu icon means "close this window." A double-click on a program icon in the Program Manager means "start this program." In general, a double-click should extend the action that was started by a single click.

Clicking with a shift key involves holding down one of the shift keys (Shift or Ctrl) while clicking a mouse button. The shift key modifies the mouse click, in the same way that a shift key modifies a keyboard key. Shift key + A key, for example, gives us a capital A. The meaning of Shift + Click or Ctrl + Click will depend on the program. In general, though, Shift + Click is a request to extend a selection that was started with a single Click.

Dragging is a two-part mouse action, which starts with clicking to select an object, and then—with the mouse button still pressed— involves moving the mouse to cause the selected object to move. When the object has arrived at the desired location, the mouse button is released. Dragging is perhaps the hardest operation for new Windows users to master, since it combines mouse button action and mouse movement. But it is also a widely used action. For example, in graphic programs, dragging allows a user to directly manipulate objects on the display screen. In the Windows interface itself, dragging is an important mouse action: Dragging is used to move windows, select menu items, and operate scroll bars.

This brief introduction to mouse actions is not a substitute for your working with the Windows user interface and becoming comfortable with each of these techniques. If you are a regular Windows user, it will help make you a better Windows programmer. But now, let's roll up our sleeves and start to investigate some of the issues that will help you program for the mouse. In the same way that we traced the path of keyboard data from the hardware into our program, we're going to follow the path that mouse data takes in hopes of understanding how a Windows program can best make use of this device.

How a Windows Program Receives Mouse Input

The path that mouse data takes is illustrated in Figure 16.1. In many respects, mouse data is much simpler than keyboard data, and so this figure is correspondingly simpler than the diagram that we saw in the last chapter. Nevertheless, mouse input has some unique qualities, and understanding these qualities will help you use mouse input.

The Mouse

Although there are other pointing devices besides the mouse—including track balls, joy sticks, touch screens, and cats paws—none has experienced the same popularity as the mouse. At present, a

Figure 16.1   *The flow of mouse data*

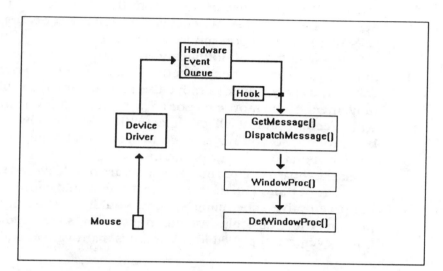

relatively small number of companies ship mice, including Hewlett-Packard, Logitech, Microsoft, and Mouse Systems. Among these companies, there aren't many differences between the mouse each provides. Some have two buttons and others have three. Some detect movement by the motion of a rubber-coated steel ball, while others use optical detection methods. There is also little variety in the way different mice connect to the computer system. Some mice use a communication port, while others connect to a special bus adapter card, and still others connect to the system through the keyboard.

When a mouse reports its location, it does so in terms of movement along the X and Y axes. And, like keyboard activity, mouse button actions are reported as button down and button up actions. When one of these events occur, a signal is sent which results in a hardware interrupt being generated. The handling of the interrupt is the job of the next component we're going to look at: the device driver.

The Mouse Device Driver

When Windows starts up, the mouse driver loads itself and goes off in search of a mouse. When Windows asks, the device driver lets Windows know whether a mouse is present in the system. If so,

Windows calls the driver to provide an address of a procedure to be called to report mouse events. From that point on, the job of the device driver is simple: Whenever a mouse event occurs, the driver calls Windows to report mouse actions.

When Windows is notified of a mouse event, one of the first things it does is to check whether the mouse has moved. If so, it calls the display driver to move the mouse cursor. In this way, the movement of the mouse cursor always occurs at interrupt time, and will preempt almost all other activities. But this happens in the background, so you never need to worry that it might disrupt the proper operation of your programs.

Like keyboard events, mouse events are not delivered to programs at interrupt time. The disruption that this would cause to Windows' nonpreemptive scheduling system would make writing Windows programs very difficult. Instead, mouse events are handled like keyboard events and placed into Windows' hardware event queue.

The Hardware Event Queue

Mouse events are written into the hardware event queue, where they wait for delivery to the message loop of a program. When we introduced the hardware event queue in our discussion of keyboard input, we mentioned that it had room for 120 events. While this is easily enough to keep ahead of most typists, you might be concerned that the queue can overflow if the mouse were to be quickly moved across the screen.

In anticipation of this problem, Windows regards mouse movement in a very special way. Before a new mouse move event is written to the hardware event queue, a check is made to see if the previous hardware event was also reporting mouse movement. If so, the previous event is overwritten with the latest mouse move information. After all, when the user is moving the mouse, the destination is more important than every point traversed by the mouse.

The events in the hardware event queue don't yet belong to any particular program, until they are claimed by the GetMessage routine. This is necessary for the proper operation of the system. After all, one mouse message might cause a window to move or to close. This would change the way that subsequent mouse messages are handled, since mouse input is based on mouse cursor location. That decision is made by the next link in the mouse handling chain: the GetMessage loop.

The GetMessage Loop

Every program has a GetMessage loop, which serves as one of the gateways for messages to enter a program for processing. As discussed earlier, this message passing mechanism also serves to keep Windows' multitasking system working properly.

When a program calls GetMessage, it opens the possibility that Windows may decide to put the program to sleep and wake up another program. This is precisely what happens when GetMessage finds that the hardware event queue contains a mouse event for another program. It puts the first program to sleep, and wakes up the second program. The second program can then return from its own call to GetMessage, where it has been sleeping, with a mouse message to process.

GetMessage decides which program should receive a mouse message by finding out which program owns the window where the mouse cursor resides. For now, though, let's set aside these multitasking issues and concentrate on the way GetMessage operates once it has decided that a specific program should receive a mouse message.

Even after GetMessage has found a mouse event for one of our windows, it still isn't ready to bring a message back to our program. The problem is simple: There are two types of mouse messages, depending on where the cursor is resting. Table 16.1 provides a list of the two types: client area and non-client area messages. The dis-

Table 16.1 *Windows mouse messages*

Client Area Messages	Non-Client Area Message
WM_LBUTTONDOWN	WM_NCLBUTTONDOWN
WM_LBUTTONUP	WM_NCLBUTTONUP
WM_LBUTTONDBLCLK	WM_NCLBUTTONDBLCLK
WM_MBUTTONDOWN	WM_NCMBUTTONDOWN
WM_MBUTTONUP	WM_NCMBUTTONUP
WM_MBUTTONDBLCLK	WM_NCMBUTTONDBLCLK
WM_RBUTTONDOWN	WM_NCRBUTTONDOWN
WM_RBUTTONUP	WM_NCRBUTTONUP
WM_RBUTTONDBLCLK	WM_NCRBUTTONDBLCLK
WM_MOUSEMOVE	WM_NCMOUSEMOVE

tinction is important, since Windows itself takes care of mouse messages in the non-client area of the window, and lets our program handle client area mouse messages.

As you can tell by looking at the messages in Table 16.1, Windows has messages for up to three mouse buttons, which are called the left, middle, and right buttons. Since some mice have only two buttons, few programs rely on the middle button for mouse input. In addition, Windows itself relies exclusively on the left button, and many programs follow this practice.

In case you are worried that this is unfair to users who prefer the right mouse button, Windows has a built-in solution. The Control Panel lets a user swap the left and right mouse buttons. When this is done, Windows automatically converts all right button messages into left button messages. Therefore, if a program uses only one mouse button, it can safely rely on left button messages and still satisfy users who prefer to use the right button.

To determine where the mouse cursor is resting in a window, and therefore what type of message is needed, the GetMessage routine sends a message to the window procedure: WM_NCHITTEST. To understand how this works, we need to review Windows' message passing mechanisms.

In Chapter 4, we introduced two types of message processing: push-model and pull-model processing. At the time, we said that the GetMessage routine takes care of pull-model processing to read hardware event information. And yet, to determine the location of the mouse cursor, GetMessage relies on push-model processing. In more familiar terms, the GetMessage routine calls your window procedure as if it were a subroutine.

It does so using a Windows library routine that we have not yet encountered: SendMessage. A window procedure cannot be called directly. The reason has to do with the way that a window procedure is connected to Windows' push-model message mechanism. Instead, the SendMessage routine calls a window procedure for us. In other words, if you want to call a window procedure named MinWindowProc, you would never do this:

```
/* Do not call a window procedure like this.  */
MinWindowProc (hwnd, msg, wValue, lValue);
```

Instead, you would use the SendMessage routine like this:

```
lRetVal = SendMessage (hwnd, msg, wValue, lValue);
```

This is exactly like a function call. The window procedure is called immediately, using the four parameters specified. And like a function call, we get back whatever return value the window procedure has decided to give us.

The return value is very important in the context of the WM_NCHITTEST message that GetMessage sends to our window procedure. This message asks the window procedure to identify where the mouse cursor is resting. Most programs pass this message on to the default window procedure, which studies the location of the mouse cursor, and provides a **hit-test code** as a return value. The hit-test codes are shown in Figure 16.2.

Most of the hit-test codes describe a location on the window border, like HTTOP and HTTOPLEFT. Others identify different non-client area objects like scrollbars and menus. One of the hit-test codes, HTCLIENT, refers to the window's client area. GetMessage uses the hit-test code to decide the type of mouse message to generate. When the hit-test code is equal to HTCLIENT, a client area message is generated; all other hit-test codes cause non-client area mouse messages to be generated.

Before GetMessage returns a mouse message to our program, there is still one more thing it does: It makes sure the shape of the

Figure 16.2   *Windows hit-test codes*

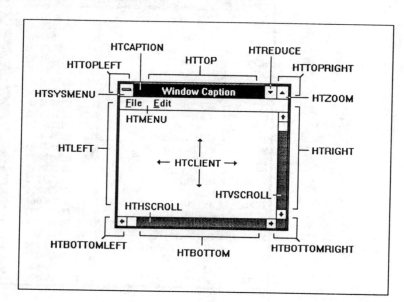

mouse cursor is correct for the location of the mouse. To do this, it sends yet another message to our window procedure: WM_SETCURSOR. Like the WM_NCHITTEST message, most programs ignore this message and allow the default window procedure to do the right thing. The hit-test code is included with the message as the low word of the lParam parameter, so that the default window procedure knows how to correctly set the cursor shape. For example, the HTTOP hit-test code indicates that a two-headed arrow cursor is needed to show the user that window resizing is available, while the HTMENU code summons the normal arrow cursor.

Figure 16.3 shows an example of SPY listening to mouse messages. This is typical mouse message traffic. With one exception, which we'll cover when we discuss *mouse capture*, the WM_NCHITTEST and WM_SETCURSOR messages always precede a mouse message. The reason now should be evident: Windows must first find the location of the mouse cursor to know whether to generate a client area or a non-client area message. Once the location is known, Windows makes sure that the user knows by setting the mouse cursor to the correct shape.

Figure 16.3   *SPY listening to mouse messages*

When we discussed keyboard input, we mentioned that Windows allows for the installation of message hooks, which can be used to alter the flow of messages. While we aren't going to take the time now to describe how to install a hook, you should be aware that a WH_GETMESSAGE hook can alter the flow of any client area or non-client area mouse message. Once GetMessage is ready to bring a message into our program, it makes a call to the hook to see if any changes need to be made before the message itself is delivered to a program.

Once GetMessage has brought a mouse message into our program, the message is sent on to the correct window procedure by the DispatchMessage routine. From the point of view of our program, the window procedure is where all the action is. So, let's take a look at how a window procedure can handle mouse traffic.

The Window Procedure

Of the 20 mouse messages that exist in Windows, 10 are non-client area messages and can be safely ignored by a window procedure. After all, the non-client area of a window is maintained by Windows. Among the 10 client area messages, one lets our program know the location of the mouse in our client area: WM_MOUSEMOVE. Of the other nine, three are for the left button, three for the middle button, and three for the right button. Since the processing for each set of messages is the same, and because most programs ignore the middle and right buttons, we're going to focus our attention on the left mouse button and its three messages: WM_LBUTTONDOWN, WM_LBUTTONUP, and WM_LBUTTONDBLCLK.

The WM_LBUTTONDOWN Message. When the user pushes the left mouse button with the cursor in our client area, our window procedure receives a WM_LBUTTONDOWN message. Besides telling us that a click has occurred in our client area, the two window procedure parameters, wParam and lParam, tell us quite a bit more about the message. Incidentally, the wParam and lParam values are the same for all client area mouse messages.

The lParam value in a mouse message contains the location of the mouse cursor, in client area coordinates. We introduced client area coordinates in Chapter 6. This coordinate system places the origin in the upper-left corner of the client area, with one unit equal to one pixel. Figure 16.4 shows how client area coordinates flip the normal Cartesian coordinate system upside-down, with the Y axis positive going downward.

Figure 16.4 *Client area coordinates*

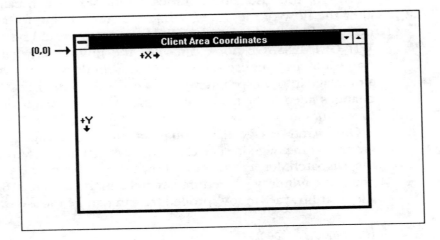

The X value is in the low word of lParam and the Y value is in the high word. One way to extract these values is to use the HIWORD and LOWORD macros, as shown here:

```
long FAR PASCAL WindowProc (...)
    {
    int xValue, yValue;

    switch (msg)
        {
        case WM_LBUTTONDOWN:
            xValue = LOWORD(lParam);
            yValue = HIWORD(lParam);
                .
                .
                .
```

But often it's more convenient to store the location of the mouse in a variable of type POINT. POINT is defined in Windows.h as

```
typedef struct tagPOINT
    {
    int    x;
    int    y;
    } POINT;
```

so that it has a place for a pair of integer values, x and y. There's a special macro, MAKEPOINT, which converts lParam into a POINT value. Here is how it is used:

```
long FAR PASCAL WindowProc (...)
    {
    POINT pt;

    switch (msg)
        {
        case WM_LBUTTONDOWN:
            pt = MAKEPOINT (lParam);
            .
            .
            .
```

We can then conveniently refer to pt.x and pt.y as the coordinate pair that tells us where the user is pointing in our client area.

The wParam value in a mouse message is a set of flags that describes the state of all three mouse buttons as well as the state of the Shift key and the Ctrl key. Figure 16.5 shows the layout of these flags.

The value of a field is 1 if the corresponding mouse button or keyboard key is down, otherwise the value is 0. To test whether a specific field is down, you can use the C language bitwise-AND operator, "&." Here is how to see if the shift key is down in response to a left-button down message:

```
long FAR PASCAL WindowProc (...)
    {

    switch (msg)
        {
        case WM_LBUTTONDOWN:
            if (wParam & MK_SHIFT)
                {
                /* Shift key is down.  */
                }
            .
            .
            .
```

The WM_LBUTTONUP Message. This message signals that the left mouse button has been released. In many ways, this message is

Figure 16.5 *Five fields of wParam for client area mouse messages*

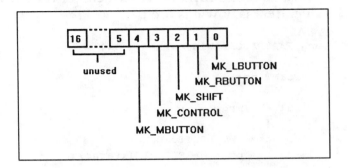

analogous to the WM_KEYUP keyboard message. And yet, Windows programs rarely pay attention to the WM_KEYUP message when handling keyboard input. The WM_LBUTTONDOWN message, on the other hand, is quite important. If you are writing a program that uses the mouse to draw, for example, this message will tell you when to stop drawing. In the enhanced rectangle drawing program that you'll find later in this chapter, this message is used both to finish drawing rectangles and to finish the job when we drag a rectangle across the window.

The WM_LBUTTONDBLCLK Message. At the beginning of this chapter, we introduced double-clicking as a common user action. To be effective, a program that responds to a double-click should be careful that the double-click is an extension of a single click. The reason is that a single click message will always be received before a double-click message.

For a window to receive double-click messages, it must have been defined with a special class style: CS_DBLCLKS. Here is a code fragment that shows how this is done:

```
.
.
.
wndclass.style = CS_DBLCLKS;
.
.
.
RegisterClass (&wndclass);
```

When a window has this bit set in its style definition, it changes the way that button down messages are handled: A button down message causes a timer to be started. This causes the system to incur some additional overhead. Even though this overhead is small, programs that don't plan to use double-click messages should avoid setting this style bit.

If a second button down message is received within a short (1/2 second) period of time, a double-click message is substituted for the second button down message. Here is the sequence of messages that will be sent when the user performs a double-click on the left mouse button:

Message	Comment
WM_LBUTTONDOWN	First button down message
WM_LBUTTONUP	
WM_LBUTTONDBLCLK	Replaces second button down message
WM_LBUTTONUP	

The WM_MOUSEMOVE Message. The fourth and final message that we're going to look at is the mouse movement message. As we mentioned earlier, Windows has a built-in mechanism to prevent mouse move messages from overflowing the hardware event queue. Thus, the mouse movement messages that a program receives might only provide a sampling of all of the places that mouse visited. But this sampling is sufficient for most programs to track the movement of this pointing device.

In a moment, we'll look at some sample programs that show the use of each of these mouse messages. But first, let's look at the last component that plays an important role in handling mouse messages, the default window procedure.

The Default Window Procedure

When we first introduced the default window procedure, we described it as the central reason that Windows programs behave in such a uniform manner. It provides all the basic, minimum processing that allows a common set of user actions to produce the same results from different Windows programs. Menus, scroll bars, and windows can all be accessed using the same set of user actions. This uniformity assumes, of course, that Windows programmers pass along all their "extra" messages. In the case of mouse messages, the default window procedure ignores the client area messages and instead relies on non-client area messages.

The default window procedure is also responsible for providing a common mouse and keyboard interface. It does this by translating input into a set of system commands, which show up as WM_SYS-COMMAND messages. And finally, the default window procedure handles the WM_NCHITTEST and WM_SETCURSOR messages which pave the way for almost all mouse messages.

When a mouse message gets to the default window procedure, it has arrived at its final destination. Starting at the mouse itself, mouse input follows a pretty direct route into a program. But, as we've seen, that route may cause Windows' multitasking switcher to stop feeding messages to one program and start feeding them to another. And finally, we've seen that half of the mouse messages that occur can be safely ignored—that is, assuming we pass our ignored messages on to the default window procedure.

For all this mouse theory to be helpful to you in building Windows programs, it would help to see some practical examples. In this chapter, we're going to show you three such examples. The first program, CARET2, will show how a mouse click can be used in a text input window to move a caret. Our second program, RECT2, is a revision of the rectangle drawing program we first encountered in Chapter 9. We'll explore the application of GDI raster operations to create stretchable rectangles and draggable objects. Our final program, DYNACURS, creates a mouse cursor "on the fly." It echoes the mouse location, using the cursor, and in the process shows how to use a Windows library routine that is new with Windows 3.0: CreateCursor.

A Mouse Input Sample: Caret2

In the last chapter, we introduced a program that receives keyboard input. We then enhanced this program with a caret so that the user could always see the current text entry position. Using the keyboard cursor keys, the user moves the caret to different positions in the text. Now that we've been discussing the use of the mouse, the time has come to enhance our program one more time so that the mouse can be used to move the caret.

CARET2.MAK

```
caret2.res: caret2.rc caret2.cur caret2.ico
    rc -r caret2.rc

caret2.obj: caret2.c
```

```
    cl -AM -c -d -Gsw -Ow -W2 -Zpi caret2.c

caret2.exe: caret2.obj caret2.def
    link caret2,/align:16,/map, mlibcew libw/NOD/NOE/CO,
caret2.def
    rc caret2.res caret2.exe

caret2.exe: caret2.res
    rc caret2.res caret2.exe
```

CARET2.C

```
/*------------------------------------------------------------*\
|    CARET2.C -- Shows keyboard caret and mouse input.        |
\*------------------------------------------------------------*/
#include <Windows.H>


/*------------------------------------------------------------*\
|                    Function Prototypes.                     |
\*------------------------------------------------------------*/
long FAR  PASCAL MinWndProc (HWND, WORD, WORD, LONG);
void NEAR PASCAL CrtSetCaretPos (HWND, int, char *, int *,
                                 int *, int);


/*------------------------------------------------------------*\
|                  Main Function:  WinMain.                   |
\*------------------------------------------------------------*/
int PASCAL WinMain (HANDLE hInstance,
                    HANDLE hPrevInstance,
                    LPSTR  lpszCmdLine,
                    int    cmdShow)
    {
    HWND     hwnd;
    MSG      msg;
    WNDCLASS wndclass;

    if (!hPrevInstance)
        {
        wndclass.lpszClassName = "MIN:MAIN";
        wndclass.hInstance     = hInstance;
        wndclass.lpfnWndProc   = MinWndProc;
```

```
        wndclass.hCursor        = LoadCursor (NULL, IDC_IBEAM);
        wndclass.hIcon          = LoadIcon (hInstance,"snapshot");
        wndclass.lpszMenuName   = NULL;
        wndclass.hbrBackground  = COLOR_WINDOW+1;
        wndclass.style          = CS_HREDRAW | CS_VREDRAW;
        wndclass.cbClsExtra     = 0;
        wndclass.cbWndExtra     = 0;

        RegisterClass( &wndclass);
        }

    hwnd = CreateWindow("MIN:MAIN",          /* Class name.  */
                        "Caret Demo 2",      /* Title.       */
                        WS_OVERLAPPEDWINDOW, /* Style bits.  */
                        CW_USEDEFAULT,       /* x - default. */
                        0,                   /* y - default. */
                        CW_USEDEFAULT,       /* cx - default. */
                        0,                   /* cy - default. */
                        NULL,                /* No parent.   */
                        NULL,                /* Class menu.  */
                        hInstance,           /* Creator      */
                        NULL                 /* Params.      */
                        ) ;
    ShowWindow (hwnd, cmdShow);
    while (GetMessage(&msg, 0, 0, 0))
        {
        TranslateMessage(&msg);         /*  Keyboard input.   */
        DispatchMessage(&msg);
        }
    return 0;
    }


/*-------------------------------------------------------------*\
|              Window Procedure:  MinWndProc.                   |
\*-------------------------------------------------------------*/
long FAR PASCAL MinWndProc (HWND hwnd,   WORD wMsg,
                            WORD wParam, LONG lParam)


    {
#define BUFSIZE 40
    static unsigned char acInput[BUFSIZE];/* Input array.    */
```

```
static int  cc = 0;                        /*  Character count. */
static int  icc = 0;                       /*  Array index.     */
static int  yLineHeight;
static int  xLeftMargin;
static int  xCaretPos, yCaretPos;
static RECT rHit;

switch (wMsg)
    {
    case WM_CHAR:
        {
        DWORD dw;
        HDC hdc;
        int i;

        /*  Backspace.  */
        if (wParam == VK_BACK)
            {
            if (icc == 0)
                MessageBeep(0);
            else  /*  Remove a character.  */
                {
                icc--;
                CrtSetCaretPos (hwnd, icc, acInput,
                    &xCaretPos, &yCaretPos, xLeftMargin);

                for (i=icc;i<cc;i++)
                    acInput[i]=acInput[i+1];
                cc--;
                InvalidateRect (hwnd, NULL, TRUE);
                }
            break;
            }

        /*  Filter out unwanted character codes.  */
        if (wParam <= VK_ESCAPE)
            {
            MessageBeep(0);  /* Complain.  */
            break;
            }
```

```
        /*  Complain if buffer is full.  */
        if (cc >= BUFSIZE)
            {
            MessageBeep (0);
            break;
            }

        /*  Make room for a new character.  */
        for (i=cc;i>icc;i--)
            acInput[i]=acInput[i-1];

        /*  Put new character in buffer.  */
        acInput[icc] = (unsigned char)wParam;;

        icc++;
        cc++;
        CrtSetCaretPos (hwnd, icc, acInput,
              &xCaretPos, &yCaretPos, xLeftMargin);

        InvalidateRect (hwnd, NULL, TRUE);
        }
        break;

    case WM_CREATE:
        {
        HDC hdc;
        TEXTMETRIC tm;

        hdc = GetDC (hwnd);
        GetTextMetrics (hdc, &tm);
        yLineHeight = tm.tmHeight + tm.tmExternalLeading;
        xLeftMargin = tm.tmAveCharWidth;
        ReleaseDC (hwnd, hdc);
        }
        break;

    case WM_DESTROY:
        PostQuitMessage(0);
        break;

    case WM_KEYDOWN:
```

```
                {
                DWORD dw;
                HDC hdc;
                int i;

                switch (wParam)
                    {
                  case VK_DELETE:
                      /*  If end of buffer, complain.  */
                      if (icc == cc)
                          MessageBeep(0);
                      else  /*  Remove a character.  */
                          {
                          for (i=icc;i<cc;i++)
                              acInput[i]=acInput[i+1];
                          cc--;
                          InvalidateRect (hwnd, NULL, TRUE);
                          }
                      break;
                  case VK_END:
                      icc = cc;
                      CrtSetCaretPos (hwnd, icc, acInput,
                          &xCaretPos, &yCaretPos, xLeftMargin);
                      break;
                  case VK_HOME:
                      icc = 0;
                      CrtSetCaretPos (hwnd, icc, acInput,
                          &xCaretPos, &yCaretPos, xLeftMargin);
                      break;
                  case VK_LEFT:
                      if (icc > 0)
                          {
                          icc--;
                          CrtSetCaretPos (hwnd, icc, acInput,
                              &xCaretPos, &yCaretPos,
xLeftMargin);
                          }
                      else MessageBeep(0);
                      break;
                  case VK_RIGHT:
                      if (icc < cc)
```

```
                              {
                              icc++;
                              CrtSetCaretPos (hwnd, icc, acInput,
                                   &xCaretPos, &yCaretPos,
xLeftMargin);

                              }
                      else MessageBeep(0);
                      break;
                }
            }
            break;

        case WM_KILLFOCUS:
            DestroyCaret();
            break;

        case WM_LBUTTONDOWN:
            {
            DWORD dw;
            HDC hdc;
            int i;
            int xTotWidth;
            int xPrevHalfWidth;
            int xNextHalfWidth;
            POINT pt;

            pt = MAKEPOINT (lParam);

            /*  First check:  is it in our hit area?  */
            if (PtInRect(&rHit, pt))
                {
                hdc = GetDC (hwnd);
                xTotWidth = xLeftMargin;
                xPrevHalfWidth = xLeftMargin;

                icc = cc;  /* Default = end of string.  */

                /*  Next: loop through characters.  */
                for (i=0;i<cc;i++)
                    {
                    dw = GetTextExtent (hdc, &acInput[i], 1);
```

```
                    xNextHalfWidth = LOWORD(dw)/2;
                    if ((xTotWidth - xPrevHalfWidth) <= pt.x &&
                        (xTotWidth + xNextHalfWidth) >  pt.x)
                        {
                        /*  A hit!  Set caret position.  */
                        icc = i;
                        break;
                        }
                    xPrevHalfWidth = xNextHalfWidth;
                    xTotWidth += LOWORD(dw);
                    }

            /*  Any mousing around in the hit rectangle   */
            /*     will cause caret to move.               */
            CrtSetCaretPos (hwnd, icc, acInput,
                &xCaretPos, &yCaretPos, xLeftMargin);

            ReleaseDC (hwnd, hdc);
            }
        }
        break;

    case WM_PAINT:
        {
        DWORD dw;
        HDC hdc;
        PAINTSTRUCT ps;

        hdc = BeginPaint (hwnd, &ps);
        TextOut (hdc, xLeftMargin, yLineHeight,
                acInput, cc);

        /* Calculate and save hit rectangle.  */
        GetClientRect (hwnd, &rHit);
        rHit.top     = yLineHeight,
        dw = GetTextExtent (hdc, acInput, cc);
        rHit.bottom = rHit.top + HIWORD (dw);

        EndPaint (hwnd, &ps);
        }
        break;
```

```
        case WM_SETFOCUS:
            {
            DWORD dw;
            HDC hdc;

            hdc = GetDC (hwnd);
            dw = GetTextExtent (hdc, acInput, icc);
            xCaretPos = xLeftMargin + LOWORD(dw);
            yCaretPos = yLineHeight;
            ReleaseDC (hwnd, hdc);
            CreateCaret(hwnd, 0, 0, yLineHeight);
            SetCaretPos (xCaretPos, yCaretPos);
            ShowCaret (hwnd);
            }
            break;

        default:
            return(DefWindowProc(hwnd,wMsg,wParam,lParam));
            break;
        }
    return 0L;
    }


void NEAR PASCAL CrtSetCaretPos (HWND hwnd,
                                 int icc,
                                 char * acInput,
                                 int *pxCaretPos,
                                 int *pyCaretPos,
                                 int xLeftMargin)

    {
    DWORD dw;
    HDC hdc;

    hdc = GetDC (hwnd);
    dw = GetTextExtent (hdc, acInput, icc);
    ReleaseDC (hwnd, hdc);
    *pxCaretPos = LOWORD(dw) + xLeftMargin;
    SetCaretPos (*pxCaretPos, *pyCaretPos);
    }
```

CARET2.RC

```
snapshot icon min.ico
```

CARET2.DEF

```
NAME CARET2

EXETYPE WINDOWS

DESCRIPTION 'Caret and Mouse Demo'

CODE      MOVEABLE DISCARDABLE
DATA      MOVEABLE MULTIPLE

HEAPSIZE      512
STACKSIZE    5000

EXPORTS
    MinWndProc
```

System Cursors

All of the programs that we've seen up to now have used the hand cursor that we created for the MIN program back in Chapter 2. But since CARET2 uses the mouse to point at text, we're going to take advantage of a predefined system cursor that is more suitable for working with text: the I-Beam cursor. This tall, skinny cursor is well suited for working in the narrow space between text characters.

Figure 16.6 shows Windows' eleven predefined system cursors. In many ways, these cursors are like the stock objects that we encountered in our discussion of GDI programming. To use a system cursor, you need a handle to the cursor. The LoadCursor routine does the job for us, and is defined as follows:

```
HCURSOR LoadCursor (hInstance, lpCursorName)
```

- hInstance is the instance handle of the module that owns the cursor, or NULL for a system cursor.
- lpCursorname is the name of the cursor in the resource file. Or, for system cursors, is one of the identifiers shown in Figure 16.6

The easiest way to incorporate a system cursor into a program is to make the cursor part of the class definition during program initialization. This is just what we did to get the I-Beam cursor into CARET2. Here are the lines of code that attached this cursor to the window class of our program's main window:

```
.
.
wndclass.hCursor = LoadCursor (NULL, IDC_IBEAM);
.
.
RegisterClass( &wndclass);
```

Figure 16.6 *Windows predefined system cursors*

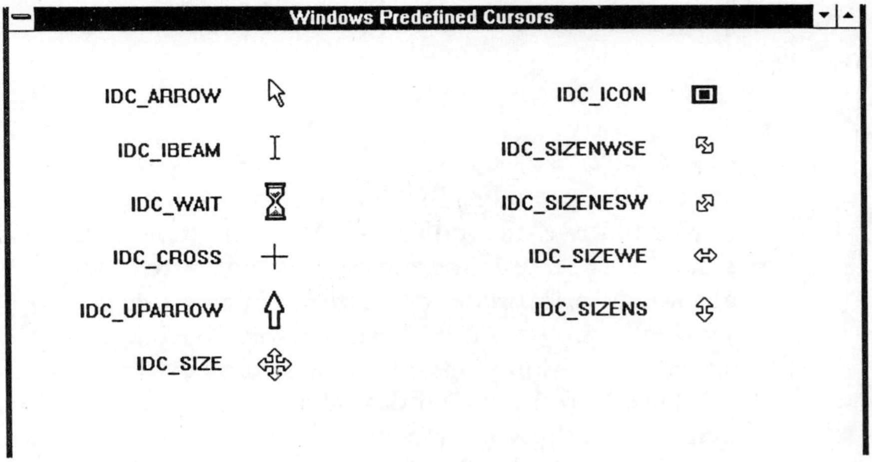

But suppose our program was going to be busy for a moment or two and wanted to display the hourglass cursor to let the user know that an operation is going to take an extended amount of time. This is typical when saving a file, or performing another lengthy operation. It's a simple matter to change the cursor for a moment using the SetCursor routine. SetCursor takes a single parameter: a cursor handle. First, of course, we'll need to get a handle to the hourglass cursor. Here is code that does this:

```
WindowProc (...)
    {
    static HCURSOR hcrWait;

    switch(msg)
        {
        case WM_CREATE:
            hcrWait = LoadCursor (NULL, IDC_WAIT);
            .
            .
            .
```

Here is how to change the cursor:

```
{
int hcrOld;

hcrOld = SetCursor (hcrWait);
.
.
/*  Lengthy operation.  */
.
.
SetCursor (hcrOld);
}
```

Another way to switch cursors involves responding to the WM_SETCURSOR message. This is useful when we wish to use a different cursor to show the user that we're working in a different mode. For example, a drawing program might use an I-Beam to show that text input is expected, and a Cross cursor to show that rectangle drawing is expected. Of course, we need to start by getting a handle to these two system cursors, which we do as follows:

```
WindowProc (...)
    {
    static HCURSOR hcrIBeam;
    static HCURSOR hcrCross;

    switch(msg)
        {
        case WM_CREATE:
            hcrIBeam = LoadCursor (NULL, IDC_IBEAM);
            hcrICross= LoadCursor (NULL, IDC_CROSS);

            .
            .
```

In response to the WM_SETCURSOR message, here is how we would set the cursor properly:

```
        .
        .
        case WM_SETCURSOR:
            if (LOWORD(lParam) == HTCLIENT)
                {
                if (fType == TEXT)
                    SetCursor (hcrIBeam);
                else
                    SetCursor (hcrCross);
                }
            else
                DefWindowProc (hwnd, msg,
                                wParam, lParam);
            break;
        .
        .
```

When processing the WM_SETCURSOR message, it is important to check the hit-test code that is passed in the low word of lParam. After all, we're only interested in client area mouse messages. All other messages should be passed on to the default window procedure.

Later in this chapter, we're going to investigate other alternatives for changing a program's cursor, including the creation of cursor's "on the fly."

Hit-Testing

Besides using the I-Beam system cursor, the primary difference between CARET2 and CARET has to do with the way that the WM_LBUTTONDOWN message is handled. CARET ignores this message, and CARET2 uses it to detect where to place the mouse cursor.

Connecting mouse input to objects that are drawn on the display is called **hit-testing**. There are two Windows library routines for hit-testing: PtInRegion and PtInRect. Both routines tell you if a point lies inside a specified area. The PtInRect routine lets you define the area in terms of a simple rectangle, while PtInRegion lets the area be defined in terms of a region. As you may recall from our discussion of clipping in Chapter 10, a region is defined by a set of rectangles. Let's take a closer look at PtInRect, which is the routine that CARET2 used.

The PtInRect routine is defined as follows:

```
BOOL PtInRect (lpRect, Point)
```

- lpRect is a long pointer to a RECT data structure that contains the rectangle against which the hit-testing is performed.
- Point is a variable of type POINT. That is, it is an X and a Y value.

The return value is TRUE if the point is inside the rectangle, otherwise it returns FALSE.

CARET2 uses the PtInRect routine to determine if the cursor is located within a hit rectangle. The hit rectangle is defined when the text is displayed, that is, in response to the WM_PAINT message. It makes sense to define the hit areas during the WM_PAINT message, since the coordinates of the output need to be calculated to handle the requirements of output. It's a simple matter to store these values away so that they can be useful to test mouse input.

The PtInRect routine is only used for preliminary hit-testing to see if the cursor is located anywhere inside an imaginary rectangle that bounds the text and extends to the left and right borders of the window. But we need to do some more work to determine exactly where the cursor is resting to properly place the caret.

Actually, since a caret should always be placed between two characters, the real issue involves figuring out the letter break that lies closest to the cursor. CARET2 has it easy, since the caret position is defined in terms of character cells by the variable `icc`. CARET2 calculates the hit area by looping through the array of characters, `acInput`.

The key to understanding the character hit-test loop lies with three variables: xTotWidth, xPrevHalfWidth, and xNextHalfWidth, visually depicted in Figure 16.7. Notice first of all that we're only interested in X values. The reason is simple: The PtInRect test has already determined that we're in the proper Y range. The value of xTotWidth is the total width of the text, including the margin. This means that xTotWidth is the distance from the left border measured in client area coordinates. The xPrevHalfWidth variable holds a value equal to one-half the width of the previous character. xNextHalfWidth holds a value of one-half the width of the next character. As we loop through the array of characters, hit-testing becomes simple: We test whether the point is between the beginning of the previous character and the end of the next character, as shown here:

```
if ((xTotWidth - xPrevHalfWidth) <= pt.x &&
    (xTotWidth + xNextHalfWidth) >  pt.x)
    {
    /*  A hit!  Set caret position.  */
    icc = i;
    break;
    }
```

Once a hit is made, it's a simple matter to set the current character position variable, icc, break out of the loop, and call our private

Figure 16.7   *Hit testing characters in CARET2*

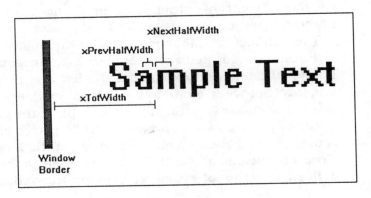

caret moving routine, CrtSetCaretPos. Of course, this routine calls the Windows routine, SetCaretPos, to do the actual work.

CARET2 has shown a number of things: the use of predefined system cursors, and one approach to take in combining mouse input with text. Of course, part of the challenge in working with the system font is the fact that it is nonproportional. Hit-testing a fixed pitch font, after all, would be quite a bit easier. But Windows gives you all the tools you need to make the hit-testing work.

There is certainly room for improvement in this program. For example, it would probably be more efficient to calculate the width of each character cell ahead of time. Once stored away, much of the hit-testing and caret movement becomes simpler. Of course, this improvement has its trade-off in memory used.

Now let's look at our second sample program. This time, we've improved on the rectangle drawing program from Chapter 14.

Dragable Objects and Stretchable Rectangles

As the mouse cursor travels across the system display, it seems to perform a little magic. It can go anywhere on the display screen, and yet it never causes any damage to any of the objects it walks over. In most cases, this magic is the result of software. A well-written device driver gives the illusion that the mouse cursor isn't part of the rest of the display. In other cases, the magic is part of the hardware. Some display adapters have a built-in ability to support cursors. Whichever approach is taken, the result is the same: the cursor never causes any damage to any objects on the display screen.

A similar effect is seen when a window is moved. If the user clicks on the caption bar of a window (or selects the Move item on the system menu), a dotted outline of the window lets the user see the proposed location for the window as it is moved. Thus, the user can preview the results of the move before actually committing to the move.

These same type of "floating images" can be very useful in a Windows program. They can be used to help the user reposition objects in a window. Since they don't damage other objects in the window, the user can arrange objects in different ways before committing to one arrangement or another.

These effects can be achieved using GDI **raster operation (or ROP) codes**. We first discussed the topic of ROP codes in Chapter 13. We did not provide a programming example then, however, since ROP codes are most easily understood in the context of the mouse.

As you may recall, a raster operation is a combination of one or more Boolean operations applied between a source, which might be a pen or a brush, and a destination. Some of the raster operations ignore the source and simply change the destination. In a moment, we're going to look at a sample program, RECT2, which uses the NOT operator to produce the effect of dragable and stretchable rectangles.

A dragable rectangle can be grabbed (using the mouse) and placed in a new position. Although our demonstration program uses rectangles, the principle is the same if you wish to drag any object that is drawn using GDI's pixel, line, or filled area routines. Figure 16.8 shows an example of a rectangle being dragged in our sample program. Notice how the outline of the rectangle is always visible, no matter what color is part of the background. Also, as it is moved, it doesn't damage the other rectangles. Both of these qualities are achieved using raster operations.

A stretchable rectangle is also drawn using raster operations. A stretchable rectangle lets you preview the rectangle as it is drawn. By providing this feedback, the rectangle drawing program makes it easy to avoid unwanted effects. Figure 16.9 shows how a stretchable

Figure 16.8 *A dragable rectangle*

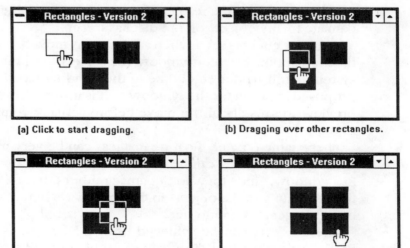

[a] Click to start dragging.

[b] Dragging over other rectangles.

[c] Still dragging.

[d] Release to place rectangle.

Figure 16.9   *A stretchable rectangle*

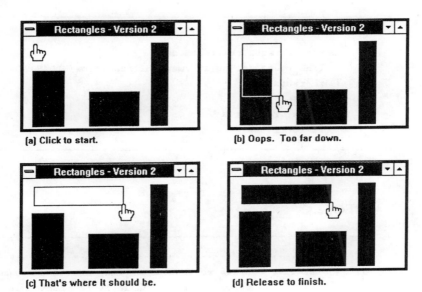

(a) Click to start.   (b) Oops. Too far down.

(c) That's where it should be.   (d) Release to finish.

rectangle helps position a rectangle as it is drawn. In the (b) panel, this preview capability helps us see that we've made a mistake. But this mistake is easily corrected before we commit to our final rectangle.

Like our first rectangle drawing program, RECT2 draws rectangles in response to mouse button activity. The first corner of a rectangle is selected by pressing the mouse button. The second, opposing corner is selected by releasing the mouse button. As the mouse is dragged from the first corner to the second corner, a stretchable rectangle outline is echoed to the user to let them know where the final rectangle is to be placed. RECT2 has also been enhanced to allow the user to drag rectangles. The drag action is differentiated from a drawing operation by the use of the Shift key to accompany a button click.

RECT2.MAK

```
rect2.res: rect2.rc rect2.cur rect2.ico
    rc -r rect2.rc
```

```
cl -AM -c -d -Gsw -Od -W2 -Zp1 rect2.c
```

```
rect2.exe: rect2.obj rect2.def
    link rect2,/align:16,/map, mlibcew libw/NOD/NOE/CO, rect2.def
    rc rect2.res

rect2.exe: rect2.res
    rc rect2.res
```

RECT2.C

```
/*--------------------------------------------------------------*\
|    RECT2.C - Draws rectangles in response to mouse messages, |
|              echoing a stretchable rubber rectangle.         |
|              A rectangle can be moved when it is clicked     |
|              with the SHIFT key depressed.                   |
\*--------------------------------------------------------------*/
#include <Windows.H>


/*--------------------------------------------------------------*\
|                    Function Prototypes.                      |
\*--------------------------------------------------------------*/
long FAR  PASCAL RecWndProc (HWND, WORD, WORD, LONG);
void NEAR PASCAL Rect2DrawNotRect (HWND, int, int, int, int);


/*--------------------------------------------------------------*\
|                    Main Function:  WinMain.                  |
\*--------------------------------------------------------------*/
int PASCAL WinMain (HANDLE hInstance,
                    HANDLE hPrevInstance,
                    LPSTR  lpszCmdLine,
                    int    cmdShow)

    {
    HWND      hwnd;
    MSG       msg;
    WNDCLASS  wndclass;
```

```
    if (!hPrevInstance)
        {
        wndclass.lpszClassName = "RECT:MAIN";
        wndclass.hInstance     = hInstance;
        wndclass.lpfnWndProc   = RecWndProc;
        wndclass.hCursor       = LoadCursor (hInstance, "hand");
        wndclass.hIcon         = LoadIcon (hInstance,"snapshot");
        wndclass.lpszMenuName  = NULL;
        wndclass.hbrBackground = COLOR_WINDOW+1;
        wndclass.style         = CS_HREDRAW | CS_VREDRAW;
        wndclass.cbClsExtra    = 0;
        wndclass.cbWndExtra    = 0;

        RegisterClass( &wndclass);
        }

    hwnd = CreateWindow("RECT:MAIN",          /* Class name.  */
                                              /* Title.       */
                    "Rectangles - Version 2",
                    WS_OVERLAPPEDWINDOW,      /* Style bits.  */
                    CW_USEDEFAULT,            /* x - default. */
                    0,                        /* y - default. */
                    CW_USEDEFAULT,            /* cx - default. */
                    0,                        /* cy - default. */
                    NULL,                     /* No parent.   */
                    NULL,                     /* Class menu.  */
                    hInstance,                /* Creator.     */
                    NULL                      /* Params.      */
                    ) ;

ShowWindow (hwnd, cmdShow);

while (GetMessage (&msg, 0, 0, 0))
    {
    TranslateMessage (&msg);         /* Keyboard input.   */
    DispatchMessage (&msg);
    }
```

```
}
```

```
/*--------------------------------------------------------------*\
|                  Window Procedure:  RecWndProc.              |
\*--------------------------------------------------------------*/
long FAR PASCAL RecWndProc (HWND hwnd,    WORD msg,
                            WORD wParam, LONG lParam)

    {
#define MAXRECTS 50
    static BOOL    fCapture = FALSE;
    static BOOL    fDrag    = FALSE;
    static int     cRects = 0;
    static int     iDrag  = -1;
    static POINT   ptDrag;
    static RECT    r[MAXRECTS];

    switch (msg)
        {
        case WM_DESTROY:
            PostQuitMessage(0);
            break;

        case WM_LBUTTONDOWN:
            {
            int i;
            POINT pt;

            SetCapture (hwnd);
            fCapture = TRUE;

            pt = MAKEPOINT (lParam);

            /*  Always record starting point.  */
            r[cRects].left = r[cRects].right  = pt.x;
            r[cRects].top  = r[cRects].bottom = pt.y;

            /*  If not dragging, exit.  */
            if (!(MK_SHIFT & wParam))
                break;

            /*  Loop through all rectangles.  */
            for (i=cRects-1;i>=0;i--)
                {
```

```
            if (PtInRect (&r[i], pt))

                            {
                            ptDrag = pt;
                            fDrag = TRUE;
                            iDrag = i;
                            InvalidateRect (hwnd, &r[i], TRUE);
                            UpdateWindow (hwnd);
                            Rect2DrawNotRect (hwnd, r[iDrag].left,
                                                    r[iDrag].top,
                                                    r[iDrag].right,
                                                    r[iDrag].bottom);

                            break;
                            }
                    }
            }
        break;

    case WM_LBUTTONUP:
        if (!fCapture)
            break;

        ReleaseCapture ();
        fCapture = FALSE;

        if (fDrag)
            {
            Rect2DrawNotRect (hwnd, r[iDrag].left,
                                    r[iDrag].top,
                                    r[iDrag].right,
                                    r[iDrag].bottom);
            InvalidateRect (hwnd, &r[iDrag], TRUE);

            fDrag = FALSE;
            iDrag = -1;
            }
        else
            {
            int i;

            Rect2DrawNotRect (hwnd, r[cRects].left,
                                    r[cRects].top,
```

```
                                      r[cRects].right,

                                        r[cRects].bottom);

            /*  Make sure order is correct: left < right.  */
            if (r[cRects].left > r[cRects].right)
                {
                i = r[cRects].left;
                r[cRects].left = r[cRects].right;
                r[cRects].right = i;
                }

            /*  Top should be less than bottom.  */
            if (r[cRects].top > r[cRects].bottom)
                {
                i = r[cRects].top;
                r[cRects].top = r[cRects].bottom;
                r[cRects].bottom = i;
                }

            InvalidateRect (hwnd, &r[cRects], TRUE);

            cRects++;
            if (cRects == MAXRECTS) cRects = 0;
            }
        break;


    case WM_MOUSEMOVE:
        {
        POINT pt;

        if (!fCapture)
            break;

        pt = MAKEPOINT (lParam);

        if (fDrag)
            {
            /* Remove previous rectangle.  */
            Rect2DrawNotRect (hwnd, r[iDrag].left,
                                    r[iDrag].top,
```

```
                                    r[iDrag].right,

                                            r[iDrag].bottom);

            /*  Calculate relative movement.  */
            ptDrag.x = ptDrag.x - pt.x;  // X-offset
            ptDrag.y = ptDrag.y - pt.y;  // Y-offset

            r[iDrag].left    -= ptDrag.x;
            r[iDrag].top     -= ptDrag.y;
            r[iDrag].right   -= ptDrag.x;
            r[iDrag].bottom  -= ptDrag.y;

            /*  Remember drag point for next time.  */
            ptDrag = pt;

            /* Draw next rectangle.  */
            Rect2DrawNotRect (hwnd, r[iDrag].left,
                                    r[iDrag].top,
                                    r[iDrag].right,
                                    r[iDrag].bottom);
        }
    else
        {
        /* Remove previous rectangle.  */
        Rect2DrawNotRect (hwnd, r[cRects].left,
                                r[cRects].top,
                                r[cRects].right,
                                r[cRects].bottom);

        r[cRects].right  = pt.x;
        r[cRects].bottom = pt.y;

        /* Draw a new rectangle.  */
        Rect2DrawNotRect (hwnd, r[cRects].left,
                                r[cRects].top,
                                r[cRects].right,
                                r[cRects].bottom);
        }
    }
break;
```

```
        case WM_PAINT:

            {
            PAINTSTRUCT ps;
            HDC hdc;
            int i;

            hdc = BeginPaint (hwnd, &ps);
            SelectObject (hdc, GetStockObject (BLACK_BRUSH));

            for (i = 0; i < cRects ; i++ )
                {
                if (i == iDrag)
                    continue;
                Rectangle (hdc, r[i].left, r[i].top,
                                r[i].right, r[i].bottom);

                }

            EndPaint (hwnd, &ps);
            }
            break;

        default:
            return(DefWindowProc(hwnd,msg,wParam,lParam));
            break;
        }
    return 0L;
    }

/*-----------------------------------------------------------*\
 |           Rect2DrawNotRect: Draw a NOT Rectangle.          |
\*-----------------------------------------------------------*/
void NEAR PASCAL Rect2DrawNotRect (HWND hwnd, int x1, int y1,
                                   int x2, int y2)

    {
    HDC hdc;

    hdc = GetDC (hwnd);
    SelectObject (hdc, GetStockObject (NULL_BRUSH));
    SetROP2 (hdc, R2_NOT);
    Rectangle (hdc, x1, y1, x2, y2);
    ReleaseDC (hwnd, hdc);
```

}

RECT2.RC

```
snapshot icon rect2.ico

hand   cursor rect2.cur
```

RECT2.DEF

```
NAME      RECT2

EXETYPE WINDOWS

DESCRIPTION 'Rectangles/Mouse Demo.   (c)Copyright Paul Yao, 1990'

CODE      MOVEABLE DISCARDABLE
DATA      MOVEABLE MULTIPLE

HEAPSIZE      512
STACKSIZE    5000

EXPORTS
```

```
RecWndProc
```

Dragging and Stretching

Any program that does any dragging or stretching will be interested in three mouse messages: button down, mouse move, and button up. In response to the button down message, the window procedure does whatever initialization it needs to do to make the dragging or stretching work. The mouse move message means the mouse cursor has moved, and that the dragged or stretched object needs to be modified to reflect that movement. The simplest way to handle this is to erase the image of the object at the old location and create a copy of the object at the new location. The button up message means that no more movement is required, so dragging or stretching can be turned off and the object made permanent.

While movement is going on, the raster operations provide a convenient manner to quickly draw and erase the moveable/stretchable rectangles. The particular raster operation that we use is the one associated with the NOT operation, R2_NOT. A nice feature of this raster operation is that it virtually guarantees that the object you draw will appear. Every white pixel encountered will turn black and every black pixel encountered will turn white. Pixels that have colors other than black and white will be changed to the logical inverse color. You'll find that this produces some slightly unexpected results—like the fact that R2_NOT of Blue on a 16-color VGA adapter gives Yellow (instead of Orange). This is a limitation of the hardware, and a compromise to allow a reasonable set of colors to be available on this device.

In spite of this odd behavior with color, the second—and most important—advantage of the R2_NOT raster operation is that everything is easily reversible. Let's look at the two-color monochrome case to convince ourselves that this is true. The *first* time a figure (say a rectangle) is drawn, every white pixel turns black and every black pixel turns white. The *second* time the same figure is drawn, every white pixel turns black and every black pixel turns white. But after the figure is drawn the second time, the figure itself disappears. Put together, the two advantages of the R2_NOT raster operation are ideal for drawing dragable and stretchable rectangles.

In RECT2, the routine that draws all of the R2_NOT rectangles is Rect2DrawNotRect. It calls GetDC for a DC that can draw anywhere in the client area. It selects the stock null brush into the DC, so that we only draw the outline of the rectangle. It sets the raster operation to R2_NOT by calling the SetROP2 routine, then draws a rectangle. The routine itself doesn't know (or care) whether it is drawing the first rectangle—to make one appear—or the second rectangle—to make it disappear.

A second issue that is raised by the RECT2 program is that of the mouse capture, which we're going to discuss next.

The Mouse Capture

Mouse messages are always sent to the window lying under the mouse cursor. In this way, the user is free to move the cursor to the desired program and start it running with a mouse click. But there are times when it makes sense to restrict all mouse messages to one window. In particular, it is useful when some operation has started that must be completed in order to leave the program in a stable, known state. Rectangle dragging and stretching are two such times.

In RECT2, when the WM_LBUTTONDOWN message is received, the program gets set up to draw a new rectangle or to move an existing rectangle. The program expects to receive another message—a WM_LBUTTONUP—before things are returned to "normal." If a second WM_LBUTTONDOWN message is received before a WM_LBUTTONUP message, it will cause some confusion in the program and a mess in the window.

To make sure that our window gets the expected sequence of messages, the window procedure **captures** the mouse. This is done by making a call to SetCapture, which takes a single parameter: a window handle. A call is made to SetCapture in response to the WM_LBUTTONDOWN message, which guarantees that no other window will get a mouse message until the capture is released.

Releasing the capture is done by making a call to ReleaseCapture, which is a Windows library routine that takes no parameters. RECT2 calls ReleaseCapture in response to a WM_LBUTTONUP message, to allow other programs to receive mouse messages from the user.

In Chapter 7, we introduced the Windows sandwich. The idea is that the use of a system resource is sandwiched between two calls: The first call obtains the resource and the second call releases the resource. This is certainly an accurate description of the way the mouse capture is handled. In culinary terms:

The Windows Sandwich	Applied to Mouse Capture
Top Slice of Bread	SetCapture() called at WM_LBUTTONDOWN time
Filling	Mouse events used during WM_MOUSEMOVE
Bottom Slice of Bread	ReleaseCapture() called at WM_LBUTTONUP time

The final point to be made about the mouse capture is that the hit-testing and cursor setting messages are disabled when the mouse is captured. That is, you will not encounter the WM_NCHITTEST or WM_SETCURSOR messages when the mouse is captured. The hit-testing message, WM_NCHITTEST, after all, tests whether a client area or non-client area message should be sent, and only client area messages are sent when the mouse is captured. And the WM_SETCURSOR is not sent since Windows doesn't expect the cursor to change when one window has reserved all mouse input for itself.

At this point, we're going to turn our attention to the third sample program of this chapter. It creates a mouse cursor on the fly, which is a capability that is new with Windows 3.0.

Creating Dynamic Cursors

In Chapter 2, when we introduced the minimum Windows program, we created a custom cursor in the shape of a hand. As you may recall, we used two tools: the Paintbrush program, which drew the basic outline of a hand, and SDKPaint, which we used to fine-tune the bits in the cursor. Once the cursor was created, it was saved to a file, MIN.CUR, which was referenced in the resource file for our minimum Windows program, MIN.RC.

While a static custom cursor like this will serve most of your needs, there may be times when you need to create a dynamic cursor. A dynamic cursor is one that is created by a Windows program at execution time, instead of during program development time. One way to create a dynamic cursor is to create a GDI bitmap and then use GDI routines to draw the desired shape. This is the approach we will take. This simple description hides the fact that quite a bit of shuffling is required to create a custom cursor.

The DYNACURS Program

Our dynamic cursor program echoes the current mouse location.

Figure 16.10   *The cursor in DYNACURS echoes the mouse location*

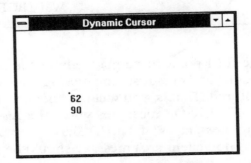

Figure 16.10 shows a sample of its output. The "hot-spot" of the cursor is in the upper-left corner, marked by a dot. The top number is the X-location of the cursor, and the bottom number is the Y-location.

One of the first things you notice when you run this program is the way the cursor seems to blink a lot. That is, as the mouse moves and the cursor changes, the dynamic cursor doesn't have the smooth quality that we associate with a normal cursor. The reason has to do with the fact that the background—the area "behind" the cursor—must be restored every time the cursor changes. While this would be a very annoying feature in a commercially released Windows product, it's only a minor flaw in a program that demonstrates the creation of dynamic cursors.

DYNACURS.MAK

```
dynacurs.res: dynacurs.rc dynacurs.ico
    rc -r dynacurs.rc

dynacurs.obj: dynacurs.c
    cl -AM -c -d -Gsw -Ow -W2 -Zpi dynacurs.c

dynacurs.exe: dynacurs.obj dynacurs.def
    link dynacurs,/align:16,/map, mlibcew libw/NOD/NOE/CO, \
        dynacurs.def
    rc dynacurs.res

dynacurs.exe: dynacurs.res
    rc dynacurs.res
```

DYNACURS.C

```
/*-------------------------------------------------------------*\
|    DYNACURS - Creates a dynamic cursor on the fly.           |
\*-------------------------------------------------------------*/
#include <Windows.H>


/*-------------------------------------------------------------*\
|                    Function Prototypes.                      |
\*-------------------------------------------------------------*/
long FAR PASCAL MinWndProc (HWND, WORD, WORD, LONG);
```

```
/*------------------------------------------------------------*\
|                  Main Function:  WinMain.                   |
\*------------------------------------------------------------*/


int PASCAL WinMain (HANDLE hInstance,
                    HANDLE hPrevInstance,
                    LPSTR  lpszCmdLine,
                    int    cmdShow)
    {
HWND     hwnd;
MSG      msg;
WNDCLASS wndclass;

if (!hPrevInstance)
    {
    wndclass.lpszClassName = "MIN:MAIN";
    wndclass.hInstance     = hInstance;
    wndclass.lpfnWndProc   = MinWndProc;
    wndclass.hCursor       = NULL;
    wndclass.hIcon         = LoadIcon (hInstance,"snapshot");
    wndclass.lpszMenuName  = NULL;
    wndclass.hbrBackground = COLOR_WINDOW+1;
    wndclass.style         = NULL;
    wndclass.cbClsExtra    = 0;
    wndclass.cbWndExtra    = 0;

    RegisterClass( &wndclass);
    }

hwnd = CreateWindow("MIN:MAIN",            /* Class name.  */
                    "Dynamic Cursor",      /* Title.       */
                    WS_OVERLAPPEDWINDOW,   /* Style bits.  */
                    CW_USEDEFAULT,         /* x - default. */
                    0,                     /* y - default. */
                    CW_USEDEFAULT,         /* cx - default. */
                    0,                     /* cy - default. */
                    NULL,                  /* No parent.   */
                    NULL,                  /* Class menu.  */
                    hInstance,             /* Creator      */
                    NULL                   /* Params.      */
                    ) ;
    ShowWindow (hwnd, cmdShow);
```

```
    while (GetMessage(&msg, 0, 0, 0))
        {
        TranslateMessage(&msg);            /*  Keyboard input.      */

        DispatchMessage(&msg);
        }
    return 0;
    }


/*-------------------------------------------------------------------*\
  |                 Window Procedure:  MinWndProc.                    |
\*-------------------------------------------------------------------*/
long FAR PASCAL MinWndProc (HWND hwnd,      WORD wMsg,
                            WORD wParam, LONG lParam)

    {
    static HCURSOR hcr = 0;
    static HBITMAP hbm;
    static HBITMAP hbmOld;
    static HBRUSH  hbrWhite;
    static HBRUSH  hbrBlack;
    static HDC hdcBitmap;
    static HANDLE hmemAND;
    static HANDLE hmemXOR;
    static int cbSize;
    static int cxCursor;
    static int cyCursor;

    switch (wMsg)
        {
        case WM_CREATE:
            {
            HDC hdc;

            /*  Find out expected size of cursor.  */
            cxCursor = GetSystemMetrics (SM_CXCURSOR);
            cyCursor = GetSystemMetrics (SM_CYCURSOR);

            /*  Create some scratch objects:  */

                /*  A bitmap.  */
            hbm = CreateBitmap (cxCursor,  // width
```

```
                                  cyCursor,    // height
                                  1,           // planes
                                  1,           // bits per pixel
```

```
                               NULL);      // initial data

                /*   A DC for the bitmap.  */
        hdc = GetDC (hwnd);
        hdcBitmap = CreateCompatibleDC (hdc);
        ReleaseDC (hwnd, hdc);

                /*   Connect the bitmap to the DC.  */
        hbmOld = SelectObject (hdcBitmap, hbm);

                /*   Some memory scratch space.  */
        cbSize = (cxCursor/8) * cyCursor;
        hmemAND = GlobalAlloc (GMEM_MOVEABLE,   // flags
                              (DWORD)cbSize); // size

        hmemXOR = GlobalAlloc (GMEM_MOVEABLE,   // flags
                              (DWORD)cbSize); // size

        /*  Get GDI objects to use.  */
        hbrWhite = GetStockObject (WHITE_BRUSH);
        hbrBlack = GetStockObject (BLACK_BRUSH);

        /* Error checking.  */
        if (hbm == NULL      || hdcBitmap == NULL ||
            hmemAND == NULL || hmemXOR == NULL      ||
            cxCursor%8 != NULL)
            {
            MessageBox (hwnd, "Unable to Initialize",
                        "Dynamic Cursor", MB_OK);
            DestroyWindow (hwnd);
            break;
            }
        }
        break;

    case WM_DESTROY:
        SelectObject (hdcBitmap, hbmOld);
        DeleteDC (hdcBitmap);
```

```
            DeleteObject (hbm);
            DestroyCursor(hcr);
            GlobalFree (hmemAND);
```

```
          GlobalFree (hmemXOR);

          PostQuitMessage(0);  /* Say good-bye Gracie.  */
          break;

      case WM_SETCURSOR:
          {
          char acLine1[8];
          char acLine2[8];
          int  cc1;
          int  cc2;
          LPSTR lpAND;
          LPSTR lpXOR;
          POINT pt;

          /* Ignore all non-client area messages.  */
          if (LOWORD(lParam) != HTCLIENT)
              goto DefaultExit;

          /*  Set up AND Mask.  */
          SelectObject (hdcBitmap, hbrWhite);
          PatBlt (hdcBitmap, 0, 0, cxCursor, cyCursor,
                  PATCOPY);

          /* Light up the hot-spot.  */
          SetPixel (hdcBitmap, 0, 0, 0L);
          SetPixel (hdcBitmap, 0, 1, 0L);
          SetPixel (hdcBitmap, 1, 0, 0L);
          SetPixel (hdcBitmap, 1, 1, 0L);

          /*  Where is the mouse cursor?  */
          GetCursorPos (&pt);
          ScreenToClient (hwnd, &pt);

          cc1 = wsprintf (acLine1,"%d", pt.x);
          cc2 = wsprintf (acLine2,"%d", pt.y);

          /*  Write coordinates onto bitmap.  */
```

```
            TextOut (hdcBitmap, 3, 0, acLine1, cc1);
            TextOut (hdcBitmap, 3, cyCursor/2, acLine2, cc2);
```

```
            /*  Set up memory to grab bits.  */
            lpAND = GlobalLock (hmemAND);
            if (lpAND == NULL) goto DefaultExit;
            GetBitmapBits (hbm, (DWORD)cbSize, lpAND);

            /*  Set up XOR Mask.  */
            SelectObject (hdcBitmap, hbrBlack);
            PatBlt (hdcBitmap, 0, 0, cxCursor, cyCursor,
                    PATCOPY);

            /*  Set up memory to grab bits.  */
            lpXOR = GlobalLock (hmemXOR);
            if (lpXOR == NULL) goto DefaultExit;
            GetBitmapBits (hbm, (DWORD)cbSize, lpXOR);

            /*  Remove old cursor.  */
            if (hcr != NULL) DestroyCursor(hcr);

            /*  Spin a cursor on the fly.  */
            hcr = CreateCursor (
                GetWindowWord (hwnd, GWW_HINSTANCE),
                0,          // X-hotspot
                0,          // Y-hotspot
                cxCursor,   // width
                cyCursor,   // height
                lpAND,      // AND bitmask
                lpXOR);     // XOR bitmask

            GlobalUnlock (hmemAND);
            GlobalUnlock (hmemXOR);

            SetCursor (NULL);  // Turn off cursor.
            SetCursor (hcr);   // Set to our new cursor.
            }
            break;

        default:
DefaultExit:
            return(DefWindowProc(hwnd,wMsg,wParam,lParam));
            break;
```

```
        }
    return OL;
    }
```

DYNACURS.RC

```
snapshot icon dynacurs.ico
```

DYNACURS.DEF

```
NAME      DYNACURS

EXETYPE WINDOWS

DESCRIPTION 'Dynamic Cursor'

CODE      MOVEABLE DISCARDABLE
DATA      MOVEABLE MULTIPLE

HEAPSIZE       512
STACKSIZE     5000

EXPORTS
    MinWndProc
```

DYNACURS is interested in three messages: WM_CREATE, WM_DESTROY, and WM_SETCURSOR. In response to the WM_CREATE message, several objects are created and initialized that will be needed to support the cursor creation. This includes a monochrome memory bitmap, a device context to connect to the bitmap, and some dynamically allocated memory. The WM_SETCURSOR message triggers the dynamic cursor creation, which involves determining the mouse cursor location, calling GDI routines to write this location to the memory bitmaps, and then calling the CreateCursor routine to convert this data into a full-fledged cursor. In response to the third message, WM_DESTROY, DYNACURS cleans up and deallocates the objects that were created in response to the WM_CREATE message. To understand why these objects are needed, it will help to explore the insides of a cursor, so that you'll know what makes it tick.

Table 16.2   *Truth table for cursor creation*

AND Mask	XOR Mask	Cursor
0 (Black)	0 (Black)	Black
0 (Black)	1 (White)	White
1 (White)	0 (Black)	Display
1 (White)	1 (White)	Not Display

How Cursors Work

A cursor is a data object that consists of two parts. Each part is a monochrome bitmap that is combined with the pixels of the display surface to create the cursor image. The first part is called the AND mask, to reflect the fact that the pixels of this bitmap are combined with the surface using the logical AND operation. The second part of the cursor is called the XOR mask, which again reflects the fact that a logical operation, XOR, is used to combine this bitmap with the display surface.

When the display driver draws a cursor, it starts by making a copy of the pixels that are already on the display surface. This insures that the old image can be restored, and is key in maintaining the integrity of the image on the display surface. Once the copy has been made, the AND mask is applied to the surface, followed by the XOR mask. Through the magic of Boolean operations, this two-step process allows four different effects: black, white, display, and not-display. By "display," we mean that the cursor is transparent and allows the background to show through. By "not-display," we mean the pixels on the background are inverted. This is a rarely used combination, but it can provide some interesting effects. For example, the not-display effect might be used on a cursor in the shape of a magnifying glass to help suggest the fuzzy distortion of the lens surface. Table 16.2 has a truth table that shows how pixels of the AND mask and XOR mask combine to create the four effects.

To create an all black cursor, you need to set both masks to black. An all white cursor would result from an all black AND mask and an all white XOR mask. DYNACURS creates black text on a transparent (display colored) background by combining an AND mask of black text on a white background with an all black XOR mask.

The routine that creates a dynamic cursor is CreateCursor, defined as

```
CreateCursor (hInstance, xHotSpot, yHotSpot, nWidth,
              hHeight, lpANDbitPlane, lpXORbitPlane);
```

- hInstance is the instance handle that was passed to our program as a parameter to WinMain. If you don't want to store this value in a global variable and if you have a window handle, you can call GetWindowWord like this to get the instance handle:

```
GetWindowWord (hwnd, GWW_HINSTANCE)
```

- xHotSpot is the X coordinate for the cursor hot-spot.
- yHotSpot is the Y coordinate for the cursor hot-spot.
- nWidth is the width in pixels of the cursor. If the size we provide doesn't match the size desired by the display driver, our cursor will be stretched (or shrunk). To make sure we have a match, we ask Windows to provide the size that the display driver expects. The following call provides the correct width value:

```
GetSystemMetrics (SM_CXCURSOR);
```

- nHeight is the height in pixels of the cursor. We set this value to match the size desired by the display driver by calling the following routine:

```
GetSystemMetrics (SM_CYCURSOR);
```

- lpANDbitPlane is a LPSTR (char far *) pointer to the bits that make up the AND mask.
- lpXORbitPlane is a LPSTR (char far *) pointer to the bits that make up the XOR mask.

Here is the call that DYNACURS makes to create the dynamic cursor:

```
hcr = CreateCursor (
    GetWindowWord (hwnd, GWW_HINSTANCE),
    0,          // X-hotspot
    0,          // Y-hotspot
    cxCursor,   // width
    cyCursor,   // height
    lpAND,      // AND bitmask
    lpXOR);     // XOR bitmask
```

Most of the work that we need to do to create a custom cursor involves creating the two bit masks. Understanding what DYNACURS does to get these two bit masks requires an understanding of two topics, GDI Bitmaps and dynamic memory allocation. Since these two topics will be the subject of later chapters, we're going to limit our discussion to a brief introduction.

Creating a GDI Bitmap

In our introduction to GDI in Chapter 10, we described a bitmap as a type of pseudo device that is used primarily to store pictures. If you think of a bitmap as nothing more than a type of device, you will be half way to understanding how to use them. The other half involves understanding how to get a handle to a DC that will allow you to write on a bitmap. The following calls accomplish that:

```
/*  Create some scratch objects:  */

      /*  A bitmap.  */
hbm = CreateBitmap (cxCursor,   // width
                    cyCursor,   // height
                    1,          // planes
                    1,          // bits per pixel
                    NULL);      // initial data

      /*  A DC for the bitmap.  */
hdc = GetDC (hwnd);
hdcBitmap = CreateCompatibleDC (hdc);
ReleaseDC (hwnd, hdc);

      /*  Connect the bitmap to the DC.  */
hbmOld = SelectObject (hdcBitmap, hbm);
```

The first routine, CreateBitmap, requests GDI to allocate the memory that will be used to store the bits of our bitmap. The width and height values, cxCursor and cyCursor, come from Windows itself, which tells us, via the GetSystemMetrics routine, the size of the cursor that the current display driver expects to use:

```
/*  Find out expected size of cursor.  */
cxCursor = GetSystemMetrics (SM_CXCURSOR);
cyCursor = GetSystemMetrics (SM_CYCURSOR);
```

To build a cursor, we need a monochrome bitmap, which is the reason we set the number of planes to 1 and the bits per pixel to 1. The CreateBitmap routine returns a handle to a bitmap, of the type HBITMAP, which we store in the variable hbm.

By itself, a bitmap is just a block of memory. We need to create a connection to the memory, and also a set of drawing tools that will allow us to send output to the bitmap just like we send output to the display device. We need a device context. The simplest way to create a DC is to ask GDI to make a copy of an existing DC for us. This is accomplished with the following calls:

```
hdc = GetDC (hwnd);
hdcBitmap = CreateCompatibleDC (hdc);
ReleaseDC (hwnd, hdc);
```

We borrow and return a DC with a GetDC/ReleaseDC pair, and create a new DC with the call to CreateCompatibleDC. The value returned by CreateCompatibleDC is a handle to a DC. But by itself, it has no connection to our bitmap (or any device, for that matter), so we need to create a connection. We do this by calling SelectObject:

```
hbmOld = SelectObject (hdcBitmap, hbm);
```

As you may recall, we use the SelectObject routine to install pens, brushes, and other drawing objects into a DC. But the bitmap is more than just a drawing object—it is a full-fledged drawing surface. Or, as we have said earlier, a *pseudo device*. Once the bitmap and DC are connected, we draw to the bitmap by calling any GDI drawing routine and providing the DC handle as a parameter. When the bitmap is connected to the DC SelectObject provides, we save the value returned by SelectObject so that we can later disconnect the bitmap from the DC. At cleanup time, this will make it easy to destroy both objects.

At this point, we've seen how to create a bitmap. Let's look at how DYNACURS uses the bitmap.

Using the GDI Bitmap

When DYNACURS receives a WM_SETCURSOR message, it draws into our bitmap to create the desired pixel patterns for the AND and XOR bit masks. The bits are then copied from the bitmap into two dynamically allocated pieces of memory, since CreateCursor does not read a bitmap directly but instead reads the bit masks as blocks of memory. These bit masks are passed to CreateCursor via the two pointers that make up CreateCursor's last two parameters.

The first bit mask that gets set up is the AND mask. First, we set all the bits to white, using a routine called PatBlt. This GDI routine fills a rectangular area on a drawing surface using the currently selected brush. Here is the code that does this for us:

```
SelectObject (hdcBitmap, hbrWhite);
PatBlt (hdcBitmap, 0, 0, cxCursor, cyCursor,
        PATCOPY);
```

Drawing the four pixel square hot spot involves four calls to Set-Pixel:

```
SetPixel (hdcBitmap, 0, 0, 0L);
SetPixel (hdcBitmap, 0, 1, 0L);
SetPixel (hdcBitmap, 1, 0, 0L);
SetPixel (hdcBitmap, 1, 1, 0L);
```

DYNACURS then makes a call to GetCursorPos, which finds out the location of the mouse cursor in **screen coordinates**. Like client area coordinates, screen coordinates are pixel units. But they differ from client area coordinates in that the origin (0,0) is at the upper-left corner of the entire screen instead of the upper-left corner of the client area. To convert from one to the other, a call is made to ScreenToClient. Then, the coordinates are converted from integer values to a character string, and the two lines are written onto the bitmap:

```
GetCursorPos (&pt);
ScreenToClient (hwnd, &pt);

cc1 = wsprintf (acLine1,"%d", pt.x);
cc2 = wsprintf (acLine2,"%d", pt.y);

/*  Write coordinates onto bitmap.  */
TextOut (hdcBitmap, 3, 0, acLine1, cc1);
TextOut (hdcBitmap, 3, cyCursor/2, acLine2, cc2);
```

At this point, the bitmap contains the image that we want to use for the AND mask on the cursor. But we have to ask GDI to make a copy of the bits in a form that CreateCursor will accept. This is the job of the GetBitmapBits routine. GetBitmapBits is defined as follows:

```
DWORD GetBitmapBits (hBitmap, dwCount, lpBits)
```

- hBitmap is a handle to a bitmap.
- dwCount is a DWORD value for the size of the storage area.
- lpBits is a char far * (LPSTR) flag that points to the data area to hold the bits.

The following line of code from DYNACURS copies the bits from the bitmap into a block of dynamically allocated memory, suitable for passing to CreateCursor:

```
GetBitmapBits (hbm, (DWORD)cbSize, lpAND);
```

The creation of the XOR bit mask is similar, but much simpler. The PatBlt routine is called to set every pixel in the bitmap to black. Once this is done, a call is made to GetBitmapBits to copy the bits from the bitmap to a piece of dynamically allocated memory. To fully understand how DYNACURS works, we need to explore further the allocation and use of dynamically allocated memory.

Dynamically Allocating Memory

The reason that dynamically allocated memory is necessary is that there is no way to anticipate the amount of memory that may be required to hold the bits of a cursor. For example, here are the cursor sizes and memory requirement for some of today's popular display adapters:

Display Adapter	Cusor Size	Memory Required
CGA	32 x 16	64 bytes
EGA/VGA	32 x 32	128 bytes
8514/a	64 x 64	512 bytes

New display adapters may come along tomorrow that require larger blocks of memory to store the AND and XOR bit masks, so, to be safe, we depend upon dynamic memory allocation to provide the memory we need.

If you've done a lot of C language programming, you're probably familiar with `malloc`, the C-runtime library routine which dynamically allocates memory. For reasons that we'll describe in Chapter 18, Windows programmers don't use this routine, but instead will rely on two sets of memory allocating routines that are built into Windows. Here are the routines that DYNACURS uses:

Routine Name	Description
GlobalAlloc	Allocates a block (segment) of memory.
GlobalLock	Locks the memory in place and provides a far pointer.
GlobalUnlock	Unlocks the memory to allow it to move.
GlobalFree	Deallocates a block of memory.

To determine the amount of memory that is required, we start by asking Windows for the cursor size that the display adapter requires:

```
cxCursor = GetSystemMetrics (SM_CXCURSOR);
cyCursor = GetSystemMetrics (SM_CYCURSOR);
```

Since cxCursor is the width in pixels and cyCursor is the height in pixels, we can get the total size in bytes necessary to store this object by dividing cxCursor by eight and then multiplying by cyCursor, like this:

```
cbSize = (cxCursor/8) * cyCursor;
```

We allocate two blocks of memory: one for the AND mask and one for the XOR mask using the GlobalAlloc routine, as shown here:

```
hmemAND = GlobalAlloc (GMEM_MOVEABLE,    // flags
                       (DWORD)cbSize); // size
```

```
hmemXOR = GlobalAlloc (GMEM_MOVEABLE,    // flags
                       (DWORD)cbSize); // size
```

The GMEM_MOVEABLE flag tells Windows that it can move the object when we aren't using it. This is necessary because Windows runs in the real mode of the Intel-86 family of CPUs. This particular mode doesn't provide any hardware assistance to manage memory. And so Windows programs must manage memory in a way that cooperates with Windows and with other Windows programs. The GMEM_MOVEABLE flag offers a reasonable compromise between usefulness and cooperativeness. We'll explore the use of this and other flags more fully in Chapter 18.

GlobalAlloc returns a handle to the memory block, which serves to identify a block of memory, although it does not tell us where movable memory is located. To find that out, we must lock the memory down using the GlobalLock routine. This routine returns a far pointer to the memory block, which is how we can access it. GlobalLock is defined as follows:

```
LPSTR GlobalLock (hMem)
```

- hMem is a handle to a global memory object, allocated with the GlobalAlloc routine.

Here are the lines of code from DYNACURS that lock the memory so it can be accessed. Notice that we check the return value to make sure that we have retrieved a valid pointer. This is a good habit to get into, since a NULL pointer can cause problems depending on Windows' operating mode. In real mode, it allows you to trash the interrupt vectors located at the very low end of memory. In protect mode, it causes a protection violation which results in the termination of your program. Neither alternative is attractive, and it is quick and easy to avoid these problems.

```
lpAND = GlobalLock (hmemAND);
if (lpAND == NULL) goto DefaultExit;

lpXOR = GlobalLock (hmemXOR);
if (lpXOR == NULL) goto DefaultExit;
```

After we are done using a block of dynamically allocated memory, we unlock the memory objects by calling GlobalUnlock. The primary reason we do this is to allow our programs to behave nicely when Windows is running in real mode:

```
GlobalUnlock (hmemAND);
GlobalUnlock (hmemXOR);
```

The final issue that we need to address is the freeing of our memory objects when DYNACURS gets a WM_DESTROY message. That is the job of the GlobalFree routine. Windows is smart enough to reclaim unused memory when a program exits, but we think it's a good programming practice to clean up after yourself. After all, someone may later use your code as part of a larger programming project and may not check to make sure that you have cleaned up properly. And since GDI objects do not automatically get cleaned up, you must make sure to destroy the GDI objects that you have created. Here is how DYNACURS cleans up the memory, the leftover cursor, and GDI objects that it created:

```
    .
    .
case WM_DESTROY:
    SelectObject (hdcBitmap, hbmOld);
    DeleteDC (hdcBitmap);
    DeleteObject (hbm);
    DestroyCursor(hcr);
    GlobalFree (hmemAND);
    GlobalFree (hmemXOR);

    PostQuitMessage(0);  /* Say good-bye Gracie. */
    break;
    .
    .
```

While creating a dynamic cursor takes a lot of work, it provides a way to create custom cursors at run time. You might create a cursor in the shape of a clock face or a timer to count down a lengthy operation. You can even let the user define their own private, custom cursors. And any cursor you create can be used as an icon as well, since the two user interface objects share the exact same format.

Figure 16.11   *Another dynamic cursor*

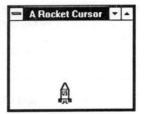

We're going to step back a moment and look at a cursor created with the CreateCursor routine that doesn't involve GDI bitmaps or dynamically allocated memory. If you found the earlier example to be somewhat long and involved, this might help you appreciate exactly what is happening when a cursor is created on the fly.

A Simpler Dynamic Cursor

A simpler way to create a dynamic cursor involves figuring out the layout of the AND mask and XOR mask ahead of time by hand, and passing a pointer to these masks to the CreateCursor routine. A serious drawback to this approach is that it is horribly device-dependent. But it illustrates the creation of a dynamic cursor in a somewhat simpler fashion that may help clarify exactly what was happening in our last example. Figure 16.11 shows our dynamic cursor, which is in the shape of a rocket.

Here is the window procedure of the program that created this:

```
/*----------------------------------------------------------------*\
|              Window Procedure:  MinWndProc.                      |
\*----------------------------------------------------------------*/
long FAR PASCAL MinWndProc (HWND hwnd,    WORD wMsg,
                            WORD wParam, LONG lParam)

    {
    static char acAND[] = {0xff, 0xff, 0xff, 0xff,   // Scan 1
                           0xff, 0xfe, 0x3f, 0xff,   // Scan 2
                           0xff, 0xfc, 0x1f, 0xff,   // Scan 3
                           0xff, 0xfc, 0x9f, 0xff,   // Scan 4
                           0xff, 0xf8, 0x8f, 0xff,   // Scan 5
```

```
                              0xff, 0xf9, 0xcf, 0xff,   // Scan 6
                              0xff, 0xf1, 0xc7, 0xff,   // Scan 7
                              0xff, 0xf3, 0xe7, 0xff,   // Scan 8
                              0xff, 0xe3, 0xe3, 0xff,   // Scan 9
                              0xff, 0xe7, 0xf3, 0xff,   // Scan 10
                              0xff, 0xc0, 0x01, 0xff,   // Scan 11
```

```
                              0xff, 0xcf, 0xf9, 0xff,   // Scan 12
                              0xff, 0xca, 0x89, 0xff,   // Scan 13
                              0xff, 0xca, 0x89, 0xff,   // Scan 14
                              0xff, 0xca, 0xb9, 0xff,   // Scan 15
                              0xff, 0xca, 0x89, 0xff,   // Scan 16
                              0xff, 0xca, 0x89, 0xff,   // Scan 17
                              0xff, 0xca, 0xe9, 0xff,   // Scan 18
                              0xff, 0xc8, 0x89, 0xff,   // Scan 19
                              0xff, 0xc8, 0x89, 0xff,   // Scan 20
                              0xff, 0xcf, 0xf9, 0xff,   // Scan 21
                              0xff, 0xcf, 0xf9, 0xff,   // Scan 22
                              0xff, 0xcf, 0xf9, 0xff,   // Scan 23
                              0xff, 0xcf, 0xf9, 0xff,   // Scan 24
                              0xfe, 0x00, 0x00, 0x3f,   // Scan 25
                              0xfe, 0x00, 0x00, 0x3f,   // Scan 26
                              0xfe, 0x4f, 0xf9, 0x3f,   // Scan 27
                              0xfe, 0x4d, 0x59, 0x3f,   // Scan 28
                              0xfe, 0x0d, 0x58, 0x3f,   // Scan 29
                              0xfe, 0x0d, 0x58, 0x3f,   // Scan 30
                              0xff, 0xfd, 0x5f, 0xff,   // Scan 31
                              0xff, 0xf1, 0xc7, 0xff};  // Scan 32

static char acXOR[] ={0, 0, 0, 0, 0, 0, 0, 0,
                      0, 0, 0, 0, 0, 0, 0, 0,
                      0, 0, 0, 0, 0, 0, 0, 0,
                      0, 0, 0, 0, 0, 0, 0, 0,
                      0, 0, 0, 0, 0, 0, 0, 0,
                      0, 0, 0, 0, 0, 0, 0, 0,
                      0, 0, 0, 0, 0, 0, 0, 0,
                      0, 0, 0, 0, 0, 0, 0, 0,
                      0, 0, 0, 0, 0, 0, 0, 0,
                      0, 0, 0, 0, 0, 0, 0, 0,
                      0, 0, 0, 0, 0, 0, 0, 0,
                      0, 0, 0, 0, 0, 0, 0, 0,
                      0, 0, 0, 0, 0, 0, 0, 0,
```

```
                         0, 0, 0, 0, 0, 0, 0, 0,
                         0, 0, 0, 0, 0, 0, 0, 0,
                         0, 0, 0, 0, 0, 0, 0, 0};

        static HCURSOR hcr;


        switch (wMsg)
            {
          case WM_CREATE:
            hcr = CreateCursor (
                    GetWindowWord (hwnd, GWW_HINSTANCE),
                    0,          // X-hotspot
                    0,          // Y-hotspot
                    32,         // width
                    32,         // height
                    acAND,      // AND bitmask
                    acXOR);     // XOR bitmask
                break;


          case WM_DESTROY:
                PostQuitMessage(0);
                break;


          case WM_SETCURSOR:
                if (LOWORD(lParam) == HTCLIENT)
                    SetCursor (hcr);
                else
                    return(DefWindowProc(hwnd,wMsg,wParam,lParam));
                break;


          default:
                return(DefWindowProc(hwnd,wMsg,wParam,lParam));
                break;
            }
        return 0L;
        }
```

While this shows a simple way to create a dynamic cursor, there are several problems. First, the cursor is very device-dependent. This cursor works properly with EGA and VGA display adapters, both of which use a 32x32 bit cursor, but will not work on devices which take a different sized cursor. In addition, this is not a very dynamic cursor. You would be better off creating a regular static cursor than using this approach. What this does do, we hope, is provide a simpler framework for understanding the way that dynamic cursor creation works.

This concludes our look at how a Windows program receives keyboard and mouse input from the user. In the next section, we'll be looking at how different Windows user interface objects—like menus, windows, and dialog boxes—can be blended into a Windows program.

Part 6

Operating System Considerations

17

Memory, Part I: System Memory Management

To fully appreciate the way that Windows manages memory, you need to look at the hardware on which Windows runs: the Intel-86 family of CPUs. Among the members of this family are the 8086, 8088, 80186, 80188, 80286, 80386-SX, 80386-DX, and 80486 microprocessors. One reason that Windows runs on all these processors is that Intel designed each new CPU with an eye toward creating a migration path from the older processors. As advanced capabilities were introduced in new processors, doors were always left open to help migrate software from older chips.

From the start, Windows was built with the more advanced chips in mind. The architect of memory management in Windows 1.x was Steve Wood, a former Yale graduate student who started working for Microsoft in June of 1983. He laid the foundation for Windows' memory management, which he modeled after the protect mode of the Intel 286 processor. In those days, Microsoft was contemplating a successor to DOS, and planned for Windows to run with the new operating system. Of course, today we know that OS/2 is that operating system and, with the help of Microsoft's Software Migration Kit (SMK), Windows programs can be run inside the OS/2 Presentation Manager graphical user interface.

Each subsequent version of Windows built on the original design to improve memory use. The architect of Windows' memory management for Windows 2.x and 3.x, David Weise, was also one of the designers of the EMS 4.0 Memory Specification. This allowed him to build EMS support into Windows 2.x and to continue that support in Real-Mode Windows 3.0. This latest version of Windows has a flexible approach to memory use that allows it to push the limits of whatever processor it finds itself running with.

In this chapter, we're going to discuss the three operating modes that Windows 3.0 uses to manage memory across the wide range of capabilities that exist in the Intel-86 family of CPUs. We're going to discuss how memory is managed from the point of view of Windows—that is, from the point of view of the *operating system*. In the next chapter, we'll continue our discussion of memory by looking at how *programs* manage memory. Let's start our discussion by getting down to bare metal: Let's start by looking at the processors.

The Intel-86 Family of Processors

We're going to limit our discussion to the processors that represent the three memory modes in which Windows operates: the 8088, 80286, and 80386. These represent the most widely used chips and most significant milestones in the development of this processor family.

The Physical Address Space

One important aspect worth considering with any microprocessor is the maximum amount of memory that it can access—that is, the size of its address space. One way to determine this is to count the number of memory addressing lines that connect the processor to system memory. That number raised to a power of 2 is the size of the address space. For example, the 8088 has 20 address lines, which translates into a 2^{20} or 1 megabyte (1,048,576 bytes) address space. With 24 address lines, the 80286 can address 2^{24} or 16 megabytes (16,777,216 bytes) of physical RAM. And finally the 80386, with its 32 address lines, can use up to 2^{32} or 4 gigabytes (4,294,967,296 bytes) of system memory.

Every byte of memory in the system has its own unique physical address, starting at zero on up to n-1 for a system with n bytes of memory. For example, the 8088 has a memory address range from 0 to 1,048,575. In this regard, the Intel-86 family of processors is like any other processor. The physical address allows the CPU to communicate with the memory addressing hardware. But this is not how software communicates an address to the CPU. Instead, to application software, the address space is only available through a segmented memory addressing scheme.

Segmented Memory

All members of the Intel-86 family use segmented memory addressing. As we mentioned in an earlier chapter, it may help to understand this if you think about building addresses in the physical world. The Prime Minister of Great Britain, for example, lives at Number 10 Downing Street; the President of the United States lives at 1600 Pennsylvania Avenue. A two-part logical address gives each program the freedom to divide its address space into many small "streets" or *segments*, each of which can hold from one to 65,535 "houses" or *bytes*. And, if we may push the analogy further, this approach permits operating system software to give each program its own "city"—that is, its own private address space.

To programmers unaccustomed to the Intel-86 family of processors, segmented addressing can be both confusing and frustrating. But it provides some benefits worth considering. For experienced DOS and OS/2 programmers, segmented addressing will be very familiar, although you should pay attention to the particular way that Windows operates in this environment.

A key benefit of segmented addressing is software migration. This architecture was first selected by Intel to allow software to migrate from the older 8-bit 8080 processor to the first member of this family, the 8086. The continued adoption of this addressing scheme has allowed DOS to run on all members of the Intel-86 family when they run in real-mode. It is also one of the reasons that DOS programs can run under the various Intel-86 based operating systems, like Windows, OS/2 and UNIX. And finally, it gives properly written Windows programs a migration path from the earlier versions of Windows to the protect mode operation of Windows 3.x, and on into future versions.

From the point of view of software development, segmented addressing is helpful in program debugging. A program can be divided into multiple code and data segments to create "fire-walls" between different parts of an application. Fire-walls prevent bad memory references in one part of an application from contaminating the data in another part of the application, and therefore make programs easier to debug. In protect mode, the processor complains loudly when an invalid segment reference is made, or when a program tries to read or write beyond the end of a memory segment.

And finally, a benefit of segmented programs is that they provide the operating system with hints about the **working sets** of a program. These hints can result in improved performance and lower memory requirements. A working set is a division of a program that performs a task or a set of tasks for the user. Since Windows incorporates an overlay facility called **dynamic linking**, at any given moment only *part* of a program has to be loaded into memory (see Chapter 19 for details on dynamic linking). If each working set in a program is a cleanly defined set of code segments, memory use is optimized. In a low-memory situation, Windows discards code segments from the current working set *last*. In this way, a program with well-defined working sets—what Windows programmers call "well-tuned"—will have lower memory requirements than the same program that hasn't been tuned. The latter program will slow down in a low-memory situation, since Windows will have to continually re-read previously discarded code segments from disk: a situation commonly called **disk-thrashing**.

Microsoft includes a swap-tuning utility with the Windows Software Development Kit to help determine the working sets of a program. The information generated by this facility will help you restructure your program to optimize code structure and memory use. In the next chapter, we'll discuss issues related to the segmenting of a Windows program.

The Logical Address

While a CPU uses a physical address to read and write in physical memory, programmers use a higher level abstraction called a **logical address**. It's the job of the CPU to translate logical addresses into physical addresses to access memory locations in the physical address space. This is illustrated in Figure 17.1.

The translation process that takes place in the CPU might be very simple or very involved, depending on the current operating mode of the CPU. In *real mode*, for example, simple bit shifting and addition is involved. In the various *protect modes*, however, the CPU uses a lookup table to determine how to map a logical address into a physical address. This lookup table allows the operating system to move memory objects so that it can minimize fragmentation of physical memory. The operating system can even play tricks like writing memory to disk to implement virtual memory. If you are familiar with the operation of OS/2 version 1.x, you know that its virtual memory manager writes segments to disk. And finally, the higher end 80386 and 80486 chips have special hardware that, when enabled, provides an additional level of indirection that divides memory into four K-byte pages. This paging mechanism is particularly

Figure 17.1 *The Translation of a logical address to a physical address*

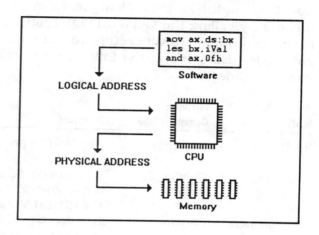

useful in creating a very efficient virtual memory system, which is how the Windows memory manager implements virtual memory in 386 Enhanced Mode.

In a moment, we're going to take a close look at each of the operating modes that Windows uses. But first, let's look at the pieces that make up a logical address. Every processor in the Intel-86 family uses a two-part logical address, made up of a **segment identifier** and an **offset**.

The *segment identifier* specifies the segment of memory that we are interested in. The segment identifier is a 16-bit value that is the "street name" that we're working on. In the logical-to-physical address translation process, it answers the question "where in the world is the segment." The answer might be within the physical address space of the CPU, or, in a virtual memory system, swapped out to disk.

The second part of a logical address, the *offset*, indicates the number of bytes into a specific segment to look for the bytes we want to work with. If the segment identifier is the street name, then the offset is the house number. Or, you can think of a segment as an array and the offset as an array index. In any event, both segment identifier and offset are used together to address specific bytes in system memory.

With this introduction to the basics of memory addressing for the Intel-86 family, let's take a look at how the Intel-86 family supports Windows' operating modes: Real Mode, Standard Mode, and 386

Enhanced Mode. To check the current mode, a user can look at the About box in the Program Manager. From a program, you can find this out by calling the **GetWinFlags** routine. Also, providing you have the proper hardware setup, you can manually start the different modes using one of the following switches on the Windows' command line:

Mode	Windows Command Line	Comment
Real	C> win /r	Any Intel-86 processor with 640K of RAM.
Standard	C> win /2	Requires 80286 or 80386 CPU with 640K plus 192K extended memory and the HIMEM.SYS driver.
386-Enhanced	C> win /3	Requires 80386 CPU with 640K plus 1 megabyte extended memory and the HIMEM.SYS driver.

Real Mode Operation

While all members of the Intel-86 family can operate efficiently in real mode, it is usually associated with the oldest members of this family, the 8086 and 8088. With 20 address lines, these chips have a one-megabyte address space. To maintain complete compatibility, the other processors in this family share this same address space when emulating real-mode.

Real-mode gets its name from the fact that a logical address is equivalent to the *real* physical address. To convert a logical address to the physical address, the CPU starts by shifting the 16-bit segment value left by four bits to create a 20-bit value. To this, it adds the 16-bit offset. Figure 17.2 illustrates this process.

Because the segment value is shifted left by four bits, which effectively multiplies it by 16, the smallest segment in real-mode is 16 bytes long. Intel call this a **paragraph**. Because of the way Windows operates in real-mode, the granularity of segments is actually two paragraphs, or 32 bytes. Another way to visualize the logical-to-physical address conversion is shown in Figure 17.3.

The Real Mode Address Space

Since Windows runs as an extension to DOS, it inherits the DOS environment. In memory terms, this means the one-megabyte ad-

Figure 17.2   *Real mode address calculation*

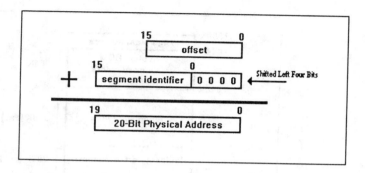

dress space of real mode, divided into several parts as depicted in Figure 17.4.

In this figure, the dotted lines dividing the three pieces in the 0–640K range is meant to suggest that the size of each piece can vary somewhat. DOS, its device drivers, and terminate-and-stay-resident (TSR) programs get first crack at the lowest end of memory. When Windows starts up, it requires a minimum of 200K or so for its device drivers, resident fonts, and the fixed code and data used by the Windows' core components: Kernel, User, and GDI. The space marked as "application area" is used for both Windows programs and for the discardable parts of Windows over and above the minimum set needed.

The well-publicized "640K Limit" on DOS applications results from the design of the DOS address space, which reserves the area between 640K and 1024K for system uses: video adapter cards,

Figure 17.3   *Real mode addressing uses physical addresses to reference system memory*

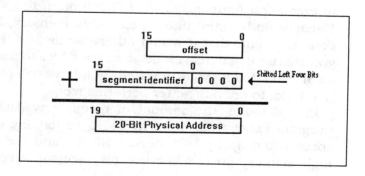

Figure 17.4 *The real mode address space*

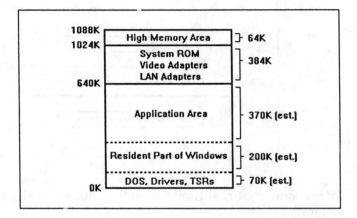

ROM, and other uses. Since this memory area is occupied by hardware, Windows can't do anything to make it available for its own use, except in Real Mode, when it is used for EMS support.

However, on 80286 and 80386 CPUs, Windows gets an extra 64 Kbytes of memory from the **High Memory Area** (HMA), located just above the one-megabyte address line, when an XMS (eXtended Memory Specification) driver is installed, such as HIMEM.SYS. This is the beginning of the extended memory area, which is usually only available in protect mode. But this memory is available in real mode through tricks that an XMS driver plays. When it is available, HMA memory can be used by Windows itself.

Above and beyond the HMA, real-mode Windows is able to make other uses of extended memory. The SMARTDRV disk-caching device driver, for example, can be set up to optimize disk transfer operations. And the RAMDRIVE driver emulates a disk drive in RAM, to create fast temporary files. In addition, if the Windows Memory Manager finds extra, unused extended memory, it uses it to store code segments that it would otherwise discard. For this reason, if you are running in real mode, it's a good idea to leave about 256K or so of extended RAM unallocated. Windows will put this memory to good use, to provide better performance.

In real mode, the amount of memory available to a Windows program varies from 300K to 450K, depending on the amount of space taken up by DOS device drivers, and the availability of the high memory area. While this may seem a very small amount of memory, Windows' dynamic linking facility allows a program 10 times this size (or *larger*) to run. In such situations, the performance might be sluggish, which would encourage a hardware upgrade to accommodate one of Windows' more advanced operating modes. But, such a program *can* run.

Real Mode and Windows

Prior to Windows 3.0, all versions of Windows ran exclusively in real mode. Windows was limited to real mode for marketing reasons: The installed base of microcomputers was dominated by machines that could only be run in real mode—computers based on the Intel 8088 and 8086 CPUs. The memory manager was first built for real mode, but it was designed with the protect modes of the higher-end chips in mind, which is one of the reasons that Windows 3.0 is able to operate in all of its different modes.

Real-mode addressing is fast and efficient, since there is very little overhead involved in translating logical addresses to physical addresses. To seasoned DOS programmers, it may seem like the most open, accessible way to work. And it is, until you try to create a multitasking operating system.

The job of an operating system is to manage and distribute resources. This is true whether the resource is processor time, disk space, or memory. The problem with real-mode addressing is that it makes it very difficult for an operating system to manage memory. It's easy enough to allocate memory to a program—the operating system carves off a piece of system memory and assigns it to a program—great care must be taken in the *way* memory is assigned. If a real-mode operating system assigns memory by providing an address, it is almost impossible for the operating system to move that block of memory. But memory movement is precisely what an operating system must do in order to avoid the problems associated with memory fragmentation. To circumvent this problem, real-mode Windows uses a handle-based approach to allocating memory.

Movable Memory

When a block of memory is allocated, a program does not receive an addresss, but a handle that identifies the memory. Like the handles that we encountered in our discussion of GDI drawing objects, the value of a handle has no meaning to anyone but the subsystem that issued the handle. Like a claim check at a restaurant coat room, a program can trade the memory handle for a memory address whenever it needs to access the memory. At that time, Windows provides a pointer to the memory and locks the segment in place. All other times, the Windows Memory Manager is free to move and compact system memory to reduce fragmentation. Or, in coat room terms, your hat and coat can be moved to another room or even to another floor when the main coat room gets too crowded.

A handle-based, movable memory system helps the Windows' memory manager to avoid memory loss due to fragmentation. But another mechanism is needed to deal with the problem of running out of physical memory: a situation sometimes referred to as "memory overcommit." In the world of mainframe computers, virtual memory systems solve this problem by copying portions of memory to disk. But this requires fast disks and, in the best of cases, hardware support for memory management. When the first version of Windows was being created, neither was available on the computers for which Windows was being written.

The first version of Windows was targeted to run on a 4.77 MHz 8088-based system with 256K of memory and two floppy diskette drives. When Microsoft started building Windows in 1983, hard disks were not widely used, and the 80286-based PC/AT had not yet been introduced. Given the low power of this target machine, even if the 8088 had any sophisticated memory management capabilities (which it doesn't), the two floppy drives of a minimally configured system did not provide fast enough response or a large enough capacity for implementing a virtual memory system. Instead, Microsoft implemented what some might call a "poor-man's" virtual memory system: dynamic linking. This facility depends on the second type of memory that we're going to discuss: discardable memory.

Discardable Memory

To help ease the memory crunch, the Windows memory manager can do more than just move memory around. If it needs to, it can **discard** objects from memory. A discarded object is purged from memory and is overwritten by whatever objects are allocated in its place. The most obvious type of discardable memory object is code. In most cases, code is not modified. So code that is not needed can be discarded, and re-read when it is needed again.

Discardable, read-on-demand code is the basis of Windows' dynamic link mechanism. This is a very flexible mechanism that allows code to be removed from system memory when it is not used. In some ways, this mechanism has a lot in common with memory overlay facilities that are used by some DOS programs, and even in some very old mainframe systems. But the difference between Windows' dynamic linking mechanism and overlays is that dynamic linking is transparent to the application programmer. Overlays, on the other hand, typically must be designed with great care to avoid a deadlock—a situation in which the system must halt because it cannot read in the next overlay that it needs to continue operating properly. Windows dynamic-link mechanism does the work to insure that deadlocks do not occur.

Besides code, another type of object is commonly placed into discardable memory objects: **resources**. To the Windows Memory Manager, a resource is a block of read-only data. When a resource is needed, it is ordinarily read from disk into a discardable memory block. Later, when system memory gets crowded, the Memory Manager can discard resources to allow other objects to take its place.

There are quite a few kinds of resources in Windows. Some are used to support the user interface, like menu and dialog box templates, icons, and cursors. Others are used to store GDI objects like fonts and bitmaps. Beyond these, programmers can create custom resources for private read-only data if they wish. Like discardable code, discardable resources give the Windows memory manager the freedom to purge objects that might otherwise clog system memory.

We've looked at two types of memory objects that can be allocated in Windows: movable and discardable. Both types allow a flexible, dynamic memory management system to be implemented on top of the relatively inflexible addressing of real mode. Windows supports a third type of memory, which application programmers should avoid, but which is important for the well-being and overall efficient operation of certain parts of the system: fixed memory.

Fixed Memory

While movable and discardable memory objects are necessary for the Memory Manager to meet the demands of Windows' multitasking, there are situations that require memory that won't be moved or discarded. For example, an interrupt-handler will require a fixed location in memory since it must always be ready to process an interrupt. For such uses, the Windows memory manager allows the allocation of segments that reside at a fixed location.

Of course, the use of fixed memory should be limited to special cases like device drivers. If a Windows program allocated fixed memory for regular uses, it would quickly use up this scarce resource and cause the system to slow down. When we talk about dynamic memory allocation in the next chapter, you'll see that a program *can* allocate as many fixed memory objects as it requires. But, before you do this, be sure that the other types of memory truly cannot satisfy your requirements.

EMS and Real Mode Windows

Microsoft's second major revision of Windows, version 2.x, introduced support for EMS memory, which is memory that is made available according to the **expanded memory specification**. EMS describes a software interface for bank-switching memory to increase the total amount of memory that DOS programs can access. Since Windows runs on top of DOS, Windows is able to take advantage of EMS. In fact, Windows programs can directly communicate with the expanded memory manager to allocate pages just like their DOS counterparts. But Windows programs don't have to do anything special to benefit from the presence of EMS memory. Instead, the Windows Memory Manager does all the work behind the scenes to increase total available system memory.

EMS does not increase the size of the hardware address space. Instead, it switches extra memory into unused parts of the DOS address space. In this way, EMS allows up to 32 additional megabytes of memory to be accessible in the DOS address space. At first glance, this seems to be enough memory to satisfy the needs of *any* DOS or Windows program. However, because its gobs of memory are not *simultaneously* accessible, EMS is only a limited solution to the memory crunch.

For example, in one configuration, a 64K memory window serves as the only access point for all of the memory on an EMS card. This memory window, which is also called the **EMS page frame**, is typically divided into pages that are 16K bytes. Thus, our 64K memory window consists of four 16K memory pages. If a program wanted to access more than 64K of EMS memory at a time, it would have to decide which EMS pages to use and which pages to ignore. With its tiny memory window, EMS cannot be a general-purpose memory management solution. But there is no denying that it has helped ease the memory shortage of real-mode systems. Figure 17.5 illustrates the relationship of the real-mode address space to EMS memory pages.

Windows' use of EMS is transparent to Windows programs. When a Windows program starts running, the program receives a private

Figure 17.5   *EMS lets real-mode programs peek at a larger address space*

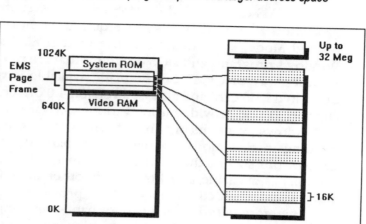

EMS bank. The program is guaranteed to have private use of this memory, free from competition with other programs. As Windows' multitasking switcher lets other programs run, it communicates with the EMS memory manager to map the correct EMS bank into the EMS page frame. The net result is reduced competition for memory between different programs, more total available memory, and better overall performance. The improved performance comes from postponing low-memory situations, when code must be discarded and reread from disk.

When running in Real Mode, Windows 3.x allocates EMS memory for programs in the same way that Windows 2.x did. But in its other operating modes, Windows ignores EMS memory. That is, Windows does not use EMS memory for Windows programs in either Standard Mode or 386-Enhanced Mode. These other modes have access to extended memory, which doesn't suffer the same shortcomings of EMS memory. Extended memory, after all, is accessible without bank switching and has the added advantage of virtual memory support in 386-Enhanced Mode.

Under Windows 2.x, a program could ask Windows to step aside so that the program can directly allocate and manage its own EMS memory. This capability is also available in Windows 3.0. Programs that wish to do this must have the -l switch set when the resource compiler is run (rc.exe) so that the proper flag gets set in the program's executable file.

EMS support can be provided in several ways. Windows comes with an EMS driver called EMM386.SYS for systems with an 80386 processor. However, this is not required when running in 386-Enhanced Mode, since this mode has built-in EMS support for both Windows programs and DOS programs that are run under Windows. Another way that EMS can be made available is with the use of a dedicated EMS card and at least a version 4.0 driver. And finally, EMS support can be provided using various software emulations.

Windows programs only benefit from the presence of EMS when running in real mode. In real mode, bank-switched memory increases the size of the total address space, but only one bank of memory is available at a time. In its other operating modes, Windows uses extended memory, which provides the same amount of extra memory *without* the need for bank-switching. For this reason, Windows 3.0 ignores EMS when running in either of the two protect modes. There is no question, however, that EMS support provided an important improvement for Windows 2.x, and that it can benefit users who need to run Windows 3.0 in real mode.

EMS is important in another way. It represents the first time that Windows' memory management supported the concept of a private address space for application programs. A private address space helps protect applications from the misbehavior of other applications, since a private address space can only be accessed by its owner. In Windows 3.0 protect mode, which we're going to discuss in a moment, the idea of a private address space is also starting to be implemented with the memory protection that is provided. Future versions of Windows will continue to enhance and enforce the concept of private address spaces to help protect programs from the problems that arise when memory addressing errors occur. For the present, in both Standard Mode and 386-Enhanced Mode, Windows takes advantage of the memory protection features of the 80286 and higher processors. Let's take a look at those two modes, and at the way that they operate.

Standard and Enhanced Mode

As we mentioned earlier, when Windows' memory management system was first being designed, it was with an eye toward someday moving Windows to the protect modes of the Intel-86 family. With Windows 3.0, this vision is realized in not one but *two* operating modes: Windows Standard Mode and 386-Enhanced Mode.

Standard Mode gives Windows the benefits of protect mode on the 80286 and 80386 processors. In this mode, Windows programs get a physical address space that breaks the one-megabyte boundary of real mode and can be as large as 16 megabytes. Unlike the bank-switched memory of EMS, in protect mode the additional memory is **extended memory**—that is, the memory is a directly addressable extension to the real-mode address space. Protect mode provides special memory management support that is not available in real mode. This support includes the enforcement of memory access rules that helps preserve the integrity of each program, of each program's data, and of the system itself.

In 386-Enhanced Mode, Windows gets all the benefits of Standard Mode, plus an even larger address space. When running in this mode, don't be alarmed when the Program Manager tells you that the system has more *free* memory than you have RAM installed in your system. Someone at Microsoft, during the development of Windows, complained about this problem in a bug report, and was told simply: *"Welcome to the world of virtual memory!"*

The virtual memory of 386-Enhanced Mode is provided by a 386 control program, WIN386.EXE, that works with the memory paging hardware built into the 80386 processor. In this mode, the address space can grow to a size that is up to four times the available physical memory. For example, five megabytes of physical memory can support a virtual address space of 20 megabytes. And 16 megabytes of RAM can support a 64-megabyte virtual memory address space. These examples assume, of course, that there is enough disk space to hold the memory pages that have been swapped out.

Protect Mode

The term *protect mode* refers to a state of the processor in which certain rules are enforced when memory is addressed. These rules minimize the risk that a program will overwrite—either accidentally or intentionally—memory that doesn't belong to it. A program that violates these rules is subject to a serious penalty: It is terminated.

This harsh treatment contrasts sharply with the way a similar action is treated in real mode. For example, it's quite common for a DOS program to busy itself poking around the DOS data areas, installing private interrupt handlers, and in general making itself at home. Since DOS is a single-tasking system, such liberties are allowable since they don't interfere with the operation of other programs.

But Windows is a multitasking system, and even though programs can fiddle with any part of system memory in Real Mode Windows, this should be avoided. Programs should refrain from actions that might have adverse side effects for other programs. Such actions may cause a program to be incompatible with protect mode Windows.

And yet, an otherwise "well-behaved" program might mistakenly overwrite memory belonging to another program—or even memory that belongs to Windows itself. Without the memory protection of protect mode, such actions can lead to data corruption and even a system crash. Protect mode provides increased system integrity because of its memory protection features.

Memory Addressing in Protect Mode

When a program addresses memory in protect mode, it uses a two-part segment address just like a program in real-mode, with a segment identifier and an offset. But in protect mode, the logical-to-physical addresss conversion is not simply a shift and add operation. Instead, the processor relies on special tables called **descriptor tables** that are created and maintained by the operating system. There are two types of descriptor tables: **Global Descriptor Tables** (GDT), and **Local Descriptor Tables** (LDT). (A third type of descriptor table, the Interrupt Descriptor Table or IDT, is used to hold interrupt vectors. But its use is beyond this discussion.)

Intel designed its protect mode with a lot of flexibility in the way that descriptor tables can be used by different operating systems. In general, a descriptor table contains an array of segment information records, known as **segment descriptors**. In protect mode, the part of a memory address that we have been calling a "segment identifier" is referred to as a **segment selector**. A segment selector is an index into the array of descriptors that make up a descriptor table. It identifies the segment descriptor that provides the detail needed to access the segment data. Here is what a segment descriptor contains:

Segment Descriptor Field	80286 Size	80386 Size
Segment Location (aka Base Address)	3 bytes	4 bytes
Segment Size (aka Segment Limit)	2 bytes	2 1/2 bytes
Flags	1 byte	1 1/2 bytes
Unused	2 bytes	0 bytes
	8 bytes	8 bytes

Figure 17.6 *The segment value is an index into a descriptor table*

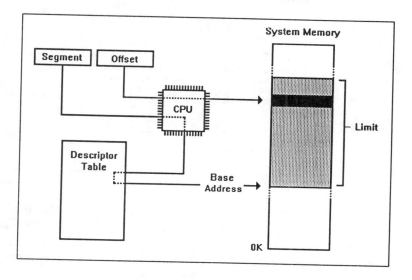

When a program references a memory location, the CPU loads the segment descriptor into special registers for use in determining the physical address of the segment. The offset is added to the base address, to access the desired bytes of memory. This process is illustrated in Figure 17.6.

Actually, only 13 of the 16 bits in a segment value are used as a descriptor table index. As shown in Figure 17.7, the other three bits are two additional fields that play an important part in the addressing scheme and protection mechanism of protect mode. Bit 2 is a flag that indicates which descriptor table to use. This field allows an operating system to set up an address space of a program using two descriptor tables: one GDT and one LDT. The idea is that the GDT contains all the memory that is shared system wide. The LDT, on the other hand, represents a program's private address space.

Bits 0 and 1 describe the segment's **requested privilege level** (RPL). These bits are set by operating system software to create and enforce a memory protection scheme with four privilege levels, 0 to 3. 0 is the highest privilege level, and is reserved for the most trusted operating system software. In Windows Standard Mode, the DOS Protect Mode Interface (DPMI) code has the highest privilege level, which is also known as ring 0.

The DPMI support code resides in the HIMEM.SYS driver, which is referenced in the CONFIG.SYS file. DPMI provides access to mem-

Figure 17.7 *Structure of a protect mode selector*

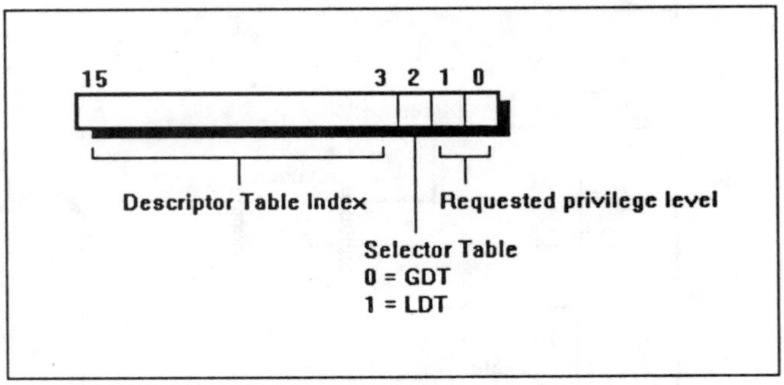

ory above the 640K line. Memory in the range 640K to 1024K is known as **upper memory blocks (UMB)**. The 64K from 1024K to 1088K is called the **high memory area (HMA)**. And finally, memory allocated above the 1088K line is called **extended memory blocks** (EMBs). In 386-Enhanced Mode, the 386 control program has ring 0 privileges.

In this architecture, memory protection is enforced in the following way. A memory error causes an exception to occur—that is, a CPU interrupt. In Windows, this results in the offending program being terminated with an error message like that shown in Figure 17.8. If you ran some of the earliest, prerelease versions of Windows 3.0, you'd see the word "Trayf"—Yiddish for "Not Kosher"—in this message. An apt description for an invalid memory reference.

Several types of errors cause this message to appear. For example, if a program tries to address memory using an invalid segment selector, the CPU catches the error and reports it to the operating system. Of, if a program tries to access memory beyond the end of a segment—that is, if the offset value is greater than the segment limit—the memory management hardware prevents the program from accessing memory that does not belong to it. It notifies the operating system that a program has violated the rules for the proper use of memory.

When such an error occurs and a debugger like CodeView is present, Windows refrains from displaying the error message. Instead, it passes control to the debugger. At that time, CodeView shows you where the error occurred. If it is within your program, CodeView shows you the source code line that caused the error. But if it was not in your code—for example, if the error occurred in a

Figure 17.8 *Windows' fatal error message*

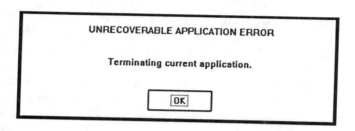

```
UNRECOVERABLE APPLICATION ERROR

Terminating current application.

      [ OK ]
```

device driver or in one of Windows' libraries—CodeView simply shows you the machine instruction that was responsible for the error.

Windows and Protect Mode

In Windows 3.0, all Windows programs and the Windows library code itself reside at ring 1; that is, they run with a privilege level of 1. This will change in a future version of Windows, when Windows programs and the Windows libraries are made to reside at the lowest privilege level, ring 3. This would give future versions of Windows the freedom to use the higher privilege levels for other operating system components. In addition, if Windows puts applications at ring three, that means that Windows programs will be running at the same privilege level as OS/2 Presentation Manager programs. No doubt, this will minimize any possible compatibility differences between Windows and OS/2, to help Windows programs to be binary compatible with OS/2 version 2.0.

The current version of Windows, version 3.0, uses a single LDT for all of its own memory and that of every Windows program running in the system. This means that the maximum number of segments that can exist in the system at any moment is 2^{13} or 8192, since that is the maximum number that will fit in an LDT. In a future version, Microsoft is planning to provide an LDT for each program that runs. This provides several benefits. First, it strengthens the idea of a private address space, to help protect programs from the memory errors of other programs. Next, it increases the total number of memory objects that any one program can create. And finally, it is another step toward making the environment of a Windows program as similar as possible to that of OS/2, to help in the migration of Windows programs to the OS/2 Presentation Manager.

When we described real-mode memory management, we talked about the three types of memory objects: movable, discardable, and fixed. An operating system needs all three types of objects to be able to do an effective job of managing system memory. For this reason, real-mode Windows implements these types of memory objects in software, since there wasn't any hardware support for them.

When running in protect mode, things operate a little more efficiently because Windows has help from the processor's memory management hardware. Since programs don't have access to physical addresses as they do in real mode, the Windows Memory Manager can reorganize memory whenever it needs to. The only thing it has to worry about is updating the descriptor table to reflect the new location of a memory object. From a program's point of view, even if an object is moved in physical memory, it still appears at the same logical address, since the address references a descriptor table entry and not a physical address. In protect-mode Windows, discardable objects behave in the same way that they do under real-mode Windows. After all, discarding is a very efficient way to make more memory available when more memory is needed.

Fixed memory objects, which are the third type of memory object that Windows supports, are treated much the same as they are under real mode. But, just like movable objects, a fixed object can move. The reason is that, even though the fixed object will maintain its logical address, Windows can move the object in the physical address space. Of course, certain operations require that fixed objects do not move in physical memory, such as an interrupt handler in a device driver DLL. For such uses, Windows allows segments to have a fixed logical address as well as a fixed physical address.

Thirty-Two Bit Addressing

When the Intel 80386 and higher chips are run in protect mode, 32-bit registers can be used to address segments that either one megabyte or four gigabytes (depending on how the addressing granularity is used). When running the 386-Enhanced Mode, the Windows KERNEL memory manager itself uses 32-bit addressing. When it does this, it packs objects that otherwise would have their own segment into larger arrays, to get the faster performance that comes from minimizing the number of different segments that must be referenced.

Microsoft provides some limited support for programs that wish to use 32-bit addressing, mostly in the form of some documentation and a dynamic link library that is supplied in the Windows SDK. While a program written for 32-bit addressing will only be able to run under 386-Enhanced Mode, this may be suitable for certain vertical market and turn-key applications, and other applications targeted toward running only in 386-Enhanced Mode.

Windows Virtual Memory Support

All that we have said about protect mode operation applies equally to Standard Mode and to 386-Enhanced Mode. But there is an important capability that is only available in 386-Enhanced Mode: support for virtual memory.

Virtual memory support works alongside the protect mode addressing mechanism that we have been discussing. In other words, the segment value in an address is still used as an index into a descriptor table to determine the base address of a segment. And the offset is added to this base address to determine the exact bytes to be worked on.

The difference between regular protect mode and the virtual-memory protect mode on the 386 has to do with how this base + offset address is interpreted. In regular protect mode, it is interpreted as a physical memory address. But in Enhanced Mode, the paging hardware built into the Intel 80386 processor is enabled, allowing addresses to be treated as virtual memory addresses. Figure 17.9 illustrates how this translation is done.

This figure shows how the segment and offset values are decoded into an address in the virtual address space. This address space is divided into 4K pages, each of which resides in either physical memory or in a swapfile on disk. When a reference is made to a location that resides on disk, a page fault is triggered, which is simply an internal CPU interrupt. At such times, the virtual memory manager reads the desired page from disk to provide access to the required code or data. The instruction that triggered the page fault is then restarted so that paging is entirely transparent to software.

The virtual memory manager packs segments into the virtual address space as tightly as it can. In other words, as suggested in Figure 17.9, the beginning and end of a segment do not have to coincide with a page boundary. The net result is that the virtual memory manager avoids wasting even a single byte. The paging hardware behaves in a traditional manner, so that part of a segment can be on disk while another part is in physical memory. As you might expect,

Figure 17.9 *Virtual memory addressing*

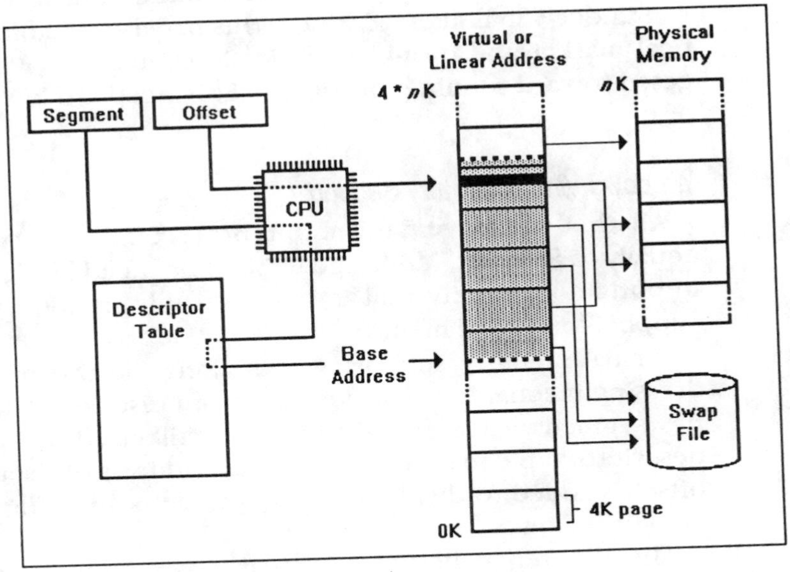

the portions that are in physical memory do not have any special relationship with each other. Instead, the virtual memory manager can relocate a page of memory anywhere that is convenient.

Even when virtual memory is available, Windows can still discard segments when it starts running out of memory. However, in Windows 3.0, discarding only occurs when the Windows Memory Manager has used up the virtual address space. For this reason, the current implementation of 386-Enhanced Mode has a slight inefficiency built in: It *swaps* discardable code and resources instead of *discarding* them.

The reason this happens is that 386-Enhanced Mode uses two different memory managers: Windows' protect mode global heap manager and the 386 control program's virtual memory manager. Windows global heap manager allocates segments in Windows' address space. The 386 control program provides virtual memory support, EMS emulation, and management of the 8086 virtual machines in which DOS programs run.

When Windows' global heap manager needs memory, it makes a call to the 386 control program. Windows' memory manager discards memory objects only when the 386 control program runs out of virtual memory. In a future version, the two memory managers will be more tightly integrated to run more efficiently. At that time, instead of swapping discardable memory objects, the Windows memory manager will direct the virtual memory manager to purge discardable segments.

How Windows Selects a Segment for Discarding

In all of its operating modes, Windows can purge code and data segments that are marked as *discardable* when it runs out of free memory. Understanding how Windows chooses to discard one segment over another will help you understand Windows' behavior in a low-memory situation. This, in turn, will help you write programs that can operate effectively even when memory is scarce, either because many programs are running or because Windows is operating in Real Mode.

Windows discards segments on a *least recently used* basis. That is, when it needs to discard a segment, it picks a segment that has resided in system memory the longest without being used. To determine the least recently used segment, Windows maintains a table of discardable segments known as the **LRU List**. Every discardable code and data segment has an entry on the LRU List.

Every one-quarter second, on a hardware timer tick, Windows scans an access flag associated with each discardable code segment in the system. If the segment has been accessed since the last time the flag was checked, the segment gets moved to the bottom of the LRU list. That is, it gets promoted to the most recently used position in the table. Once a segment has been promoted, the access flag gets cleared so that it is ready to be tripped again if the segment is used again.

A drawback to this approach is that it isn't exact. In other words, it doesn't distinguish between a segment that was accessed 30 times and one that was accessed just once. But this approach was chosen because it is quite fast.

The access flags for discardable code segments reside in different places depending on whether the system is running in real or protect mode. In real mode, the Windows memory manager supports a data structure called a **module database** for every program and dynamic link library (we'll take a closer look at this data structure later in this chapter). The access flags are stored as an array of bytes in the module database, with one byte per discardable code segment.

In protect mode, the Intel-86 family provides support for an access flag in hardware. To be more precise, the access flag is a one-bit field of the segment descriptor in the descriptor tables (in the LDT). The memory management hardware automatically sets this bit when a segment has been accessed. Windows checks this bit when it scans all discardable segments to update the LRU List.

Data segments are treated a little differently, but the idea is the same. Windows doesn't keep an access flag for data segments. Instead, the LRU List is automatically updated by the locking and unlocking mechanism that is used to access discardable data objects. After all, a segment must be locked to access it. Then, when it is unlocked, the segment gets automatically promoted to the bottom of the LRU List, to make it the most recently used segment.

You might find yourself working on an application that doesn't work well with the "least recently used" discarding algorithm. Consider, for example, a database program that walks a circular linked-list of data segments. As it makes the round of these segments, the very next segment that the program wants to use will also be the least recently used and therefore the one most likely to be discarded. In such cases, there are Windows library routines that can be used to directly modify the LRU tables: GlobalLRUNewest, which makes a segment the least likely to be discarded, and GlobalLRUOldest, which makes a segment the most likely to be discarded.

The LRU mechanism is largely transparent to Windows programs running in protect mode. In real mode, if you run the SYMDEB debugger, you might run across a single machine instruction that is added to help update the LRU List. This instruction is embedded in a piece of dynamic link code called a *thunk*, which we discuss in more detail in Chapter 19:

```
SAR   CS:[xxxx], 1
```

This *shift arithmetic right* instruction trips the access byte of a discardable code segment. Segments that are fixed or that are not present have a value of FFh. Segments that haven't been accessed since the last LRU timer tick have a value of 01h. This instruction leaves the FFh value unchanged, while it changes the value of 01h to 00h. The bytes that are modified by this instruction are scanned by Windows as it updates the LRU List.

Now that we've looked at the way that Windows manages memory, let's take a look at the data objects that Windows itself allocates. In this chapter, we're going to focus on the data objects that the

Windows Kernel allocates. In the next chapter, when we discuss application memory use, we'll look at the memory used by Windows' other two core components: USER.EXE and GDI.EXE.

The KERNEL's Private Memory Use

When Windows' three main components are doing work for Windows programs, they consume memory. For the most part, a Windows programmer doesn't have to know how this memory is consumed. But it can help if you're interested in knowing what makes Windows' tick. Also, there are certain system limits that you will understand only when you know how Windows uses memory.

We're going to start with a look at the memory used by Windows' KERNEL, which is the part of Windows that is responsible for memory management, dynamic linking, and other functions that are traditionally associated with operating systems. In the next chapter, we'll look at the memory that is used by the other two components of Windows: USER and GDI. We're going to wait until the next chapter to discuss the memory used by the other two components, since the memory used is allocated as a direct result of a request for services that have been made by application programs.

KERNEL Data Objects

The KERNEL is responsible for dynamic linking, memory management, and interacting with DOS when Windows programs require DOS system services. Although there are many tiny data structures tucked away throughout the system that the KERNEL uses, we're going to limit our discussion to three of the most important: the Burgermaster, the task database, and the module databases. These objects are visible using the HEAPWALK utility when Windows is running in Real Mode, as shown in Figure 17.10. In protect mode, the Burgermaster goes away because its job is taken over by the protect mode descriptor tables, and other internal data structures.

The Burgermaster. The Burgermaster gets its name from a fast-food restaurant that is next door to the building where Windows was first developed. In those days, two numbers were programmed into the telephone auto-dialer at Microsoft; one was the number of the take-out service at Burgermaster. (The other was the number of the athletic club to which Microsoft employees were given memberships.) This object was named in honor of this restaurant, because

Figure 17.10   *HEAPWALK in Real Mode showing a snapshot of Windows' global heap*

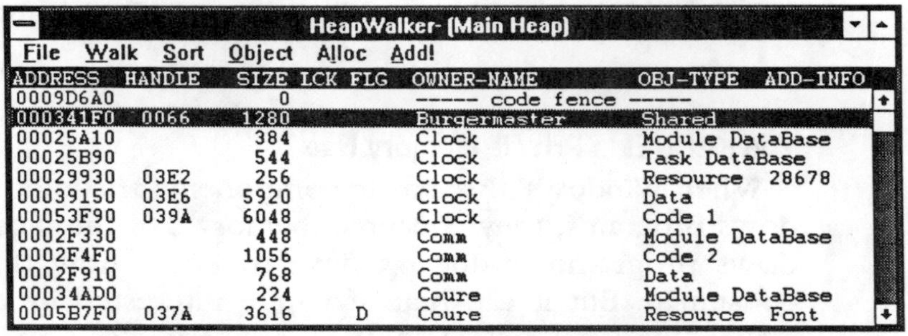

```
═                          HeapWalker- [Main Heap]                    ▼ ▲
 File   Walk   Sort   Object   Alloc   Add!
ADDRESS  HANDLE   SIZE LCK FLG  OWNER-NAME            OBJ-TYPE   ADD-INFO
0009D6A0            0           ----- code fence -----                   ↑
000341F0  0066    1280          Burgermaster         Shared
00025A10            384         Clock                Module DataBase
00025B90            544         Clock                Task DataBase
00029930  03E2     256          Clock                Resource   28678
00039150  03E6    5920          Clock                Data
00053F90  039A    6048          Clock                Code 1
0002F330            448         Comm                 Module DataBase
0002F4F0           1056         Comm                 Code 2
0002F910            768         Comm                 Data
00034AD0            224         Coure                Module DataBase
0005B7F0  037A    3616      D   Coure                Resource   Font    ↓
```

the members of the development team that worked on the KERNEL ate lunch at Burgermaster almost every day.

The Burgermaster is the master memory handle table for movable and discardable objects in Windows. In other words, like the descriptor tables in protect mode, the Burgermaster maintains the physical addresses of movable memory objects. When a program needs to get the address of such a segment, it makes a calls to one of several Windows library routines, which look it up in the Burgermaster.

The Task Database. A Task Database (or TDB) is created for every instance of every program that runs in Windows. In our example, a single copy of CLOCK is running, so there is a single TDB. A TDB always sits in a fixed segment and contains pointers to all of the things that make an instance of a program unique. Here is a partial list of some of the things that are stored in the TDB:

TDB Field	Comment
Array of Instance Thunks	Created by MakeProcInstance routine for use by dialog box procedures and other "call-back" procedures, but *not* for window procedure.
Current MS-DOS Disk & Directory	On a task switch, Windows sets up the current disk and directory for the active program.
EMS Allocation Data	Real Mode only.

(Continued)

TDB Field	Comment
Application Message Queue	Keeps private messages that have been posted to a program (using the PostMessage routine).
Module Database Handle	Memory object that contains directory of objects in the module's .EXE or .DLL file.
Private Interrupt Vector Table	Contains the private interrupts that a program has installed. Only a small set can be installed, including interrupts 0, 2, 4, 6, 7. These deal with errors in arithmetic functions. Can be changed by calling interrupt 21h (DOS Services), function number 25h.
Pointer to DOS Program Database	Also known as the DOS Program Segment Prefix or PSP. Windows provides a copy of this data structure for each Windows program that runs. A program can get the address of this by calling GetCurrentPDB.
Task-Switch Save Area	Saves CPU registers between task switches.

This list is not complete, nor is this the order of the actual TDB. Microsoft has not documented the contents of the TDB, which means it may change in a future version. But it's included here to give you an idea of the type of data that Windows saves for every instance of every program. For example, from the list you can see that Windows keeps track of the current disk and directory for each program. A program can freely change these and not be worried about any adverse effects on other programs. Also, in case you wondered where the application's private message queue lives, it lives in the TDB. Notice that the TDB has a private interrupt vector table. If you want to trap the interrupts that are generated when certain arithmetic errors occur, you can install your own interrupt handler. For example, interrupt vector 0 is issued when a divided-by-zero error occurs. Programs that don't handle those interrupts themselves are terminated when such errors occur.

Windows always creates one TDB per instance of every program that runs. When an instance of a program terminates, the TDB is removed from memory. Knowing this, you should check that your Windows programs terminate properly. How? It's easy. Run HEAP-WALK, and check that there are no unexpected objects labeled "Task Database" when you think your program should have terminated. If you do find such objects, you'll know that your program has not exited properly.

The Module Database. There is an entry in the TDB that points to another data object that the KERNEL uses: the module database. The module database contains an abbreviated version of the header to an EXE file, known more simply as an EXE header. A utility in the Windows software development kit lets you read this header, called EXEHDR.EXE. Appendix E contains a complete discussion of the file format of executable files.

Windows uses the module database whenever it needs to load anything from an executable file. This includes code, resources, and data. When we discuss dynamic linking in Chapter 19, you'll see that Windows sets up tiny code fragments called *thunks* to make dynamic linking work. In Real Mode, thunks allow code to be discarded and moved with a minimum of overhead. The module database is basically a directory of segments that can be read from an executable file.

Programs have module databases, but so do dynamic link libraries. If you run HEAPWALK, you'll notice that KERNEL, USER, and GDI each have a module database. There is even a module database for fonts, which are simply dynamic link libraries that have no code.

In this chapter, we have looked at the way that Windows is able to take advantage of the memory capabilities of the entire family of Intel-86 processors. In the next chapter, we're going to look at application-specific memory use issues. We're going to address all the different types of memory that are available to a Windows program.

18

Memory, Part II:
Application Memory Use

When a programmer starts to think about how to pack a Windows program's data into memory, it can be compared to what a traveler thinks about when packing for a trip. The first question is: What bags do I take? For a weekend, a small suitcase might do. For a two-week vacation, several suitcases might be needed. In the context of a program, the question is "What kinds of containers can a Windows program use to store data?"

In designing the approach that your programs will take in using memory, there are a number of basic issues to deal with. These include allocation, visibility, lifetime, and overhead. As we look at the different types of memory that are available to a Windows program, we'll consider each of these issues, and weigh their importance. Table 18.1 summarizes these issues for the many types of memory available to a Windows application.

The issue of **allocation** involves *who* allocates a given piece of memory. The compiler allocates some memory for you, which is the case with static and automatic variables. In other cases, you must explicitly allocate memory. For example, to allocate memory using one of Windows' dynamic memory allocation packages, you make explicit calls to either LocalAlloc or GlobalAlloc. In some cases, memory allocation is a side-effect of creating certain types of system objects. For example, when you create a device context (DC) in GDI, objects are allocated in GDI's local heap space.

The issue of **visibility** has to do with who can see the memory. Some objects have a very limited visibility, like automatic variables declared inside a function. Others have a visibility that is system wide, like GDI drawing objects and certain objects allocated from the global heap. Such objects can be shared between programs, but

641

Table 18.1 *A summary of application memory use*

Memory Type	Allocation	Visibility	Lifetime	Overhead
Static variables	C compiler	in a program	program	none
Automatic variables	C compiler	in a function	function	none
Local Heap	calls to LocalAlloc	in a program	program	4 or 6 bytes
Global Heap	calls to GlobalAlloc	program/ system	program/ system	24 bytes
Resources	Resource manager	program/ system	owner	24 bytes
GDI Objects	GDI routines	system	system	varies
USER Objects	USER routines	system	owner	varies

be careful to clean up such objects when you are done. Windows doesn't automatically clean them up for you.

The issue of **lifetime** describes how memory is reclaimed. With some objects, memory is reclaimed automatically when a program terminates. This is the case with static and automatic variables, as well as objects allocated from the local heap. Other objects must be explicitly deallocated to free up this memory for other uses. In general, it is a good programming practice to free memory when it is no longer needed, whether or not that memory will be automatically freed.

And finally, the issue of **overhead** describes what extra costs are associated with allocating a piece of memory beyond the actual bytes that are used. This issue is especially important when deciding how to use dynamic memory allocation—allocation from the local and global heaps. For example, every global memory object has an overhead of 24 bytes *minimum*. If you are in the habit of allocating hundreds of tiny (12-byte) objects, you'll want to think again before putting them into a global memory object.

Let's begin by looking at each of the different types of memory that is available. We'll then discuss issues relating to the allocation of memory from the global heap—the most flexible and useful type of dynamic memory allocation. We'll look at how code structure affects memory use, then look at allocation from the local heap, the use of custom resources, and some tricks that will allow you to perform local heap allocation in a dynamically allocated segment. We'll provide you with a lot of sample code, so you can examine in detail all of the pieces that are necessary to make each type of memory work properly.

Overview of Application Memory Use

In the last chapter, we described how the Intel-86 family of processors uses a segmented addressing scheme. Since Windows is built on top of this architecture, Windows programmers should keep in mind that the segment is the fundamental unit of memory. This being the case, our discussion of memory is organized in terms of segments. We'll start with the default data segment, which holds three types of data objects: static variables, automatic variables, and the local heap.

Default Data Segment

Windows' works best with programs that have a *single* data segment. This is another way of saying that you should use the small or medium compiler models, since these create a single data segment by default. A single data segment is best because of the way that Windows' dynamic linking works. As we'll describe in Chapter 19, when we describe the dynamic link mechanism, Windows can fix up the data segment register when a Windows library routine calls a function in your program. This call-back mechanism is used for window procedures, and therefore is fundamental to the way that Windows works. For each program, Windows internally stores only *one* data segment value.

Programs that *must* have more than one default data segments can do so—that is, you can use the compact, large, or huge compiler models. But your program is subject to certain restrictions. For one thing, Windows will only allow one instance of your program to run at a time. And, to operate properly in Real Mode, Windows will automatically load extra data segments as FIXED segments. This can cause problems with your program's use of your local heap. In brief, if at all possible, you should build your program around a single default data segment, since doing otherwise can cause more grief than benefit.

In Figure 18.1, HEAPWALK shows the default data segment that belongs to MIN, the minimum Windows program we developed

Figure 18.1 *HEAPWALK shows MIN's default data segment*

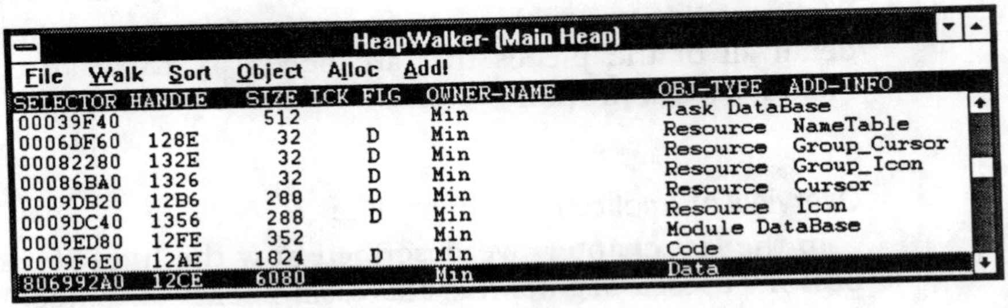

```
┌─────────────────────── HeapWalker- (Main Heap) ───────────────── ▼ ▲ ┐
│ File  Walk  Sort  Object  Alloc  Addl                                 │
│ SELECTOR HANDLE   SIZE LCK FLG OWNER-NAME    OBJ-TYPE  ADD-INFO      ▲ │
│ 00039F40          512          Min          Task DataBase             │
│ 0006DF60  128E     32  D       Min          Resource  NameTable       │
│ 00082280  132E     32  D       Min          Resource  Group_Cursor    │
│ 00086BA0  1326     32  D       Min          Resource  Group_Icon      │
│ 0009DB20  12B6    288  D       Min          Resource  Cursor          │
│ 0009DC40  1356    288  D       Min          Resource  Icon            │
│ 0009ED80  12FE    352          Min          Module DataBase           │
│ 0009F6E0  12AE   1824  D       Min          Code                    ▼ │
│ 806992A0  12CE   6080          Min          Data                      │
└───────────────────────────────────────────────────────────────────────┘
```

earlier in this book. In many respects, a program's default data segment is just another segment in the global heap: The Windows' loader allocates the segment from the global heap using the global heap allocation routine, GlobalAlloc.

The default data segment is unique in some respects. For one thing, it is automatically **locked** whenever a message is delivered to your program. When we discuss global heap allocation, you'll see that programs must explicitly lock dynamically allocated data segments. But not the default data segment, which Windows locks for you. The default data segment is also special in that Windows is careful to set up the correct value in the DS (data segment) register when a message is delivered to a program. When we discuss dynamic linking in Chapter 19, you'll see how important this is. Every program and some dynamic link libraries will have a default data segment (dynamic link libraries aren't required to have a data segement). The dynamic link mechanism is set up to support this and to make sure that your program always has access to its required data.

As the gateway to many messages that are sent to your program, the `GetMessage` routine locks and unlocks your default data segment at the proper time. Also, when another program directly calls one of your window procedures with the `SendMessage` routine, your default data segment is also locked. Among the routines that *may* cause your data segment to become momentarily unlocked are the local heap allocation routines (LocalAlloc and LocalReAlloc) and the atom table allocation routines, since they call the local heap allocation routines. To avoid the problems that this can cause, avoid writing code like this:

```
LPSTR lp;
lp = &static_or_stack_object;
```

```
hMem = LocalAlloc (...);
/*  After a call to LocalAlloc or LocalReAlloc, previously  */
/*  constructed far pointers to local data or              */
/*  to the stack may be invalie.                           */
```

As the comment in the code suggests, if you construct a far pointer to any object in your default data segment, and then call LocalAlloc or LocalReAlloc, the far pointer may be invalid. It will be, in fact, when your program is running in real mode and the default data segment has to be grown—and moved—to satisfy the allocation request. On the other hand, if you increment the lock count on your default data segment (by calling LockData()), the segment will not move, although this may cause calls to LocalAlloc / LocalReAlloc to fail.

A program's data segment is divided into four or five parts: a header, static data area, stack, local heap, and an optional atom table. Figure 18.2 shows a typical program's data segment, with each part labeled. For the sake of comparison, it's interesting to note that a dynamic link library's data segment may contain all of these same elements, except DLLs ordinarily do not have a stack. Instead, DLLs use the stack of the programs that call the library routines. Figure 18.3 shows a typical DLL data segment. Let's look at each element in a typical program's data segment, one at a time starting with the segment header.

Figure 18.2 *A typical program's local data segment*

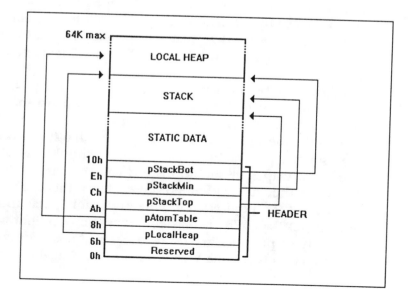

Figure 18.3 *A typical dynamic link library's data segment*

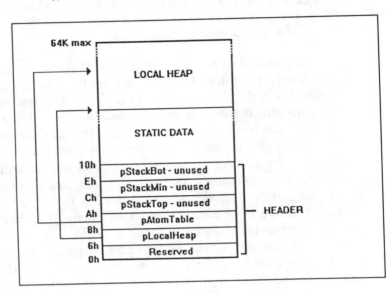

Default Data Segment Header. The header is a 16-byte area that contains pointers used by the KERNEL to manage the local data segment. A Windows program should leave this area alone, since it is automatically allocated at compile/link time and managed by the KERNEL at runtime. When allocating a local heap on a dynamically allocated segment, however, you'll need to set aside the first 16 bytes for use by the KERNEL. We'll show how this is done later in this chapter. Other than that, our primary interest in this data area rests in what we can learn about Windows' management of a local data segment.

Of the five pointers in the segment header, by far and away the most important is the pointer to the local heap, pLocalHeap. It is used by the local heap management routines to find the local heap so that the local heap doesn't interfere with other data objects in the data segment. Your Windows program should not directly modify the local heap, but should instead call the various local heap routines—another subject we'll discuss later in this chapter.

Three of the pointers reference the stack: pStackBot, pStackMin, and pStackTop. When the debug version of Windows is installed, these three pointers are used to check for stack overflows. It's a good idea to test your Windows programs against this special version, since it will help you find errors that might otherwise go undetected.

The fifth and final pointer, pAtomTable, points to an atom table if a program has created one. Atom tables are created from memory allocated out of the local heap and are managed by the various atom management routines. Notice that the segment header doesn't have any pointer to the static data area. It's the compiler's job to define the static data area and generate the correct code to use it.

The Static Data Area. The static data area holds a program's "global" data. This includes all variables declared outside of functions, all variables declared with the `static` keyword, all static strings, and the static data allocated for use by various C library routines.

In the following code fragment, four different objects are allocated in the static data area, and five are not. Can you identify the static data objects?

```
char pch[] = "String of Characters";
int  i;

long FAR PASCAL WndProc (HWND hwnd,
                         WORD wMsg,
                         WORD wParam,
                         LONG lParam)
  {
  static int iCount;
  long       lValue;
```

As you might expect, the two variables defined outside any function—pch and i—are allocated in the static data area. So is iCount, which uses the `static` keyword. This declaration, since it's inside the bounds of a function, limits the **scope** of this variable to the WndProc function. In other words, iCount is only visible to code *inside* this function. But, as a static object, it has a lifetime as long as the program itself, which means that it resides in the static data area.

The fourth object placed in the static area is the string: "String of Characters." Because strings can take up quite a bit of space, you can reduce the size of the static data area by putting all strings into a string resource. When a string is needed, it can be loaded and used.

When it is not needed, string resources can be discarded from memory to reduce the overall demand for system memory.

The Stack. The stack is a dynamic data area that is managed for you through a high-level language like C. Stacks are so central to software that the Intel processors have a set of registers that are dedicated to the use and maintenance of the stack area. These include the SS (stack segment) register, and the BP (base pointer) and SP (stack pointer) offset registers. Stack use is even built into the processor's hardware. When it makes a function call, the processor automatically pushes return address on the stack. When returning from a function, a return address is automatically popped off the stack as the location of the next instruction to be executed.

The C compiler and the processor store three things on the stack: local variables, arguments passed to called functions, and return addresses. As you may recall, the STACKSIZE statement in the module definition (.DEF) file defines the amount of space reserved for the stack, with a *minimum* stack size of 5Kbytes. You'll want to understand how your program uses this stack, so that you can allocate the proper amount of stack space.

Variables declared inside a function that don't use the `static` keyword are local variables, such as the `lValue` variable in the code fragment we looked at a moment ago. Space on the stack for local variables is allocated when a function is called, and freed when returning from a function. If you are writing a program that allocates a lot of local variables, you may wish to use a higher STACKSIZE value to reflect the additional memory that is needed. A higher stack size should also be requested for programs that do a lot of recursive calling, since local variables are allocated for *each* call made into functions. The accompanying boxed discussion provides some additional details on the use of the stack for the three basic stack objects.

The accompanying figure shows the relationship of the three main types of stack objects: arguments, return address, and local variables.

Also shown is the C-language call, and the resulting assembly language instructions that support this stack structure. The `push` *instruction puts arguments on the stack for called functions. The* `call` *instruction places a return address on the stack, and passes control to the called function. Inside the called function, the compiler creates the code to adjust the base pointer, BP, and the stack pointer, SP, to access both the passed arguments and the local variables on the* **stack frame.** *Notice that the variable defined with the* `static` *keyword,* `j`, *is not allocated on the stack. Instead, as a static data object, it is allocated in the static data area.*

```
C-LANGUAGE              MASM                        STACK

x(...)                  push a
    {                   push b                        a
    y(a,b,c);           push c                        b
RetAddr:                call y                        c
    }                                             x-RetAddr
                                          bp →    old bp value
NEAR PASCAL y                                        x
    (int a,                                          y
        int b,          y proc near       sp →       z
        int c)          push bp
    {                   mov  bp,sp
    int x,y,z;          sub  sp,6
    static int j;       .
    .                   .
    .                   .
    .                   mov  sp,bp
    }                   pop  bp
                        ret  6
```

The BP, or base-pointer, register, is set up to allow arguments and the local variables to be referenced from a fixed location. If you run a debugger like Codeview, you can see the machine language references to arguments as positive offsets from BP. Here is an assembly language instruction that references the third passed argument in our example:

```
MOV    AX, [BP+04]
```

Local variables are referenced as negative offsets from BP. For example, here is how the third local variable might be accessed:

```
MOV    AX, [BP-06]
```

> *Because the PASCAL calling convention has been selected, the called function cleans up the stack. This is actually built into the return instruction, which is one reason that this calling convention creates smaller, faster code:*
>
> ```
> RET    6
> ```
>
> *If this seems somewhat esoteric and complex to you, don't worry too much. Fortunately, the details of stack management are mostly the concern of assembly language programmers and compiler writers. The compiler takes care of everything, so that you don't have to think about it. The important things to keep in mind are the three uses of the stack, so that you can be sure to adjust your stack size when you write a Windows program that uses either a lot of local variables or deeply nested recursive calls.*

The Debug Version of Windows and Stack Checking. Under ordinary circumstances, a stack overflow will go unnoticed. Or, it will result in mysterious and untraceable problems with your program. To prevent this problem, you must test your programs under very special circumstances, since the normal C stack checking is disabled under Windows. Here's what you need. First, you must compile your programs with stack checking *enabled*, which means compile *without* the -Gs switch. Next, you must have a special version of Windows installed on your system that is known as the **debug version**. The debug version of Windows is created by copying a set of dynamic link library files from the Windows software development kit into the system subdirectory (\windows\system). The special set of DLLs perform additional error checking, including a check for a stack overflow. And finally, you need to have an extra monitor hooked up to your system. This allows you to receive debugging information (and to communicate with debuggers like CodeView and Symdeb) without disturbing the graphic display screen.

The Local Heap. Local heaps are one of two places from which programs can perform dynamic memory allocation (the other is the global heap). Local heaps are always set up inside a single data segment. A local heap is automatically set up for a program's use in the default data segment. In addition, a program can allocate other

Table 18.2 *Windows local heap management routines*

LocalAlloc *	Allocates memory from a local heap.
LocalCompact	Reorganizes a local heap.
LocalDiscard	Discards an unlocked, discardable object.
LocalFlags	Provides information about a specific memory object.
LocalFree *	Frees a local memory object.
LocalHandle	Provides the handle of a local memory object associated with a given memory address.
LocalInit *	Initializes a local heap.
LocalLock *	Increments the lock count on a local memory object, and returns its address.
LocalReAlloc *	Changes the size of a local memory object.
LocalShrink	Reorganizes a local heap and reduces the size of the heap (if possible) to the initial, starting size. If this routine is successful, it reduces the size of the data segment that contains the heap, so that the memory can be reclaimed by the global heap.
LocalSize	Returns the current size of a local memory object.
LocalUnlock *	Decrements the lock count on a local memory object.

segments in which a local heap can be created. We'll describe how this is done later in this chapter.

Without requiring any special effort on your part, every program has one local heap, which resides at the end of the default data segment. The initial size of the heap depends on the value defined in the module definition (.DEF) file with the HEAPSIZE statement. The heap can grow beyond this size, though. And when it does, the segment that contains the local heap will grow as well. A local heap can continue to grow until its segment reaches a maximum size of 64K.

Programs allocate memory from a local heap using one of the twelve local heap management routines. You can easily tell one of these routines, since the name of each routine starts with the word "Local." For example, LocalAlloc is the name of the routine that allocates memory from a local heap. LocalFree releases memory that has been allocated in a local heap. Table 18.2 provides a complete list of the local heap management routines. Later in this chapter, we'll take a closer look at local heap management, and provide some more detail on the routines marked with a "*".

In the preceding chapter, we described how three types of segments can be allocated on the global heap: moveable, discardable, and fixed. The local heap also supports these three types. Moveable objects can be allocated to help minimize memory fragmentation, and discardable objects can be allocated to give the local memory manager the freedom to purge unneeded objects when memory is low. By comparison, the standard C library routines only allocate fixed objects and do not support moveable or discardable objects. In this way, the local memory manager provides quite a bit more sophistication than the C library's `malloc` routine in allocating and managing a heap space.

To support moveable and discardable memory objects, the local heap manager provides a **memory handle** when it allocates a local memory object. Like the handles that we encountered in the context of GDI objects, a memory handle is simply an identifier that can be traded in to access the real object. When a memory handle is passed to the LocalLock routine, a memory pointer is provided. As we'll see later, this means that code like the following is required to access a local memory object:

```
HANDLE hMem;
PSTR   pstr;

/*  Allocate a 15 byte moveable object.  */
hMem = LocalAlloc (LMEM_MOVEABLE, 15);

/*  Lock the object, getting a pointer.  */
pstr = LocalLock (hMem);

lstrcpy (pstr, "Hello World");

/*  Unlock the object.  */
LocalUnlock (hMem);
```

Later in this chapter, we'll provide you a full-blown example of a program that uses local heap allocation. Let's continue our tour of program memory management by looking at the last item in the default data segment, the atom table.

Atom Tables. Optionally, a program can create an atom table in its local data segment. An atom table provides a way to store and retrieve variable-length character strings. When an atom is created, a handle is issued that uniquely identifies the string. At two bytes, a handle is a small, fixed-size value that can easily and conveniently be

placed into fixed length data structures with a minimum of overhead. And atom tables are efficient, since duplicate requests create
the same atom value. The USER module uses atoms to store the
names of window classes, clipboard formats, and application-defined messages. You may wish to use them to help you deal efficiently with variable-length strings.

In addition to the private atom table that resides in the local data
segment, Windows provides a global atom table. Windows' Dynamic Data Exchange (DDE) protocol relies on the global atom table
to pass the ASCII names of data topics between programs. Since
DDE uses messages to relay requests for data, an atom provides a
compact way to store the name of a desired data element in a very
small space.

Dynamically Allocated Segments

Dynamically allocated segments provide the most flexible type of
read/write memory for an application to use. Up to the limit of
available system memory, you can have as many as you want, and
each segment you allocate can be as large as 64K. In fact, you can
allocate segments larger than 64K, although the methods required
to support this are beyond the scope of this book.

How many dynamically allocated segments *can* a program create?
There are three factors: available system memory, the size of a handle table, and whether Windows is running in Real, Standard, or
386-Enhanced Mode. Real Mode has a maximum address space of
one megabyte, Standard Mode has a maximum of 16 megabytes, and
386-Enhanced Mode has a maximum of 64 megabytes. In all three
modes, the maximum size of a handle table is 8192 entries, which
means that a maximum of 8192 segments can be created. However,
Standard Mode uses *two* table entries for each segment, so the system-wide maximum for Standard Mode is 4096 segments. Future
versions of Windows will probably fix Standard Mode, so that 8192
segments can be allocated. In addition, in future versions of Windows these protect mode limits will most likely become a *per task*
limit. In Windows 3.0, however, these limits apply on a system-wide
basis.

Programs allocate and manage dynamic segments using Windows'
global heap management routines. This is a set of 21 routines that
start with the word "Global." GlobaAlloc, for example, allocates a
dynamic segment and GlobalFree deallocates a segment. When you
look for dynamically allocated segments using HEAPWALK, you'll

Figure 18.4 *Dynamically allocated segment as seen by HEAPWALK*

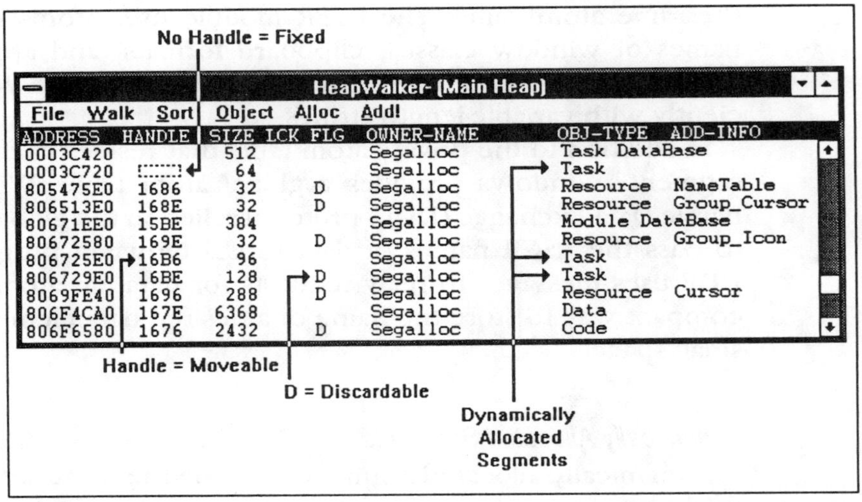

need to keep in mind that it uses the type "Task" and "Shared" to distinguish such segments, as shown in Figure 18.4.

There are three basic types of segments: fixed, moveable, and discardable. The use of fixed segments tends to be limited to device drivers, which require that a memory object always stays in one place. The reason is that fixed segments prevent the memory manager from compacting memory when it needs to, so that most programs use moveable segments to store data. From the memory manager's point of view, the most "friendly" kind of object is a discardable one. It can be moved or discarded, as the memory manager sees fit, when system memory starts to get a little cramped. Code and resource segments are usually discardable segments, although a program could store data in a discardable segment to implement a type of virtual memory system under Real and Standard Mode Windows.

Just like the local memory manager, the global memory manager provides a handle when it allocates a block of memory. The use of a handle instead of a pointer allows moveable and discardable objects to be moved or discarded. When a program wishes to access the memory, it calls a special routine which locks the object in place and provides a pointer: GlobalLock. When a program has finished using a block of memory, it releases the object by calling Global-

Unlock. Here is a sample code fragment that shows how a segment from the global heap can be allocated so that a string can be copied into the segment:

```
HANDLE hMem;
LPSTR   lpstr;

/*  Allocate a 15 byte moveable object.  */
hMem = GlobalAlloc (GMEM_MOVEABLE, 15L);

/*  Lock the object, getting a pointer.  */
lpstr = GlobalLock (hMem);

lstrcpy (lpstr, "Hello World");

/*  Unlock the object.  */
GlobalUnlock (hMem);
```

If you compare this code fragment to the one we looked at during our discussion of the local heap routines, you'll find that the two sets of dynamic memory allocation routines look very similar. This is no accident. The two subroutine packages were developed at the same time, to provide similar services but at two different levels: One manages the system-wide global heap and the other manages the private local heap that each program is given by default.

Later in this chapter, we'll provide a complete program to demonstrate the use of the global heap management routines. For now, let's move on to discuss another place that programs can store data: resources.

Resources

An important type of memory object often overlooked for their memory management qualities are resources. A resource is a read-only data object that has been merged into a program's .EXE file by the resource compiler. When the data is needed, the resource manager reads it from disk and places it into a discardable memory object. And when the memory manager needs to reclaim the memory for another use, a resource can typically be discarded or purged from system memory. As allocated segments, resources can be allocated as fixed, moveable, or discardable segments. Since discardable resources are the most flexible, they are the most common.

Figure 18.5 *HEAPWALK lets you see resource-type objects*

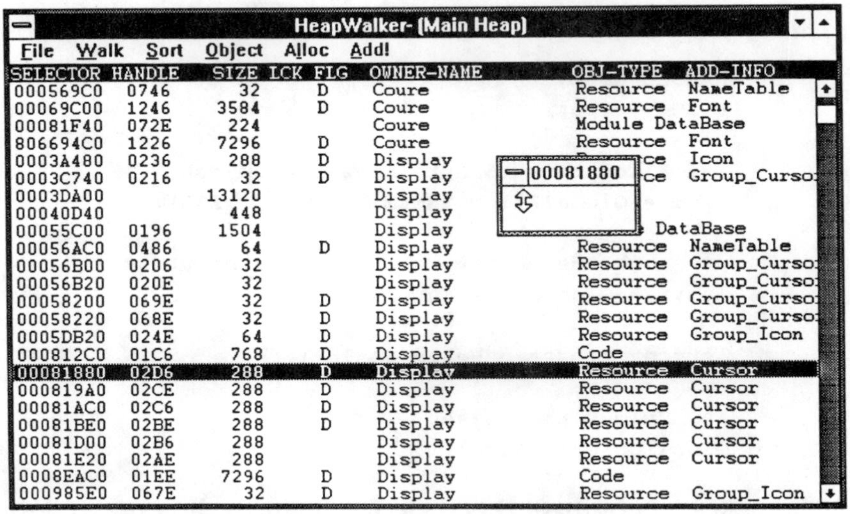

```
                 HeapWalker- [Main Heap]
 File  Walk  Sort  Object  Alloc  Add!
SELECTOR HANDLE   SIZE LCK FLG  OWNER-NAME        OBJ-TYPE  ADD-INFO
000569C0  0746     32      D    Coure             Resource  NameTable
00069C00  1246   3584      D    Coure             Resource  Font
00081F40  072E    224           Coure             Module    DataBase
806694C0  1226   7296      D    Coure             Resource  Font
0003A480  0236    288      D    Display                  ce  Icon
0003C740  0216     32      D    Display    00081880 ce  Group_Curso
0003DA00         13120          Display
00040D40          448           Display
00055C00  0196   1504           Display                   DataBase
00056AC0  0486     64      D    Display           Resource  NameTable
00056B00  0206     32           Display           Resource  Group_Curso
00056B20  020E     32           Display           Resource  Group_Curso
00058200  069E     32      D    Display           Resource  Group_Curso
00058220  068E     32      D    Display           Resource  Group_Curso
0005DB20  024E     64      D    Display           Resource  Group_Icon
000812C0  01C6    768      D    Display           Code
00081880  02D6    288      D    Display           Resource  Cursor
000819A0  02CE    288      D    Display           Resource  Cursor
00081AC0  02C6    288      D    Display           Resource  Cursor
00081BE0  02BE    288      D    Display           Resource  Cursor
00081D00  02B6    288           Display           Resource  Cursor
00081E20  02AE    288           Display           Resource  Cursor
0008EAC0  01EE   7296      D    Display           Code
000985E0  067E     32      D    Display           Resource  Group_Icon
```

Using HEAPWALK, it's easy to find the resource segments: They are labeled "Resource." HEAPWALK knows the difference between different types of resources, so it tells whether a specific object is a menu, dialog box template, cursor, icon, or whatever. In addition, if you double-click on a resource which contains a graphic image (such as an icon or a cursor), HEAPWALK displays the object for you. Figure 18.5 shows HEAPWALK listing several resources and displaying the image of one of GDI's cursors.

Table 18.3 provides a list of the different types of resources that Windows supports, along with the chapter in this book that discusses the use of each type. As you can see, resources play a key role in how certain data objects are packaged for use. Resources are used for user-interface objects, GDI objects, and space-saving objects like string-tables, and custom resources.

From a memory use point of view, each resource resides in a separate segment. In other words, a program with one accelerator table, two menu templates, and four dialog box templates has a total of seven different segments worth of resources. The advantage of having each resource packed in its own segment is that each can be loaded and discarded in a manner that is completely independent of other resources.

Table 18.3   *Windows' predefined resources*

Resource Type	Covered In Depth
Accelerator Table	Chapter 11
Bitmaps	
Cursors	Chapter 17
Custom Resources	Chapter 18
Dialog Box Templates	Chapter 14
Fonts	Chapter 10
Icons	
Menu Templates	Chapter 11
String Tables	Chapter 18

GDI Data Segment

Whenever a program creates a GDI object, space is allocated out of GDI's data segment. Or more specifically, space is allocated from GDI's local heap. While there's no doubt that programs will need to use such objects, care should be taken to avoid creating too many of these types of objects. In addition, programs that create GDI drawing objects should be careful to destroy the objects when they are not needed. Otherwise, if GDI's heap gets full, it will prevent other programs from being able to run properly. In a future version of Windows, Microsoft plans to delete GDI objects when the application that allocated the object quits. In the meantime, you should allocate only the minimum number of objects that you need, and be sure to destroy objects when you are done using them.

Table 18.4 provides a list of GDI objects and the size that each takes from GDI's data segment. These sizes are subject to change;

Table 18.4   *Space taken in GDI's local heap by various GDI drawing objects*

Object	Size
Brush	32 bytes
Bitmap	28–32 bytes
Font	40–44 bytes
Pen	28 bytes
Region	28 bytes to several Kbytes
Palette	28 bytes

Figure 18.6 *HEAPWALK showing GDI's data segment*

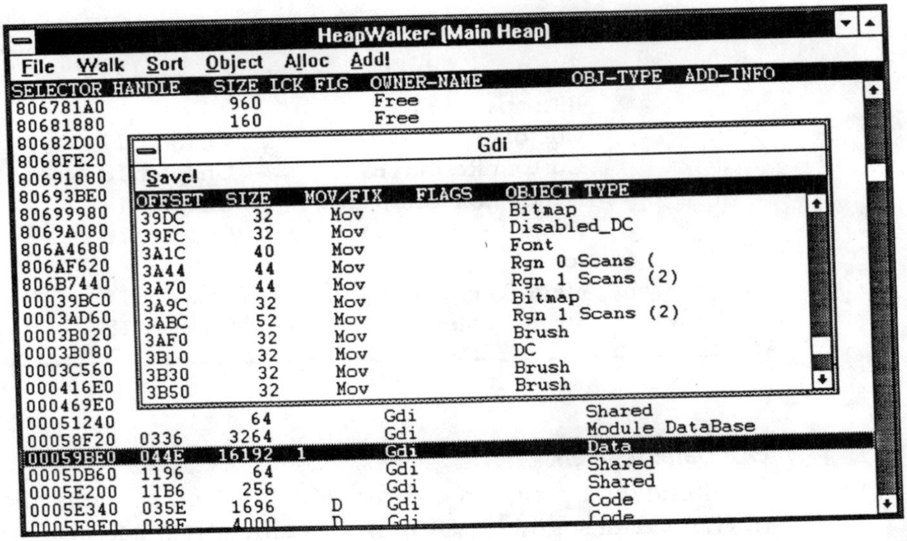

they are provided to help you get a sense for the demands that each object places on system memory. These sizes were determined using HEAPWALK, which can show the contents of GDI's data segment. Two of these objects reside in their own segment: fonts and bitmaps. The local heap object contains a pointer to the larger object.

If you'd like to see for yourself, you can run HEAPWALK and select the Object–GDI LocalWalk menu selection. It provides a window showing the various objects that are in GDI's data segment, as shown in Figure 18.6. It's interesting to note that GDI's data segment starts out relatively small. In this figure, it is 16 Kbytes—so there is a lot of room to grow to meet the demands that applications make for GDI drawing objects.

One other data area can get filled by the actions that programs take, and should be monitored carefully: the USER library's data segment.

USER Data Segment

Windows' USER module provides the support for Windows' user interface objects. This includes windows, menus, dialog boxes, and accelerator tables. Unlike GDI objects, USER objects in general are not shared between programs. For this reason, when a Windows

Table 18.5 *Approximate size of various USER data objects*

Object	Size
menus	20 bytes/ menu plus 20 bytes/ menu item
window class	40–50 bytes
window	60–70 bytes

program terminates, USER can free the data objects that were created. Nonetheless, the wise Windows programmer makes frugal use of memory and will destroy objects when done using them.

Quite a few user interface objects are stored as resources, and therefore reside in their own segments. Included in this group are cursors, icons, dialog box templates, and menu templates. Other objects take up USER heap space, including those shown in Table 18.5.

Unfortunately, HEAPWALK doesn't show the size of individual objects in USER's data segment as it does for GDI's data segment. So the estimates in this table were created by looking at the size of data structures in the Microsoft documentation and adding 50% for internal overhead. Of course, the exact size is not as important (since it can change from version to version) as the simple fact that your use of these objects takes up space which, at least for now, is in short supply. For example, if you define 10 window classes and create 100 windows of each class, you consume about 7500 bytes of USER heap space. Since USER's heap is also used by other programs, including the Program Manager, File Manager, etc., you need to be careful to not create too many objects that may cause this heap space to be overrun.

Assuming you don't create too many objects and overload USER's heap space, there are two often overlooked types of memory areas: class extra bytes and window extra bytes. These are small data areas that reside in USER's data segment, but which are attached to a specific window or window class. A program might put flags, or even a memory handle, into these extra bytes. Then they can be accessed by simply providing the window handle. Here is a list of the routines that access window and class extra bytes:

Class Extra Bytes	Window Extra Bytes
SetClassWord	SetWindowWord
SetClassLong	SetWindowLong
GetClassWord	GetWindowWord
GetClassLong	GetWindowLong

The advantage of these extra bytes is that they allow you, for example, to store the head of a linked list in an area that is directly related to a window. Or, you can store a memory handle, to give each window—in effect—its own private data area. The most obvious use of this type of memory is in implementing custom dialog box controls. But it is equally useful in implementing applications that support the multiple document interface (MDI).

With this brief introduction to the different types of memory available to Windows applications, you have a reasonably complete picture of the choices you can make. Now it's time to roll up our sleeves and look at the implementation details for using different types of memory. The rest of this chapter provides five complete code examples to answer any further questions you might have regarding an application's use of memory. Here is a list of the code examples and the topics that each focuses on:

1. SEGALLOC This sample program demonstrates how to use memory allocated out of the global heap. The accompanying discussion provides more details on the various global heap management routines.
2. MIN2 We're going to take a second look at the minimum Windows program to support a discussion of code structure and memory use. This program demonstrates how a Windows program can be divided into multiple code segments to improve memory use.
3. LOCALMEM This program provides an example of using the local heap management routines to allocate objects from a program's default data segment. This program also demonstrates the use of string tables.
4. SUBSEG This program shows how the local heap management routines can be used with a segment that is dynamically allocated from the global heap. This program combines global heap management routines and local heap management routines.

5. CUSTRES This program demonstrates the creation of a custom resource. A sine table is stored as a resource and used to calculate sine and cosine values, which are used to draw a circle.

Let's get started, then, with a look at using the global heap management routines.

Global Heap Allocation

When a program allocates memory from Windows' global heap, it is allocating a segment. Segments can be allocated that are fixed, moveable, or discardable, depending upon what a program needs. In general, though, programmers should keep in mind the words of John Pollock, who worked on Windows' first KERNEL and was the first Windows instructor for many Windows programmers. He urged programmers to keep dynamically allocated segments "as *few* as possible, as *small* as possible, and as *discardable* as possible."

As Few as Possible. You'll want to keep your segments as *few* as possible because of the overhead of a segment. Segments are expensive. Each incurs 24 bytes of overhead: a 16-byte invisible header that links all segments together and an 8-byte entry in a master segment table. In Real Mode, this segment table is called the Burger-Master. In protect mode, the segment table is the local descriptor table (LDT). See Chapter 17 for more details.

Because of this high overhead, you'll probably want to minimize the number of segments you allocate. For example, with an overhead of 24 bytes, if you allocate a segment to hold a 24-byte data object, it really costs you 48 bytes. That's a lot like having a sales tax of 100% on everything you buy. But since this is a fixed cost, you can effectively lower your "memory-use tax" by putting many objects into a single segment. For example, if you put 2400 bytes of data into a single object, you have effectively lowered your taxes to a mere 1%. When you start to think about how to make the best use of dynamically allocated segments, think about using arrays of records instead of working with a linked list of segments. It will help you get your money's worth from the memory manager.

A second issue that relates to segment overhead involves **granularity**. This refers to the actual pieces of memory that Windows carves out when you allocate a segment. Dynamically allocated segments have a granularity of 32 bytes—or, in real-mode memory terms, two paragraphs. (Recall that in real mode the smallest segment is 16 bytes, which is called a paragraph. Even though protect mode allows for smaller segments, Windows doesn't.) In Real and Standard Modes, 16 bytes of every object is used as a header. In either of these modes, if you ask for a segment that is between one and 16 bytes long, it costs you 32 bytes. This table shows how a 32-byte granularity affects the size of the *actual* versus the *requested* memory.

Requested Size	Actual Size	Header	Actual Data Area
1–16 bytes	32 bytes	16 bytes	16 bytes
17–48	64	16	48
49–80	96	16	80
81–112	128	16	112

Notice that the size of the actual data area jumps in odd-paragraph increments, so that every segment request is an odd multiple of 16 bytes (1, 3, 5, 7, etc.).

In 386-Enhanced Mode, a 32-byte granularity is also used. However, the implementation is a little different since this mode is able to take advantage of features of the Intel 80386. The granularity is in terms of evenparagraphs. Here is a table that demonstrates this:

Requested Size	Actual Size	Header	Actual Data Area
1–32 bytes	32 bytes	32 bytes (hidden)	32 bytes
33–64	64	32 bytes (hidden)	64 bytes
65–96	96	32 bytes (hidden)	96 bytes
97–128	128	32 bytes (hidden)	128 bytes

Since the 386-Enhanced Mode runs in protect mode, just like Standard Mode, a reference beyond the limit of a segment causes a program to terminate with a UAE error. However, since this mode has a different alignment from Standard Mode, it is possible that a bug that causes a UAE error in one of the protect modes might not cause the same error in the other protect mode. You should advise the people who test your programs to be sure to run a full set of tests in both modes. A small difference like this can cause a stable program in one environment to crash in the other.

As Small as Possible. Keep your segments as small as possible, because Windows is a multitasking system, and memory that you allocate is not available for other Windows programs. This is particularly an issue in Real Mode, with its tiny, one-megabyte address space. But even in other modes, only allocate the amount of memory you need and no more.

One reason that John Pollock made this recommendation has to do with the way some DOS programs behave. Since DOS is a single-tasking operating system, the first thing that many DOS programs do is to allocate all of system memory. If a Windows program tried to do this, it would effectively lock out other programs from being able to run.

So, whether you are moving to Windows from DOS or from some other programming environment, keep in mind that memory is a shared and in some cases, a scarce resource. Allocate only what you need, when you need it. And, when you are done using a block of memory, free it so that other Windows programs can use it.

As Discardable as Possible. In the last chapter, we talked about the three types of memory objects: fixed, moveable, and discardable. To the Windows memory manager, fixed is the least flexible and therefore least desirable type of memory object, and discardable is the most desirable. But programmers new to Windows tend to see things just the opposite way: Fixed memory seems the most comfortable, discardable seems the most disastrous, and moveable only slightly less so. After all, what programmer in his right mind wants to deal with data that keeps wiggling away, or disappears completely?

John Pollock's recommendation to make memory as discardable as possible reflects the fact that memory should be treated as a scarce resource. Programs with moderate requirements for memory usually keep data in moveable data segments. After all, a moveable segment gives the memory manager the freedom to shuffle memory so it can minimize fragmentation.

Programs with a large or unlimited need for memory, like word processing programs or spreadsheet programs, require their own mechanism to transfer data between main system memory and disk. After all, even a virtual memory system can run out of memory. And when Windows is without virtual memory in the Standard and Real Modes, such programs will run out of "real memory" sooner. Discardable memory provides a way for such programs to volunteer objects to be purged. When memory is plentiful, discardable objects don't have to be purged. But when memory is scarce, the memory manager can exercise its option to remove discardable objects.

Global Heap API

Table 18.6 shows all of Windows' global heap management routines. This table is set up to show how 12 of these routines must be paired together to create a sandwich construction that we first introduced in Chapter 7. The other nine routines act either on a specific global memory object or on the global heap as a whole.

For the most common uses, programs can get by with just five of these routines: GlobalAlloc, GlobalReAlloc, GlobalLock, GlobalUnlock, and GlobalFree. We're going to take a close look at these routines, to provide you with enough information so you can start using them in your Windows programming.

GlobalAlloc. The GlobalAlloc routine allocates memory from the global heap. It is defined as

```
HANDLE GlobalAlloc (wFlags, dwBytes)
```

- wFlags is a combination of one or more global memory allocation flags, discussed below.
- dwBytes is an unsigned long value for the number of bytes to allocate.

GlobalAlloc returns the handle that identifies the segment you've allocated. Be sure to *always* check the return value from this function, since there is no guarantee that your request can be satisfied. When an allocation request cannot be met, GlobalAlloc lets you know by returning a NULL handle.

The value of wFlags can be a combination of nine different flags, depending on the type of memory you wish to allocate (fixed, moveable, or discardable), whether the memory is going to be shared or not, and other considerations. Here are the nine flags:

Description	Flag
Fixed memory object	GMEM_FIXED
Moveable memory object	GMEM_MOVEABLE
Discardable memory object	GMEM_DISCARDABLE | GMEM_MOVEABLE
Initialize with zeros.	GMEM_ZEROINIT

(Continued)

Description	Flag
Segment will be shared	GMEM_DDESHARE
Do not compact	GMEM_NOCOMPACT
Do not discard	GMEM_NODISCARD
Tag a discardable segment so that a notification routine is called *before* the segment is discarded	GMEM_NOTIFY
Do not put in EMS memory	GMEM_NOT_BANKED

Table 18.6 *Windows' global heap management routines*

Top Slice	Bottom Slice	Description
GlobalAlloc	GlobalFree	Allocates a segment from the global heap.
GlobalCompact	na	Reorganizes the global heap to determine the largest block of available free memory.
GlobalDiscard	na	Purges an unlocked, discardable segment from memory.
GlobalDosAlloc	GlobalDosFree	Allocates a block of memory in the DOS address space, that is, below the one-megabyte line, so that a Windows program can share a data area with a DOS program or a DOS device driver.
GlobalFix	GlobalUnfix	Prevents an object from moving in the linear address space. Notice that this doesn't keep an object from being swapped to disk—only the GlobalPageLock routine can do that.
GlobalFlags	na	Retrieves the flags associated with a global memory object.

(Continued)

Table 18.6   *Continued*

Top Slice	Bottom Slice	Description
GlobalHandle	na	Provides the global handle associated with a specific segment address.
GlobalLock	GlobalUnlock	Retrieves the address of a global memory object. In Real Mode, it also increments the lock count to prevent it from moving in physical memory. In all modes, it prevents a discardable object from being discarded.
GlobalLRUNewest	na	Changes a segment's priority in the LRU discarding table to make it *least* likely to be discarded.
GlobalLRUOldest	na	Changes a segment's priority in the LRU discarding table to make it the *most* likely to be discarded.
GlobalNotify	na	Sets up a call-back procedure through which the global heap manager notifies a program *before* a segment is discarded. A program can implement a virtual memory management scheme using this routine, that will work in all Windows' different operating modes.
GlobalPageLock	GlobalPageUnlock	Fixes a segment's location in the linear address space, and also prevents the virtual memory pages from being swapped out to disk. This provides the maximum protection against any movement of a segment, which is required for certain types of device drivers. However, programs should avoid using this since overuse of page locking can be severely detrimental to overall system performance.

(Continued)

Table 18.6 *Continued*

Top Slice	Bottom Slice	Description
GlobalReAlloc	na	Changes the size of a segment on the global heap. Both locked and unlocked segments can be resized, although a special flag must be set if you want to allow a locked segment to move if it is necessary to satisfy the allocation request.
GlobalSize	na	Returns the size of a segment on the global heap.
GlobalWire	GlobalUnwire	In Real-Mode Windows, moves a segment to a very low memory position for segments that are going to be locked for an unusually long period of time. This measure helps avoid serious fragmentation that otherwise occurs when movable or discardable memory objects are left locked for longer periods of time than to process a single message.

The first four sets of flags are the most important, and most useful. Most of the time, you'll start by deciding the disposition of your memory object: fixed, moveable, or discardable. Next, you'll decide whether to initialize the data area with zeros or not, and your job is done. The other flags have more specialized uses, which we'll review briefly to help you decide when one might be useful to you.

The second parameter, dwBytes, is the number of bytes to allocate. Since this is an unsigned long value, you'll often have to supply a type-cast if you have calculated the size of an object using regular integer values. For example, here is how to allocate a 200-byte, moveable segment:

```
hMem = GlobalAlloc (GMEM_MOVEABLE, (DWORD)200);
```

This routine accepts an unsigned long value for the size of a memory object because it supports memory objects that are larger than 64K. Since this is the limit on the size of a segment, Windows allocates objects larger than 64K by setting aside multiple segments to satisfy your memory request. If you wish to allocate objects larger than 64K, you'll have to do some special **segment arithmetic** to allow segment boundaries to be crossed correctly.

One approach to handling the segment arithmetic that is required for objects larger than 64K is to rely on the built-in support that some C Compilers provide. Pointers to such objects are referred to as **huge** pointers. However, this approach involves taking on quite a bit of overhead for even the simplest pointer operations. A more efficient approach is to use the __AHINCR symbol that Windows provides, which you can add to a segment address yourself if a segment boundary has been crossed. A simpler approach involves avoiding the allocation of memory objects that are larger than 64K.

The remaining flags are used for special circumstances. For example, the GMEM_DDESHARE flag marks a segment as one that may be shared between different programs. The "DDE" in the flag name is the acronym for the **dynamic data exchange (DDE),** a data sharing protocol built on top of Windows' message passing system. This flag should be used when sharing data using either DDE, or the Clipboard. In general, programs should use one of these two mechanisms to share data, and not simply share memory handles. The reason is that certain configurations of Windows are built around the idea of private address spaces. As time goes on, this will be the case for all protect mode implementations of Windows, but for now, it is limited to Windows running with EMS memory. All data sharing *must* be based on a client-server model. That is, one program *writes* the data, a second one *reads* the data and makes a copy for its own use. Two programs can never share the same dynamically allocated segment with both having read/write privileges.

The GMEM_NOCOMPACT flag tells the memory manager not to move memory to satisfy the memory request. The GMEM_NODISCARD flag says the same thing, and adds an additional condition: No segments should be discarded to satisfy the allocation request. These are useful for programs that want to avoid disturbing the global heap. For a program that is very sensitive to performance issues, memory movement is expensive. These flags tell the memory manager that memory should be allocated *only* if it can be done quickly from an existing free block.

The GMEM_NOTIFY flag is used for discardable segments to request the memory manager to notify you before it discards your segments. When the time comes to discard a segment, the memory manager calls a function that you have defined as a notification call-back function. The notification routine is assigned using the GlobalNotify routine. It is useful for implementing a virtual memory system that works in all of Windows' operating modes.

The final flag, GMEM_NOT_BANKED, is primarily for the use of optimizing device drivers for Real Mode when EMS memory is present. EMS was a very important addition to Windows 2.x; but with the advent of protect mode and the use of extended memory, EMS is something that will become less and less useful over time. In fact, some people wonder why Microsoft doesn't give up Real Mode support entirely and run Windows solely in protect mode. For device driver writers, this flag might be important. For everybody else, it's not that useful.

GlobalLock. The GlobalLock routine provides the address of a global segment, and increments the lock count for certain types of segments. It is defined as

```
LPSTR GlobalLock (hMem)
```

- hMem is a memory handle of a segment allocated with Global-Alloc.

Programs make calls to GlobalLock to get the address of a moveable or discardable segment. In addition, this routine increments the lock count for discardable objects, to prevent them from being discarded. Using moveable or discardable segments requires a two-step process. The first step is to allocate the memory itself. The second step involves calling GlobalLock to retrieve a far pointer that can be used to access the memory. For example, here is how to allocate a moveable segment that can accommodate a 274-byte object, and lock it for use:

```
HANDLE hMem;
LPSTR lp;

hMem = GlobalAlloc (GMEM_MOVEABLE, (DWORD)274));
if (!hMem)
    goto ErrorExit1;

lp = GlobalLock (hMem);
if (!lp)
    goto ErrorExit2;
```

Notice the two sets of error checking in this code fragment. The first check makes sure that the allocation was successful. Most programmers agree that this is reasonable. The second check is to make sure that the lock is successful. Many programmers are hesitant to check every time they lock an object. It's a little extra effort, but it prevents a program from unpleasant surprises. For one thing, a program that tries to use a null pointer will cause a general protection error—sometimes known as a GP Fault. Then, Windows will terminate the program with an "Unexpected Application Error" message.

To help you understand the necessity for this message, here is a list of the things that cause a call to GlobalLock to fail:

1. A discardable object that has been discarded.
2. Inability to copy a Clipboard or DDE object to the local address space. At present, this is only a concern in Real Mode Windows when running with EMS. But this will likely be an issue in protect mode in a future version of Windows.
3. Invalid memory handle. This can happen if an object has already been freed, or if the memory location that the program has been using to store the memory handle has been overwritten.

At first glance, it may appear as if GlobalLock only fails in the most extreme circumstances. You might wonder whether you can avoid checking for a failed return for moveable objects that are not being used in the context of the Clipboard and DDE. Unfortunately, the third set of causes is the "catch-all" that makes it necessary to always check the return value of GlobalLock. A memory handle can get overwritten, which will likely cause GlobalLock to fail.

When a program allocates a fixed object, there is no need to call GlobalLock. The reason is that the handle of fixed objects is always the segment address of the allocated memory. Here is how to allocate a fixed block of memory and convert the memory handle into a pointer:

```
HANDLE hMem;
LPSTR lp;

hMem = GlobalAlloc (GMEM_FIXED, (DWORD)200);
lp = (LPSTR)MAKELONG (0, hMem);
```

The MAKELONG macro packs two-word (two-byte) values into a long (four-byte) value, which can be cast to a far pointer. Of course, to work well in all of Windows' operating modes, you should probably avoid allocating fixed memory objects. But we are showing you this to give you a peek at something that you *can* do quite freely in the context of local heaps. But more on that later on.

GlobalReAlloc. The GlobalReAlloc routine changes the size of a memory object on the global heap, and is defined as

```
HANDLE GlobalReAlloc (hMem, dwBytes, wFlags)
```

- hMem is a memory handle, obtained by calling GlobalAlloc.
- dwBytes is an unsigned long value for the number of bytes to allocate, or zero if the GMEM_MODIFY flag is being used to change the memory disposition of a memory object.
- wFlags is one or more flags, or zero if the object is just changing sizes.

The GlobalReAlloc routine can be used to do two different things: change the size of a global memory object, and change the memory disposition of a memory object. It takes all the same flags as the GlobalAlloc routine plus one new one: GMEM_MODIFY. This flag indicates when the memory disposition is being changed—for example, when a moveable object is being made discardable, or when a discardable object is being made moveable. Aside from this, the GlobalReAlloc routine can pretty much be treated as an extension of the GlobalAlloc routine. Here are some examples of its usage:

```
/*  Make an object moveable.  */
GlobalReAlloc (hMem, 0, GMEM_MODIFY | GMEM_MOVEABLE);

/*  Resize an object.  */
GlobalReAlloc (hMem, (DWORD)1843, 0);

/*  Resize an object, filling new area with zeroes. */
GlobalReAlloc (hMem, (DWORD)dwSize, GMEM_ZEROINIT);
```

GlobalUnlock. The GlobalUnlock routine decrements the lock count for certain types of segments, and is defined as

```
BOOL GlobalUnlock (hMem)
```

- hMem is a memory handle allocated with the GlobalAlloc routine.

In general, you'll call GlobalUnlock as the second part of a sandwich construction whenever you call GlobalLock. For example, here is a typical usage in response to a WM_LBUTTONDOWN message, to retrieve the mouse location from the lParam:

```
long far PASCAL WndProc (...)
    {
    LPPOINT lp;

    switch (msg)
        {
        case WM_LBUTTONDOWN:
            lp = (LPPOINT)GlobalLock (hmem);
            *lp[cp] = MAKEPOINT(lParam);
            GlobalUnlock(hmem);
            .
            .
```

The key issue that this code fragment demonstrates is the need to keep a memory segment locked for only a very brief period of time. Otherwise, you risk fragmenting the global heap and wasting memory. This will affect the performance of your program, as well as all other programs currently running in the system. In short, locks should be very short term.

GlobalFree. The GlobalFree routine frees an unlocked global memory object that was allocated with the GlobalAlloc routine. It is defined as

```
HANDLE GlobalFree (hMem)
```

- hMem is a global memory handle that was allocated by calling GlobalAlloc.

GlobalFree releases the segment and all internally created data structures that are associated with a given memory handle. Even though Windows frees all memory segments when a program terminates, it's a good practice to explicitly free every object when you are done using it.

This in-depth introduction to Windows' global heap management routines has almost gotten us ready to look at some sample programs. But first, we're going to look at an issue that should give you another perspective on the way that memory is managed in Windows. Even if you never use any of these routines in any of your

Windows programs, understanding where they might be useful will help you better understand Windows' memory management. What we're referring to is the various sets of routines that lock, wire, fix, and otherwise coerce a global segment to reside in a fixed location.

Locked, Wired, Fixed, and Page Locked

In our discussion of Windows global heap management routines, we identified GlobalLock as the routine that programs use to **dereference** a handle to get a pointer. By dereference, we simply mean to convert into a pointer. GlobalLock has a second role: When needed, it keeps objects from moving. Because of the difference in real and protect modes, the exact meaning of this depends on the current operating mode. For example, in protect mode, GlobalLock doesn't prevent a moveable object from being relocated, or even from being swapped to disk. In real mode, however, which doesn't have special hardware memory management support, GlobalLock *does* prevent such objects from moving. And in all modes, it prevents discardable objects from being purged. Windows supports three other ways to influence the movement of a memory segment besides locking. A segment can also be wired, fixed, or page locked. Let's explore the meaning of each of these.

Wired Segments. When a program asks Windows to allocate a segment from the global heap, Windows searches through its free list. The free list is a set of doubly linked lists that can be walked from either end. When allocating a fixed or moveable object, the memory manager always starts at the low-memory end of the free list. When allocating a discardable object, the search starts at the high-memory end. As depicted in Figure 18.7, this tends to group fixed and moveable objects at the bottom of memory, and discardable objects at the top of memory.

In addition, when allocating a fixed object, the global memory manager works quite hard to move moveable objects so that fixed objects can be as low as possible. This accentuates the layering of the global heap even more, so that—ideally at least—all fixed objects will be allocated lower than any moveable object. With fixed objects at the bottom of memory, moveable objects in the middle, and discardable objects at the top, fragmentation among moveable objects can be minimized. In a low-memory situation, Windows can purge several discardable objects at once, freeing up space for other uses.

For the most part, programs will allocate moveable or discardable objects. However, it is easy to change the disposition of a moveable

Figure 18.7　*The layout of the global heap*

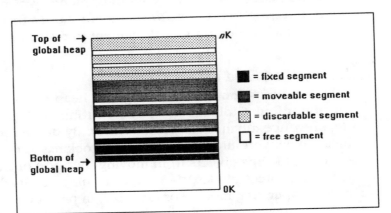

object to be discardable and vice versa. On the other hand, it is not possible to change either of these objects into a fixed memory object. In fact, from the point of view of the global heap manager, this would not be a good thing. If a program were able to change a moveable or discardable segment into a fixed segment, it would create a memory sandbar. In other words, it would create a block in the middle of memory that would prevent the global heap manager from being able to freely move objects around.

However, there are times when an application may wish to lock a piece of memory down over a longer period of time than is normal. The GlobalWire/ GlobalUnwire pair of routines provides the necessary support for this kind of operation. The GlobalWire routine first *moves* a moveable or discardable object to a very low memory location. This allows such objects to be fixed, without the fragmentation that would otherwise occur if the GlobalLock routine were to be used, for example. When a wired object does not have to be fixed any more, the GlobalUnwire routine can be used to let it rejoin the ranks of moveable and discardable objects.

Fixed Segments. In the two protect modes, a global memory object might be "locked," but may still be able to move. In fact, it can even be swapped to disk (although it will not be discarded). As described in the preceding chapter, this movement is possible because of the hardware memory management that is built into protect mode. The LDT table, for example, allows a memory segment to move in physical memory without a change in its logical address.

Certain device drivers, however, don't operate on the logical address. Instead, they use the physical address. For their use, the global heap management routines include the GlobalFix/ GlobalUnfix pair. The GlobalFix routine forces a segment to remain at the same physical address. In the same way that programs shouldn't lock down segments for lengthy periods of time, segments should not be fixed for lengthy periods of time. This can cause fragmentation of the physical address space, which makes overall system memory management less efficient. But for device drivers and other uses that require a fixed physical addresss, the GlobalFix routine can be used. To counter the effect of the GlobalFix routine, a call to GlobalUnfix is required.

Page-Locked Segments. Even though GlobalFix can prevent an object from moving in the physical address space, it can still be swapped to disk. The reason is that there are two memory mangers at work—one that manages the linear, "virtual" address space, and another one that supports this address space by moving blocks of memory—also known as "pages"—to disk. When a page is referenced that is not present, a page fault is created that causes the virtual memory manager to bring the required page into memory.

While GlobalFix prevents an object from moving in the virtual address space, there are times when even more control is needed. In particular, for time-critical device drivers, it may be necessary to select certain segments and designate them as **page-locked**. A page-locked segment is the most securely attached segment that Windows 3.0 can provide. Such segments cannot move in the virtual address space, so their "physical" address stays the same. But also, such segments cannot be swapped to disk—so that response time to access that memory is always the best it can be. Even if you never write a device driver that requires page-locking, it's nice to know that Windows has this capability to allow time-critical operations— like keyboard and mouse driver code, for example—to be serviced as quickly as possible.

From earlier versions of Windows, some programmers have gotten into the habit of using a segment's lock-count to determine whether it needed to be unlocked or not. However, in Windows 3.0, with its sophisticated memory management, certain things have changed. If you are new to Windows programming, or if you are starting a new programming project, you may not need to worry about this practice. But if you are planning to work on some older Windows code, be on the lookout for code that relies on the lock count.

Hint
••••

Avoid depending on using the lock count to determine whether GlobalLock has locked a segment. In both protect modes, GlobalLock does not affect the lock count of a moveable segment.

With this under our belt, it's time to take a look at a sample Windows program that allocates memory from the global heap.

A Sample Program: SEGALLOC

This sample program allocates three different segments from the global heap and displays information about each segment. Figure 18.8 shows the output from our program, SEGALLOC. As you can see, SEGALLOC allocates one fixed, one moveable, and one discardable segment. Also displayed are the bytes requested, the actual size of the allocated object, the handle, and the address of the segment.

If you compare the handle and the address for the fixed memory object, you'll notice that the handle *is* the segment address. This is true for all fixed segments, in all of Windows' operating modes. Notice that the offset portion of every address is zero. When you allocate a segment from the global heap, you get to start writing your own data at the beginning of the segment, which is what this address tells you. This will be the case for all types of segments in all operating modes.

If you compare the handle and the address for the moveable and discardable objects, you'll notice some similarity. It seems that this formula can be used to find a segment address:

```
segment_address = handle - 1; /* Don't do this! */
```

Figure 18.8   *SEGALLOC displays information about the segments it allocates*

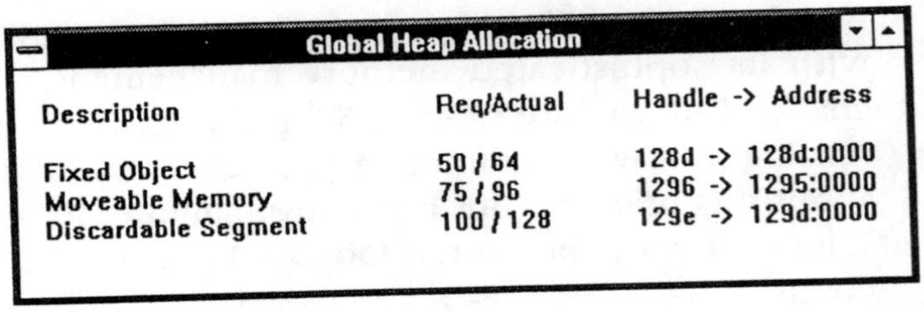

Global Heap Allocation		
Description	Req/Actual	Handle -> Address
Fixed Object	50 / 64	128d -> 128d:0000
Moveable Memory	75 / 96	1296 -> 1295:0000
Discardable Segment	100 / 128	129e -> 129d:0000

This formula works in protect mode for Windows 3.0; but don't do this, and don't depend on this working in future versions of Windows. Microsoft plans to continue enhancing Windows. If you rely on this particular quirk, your programs may stop working in a future version of Windows.

SEGALLOC.MAK

```
segalloc.res: segalloc.rc segalloc.cur segalloc.ico
    rc -r segalloc.rc

segalloc.obj: segalloc.c
    cl -AM -c -d -Gsw -Ow -W2 -Zpi segalloc.c

segalloc.exe: segalloc.obj segalloc.def
    link segalloc,/align:16,/map, mlibcew libw/NOD/NOE/CO,\
        segalloc.def
    rc segalloc.res


segalloc.exe: segalloc.res
    rc segalloc.res
```

SEGALLOC.C

```
/*----------------------------------------------------------*\
 |   SEGALLOC - Sample program showing global heap allocation  |
 |              in Microsoft Windows.                          |
 \*----------------------------------------------------------*/
#include <Windows.H>


/*----------------------------------------------------------*\
 |                  Function Prototypes.                       |
 \*----------------------------------------------------------*/
long FAR  PASCAL SegallocWndProc (HWND, WORD, WORD, LONG);


/*----------------------------------------------------------*\
 |                  Main Function:  WinMain.                   |
 \*----------------------------------------------------------*/
int PASCAL WinMain (HANDLE hInstance,
                    HANDLE hPrevInstance,
                    LPSTR  lpszCmdLine,
```

```
                          int     cmdShow)
{
HWND       hwnd;
MSG        msg;
WNDCLASS   wndclass;

if (!hPrevInstance)
    {
    wndclass.lpszClassName = "Segalloc:MAIN";
    wndclass.hInstance     = hInstance;
    wndclass.lpfnWndProc   = SegallocWndProc;
    wndclass.hCursor       = LoadCursor (hInstance, "hand");
    wndclass.hIcon         = LoadIcon (hInstance,"snapshot");
    wndclass.lpszMenuName  = NULL;
    wndclass.hbrBackground = COLOR_WINDOW+1;
    wndclass.style         = NULL;
    wndclass.cbClsExtra    = 0;
    wndclass.cbWndExtra    = 0;

    RegisterClass( &wndclass);
    }

hwnd = CreateWindow("Segalloc:MAIN",       /* Class name.  */
                                           /* Title.       */
                  "Global Heap Allocation",
                  WS_OVERLAPPEDWINDOW,     /* Style bits.  */
                  CW_USEDEFAULT,           /* x - default. */
                  0,                       /* y - default. */
                  CW_USEDEFAULT,           /* cx - default. */
                  0,                       /* cy - default. */
                  NULL,                    /* No parent.   */
                  NULL,                    /* Class menu.  */
                  hInstance,               /* Creator      */
                  NULL                     /* Params.      */
                  ) ;
ShowWindow (hwnd, cmdShow);
while (GetMessage(&msg, 0, 0, 0))
    {
    TranslateMessage(&msg);              /* Keyboard input.  */
    DispatchMessage(&msg);
    }
```

```
        return 0;
        }

#define STRSIZE 30
typedef struct tagSEGDATA
    {
    char  achDesc[STRSIZE];   /*  Description of data.  */
    DWORD dwAlloc;            /*  Amount asked for.     */
    DWORD dwActual;           /*  Actually allocated.   */
    WORD  wFlags;             /*  Allocation flags.     */
    } SEGDATA;

typedef SEGDATA FAR *LPSEGDATA;

#define COUNT        3

/*-------------------------------------------------------------*\
|                Window Procedure: SegallocWndProc.             |
\*-------------------------------------------------------------*/
long FAR PASCAL SegallocWndProc (HWND hwnd,   WORD wMsg,
                                 WORD wParam, LONG lParam)
    {
    static char Label1[] = "Description";
    static char Label2[] = "Req/Actual";
    static char Label3[] = "Handle  ->  Address";

    static int  cb1 = sizeof (Label1) - 1;
    static int  cb2 = sizeof (Label2) - 1;
    static int  cb3 = sizeof (Label3) - 1;

    static HANDLE h[COUNT];
    static SEGDATA sd[COUNT] =
        {
        "Fixed Object",            50, 0, GMEM_FIXED,
        "Moveable Memory",         75, 0, GMEM_MOVEABLE |
                                          GMEM_ZEROINIT,
        "Discardable Segment",    100, 0, GMEM_DISCARDABLE |
                                          GMEM_MOVEABLE,
        };
    static TEXTMETRIC tmSys;
```

```
        switch (wMsg)
            {
            case WM_CREATE:
                {
                HDC hdc;
                int i;
                LPSEGDATA lpsd;

                for (i=0;i<COUNT;i++)
                    {
                    h[i] = GlobalAlloc(sd[i].wFlags,
                                       sd[i].dwAlloc);
                    if (!h[i])
                        goto ErrorExit;

                    lpsd = (LPSEGDATA)GlobalLock (h[i]);
                    if (!lpsd)
                        goto ErrorExit;

                    lstrcpy (lpsd->achDesc, sd[i].achDesc);
                    lpsd->dwAlloc = sd[i].dwAlloc;
                    lpsd->dwActual = GlobalSize (h[i]);
                    lpsd->wFlags = sd[i].wFlags;
                    GlobalUnlock (h[i]);
                    } /* [for] */

                hdc = GetDC (hwnd);
                GetTextMetrics (hdc, &tmSys);
                ReleaseDC (hwnd, hdc);
                break;
                }
ErrorExit:
                MessageBox (GetFocus(),
                            "Not enough memory",
                            "SegAlloc", MB_OK);
                DestroyWindow (hwnd);
                break;

            case WM_DESTROY:
                {
                int i;
```

```
        for (i=0;i<COUNT;i++)
            GlobalFree (h[i]);
        }
        PostQuitMessage(0);
        break;

    case WM_PAINT:
        {
        char buff[30];
        int i;
        int xText1;
        int xText2;
        int xText3;
        int yText;

        LPSEGDATA lpsd;
        PAINTSTRUCT ps;

        BeginPaint (hwnd, &ps);

        /*  Calculate text positioning variables.      */
        xText1 = tmSys.tmAveCharWidth * 2;
        xText2 = xText1 + (STRSIZE * tmSys.tmAveCharWidth);
        xText3 = xText2 + ((cb2+5) * tmSys.tmAveCharWidth);
        yText = tmSys.tmHeight;

        /*  Print titles.                              */
        TextOut (ps.hdc, xText1, yText, Label1, cb1);
        TextOut (ps.hdc, xText2, yText, Label2, cb2);
        TextOut (ps.hdc, xText3, yText, Label3, cb3);

        yText += tmSys.tmHeight * 2;

        for (i=0;i<COUNT;i++)
            {
            lpsd = (LPSEGDATA)GlobalLock (h[i]);

            /*  Print description.                     */
            TextOut (ps.hdc, xText1, yText,
                    lpsd->achDesc, lstrlen(lpsd->achDesc));
```

```
                    /*   Print allocated vs actual size.          */
                    wsprintf (buff, "%ld / %ld", lpsd->dwAlloc,
                                                  lpsd->dwActual);
                    TextOut (ps.hdc, xText2, yText,
                            buff, lstrlen (buff));


                    /*   Print handle and actual address.          */
                    wsprintf (buff, "%04x  ->  %04x:%04x", h[i],
                            HIWORD(lpsd), LOWORD(lpsd));
                    TextOut (ps.hdc, xText3, yText,
                            buff, lstrlen (buff));


                    GlobalUnlock (h[i]);


                    /*   Advance to next line.                     */
                    yText += tmSys.tmHeight +
tmSys.tmExternalLeading;
                    }

            EndPaint (hwnd, &ps);
            }
            break;

        default:
            return(DefWindowProc(hwnd,wMsg,wParam,lParam));
            break;
        }
    return 0L;
    }
```

SEGALLOC.RC

```
snapshot icon segalloc.ico

hand   cursor segalloc.cur
```

SEGALLOC.DEF

```
NAME      SEGALLOC

EXETYPE WINDOWS

DESCRIPTION 'Segment Allocation Demo'

CODE      MOVEABLE DISCARDABLE
DATA      MOVEABLE MULTIPLE

HEAPSIZE      512
STACKSIZE    5000

EXPORTS
   SegallocWndProc
```

Perhaps the most important aspect of this code involves the error checking that is performed when a global memory object is allocated and locked. It is important to check the return value from the various allocation and locking routines, because there is no guarantee that you will get the memory you have asked for. And even if you get the memory you ask for, you must guard against the possibility that a memory handle will become invalid. In a large program, with many different pieces, it's always possible that a memory handle can get overwritten, or inadvertently freed.

Another important aspect of global heap allocation has to do with the length of time that a memory object is left locked. A general rule of thumb is that such memory objects should only stay locked for the duration of a single message. This gives the global heap manager the freedom to reorganize memory to minimize fragmentation. Of course, this issue is of primary importance in real-mode operation. With its hardware support of moveable addresses, a call to Global-Lock in protect mode does not carry with it the danger of fragmenting the global heap. However, unless you write special-case code for protect mode, it's often easiest to follow the rule of thumb, which allows a program to operate in a "friendly" manner in all modes.

Our next sample program looks at the relationship between the structure of a program's code and good memory usage. The recommendation that a program be divided into multiple, small code segments goes against the grain of many DOS programmers. But since DOS is a single-tasking system, with no built-in support for dynamic overlays, DOS programmers can get away with creating monolith programs with large code segments. Efficient operation under Windows, on the other hand, requires a different approach.

Code Structure and Memory Use

Most of the material in this chapter deals with the data used by a program. But an equally important issue is the memory used by a program's code. Because of the magic of dynamic linking, Windows can run with only part of a program loaded into memory at any given time. Dynamic linking gives you all the benefits of a sophisticated overlay manager, without requiring you to carefully design each overlay.

While care is not *required* in putting together the different overlay working sets that make up a program, some effort is required to get the best performance in a low-memory situation. Even in protect mode, when there are megabytes and megabytes of memory, a program can encounter a low-memory situation when there are lots of other programs running. To help you create programs that run well in low memory situations, we're going to provide two basic recommendations: one easy and one requiring a little more effort. The approach you take will depend on the size of your program, and the need to perform well in low-memory situations.

The simple approach involves dividing your program into multiple, small (4K or so) code segments. When working with the Microsoft C Compiler, this requires that you first divide your code between multiple source files. But beyond that, you must make entries into your program's module definition (.DEF) file. This is necessary because the linker (LINK.EXE) will try to pack smaller code segments into larger code segments. But hopefully, by restructuring your application, you'll be able to define your own PRELOAD segments, so that the Windows loader can be sure to load the minimum required set of segments to make your program's start-up perform quickly.

The second approach that you can take to improve your program's performance in low-memory situations involves running the **swap-tuner** to test the memory activity associated with your program. This is also known as the Windows profiler. Basically, it involves using a special version of the Windows kernel (SKERNEL.EXE) that records all memory loading and discarding activity. By reviewing the output of the swap kernel, you can get a better idea of the actual **working sets** of your program. A working set is defined as the groupings of code segments that are required to perform a specific task or set of tasks. The swap tuner helps you see the actual memory activity of your program, so that you can adjust the code that each code segment contains to minimize thrashing—the need to reread many different segments from disk in order to accomplish a specific task.

A Sample Segmented Program

We're going to start by showing a simple example of a segmented program. This is hardly going to be a "realistic example," since we're just going to divide our minimum Windows program, MIN, into three segments. However, our experience shows that some of the trouble with segmenting applications stems from little quirks in the development tools. Therefore, this example will show you how to overcome these quirks to successfully divide a program into multiple code segments.

We're going to call this program MIN2, although you can call it "Son of Min," if you'd like. To start off, the Microsoft C Compiler requires the code from each segment to be in a different source file. MIN2 will have two source files: MIN2.C and MIN2INIT.C. Here is the source code:

MIN2.MAK

```
min2.res: min2.rc min2.cur min2.ico
    rc -r min2.rc

min2.obj: min2.c
    cl -AM -c -d -Gsw -Ow -W2 -Zpi min2.c

min2init.obj: min2init.c
    cl -AM -c -d -Gsw -Ow -W2 -Zpi min2init.c

min2.exe: min2.obj min2.def
    link min2+min2init,/align:16,/map, mlibcew libw/NOD/NOE/CO,\
        min2.def
    rc min2.res
```

```
min2.exe: min2.res
    rc min2.res
```

MIN2.C

```
/*-------------------------------------------------------------*\
|   MIN2.C - A minimum Windows program that demonstrates       |
|            principles of segmenting code in an application.   |
\*-------------------------------------------------------------*/
#include <Windows.H>


/*-------------------------------------------------------------*\
|                    Function Prototypes.                       |
\*-------------------------------------------------------------*/
long FAR  PASCAL Min2WndProc (HWND, WORD, WORD, LONG);
VOID FAR  PASCAL Min2Init (HANDLE, HANDLE, int);


/*-------------------------------------------------------------*\
|                 Main Function:  WinMain.                      |
\*-------------------------------------------------------------*/
int PASCAL WinMain (HANDLE hInstance,
                    HANDLE hPrevInstance,
                    LPSTR  lpszCmdLine,
                    int    cmdShow)

    {
    MSG     msg;

    Min2Init (hInstance, hPrevInstance, cmdShow);

    while (GetMessage(&msg, 0, 0, 0))
        {
        TranslateMessage(&msg);          /* Keyboard input.     */
        DispatchMessage(&msg);
        }
    return 0;
    }


/*-------------------------------------------------------------*\
|                Window Procedure:  Min2WndProc.                |
\*-------------------------------------------------------------*/
```

```
long FAR PASCAL Min2WndProc (HWND hwnd,     WORD wMsg,
                                WORD wParam, LONG lParam)
    {
    switch (wMsg)
        {
        case WM_DESTROY:
            PostQuitMessage(0);
            break;

        default:
            return(DefWindowProc(hwnd,wMsg,wParam,lParam));
            break;
        }
    return 0L;
    }
```

MIN2INIT.C

```
/*------------------------------------------------------------*\
|    Min2Init.C - Initialization routine for MIN2.             |
\*------------------------------------------------------------*/
#include <Windows.H>


/*------------------------------------------------------------*\
|                    Function Prototypes.                      |
\*------------------------------------------------------------*/
long FAR  PASCAL Min2WndProc (HWND, unsigned, WORD, LONG);


/*------------------------------------------------------------*\
|           Min2Init - MIN2 Initialization Function.           |
\*------------------------------------------------------------*/
VOID FAR PASCAL Min2Init (HANDLE hInstance,
                          HANDLE hPrevInstance,
                          int    cmdShow)
    {
    HWND     hwnd;
    WNDCLASS wndclass;

    if (!hPrevInstance)
        {
        wndclass.lpszClassName = "Min2:MAIN";
```

```
        wndclass.hInstance      = hInstance;
        wndclass.lpfnWndProc    = Min2WndProc;
        wndclass.hCursor        = LoadCursor (hInstance, "hand");
        wndclass.hIcon          = LoadIcon (hInstance,"snapshot");
        wndclass.lpszMenuName   = NULL;
        wndclass.hbrBackground  = COLOR_WINDOW+1;
        wndclass.style          = NULL;
        wndclass.cbClsExtra     = 0;
        wndclass.cbWndExtra     = 0;

        RegisterClass( &wndclass);
        }

    hwnd = CreateWindow("Min2:MAIN",         /* Class name.   */
                        "Minimum",           /* Title.        */
                        WS_OVERLAPPEDWINDOW, /* Style bits.   */
                        CW_USEDEFAULT,       /* x - default.  */
                        0,                   /* y - default.  */
                        CW_USEDEFAULT,       /* cx - default. */
                        0,                   /* cy - default. */
                        NULL,                /* No parent.    */
                        NULL,                /* Class menu.   */
                        hInstance,           /* Creator       */
                        NULL                 /* Params.       */
                        ) ;
    ShowWindow (hwnd, cmdShow);
    }
```

MIN2.RC

```
snapshot icon min2.ico

hand   cursor min2.cur
```

MIN2.DEF

```
NAME    MIN2

EXETYPE WINDOWS
```

```
DESCRIPTION 'Segmented Code Demo'

DATA      MOVEABLE MULTIPLE

HEAPSIZE      512
STACKSIZE     5000

SEGMENTS
    MIN2_TEXT          MOVEABLE DISCARDABLE
    MIN2INIT_TEXT      MOVEABLE DISCARDABLE PRELOAD
    _TEXT              MOVEABLE DISCARDABLE

EXPORTS
    Min2WndProc
```

Even though this program has only two source files, there are actually three code segments. The third code segment contains a program's start-up code and other support routines that are automatically linked in at program creation time. These items reside in a segment named _TEXT. The names of the other segments are created by the C compiler using the filename plus _TEXT. For example, the source file MIN2.C creates a code segment with the name MIN2_TEXT.

Each segment of our program is listed in the module definition file under the SEGMENTS keyword. If running in Real Mode with EMS is important to your application, the order in which segments are listed is important. In brief, in certain EMS configurations, code segments are not discarded from EMS memory. Therefore, since segments are loaded first into EMS memory, the order of segments should be with the most important segments first. That is, the segments that your program will need the *most* should be placed *highest* in the SEGMENTS statement of the module definition file.

Notice the use of the four keywords in MIN2's module definition file: PRELOAD, MOVEABLE, DISCARDABLE, and LOADONCALL. As the names suggest, each keyword gives a memory attribute to a segment. While the FIXED keyword can also be used, it should be avoided. There is a bug in version 3.0 of Windows that makes such segments fixed and page-locked. While this will be corrected in a future version, you should avoid this keyword for now. While the use of this keyword is suitable for device drivers, it is not suitable for application programs because of the constraints its use puts on the global heap manager.

The next step to tuning MIN2, of course, involves running it through the swap-tuner. This would allow us to see when segments are loaded and discarded. Of course, there are only a few routines in the two segments that make up MIN2. In a larger program, the swap-tuner would help to restructure a program to improve the performance in a low-memory situation.

The results of swap tuning can seem paradoxical at times. For example, to make the best use of memory, it may be necessary to duplicate certain routines that are used in several different places. Instead of centralizing the "helper" routines in a program, it may make sense to create multiple copies of each, with a local copy in the code segments where the service is needed. Another alternative involves proving each function with its own code segment. Of course, the trade-off here is that far calls are quite a bit more expensive than near calls.

We hope this introduction to the effect of code structure on memory use will help you start thinking about code in a different way. Code structure *can* affect the performance of a Windows program, just as surely as the structure of a program's data will affect its performance. It's time to look at our next sample program, which provides an example of using the local heap that is automatically provided as part of every program's default data segment.

Local Heap Allocation

Let's take a look at Windows' local heap allocation routines. Table 18.7 lists all of the routines that are provided for local heap management. We're going to focus our attention on six of them: LocalInit, LocalAlloc, LocalReAlloc, LocalLock, LocalUnlock, and LocalFree.

LocalInit. The LocalInit routine initializes a local heap. LocalInit takes three parameters:

```
BOOL LocalInit (wSegment, pStart, pEnd)
```

- wSegment is the segment address of the heap to be initialized. Or, if it is zero, the data segment referenced by the DS register is initialized.
- pStart is the beginning offset of the heap in the segment.
- pEnd is the offset of the end of the heap in the segment. *Or*, if pStart is zero, then pEnd is the size of the heap, and a heap is created at the *end* of the designated segment.

Table 18.7 *Windows local heap management routines*

LocalAlloc	Allocates memory from a local heap.
LocalCompact	Reorganizes a local heap.
LocalDiscard	Discards an unlocked, discardable object.
LocalFlags	Provides information about a specific memory object.
LocalFree	Frees a local memory object.
LocalHandle	Provides the handle of a local memory object associated with a given memory address.
LocalInit	Initializes a local heap.
LocalLock	Increments the lock count on a local memory object, and returns its address.
LocalReAlloc	Changes the size of a local memory object.
LocalShrink	Reorganizes a local heap and reduces the size of the heap (if possible) to the initial, starting size. If this routine is successful, it reduces the size of the data segment that contains the heap, so that the memory can be reclaimed by the global heap.
LocalSize	Returns the current size of a local memory object.
LocalUnlock	Decrements the lock count on a local memory object.

LocalInit installs the necessary data structures that are required to support local heap allocation in a segment. Windows programs do not need to initialize their default data segment, since LocalInit is called automatically for you. However, LocalInit *can* be called to set up a local heap in another segment. As we'll detail later in this chapter, this allows you to have access to as many local heaps as you need.

Unlike application programs, Windows dynamic link libraries must explicitly call LocalInit in order to have a local heap. We'll discuss how this is done in Chapter 19, when we describe how to write dynamic link libraries.

LocalAlloc. The LocalAlloc routine allocates memory from a local heap. It is defined as

```
HANDLE LocalAlloc (wFlags, wBytes)
```

- wFlags is a combination of one or more local memory allocation flags, discussed below.
- wBytes is an unsigned integer value of the size of the object to allocate.

LocalAlloc returns a handle that identifies the object you've allocated. Be sure that you *always* check the return value, since there is never a guarantee that you'll get the memory you requested. A NULL handle is returned when a memory allocation request fails.

The value of wFlags can be a combination of five flags, depending on the type of memory object you wish to allocate (fixed, moveable, or discardable), whether to avoid disturbing the heap, and whether to initialize with zeros. This table lists your choices:

Description	Flags
Fixed memory object	LMEM_FIXED
Moveable memory object	LMEM_MOVEABLE
Discardable memory object	LMEM_MOVEABLE | LMEM_DISCARDABLE
Do not compact or discard	LMEM_NOCOMPACT
Initialize with zeros	LMEM_ZEROINIT

As this table suggests, if you wish to allocate a discardable object, you use *both* the moveable and the discardable flag. This makes sense, since a discardable object must also be moveable. The LMEM_NOCOMPACT flag tells the local memory manager that your need for memory can be satisfied some other way, and that if there isn't an available free block, no moving or discarding should be done to satisfy the memory allocation. When you wish to use more than one flag, you combine them using the OR operator "|". For example, to allocate a five-byte moveable object that is initialized with zeros, you say:

```
hMem = LocalAlloc (LMEM_MOVEABLE | LMEM_ZEROINIT, 5);
```

Be careful to avoid the LMEM_NODISCARD flag, which is mentioned in the Microsoft documentation but doesn't seem to have the effect that the documentation says it should. The documentation says that it should prevent discarding, but it seems to have no effect at all.

LocalAlloc returns a memory handle. For moveable and discardable memory objects, you obtain a pointer by calling the LocalLock routine, which we'll discuss shortly. For fixed objects, the handle itself is a pointer. In this way, LocalAlloc can be used in exactly the same manner as the C library's malloc. In other words, here is how to allocate and use a fixed memory object:

```
char * pch;
pch =(char *)LocalAlloc (LMEM_FIXED|LMEM_ZEROINIT, 15);
lstrcpy (pch, "Hello World");
```

For the sake of clarity, this code uses the normal C type, `char *`, instead of the more precise Windows type, `PSTR`. You may have already noticed that this code casts the return value from LocalAlloc. This prevents the compiler from complaining about assigning a HANDLE value (unsigned int) to a pointer. We know it's correct. The cast tells the compiler to save its error messages for real problems.

LocalLock. The LocalLock routine increments the lock count on a local memory object, and returns its address.

```
PSTR LocalLock (hMem)
```

- hMem is a handle to a memory object, returned by a call to LocalAlloc.

Programs call LocalLock to get the address of a moveable or discardable object. At the same time, this routine makes sure that the object won't get moved or discarded so that the address will be valid until a call is made to LocalUnlock. In general, it's a good idea to keep all objects unlocked until the precise time that they are needed. This gives the local heap manager the freedom to move memory as it needs to so that it can optimize the use of the local heap.

According to the prototype in Windows.H, LocalLock returns a near pointer to a character string. However, this doesn't mean that only character values can be placed into a memory object. You put the return value from LocalLock into any type of pointer, to provide you with a convenient way to access any type of dynamically allocated data. The following example makes it easy to store an array of integers into a local memory object:

```
int * pi;

pi = (int near * )LocalLock (hmem);
if (pi)
    {
    pi[0] = 1;
    pi[1] = 2;
```

```
        LocalUnlock (hmem);
        }
else
    {
    /* Error. */
    }
```

It's very important to check the return value from LocalLock, as we've done in this example. A null pointer indicates that the lock has failed. There are several things that could make this happen. If we are trying to lock a discardable object, it's possible that the object has been discarded. Or, perhaps the memory handle has been accidentally overwritten. Whatever the cause, you don't want to write using a null pointer. You will overwrite the memory locations at the bottom of your data segment, which means the data area that is used to maintain your data segment.

LocalReAlloc. The LocalReAlloc routine changes the size of a local memory object. LocalReAlloc is defined as

```
HANDLE LocalReAlloc (hMem, wBytes, wFlags)
```

- hMem is a memory handle returned by the LocalAlloc routine.
- wBytes is the new size. When you make an object smaller, it truncates (and loses) the data from the end of the object. When you make an object larger, it preserves the previous contents of the object.
- wFlags is a combination of one or more local allocation flags.

LocalReAlloc returns a HANDLE, which is one of three values. If the reallocation fails, the return value is NULL. For moveable and discardable objects, if the allocation is successful, the return value is the same handle value that was passed into the routine. For fixed objects, the handle may be the same or may be different, depending on whether the object must be moved to satisfy the allocation request.

To understand why, recall from our earlier discussion that the handle to a fixed memory object is actually a pointer to the object itself. If the object must be moved to satisfy a memory allocation request, it follows that the pointer must change as well. To prevent the local memory manager from mysteriously moving a fixed object, a fixed object will only be moved by the LocalReAlloc call if the

LMEM_MOVEABLE flag is specified. For example, here is how to reallocate a fixed memory object, allowing it to move:

```
/*  Enlarge a fixed object, and let it move.     */
hNew = LocalReAlloc (hOld,
                        cbSize,         /* New size.    */
                        LMEM_MOVEABLE);/* Ok to move.   */
if (!hNew)
    {
    /* Error.  */
    }
else
    hOld = hNew;
```

The LMEM_MOVEABLE flag has another use. This flag allows a moveable or discardable memory object that is *locked* to be moved if needed to satisfy an allocation request. In most cases, you'll only change the size of a moveable or discardable memory object when it is unlocked. At such times, the memory manager is free to relocate the object. But, if you wish to make a locked object larger, you'll need to include the LMEM_MOVEABLE flag in case the object must be moved.

If you want to change the *size* of a local memory object and *not* its memory disposition (fixed, moveable, discardable), you can set wFlags to zero. Or, use the LMEM_ZEROINIT flag to ask for a larger object with the newly allocated space zero initialized. For example, even though the wFlags field is set to zero in this example, it doesn't change the memory disposition—only the size:

```
h = LocalReAlloc (hMem,
                28,         /*  New size.      */
                0);         /*  Ignore flags.  */
```

To change the memory disposition of a memory object, use the LMEM_MODIFY flag. You can't change the disposition of a fixed memory object. However, you *can* make a moveable object discardable, or make a discardable object into a moveable object. To make a moveable object discardable, you say:

```
LocalReAlloc (hMem,
                0,              /* Ignore the size.  */
                LMEM_MODIFY   | /* Just change flags. */
                LMEM_MOVEABLE |
                LMEM_DISCARDABLE);
```

and to make a discardable object moveable, you say:

```
LocalReAlloc (hMem,
              0,                  /* Ignore the size.    */
              LMEM_MODIFY |       /* Just change flags. */
              LMEM_MOVEABLE);
```

When you change the memory disposition like this, the reallocation size is ignored. In these examples, even though we request a reallocation size of zero, the LMEM_MODIFY flag has precedence; so we can safely use a value of zero, to avoid having to figure out the current size of the object and pass it in to LocalReAlloc.

LocalUnlock. The LocalUnlock routine decrements the lock count on a local memory object.

```
BOOL LocalUnlock (hMem)
```

- hMem is a local memory handle, as provided by the LocalAlloc routine.

The LocalUnlock routine is the second slice to a Windows sandwich. To give the local memory manager the greatest freedom to manage the local heap, you should lock memory objects for only the briefest period of time. For example, to store character values that a program receives from a WM_CHAR message, you would say:

```
WndProc (...)
    {
    switch (msg)
        {
        case WM_CHAR:
            pch = LocalLock (hmem);
            pch[iNextChar] = (unsigned char) wParam;
            LocalUnlock (hmem);
            break;
            .
            .
            .
```

In this case, the memory object identified by the handle hmem is only kept locked for as long as it takes to copy a character into the memory object.

LocalFree. The LocalFree routine frees a local memory object.

```
HANDLE LocalFree (hMem)
```

- hMem is a memory handle returned by LocalAlloc.

Any time a dynamic memory object is allocated, it consumes memory that cannot be used for other purposes. Therefore, care should be taken to free memory that is not needed. The LocalFree routine is provided for this purpose.

Of course, Windows has *some* safeguards to keep memory from going away permanently. For example, when a program terminates, all of the dynamic memory that it allocated is automatically freed. This helps prevent the global heap from becoming congested with unnecessary blocks of memory that programs forgot to free. In spite of this, Windows programmers should be careful to always free memory that is no longer needed.

LOCALMEM: A Sample Heap Allocation Program

Let's take a look at a sample Windows program that shows some basic techniques in dealing with local memory. This program actually shows how to use two different types of application memory: the local heap and string resources. This program reads in a list of cities that are saved as string resources. These are stored in moveable memory objects that have been allocated from the local heap. Figure 18.9 shows the program running.

Figure 18.9 *Sample program showing local heap allocation*

```
┌──────────────────────────────────────────────────────────┐
│ ═         Local Memory Allocation              ▼ ▲        │
├──────────────────────────────────────────────────────────┤
│                                                          │
│  The World's Largest Cities (pop. in thous.)             │
│                                                          │
│  Tokyo-Yokahama, Japan        25,434                     │
│  Mexico City, Mexico          16,901                     │
│  Sao Paolo, Brazil            14,911                     │
│  New York, U.S.               14,598                     │
│  Seoul, South Korea           13,665                     │
│  Osaka-Koba-Kyoto, Japan      13,562                     │
│  Buenos Aires, Argentina      10,750                     │
│  Calcutta, India              10,462                     │
│                                                          │
└──────────────────────────────────────────────────────────┘
```

LOCALMEM.MAK

```
localmem.res: localmem.rc localmem.cur localmem.ico
    rc -r localmem.rc

localmem.obj: localmem.c
    cl -AM -c -d -Gsw -Ow -W2 -Zpi localmem.c

localmem.exe: localmem.obj localmem.def
    link localmem,/align:16,/map, mlibcew libw/NOD/NOE/CO,\
        localmem.def
    rc localmem.res

localmem.exe: localmem.res
    rc localmem.res
```

LOCALMEM.C

```
/*---------------------------------------------------------------*\
 |   LOCALMEM.C - Demonstration of local memory allocation, and |
 |                the use of string tables.                      |
 \*---------------------------------------------------------------*/
#include <Windows.H>
#include "localmem.h"


/*---------------------------------------------------------------*\
 |                     Function Prototypes.                       |
 \*---------------------------------------------------------------*/
long FAR  PASCAL LocalWndProc (HWND, WORD, WORD, LONG);
BOOL NEAR PASCAL LocalCreate (HWND hwnd);
BOOL NEAR PASCAL LocalPaint (HWND hwnd);


/*---------------------------------------------------------------*\
 |                   Static Data Definitions.                    |
 \*---------------------------------------------------------------*/
HANDLE hInst;
HANDLE ahCities;
PSTR   pchTitle;
PSTR   pchNoMem;
```

```
TEXTMETRIC tmSys;

/*--------------------------------------------------------------------*\
|                    Main Function:  WinMain.                          |
\*--------------------------------------------------------------------*/
int PASCAL WinMain (HANDLE hInstance,
                    HANDLE hPrevInstance,
                    LPSTR  lpszCmdLine,
                    int    cmdShow)
    {
    HWND      hwnd;
    int       ccSize;
    MSG       msg;
    WNDCLASS  wndclass;

    if (!hPrevInstance)
        {
        wndclass.lpszClassName = "MIN:MAIN";
        wndclass.hInstance     = hInstance;
        wndclass.lpfnWndProc   = LocalWndProc;
        wndclass.hCursor       = LoadCursor (hInstance, "hand");
        wndclass.hIcon         = LoadIcon (hInstance,"snapshot");
        wndclass.lpszMenuName  = NULL;
        wndclass.hbrBackground = COLOR_WINDOW+1;
        wndclass.style         = CS_HREDRAW | CS_VREDRAW;
        wndclass.cbClsExtra    = 0;
        wndclass.cbWndExtra    = 0;

        RegisterClass( &wndclass);
        }

    hInst = hInstance;

    /*  Load application title from string table.            */
    pchTitle = (PSTR)LocalAlloc (LMEM_FIXED, MAXSTRLEN);
    if (!pchTitle) goto ErrExit;  /* Fail?  Exit program.    */

    ccSize = LoadString (hInst, IDS_TITLE, pchTitle, MAXSTRLEN);
    LocalReAlloc ((HANDLE)pchTitle, ccSize+1, 0);
```

```
    /*  Load 'out of memory' message from string table.          */
    pchNoMem = (PSTR)LocalAlloc (LMEM_FIXED, MAXSTRLEN);
    if (!pchNoMem) goto ErrExit;  /* Fail?  Exit program.        */

    ccSize = LoadString (hInst, IDS_NOMEM, pchNoMem, MAXSTRLEN);
    LocalReAlloc ((HANDLE)pchNoMem, ccSize+1, 0);


    hwnd = CreateWindow("MIN:MAIN",             /* Class name.    */
                        pchTitle,               /* Title.         */
                        WS_OVERLAPPEDWINDOW,    /* Style bits.    */
                        CW_USEDEFAULT,          /* x - default.   */
                        0,                      /* y - default.   */
                        CW_USEDEFAULT,          /* cx - default.  */
                        0,                      /* cy - default.  */
                        NULL,                   /* No parent.     */
                        NULL,                   /* Class menu.    */
                        hInstance,              /* Creator        */
                        NULL                    /* Params.        */
                        ) ;
    ShowWindow (hwnd, cmdShow);

    while (GetMessage(&msg, 0, 0, 0))
        {
        TranslateMessage(&msg);             /*  Keyboard input.   */
        DispatchMessage(&msg);
        }
ErrExit:
    return 0;
    }

/*------------------------------------------------------------*\
 |             Window Procedure:  LocalWndProc.               |
 \*------------------------------------------------------------*/
long FAR PASCAL LocalWndProc (HWND hwnd,    WORD wMsg,
                              WORD wParam, LONG lParam)


    {
    switch (wMsg)
        {
        case WM_CREATE:
```

```
                    if (!LocalCreate(hwnd))
                        {
                        MessageBox (GetFocus(), pchNoMem,
                                     pchTitle, MB_OK);
                        DestroyWindow (hwnd);
                        }
                    break;

                case WM_DESTROY:
                    PostQuitMessage(0);
                    break;

                case WM_PAINT:
                    LocalPaint (hwnd);
                    break;

                default:
                    return(DefWindowProc(hwnd,wMsg,wParam,lParam));
                    break;
                }
            return 0L;
            }


/*-------------------------------------------------------------*\
|               LocalCreate - Process WM_CREATE messages.        |
\*-------------------------------------------------------------*/
BOOL NEAR PASCAL LocalCreate (HWND hwnd)
    {
    HDC      hdc;
    int      i;
    int      cbSize;
    PHANDLE  pah;
    PSTR     pstr;

    /* Allocate and lock memory for array of handles.        */
    ahCities = LocalAlloc (LHND, sizeof(HANDLE) * CITYCOUNT);
    pah = (PHANDLE)LocalLock (ahCities);

    /* Error checking:  if lock fails, exit.                 */
    if (!pah)
        goto ErrExit2;
```

```c
                    /* Loop to read city names.                          */
                    for (i=0;i<CITYCOUNT ;i++)
                        {                                                 */
                        /*  Allocate and lock memory.
                        pah[i] = LocalAlloc (LMEM_MOVEABLE, MAXSTRLEN);
                        pstr = LocalLock (pah[i]);

                        /*  If lock fails, exit.                          */
                        if (!pstr)
                            goto ErrExit2;

                        /*  Copy string into dynamic memory object.       */
                        cbSize = LoadString (hInst, i+IDS_CITY, pstr, MAXSTRLEN);

                        /*  Unlock and resize memory to exact string size.  */
                        LocalUnlock (pah[i]);
                        LocalReAlloc (pah[i], cbSize+1, 0);

                        } /* [for i] */

                LocalUnlock (ahCities);

                hdc = GetDC (hwnd);
                GetTextMetrics (hdc, &tmSys);      /*  Save for later.     */
                ReleaseDC (hwnd, hdc);

                return TRUE;    /*  All went well.  Indicate sucess.       */

        ErrExit2:

                /*  Out of memory.  Free everything.                       */
                for (i--;i>=0;i--)
                    LocalFree (pah[i]);
                LocalUnlock (ahCities);
                LocalFree(ahCities);

        ErrExit1:
                return FALSE;  /*  Unable to complete - indicate failure.  */
                }
```

```
/*--------------------------------------------------------------*\
  |               LocalPaint - Process WM_PAINT messages.         |
  \*--------------------------------------------------------------*/
BOOL NEAR PASCAL LocalPaint (HWND hwnd)
    {
    int i;
    int xText;
    int yText;
    int xTabPosition;
    PAINTSTRUCT ps;
    PHANDLE pah;
    PSTR    pstr;
    RECT    r;

    BeginPaint (hwnd, &ps);

    /*  Initialize values for writing lines of text.            */
    xText = tmSys.tmAveCharWidth * 4;
    yText = tmSys.tmHeight * 2;
    GetClientRect (hwnd, &r);
    xTabPosition = r.right/2;


    /*  Lock array of handles.  If fail, exit.                  */
    pah = (PHANDLE)LocalLock (ahCities);
    if (!pah)
        goto ErrExit;

    for (i=0;i<CITYCOUNT;i++)
        {
        pstr = LocalLock (pah[i]);
        TabbedTextOut (ps.hdc,
                       xText,
                       yText,
                       pstr,
                       lstrlen(pstr),
                       1,
                       &xTabPosition,
                       0);

        LocalUnlock (pah[i]);
```

```
            /*  Increment for next line.                            */
            yText += tmSys.tmHeight + tmSys.tmExternalLeading;
            }
        LocalUnlock (ahCities);


ErrExit:
    EndPaint (hwnd, &ps);
    }
```

LOCALMEM.RC

```
#include "localmem.h"

snapshot icon localmem.ico

hand  cursor localmem.cur

stringtable
  {
  IDS_TITLE, "Local Memory Allocation"
  IDS_NOMEM, "Unable to Initialize Program - Out of Memory"
  IDS_CITY     "The World's Largest Cities (pop. in thous.)"
  IDS_CITY+1, " ";
  IDS_CITY+2, "Tokyo-Yokahama, Japan\t25,434"
  IDS_CITY+3, "Mexico City, Mexico\t16,901"
  IDS_CITY+4, "Sao Paolo, Brazil\t14,911"
  IDS_CITY+5, "New York, U.S.\t14,598"
  IDS_CITY+6, "Seoul, South Korea\t13,665"
  IDS_CITY+7, "Osaka-Koba-Kyoto, Japan\t13,562"
  IDS_CITY+8, "Buenos Aires, Argentina\t10,750"
  IDS_CITY+9, "Calcutta, India\t10,462"
  }
```

LOCALMEM.DEF

```
NAME    LOCALMEM

EXETYPE WINDOWS
```

```
DESCRIPTION 'Local Memory Sample'

CODE      MOVEABLE DISCARDABLE
DATA      MOVEABLE MULTIPLE

HEAPSIZE      512
STACKSIZE    5000

EXPORTS
     LocalWndProc
```

Most of the action in LOCALMEM occurs in response to two messages: WM_CREATE and WM_PAINT. Memory is allocated and string tables read in response to WM_CREATE. All of this is displayed when the WM_PAINT message is received.

If there is any one issue in local memory management that is more critical than any other, it involves error checking. In order for a Windows program to be robust and error free, it must respond properly to failed memory allocation requests. The point is simple: Not every allocation request can be satisfied. When an allocation fails, a program must be ready to take corrective action to avoid losing data.

For this reason, every dynamic allocation request in LOCALMEM is followed by a check for a valid memory handle. For example:

```
/*  Load application title from string table.      */
pchTitle = (PSTR)LocalAlloc (LMEM_FIXED, MAXSTRLEN);
if (!pchTitle) goto ErrExit; /* Fail?  Exit program. */
```

Since a fixed memory object is being allocated, the handle is a pointer to a character string. In the terms of Windows.h definitions, PSTR is the same as char near *. If LocalAlloc fails, it returns a null value. On receipt of a null, this code jumps to the error handling portion of the function. While advocates of structured programming may dislike the use of goto statements, they provide an excellent way to provide error handling when a memory allocation request fails.

If the above lines of code are successful, the LoadString routine is called to copy a string from a string table resource into the memory that is allocated. The object is then shrunk so that it is just large enough to hold the number of characters that LoadString reports as having been copied.

```
ccSize = LoadString (hInst, IDS_TITLE, pchTitle,
                     MAXSTRLEN);
LocalReAlloc ((HANDLE)pchTitle, ccSize+1, 0);
```

The LoadString routine is defined as follows:

```
LoadString (hInstance, wID, lpBuffer, nBufferMax)
```

- hInstance is an instance handle.
- wID is an integer identifier of the string to be retrieved.
- lpBuffer is a long pointer to a character string buffer.
- nBufferMax is the maximum number of characters to copy to lpBuffer.

Later in this chapter, we're going to discuss some of the memory implications of using resources. In brief, it provides a great deal of flexibility in moving read-only data out of a program's data segment and onto disk. As they are needed, resources—like the strings from the string table resource—can be read into memory and accessed. Resources provide another type of data container that should be considered as part of a Windows program's total memory management picture. For now, let's get back to LOCALMEM.

Another approach that you can take to error checking involves testing only the return value of LocalLock and not LocalAlloc. Here is an example:

```
/*  Allocate and lock memory.                     */
pah[i] = LocalAlloc (LMEM_MOVEABLE, MAXSTRLEN);
pstr = LocalLock (pah[i]);


/*  If lock fails, exit.                          */
if (!pstr)
    goto ErrExit2;
```

In this case, a single line of error checking does the work that might otherwise require two checks: for a valid pointer *as well as* a valid memory handle. Programmers are often eager to omit error checking, but this is unwise. After all, an "invalid" pointer is still usable from the point of view of the C programming language: It points to the bottom of the data segment, which is where the segment header lives. A single write to the right byte in this area can cause otherwise robust programs to come crashing down.

A program can have more than one local heap. This capability is often overlooked by Windows programmers. The primary reason is probably the lack of a well-documented approach, plus the need to write some assembly language code. If you are using Microsoft's C Compiler, version 6.0, you may know that it has support for embedded assembly language. We're going to take advantage of this capability to show you how a program can create as many local heaps as it wishes. Each local heap resides in its own dynamically allocated segment, which the local heap manager will grow until it reaches a maximum of 64K.

Local Heap Allocation in a Dynamically Allocated Segment

As you know, there are two dynamic memory allocation packages in Windows: local heap allocation and global memory allocation. By default, every Windows program has a local heap. The heap is created by a routine called InitApp, which is not documented anywhere but is part of the standard (but hidden) startup sequence of every program. The advantage of the local heap is that the overhead for objects is fairly low and, with an alignment of four bytes, wastage is at a minimum. The only problem with the default local heap, however, is that it is too small for many uses. At most, depending on the size of your stack and static data, a default local heap might be 30–50K.

The problem of size can be solved by using the global heap. The global heap, after all, is the sum total of the address space in the system. On systems with an 80386, this means disk space in addition to physical RAM. The problem with the global heap, however, is that the overhead per object is very high. And, at 32 bytes, the granularity of segments is too high to be used for very small objects. Only large objects, or arrays of small objects, are suitable for storage in objects allocated from the global heap.

To get the benefits of both local and global heap management routines, it's possible to create a local heap in a dynamically allocated global segment. From this heap, small objects can be allocated which can efficiently share the segment with the other objects, all managed by the local heap manager. Doing this requires a little sleight of hand and a little assembly language programming, but the results can be well worth the effort.

The first thing to think about is the fact that the first 16 bytes of the segment are reserved. The local heap manager uses various bytes in this area for its own purposes. If you use this space for something else, you risk overwriting the pointers into your local heap. So, whatever you do, make sure the first 16 bytes are initialized to zero.

The second issue is the initialization of the local heap. This is easily done with the LocalInit routine. Here is one way to initialize a local heap in a dynamically allocated segment:

```
HANDLE hMem;
int    pStart, pEnd;
LPSTR lp;
WORD  wSeg;

hMem = GlobalAlloc (GMEM_MOVEABLE|GMEM_ZEROINIT, 4096L);
if (!hMem)
    goto ErrorOut;

lp = GlobalLock (hMem);
wSeg = HIWORD (lp);

pStart = 16;
pEnd   = (int)GlobalSize (hMem)-1;
LocalInit (wSeg, pStart, pEnd);
GlobalUnlock(hMem);
GlobalUnlock (hMem);
```

Notice that two calls to GlobalUnlock are required. The first is to counteract the lock of our own call to GlobalLock—it's the second slice in a code sandwich. The second call to GlobalUnlock is required because LocalInit leaves a segment locked. Without this second call, the data segment would be locked in memory. This would prevent the segment from growing, and would create a memory sandbar in the global heap.

As always, GlobalAlloc's return value should always be checked to make sure that the requested memory is available. Even though we asked for a 4096-byte segment, because different operating modes align on different segment boundaries, we call GlobalSize to make sure we know the exact size of the segment. pStart is set to 16 to make room for the header. pEnd is set to the offset of the last byte in the segment, which is the segment size minus one.

Incidentally, a slightly shorter way to do the same thing involves setting pStart to zero and setting pEnd to the actual *size* of the local heap. Here's the code that does that:

```
pEnd   = (int)GlobalSize (hMem)-16;
LocalInit (wSeg, 0, pEnd);
```

In this case, notice that we're subtracting 16 from the size of the segment rather than just one. The reason is simple: We must set aside the first 16 bytes for the segment header.

Accessing the local heap requires a little assembly language programming. We're going to cheat a little, and use a capability of Microsoft's C Compiler, version 6.0, that lets us embed assembler into C code. If your compiler doesn't support this, you will have to write stand-alone assembly language subroutines. We can call any local heap management routine. The only difference is that before and after each call, we must change the value in the DS register to hold the address of our local heap. Here's how to do it:

```
LPSTR lp;
HANDLE hmem;
WORD  wHeapDS;  /*  Must be a stack variable!  */

lp = GlobalLock (hmem);   /* Where local heap lives. */
wHeapDS = HIWORD (lp);

_asm{
    push  DS

    mov   AX, wHeapDS
    mov   DS, AX

    }

hmem = LocalAlloc (LMEM_MOVEABLE, 16);

_asm{
    pop   DS
    }

GlobalUnlock (hmem);
```

While this may look rather complex and bizarre, this approach allows a Windows program to derive the benefits of both memory management packages, and to surmount some of the drawbacks of each.

Of course, to use a memory object, you must call two lock routines: one for the segment and one for the local heap object. And, to keep either of these data areas from becoming too fragmented, you will probably want to unlock at both levels. There are compromises, of course. For example, a program might make all local heap objects *fixed*, which removes the need to do the second lock. And, for the most effective use, it probably makes sense to build a small subroutine library to manage the two-level allocation scheme. This might be as simple as creating 32-bit handles, with half for the local handle and half for the global handle. That, in fact, is the approach taken by our sample program. Or, a subroutine package could issue its own, private 16-bit handles that it would then use to find the right segment and the right local memory object. There are several approaches to take, and we hope this brief introduction has provided you with enough information to find one that will work for you.

If you're like many programmers, all this theoretical discussion and bits of code are not as interesting as a full-blown working program that demonstrates how to put the theory into practice. So, without further ado, here is our sample program: SUBSEG.

SUBSEG: A Combined Local/Global Heap Allocation Program

SUBSEG demonstrates how to perform subsegment allocation in a dynamically allocated segment. We borrow the term "subsegment allocation" from the world of OS/2, since it seems to be more suggestive of what we are doing than the term "local allocation." To help you get the most from this example, we have written a set of subsegment allocation routines that mirrors the format of the routines in Windows' standard memory allocation routines. In other words, we've written a routine called SubAlloc which takes all the same parameters as the LocalAlloc routine. Four other routines provide the basic allocation services to get you started in writing a complete sub allocation library. There is one additional function, SubInitialize, which allocates a segment from the global heap and initializes the segment to hold a local heap.

SUBSEG is adapted from SEGALLOC, which is the segment allocation sample we presented earlier in this chapter. SUBSEG displays information about the allocated data objects. To convince you that it

Figure 18.10 *SUBSEG shows information about the objects it allocates.*

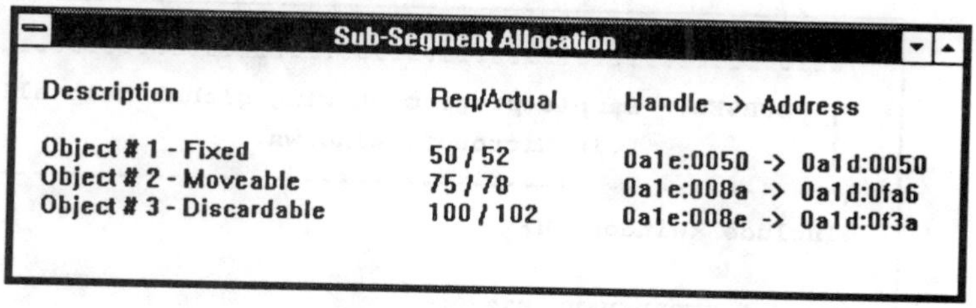

Description	Req/Actual	Handle -> Address
Object # 1 - Fixed	50 / 52	0a1e:0050 -> 0a1d:0050
Object # 2 - Moveable	75 / 78	0a1e:008a -> 0a1d:0fa6
Object # 3 - Discardable	100 / 102	0a1e:008e -> 0a1d:0f3a

works as advertised, it reads this information from the data object itself. Figure 18.10 shows SUBSEG running. If you compare this program to the SEGALLOC program, one thing you may notice is that the overhead of objects are much lower in this program. That is because segments allocated from the global heap are aligned on 32-byte boundaries, whereas objects allocated from a local heap are allocated on four-byte boundaries. The wastage due to "rounding" is much less in local heaps.

SUBSEG.MAK

```
subseg.res: subseg.rc subseg.cur subseg.ico
    rc -r subseg.rc

submem.obj: submem.c
    cl -AM -c -d -Gsw -Od -W2 -Zpi submem.c

subseg.obj: subseg.c
    cl -AM -c -d -Gsw -Od -W2 -Zpi subseg.c

subseg.exe: subseg.obj submem.obj subseg.def
    link subseg+submem,/align:16,/map, mlibcew libw/NOD/NOE/CO,\
        subseg.def
    rc subseg.res

subseg.exe: subseg.res
    rc subseg.res
```

SUBSEG.C

```
/*------------------------------------------------------*\
 | SUBSEG - Sample program showing global heap allocation |
 |            in Microsoft Windows.                       |
\*------------------------------------------------------*/
#include <Windows.H>

typedef DWORD HANDLE32;

/*------------------------------------------------------*\
 |                 Function Prototypes.                   |
\*------------------------------------------------------*/
long FAR  PASCAL SubsegWndProc (HWND, WORD, WORD, LONG);

BOOL     FAR PASCAL SubInitialize(VOID);
HANDLE32 FAR PASCAL SubAlloc(WORD, WORD);
HANDLE32 FAR PASCAL SubFree(HANDLE32);
LPSTR    FAR PASCAL SubLock(HANDLE32);
WORD     FAR PASCAL SubSize(HANDLE32);
BOOL     FAR PASCAL SubUnlock(HANDLE32);


/*------------------------------------------------------*\
 |                 Main Function:  WinMain.               |
\*------------------------------------------------------*/
int PASCAL WinMain (HANDLE hInstance,
                    HANDLE hPrevInstance,
                    LPSTR  lpszCmdLine,
                    int    cmdShow)

    {
    HWND     hwnd;
    MSG      msg;
    WNDCLASS wndclass;

    if (!hPrevInstance)
        {
        wndclass.lpszClassName = "Subseg:MAIN";
        wndclass.hInstance     = hInstance;
        wndclass.lpfnWndProc   = SubsegWndProc;
        wndclass.hCursor       = LoadCursor (hInstance, "hand");
        wndclass.hIcon         = LoadIcon (hInstance,"snapshot");
```

```
            wndclass.lpszMenuName  = NULL;
            wndclass.hbrBackground = COLOR_WINDOW+1;
            wndclass.style         = NULL;
            wndclass.cbClsExtra    = 0;
            wndclass.cbWndExtra    = 0;


            RegisterClass( &wndclass);
            }

    hwnd = CreateWindow("Subseg:MAIN",      /* Class name.  */
                                            /* Title.       */
                        "Sub-Segment Allocation",
                        WS_OVERLAPPEDWINDOW, /* Style bits.  */
                        CW_USEDEFAULT,       /* x - default. */
                        0,                   /* y - default. */
                        CW_USEDEFAULT,       /* cx - default. */
                        0,                   /* cy - default. */
                        NULL,                /* No parent.   */
                        NULL,                /* Class menu.  */
                        hInstance,           /* Creator      */
                        NULL                 /* Params.      */
                        ) ;
    ShowWindow (hwnd, cmdShow);

    while (GetMessage(&msg, 0, 0, 0))
        {
        TranslateMessage(&msg);             /*  Keyboard input.  */
        DispatchMessage(&msg);
        }
    return 0;
    }

#define STRSIZE 30
typedef struct tagSEGDATA
    {
    char   achDesc[STRSIZE];  /*  Description of data.  */
    DWORD  dwAlloc;           /*  Amount asked for.     */
    DWORD  dwActual;          /*  Actually allocated.   */
    WORD   wFlags;            /*  Allocation flags.     */
    } SEGDATA;
```

```
typedef SEGDATA FAR *LPSEGDATA;

#define COUNT      3

/*------------------------------------------------------------*\
 |                Window Procedure:  SubsegWndProc.          |
\*------------------------------------------------------------*/
long FAR PASCAL SubsegWndProc (HWND hwnd,    WORD wMsg,
                                   WORD wParam, LONG lParam)
    {
    static char Label1[] = "Description";
    static char Label2[] = "Req/Actual";
    static char Label3[] = "Handle ->  Address";

    static int  cb1 = sizeof (Label1) - 1;
    static int  cb2 = sizeof (Label2) - 1;
    static int  cb3 = sizeof (Label3) - 1;

    static HANDLE32 h[COUNT];
    static SEGDATA sd[COUNT] =
        {
        "Object # 1 - Fixed",        50, 0, LMEM_FIXED,
        "Object # 2 - Moveable",     75, 0, LMEM_MOVEABLE |
                                            LMEM_ZEROINIT,
        "Object # 3 - Discardable", 100, 0, LMEM_DISCARDABLE |
                                            LMEM_MOVEABLE,

        };
    static TEXTMETRIC tmSys;

    switch (wMsg)
        {
        case WM_CREATE:
            {
            HDC hdc;
            int i;
            LPSEGDATA lpsd;

            if (!SubInitialize())
                goto ErrorExit;

            for (i=0;i<COUNT;i++)
```

```
                        {
                        h[i] = SubAlloc(sd[i].wFlags,
                                        sd[i].dwAlloc);
                        if (!h[i])
                            goto ErrorExit;

                        lpsd = (LPSEGDATA)SubLock (h[i]);
                        if (!lpsd)
                            goto ErrorExit;

                        lstrcpy (lpsd->achDesc, sd[i].achDesc);
                        lpsd->dwAlloc = sd[i].dwAlloc;
                        lpsd->dwActual = SubSize (h[i]);
                        lpsd->wFlags = sd[i].wFlags;
                        SubUnlock (h[i]);
                        } /* [for] */

                    hdc = GetDC (hwnd);
                    GetTextMetrics (hdc, &tmSys);
                    ReleaseDC (hwnd, hdc);
                    break;

ErrorExit:
                    MessageBox (GetFocus(), "Not enough memory",
                                "Subseg", MB_OK);
                    DestroyWindow (hwnd);
                    }
                    break;

            case WM_DESTROY:
                    PostQuitMessage(0);
                    break;

            case WM_PAINT:
                    {
                    char buff[30];
                    int i;
                    int xText1;
                    int xText2;
                    int xText3;
                    int yText;
```

```
            LPSEGDATA lpsd;
            PAINTSTRUCT ps;

            BeginPaint (hwnd, &ps);

            /*  Calculate text positioning variables.          */
            xText1 = tmSys.tmAveCharWidth * 2;
            xText2 = xText1 + (STRSIZE * tmSys.tmAveCharWidth);
            xText3 = xText2 + ((cb2+5) * tmSys.tmAveCharWidth);
            yText = tmSys.tmHeight;

            /*  Print titles.                                    */
            TextOut (ps.hdc, xText1, yText, Label1, cb1);
            TextOut (ps.hdc, xText2, yText, Label2, cb2);
            TextOut (ps.hdc, xText3, yText, Label3, cb3);

            yText += tmSys.tmHeight * 2;

            for (i=0;i<COUNT;i++)
                {
                lpsd = (LPSEGDATA)SubLock (h[i]);

                /*  Print description.                           */
                TextOut (ps.hdc, xText1, yText,
                        lpsd->achDesc, lstrlen(lpsd->achDesc));

                /*  Print allocated vs actual size.              */
                wsprintf (buff, "%ld / %ld", lpsd->dwAlloc,
                                            lpsd->dwActual);
                TextOut (ps.hdc, xText2, yText,
                        buff, lstrlen (buff));

                /*  Print handle and actual address.             */
                wsprintf (buff, "%04x:%04x  ->  %04x:%04x",
                        HIWORD(h[i]), LOWORD(h[i]),
                        HIWORD(lpsd), LOWORD(lpsd));
                TextOut (ps.hdc, xText3, yText,
                        buff, lstrlen (buff));

                SubUnlock (h[i]);
```

```
                    /*  Advance to next line.                    */
                    yText += tmSys.tmHeight +
tmSys.tmExternalLeading;
                    }

             EndPaint (hwnd, &ps);
             }
             break;

        default:
            return(DefWindowProc(hwnd,wMsg,wParam,lParam));
            break;
        }
    return 0L;
    }
```

SUBMEM.C

```
/*------------------------------------------------------------*\
 |   SUB.C  -  Sub-segment allocation routines, for creating   |
 |            local heaps in dynamically allocated segments.   |
 \*------------------------------------------------------------*/
#include <Windows.H>

typedef DWORD HANDLE32;


/*------------------------------------------------------------*\
 |                      Static Data Definitions.               |
 \*------------------------------------------------------------*/
HANDLE hSegment;


/*------------------------------------------------------------*\
 |   SubInitialize - Call first to allocate a segment from the |
 |                   global heap.                              |
 \*------------------------------------------------------------*/
BOOL      FAR PASCAL SubInitialize(VOID)
    {
    BOOL  bRetVal;
```

```
    LPSTR  lp;
    WORD   wSeg;
    WORD   wSize;

    hSegment = GlobalAlloc (GMEM_MOVEABLE | GMEM_ZEROINIT,
                            4096L);
    if (!hSegment)
        return FALSE;

    lp = GlobalLock (hSegment);
    if (!lp)
        return FALSE;

    wSeg = HIWORD (lp);
    wSize = (WORD)GlobalSize (hSegment) - 16;

    bRetVal = LocalInit (wSeg, 0, wSize);

    GlobalUnlock (hSegment);
    GlobalUnlock (hSegment);  /*  Undo LocalInit's GlobalLock. */

    return bRetVal;
    }


/*-------------------------------------------------------------*\
|   SubAlloc - Allocate a subsegment.                           |
|                                                               |
|   Input:  wFlags = local heap allocation flags.              |
|           wBytes = number of bytes to allocate.             |
|                                                               |
|   Returns:  A 4-byte "handle", put together as:             |
|             HIWORD = Handle to global segment.              |
|             LOWORD = Handle to local object.                |
\*-------------------------------------------------------------*/
HANDLE32 FAR PASCAL SubAlloc(WORD wFlags, WORD wBytes)
    {
    HANDLE hMem;
    LPSTR  lp;
    WORD   wSeg;
```

```
    lp = GlobalLock (hSegment);
    if (!lp)
        return 0L;

    wSeg = HIWORD (lp);

    _asm { push    ds
           mov     ax, wSeg
           mov     ds, ax   }

    hMem = LocalAlloc (wFlags, wBytes);

    _asm { pop     ds }

    GlobalUnlock (hSegment);

    if (!hMem)
        return 0L;
    else
        return MAKELONG (hMem, hSegment);
    }


/*------------------------------------------------------------------*\
 |  SubFree - Free a subsegment.                                    |
 |                                                                  |
 |  Input:  A 4-byte "handle", put together as:                     |
 |             HIWORD = Handle to global segment.                   |
 |             LOWORD = Handle to local object.                     |
 |                                                                  |
 |  Returns:  The original handle, if successful.  Otherwise,       |
 |             returns NULL.                                        |
\*------------------------------------------------------------------*/
HANDLE32 FAR PASCAL SubFree(HANDLE32 hSubMem)
    {
    HANDLE hSeg;
    HANDLE hMem;
    LPSTR lp;
    WORD  wSeg;

    hSeg = HIWORD (hSubMem);
    hMem = LOWORD (hSubMem);
```

```
        lp = GlobalLock (hSeg);
        if (!lp)
            return 0L;

        wSeg = HIWORD (lp);

        _asm { push    ds
               mov     ax, wSeg
               mov     ds, ax  }

        hMem = LocalFree (hMem);

        _asm { pop     ds }

        GlobalUnlock (hSeg);

        if (!hMem)
            return 0L;
        else
            return MAKELONG (hMem, hSeg);
        }

/*----------------------------------------------------------*\
 |  SubLock - Lock a subsegment and the segment it lives in.  |
 |                                                           |
 |  Input:  A 4-byte "handle", put together as:              |
 |                 HIWORD = Handle to global segment.        |
 |                 LOWORD = Handle to local object.          |
 |                                                           |
 |  Returns: A far pointer to the object.                    |
\*----------------------------------------------------------*/
LPSTR    FAR PASCAL SubLock(HANDLE32 hSubMem)
        {
        HANDLE hSeg;
        HANDLE hMem;
        LPSTR lp;
        PSTR  p;
        WORD  wSeg;

        hSeg = HIWORD (hSubMem);
```

```
         hMem = LOWORD (hSubMem);

         lp = GlobalLock (hSeg);
         if (!lp)
             return 0L;

         wSeg = HIWORD (lp);

         _asm { push    ds
                mov     ax, wSeg
                mov     ds, ax    }

         p = LocalLock (hMem);

         _asm { pop     ds }

         /*  No Matching GlobalUnlock -- leave segment locked     */
         /*  for caller to use.  We'll unlock twice in SubUnlock. */

         if (!p)
             return (LPSTR)0;
         else
             return (LPSTR)MAKELONG (p, wSeg);
         }


/*-------------------------------------------------------------*\
 |  SubSize - Returns the size of a subsegment.                |
 |                                                             |
 |  Input:  A 4-byte "handle", put together as:                |
 |              HIWORD = Handle to global segment.             |
 |              LOWORD = Handle to local object.               |
 |                                                             |
 |  Returns: a WORD value with the subsegment size, or zero    |
 |           if the handle is invalid.                         |
\*-------------------------------------------------------------*/
WORD    FAR PASCAL SubSize(HANDLE32 hSubMem)
     {
     HANDLE hSeg;
     HANDLE hMem;
     LPSTR lp;
     WORD  wSeg;
```

```
    WORD   wSize;

    hSeg = HIWORD (hSubMem);
    hMem = LOWORD (hSubMem);

    lp = GlobalLock (hSeg);
    if (!lp)
        return 0;

    wSeg = HIWORD (lp);

    _asm { push     ds
           mov      ax, wSeg
           mov      ds, ax    }

    wSize = LocalSize (hMem);

    _asm { pop      ds }

    GlobalUnlock (hSeg);

    return wSize;
    }
```

```
/*----------------------------------------------------------------*\
 |  SubUnlock - Unlock a subsegment, and the segment it lives   |
 |              in.                                             |
 |  Input: A 4-byte "handle", put together as:                 |
 |              HIWORD = Handle to global segment.             |
 |              LOWORD = Handle to local object.               |
 |                                                             |
 |  Returns: The LocalUnlock return value, which is zero if    |
 |           the block's reference count was decreased to      |
 |           zero, otherwise it is non-zero.                   |
\*----------------------------------------------------------------*/
BOOL    FAR PASCAL SubUnlock(HANDLE32 hSubMem)
    {
    BOOL   bRetVal;
    HANDLE hSeg;
    HANDLE hMem;
    LPSTR  lp;
```

```
        WORD    wSeg;

        hSeg = HIWORD (hSubMem);
        hMem = LOWORD (hSubMem);

        lp = GlobalLock (hSeg);
        if (!lp)
            return 0L;

        wSeg = HIWORD (lp);

        _asm { push    ds
               mov     ax, wSeg
               mov     ds, ax    }

        bRetVal = LocalUnlock (hMem);

        _asm { pop     ds }

        GlobalUnlock (hSeg);
        GlobalUnlock (hSeg);

        return bRetVal;
        }
```

SUBSEG.RC

```
snapshot icon subseg.ico

hand  cursor subseg.cur
```

SUBSEG.DEF

```
NAME    SUBSEG

EXETYPE WINDOWS
```

```
DESCRIPTION 'Sub-Segment Allocation Demo'

CODE      MOVEABLE DISCARDABLE
DATA      MOVEABLE MULTIPLE


HEAPSIZE     512
STACKSIZE    5000


EXPORTS
    SubsegWndProc
```

The first thing you may notice about this program is that very little is different from the SEGALLOC program from which it was derived. This is intentional, since the allocation routines that we have created are meant to exactly mirror both the local and global heap management routines. So, the SubAlloc routine takes the place of Global-Alloc or LocalAlloc, and the SubLock routine takes the place of GlobalLock or LocalLock. However, when you look at the code to the subsegment routines, you'll find that calls are made to *both* local and global heap management routines.

There is also an important difference in the handle that SubAlloc returns. Instead of the normal 16-bit handle, it returns a 32-bit handle. This is really two handles in one: The high-word contains the handle of the segment, and the low-word contains the handle of the local heap object. This allows the routines to be extended to support several local heaps in several different segments. The only requirement is that LocalInit be called to initialize each segment. This program only uses one segment for the sake of simplicity.

Another limitation of this program is that the segment that contains the local heap is never freed. While this may be reasonable for a tiny, sample program, this is clearly a case of "do as I say, and not as I do." In other words, please be sure to free any memory you allocate, unlock any memory you lock, and in general undo whatever needs undoing to free any resource you use.

Let's move on to our next and final sample program, which creates a custom resource.

Custom Resources

Although Windows provides built-in support for several different types of resources, you may wish to create your own custom resource types. This lets you take advantage of the built-in memory management features of resources, with a minimum of effort on your part. The best candidates for custom resources are data objects that won't change. We're going to show an example of a resource that will be used to calculate sine and cosine values. This table allows a calculation of an integer sine value, which is simply a sine value multiplied by 10,000. The advantage of using a lookup table is that it is faster than calculating "on-the-fly." In addition, since the low-end members of the Intel-86 family (80386 and earlier) do not have built-in floating point support, you'll get faster overall performance if you limit your calculations to integer arithmetic. It may interest you to know that this factor influenced Microsoft enough to build Windows without *any* use of floating point arithmetic.

We're going to write two routines that will provide sine and cosine values for an angle entered in degrees. Roughly speaking, then, with two functions and 360 degrees, 720 different values are required for our lookup table. But we're going to take advantage of the symmetry of this table to play a few tricks, do a little folding and rotating, and produce the same results with a single table of 90 sine values. To see how we're going to pull this off, read on!

The first thing we'll need to do is to create a table of values. There are many ways to do this, but the most straightforward involves writing a small C program that calculates our sine values and writes them as ASCII text to a data file. Why ASCII text? We're going to show you a trick that will allow you to build complex binary data objects from ASCII text files. The only tools that are required are the macro assembler (MASM), the linker, and a special converter called EXE2BIN.EXE which comes with DOS. Here are the program files that we use to create our table of sine values:

SINE.MAK

```
sine.obj: sine.c
    cl -c sine.c

sine.exe: sine.obj
    link sine;

sinedata.asm: sine.exe
    sine
```

```
sinedata.bin: sinedata.asm
    masm sinedata.asm, sinedata.obj;
    link sinedata, sinedata.exe;
    exe2bin sinedata.exe
```

SINE.C

```
/*-----------------------------------------------------------*\
|  SINE.C - Creates a .ASM data file containing sine values   |
|                from 0 to 90 degrees.  This file is suitable  |
|                for creating a custom Windows resource.       |
\*-----------------------------------------------------------*/

#include "stdio.h"
#include "math.h"

char achFileHeader[] =
     ";\n"
     "; Sine/Cosine Data Table\n"
     ";\n"
     ";\n"
     "; Table of Sine values from 0 to 90 degrees\n"
     ";\n"
     "SINDATA segment public\n";

char achFileFooter[] =
     "\n"
     "SINDATA ends\n"
     "END\n";


main()
    {
    double dbPI  = 3.1415926536;
    double dbRad;
    FILE   * fp;
    int    iAngle;
    int    iSin;
```

```
    if (!(fp = fopen("sinedata.asm", "w")))
        {
        printf("Can't create sinedata.asm.\n");
        exit(1);
        }

    fprintf (fp, achFileHeader);
    fprintf (fp, "DW ");

    for (iAngle = 0; iAngle <= 90; iAngle++)
        {
        dbRad = (((double)iAngle) * dbPI) / 180.0;
        iSin = sin(dbRad) * 10000.0 + 0.5;
        fprintf(fp, " %5d", iSin);

        if (iAngle % 8 == 7)
            fprintf (fp, "\nDW ");
        else if (iAngle != 90)
            fprintf (fp, ",");
        }

    fprintf(fp, achFileFooter);

    fclose(fp);
    }
```

The data file created by this program is essentially a MASM language file, containing the data definitions suitable for use as a data segment. But we're not going to write any MASM code to support it. Instead, we're going to let MASM convert the data definitions into binary format. Here is the MASM file that is created, SINEDATA.ASM:

```
;
; Sine/Cosine Data Table
;
;
; Table of Sine values from 0 to 90 degrees
```

```
;
SINDATA segment public
DW       0,    175,    349,    523,    698,    872,   1045,   1219
DW    1392,   1564,   1736,   1908,   2079,   2250,   2419,   2588
DW    2756,   2924,   3090,   3256,   3420,   3584,   3746,   3907
DW    4067,   4226,   4384,   4540,   4695,   4848,   5000,   5150
DW    5299,   5446,   5592,   5736,   5878,   6018,   6157,   6293
DW    6428,   6561,   6691,   6820,   6947,   7071,   7193,   7314
DW    7431,   7547,   7660,   7771,   7880,   7986,   8090,   8192
DW    8290,   8387,   8480,   8572,   8660,   8746,   8829,   8910
DW    8988,   9063,   9135,   9205,   9272,   9336,   9397,   9455
DW    9511,   9563,   9613,   9659,   9703,   9744,   9781,   9816
DW    9848,   9877,   9903,   9925,   9945,   9962,   9976,   9986
DW    9994,   9998,  10000
SINDATA ends
END
```

After this data file has been run through the macro assembler and the linker, the result is an .EXE file that is almost ready to run as a DOS program. Well, not really, since it doesn't have any code. It's just an executable file with a data segment. To isolate the data into a pure binary object, we run the EXE2BIN program. This program is ordinarily used to create .COM files from .EXE files. COM files are simply memory images that can be loaded and run "as-is." Since that's exactly what we want—a pure, binary image—EXE2BIN does the trick to create our sine table resource.

To test that the sine and cosine functions are providing accurate values, our sample program, CUSTRES, connects 359 points together to draw a circle with a radius of 100 pixels. The drawing appears in Figure 18.11. While this is quite a bit slower, and rougher than you would expect from calling GDI's Ellipse routine, it demonstrates quite nicely that the sine and cosine values that we generate at least *look* right in the range 0 to 360 degrees.

Here is the code for our custom resource program, CUSTRES.EXE, that used the sine table information to calculate sines and cosines that were used to actually draw the circle shown in the figure.

Figure 18.11 *Circle drawn by CUSTRES*

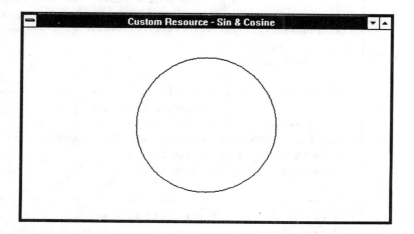

CUSTRES.MAK

```
custres.res: custres.rc custres.cur custres.ico sinedata.bin
    rc -r custres.rc

custres.obj: custres.c
    cl -AM -c -d -Gsw -Ow -W2 -Zpi custres.c

custres.exe: custres.obj custres.def
    link custres,/align:16,/map, mlibcew libw/NOD/NOE/CO, \
        custres.def
    rc custres.res

custres.exe: custres.res
    rc custres.res
```

CUSTRES.C

```
/*---------------------------------------------------------------*\
 |    CUSTRES.C - Creating a custom resource in Windows.  This    |
 |                program creates a resource that contains        |
```

```
|                    a Sin and Cosine table.  It uses this table  |
|                    to calculate from both degrees and radians.  |
\*----------------------------------------------------------------*/
#include <Windows.H>
#include "custres.h"


/*--------------------------------------------------------------*\
|                     Function Prototypes.                       |
\*--------------------------------------------------------------*/
long FAR  PASCAL MinWndProc (HWND, WORD, WORD, LONG);
int NEAR PASCAL intSin (int iValue);
int NEAR PASCAL intCos (int iValue);


/*--------------------------------------------------------------*\
|                     Static Data Allocation.                   |
\*--------------------------------------------------------------*/
HANDLE hInst;
HANDLE hresSinData;


/*--------------------------------------------------------------*\
|                     Main Function:  WinMain.                   |
\*--------------------------------------------------------------*/
int PASCAL WinMain (HANDLE hInstance,
                    HANDLE hPrevInstance,
                    LPSTR  lpszCmdLine,
                    int    cmdShow)
    {
    HWND      hwnd;
    MSG       msg;
    WNDCLASS wndclass;

    if (!hPrevInstance)
        {
        wndclass.lpszClassName = "MIN:MAIN";
        wndclass.hInstance     = hInstance;
        wndclass.lpfnWndProc   = MinWndProc;
        wndclass.hCursor       = LoadCursor (hInstance, "hand");
        wndclass.hIcon         = LoadIcon (hInstance,"snapshot");
        wndclass.lpszMenuName  = NULL;
        wndclass.hbrBackground = COLOR_WINDOW+1;
        wndclass.style         = CS_HREDRAW | CS_VREDRAW;
```

```
        wndclass.cbClsExtra    = 0;
        wndclass.cbWndExtra    = 0;

        RegisterClass( &wndclass);
        }

    hInst = hInstance;

    hwnd = CreateWindow("MIN:MAIN",            /* Class name.  */
                                               /* Title.       */
                    "Custom Resource - Sin & Cosine",
                    WS_OVERLAPPEDWINDOW,  /* Style bits. */
                    CW_USEDEFAULT,        /* x - default. */
                    0,                    /* y - default. */
                    CW_USEDEFAULT,        /* cx - default. */
                    0,                    /* cy - default. */
                    NULL,                 /* No parent. */
                    NULL,                 /* Class menu. */
                    hInstance,            /* Creator     */
                    NULL                  /* Params.     */
                    ) ;
    ShowWindow (hwnd, cmdShow);
    while (GetMessage(&msg, 0, 0, 0))
        {
        TranslateMessage(&msg);         /* Keyboard input.    */
        DispatchMessage(&msg);
        }
    return 0;
    }

/*------------------------------------------------------------*\
|                Window Procedure:  MinWndProc.               |
\*------------------------------------------------------------*/
long FAR PASCAL MinWndProc (HWND hwnd,   WORD wMsg,
                           WORD wParam, LONG lParam)
    {

    switch (wMsg)
        {
        case WM_CREATE:
            {
```

```
            HANDLE hRes;
            hRes = FindResource (hInst,
                    MAKEINTRESOURCE(SIN),        /* Name. */
                    MAKEINTRESOURCE(TABLE));     /* Type. */
            hresSinData = LoadResource (hInst, hRes);
            }
            break;

    case WM_DESTROY:
            FreeResource (hresSinData);
            PostQuitMessage(0);
            break;

    case WM_PAINT:
            {
            int i;
            int x, y;
            PAINTSTRUCT ps;
            RECT r;

            BeginPaint (hwnd, &ps);
            GetClientRect (hwnd, &r);
            SetViewportOrg (ps.hdc, r.right/2, r.bottom/2);

            x = intCos (0)/100;
            y = intSin (0)/100;
            MoveTo (ps.hdc, x, y);

            for (i=0;i<=360;i++)
                {
                x = intCos (i)/100;
                y = intSin (i)/100;
                LineTo (ps.hdc, x, y);
                }

            EndPaint (hwnd, &ps);
            }
            break;

    default:
            return(DefWindowProc(hwnd,wMsg,wParam,lParam));
```

```
            break;
        }
    return 0L;
    }



/*-----------------------------------------------------------------*\
|  intSin  -  Calculates an integer sin value in units equal  |
|             to 10,000th for any degree entered, using a     |
|             value derived from a custom sin resource.       |
\*-----------------------------------------------------------------*/
int NEAR PASCAL intSin (int iValue)
    {
    int iSign;

    int FAR * fpSin;

    fpSin = (int FAR *)LockResource (hresSinData);
    if (fpSin == NULL)
        return (0);

    while (iValue < 0)   iValue +=360;
    while (iValue > 360) iValue -=360;

    iSign = 1;

    if (iValue > 90 && iValue <=180)
        {
        iValue = 180 - iValue;
        }
    else if (iValue > 180 && iValue <= 270)
        {
        iSign = -1;
        iValue = iValue - 180;
        }
    else if (iValue > 270 && iValue <= 360)
        {
        iSign = -1;
        iValue = 360 - iValue;
        }
```

```
        /*  Adjust pointer to correct table entry.  */
        fpSin += iValue;

        iSign = *fpSin * iSign;
        UnlockResource (hresSinData);

        return (iSign);
        }


/*------------------------------------------------------------------*\
 |  intCos  -  Calculates an integer cosine value in units          |
 |             equal to 10,000th for any degree entered, using      |
 |             a value derived from a custom sin resource.          |
\*------------------------------------------------------------------*/
int NEAR PASCAL intCos (int iValue)
    {
    return (intSin (iValue-90));
    }
```

CUSTRES.H

```
#define TABLE  100  /*  Custom resource type.  */
#define SINE   100  /*  ID of sine table.      */
```

CUSTRES.RC

```
#include "custres.h"

snapshot icon custres.ico

hand  cursor custres.cur

SIN   TABLE  sinedata.bin DISCARDABLE
```

CUSTRES.DEF

```
NAME      CUSTRES

EXETYPE WINDOWS

DESCRIPTION 'Custom Resource'

CODE      MOVEABLE DISCARDABLE
DATA      MOVEABLE MULTIPLE

HEAPSIZE      512
STACKSIZE    5000

EXPORTS
    MinWndProc
```

CUSTRES does all its work during three messages: WM_CREATE, WM_PAINT, and WM_DESTROY. All of the sine and cosine information is provided in two routines: intSin and intCos. The second function actually cheats: Since a cosine is always 90 degrees out of phase with a sine, the intCos function subtracts 90 degrees from the actual angle and calls the intSin function—just a little trigonometric sleight of hand to make Mom proud.

To use a custom function, you must call three routines: FindResource, LoadResource, and LockResource. In response to the WM_CREATE message, the first two are called. The result is a memory handle that is stored in `hresSinData`. The FindResource searches for the reference to a resource in the module database, which, as we mentioned earlier, is simply an abbreviated memory image of the module's file header. FindResource takes three parameters:

```
FindResource (hInstance, lpName, lpType)
```

- hInstance is an instance handle.
- lpName is a long pointer to a character string with the resource name.
- lpType is a long pointer to a character string with the resource type.

Even though lpName and lpType are pointers to character strings, this is not the most efficient way to identify a resource. The reason is simple: A string comparison is more expensive than an integer comparison. For this reason, we use a macro, MAKEINTRESOURCE, which lets us define integers and use them in place of a character string. Here are the two integers we defined in CUSTRES:

```
#define  TABLE  100  /*  Custom resource type.  */
#define  SINE   100  /*  ID of sine table.      */
```

which we use in the call to FindResource, as follows:

```
hRes = FindResource (hInst,
          MAKEINTRESOURCE(SIN),        /* Name. */
          MAKEINTRESOURCE(TABLE));     /* Type. */
```

The MAKEINTRESOURCE macro creates a pseudo-pointer, with zero for a segment identifier and the integer value for the offset value. It casts this value as an LPSTR, which is how this routine is defined, so that the C compiler doesn't complain. When the Find-Resource routine sees this value, it does not treat it as a pointer (this would be a fatal error!). Instead, it uses the two-byte integer value to find the resource definition. It can find it, because the resource file, CUSTRES.RC, has the following line:

```
SIN   TABLE  sinedata.bin DISCARDABLE
```

This causes the data in the resource file, sinedata.bin, to be copied entirely into CUSTRES.EXE at compile/link time. This means that CUSTRES is a stand-alone program and doesn't need the original resource data file to be present at run time.

Once FindResource has identified the specific resource that we are interested in, it provides a resource identifier: a handle that must be provided to the LoadResouce routine to be useful. LoadResource is the next routine called, and it is defined as

```
LoadResource (hInstance, hresInfo)
```

- hInstance is the instance handle.
- hresInfo is the handle returned by the FindResource routine.

In spite of its name, LoadResource does *not* cause the resource to be loaded into memory. Instead, it allocates a memory object from the global heap with a size of zero. This doesn't actually cause any memory to be allocated, but does cause a global memory handle to be assigned for our use. LoadResource provides this memory handle as a return value, which CUSTRES stores in hresSinData.

The routine that actually causes a resource to be loaded into memory is LockResource. But CUSTRES doesn't call this routine until it actually needs to use the data in the sine table. By postponing the loading of such a memory object, CUSTRES helps minimize the demand it makes on system memory. LockResource does several things: It loads the resource into memory, locks it in place, and returns a pointer to the data. LockResource is defined as

```
LPSTR LockResource (hResData)
```

- hResData is the handle returned by the LoadResource function.

LockResource returns a long pointer to a string. But if you're not storing characters in a resource, it's a simple matter to define the desired string and cast the results of LockResource to the right thing.

Here is how CUSTRES handles its need for a pointer to integer data:

```
int FAR * fpSin;

fpSin = (int FAR *)LockResource (hresSinData);
if (fpSin == NULL)
    return (0);
```

As we have mentioned elsewhere, casting the return value to routines like LockResource keep the compiler complaining about an alleged type-mismatch. We know better, and we let the compiler know it. Also, we check the return value from LockResource, in case it wasn't able to load the resource into memory.

The LockResource routine should never be discussed alone, but always in the context of an UnlockResource, with which it creates a *Windows sandwich*. We discussed this code construction earlier as a way to organize the use of a shared resource. In this case, the resource is memory. Calls to LockResource must be paired with calls to UnlockResource. The first loads the resource and ties it down in memory. The second unties the resource, allowing it to be moved in memory or even discarded, if the memory manager sees fit to do so. In CUSTRES, the `intsin` function uses these two routines to bracket its use of the sine data, creating a Windows sandwich that insures that the object is locked when we need it, and unlocked when we don't. The UnlockResource function is defined as

```
BOOL UnlockResource (hResData)
```

- hResData is the handle returned by the LoadResource function.

The final routine that plays a role in the handling of the custom resource is FreeResource. This frees all the memory associated with our custom resource. FreeResource is defined as

```
FreeResource (hResData)
```

- hResData is the handle returned by the LoadResource function.

This routine is called in response to the WM_DESTROY message, to deallocate the sine data memory. In this program, we don't actually need to call FreeResource, since the resource will be freed when our program terminates. But, as mentioned elsewhere in this book, it is a good programming practice that will help your code survive future programmers who fix, update, modify, and in other ways use your code in their projects.

It's worth noting that this program draws pixel coordinates using the default MM_TEXT mapping mode. In Chapter 20, when we discuss coordinate mapping, you'll see that there are better ways to make sure you can get a round circle. The only reason the circle you saw in Figure 18.11 was perfectly round is that the screen shot was taken on a device with a 1:1 aspect ratio, a VGA. We give you a brief preview of coordinate mapping, though, by moving the drawing origin from the upper-left corner to the very middle of the window:

```
GetClientRect (hwnd, &r);
SetViewportOrg (ps.hdc, r.right/2, r.bottom/2);
```

A complete look at the issues relating to coordinate transformations are provided in Chapter 20.

From our discussion, you can see that Windows provides many choices in how program uses memory for its code and data. Understanding these choices will help you tune your program to work optimally in all of Windows operating modes, and for compatibility with future versions of Windows.

19
Dynamic Linking

In all its operating modes, Real, Standard, and 386-Enhanced, Windows uses dynamic linking. Dynamic linking is several things rolled into one. First of all, it is a memory management technique that allows code to be loaded from disk on demand. Dynamic linking allows code to be discarded to free memory for other uses. When running in protect mode, Windows' dynamic linking depends on the built-in memory management features of the Intel-86 family of CPUs to trigger the loading process. And when running in real mode, even without the hardware support, Windows is able to provide dynamic linking that is just as efficient as its protect mode counterpart with a mechanism that is implemented entirely in software.

Second, dynamic linking provides a way to connect subroutine libraries to programs at *run time*. This contrasts sharply with static linking, in which routines from a subroutine library are copied to a program's executable file at program *creation time*. For example, if a Windows program uses the `memset` C-runtime routine, a copy of the routine is stored in the program's .EXE file. This is **static linking**. For the program to be able to access a new version of the memset routine (if it were made smaller, faster, more bug-free, or whatever), the program file must be recreated. Thus, a statically linked routine doesn't allow automatic upgrades when library functions are improved. But dynamic linking does, since the functions in a dynamic link library are not copied to a program's executable file at program creation time, but are linked to the program at run time. This is why, for example, Windows programs will be able to run unchanged in a future version of OS/2.

Third, dynamic linking provides an efficient mechanism for sharing code and data between application programs. For example, a single copy of the code for the subroutines in Windows graphic library, GDI.EXE, is shareable between all the different Windows

741

programs that wish to use them. When your program runs alongside Aldus PageMaker, for example, both programs use the same copy of the TextOut routine. The net result is a much lower demand on system memory. An example of *data* sharing occurs whenever text appears on a display screen. GDI fonts are implemented in dynamic link libraries, which means that they are shared by whichever programs wish to use them. Even with many programs accessing a font, only a single copy of the font data is present in the system.

The most obvious examples of dynamic linking occur between Windows programs and the main Windows dynamic link libraries: KERNEL.EXE (or KRNL286.EXE for Standard Mode, KRNL386.EXE for 386-Enhanced Mode), USER.EXE and GDI.EXE. When a Windows program is running, it relies on dynamic linking to make the proper connections to the various Windows library routines. Dynamic links are also created between the three main Windows dynamic link libraries and Windows' device drivers. For example, when GDI accesses a printer, it dynamically links to a printer driver. Dynamic linking makes it easy to upgrade or replace different parts of Windows—fonts, device drivers, or even the main libraries themselves.

The Dynamic Linking Mechanism

Let's take a moment to look at the nuts and bolts of Windows' dynamic linking mechanism. Even though dynamic linking occurs without requiring you to know how it works, there are several reasons why it is helpful to understand the mechanism itself. First of all, you might not be convinced that you can build programs that are bigger than your address space on a microcomputer. Even if you're comfortable with this idea, you might be concerned that the mechanism isn't efficient or has unexpected side-effects. You might want to know if you can build your own dynamic link libraries, and understanding the mechanism can help you decide when they are appropriate and when they are not. Or you might just be the kind of person who wants to know how things really work. Whatever your motivation, we think you'll find that—in all its operating modes—Windows' dynamic link mechanism is a fast, efficient, and very elegant approach to the problems of managing the dynamic loading and linking of code.

The architect of Windows' dynamic link mechanism is Steve Wood, who joined Microsoft in 1983. While a graduate student at Yale University, Steve had been involved with some systems programming projects on DEC-20 computers. One project involved the creation of a mechanism to share library code between different processes. This was accomplished by mapping the address space of different processes into the same physical address space. The net result was a reduction in required memory to support shared code.

This sounds a lot like dynamic linking. But the difference is that, when he started to work on building the dynamic link mechanism, Steve and the other members of the first KERNEL team were working on a machine with minimal capabilities. The target machine for the first version of Windows, after all, was to have an Intel 8088 CPU, two floppy disk drivers, and 256K of RAM. Dynamic linking could only require a minimum of overhead and had to be a software-only solution to a problem that had been solved elsewhere using dedicated hardware.

With a minimum amount of memory, the solution was to make much of the system reside in code segments that could be discarded. After all, if code resided on disk instead of in memory, there would be more room for applications to do their work. The trick was to figure out how to bring a code segment into memory. One of the things that was quickly apparent was that a whole new set of tools would have to be forged in order to get dynamic linking to work properly.

For example, a new linker had to be built to support the new .EXE file format that was required to support dynamic linking. A new program loader had to be built, to accommodate the fact that not all segments would necessarily be present when a program was running. And finally, a new compiler had to be built to generate code that would seamlessly connect programs and dynamic link libraries together in a working system. The first Windows development team discovered quite quickly that one of the challenges to working with new tools was determining when a bug was caused by the tools and when it was caused by your own code.

The program loader that was built into the first version of Windows served as the foundation on which all later loaders were built. To describe its operation, we need to look at how code segments are dynamically loaded and routines linked for discardable, movable, and fixed code segments. We'll start with the hardest case: discardable code.

Dynamic Linking and Discardable Code Segments

When you are building a dynamic link mechanism like the one Windows uses, the hardest aspect of dealing with discardable code segments is the fact that you never know when a code segment is present in memory or not. Without the hardware memory magic of protect mode, Real Mode Windows creates a tiny code stub for every FAR routine in programs and dynamic link libraries. These code stubs are called **loader thunks** or **call thunks** and reside in the module database.

Consider the case of a program that uses GDI's Rectangle routine, which for this example we'll suppose is in a discardable code segment. We'll call our program DRAWRECT. Before this program starts running, Windows will already have created a module database for GDI. Inside GDI's module database, there is one call thunk for every FAR routine in GDI, including Rectangle. Figure 19.1 depicts GDI's module database in memory. In real mode, a call thunk for routines in discardable segments have one of two states: an interrupt to the loader, as depicted in Figure 19.1, or a jump to the routine in memory, depicted in Figure 19.3.

When the first instance of DRAWRECT starts running, the Windows loader starts the load process by creating a DRAWRECT's module database. The module database is used to resolve calls *into* DRAWRECT, and so is not interesting to us in the context of linking DRAWRECT to GDI's Rectangle routine. However, DRAWRECT's module database *is* needed to locate DRAWRECT's entry point. After

Figure 19.1 *Memory before the dynamic link*

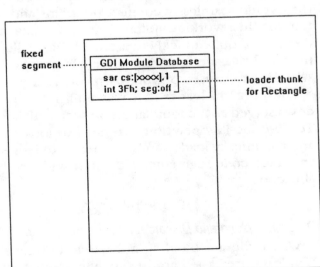

loading all of DRAWRECT's preload segments, control is passed to this entry point.

The dynamic link from DRAWRECT to GDI's **Rectangle** routine occurs when Windows loads a code segment that actually calls **Rectangle**. Appended to the end of such a code segment is a **relocation table**, which contains the fix-up information needed to create the first half of a dynamic link.

There are basically two types of relocation table entries: internal references and external references. The internal references define far calls to routines inside DRAWRECT. Part of dynamic linking, then, involves creating connections between a newly loaded code segment and other code segments in the same program or dynamic link library.

The external references define calls to dynamic link library routines, such as GDI's `Rectangle`. When DRAWRECT's code segment is loaded into memory, the far call to the **Rectangle** routine is fixed up to the address of the Rectangle routine's alias—that is, to the call thunk—in GDI's module database, as depicted in Figure 19.2.

When the Windows loader has finished creating all of the fix-ups described in the segment's relocation table, it frees the memory associated with the relocation table. When the relocation information is needed again, it will be reread from disk along with the code segment.

Figure 19.2 *DRAWRECT fix-up to GDI's module database*

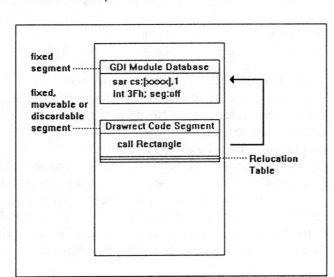

When a code segment is loaded into memory, it is patched once for every far call in the segment, including far calls to internal as well as external routines. This means simply that the code in the newly loaded code segment has been modified so that every far call points to *something*. In the Windows programs that you write, you'll want to keep your code segments small and the number of far calls to a minimum because of the overhead incurred when a code segment is loaded into memory.

Getting back to our example program, an interesting aspect of the dynamic link is that, even though DRAWRECT's code segment has been fixed up to call into GDI's module database, the code segment that actually holds the Rectangle routine does not have to be present in memory. As you'll see in a moment, when the code segment is not present, code in Rectangle's call thunk causes the code segment containing Rectangle to actually be loaded into memory.

The next step in the dynamic link process occurs when DRAWRECT actually calls Rectangle. Of course, it calls into the call thunk in the module database. As we mentioned earlier, the call thunk is a tiny code stub that will have one of two states, depending on whether Rectangle is open for business or out to lunch. Let's assume that it is out to lunch, to see how the call thunk responds. In such cases, the call thunk will have code that looks like the following:

```
                        ; --> "Out-To-Lunch"
SAR   CS:[00B4h],1      ; update access flag
INT   3Fh               ; Call to the Windows' loader
DB    seg               ; Code segment number
DW    off               ; Offset to Rectangle routine
```

When DRAWRECT calls into this piece of code, it triggers a software interrupt which calls the Windows loader, interrupt 3F. The Windows loader reads the next three bytes of information, which contain the segment number (from 1 to 255) and the offset into the code segment (0 to 65535). Since there is only a single byte for the segment number, the total number of segments that can exist in any .EXE or .DLL file is 255 (segment zero is reserved for return thunks, to be covered later). This limitation is intrinsic to the format of the EXE file itself, and therefore you can't create an EXE file with more than 255 segments. However, you can create a dynamic link library that allows a program to easily overcome this limitation.

Once the Windows loader has read the necessary code segment from disk, it modifies the module database so that the thunk associated with the Rectangle routine has machine instructions represented by the following assembly language:

```
                    ; --> "Open For Business"
SAR  CS:[00B4h],1   ; Update access flag
JMP  Rectangle
```

Not only are fix-ups performed for the Rectangle routine's call thunk, but also for the thunks of all *other* far routines that reside in Rectangle's code segment. And if Rectangle makes far calls to other code segments, those calls are fixed up along with any other far calls *from* Rectangle's code segment. That is, both inward bound and outward bound far calls are patched. Once the code segment has been loaded into memory and the module database fixed up, the dynamic link is complete. The Rectangle routine can retrieve its parameters off the stack and do its job. The complete dynamic link, from DRAWRECT through GDI's module database and into Rectangle, is depicted in Figure 19.3.

All calls to Rectangle are fixed up to call Rectangle's alias in the module database, which serves as a kind of switchboard operator for

Figure 19.3 *Final fix-up from GDI's module database to Rectangle's code segment*

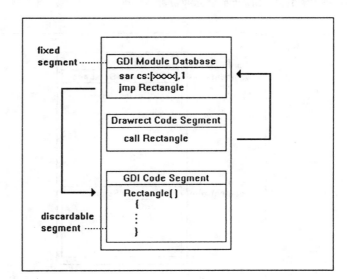

this routine. Notice that the Windows memory manager can move Rectangle's segment at any time. When it does so, it does not have to patch every program's code segment that calls Rectangle. Instead, it simply patches Rectangle's call thunk (and the call thunk of other far routines that might be in the same code segment). The code segment can also be discarded from memory at any time. When this occurs, the dynamic linker simply fixes up the call thunks with an INT 3F instruction to call the Windows loader to restore the code segment into memory. Of course, fixups are not free. But the dynamic link mechanism allows a code segment to be removed from memory, and reloaded later to give the greatest flexibility in how memory is used.

Dynamic Linking and Fixed Code Segments

Once you understand how a dynamic link to a discardable code segment is created, you'll see that dynamic links to fixed code segments are even simpler. Dynamic links to fixed code segments are not routed through a call thunk, but instead link a caller directly to the called routine. One reason for this is that fixed code segments are always treated as preload segments, so that they are always resident in memory and never move.

Figure 19.4 *GDI immediately after loading*

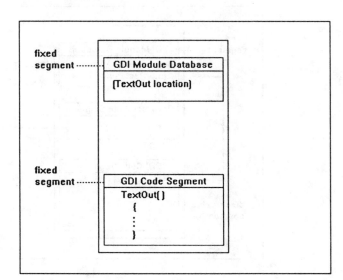

Consider a program that calls GDI's **TextOut** routine, which we'll assume for the moment is in a fixed code segment. For this example, we'll call our program DOTEXT, calls TextOut. As before, when GDI is first brought into memory, the Windows loader creates GDI's module database. Once this is done, the loader reads all fixed code segments into memory. Figure 19.4 shows the state of two objects that are in memory after GDI has been loaded: the module database and the fixed code segment that contains TextOut.

Since the fixed code segment is loaded when GDI starts running, it will never need a loader thunk. However, to locate the routine itself, the module database lists the address of far routines. The loader will require this information when it loads DOTEXT into memory. At that time, a dynamic link is created that directly connects DOTEXT to TextOut, as depicted in Figure 19.5. Unlike the fix-up to a movable or discardable segment, the fix-up to a *fixed* code segment always goes directly from the caller to the called routine.

In protect mode, the memory management hardware can move memory objects without changing the logical address. For this reason, all dynamic link fix-ups in protect mode are treated just like the dynamic link we just described. In other words, all fix-ups in protect

Figure 19.5 *Direct fix-up from DOTEXT to TextOut*

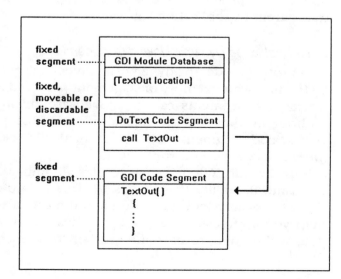

mode are treated as if every code segment were fixed. Far calls are patched up by the Windows loader to directly connect a caller to the called routine. This is true for movable segments as well as discardable segments.

Since protect mode doesn't have call thunks in the module database, you might wonder how discardable code segments get reloaded. In real mode, as you'll recall, the loader thunk in the module database triggers a code segment reload:

```
SAR    CS:[00B4h],1    ; Update access flag
INT    3Fh             ; Call to the Windows' loader
DB     seg             ; Code segment number
DW     off             ; Offset to Rectangle routine
```

In protect mode, when an absent code segment is called, a segment fault occurs. As you may recall from our discussion of protect mode operation in Chapter 17, every segment identifier contains an index into a protect mode descriptor table. Among the information that is kept in these tables is a flag that lets the system know whether a segment is actually present in memory or not. When it is not present, the segment fault—which is simply a software interrupt—notifies the memory manager that it must load the missing segment. Windows' memory manager loads the code segment into memory and then causes the instruction that triggered the segment fault to be restarted. In this way, the memory management hardware that operates in protect mode is able to operate in a manner that is transparent to application software.

Other Real Mode Dynamic Linking Considerations

In protect mode, the dynamic link mechanism is greatly simplified by the hardware memory management provided by the various Intel processors. Segments can be moved around in physical memory without invalidating the logical address that programs use. Discarded code segments can be automatically reloaded when a *segment not present* interrupt occurs.

In real mode, Windows has to play a number of tricks to achieve the same flexibility that comes for free in protect mode. Two of these tricks are **stack patching** and the use of **return thunks**. To help you appreciate the work that Real Mode Windows does for you, we're going to describe each of these mechanisms in a little detail.

Stack Patching. Stack patching involves walking the stack of a program and updating references that have been made to code segments that have moved. Earlier, we mentioned that the only thing that had to happen when a code segment was moved was to update the references to the routine in a module database. This is true most of the time. But if the address of a routine is referenced as a return address on the stack, that reference must also be fixed up.

Whenever a function is called—inside a dynamic link library or inside a regular program—a return address is placed on the stack. This address identifies the location of the machine instruction that is to be executed next when we return from the function. When a code segment referenced on the stack moves, Windows must walk the stack and patch the return address so that calls can correctly find their way back to the calling function. Windows patches the stack for every instance of every program running in the system.

Because Windows can patch stacks, it is free to move any code segment at any time. This gives the Windows memory manager the freedom to move any movable code segment at any time. This allows real mode Windows to have the same flexibility of protect-mode Windows—which is critical, given the greater memory constraints that are part of real-mode operation.

Return Thunks. In the same way that stack patching allows code segments to be *moved*, return thunks allow code segments to be *discarded*. In our discussion of dynamic linking, we mentioned that a code segment could be discarded at any time, as long as the module database was updated to call the Windows loader the next time a function in the segment was called. We mentioned that the reloading of discardable code segments is done by a tiny code stub called a call thunk.

When Windows discards a code segment that is referenced as a return address on the stack, the stack is also patched. The stack patching operation involves walking the stack of all programs, looking for a reference to the discarded code segment. Since the stack cannot be patched with the address of a discarded code segment, which has no address, it is instead patched to return to a tiny code stub called a **return thunk**. A return thunk is similar to a call thunk, except that after loading the necessary code segment, it provides a bridge for a return instruction instead of a call instruction. After the segment has been loaded, execution continues at the return address that was on the stack before the segment was discarded. Here is an example of a return thunk:

```
INT  3Fh          ; Call to the Windows' loader.
DB   0            ; Zero segment = return thunk.
DW                ; seg:IP packed into 20 bits.
DB                ; Handle to data segment packed
                  ; into 12 bits.
```

A return thunk looks a lot like a loader thunk, except that an invalid segment number is given: zero. This flags the INT 3F loader that this is a return thunk. In this case, it knows that the three bytes that follow contain all the data it needs to continue, although things are packed a little tightly. For one thing, the segment number and the code segment offset are crammed into 20 bits. This is possible since the code segment number will be a number between 0 and 255, which means it only takes one byte. That leaves 16 bits for the offset. A handle to the data segment is stored in the return thunk, since the data segment itself may have moved while memory was being jostled around. When the return thunk is run, the data segment is patched to reflect the new location of the data segment. All of this allows Windows to survive even a very low memory situation, since *any* code segment in the entire system (except the currently executing one) can be discarded if more memory is needed.

Up until now, our discussion of dynamic linking has focused on *code*. We have described the way that code can be loaded, moved, and discarded in all of Windows' operating modes. Windows takes advantage of the features of protect mode, when they are available, but also adapts to the constraints and limitation of real mode with no change in overall system capabilities. We're now going to look at the impact of dynamic linking on *data*. Windows allows every program and dynamic link library to create a default data segment, and it provides several mechanisms to make sure that every program and dynamic link library is always able to access its default data.

Dynamic Linking and Module Data Segments

When you write a stand-alone application in most operating systems, you may use functions from various static link libraries. When you do, these blend invisibly into your program so that it is almost impossible to distinguish the machine instructions created by *your* code from the machine instructions associated with library routines. If a static library routine needs to store global variables to maintain state information, the linker blends the library's global variables with your program's global variables.

When working with dynamic link libraries, the distinction between your program and the library code is more evident. For example, dynamic link libraries have their own separate executable files. GDI.EXE, for example, is the dynamic link library file where GDI routines live. The file maintains an existence that is separate from the programs that use the library routines.

Dynamic link libraries also have their own data segment that allow them to keep global variables separate from the data areas of the programs that use its routines. You can convince yourself of this by running the HEAPWALK utility and looking for the objects that are marked as "Data" owned by the USER and GDI libraries, as well as various device driver DLLs. In Figure 19.6, the data segments of the USER and the WINOLDAP dynamic link libraries are highlighted. (WINOLDAP creates a shell around DOS programs when they are running under Windows).

A Windows library makes certain functions available to Windows programs. These functions serve as a doorway into the capabilities and features of the dyamic link libraries. Such functions are given a very special flag so that Windows can help the DLL access its proper data segment. The flag marks a function as **exported**. Windows modifies the first three bytes of every exported library function to set up the library's data segment, using code like this:

```
MOV  AX, DGROUP      ; Get data segment address
PUSH DS              ; Save caller's DS
MOV  DS, AX          ; Install in DS register
```

Figure 19.6 *HEAPWALK with data segments of USER and WINOLDAP highlighted*

SELECTOR	HANDLE	SIZE	LCK	FLG	OWNER-NAME	OBJ-TYPE	ADD-INFO
0007ABE0	04BE	1280		D	User	Code	
0007B0E0	04B6	8768		D	User	Code	
0007E5C0	0256	32		D	User	Resource	Group_Cursor
000826E0	05C6	2080		D	User	Code	
00083E80	05EE	2944		D	User	Code	
00085FC0	054E	2336		D	User	Code	
0008BAA0	05FE	29952	1		User	Data	
0009C500	05AE	9728		D	User	Code	
8051D660	055E	9152		D	User	Code	
00035EE0		512			Winoldap	Task	DataBase
000360E0		992	1		Winoldap	Data	
000365C0	094E	64	1		Winoldap	Code	
00037740	09BE	32		D	Winoldap	Resource	NameTable
0005A300	09EE	32		D	Winoldap	Resource	String
0005D500	09F6	32		D	Winoldap	Resource	String
0005D620	09CE	64		D	Winoldap	Resource	Group_Icon
0005D660	09FE	32		D	Winoldap	Resource	String
0005D740	0A06	32		D	Winoldap	Resource	String

HeapWalker- (Main Heap)

File Walk Sort Object Alloc Add!

When the library's data segment moves, Windows updates the value of DGROUP for all exported routines in the library. This causes the data segment register to be correctly set whenever a program calls into one of the exported "doorway" functions. Here is the complete set of assembly language instructions used to set up the data segment of an exported far routine in a dynamic link library:

```
MOV   AX, DGROUP      ; Get data segment address
INC   BP
PUSH  BP
MOV   BP, SP
PUSH  DS             ; Save caller's DS
MOV   DS, AX
```

Earlier, when we described some of the tricks that real-mode Windows must play, we said that it must sometimes walk and patch the stack when a code segment has moved or been discarded. The PUSH BP and MOV BP,SP instructions are how the compiler ordinarily saves the old BP value and intializes it for the private use of the current function. This effectively creates a linked list of stack frames that make it easy for the stack walking to take place. The INC BP instruction is only used for far calls, and so helps the memory manager to distinguish between a near and far call.

At certain times, a Windows library routine will call functions within a Windows program. Such routines are referred to as **call-back functions**. Up until this point in this book, we have discussed two types of call-back functions: window procedures and dialog box procedures. Other types include enumeration procedures and subclass procedures. Just like a window procedure, and the special "doorway" functions in a dynamic link library, all call-back procedures must be *exported*. There are two ways to export a procedure: you can place an entry into the module definition file, like this:

```
EXPORTS
    MinWindowProc
```

Or, if you are using the Microsoft C Compiler, version 5.1 or later, you can use the _exports directive as shown here:

```
LONG FAR PASCAL _exports MinWindowProc
                    (HWND hwnd,   WORD wMsg,
                    WORD wParam, LONG lParam)
```

It is very important to export a procedure that Windows calls. The reason has to do with the fact that when Windows calls you, the data segment register will be set up for one of Windows dynamic link libraries (USER or GDI). By exporting the call-back procedures, you put in place one-half of a mechanism that sets the DS register up properly so you can access your program's data segment.

Here is what the C compiler puts at the beginning of every far function:

```
PUSH DS          ; Put DS value into
POP  AX          ; the AX register.
NOP              ; Place holder
INC  BP          ; stack-walking preparation
PUSH BP          ; stack-walking preparation
MOV  BP, SP      ; set up regular stack frame
PUSH DS          ; save caller's DS
MOV  DS, AX      ; install our own DS
```

At first glance, it looks like this routine does a lot of work for nothing. But in fact this somewhat complicated piece of code makes sure that every far call saves a copy of the caller's data segment on the stack. Why? This allows Windows to patch the address of *data segments* that are moved at the same time that it patches code segment addresses. Anytime any code or segment address moves, Windows has no problem patching this up correctly.

At the moment a code segment is loaded into memory, the Windows loader checks for the exported functions in the segment. If it finds one, it modifies the instructions in the first three bytes to allow the DS register to be set up correctly. Windows replaces the PUSH DS, POP AX instructions that the compiler generated, and which we saw in the previous code example, with three NOP (no operation) instructions, as shown here:

```
NOP
NOP
NOP
INC  BP          ; stack-walking preparation
PUSH BP          ; stack-walking preparation
MOV  BP, SP      ; set up regular stack frame
PUSH DS          ; save caller's DS
MOV  DS, AX      ; install our own DS
```

This allows an exported function to receive its data segment value in the AX register. But wait—how does the data segment value get into the AX register? That depends on the type of call-back function: Window procedures use one mechanism, and all other call-back functions use another.

A window procedure receives its data segment fix-up value as part of Windows' message delivery mechanism. When you call Create-Window (or CreateWindowEx) to create a window, you pass an instance handle that identifies the data segment that is to be associated with the window. The message delivery mechanism uses this value to set up the proper AX value for window procedures.

All other call-back functions must use another mechanism that requires a little work on your part, but insures that the AX register will be set up properly with the address of the data segment. The mechanism is called an **Instance thunk**.

The Instance Thunk

The dynamic link mechanism allows the code from different **modules**—executable programs and dynamic link libraries—to be linked together efficiently at run time. Every module can have its own data segment, which allows programs and dynamic link libraries to store global variables that they need to do their work. The rule about data fix-ups is that *a data segment (DS) fix-up is required every time a module boundary is crossed*. We have already described how this is done for dynamic link libraries, and for window procedures in applications. The third type of data segment fix-up must be setup and managed by a Windows program.

Here is a list of the different call-back procedures that can be created in Windows. As you can see, call-backs play many different roles in Windows. A call-back provides a way for Windows to deliver information to a Windows program in a fairly efficient manner.

Call-Back Function	Description
Dialog box procedure	Used to initialize and maintain a dialog box.
Enumeration procedure	When a program wants to query Windows about certain types of objects, an enumeration procedure is used. Windows calls the enumeration procedure once for each object. Objects that are enumerated include windows, fonts, GDI drawing objects, clipboard formats. *(Continued)*

Call-Back Function	Description
Hook	Allows a program to eavesdrop and change message traffic in the system. A keyboard hook, for example, lets a program respond to any "hot-key," even if the program isn't currently active.
Memory discarding notification procedure	GlobalNotify lets a program set up a call-back procedure that is called before the Windows memory manager discards a memory object.
Sub-class procedure	Provides a means of eavesdropping in and modifying the message traffic for a particular window.
Timer	A timer procedure allows a program to specify an alternative method for receiving timer notifications other than by a WM_TIMER message.

An important issue to keep in mind is that an Instance thunk is only required if one of these procedures resides in a Windows program. When these call-back procedures are implemented in a dynamic link library, an Instance thunk is not needed.

An Instance thunk is a very small piece of code. Here is an example of one:

```
MOV  AX, DSvalue
JMP  DialogBoxProc
```

If the routine, DialogBoxProc, resided in a fixed code segment, this fix-up would jump directly to the code itself. Figure 19.7 shows the relationship of the different pieces to one another, and shows the flow of control through an instance thunk for all protect mode and for fixed code segments in real mode.

There is another case worth looking at briefly, since it helps to bring the complexity of real-mode operation into perspective. Earlier, we mentioned that in real mode, calls into movable and discardable code segments are always routed through a module database call thunk. When you add an instance thunk, you get an arrangement like that depicted in Figure 19.8. That is, the instance thunk is first called to put the data segment value into the AX register. Then, control passes to the call thunk to load an absent segment, or to jump to the segment when it's present.

Figure 19.7 *An Instance Thunk and a fixed code segment*

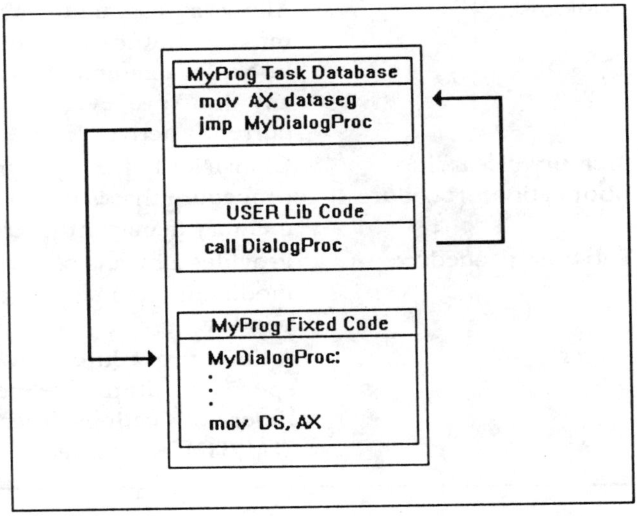

Notice that the call gets routed through both the task database and the module database of the program. In the task database, the instance thunk puts the value of the program's data segment into the AX register. If the data segment moves, the memory manager walks through all the active thunks in the task database to insure that these thunks stay current. From the task database, a jump is made into the module database. It arrives at the loader thunk that we described earlier. After all, this is the mechanism that allows a code segment to be discarded or moved in real mode. And finally, control arrives at our call-back procedure. Of course, as we saw in the earlier code fragments, one of the first instructions in the call-back procedure will establish the data segment address by copying the value in the AX register into the DS register.

A program creates an instance thunk by calling the **MakeProc-Instance** routine, which we have seen already in our discussion of dialog boxes in Chapter 14. This routine takes as one of its parameters a procedure address—which, in real-mode operation, is the address of a module database call thunk for functions that reside in movable or discardable segments. It returns an instance thunk, which can then be provided as the address of a far procedure for

Figure 19.8   *An Instance Thunk and a movable or discardable code segment*

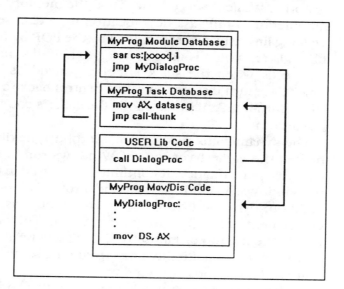

those Windows library routines which require the address of call-back procedures.

Clean Up Before You Go Home

We have described three different sets of entries that can be made into far functions: exported library entries, unexported program entries, and exported program entries. The first reflects how the Windows loader sets up a dynamic link library's data segment. The second is simply what the C Compiler creates to allow the other two entries to work properly. And the third is for call-back functions like window procedures and dialog box procedures.

Although there are three different entries for far functions, all far functions in Windows clean up the stack in the same way, with the following instructions:

```
MOV  SP, BP    ; restore caller's stack frame
POP  DS        ; restore caller's DS
POP  BP        ; clear off stack-walking link list
DEC  BP        ; flip even/odd far call bit
RETF 0002      ; far return
```

In other words, the caller's data segment value—the DS register—is restored. While it was on the stack, the memory manager may have modified it to reflect a new location for a data segment. The stack-walking link list value is removed by the POP BP instruction, and the BP register, which is used as a flag to help distinguish far calls from near calls when the stack is being walked, is decremented. And finally, a return instruction sends control back to the caller (or back to a return-thunk, if in real mode the caller's code segment had to be discarded).

The dynamic link mechanism is a robust, flexible mechanism that helped the earliest versions of Windows run in real mode with acceptable performance. It continues to be used in the present version of Windows, in both its real and protect modes of operation. In addition, dynamic linking has been adopted as a key architectural component of the OS/2 operating system. This is one of the reasons that in the not too distant future, OS/2 will be able to accommodate a "Windows compatibility box" to run the same Windows programs that can be run today in Windows 3.

As you've seen, dynamic linking has both a code and a data aspect. The code aspect allows a program to be linked to library code at run time instead of at link time. This has allowed programs written for previous version of Windows to run (almost) effortlessly in Windows 3, and will allow the programs that you write today to run unmodified in future versions of Windows and on OS/2. The data aspect of dynamic linking is invisible to a program for its window procedures, and involves a call to **MakeProcInstance** for all other call-back procedures. While the data side of dynamic linking is not as transparent as is the code side, both parts work together with relatively little effort on your part.

Part 7

More Topics in GDI Programming

20

Coordinate Transformation and Scrolling

The creation and use of graphical output is a vast subject area, about which much has been written and much will continue to be written. This chapter and the one that follows are going to return to the subject of graphics to insure that we have covered the basics you'll need to know to build a full-blown Windows application.

In this chapter, we cover two topics: coordinate transformation and scrolling. Coordinate transformation has to do with GDI's facilities for using other coordinates besides the pixel-based client area coordinates that we have used up until now. Scrolling is the process by which a program whose data does not fit in a window can make that data available to users. The user interface portion of scrolling is, of course, scroll bars. But making the best use of the programming interface involves understanding the help that Windows gives you when you scroll pixels on the display.

Coordinate Transformation

Coordinate transformation refers to the way GDI interprets the drawing coordinates that you provide to describe the location and shape of geometric figures and text. Up to now, we haven't used coordinate transformations but have used only pixel coordinates. But GDI does not restrict you to pixel coordinates. For example, you can tell GDI to interpret drawing coordinates in inches or millimeters. Or, you can define your own coordinate system to scale—for example, 10 units per pixel, one unit per 18 pixels, or whatever arbitrary scaling factors you wish to apply.

Like many of GDI's other features, coordinate transformations are controlled by making changes to the drawing attributes in a DC. Here is a list of the DC attributes that play a part in coordinate transformation:

DC Attribute	Description
Mapping mode	Determines the units. See Table 20.1.
Viewport extent	Pixel units for scaling in MM_ANISOTROPIC and MM_ISOTROPIC mapping modes.
Viewport origin	Pixel units for coordinate translation.
Window extent	Real world units for scaling in MM_ANISOTROPIC and MM_ISOTROPIC mapping modes.
Window origin	Real world units for coordinate translation.

In the world of graphics programming, there are three types of coordinate transformation: **translation**, **scaling**, and **rotation**. GDI supports translation and scaling, but has no built-in support for rotation. This does not mean that a program cannot rotate a drawing, but doing so requires a program to calculate the rotated coordinate values itself.

Table 20.1   *GDI mapping modes*

Mapping Mode Name	One Logical Unit	Inches	Millimeters
MM_TEXT	1 pixel	-	-
MM_HIMETRIC	0.01 mm	0.000394	0.01
MM_TWIPS	1/1440 inches	0.000694	0.0176
MM_HIENGLISH	0.001 inches	0.001	0.0254
MM_LOMETRIC	0.1 mm	0.00394	0.1
MM_LOENGLISH	0.01 inches	0.01	0.254
MM_ISOTROPIC	} Scaling based on ratio between two DC		
MM_ANISOTROPIC	} attribute values: window extent and viewport extent		

As depicted in Figure 20.1(b), translation involves sliding an image to a new location. This is sometimes referred to as **scrolling** or **panning**. Translation by itself does not change the size of a picture, nor does it cause the picture to appear at a different angle; translation just changes the picture's location. In terms of how the coordinates are interpreted, translating involves one or more of the following operations: adding or subtracting an X-translation value to x-coordinates, and adding or subtracting a Y-translation value to y-coordinates.

Figure 20.1(c) shows an example of scaling. Scaling, also referred to as **zooming**, causes a picture to change size. When **uniform scaling** takes place, the changes to the x-coordinates are proportional to the changes to the y-coordinates. **Differential scaling**, on the other hand, means that the scaling factor for x-coordinates is different from the scaling factor that is applied to the y-coordinates. In addition to changing the *size* of a picture, scaling also changes the distance from the origin. In other words, a coordinate transformation that causes scaling also causes translation (sliding) either toward or away from the origin.

In the same way that you can think of translations in terms of adding or subtracting values to coordinates, scaling involves multiplying by a scaling factor. In common parlance, it's pretty common

Figure 20.1 *Coordinate transformation: (a) the original drawing; (b) translation; (c) scaling; and (d) rotation.*

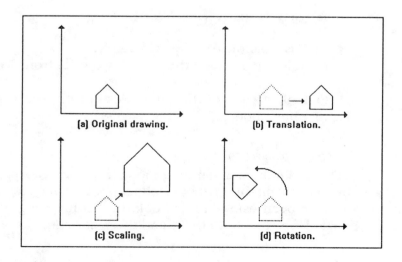

to hear people describe scaling in terms of a multiplier. Something might be twice as large as something else, or only half as large.

Figure 20.1 (d) shows an example of a rotated picture. GDI does not provide any rotation for you, but for the sake of completeness we'll explore what rotation involves in the world of graphics programming. Rotation is usually described in terms of rotation around a point. The simplest rotation uses the origin (0,0) as the rotation point. The illustration shows this type of rotation, in which the picture seems to behave like a constellation in the sky: although it has traveled some distance, the angle of the image itself doesn't seem to have rotated very much. On the other hand, if we place the rotation point somewhere in the middle of an object, it rotates around the rotation point like a phonograph record rotates on a turntable.

GDI's eight mapping modes can be divided into four categories: device, fully constrained, partially constrained, and fully unconstrained. The mapping modes that belong in each category are listed in Table 20.2. To determine the active mapping mode in a DC, you call **GetMapMode**, which is defined:

```
int GetMapMode (hDC)
```

- hDC is a handle to a device context.

Setting a mapping mode requires a call to **SetMapMode**, which is defined:

```
int SetMapMode (hDC, nMapMode)
```

- hDC is a handle to a device context.
- nMapMode is one of the mapping modes from Table 20.2.

Let's look at each of the categories in turn, starting with the device mapping mode.

Device Mapping Mode

There is only one mapping mode in this category, MM_TEXT. As you may recall, this is the default mapping mode and is the only one we have been using in this book. In this mapping mode, one unit equals 1 pixel, in both the X and the Y direction.

Table 20.2   *Categories of mapping modes*

Category	Mapping Modes	One Unit Equals
Device	MM_TEXT	One pixel.
Fully constrained	MM_HIMETRIC	One-hundredth of a millimeter.
	MM_TWIPS	Approx. 1/1440 of a point.
	MM_HIENGLISH	One-thousandth of an inch.
	MM_LOMETRIC	One-tenth of a millimeter.
	MM_LOENGLISH	One-hundredth of an inch.
Partially constrained	MM_ISOTROPIC	Arbitrary units, but uniform scaling is applied to X and Y, which means that X units and Y units are identical.
Fully unconstrained	MM_ANISOTROPIC	Arbitrary units. Differential scaling is allowed; X and Y can be independently scaled.

The advantage of this mapping mode is that it is the most accurate one. When you are writing applications in which you must have pixel-perfect drawing, you may wish to limit yourself to this mapping mode. It is also the most portable mapping mode. If you are writing code that you plan to port to other environments (like the Apple Macintosh and the various X-Window systems), you will probably want to limit yourself to this mapping mode, since pixel-based coordinates are available in all GUI systems. The OS/2 Presentation Manager, on the other hand, incorporates all of Windows' coordinate transformations and more. If you plan to port your Windows applications to this environment, you can use any of GDI's mapping modes with wild abandon.

Since drawing units are pixels, this mapping mode supports no scaling. But it does support translation—that is, scrolling. In GDI, translation is defined in terms of where the origin is located. There are two GDI routines that change the origin: **SetViewportOrg** and **SetWindowOrg**. Two routines are needed for mapping modes that scale: **SetWindowOrg** defines a translation *before* the scaling, and **SetViewportOrg** defines a translation to be applied after scaling. As you'll see, this latter routine always refers to pixels, so it is the one we're going to use in our translation of MM_TEXT coordinates. **SetViewportOrg** is defined:

```
DWORD SetViewportOrg (hDC, X, Y)
```

- hDC is a handle to a device context.
- X is the x-coordinate of the new origin.
- Y is the y-coordinate of the new origin.

When drawing on the display, the following code sets the origin in the middle of a window's client area. Figure 20.2 provides a more graphic depiction of the new location of the origin.

```
{
RECT r;

GetClientRect (hwnd, &r);
SetViewportOrg (hdc, r.right/2, r.bottom/2);
   .
   .
   .
}
```

To set the origin in the middle of the page on a printer, here is what we could say:

```
{
int cxWidth;
int cyHeight;

cxWidth  = GetDevicecaps (hdcPrinter, HORZSIZE);
cyHeight = GetDevicecaps (hdcPrinter, VERTSIZE);

SetViewportOrg (hdcPrinter, cxWidth/2, cyHeight/2);
   .
   .
   .
}
```

hdcPrinter is a handle to a printer DC. We're getting a little ahead of ourselves here, since we haven't yet discussed the creation of a printer DC. But a printer DC is a lot like a display DC. Both provide a set of drawing attributes and a connection to their respective

Figure 20.2 *The origin in the center of the client area, in device coordinates*

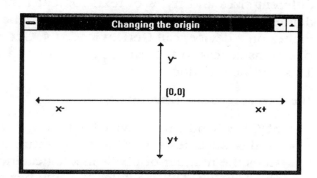

devices. As you probably guessed, the two calls to **GetDeviceCaps** provide the width and height of a printed page.

A potential problem with the MM_TEXT mapping mode is that you may inadvertently create device *dependent* code. For example, you may decide that some graphic object should be 100 pixels wide by 100 pixels tall. After all, if you developed your program on a VGA display, you'd find that this size creates an image that occupies a little more than one square inch. While you might be satisfied with the image on a VGA display, the object would change sizes when drawn on a different device. For example, on a 300 dots per inch laser printer, the same drawing occupies an area one-tenth as big.

There are several solutions to this problem. You can call **GetSystemMetrics** to determine the size of various objects on the display screen. For example, in Chapter 13, we used this method to determine how big to make a top-level window. Of course, this routine can only be used to determine the size of objects on the display screen; it doesn't tell us how to size objects on other devices.

If you are dealing with text, you can call **GetTextMetrics** to retrieve text measurement information and use these values to place text in a device-independent manner. We first used this in Chapter 10, when we discussed drawing text. You may also recall that dialog box coordinates are defined in terms of system font metrics, which allows them to achieve a large degree of device independence.

You'll want to consider a third solution if you plan to work with different sizes and styles of text: **logical inches**. A logical inch is defined in terms of an (x,y) pair. To retrieve the values for the logical inches on a device, call **GetDeviceCaps**. **GetDeviceCaps** gives applications access to the capability of bits and metrics for a device. This routine is defined:

```
int GetDeviceCaps (hDC, nIndex)
```

- hDC is a handle to a device context.
- nIndex specifies the value to be returned. LOGPIXELSX provides the number of pixels in a logical inch in the X direction, and LOGPIXELSY provides the number of pixels in a logical inch in the Y direction.

To retrieve the number of pixels per logical inch along both the X and Y axes, you say:

```
int cxInch, cyInch;

cxInch = GetDeviceCaps (hdc, LOGPIXELSX);
cyInch = GetDeviceCaps (hdc, LOGPIXELSY);
```

A logical inch is a fudge factor for scaling fonts on display screens. Its primary purpose is to improve the readability of fonts on displays. The range of font sizes that are used for **text type**—the type that makes up the main body of printed documents—varies from eight to twelve points (a point is approximately 1/72 of an inch). Since a primary use of the display screen is to preview text copy before it is sent to the printer, this fudge factor simplifies the process of emulating the printed page on a display screen—a capability sometimes called "what you see is what you get," or WYSIWYG, output.

On lower resolution devices, if fonts were scaled according to a ruler inch, eight-point type would be unreadable. Consider, for example, a CGA display, which has 28 pixels per Y-axis ruler inch. An eight-point font on this device would only be (8 x 28) / 72 or about 3 pixels high. Even on an EGA display, with its 51 pixels per Y-axis ruler inch, an eight-point font would only be (8 x 51) / 72 or six pixels high. Depending on the display device, a logical inch may be anywhere between 25 and 70 percent larger than a ruler inch.

Programs that depend heavily on different sizes of text can use a logical inch for both text and graphics. In this case, such a program can use the MM_TEXT mapping mode and still achieve a very high level of device independence. Of course, this requires that you do all of the scaling yourself. An alternative is to use GDI's mapping modes, which map directly to ruler inches on both the display screen and on printers. We are referring, of course, to the fully constrained mapping modes, which we are going to discuss next.

Fully Constrained Mapping Modes

GDI's fully constrained mapping modes are referred to as "fully constrained" because each limits you to a single scaling factor. Depending on the mode you choose, these mapping modes allow you to draw using inch, millimeter, or printer's point coordinates. The scaling of each is fixed, then, to various "real world" measuring units.

To understand this set of mapping modes, you need to understand the way GDI does arithmetic. GDI uses exclusively integer arithmetic for all its calculations, instead of floating-point coordinates which are, in some respects, more suitable coordinates. The problem with floating-point arithmetic is that the Intel-86 family of processors has no built-in floating-point support. Accurate floating-point arithmetic would require quite a bit of work, all of which would have to be done in software. For reasons of performance, then, GDI limits itself to integer arithmetic. What's more, it uses only 16-bit short integers instead of the more accurate, but slower, 32-bit integer arithmetic.

To overcome the implicit loss of precision from integer arithmetic, the fully constrained mapping modes are scaled so that units are not whole inches, millimeters, and points. Instead, units are equal to a fixed fraction of inches, millimeters, and printers points. For example, when you use the MM_HIMETRIC mapping mode, each unit is equal to 0.01 millimeter. To draw an object that is a millimeter long in this mapping mode, you specify 100 units. And in the MM_HIENGLISH mapping mode, which uses units that are equal to .001 inch, you need to specify 1000 units when drawing an object that is one inch. To give you a better idea of the relationship between the units used by these mapping modes, Figure 20.3 shows a set of 100-unit squares. For comparison sake, we've included a square whose sides are a logical inch. The last square does not have sides that are 100 units, but instead—since this figure was drawn on a VGA display—the sides are 96 pixels each. The difference that you see between the logical inch square and the MM_LOENGLISH object, which is a ruler inch on each side, demonstrates the discrepancy between a logical inch and a ruler inch.

Figure 20.3 *Squares drawn with the fully constrained mapping modes and with a logical inch*

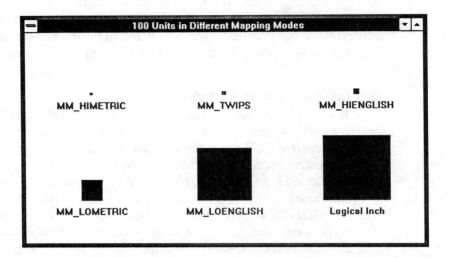

When working with these mapping modes, you must take into account the fact that the direction taken by the Y axis is different from the direction in the MM_TEXT mapping mode. In the default text mapping mode, Y coordinates increase moving down the screen (or printed page). But in all of the fully constrained mapping modes, Y coordinates increase when moving *up* the screen. In this way, these mapping modes mimic the approach taken by the Cartesian coordinate system. Figure 20.4 depicts this graphically.

When you call either **BeginPaint** or **GetDC** to borrow a display DC from the Window Manager (a topic we first introduced in Chapter 6), the DC has its origin (0,0) in the upper-left corner of the window. And, as you'll see in the next chapter, when you call **CreateDC** to obtain a DC to draw on a printer, the DC has its origin in the upper-left corner of the drawing surface. This means that if you use draw with any of these mapping modes and use positive Y coordinates, your drawing will not appear. So, if you wish to use positive Y coordinates, one of the first things you may wish to do is to move the origin to a new location. From our earlier discussion, you may recall that the **SetViewportOrg** routine can do this for us.

For example, the following code moves the origin to the lower-left corner of a window, sets the mapping mode to MM_LOENG-LISH, and then draws a rectangle that is one inch by three inches:

Figure 20.4   *Fully constrained coordinates and the Y-axis*

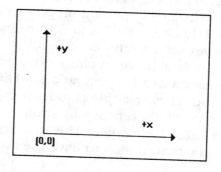

```
{
RECT r;

SetMapMode (hdc, MM_LOENGLISH);

GetClientRect (hwnd, &r);
SetViewportOrg (hdc, 0, r.bottom);

Rectangle (hdc, 0, 0, 100, 300);
}
```

Or, if you are drawing on a printer, here is how you can place the
origin at the bottom-left corner of the printed page:

```
{
int cyHeight;

cyHeight = GetDevicecaps (hdcPrinter, VERTSIZE);
SetViewportOrg (hdcPrinter, 0, cyHeight);
.
.
.
}
```

The **SetViewportOrg** routine moves the origin using pixel coordinates. Therefore, if you want to move it anywhere else on a drawing
surface, you call this routine and specify the new pixel location for
the origin.

One convenient aspect of the fully constrained mapping modes is that units in the X direction and units in the Y direction are set equal. This is particularly important on devices that do not have an **aspect ratio** of 1:1, like the CGA and EGA displays and certain types of printers. An aspect ratio describes the ratio between the distance moved in Y to achieve an equal movement in X. For example, CGA displays have a 2-to-1 aspect ratio. And EGA displays have a 1.33-to-1 aspect ratio. These mapping modes provide one way to compensate for this type of discrepancy by scaling coordinates so that X and Y units are effectively equal. This makes sense, of course, since we expect one vertical inch to have the same length as one horizontal inch.

Let's take a look at a sample program that makes use of two of these mapping modes. Our program, RULERS, draws a pair of rulers—one horizontal and one vertical—to help introduce the fully constrained mapping modes.

A Sample Program: RULERS

Our sample program, RULERS, draws two-inch rulers on the left and bottom of its client area. Figure 20.5 shows the output produced by this program. As you can see, the rulers are subdivided into eighths of an inch, with a medium-size tick to mark the half-

Figure 20.5   *The two rulers drawn by RULERS*

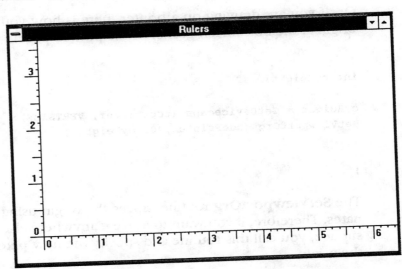

inches, and a long mark for the inches. Here is the code that produced this output.

RULERS.MAK

```
Rulers.res: Rulers.rc Rulers.cur Rulers.ico
    rc -r Rulers.rc

Rulers.obj: Rulers.c
    cl -AM -c -d -Gsw -Ow -W2 -Zpi Rulers.c

Rulers.exe: Rulers.obj Rulers.def
    link Rulers,/align:16,/map, mlibcew libw/NOD/NOE/CO,\
        Rulers.def
    rc Rulers.res

Rulers.exe: Rulers.res
    rc Rulers.res
```

RULERS.C

```c
/*-----------------------------------------------------------*\
|   RULERS.C  -  Demo program with a ruler being drawn.       |
\*-----------------------------------------------------------*/
#include <Windows.H>

#define SMALLTICK  (4)
#define MEDIUMTICK (15)
#define LARGETICK  (25)
/*-----------------------------------------------------------*\
|                    Function Prototypes.                     |
\*-----------------------------------------------------------*/
long FAR  PASCAL RulersWndProc (HWND, WORD, WORD, LONG);
void NEAR PASCAL RulersInstallCoords (HDC, HWND);
void NEAR PASCAL RulersDrawVertRuler(HDC);
void NEAR PASCAL RulersDrawHorzRuler(HDC);


/*-----------------------------------------------------------*\
|                   Main Function:  WinMain.                  |
\*-----------------------------------------------------------*/
```

```
int PASCAL WinMain (HANDLE hInstance,

                    HANDLE hPrevInstance,
                    LPSTR  lpszCmdLine,
                    int    cmdShow)
    {
HWND     hwnd;
MSG      msg;
WNDCLASS wndclass;

if (!hPrevInstance)
     {
     wndclass.lpszClassName = "Rulers:MAIN";
     wndclass.hInstance     = hInstance;
     wndclass.lpfnWndProc   = RulersWndProc;
     wndclass.hCursor       = LoadCursor (hInstance, "hand");
     wndclass.hIcon         = LoadIcon (hInstance, "snapshot");
     wndclass.lpszMenuName  = NULL;
     wndclass.hbrBackground = COLOR_WINDOW+1;
     wndclass.style         = CS_HREDRAW | CS_VREDRAW;
     wndclass.cbClsExtra    = 0;
     wndclass.cbWndExtra    = 0;

     RegisterClass( &wndclass);
     }

hwnd = CreateWindow("Rulers:MAIN",        /* Class name.  */
                    "Rulers",             /* Title.       */
                    WS_OVERLAPPEDWINDOW,  /* Style bits.  */
                    CW_USEDEFAULT,        /* x - default. */
                    0,                    /* y - default. */
                    CW_USEDEFAULT,        /* cx - default. */
                    0,                    /* cy - default. */
                    NULL,                 /* No parent.   */
                    NULL,                 /* Class menu.  */
                    hInstance,            /* Creator.     */
                    NULL);                /* Params.      */

ShowWindow (hwnd, cmdShow);

while (GetMessage(&msg, 0, 0, 0))
```

```
            {
            TranslateMessage(&msg);          /*  Keyboard input.     */
            DispatchMessage(&msg);
            }
        return 0;
        }


/*-------------------------------------------------------------------*\
 |                Window Procedure:  RulersWndProc.                | 
\*-------------------------------------------------------------------*/
long FAR PASCAL RulersWndProc (HWND hwnd,    WORD wMsg,
                                  WORD wParam, LONG lParam)
    {
    static char achTitle[80];
    static int  fCapture = FALSE;

    switch (wMsg)
        {
        case WM_DESTROY:
            PostQuitMessage(0);
            break;

        case WM_MOUSEMOVE:
            if (!fCapture)
                break;
            /*  Fall through to WM_LBUTTONDOWN.                    */

        case WM_LBUTTONDOWN:
            {
            char ach[80];
            HDC hdc;
            POINT pt1, pt2;

            /*  Get current location in device and logical        */
            /*  coordinates.                                       */
            pt1 = pt2 = MAKEPOINT (lParam);
            hdc = GetDC (hwnd);
            RulersInstallCoords (hdc, hwnd);
            DPtoLP (hdc, &pt2, 1);
            ReleaseDC (hwnd, hdc);
```

```
            /*  Do button down specific init.                */
            if (wMsg == WM_LBUTTONDOWN)
                {
                GetWindowText (hwnd, achTitle, 80);
                SetCapture (hwnd);
                fCapture = TRUE;
                }

            /*  Display location in window title bar.         */
            wsprintf (ach, "Device = (%d,%d), Logical = (%d,%d)",
                      pt1.x, pt1.y, pt2.x, pt2.y);
            SetWindowText (hwnd, ach);

            }
            break;

        case WM_LBUTTONUP:
            if (fCapture)
                {
                ReleaseCapture();
                SetWindowText (hwnd, achTitle);
                fCapture = FALSE;
                }
            break;

        case WM_PAINT:
            {
            PAINTSTRUCT ps;

            BeginPaint (hwnd, &ps);
            RulersInstallCoords (ps.hdc, hwnd);

            /*  Draw horizontal ruler.                        */
            RulersDrawHorzRuler(ps.hdc);

            /*  Draw vertical ruler.                          */
            RulersDrawVertRuler(ps.hdc);

            EndPaint (hwnd, &ps);
            }
            break;
```

```
        default:
            return(DefWindowProc(hwnd,wMsg,wParam,lParam));
            break;
        }
    return 0L;
    }




/*----------------------------------------------------------------*\
 |  RulersInstallCoords:  Install coordinate transformations.  |
\*----------------------------------------------------------------*/
void NEAR PASCAL RulersInstallCoords (HDC hdc, HWND hwnd)
    {
    RECT r;

    SetMapMode (hdc, MM_LOENGLISH);

    /*  Move pixel origin to bottom of window.                    */
    GetClientRect (hwnd, &r);
    SetViewportOrg (hdc, 0, r.bottom);

    /*  Move origin 1/2 inch up & 1/2 inch right.                 */
    SetWindowOrg (hdc, -50, -50);
    }




/*----------------------------------------------------------------*\
 |           RulersDrawVertRuler: Draw vertical ruler.         |
\*----------------------------------------------------------------*/
void NEAR PASCAL RulersDrawVertRuler(HDC hdc)
    {
    char ach[5];
    int i;
    int x, y;

    /*  Draw main axis of ruler.                                  */
    MoveTo (hdc, 0, 0);
    LineTo (hdc, 0, 500);
```

```
    /*  Draw tick marks for ruler.                               */
    for (i=0;i<=5000 ; i+=125)
        {
        /*  Width of regular ticks.                              */
        x = -SMALLTICK;

        /*  Width of half-inch ticks.                            */
        if (i%500 == 0) x = -MEDIUMTICK;

        /*  Width of whole-inch ticks.                           */
        if (i%1000 == 0) x = -LARGETICK;

        y = (i+5)/10;
        MoveTo (hdc, x, y);
        LineTo (hdc, 0, y);
        }

    /*  Draw labels for inches.                                  */
    SetTextAlign (hdc, TA_BOTTOM | TA_RIGHT);
    SetBkMode (hdc, TRANSPARENT);
    for (y=0;y<=500;y+=100)
        {
        wsprintf (ach, "%d", y/100);
        TextOut (hdc, -(2*SMALLTICK), y, ach, lstrlen(ach));
        }
    }

/*-----------------------------------------------------------------*\
|          RulersDrawHorzRuler: Draw horizontal ruler.            |
\*-----------------------------------------------------------------*/
void NEAR PASCAL RulersDrawHorzRuler(HDC hdc)
    {
    char ach[5];
    int i;
    int x, y;

    /*  Draw main axis of ruler.                                 */
    MoveTo (hdc, 0, 0);
    LineTo (hdc, 800, 0);
```

```
/*   Draw tick marks for ruler.                             */
for (i=0;i<=8000 ; i+=125)
    {
    x = (i+5)/10;
    /*   Height of regular ticks.                           */
    y = -SMALLTICK;

    /*   Width of half-inch ticks.                          */
    if (i%500 == 0) y = -MEDIUMTICK;

    /*   Width of whole-inch ticks.                         */
    if (i%1000 == 0) y = -LARGETICK;

    MoveTo (hdc, x, y);
    LineTo (hdc, x, 0);
    }

/*   Draw labels for inches.                                */
SetTextAlign (hdc, TA_TOP | TA_LEFT);
SetBkMode (hdc, TRANSPARENT);
for (x=0;x<=800;x+=100)
    {
    wsprintf (ach, "%d", x/100);
    TextOut (hdc,
            x+SMALLTICK,
            -SMALLTICK,
            ach,
            lstrlen(ach));
    }
}
```

RULERS.RC

```
snapshot icon Rulers.ico

hand   cursor Rulers.cur
```

RULERS.DEF

```
NAME      Rulers

EXETYPE WINDOWS

DESCRIPTION 'Ruler Demo Program'

CODE      MOVEABLE DISCARDABLE
DATA      MOVEABLE MULTIPLE

HEAPSIZE     512
STACKSIZE    5000

EXPORTS
    RulersWndProc
```

Perhaps the first thing worth mentioning in RULERS is a built-in debugging feature that should help you when working with any mapping mode or doing any coordinate transformation. We are referring to a feature of RULERS that echoes the location of the mouse in the title bar whenever the left button is clicked. Coordinates are provided in both device as well as in logical coordinates. Figure 20.6 shows an example of this feature in action.

This debugging aid helps determine the exact conversion that is taking place. It is particularly useful when you first begin working with mapping modes, since it is easy to request a coordinate conversion that sends your drawing hundreds of miles away from your drawing surface, or shrinks your drawing until it is only one-quarter of a pixel wide.

When a window procedure receives a mouse message, the reported location is always in client area coordinates. You may recall that these are pixel units whose origin is at the upper-left corner of the window's client area. To convert from client area coordinates to logical coordinates, you call **DPtoLP**. This GDI routine converts one or more points from device to logical units, and is defined:

Figure 20.6 *RULERS echoing the mouse location*

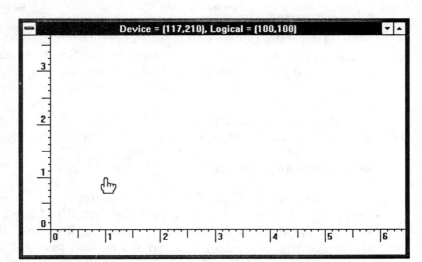

```
BOOL DPtoLP (hDC, lpPoints, nCount)
```

- hDC is a handle to a DC whose drawing attributes have been modified to reflect the desired coordinate conversion.
- lpPoints is a long pointer to an array of type POINT.
- nCount is an integer value for the number of points to be converted.

In response to either a WM_MOUSEMOVE or a WM_LBUTTONDOWN message, RULERS retrieves the location of the mouse from the lParam parameter and converts the pair of (x,y) coordinates to logical coordinates with the following code:

```
/*  Get current location in device and logical    */
/*  coordinates.                                   */
pt1 = pt2 = MAKEPOINT (lParam);
hdc = GetDC (hwnd);
RulersInstallCoords (hdc, hwnd);
DPtoLP (hdc, &pt2, 1);
ReleaseDC (hwnd, hdc);
```

The routine **RulersInstallCoords** is one of RULERS routines that sets up the necessary coordinate transformations. Our program also calls this routine in response to the WM_PAINT message, so that our painting and our mouse-location echoing both use the same conversion. We'll look at this routine in a moment.

Displaying the device and logical coordinate values in the title bar of the window involves a call to **SetWindowText**. But first, another Windows library routine, **wsprintf**, formats the values into a character string:

```
/*  Display location in window title bar.          */
wsprintf (ach, "Device = (%d,%d), Logical = (%d,%d)",
          pt1.x, pt1.y, pt2.x, pt2.y);
SetWindowText (hwnd, ach);
```

RULERS uses the MM_ENGLISH mapping mode. Requesting this mapping mode is as easy as calling the **SetMapMode** routine. This sets up the desired *scaling* so that one unit equals .01 inch. But that's not the only coordinate tranformation that RULERS uses. As shown in the code below, it also calls the **SetViewportOrg** and **SetWindowOrg** routines to install two translations to put the origin at the exact location we wish to use. Here is the RulersInstallCoords routine, which sets up the coordinate transformation that RULERS uses:

```
void NEAR PASCAL RulersInstallCoords (HDC hdc, HWND hwnd)
   {
   RECT r;

   SetMapMode (hdc, MM_LOENGLISH);

   /*  Move pixel origin to bottom of window.          */
   GetClientRect (hwnd, &r);
   SetViewportOrg (hdc, 0, r.bottom);

   /*  Move origin 1/2 inch up & 1/2 inch right.          */
   SetWindowOrg (hdc, -50, -50);
   }
```

Both **SetViewportOrg** and **SetWindowOrg** perform translations. As we mentioned earlier, translations always involve addition or subtraction. When translating between device and logical coordinates, the viewport coordinate refers to the pixel units that are added or subtracted. The window coordinate refers to the logical units (in this case, 1/100th of an inch) that are added or subtracted.

However the numbers are combined, one thing remains constant: The device and logical coordinate systems always place their origin at the same location, and all scaling radiates out from the origin.

All the fully constrained mapping modes let you draw with a pre-defined scaling factor to represent real world measurements. There are times, however, when you don't want a fixed scaling factor. For example, you may wish to set your own arbitrary scaling factor to make a graph fill a window. Or, you may wish to use a coordinate transformation to simplify the drawing of text. For each of these applications, the fully unconstrained mapping mode, which we're going to disucss next, will provide the capabilites that you need.

Fully Unconstrained Mapping Mode

In contrast to the fully constrained mapping modes, which provide a set of fixed factors for scaling, the fully unconstrained mapping mode, MM_ANISOTROPIC, lets you define any arbitrary scaling that suits you. This mapping mode lets you set scaling factors that eliminate all restrictions to allow X and Y units to be scaled independently.

Defining your own set of scaling factors requires you to call two routines: SetViewportExt and SetWindowExt. SetViewportExt, which defines the pixels to be used in a ratio for scaling, is defined:

```
DWORD SetViewportExt (hDC, X, Y)
```

- hDC is a handle to a DC.
- X defines one-half of a ratio for scaling in the X direction. The other half of the ratio is defined by the **SetWindowExt** routine.
- Y defines one-half of a ratio for scaling in the Y direction. The other half of the ratio is defined by the **SetWindowExt** routine.

SetWindowExt, which defines the "real-world" units for a scaling ratio, is defined similarly:

```
DWORD SetWindowExt (hDC, X, Y)
```

- hDC is a handle to a DC.
- X defines one-half of a ratio for scaling in the X direction. The other half of the ratio is defined by the **SetViewportExt** routine.
- Y defines one-half of a ratio for scaling in the Y direction. The other half of the ratio is defined by the **SetViewportExt** routine.

The key to understanding the scaling is to understand that each of these routines provides one-half of the needed elements that define a ratio. Of course, to use this mapping mode, we must first call SetMapMode:

```
SetMapMode (hdc, MM_ANISOTROPIC);
SetWindowOrg (hdc, 2, 2);
SetViewportOrg (hdc, 1, 1);
```

The scaling set up by this code converts two logical units to one device unit. With that scaling in place, the following code draws a rectangle with fifty pixels on each side:

```
MoveTo (hdc, 0, 0);
LineTo (hdc, 0, 100);
LineTo (hdc, 100, 100);
LineTo (hdc, 100, 0);
LineTo (hdc, 0, 0);
```

Perhaps the best way to understand the Anisotropic mapping mode is in terms of a sample program. Let's take a look at POP-CHART, which draws a graph using this mapping mode.

A Sample Program: POPCHART

Figure 20.7 shows three instances of POPCHART. This program draws a graph of the U.S. population for the years 1940 thru 1990. Notice how the client area of each instance is completely filled by the chart. One feature of the Anisotropic mapping mode is that it stretches or shrinks graphic objects to fill the available device drawing area. In a graph like this, we are less concerned about the proportions of the drawing than we are about filling the available drawing space.

Here is the code to POPCHART:

POPCHART.MAK

```
PopChart.res: PopChart.rc PopChart.cur PopChart.ico
    rc -r PopChart.rc
```

```
PopChart.obj: PopChart.c
    cl -AM -c -d -Gsw -Od -W2 -Zpi PopChart.c

PopChart.exe: PopChart.obj PopChart.def
    link PopChart,/align:16,/map, mlibcew libw/NOD/NOE/CO,\
        PopChart.def
    rc PopChart.res

PopChart.exe: PopChart.res
    rc PopChart.res
```

Figure 20.7 *ANISOTROPIC mapping mode lets a graph fill the available area.*

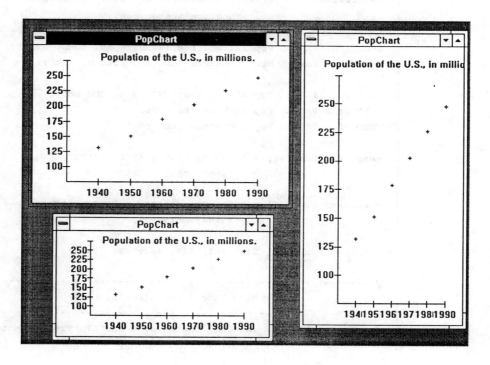

POPCHART.C

```
/*-----------------------------------------------------------*\
|  POPCHART.C  -  Population Chart showing use of the        |
|                 Anisotropic mapping mode.                  |
\*-----------------------------------------------------------*/
#include <Windows.H>
#define NUM_X_VALUES 6
#define X_START 100
#define X_STEP  100
#define X_ORIGIN  0

#define NUM_Y_VALUES 7
#define Y_START 100
#define Y_STEP    25
#define Y_ORIGIN 75

#define FLIP_Y_AXIS -1

/*-----------------------------------------------------------*\
|                   Function Prototypes.                     |
\*-----------------------------------------------------------*/
long FAR  PASCAL PopChartWndProc (HWND, WORD, WORD, LONG);
VOID NEAR PASCAL MrkDrawMarker (HDC hdc, int x, int y);

VOID NEAR PASCAL PopInitMapping(HWND hwnd, HDC hdc);
VOID NEAR PASCAL PopDrawAxis (HDC hdc);
VOID NEAR PASCAL PopDrawLabels (HDC hdc);

char *acY_Labels[] = { "100", "125", "150", "175",
                       "200", "225", "250"};

char *acX_Labels[] = { "1940", "1950", "1960", "1970",
                       "1980", "1990"};

int  popData[] = { 132, 151, 179, 203, 226, 248 };

/*-----------------------------------------------------------*\
|                   Main Function:  WinMain.                 |
\*-----------------------------------------------------------*/
int PASCAL WinMain (HANDLE hInstance,    HANDLE hPrevInstance,
```

```
                  LPSTR  lpszCmdLine, int    cmdShow)
{
HWND      hwnd;
MSG       msg;
WNDCLASS  wndclass;

if (!hPrevInstance)
     {
     wndclass.lpszClassName = "PopChart:MAIN";
     wndclass.hInstance     = hInstance;
     wndclass.lpfnWndProc   = PopChartWndProc;
     wndclass.hCursor       = LoadCursor (hInstance, "hand");
     wndclass.hIcon         = LoadIcon (hInstance,"snapshot");
     wndclass.lpszMenuName  = NULL;
     wndclass.hbrBackground = COLOR_WINDOW+1;
     wndclass.style         = CS_HREDRAW | CS_VREDRAW;
     wndclass.cbClsExtra    = 0;
     wndclass.cbWndExtra    = 0;

     RegisterClass( &wndclass);
     }

hwnd = CreateWindow("PopChart:MAIN",     /* Class name.  */
                    "PopChart",          /* Title.       */
                    WS_OVERLAPPEDWINDOW, /* Style bits.  */
                    CW_USEDEFAULT,       /* x - default. */
                    0,                   /* y - default. */
                    CW_USEDEFAULT,       /* cx - default. */
                    0,                   /* cy - default. */
                    NULL,                /* No parent.   */
                    NULL,                /* Class menu.  */
                    hInstance,           /* Creator      */
                    NULL);               /* Params.      */

ShowWindow (hwnd, cmdShow);

while (GetMessage(&msg, 0, 0, 0))
     {
     TranslateMessage(&msg);          /* Keyboard input.    */
     DispatchMessage(&msg);
     }
```

```
        return 0;
    }

/*-------------------------------------------------------------*\
  |            Window Procedure:  PopChartWndProc.              |
\*-------------------------------------------------------------*/
long FAR PASCAL PopChartWndProc (HWND hwnd,    WORD wMsg,
                                 WORD wParam, LONG lParam)
    {
    switch (wMsg)
        {
        case WM_DESTROY:
            PostQuitMessage(0);
            break;

        case WM_PAINT:
            {
            int i;
            PAINTSTRUCT ps;

            BeginPaint (hwnd, &ps);
            PopInitMapping(hwnd, ps.hdc);
            PopDrawAxis (ps.hdc);
            PopDrawLabels (ps.hdc);

            /*  Loop through data drawing markers.              */
            for (i=0; i<NUM_X_VALUES; i++)
                MrkDrawMarker (ps.hdc, (i+1)*100, popData[i]);

            EndPaint (hwnd, &ps);
            }
            break;

        default:
            return(DefWindowProc(hwnd,wMsg,wParam,lParam));
            break;
        }
    return 0L;
    }
```

```
/*-----------------------------------------------------------*\
|                        PopInitMapping                       |
\*-----------------------------------------------------------*/
VOID NEAR PASCAL PopInitMapping(HWND hwnd, HDC hdc)
    {
    RECT   r;
    DWORD dwLen;
    int    xAdjust;
    int    yAdjust;

    dwLen = GetTextExtent (hdc, acY_Labels[0],
                               lstrlen(acY_Labels[0]));
    yAdjust = HIWORD(dwLen) * 2;
    xAdjust = LOWORD(dwLen) * 2;

    SetMapMode (hdc, MM_ANISOTROPIC);

    SetWindowExt (hdc, 700, FLIP_Y_AXIS * 225);

    GetClientRect (hwnd, &r);
    r.bottom = r.bottom - yAdjust;
    r.right  = r.right - xAdjust;
    SetViewportExt (hdc, r.right, r.bottom);

    SetViewportOrg (hdc, xAdjust, r.bottom);
    SetWindowOrg (hdc, 0, 75);
    }




/*-----------------------------------------------------------*\
|                         PopDrawAxis                         |
\*-----------------------------------------------------------*/
VOID NEAR PASCAL PopDrawAxis (HDC hdc)
    {
    DWORD dw;
    int    iIndex;
    int    xHalf;
    int    yThird;

    /* Draw axis.  */
    MoveTo (hdc, 0, 275);
```

```
        LineTo (hdc, 0, 75);
        LineTo (hdc, 600, 75);

        /* Draw relative to current font.  */
        dw = GetTextExtent (hdc, "X", 1);
        xHalf = LOWORD (dw) /2;
        yThird = HIWORD (dw) /3;

        /* Draw Y Axis Tick Marks.  */
        for (iIndex = Y_START;
             iIndex < Y_START + ((NUM_Y_VALUES+1) * Y_STEP);
             iIndex+= Y_STEP)
             {
             MoveTo (hdc, X_ORIGIN - xHalf, iIndex);
             LineTo (hdc, X_ORIGIN + xHalf, iIndex);
             }

        /* Draw X Axis Tick Marks.  */
        for (iIndex = X_START;
             iIndex < X_START + NUM_X_VALUES * X_STEP;
             iIndex+= X_STEP)
             {
             MoveTo (hdc, iIndex, Y_ORIGIN - yThird);
             LineTo (hdc, iIndex, Y_ORIGIN + yThird) ;
             }
        }


/*-------------------------------------------------------------*\
|                      PopDrawLabels                            |
\*-------------------------------------------------------------*/
VOID NEAR PASCAL PopDrawLabels (HDC hdc)
    {
    DWORD dw;
    int    iIndex;
    int    iCnt;
    int    xHalf;
    int    yHalf;

    /* Graph Title.  */
    SetTextAlign (hdc, TA_TOP | TA_CENTER);
```

```
    TextOut (hdc, 350, 290, "Population of the U.S., in
millions.",
                    lstrlen ("Population of the U.S., in
millions."));

    /* Draw relative to current font.  */
    dw = GetTextExtent (hdc, "X", 1);
    xHalf = LOWORD (dw) /2;
    yHalf = HIWORD (dw) /2;

    /* Y Axis Labels.  */
    SetTextAlign (hdc, TA_TOP | TA_RIGHT);
    for (iIndex = Y_START, iCnt=0;
        iIndex < Y_START + (NUM_Y_VALUES * Y_STEP);
        iIndex+= Y_STEP, iCnt++)
      {
      TextOut (hdc,
              X_ORIGIN - xHalf,
              iIndex + yHalf,
              acY_Labels[iCnt],
              lstrlen (acY_Labels[iCnt]));
      }

    /* X Axis Labels.  */
    SetTextAlign (hdc, TA_TOP | TA_CENTER);
    for (iIndex = X_START, iCnt = 0;
        iIndex < X_START + NUM_X_VALUES * X_STEP;
        iIndex+= X_STEP, iCnt++)
      {
      TextOut (hdc,
              iIndex,
              Y_ORIGIN - yHalf,
              acX_Labels[iCnt],
              lstrlen (acX_Labels[iCnt]));
      }
    }


/*-------------------------------------------------------------*\
|                        MrkDrawMarker                          |
\*-------------------------------------------------------------*/
```

```
#define MARKERSIZE 2
VOID NEAR PASCAL MrkDrawMarker (HDC hdc, int x, int y)
    {
    int i;
    int iDC;
    POINT pt;

    /* Convert point to device coordinates.  */
    pt.x = x; pt.y = y;
    LPtoDP (hdc, &pt, 1);
    x = pt.x; y = pt.y;

    iDC = SaveDC (hdc);

    /* Restore Device Coordinate Mapping.  */
    SetMapMode (hdc, MM_TEXT);
    SetViewportExt (hdc, 1, 1);
    SetWindowExt (hdc, 1, 1);
    SetViewportOrg (hdc, 0, 0);
    SetWindowOrg (hdc, 0, 0);

    SetROP2 (hdc, R2_NOT);
    SetPixel (hdc, x, y, RGB (0, 0, 0));

    for (i=1;i<=MARKERSIZE; i++)
        {
        SetPixel (hdc, x+i, y, RGB (0, 0, 0));
        SetPixel (hdc, x-i, y, RGB (0, 0, 0));
        SetPixel (hdc, x, y+i, RGB (0, 0, 0));
        SetPixel (hdc, x, y-i, RGB (0, 0, 0));
        }

    RestoreDC (hdc, iDC);
    }
```

POPCHART.RC

```
snapshot icon PopChart.ico

hand  cursor PopChart.cur
```

POPCHART.DEF

```
NAME      PopChart

EXETYPE WINDOWS

DESCRIPTION 'Population Chart - Anisotropic Demo'

CODE      MOVEABLE DISCARDABLE
DATA      MOVEABLE MULTIPLE

HEAPSIZE      512
STACKSIZE    5000

EXPORTS
    PopChartWndProc
```

The crux of this program lies in the way the mapping mode is set, which is the job of the PopInitMapping routine. This routine starts off by determining the width and height of one of the text labels by calling **GetTextExtent**. The width and height are in pixels, which we're going to use to adjust the mapping so there is room for the text labels on the left side and the bottom of the drawing:

```
dwLen = GetTextExtent (hdc, acY_Labels[0],
                       lstrlen(acY_Labels[0]));
yAdjust = HIWORD(dwLen) * 2;
xAdjust = LOWORD(dwLen) * 2;
```

After POPCHART retrieves the size information, it sets up the mapping mode by calling **SegMapMode**:

```
SetMapMode (hdc, MM_ANISOTROPIC);
```

Anisotropic scaling has two halves: real-world or "logical" units (referred to as the "window") and pixel units (referred to as the "viewport"). POPCHART starts by setting the range of the logical units, which is the range of the values that POPCHART uses in its calls to GDI:

```
SetWindowExt (hdc, 700, FLIP_Y_AXIS * 225);
```

In the X direction, the selection of the value 700 is purely arbitrary. It allows us to plot 6 years' worth of points, spaced evenly between areas that are 100 logical units wide. The same results would have appeared had we used the value 7, which would create evenly spaced areas that were each one logical unit wide.

The value of FLIP_Y_AXIS is -1. As the name suggests, this causes the Y axis to flip. This is necessary because, by default, the direction of the Y axis in the Anisotropic mapping mode is the same as that of the MM_TEXT mapping mode: Y increases as we move down.

In the Y direction, we select 225 since this is the range of population values that we wish to graph (from 75 million to 300 million). Even though the scale on the graph only reads from 100 to 250, the extra space is used for aesthetics and to allow enough room on the top of the graph to draw the title.

Setting the other half of the Anisotropic scaling ratio, the number of pixels against which to scale, involves calling **SetViewportExt**. The X and Y extents that are passed to this routine are essentially the width and height of the client area minus an adjustment for the text labels that we plan to display:

```
GetClientRect (hwnd, &r);
r.bottom = r.bottom - yAdjust;
r.right  = r.right - xAdjust;
SetViewportExt (hdc, r.right, r.bottom);
```

The final step taken to set up the coordinate mapping involves moving the origin. As you saw earlier, this can be either a one- or two-step process, since we can change the location of the origin both in terms of pixel coordinates and in terms of logical coordinates. POPCHART does both. To move the origin to a specific location in its window's client area, POPCHART calls:

```
SetViewportOrg (hdc, xAdjust, r.bottom);
```

The call to **SetViewportOrg** moves the origin to a spot where the two axes meet on our chart. Next, POPCHART calls **SetWindowOrg** to move the origin below the bottom of the client area:

```
SetWindowOrg (hdc, 0, 75);
```

In the X direction, the value 0 is chosen, and then we advance 100 per year. Of course, we could have set this to 1930 and used the value of the year as a graphic point. The value of 75 for the Y value sets 75 million as the lowest population figure that we are interested in.

Perhaps the most challenging aspect of the Anisotropic mapping mode is that it is so flexible. In fact, you could even say that it is *too* flexible. For any particular application, there are undoubtedly several different approaches to take in setting up a logical coordinate system. Perhaps the key lies in keeping things simple and creating logical coordinate systems that allow you to use your own application's convenient coordinates.

Before we leave the Anisotropic mapping mode, it's worth mentioning a way that this mapping mode can simplify the handling of text output. It underscores the usefulness of this mapping mode, which allows the creation of any arbitrary scaling.

Text and the Anisotropic Mapping Mode

It would be easy to dismiss mapping modes as something that is of interest only for graphic images. But then, as we mentioned earlier, GDI treats text as graphic information. Therefore, there must be a way to take advantage of the mapping modes to make text easier to work with. There are many possibilites, but here is one that we think has widespread uses.

Since the anisotropic mapping mode allows you to create arbitrary scaling, it is possible to build a set of coordinates that revolve around the metrics of text. For example, here is a code fragment that sets the pixel coordinates for the Y axis so that one logical unit is equal to the height of one text line:

```
case WM_PAINT:
    {
    int cyLineHeight;
    PAINTSTRUCT ps;
    TEXTMETRIC tm;

    BeginPaint (hwnd, &ps);
    SetMapMode (ps.hdc, MM_ANISOTROPIC);

    GetTextMetrics (ps.hdc, &tm);
    cyLineHeight = tm.tmHeight + tm.tmExternalLeading;
    SetViewportExt (ps.hdc, 1, cyLineHeight);

    TextOut (ps.hdc, 10, 0, "Line 0", 6);
```

```
TextOut (ps.hdc, 10, 1, "Line 1", 6);
TextOut (ps.hdc, 10, 2, "Line 2", 6);
TextOut (ps.hdc, 10, 3, "Line 3", 6);
TextOut (ps.hdc, 10, 4, "Line 4", 6);
TextOut (ps.hdc, 10, 5, "Line 5", 6);
TextOut (ps.hdc, 10, 6, "Line 6", 6);
TextOut (ps.hdc, 10, 7, "Line 7", 6);
TextOut (ps.hdc, 10, 8, "Line 8", 6);

EndPaint (hwnd, &ps);
}
break;
```

Each unit in the Y direction is equal to the height of one line. In effect, each logical unit in the Y direction is equal to the line number. The output produced by this code fragment is shown in Figure 20.8.

When working with a fixed pitch font, you can go one step further and use the Anisotropic mapping mode to allow you to output text using coordinates that are simply character row and column values. Here is the code which does that:

```
case WM_PAINT:
    {
    int cyLineHeight;
    int cxCharWidth;
    PAINTSTRUCT ps;
    TEXTMETRIC tm;

    BeginPaint (hwnd, &ps);
    SetMapMode (ps.hdc, MM_ANISOTROPIC);

    GetTextMetrics (ps.hdc, &tm);
    cyLineHeight = tm.tmHeight + tm.tmExternalLeading;
    cxCharWidth  = tm.tmAveCharWidth;
    SetViewportExt (ps.hdc, cxCharWidth, cyLineHeight);
    .
    .
```

If you have worked with character-oriented windows, and if you don't mind limiting yourself to working with a fixed-pitch font, we think you'll find this coordinate mapping to be very useful.

Figure 20.8 *Lines of text drawn with the Anisotropic Mapping Mode*

```
┌──────────────────────────────────────────┐
│ ▬    Text & The Anistropic Mapping Mode  ▼ ▲│
│ Line 0                                      │
│ Line 1                                      │
│ Line 2                                      │
│ Line 3                                      │
│ Line 4                                      │
│ Line 5                                      │
│ Line 6                                      │
│ Line 7                                      │
│ Line 8                                      │
│                                             │
│                                             │
│                                             │
└──────────────────────────────────────────┘
```

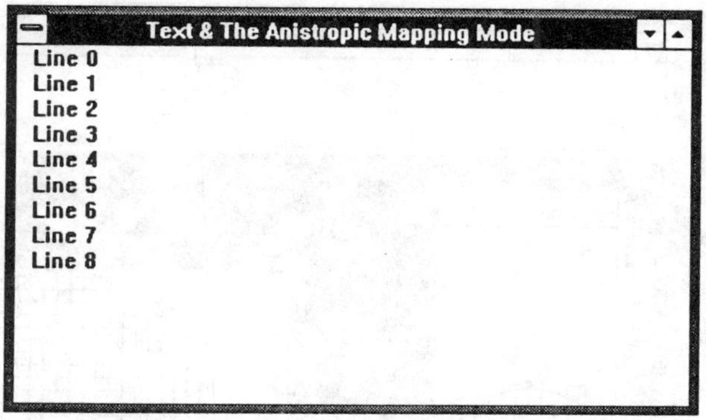

We have one more mapping mode yet to cover. This mapping mode combines some of the features of the fully constrained mapping modes and the fully unconstrained mapping modes. The next topic that we're going to cover is that of the partially constrained mapping mode, the Isotropic Mapping Mode.

Partially Constrained Mapping Mode

The Isotropic Mapping Mode is referred to as "partially constrained" because it enforces uniform scaling—X and Y units must be equal—which makes it similar to the fully constrained mapping modes. However, the choice of units is up to you. In this respect, the Isotropic Mapping Mode is like the fully *unconstrained* mapping mode. Let's look at what this mapping mode involves.

Since the Isotropic mapping mode lets you decide on a scaling factor, you call the same two routines that are used to set up scaling in the Anisotropic Mapping Mode: **SetViewportExt** and **SetWindowExt**. However, when a scaling factor has been selected, GDI modifies the viewport extent to enforce the uniform scaling of this mapping mode. The viewport extent will be modified in one of two ways: either the X value will be reduced or the Y value will be reduced.

Recall that the Viewport refers to the number of pixels on which to draw. Thus, this mapping mode guarantees that the drawing you request will fit inside the pixels that you wish it to. In addition, since this mapping mode maintains uniform scaling, it is often referred to as *shape-preserving*. In other words, perfectly round figures will

Figure 20.9   *Isotropic mode is shape retaining*

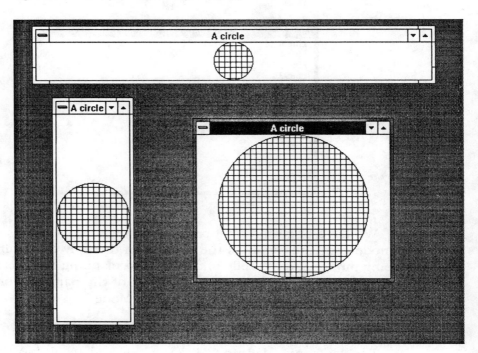

always appear perfectly round. If you wish to avoid the stretching and shrinking of the Anisotropic mapping mode but still wish to select your own coordinates, then the Isotropic mapping mode is for you.

Figure 20.9 shows how the isotropic mapping mode retains the shape of figures—in this case, a circle. Notice that when the client area is irregularly shaped, quite a bit of it is wasted. At the same time, however, we are able to see our circle completely, regardless of the shape or size of the client area. Since the picture adjusts itself to the size of the client area, the user can adjust the scaling as desired by simply changing the size of the window. Here is the code for the WM_PAINT message of the program that created the circle:

```
case WM_PAINT:
    {
    HANDLE      hbrHatch;
```

```
        PAINTSTRUCT ps;
        RECT r;

        BeginPaint (hwnd, &ps);

        /*  Install isotropic mapping mode.              */
        SetMapMode (ps.hdc, MM_ISOTROPIC);

        /*  Set up logical coordinates for 200 x 200.    */
        SetWindowExt (ps.hdc, 200, 200);

        /*  Set viewport to enclose entire client area.  */
        GetClientRect (hwnd, &r);
        SetViewportExt (ps.hdc, r.right, r.bottom);

        /*  Move origin into center of client area.      */
        SetViewportOrg (ps.hdc, r.right/2, r.bottom/2);

        /*  Create a hatch brush for drawing.            */
        hbrHatch = CreateHatchBrush (HS_CROSS, RGB (0,0,0));
        SelectObject (ps.hdc, hbrHatch);

        /*  Draw a circle.                               */
        Ellipse (ps.hdc, -100, -100, 100, 100);
        EndPaint (hwnd, &ps);

        /*  Destroy hatch brush.                         */
        DeleteObject (hbrHatch);
        }
        break;
```

As this code fragment illustrates, you should always set the window extent first before setting the viewport extent. The reason is that, in the isotropic mapping mode, GDI modifies the viewport extent to create the desired fit whenever either of the extents is changed. If you change the viewport extent *first*, then GDI may modify it to suit whatever window extent is present, thus changing the desired scaling that you are actually requesting.

Our discussion of GDI's mapping modes and coordinate transformations has gotten us ready to explore another topic: **scrolling**. Programs generally make scrolling available whenever a data object is too large to fit inside a window. The presence of scroll bars suggests to the user that this may be the case. However, scroll bars by themselves do not make scrolling happen. Instead, a program must be modified to respond to messages sent by the scroll bar. In addition, the WM_PAINT processing performed by a program must be synchronized with scrolling. Let's take a look at what this involves.

Scrolling

From the point of view of the user, scrolling solves the problem that arises when an object to be displayed extends beyond the window in which it is displayed. Scrolling can be used for wading through a very large spreadsheet or word processing document, for browsing database records, or for any operation in which only part of a data collection is visible.

Scrolling is controlled by **scroll bars**. There are two types of scroll bars: horizontal and vertical. A window can have one or both types to control scrolling. David Durant, a long-time Windows programming guru, describes a scroll bar as a visual representation of three numbers: a minimum value, a maximum value, and a current value that must lie between the minimum and the maximum.

The minimum value is represented when the **scroll thumb** rests on the top of a vertical scroll bar (or to the left of a horizontal scroll bar). The maximum value is represented when the scroll thumb rests on the bottom of a vertical scroll bar (or on the right of a horizontal scroll bar). The current position is represented by the relative position of the scroll thumb between the two. On some systems, like the OS/2 Presentation Manager, a fourth number is represented by the relative size of the scroll thumb. This indicates the relative amount of the document that is, in fact, visible. This last feature is not part of Windows, however, which instead has a fixed-size scroll thumb.

To add a scroll bar to a window, you specify additional style bits in the call to **CreateWindow**: WS_VSCROLL for a vertical scroll bar, or WS_HSCROLL for a horizontal scroll bar. Once scroll bars have been added to a window, user actions on the scroll bar are translated into messages. Horizontal scroll bars send WM_HSCROLL messages, and vertical scroll bars send WM_VSCROLL messages. Each message is accompanied by a value in the wParam parameter indicating the portion of the scroll bar on which the user has clicked. The values

Figure 20.10   *The wParam values for scroll bar messages*

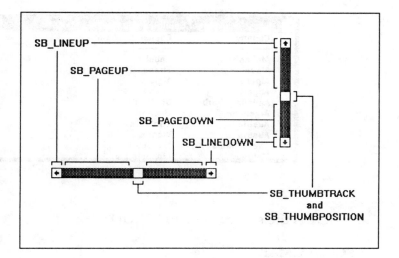

are shown in Figure 20.10 as the the symbolic constants defined in Windows.h.

When the user interacts with most parts of the scroll bar, a single message is of interest. However, when the user drags the scroll thumb directly, two types of messages are generated: one during the dragging (scroll message with wParam = SB_THUMBTRACK) and one when the dragging is completed (scroll message with wParam = SB_THUMBPOSITION). The simplest way to handle this is to ignore the messages sent during the dragging and respond only to the dragging-complete message. But programs can scroll during the dragging messages, to give the user immediate feedback about the effect of the scrolling operation.

A Sample Program: SCROLL

Figure 20.11 shows the output of our sample program, SCROLL. You may remember this program from Chapter 10, when we introduced the **TabbedTextOut** routine. SCROLL only uses a vertical scroll bar, but demonstrates the principles of scrolling that can be applied to horizontal scrolling. In addition to a scroll bar, which receives mouse input for scrolling, SCROLL also incorporates keyboard input in the scrolling process.

Figure 20.11   *The output produced by the SCROLL program.*

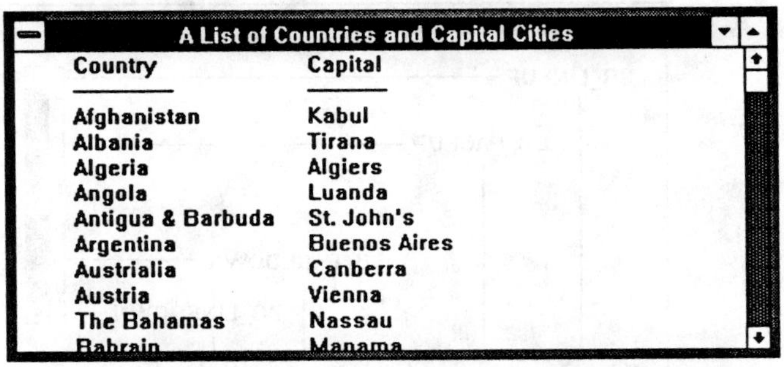

Here is the source code to SCROLL:

SCROLL.MAK

```
Scroll.res: Scroll.rc Scroll.cur Scroll.ico
    rc -r Scroll.rc

Scroll.obj: Scroll.c
    cl -AM -c -d -Gsw -Od -W2 -Zpi Scroll.c

Scroll.exe: Scroll.obj Scroll.def
    link Scroll,/align:16,/map, mlibcew libw/NOD/NOE/CO,\
        Scroll.def
    rc Scroll.res

Scroll.exe: Scroll.res
    rc Scroll.res
```

SCROLL.C

```
/*--------------------------------------------------------------*\
|    SCROLL.C  -  Sample scrolling program.                      |
\*--------------------------------------------------------------*/
#include <Windows.H>
```

```
/*------------------------------------------------------------*\
|                   Function Prototypes.                       |
\*------------------------------------------------------------*/
long FAR  PASCAL ScrollWndProc (HWND, WORD, WORD, LONG);


/*------------------------------------------------------------*\
|                   Main Function:  WinMain.                   |
\*------------------------------------------------------------*/
int PASCAL WinMain (HANDLE hInstance,   HANDLE hPrevInstance,
                    LPSTR  lpszCmdLine, int    cmdShow)
    {
    HWND     hwnd;
    MSG      msg;
    WNDCLASS wndclass;

    if (!hPrevInstance)
        {
        wndclass.lpszClassName = "Scroll:MAIN";
        wndclass.hInstance     = hInstance;
        wndclass.lpfnWndProc   = ScrollWndProc;
        wndclass.hCursor       = LoadCursor (hInstance, "hand");
        wndclass.hIcon         = LoadIcon (hInstance,"snapshot");
        wndclass.lpszMenuName  = NULL;
        wndclass.hbrBackground = COLOR_WINDOW+1;
        wndclass.style         = CS_HREDRAW | CS_VREDRAW;
        wndclass.cbClsExtra    = 0;
        wndclass.cbWndExtra    = 0;

        RegisterClass( &wndclass);
        }

    hwnd = CreateWindow("Scroll:MAIN",          /* Class name.  */
                                                /* Title.       */
                        "A List of Countries and Capital Cities",
                        WS_OVERLAPPEDWINDOW | /* Style bits.  */
                        WS_VSCROLL,
                        CW_USEDEFAULT,          /* x - default. */
                        0,                      /* y - default. */
                        CW_USEDEFAULT,          /* cx - default. */
                        0,                      /* cy - default. */
```

```
                              NULL,                /* No parent.   */
                              NULL,                /* Class menu.  */
                              hInstance,           /* Creator      */
                              NULL);               /* Params.      */


        ShowWindow (hwnd, cmdShow);

        while (GetMessage(&msg, 0, 0, 0))
            {
            TranslateMessage(&msg);        /*  Keyboard input.     */
            DispatchMessage(&msg);
            }
        return 0;
        }

/*-----------------------------------------------------------------*\
  |              Window Procedure:  TxtTabWndProc.
  |
\*-----------------------------------------------------------------*/
long FAR PASCAL ScrollWndProc (HWND hwnd,   WORD wMsg,
                                WORD wParam, LONG lParam)
        {
#define COUNT 19
        static char *apch[]= {"Country \tCapital",
                              "--------------- \t------------",
                              "Afghanistan \tKabul",
                              "Albania \tTirana",
                              "Algeria \tAlgiers",
                              "Angola \tLuanda",
                              "Antigua & Barbuda \tSt. John's",
                              "Argentina \tBuenos Aires",
                              "Austrialia \tCanberra",
                              "Austria \tVienna",
                              "The Bahamas \tNassau",
                              "Bahrain \tManama",
                              "Bangladesh \tDhaka",
                              "Barbados \tBridgetown",
                              "Belgium \tBrussels",
                              "Belize \tBelmopan",
                              "Benin \tPorto-Novo",
```

```
                                        "Bhutan \tThimphu",
                                        "Bolivia \tLa Paz"};

static int yScrollMin;
static int yScrollCurrent;
static int yScrollMax;

static int xLeftMargin;
static int xTab;
static int xTabOrigin;
static int cyLineHeight;
static int cLines;

switch (wMsg)
    {
    case WM_CREATE:
        {
        HDC hdc;
        TEXTMETRIC tm;

        /*  Init TabbedTextOut values.                        */
        hdc = GetDC (hwnd);
        GetTextMetrics (hdc, &tm);
        ReleaseDC (hwnd, hdc);
        xTab  = 20 * tm.tmAveCharWidth;
        xTabOrigin = 3 * tm.tmAveCharWidth;
        cyLineHeight = tm.tmHeight + tm.tmExternalLeading;
        xLeftMargin = tm.tmAveCharWidth * 2;

        /*  Init values needed for scrolling.                 */
        yScrollMin = 0;
        yScrollCurrent = 0;
        cLines = COUNT;
        SetScrollRange (hwnd, SB_VERT, 0, 0, FALSE);
        }
        break;

    case WM_DESTROY:
        PostQuitMessage(0);
        break;
```

```
            case WM_KEYDOWN:
                {
                WORD wScroll;
                LONG lPosition;

                wScroll = -1;
                lPosition = 0L;

                switch (wParam)
                    {
                    case VK_PRIOR:
                        wScroll = SB_PAGEUP;
                        break;
                    case VK_NEXT:
                        wScroll = SB_PAGEDOWN;
                        break;
                    case VK_UP:
                        wScroll = SB_LINEUP;
                        break;
                    case VK_DOWN:
                        wScroll = SB_LINEDOWN;
                        break;
                    case VK_HOME:
                        wScroll = SB_THUMBPOSITION;
                        lPosition = (LONG)yScrollMin;
                        break;
                    case VK_END:
                        wScroll = SB_THUMBPOSITION;
                        lPosition = (LONG)yScrollMax;
                        break;
                    }

                if (wScroll != -1)
                    SendMessage (hwnd, WM_VSCROLL, wScroll,
                                 lPosition);
                }
            break;

        case WM_PAINT:
            {
            int i;
```

```
        int yText;
        PAINTSTRUCT ps;

        BeginPaint (hwnd, &ps);

        /*  Init coordinate mapping so that 1 unit in     */
        /*  direction = 1 line.                           */
        SetMapMode (ps.hdc, MM_ANISOTROPIC);
        SetViewportExt (ps.hdc, 1, cyLineHeight);
        SetViewportOrg (ps.hdc, xLeftMargin,0);
        SetWindowOrg (ps.hdc, 0, yScrollCurrent);

        for (yText = 0; yText<COUNT; yText++)
            {
            TabbedTextOut (ps.hdc,
                          xTabOrigin,
                          yText,
                          apch[yText],
                          lstrlen(apch[yText]),
                          1,
                          &xTab,
                          xTabOrigin);
            }
        EndPaint (hwnd, &ps);
        }
        break;

    case WM_SIZE:
        {
        int cyClient;

        /*  Reset scroll bar range.                       */
        cyClient = HIWORD (lParam);
        yScrollMax = max(cLines-cyClient/cyLineHeight, 0);

        SetScrollRange (hwnd, SB_VERT,
                       yScrollMin, yScrollMax, FALSE);

        /*  Update current scroll bar position.           */
        yScrollCurrent = min (yScrollCurrent, yScrollMax);
```

```
                    /*  Update the scroll bar.                    */
                    SetScrollPos (hwnd, SB_VERT, yScrollCurrent, TRUE);
                    }
                    break;

        case WM_VSCROLL:
            {
            int yNewLine;
            int cyScroll;

            /* Determine the number of lines to scroll.           */
            switch (wParam)
                {
                case SB_PAGEDOWN:
                    yNewLine = yScrollCurrent + 4;
                    break;
                case SB_PAGEUP:
                    yNewLine = yScrollCurrent - 4;
                    break;
                case SB_LINEDOWN:
                    yNewLine = yScrollCurrent + 1;
                    break;
                case SB_LINEUP:
                    yNewLine = yScrollCurrent - 1;
                    break;
                case SB_THUMBPOSITION:
                    yNewLine = LOWORD(lParam);
                    break;
                default:
                    yNewLine = yScrollCurrent;
                }

            /*  Make sure we are still in range.                  */
            yNewLine = max (0, yNewLine);
            yNewLine = min (yScrollMax, yNewLine);
            if (yNewLine == yScrollCurrent)
                break;

            /*  Move the pixels.  A WM_PAINT message is also     */
            /*  generated to repair the 'uncovered' part of      */
            /*  the client area.                                 */
            cyScroll = (yScrollCurrent-yNewLine)*cyLineHeight;
            ScrollWindow (hwnd, 0, cyScroll, NULL, NULL);
```

```
            /*  Update the scroll bar.                    */
            yScrollCurrent = yNewLine;
            SetScrollPos (hwnd, SB_VERT, yScrollCurrent, TRUE);


            }
            break;

        default:
            return(DefWindowProc(hwnd,wMsg,wParam,lParam));
            break;
        }
    return 0L;
    }
```

SCROLL.RC

```
snapshot icon Scroll.ico

hand  cursor Scroll.cur
```

SCROLL.DEF

```
NAME      Scroll

EXETYPE WINDOWS

DESCRIPTION 'Sample scrolling program'

CODE      MOVEABLE DISCARDABLE
DATA      MOVEABLE MULTIPLE

HEAPSIZE      512
STACKSIZE   5000


EXPORTS
   ScrollWndProc
```

SCROLL defines three numbers to keep track of the three values used by the scroll bar:

```
static int yScrollMin;
static int yScrollCurrent;
static int yScrollMax;
```

In SCROLL, the scroll bar numbers represent line numbers for the text that is displayed. yScrollMin is the number of the lowest text line and is set to zero. yScrollCurrent stores the line number of the line to be displayed at the top of the window. And yScrollMax indicates the highest line number that can be displayed at the top of the window. This may or may not be equal to the number of lines (cLines), depending on the size of the client area. SCROLL calibrates its scroll bar using yScrollMin and yScrollMax by calling the **Set-ScrollRange** routine. **SetScrollRange** is defined:

```
void SetScrollRange(hWnd, nBar, nMinPos, nMaxPos, bRedraw)
```

- hWnd is a window handle of the window that contains the scroll bar.
- nBar is an integer that indicates the scroll bar of interest. It is either SB_CTL, SB_HORZ or SB_VERT.
- nMinPos is an integer value to be represented by the low end of the scroll bar.
- nMaxPos is an integer value to be represented by the high end of the scroll bar.
- bRedraw is a Boolean value that indicates whether the scroll bar should be redrawn to reflect the change.

SCROLL sets the range of its scroll bar with the following call:

```
SetScrollRange (hwnd, SB_VERT, yScrollMin, yScrollMax,
                FALSE);
```

The scroll range needs to be set twice: at window creation time in response to the WM_CREATE message and when the size of the window changes, which means in response to the WM_SIZE message. The range changes to reflect the number of lines that are not visible. When all text lines are visible, the scroll bar is removed. This happens whenever the minimum and maximum range values are set to zero. SCROLL is set up so that yScrollMin and yScrollMax are both set to zero whenever the client area is large enough to view the entire block of text, and so the removal of the scroll bar occurs automatically.

As the user interacts with the scroll bar, scroll messages are sent to SCROLL's window procedure. As these messages are received, SCROLL calculates the line to be placed at the top of the window. For the SB_LINEUP and SB_LINEDOWN messages, this means adding or subtracting a single line. For SB_PAGEUP and SB_PAGEDOWN, it involves adding or subtracting four lines. It is customary for programs to scroll one screen's worth of data for the page up and page down messages. However, since SCROLL is working with a fairly short list, it only scrolls four lines when a page up or a page down scroll message is received.

```
/* Determine the number of lines to scroll.          */
switch (wParam)
    {
    case SB_PAGEDOWN:
        yNewLine = yScrollCurrent + 4;
        break;
    case SB_PAGEUP:
        yNewLine = yScrollCurrent - 4;
        break;
    case SB_LINEDOWN:
        yNewLine = yScrollCurrent + 1;
        break;
    case SB_LINEUP:
        yNewLine = yScrollCurrent - 1;
        break;
    case SB_THUMBPOSITION:
        yNewLine = LOWORD(lParam);
        break;
    default:
        yNewLine = yScrollCurrent;
    }
```

To insure that the top and the bottom of the display area is respected, a check is made that the new line value is in range:

```
/*  Make sure we are still in range.                 */
yNewLine = max (0, yNewLine);
yNewLine = min (yScrollMax, yNewLine);
```

At that point, SCROLL updates the display to reflect the new arrangement of text lines. This involves a call to **ScrollWindow**:

```
cyScroll = (yScrollCurrent-yNewLine)*cyLineHeight;
ScrollWindow (hwnd, 0, cyScroll, NULL, NULL);
```

ScrollWindow is a fairly involved routine that does several things at once. First, it calls the **BitBlt** routine to move a rectangle of pixels on the display to a new location. Next, it calculates the area that has been "exposed" by the call to **BitBlt** and generates a WM_PAINT message so that the image in the window can be properly repaired. A third capability of **ScrollWindow** is that it can accept a clipping rectangle in which to restrict the scrolling operation. **Scroll-Window** is defined:

```
void ScrollWindow (hWnd, X, Y, lpRect, lpClipRect)
```

- hWnd is a handle to the window whose bits are to be scrolled.
- X indicates the number of device units in which to scroll in the X direction.
- Y indicates the number of device units in which to scroll in the Y direction.
- lpRect is a long pointer to a structure of type RECT, which identifies the rectangle of pixels to be scrolled, or NULL to scroll the entire client area.
- lpClipRect is a long pointer to a structure of type RECT, which identifies a clipping rectangle to be used to restrict the scrolling operation.

The last thing that SCROLL does in response to a scroll message is to update the location of the scroll bar thumb. This is accomplished with a call to **SetScrollPos**. **SetScrollPos** is defined:

```
int SetScrollPos (hWnd, nBar, nPos, bRedraw)
```

- hWnd is a window handle to the window containing the scroll bar.
- nBar is an integer which indicates the scroll bar of interest. It is either SB_CTL, SB_HORZ or SB_VERT.

- nPos indicates the new scroll thumb position, based on the minimum and maximum values defined in the call to **SetScroll-Range**.
- bRedraw is a Boolean value which indicates whether the scroll bar should be redrawn to reflect the change.

SCROLL simply moves the scroll thumb to the line number of the topmost line in the display. Since this is the value represented by yScrollCurrent, here is how SCROLL sets the position of its scroll thumb:

```
SetScrollPos (hwnd, SB_VERT, yScrollCurrent, TRUE);
```

The call to **ScrollWindow** causes a WM_PAINT message to be generated. However, the entire window is not updated, but rather **ScrollWindow** only declares the unscrolled pixels in a window to be damaged. In this way, the WM_PAINT message only repairs the part of the window that actually needs to be redrawn.

21
Printing

In this chapter, we're going to cover issues related to creating output on a printer or other hard-copy device. Windows solves some of the problems with which programmers have had to grapple under traditional programming environments. For example, Windows programmers don't have to hassle with device-specific control codes. Instead, the GDI calls that draw on displays also draw on printers. A printer driver helps GDI to convert GDI calls into the device-specific data stream needed to create graphic output on a specific printer.

GDI's device-independent drawing helps set the stage for duplicating on the printer the images on a display screen. This capability is sometimes called WYSIWYG, an acronym for "what you see is what you get." In the last chapter, we covered GDI's coordinate transformations. These go a long way toward helping create WYSIWYG output, particularly when geometric figures are drawn. WYSIWYG for text requires a little more work, since the output generated for printer fonts must be simulated using the display fonts. This is something that should be much easier in a future version of Windows, when Microsoft incorporates its *TrueType* font technology into Windows.

We're going to start this chapter by looking at the user-interface end of printing. We'll provide a sample program, PRSETUP, which demonstrates the creation of a standard set of printer setup and configuration dialog boxes. We'll then discuss the creation of a printer DC, which is the first ingredient needed to print. We'll then cover the use of the Escape function and the creation of a printer abort function, which will serve to introduce our second sample program, PRINT.

Like many of the other areas we have covered, we'll begin this discussion of printing by addressing what the user expects to see. We're going to start, then, by addressing user interface issues.

The User Interface To Printing

In Chapter 11, we introduced the standard File and Edit menus that are used in Windows programs. In particular, the "Print" menu option on the File menu is of interest to us because it initiates printing. Another menu item that was not on our standard menu, "Printer Setup...", calls up a dialog box to allow the user to configure a printer. Figure 21.1 depicts this menu item in a revised File menu.

As you might expect from the ellipsis (...), selecting "Printer Setup..." causes a dialog box to appear. A typical Printer Setup dialog box is shown in Figure 21.2. A list box displays the installed printers, along with the name of the port to which each is attached. Allowing the user to select from the available printers requires you to create and maintain a dialog like the one in the figure. In a moment, we'll show you the code required to support this dialog, and another dialog box that is used for device-specific configuration information.

As Figure 21.2 shows, a standard part of a Printer Setup dialog box is a push button marked "Setup...". When the user pushes this button, a dialog box is displayed that allows the user to configure the currently selected printer. The specific dialog box that appears depends on the selected printer.

An example of a configuration dialog box is shown in Figure 21.3. This dialog box is created by the HP Laserjet printer driver, HPPCL.DRV. Although you don't have to worry about the contents of this dialog box, your program is responsible for calling the printer driver when a configuration dialog box like this is to be displayed.

Figure 21.1 *The Printer Setup... menu item*

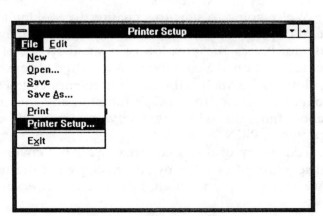

Figure 21.2 *The "Printer Setup..." dialog box*

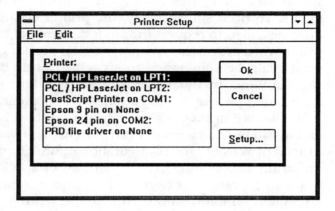

Prior to the release of Windows 3, the role of a configuration dialog box was to change a printer's default settings. In those days, printer drivers wrote all changes to one place: the system-wide configuration file, WIN.INI. This created some annoying problems for users, in particular when a user needs to use a different configuration for different types of print jobs.

Figure 21.3 *An example of a printer device driver's setup dialog box*

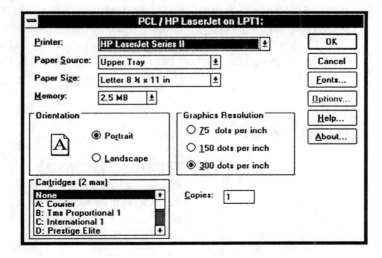

Consider, for example, a user who uses landscape mode to print spreadsheets and portrait mode to print word-processing documents. To print spreadsheets, the printer configuration dialog box must be called to request the landscape mode. Later, when the user prints word-processing documents, the printer configuration dialog must again be summoned to switch to portrait mode. Earlier versions of Windows did not provide any way for a program to connect a particular printer configuration to a document.

Windows 3 introduces several solutions to this problem. An application can instruct a printer driver to use a private configuration file instead of WIN.INI for configuration information. A private configuration file avoids interference with other applications. An application can go one step further and retrieve a memory image of the configuration information. This can be written inside a data file, to connect printer configuration data directly to a specific spreadsheet, word-processing document, or other application-specific data.

As of this writing, many of the available Windows printer drivers do not support the new Windows 3 way of saving printer configuration information. Over time, this should change as printer drivers are rewritten to conform to the latest standards.

A final user-interface issue is that users expect to be able to abort a print job after it has begun. This can take several forms: Some applications display a dialog box with a "Cancel" push button that can be clicked to abort a print job. Figure 21.4 shows an example of such a dialog box. Other applications allow the user to strike the Esc key to terminate printing. Whichever approach you decide to take, programs should always provide the user with a way to abort a print job after it has been started.

Let's look at a sample program that displays the printer setup and configuration dialog boxes we looked at in Figures 21.2 and 21.3.

Figure 21.4 *An abort print job dialog box*

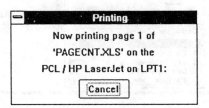

Printer Setup and Configuration

Printers are fundamentally a different type of device from display screens. For one thing, several different printers can be connected to one computer, but only one display screen can be used at any time. After a display adapter and its associated driver have been set up, there is no facility for changing the configuration of the display adapter while Windows is running. Instead, for example, a change from one resolution to another requires the user to run the Setup program and restart Windows. With a printer, however, quite a few configuration changes can be made: Output can appear in portrait or landscape mode, and it can be made to appear on letter-size or legal-size paper. While displays generally run in a single configuration, printers are able to run in many. Another difference is that a page of printed output can be ejected from a printer, while there is no comparable notion on a display screen.

To help clarify the basic ways to deal with these differences, our discussion of printing is divided into two parts. In this half of the chapter, we describe how a program can set up and configure a printer. We'll then present a fairly involved setup sample program, PRSETUP, which shows all the details needed to set up a printer in a way that takes advantage of the new features of Windows 3. The second half of this chapter details the use of printer escape calls to control print jobs, and the pagination of printer output. We'll describe what is needed to create an abort function and abort dialog box, for use when the user changes his mind and cancels a print job. Our sample program, PRINT, demonstrates the basics needed to create text and graphic output on a printer.

Printer Configuration and the Device Context

Just as you need a DC to draw on the display screen, a DC is also needed to send output to a printer. Getting a printer DC requires calling **CreateDC**. When we first discussed DCs in Chapter 6, we said that a DC represents a connection to a particular device. In the context of printers, this means a connection to a specific printer's device driver and the port to which the printer is connected. These make up two of the four parameters to **CreateDC**, which is defined:

```
HDC CreateDC (lpDriver, lpPrinter, lpPort, lpInit)
```

- lpDriver is a long pointer to a character string containing the DOS filename of a printer driver file, without an extension. For example, HPPCL identifies the HPPCL.DRV driver that is used for HP Laserjet printers.

- lpPrinter is a long pointer to a character string containing a printer description. For example, "PCL / HP Laserjet."
- lpPort is a long pointer to a character string containing a port name, such as LPT1 or COM1. It can also be the name of a file, when writing printer output to disk.
- lpInit is a long pointer to printer configuration data. If NULL, then the default configuration from WIN.INI is used.

CreateDC creates a DC for a specific printer connected to a specific port. In the second half of this chapter, when we cover the actual creation of printer output, we'll discuss this routine in more detail. For now, though, it is sufficient to say that printer setup and configuration revolves around providing the four parameters to **CreateDC**.

The Role of the WIN.INI File

When a printer is installed in Windows, an entry is made in the system configuration file, WIN.INI. There are two types of entries. One describes the default printer. The other describes all of the printers that are installed in the system at a given point in time. As you may recall, the configuration file stores strings that can be retrieved using two key words: an application name and a key name. The default printer is defined under the application name "windows" and the key name "device." For example, here is a sample WIN.INI entry for a default printer:

```
[windows]
device=PCL / HP LaserJet,HPPCL,LPT1:
```

To the right of the equal sign is the device name, the device driver, and the port.

To retrieve strings from WIN.INI, you call **GetProfileString**. This routine takes an application name and key name, and returns the string that is on the right of the equal sign. **GetProfileString** is defined:

```
int GetProfileString (lpApp, lpKey, lpDefault,
                      lpReturn, cbSize)
```

- lpApp is a long pointer to a character string containing an application name.
- lpKey is a long pointer to a character string containing a key name.
- lpDefault is a long pointer to a character string containing the default string to be returned if the desired application/keyname pair is not found.
- lpReturn is a long pointer to a character buffer for the returned string.
- cbSize is an integer defining the size of the buffer.

A character buffer is defined:

```
char achBuffer[80];
```

This code copies the default printer information into the buffer:

```
cch = GetProfileString ("windows", "device", NULL,
            achBuffer, 80);
```

The creation of a DC for the default printer requires you to parse the needed values from the character buffer. Here is a routine that does all the work, calls **CreateDC**, and returns a handle to a printer DC:

```
HDC PASCAL GetDefPrinterDC (void)
    {
    char ach[80];
    HDC  hdc;
    int  cch;
    int  i;
    PSTR pDriver;
    PSTR pPort;
    PSTR pPrinter;

    cch = GetProfileString ("windows", "device",
                    NULL, ach, 80);

    pDriver = pPrinter = &ach[0];

    for (i=0; i<cch; i++, pDriver++)
        {
        if (*pDriver == ',')
```

```
           {
           *pDriver = '\0';
           pDriver++;
           i++;
           break;
           }
      }

  for (pPort=pDriver; i<cch; i++, pPort++)
      {
      if (*pPort == ',')
          {
          *pPort = '\0';
          pPort++;
          break;
          }
      }

  hdc = CreateDC (pDriver, pPrinter, pPort, NULL);
  return (hdc);
  }
```

This routine provides a DC for the default printer, using its default settings. It provides you with enough to start experimenting with sending output to the printer. If that is your primary goal, we suggest that you skip ahead to the second half of this chapter, which starts on page 848. The next few pages, and the code sample that follows, address the role of an application in the selection of a printer and in the configuration of the printer that is selected.

If you are in the process of creating a full-blown Windows application, you may wish to give the user a choice of system printers. Lacking this, users can always go to the Control Panel to change the default printer and its configuration. But there is much to be said for providing users with a convenient solution inside your application itself, which is how most of the desktop applications that ship with Windows operate.

To find out which printers are installed, you retrieve the list from Windows' system configuration file, WIN.INI. Windows' Control Panel creates a list under the application name "device." The key name for each item in the list is, in fact, the name of the printer as supplied by each device driver. Here is an example of WIN.INI entries for installed printers:

```
[devices]
PCL / HP LaserJet=HPPCL,LPT1:,LPT2:
PostScript Printer=PSCRIPT,COM1:
Epson 9 pin=EPSON9,None
Epson 24 pin=EPSON24,COM2:
PRD file driver=D:\WINDOWS\APPS\WINWORD\PRDDRV.DRV,None
```

To retrieve the key names from a list like this, you call **GetProfile-String** with a NULL key name. The returned string contains all the key names in the list, each null terminated. For example, here is how to retrieve a list of the default printer key names:

```
char achBuff[256];

cch = GetProfileString ("windows", NULL, NULL, achBuff,
                         256);
```

This string can then be parsed and the results used in subsequent calls to GetProfileString to retrieve the rest of the information about the installed printers.

The next step in the configuration of a printer involves calling the device driver to request that it display a configuration dialog box. Although it takes care of creating and maintaining the dialog box, you'll need to find the driver, get the address of the driver's configuration function, and call the driver to make the whole operation work.

Configuring a Printer

After you have selected a printer from the Printer Setup dialog box, you may wish to configure the printer. If so, push the button marked "Setup...". In response, your program loads the device driver and calls its configuration function. At that point, the device driver takes over as it creates one or more modal dialog boxes through which it interacts with the user.

There are two configuration entry points for printer drivers: One is for drivers written for version 3.0 of Windows and later, and the other is for older, version 2.x drivers. When the time comes to call up a configuration dialog box, your program should first check for the Windows 3 configuration entry point. If this isn't available, then use version 2.x entry point. In a moment, we'll discuss the ways that the Windows 3 configuration entry point provides a wider range of services even though the dialog box appears the same. The Windows 3 entry point is named **ExtDeviceMode**, and the Windows 2.x entry point is **DeviceMode**.

Accessing these two functions first requires the driver to be loaded into memory. Since a printer driver is a dynamic-link library, calling **LoadLibrary** does the trick. **LoadLibrary** takes a single parameter: the name of the library to load. Here, for example, is how to load the HPPCL.DRV driver:

```
HANDLE hDriver;

hDriver = LoadLibrary ("HPPCL.DRV");
if (hDriver < 32)
    {
    /* Error. */
    }
else
    {
    /* Ok. */
    }
```

As suggested by this code, **LoadLibrary** returns a handle that identifies the library. If the return value is less than 32, that means an error has occurred. A program may respond by displaying a dialog box to let the user know that a problem has been encountered. If the library has already been loaded into memory, the library's reference count is incremented and **LoadLibrary** returns a handle to the library.

Once you have a valid handle to a library, you next search for a configuration function. This is the job of the **GetProcAddress** routine. **GetProcAddress** searches the module database for a function in a dynamic-link library, or in an application. This routine is defined:

```
FARPROC GetProcAddress (hModule, lpProcName)
```

- hModule is a module handle that identifies an application or a dynamic-link library. For a dynamic-link library, it is the return value from **LoadLibrary**.
- lpProcName identifies the function either as an ASCII text string or as a numeric ordinal value.

Windows 2.x Configuration Function

To retrieve the address of an old-style configuration function, start by creating two new data types for the function address:

```
typedef WORD FAR PASCAL FNOLDDEVMODE( HWND, HANDLE, LPSTR,
                                      LPSTR);
typedef FNOLDDEVMODE FAR * LPFNOLDDEVMODE;
```

These data types will recognize and enforce the function prototype for the printer configuration function to minimize the possibility of type-mismatch errors when calling the function.

Next, define a variable of type LPFNOLDDEVMODE, as shown here:

```
LPFNOLDDEVMODE lpfnProc;
```

Retrieving the address of the Windows 2.x configuration function involves calling **GetProcAddress** as follows:

```
lpfnProc = GetProcAddress (hDriver, "DeviceMode");
```

This works because the **DeviceMode** function is named in the EXPORTS section of every printer driver's module definition file. The entry looks something like this:

```
EXPORTS
    DeviceMode @ 13
```

You may recall that applications export several types of functions, including window procedures and dialog box procedures. These call-back procedures are exported to make them available to modules outside our program. In the same way, when a printer driver exports its configuration function, it allows us to call GetProcAddress and to call into the function itself.

The number in the EXPORTS statement after the @ symbol identifies a unique number—called an **ordinal identifier**. GetProcAddress allows you to retrieve a function by its ordinal identifier, so we could retrieve the Windows 2.x printer configuration address by saying:

```
lpfnProc = GetProcAddress (hDriver,
                 MAKEINTRESOURCE(13));
```

The MAKEINTRESOURCE macro creates a data object that, from the C compiler's point of view, looks like a long pointer to a character string. This is necessary because of the way that **GetProcAddress** is prototyped. Inside the four-byte value, however, the segment identifier is zero, which is always an invalid value. The number 13 is put in the offset part of the pointer, and from there it is read and used by **GetProcAddress**. This uses less memory than the example we saw a moment ago, because an integer takes less space than a character string. Also, this results in a faster lookup of the address, since ordinal values are always in memory, but string references live in a discardable resource called a **nonresident name table**, which must be loaded from disk to dereference the string.

Once you have the address of the function, calling the function is simple. The variable that contains the function address can be treated like a regular function name. Here is an example of calling a printer configuration function located at address `lpfnProc`:

```
lpfnProc (hwnd, hDriver, achPrinter, achPort);
```

Some C programmers prefer to treat the function address like other pointers and call the function like this:

```
(*lpfnProc)(hwnd, hDriver, achPrinter, achPort);
```

Both work. The old-style device mode function is defined:

```
void DeviceMode (hWnd, hModule, lpPrinter, lpPort)
```

- hWnd is a window handle. The printer driver uses this handle to identify the parent of its modal dialog box. Since this function is normally called from within a dialog box procedure, this value is often a handle to your Printer Setup dialog box.
- hModule is a module handle for the printer driver. This is the value returned by **LoadLibrary**.
- lpPrinter is a long pointer to a character string for the printer name, such as "PCL / HP Laserjet."
- lpPort is a long pointer to a character string containing the port to which the printer is attached, such as "LPT1" or "COM1," or the DOS filename when writing to a file. Whichever is used, this must be the same as the value passed in the **CreateDC** call.

When a program calls the old-style device mode function, the printer driver takes over. It reads the current setup from WIN.INI and lets the user modify the printer configuration. The user can Cancel at any time, or save the changes by pressing the Ok button. Once saved, the changes become the default printer settings, which apply to all applications the user wishes to print.

The Windows 3 configuration solves this problem in several ways: Programs can have private configuration files. A program can even get a copy of a printer's configuration information and save it away, so that each data file can have its own printer configuration information. Let's look at what is involved in the Windows 3 printer configuration function.

Windows 3 Configuration Function

Microsoft provides an include file with the Windows SDK that will help access a Windows 3 printer configuration function: DRIV-INIT.H. The first thing that you must do when accessing the configuration function is to get its address: Two data types are defined in this file, which serve as the data type for the function address:

```
typedef WORD FAR PASCAL FNDEVMODE(HWND, HANDLE, LPDEVMODE,
                                  LPSTR, LPSTR,LPDEVMODE,
                                  LPSTR, WORD);

typedef FNDEVMODE FAR * LPFNDEVMODE;
```

Retrieving the function address proceeds in the same fashion as for the Windows 2.x configuration function. When the printer driver has been brought into memory by the **LoadLibrary** function, we next call **GetProcAddress** to retrieve the address of ExtDevice-Mode, which is the Windows 3 configuration function:

```
LPFNDEVMODE lpfnMode;

lpfnExtDeviceMode = GetProcAddress (hDriver,
                                    "ExtDeviceMode");
```

Like the Windows 2.x configuration function, this function is listed in the module definition file of a printer driver with a statement like:

```
EXPORTS
    ExtDeviceMode @ 90
```

This means that the ExtDeviceMode function can be retrieved using an ordinal reference like this:

```
lpfnExtDeviceMode = GetProcAddress (hDriver,
                         MAKEINTRESOURCE (90));
```

Once we have the address of the **ExtDeviceMode** function, we can proceed to call it. First, however, let's look at how this function is defined. From there, you'll see that several options exist for how this function can be used. **ExtDeviceMode** is defined:

```
int ExtDeviceMode (hWnd, hDriver, lpDM, lpPrinter,
                   lpPort, lpInitDM, lpProfile, wMode)
```

- hWnd is a window handle used by the printer driver as the parent of its modal dialog box.
- hDriver is a handle to the printer driver, as returned by **Load-Library**.
- lpDM is a long pointer to an output buffer. When the DM_COPY mode is selected in the last parameter, the printer driver writes to this buffer a copy of the DEVMODE data for the new printer configuration.
- lpPrinter is a long pointer to a character string for a printer name, such as "PCL / HP Laserjet."
- lpPort is a long pointer to a character string for the port to which the printer is attached, or to a filename when output is being sent to disk.
- lpInitDM is a long point to an input buffer. When the DM_MODIFY mode is selected in the last parameter, the printer driver expects to find a copy of its DEVMODE data, which it uses to initialize the configuration dialog box.
- lpProfile is a long pointer to a character string. When the DM_UPDATE mode is selected in the last parameter, the printer driver updates a configuration file. If lpProfile is NULL, then WIN.INI is updated. Otherwise, the lpProfile is the name of the configuration file to be updated.
- wMode is a WORD field that can contain one or more of the following style bits, ORed together:

DM_COPY instructs the printer driver to copy the printer configuration data to the buffer referenced by lpDM.

DM_MODIFY instructs the printer driver to read the initial configuration information from the buffer referenced by lpInitDM.

DM_PROMPT instructs the printer to display a dialog box.

DM_UPDATE instructs the printer driver to modify the default settings in a configuration file. The exact configuration file to update depends on the value of lpProfile. If it is NULL, then WIN.INI is updated. Otherwise, the file referenced by lpProfile is updated.

Zero (0) instructs the printer driver simply to return the size of the buffer that is required to hold the printer configuration information.

Perhaps the most important field in this function is the last one, wMode. It provides a road map for the printer driver describing exactly what the application program needs. Let's look at several ways that this function can be called.

First of all, if an application only wants to imitate the behavior of a Windows 2.x configuration function, it would need two flags: DM_PROMPT causes the dialog box to appear and DM_UPDATE (with lpProfile set to NULL) causes WIN.INI to be updated. But the Windows 2.x way of doing things causes applications to interfere with each other. There must be a better way.

A simple way to keep applications from disrupting each other involves using a private configuration file. An application can create such a file to store other configuration information as well, such as program options that the user has selected. To get **ExtDeviceMode** to write a copy of its configuration information into MYPROF-ILE.INI, here is how it would be called:

```
lpfnExtDeviceMode (hWnd,        /*  Parent window.  */
                   hDriver,     /*  Driver handle.  */
                   NULL,        /*  Output data.
                   lpPrinter,   /*  Printer name.
                   lpPort,      /*  Port.
                   NULL,        /*  Input data.
                   "MYPROFILE",/*  Profile file.
                   DM_PROMPT |  /*  Mode
                   DM_UPDATE) ;
```

Another approach involves asking the printer driver to copy its configuration information into a buffer that you create. This data will consist of two parts: The first half corresponds to the DEVMODE data structure, defined in Windows.H as

```
typedef struct _devicemode {
    char dmDeviceName[CCHDEVICENAME];
    WORD dmSpecVersion;
    WORD dmDriverVersion;
    WORD dmSize;
    WORD dmDriverExtra;
    DWORD dmFields;
    short dmOrientation;
    short dmPaperSize;
    short dmPaperLength;
    short dmPaperWidth;
    short dmScale;
    short dmCopies;
    short dmDefaultSource;
    short dmPrintQuality;
    short dmColor;
    short dmDuplex;
} DEVMODE;
```

The second half is made up of printer-specific information, whose contents are known only to the printer driver itself. Even without knowing the meaning of this part of the data structure, however, your program can make a copy of the data, perhaps storing it along with a word-processing document, spreadsheet, or whatever other data files your application creates.

Saving the configuration information requires at least two calls to **ExtDeviceMode**. The first retrieves the size of the configuration data. This allows your program to allocate the necessary buffer. The second call involves either the DM_COPY flag, to retrieve a copy of the default configuration information, or the DM_PROMPT flag, to request a dialog box to retrieve the user's printing preferences. Here is an example of some code that retrieves the size of the data block, allocates some memory, and then calls the driver to create a dialog box:

```
HANDLE hmem;
int cbSize;
PSTR pDevModeOutput;

/*  Retrieve size of configuration data block.      */
cbSize = lpfnExtDeviceMode (NULL, hDriver, NULL,
                      lpPrinter, lpPort, NULL,
```

```
                                NULL, NULL);
hmem = LocalAlloc (LMEM_MOVEABLE, cbSize);
pDevModeOutput = LocalLock (hmem);
if (p == 0)
    goto ErrorExit;

/*  Get configuration block from user.            */
lpfnExtDeviceMode (hWnd, hDriver, pDevModeOutput,
                   lpPrinter, lpPort, NULL, NULL,
                   DM_PROMPT);
```

Later on, the printer configuration data is passed to **CreateDC** as its last parameter. The printer driver uses the configuration information at DC creation time, to make sure that the DC reflects the configuration that the user has selected.

Next, we're going to look at a sample program that shows how to deal with both types of printer configuration calls, PRSETUP. Even though PRSETUP doesn't actually print, its sheer size gives you an idea of the amount of effort required to let the user configure the printer.

A Sample Program: PRSETUP

Figure 21.5 shows the output of PRSETUP. This program lets the user configure the printer and then displays the printer name, port, and driver name, as well as the size of the buffer needed to hold the printer configuration information.

Figure 21.5   *PRSETUP*

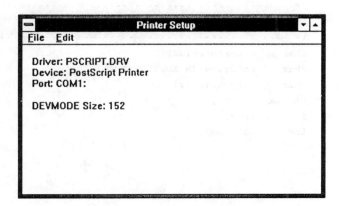

Here is the source code to our program:

PRSETUP.MAK

```
PrSetup.res: PrSetup.rc PrSetup.cur PrSetup.ico
    rc -r PrSetup.rc

PrSetup.obj: PrSetup.c
    cl -AM -c -Gsw -Od -W2 -Zip PrSetup.c

PrSetup.exe: PrSetup.obj PrSetup.def
    link PrSetup,/CO/align:16/NOD/NOE,/map, mlibcew libw,\
        PrSetup.def
    rc PrSetup.res

PrSetup.exe: PrSetup.res
    rc PrSetup.res
```

PRSETUP.C

```
/*--------------------------------------------------------------*\
 |  PrSetup.C - Demo showing dialog box to setup printer.       |
 \*--------------------------------------------------------------*/
#include <Windows.H>
#include <DrivInit.H>

#include "PrSetup.h"
#include "setupdlg.h"


/*--------------------------------------------------------------*\
 |                      Static Data.                            |
 \*--------------------------------------------------------------*/
char    achPrinter[32];
char    achDriver[MAXDRIVERNAME];
char    achPort[20];
HANDLE  hmemDM;
int     cbDM;
int     cbDMTemp;
```

```
HANDLE   hInst;
FARPROC  lpitPrSetupDialog;

/*---------------------------------------------------------------*\
|                    Function Prototypes.                         |
\*---------------------------------------------------------------*/
long FAR  PASCAL PrSetupWndProc  (HWND, WORD, WORD, LONG);
BOOL FAR  PASCAL PrSetupDialog   (HWND, WORD, WORD, LONG);
BOOL NEAR PASCAL PrSetupInit     (HWND);
int  NEAR PASCAL PrsetupParseLB  (HWND, PSTR, PSTR, PSTR);
int  NEAR PASCAL PrSetupCallDriver (HWND);
BOOL NEAR PASCAL PrSetupGetDefPrinter (PSTR, PSTR, PSTR, int);

/*---------------------------------------------------------------*\
|                    Main Function:  WinMain.                     |
\*---------------------------------------------------------------*/
int PASCAL WinMain (HANDLE hInstance,
                    HANDLE hPrevInstance,
                    LPSTR  lpszCmdLine,
                    int    cmdShow)
    {
    HWND      hwnd;
    MSG       msg;
    WNDCLASS  wndclass;

    if (!hPrevInstance)
        {
        wndclass.lpszClassName = "PrSetup:MAIN";
        wndclass.hInstance     = hInstance;
        wndclass.lpfnWndProc   = PrSetupWndProc;
        wndclass.hCursor       = LoadCursor (hInstance, "hand");
        wndclass.hIcon         = LoadIcon (hInstance,"snapshot");
        wndclass.lpszMenuName  = "#1";
        wndclass.hbrBackground = COLOR_WINDOW+1;
        wndclass.style         = NULL;
        wndclass.cbClsExtra    = 0;
        wndclass.cbWndExtra    = 0;

        RegisterClass( &wndclass);
        }
```

```
    hInst = hInstance;

    hwnd = CreateWindow("PrSetup:MAIN",        /* Class name.    */
                        "Printer Setup",       /* Title.         */
                        WS_OVERLAPPEDWINDOW,   /* Style bits.    */
                        CW_USEDEFAULT,         /* x - default.   */
                        0,                     /* y - default.   */
                        CW_USEDEFAULT,         /* cx - default.  */
                        0,                     /* cy - default.  */
                        NULL,                  /* No parent.     */
                        NULL,                  /* Class menu.    */
                        hInstance,             /* Creator        */
                        NULL);                 /* Params.        */


    ShowWindow (hwnd, cmdShow);

    lpitPrSetupDialog = MakeProcInstance (PrSetupDialog, hInst);

    while (GetMessage(&msg, 0, 0, 0))
        {
        TranslateMessage(&msg);    /*  Keyboard input.          */
        DispatchMessage(&msg);
        }
    return 0;
    }


/*-------------------------------------------------------------*\
|             Window Procedure:  PrSetupWndProc.                |
\*-------------------------------------------------------------*/
long FAR PASCAL PrSetupWndProc (HWND hwnd,    WORD wMsg,
                                WORD wParam, LONG lParam)
    {
    static int cyLineHeight;
    static int cxCharWidth;

    switch (wMsg)
        {
        case WM_COMMAND:
            {
            char buffer[80];
```

```
            switch (wParam)
                {
                case IDM_EXIT:
                    DestroyWindow (hwnd);
                    break;

                case IDM_PRINT_SETUP:
                    DialogBox (hInst,
                                MAKEINTRESOURCE (IDD_PRSETUP),
                                hwnd,
                                lpitPrSetupDialog);
                    InvalidateRect (hwnd, NULL, TRUE);
                    break;

                default:
                    wsprintf (buffer, "Command = %d", wParam);
                    MessageBox (hwnd, buffer, "WM_COMMAND",
                                MB_OK);
                    break;
                }
            }
        break;

    case WM_CREATE:
        {
        HDC hdc;
        TEXTMETRIC tm;
        hdc = GetDC (hwnd);
        GetTextMetrics (hdc, &tm);
        ReleaseDC (hwnd, hdc);
        cyLineHeight = tm.tmHeight;
        cxCharWidth  = tm.tmAveCharWidth;
        }
        break;

    case WM_DESTROY:
        PostQuitMessage(0);
        break;

    case WM_PAINT:
        {
```

```
                char ach[80];
                int x, y;
                int cb;
                PAINTSTRUCT ps;

                BeginPaint (hwnd, &ps);
                x = cxCharWidth * 2;
                y = cyLineHeight;

                cb = wsprintf (ach, "Driver: %s", (LPSTR)achDriver);
                TextOut (ps.hdc, x, y, ach, cb);
                y += cyLineHeight;

                cb = wsprintf (ach, "Device: %s", (LPSTR)achPrinter);
                TextOut (ps.hdc, x, y, ach, cb);
                y += cyLineHeight;

                cb = wsprintf (ach, "Port: %s", (LPSTR)achPort);
                TextOut (ps.hdc, x, y, ach, cb);
                y += cyLineHeight;

                y += cyLineHeight;
                cb = wsprintf (ach, "DEVMODE Size: %d", cbDM);
                TextOut (ps.hdc, x, y, ach, cb);

                EndPaint    (hwnd, &ps);
                }
                break;

        default:
                return(DefWindowProc(hwnd,wMsg,wParam,lParam));
                break;
        }
    return 0L;
    }

/*-------------------------------------------------------------------*\
|           Setup Dialog Box Procedure:  PrSetupDialog.              |
\*-------------------------------------------------------------------*/
BOOL FAR  PASCAL PrSetupDialog (HWND hdlg,    WORD wMsg,
                                 WORD wParam, LONG lParam)
```

```
        {
    switch (wMsg)
        {
        case WM_INITDIALOG:
            if (!PrSetupInit (hdlg))
                {
                MessageBox (hdlg,
                            "Out of memory.",
                            "PrSetup",
                            MB_OK);
                EndDialog (hdlg, TRUE);
                }
            return TRUE;
            break;

        case WM_COMMAND:
            {
            int    iRet;
            HCURSOR hcr;

            switch (wParam)
                {
                case IDD_OK:
                    /*  Change cursor to the hourglass.        */
                    hcr = LoadCursor (NULL, IDC_WAIT);
                    SetCursor (hcr);

                    /*  Retrieve and parse list box string     */
                    /*  for printer name,driver name and port. */
                    iRet = PrsetupParseLB (hdlg, achPrinter,
                                          achPort, achDriver);

                    if (iRet == -1)
                        goto ErrorExit;

                    /*  Free old printer data block.           */
                    if (hmemDM != 0)
                        LocalFree (hmemDM);

                    /*  Get new printer data block.            */
                    hmemDM = PrSetupGetDefPrinter (
```

```
                                    achPrinter,
                                    achPort,
                                    achDriver,
                                    0);

                    /*  Update size info for data block.        */
                    cbDM = cbDMTemp;

                    EndDialog (hdlg, TRUE);
                    break;

                case IDD_CANCEL:
                    EndDialog (hdlg, TRUE);
                    break;

                case IDD_SETUP:
                    iRet = PrSetupCallDriver (hdlg);
                    if (iRet == -1)
                        goto ErrorExit;
                    break;
                }
            return TRUE;
            }
            break;

        default:
            return FALSE;
        }
    return FALSE;

ErrorExit:
    MessageBox (hdlg, "Cannot Access Specified Driver",
                "PrSetup", MB_OK);
    return FALSE;
    }

/*----------------------------------------------------------------*\
|             Process WM_INITDIALOG for PrSetupDialog.             |
\*----------------------------------------------------------------*/
BOOL NEAR PASCAL PrSetupInit (HWND hdlg)
    {
```

```
char    achDefault[SIZETEMPBUFF];
char    ach[SIZETEMPBUFF];
HANDLE  hMem;
HWND    hwndList;
int     cch;
int     cchNext;
int     cStrings;
int     ichSearch;
int     i;
int     ich;
int     j;
LPSTR   lpKey;
PSTR    p;
WORD    wIndex;


hMem = GlobalAlloc (GMEM_MOVEABLE, MAXKEYBUFFER);
lpKey = GlobalLock (hMem);
if (!lpKey)
    return FALSE;

/* Get names of all printers installed in the system.    */
j = GetProfileString ("devices",
                        NULL,
                        NULL,
                        lpKey,
                        MAXKEYBUFFER);


hwndList = GetDlgItem (hdlg, IDD_PRINTERS);

/* Loop through key names, adding printer/port to listbox. */
for (i=0;i<j;i += cchNext)
    {
    lstrcpy (ach, &lpKey[i]);
    cchNext = lstrlen (&lpKey[i]);

    lstrcat (ach, " on ");
    cchNext += 4;

    cch = GetProfileString ("devices",
                            &lpKey[i],
```

```
                                NULL,
                                &ach[cchNext],
                                SIZETEMPBUFF - cchNext);

        /*  Set cch to NULL character at end of ach.          */
        cch += cchNext;

        /*  Skip past device driver name (ie. "HPPCL")        */
        for (ich=cchNext; ich < cch; ich++)
            {
            if (ach[ich] == ',')
                {
                ich++;
                break;
                }
            }

        /*  At this point, ach[ich]->first device, ie. "LPT1". */

        /*  Loop through each device that driver uses.        */
        for (ichSearch = ich; ichSearch <= cch; ichSearch++)
            {

            /*  If we hit a comma, or the end of the string... */
            if (ach[ichSearch] == ',' || ichSearch == cch)
                {
                ach[ichSearch] = 0;
                lstrcpy (&ach[cchNext], &ach[ich]);

                /*  Add string to list box.                    */
                SendMessage (hwndList, LB_ADDSTRING, 0,
                            (LONG)(LPSTR)ach);

                ich = ichSearch+1;
                }
            }

        cchNext = lstrlen (&lpKey[i]) + 1;
        }

    /*  Get default printer info, either the name we kept     */
    /*  or, if we don't have a printer name, from WIN.INI.     */
```

```
if (lstrlen (achPrinter) > 0)
    {
    lstrcpy (ach, achPrinter);
    lstrcat (ach, ",,");
    lstrcat (ach, achPort);
    cch = lstrlen (ach);
    }
else
    {
    /*  Get default printer information.              */
    cch = GetProfileString ("windows",
                            "device",
                            NULL,
                            ach,
                            SIZETEMPBUFF);
    }

/*  Copy printer description.                         */
for (i=0;i < cch && ach[i] != ','; i++)
    achDefault[i] = ach[i];

j = i+1;
lstrcpy(&achDefault[i]," on ");
i += 4;

/*  Skip driver name.                                 */
while (j<cch && ach[j] != ',')
    j++;

/*  Copy port name.                                   */
lstrcpy (&achDefault[i], &ach[j+1]);

/*  Search for default printer.                       */
wIndex = (WORD)SendMessage (hwndList, LB_FINDSTRING,
                            0xffff, (LONG)(LPSTR)achDefault);

/*  If found, highlight default printer in list box.  */
if (wIndex != LB_ERR)
    SendMessage (hwndList, LB_SETCURSEL, wIndex, 0L);

GlobalUnlock (hMem);
```

```
        GlobalFree (hMem);

        return TRUE;
        }


/*-----------------------------------------------------------------*\
 |      PrsetupParseLB:   Parse string returned from listbox.      |
\*-----------------------------------------------------------------*/
int  NEAR PASCAL PrsetupParseLB (HWND hdlg, PSTR achPrinter,
                                 PSTR achPort, PSTR achDriver)
        {
        char      ach[SIZETEMPBUFF];
        char      achDriverTemp[MAXDRIVERNAME];
        char      achPrinterTemp[32];
        char      achPortTemp[20];
        HWND      hCtl;
        int       cch;
        int       i;
        OFSTRUCT  of;

        /*  Get list box string.                               */
        hCtl = GetDlgItem (hdlg, IDD_PRINTERS);
        i = (int)SendMessage (hCtl, LB_GETCURSEL, 0, 0L);
        i = (int)SendMessage (hCtl, LB_GETTEXT, i, (LONG)(LPSTR)ach);

        while (ach[i] != ' ')
            i--;

        lstrcpy (achPortTemp, &ach[i+1]);

        /*  Assumes that format of list box string is:         */
        /*                                                     */
        /*      <printer description> on <port>                */
        /*                                                     */
        /*  We skip over " on ", by moving back three spaces.  */
        i -= 3;
        ach[i] = 0;

        lstrcpy (achPrinterTemp, ach);
```

```
        cch = GetProfileString ("devices",
                                achPrinterTemp,
                                NULL,
                                ach,
                                SIZETEMPBUFF);

    if (cch == 0)
        return 0;

    /*  Get driver file name.                                    */
    for (i=0; i<cch && i<MAXDRIVERNAME;i++)
        {
        if (ach[i] == ',')
            {
            achDriverTemp[i]=0;
            break;
            }
        achDriverTemp[i] = ach[i];
        }

    /*  Search for period '.' to see if we have an extension.  */
    for (;i!=0;i--)
        {
        if (achDriverTemp[i] == '.')
            break;
        }

    /*  If not, let's add an extension of .DRV              */
    if (i == 0)
        lstrcat (achDriverTemp, ".DRV");

    /*  If cannot find driver file, then fail.              */
    i = OpenFile (achDriverTemp, &of, OF_EXIST | OF_READ);
    if (i == -1)
        return -1;

lstrcpy (achDriver, achDriverTemp);
lstrcpy (achPrinter, achPrinterTemp);
lstrcpy (achPort, achPortTemp);
return 1;
}
```

```
/*--------------------------------------------------------------*\
|    PrSetupGetDefPrinter - Get printer default setup info.    |
\*--------------------------------------------------------------*/
BOOL NEAR PASCAL PrSetupGetDefPrinter (PSTR pPrinter,
                                       PSTR pPort,
                                       PSTR pDriver,
                                       int  cbData)

    {
    HANDLE      hmem;
    HANDLE      hDriver;
    LPFNDEVMODE lpfnMode;
    PDEVMODE    pdm;


    hmem = 0;


    hDriver = LoadLibrary (pDriver);
    if (hDriver < 32) goto Exit;


    lpfnMode = GetProcAddress (hDriver, "ExtDeviceMode");
    if (lpfnMode == 0)  goto Exit;


    /*  If it wasn't passed to us, query data size.            */
    if (cbData == 0)
        {
        cbData = lpfnMode (NULL,
                           hDriver,
                           NULL,
                           pPrinter,
                           pPort,
                           NULL,
                           NULL,
                           0);
        cbDMTemp = cbData;
        }


    hmem = LocalAlloc (LHND, cbData);
    pdm = (PDEVMODE)LocalLock (hmem);
    if (hmem == 0)
        goto Exit;
```

```
        /*  Get default printer setup information.                */
        lpfnMode (NULL,
                  hDriver,
                  pdm,
                  pPrinter,
                  pPort,
                  NULL,
                  "WIN.INI",
                  DM_COPY);                        /*  Return settings.      */

Exit:
    if (hmem)
       LocalUnlock (hmem);
    if (hDriver)
        FreeLibrary (hDriver);
    return hmem;
    }


/*-------------------------------------------------------------*\
|       Process Setup... push button for PrSetupDialog.         |
\*-------------------------------------------------------------*/
int  NEAR PASCAL PrSetupCallDriver (HWND hdlg)
    {
    char            ach[SIZETEMPBUFF];
    char            achDriverT[MAXDRIVERNAME];
    char            achPrinterT[32];
    char            achPortT[20];
    HANDLE          hDriver = 0;
    HANDLE          hmemDmNew = 0;
    HANDLE          hmemDmOld;
    HCURSOR         hcr;
    HWND            hCtl;
    int             cbData;
    int             cch;
    int             i;
    LPFNDEVMODE     lpfnMode;
    LPFNOLDDEVMODE  lpfnOldMode;
    PDEVMODE        pdmOld;
    PDEVMODE        pdmNew;
```

```
/*  Change cursor to the hourglass.                       */
hcr = LoadCursor (NULL, IDC_WAIT);
SetCursor (hcr);


/*  Get printer, port and driver info.                    */
i = PrsetupParseLB (hdlg, achPrinterT, achPortT, achDriverT);
if (i==-1)
    return -1;


/*  Load printer driver based on driver file name read    */
/*  from WIN.INI.                                          */
hDriver = LoadLibrary (achDriverT);
if (hDriver < 32) goto ErrorExit;


/*  Check for Win3 setup function.                         */
lpfnMode = GetProcAddress (hDriver, PROC_EXTDEVICEMODE);
if (lpfnMode == 0)  goto OldDriver;


/*  Query size of printer setup data.                      */
cbData = lpfnMode (NULL,
                   hDriver,
                   NULL,
                   achPrinterT,
                   achPortT,
                   NULL,
                   NULL,
                   0);


/*  If we don't have a printer data block, or its size     */
/*  is different from exising data block, get a new one.    */
if (hmemDM == 0 || cbData != cbDM)
    goto CreateNew;


/*  Check that existing printer data block is for the      */
/*  currently selected printer.  If not, get a new one.    */
pdmOld = (PDEVMODE)LocalLock (hmemDM);
if (pdmOld == 0)  goto ErrorExit;
if (lstrcmpi ((LPSTR)pdmOld, achPrinterT) == 0)
    {
    /*  We have a valid printer data block for currently   */
    /*  selected printer.  Give it to printer driver for   */
```

```
                /*  initial values for dialog box.                   */
                hmemDmOld = 0;
                goto GetUserData;
                }
        else
                LocalUnlock(hmemDM);


        /*  Allocate a block of memory for the default data.         */
CreateNew:
    hmemDmOld = PrSetupGetDefPrinter (achPrinterT,
                                      achPortT,
                                      achDriverT,
                                      cbData);


    pdmOld = (PDEVMODE)LocalLock (hmemDmOld);
    if (pdmOld == 0) goto ErrorExit;


    /*  Allocate a block to receive new printer data block       */
    /*  that printer driver will return from setup dialog.       */
GetUserData:
    hmemDmNew = LocalAlloc (LHND, cbData);
    pdmNew = (PDEVMODE)LocalLock (hmemDmNew);
    if (pdmNew == 0)
        goto ErrorExit;


    /*  Call printer initialization function to put up dialog    */
    /*  and allow user to change default printer settings.       */
    i = lpfnMode (hdlg,
                  hDriver,
                  pdmNew,
                  achPrinterT,
                  achPortT,
                  pdmOld,
                  "WIN.INI",
                  DM_MODIFY |
                  DM_UPDATE |
                  DM_PROMPT |
                  DM_COPY);


    /*  Clean up scratch memory, if we allocated it.             */
    if (hmemDmOld == 0)
```

```
            LocalUnlock (hmemDM);
        else
            {
            LocalUnlock (hmemDmOld);
            LocalFree (hmemDmOld);
            }

        LocalUnlock (hmemDmNew);
        LocalFree   (hmemDmNew);

        FreeLibrary (hDriver);

        return 1;


    /*  Here if the ExtDeviceMode function wasn't found, and   */
    /*  we need to ask for the DeviceMode function, which      */
    /*  indicates we have an old, pre-Win3 printer driver.     */
OldDriver:

        lpfnOldMode = GetProcAddress (hDriver, PROC_OLDDEVICEMODE);
        if (lpfnOldMode == 0)
            goto ErrorExit;

    /*  Display dialog box to get new printer settings.        */
        lpfnOldMode (hdlg,
                     hDriver,
                     achPrinterT,
                     achPortT);

    /*  We're done, and setup worked.                          */
        FreeLibrary (hDriver);
        return 1;

    /*  We're done, but setup didn't work.                     */
ErrorExit:
        if (hDriver)
            FreeLibrary (hDriver);

        if (hmemDmNew)
            {
```

```
        LocalUnlock (hmemDmNew);
        LocalFree (hmemDmNew);
        }
    MessageBox (hdlg,
              "Error in Printer Setup",
              "PrSetup",
              MB_OK);
    return 0;
    }
```

PRSETUP.H

```
/*-------------------------------------------------------------*\
|    PrSetup.h  - Include file for PrSetup.c.                  |
\*-------------------------------------------------------------*/

#define IDM_NEW          1
#define IDM_OPEN         2
#define IDM_SAVE         3
#define IDM_SAVEAS       4
#define IDM_PRINT        5
#define IDM_PRINT_SETUP 6
#define IDM_EXIT         7


#define IDM_UNDO         8
#define IDM_CUT          9
#define IDM_COPY         10
#define IDM_PASTE        11
#define IDM_CLEAR        12
#define IDM_DELETE       13



#define MAXKEYBUFFER   300
#define SIZETEMPBUFF    80
#define MAXDRIVERNAME   80

typedef WORD FAR PASCAL FNOLDDEVMODE(HWND, HANDLE, LPSTR, LPSTR);
typedef FNOLDDEVMODE FAR * LPFNOLDDEVMODE;
SETUPDLG.H
```

SETUPDLG.H

```
#define IDD_OK          1
#define IDD_CANCEL      2
#define IDD_PRSETUP     5
#define IDD_TEXT1       101
#define IDD_SETUP       102
#define IDD_PRINTERS    103
```

PRSETUP.RC

```
#include <Windows.h>
#include "PrSetup.h"
#include "setupdlg.h"

snapshot icon PrSetup.ico

hand    cursor PrSetup.cur

#include "setup.dlg"

1 MENU
    {
    POPUP "&File"
        {
        MENUITEM "&New",                IDM_NEW
        MENUITEM "&Open...",            IDM_OPEN
        MENUITEM "&Save",               IDM_SAVE
        MENUITEM "Save &As...",         IDM_SAVEAS
        MENUITEM SEPARATOR
        MENUITEM "&Print",              IDM_PRINT
        MENUITEM "P&rinter Setup...",   IDM_PRINT_SETUP
        MENUITEM SEPARATOR
        MENUITEM "E&xit",               IDM_EXIT
        }
    POPUP "&Edit"
        {
        MENUITEM "&Undo\tAlt+Backspace", IDM_UNDO
        MENUITEM SEPARATOR
```

```
        MENUITEM "Cu&t\tShift+Del",        IDM_CUT
        MENUITEM "&Copy\tCtrl+Ins",        IDM_COPY
        MENUITEM "&Paste\tShift+Ins",      IDM_PASTE
        MENUITEM SEPARATOR
        MENUITEM "Cl&ear",  IDM_CLEAR
        MENUITEM "&Delete", IDM_DELETE
        }
    }
```

SETUP.DLG

```
IDD_PRSETUP DIALOG LOADONCALL MOVEABLE DISCARDABLE
                 8, 8, 177, 82
STYLE WS_DLGFRAME | WS_POPUP
BEGIN
    CONTROL "&Printer:", IDD_TEXT1, "static",
            SS_LEFT | WS_CHILD, 7, 3, 28, 8
    CONTROL "", IDD_PRINTERS, "listbox",
            LBS_NOTIFY | WS_BORDER | WS_VSCROLL |
            WS_TABSTOP | WS_CHILD, 7, 14, 119, 57
    CONTROL "Ok", IDD_OK, "button",
            BS_DEFPUSHBUTTON | WS_TABSTOP | WS_CHILD,
            132, 6, 40, 14
    CONTROL "Cancel", IDD_CANCEL, "button",
            BS_PUSHBUTTON | WS_TABSTOP | WS_CHILD,
            132, 25, 40, 14
    CONTROL "&Setup...", IDD_SETUP, "button",
            BS_PUSHBUTTON | WS_TABSTOP | WS_CHILD,
            132, 57, 40, 14
END
```

PRSETUP.DEF

```
NAME     PRSETUP

EXETYPE WINDOWS
```

```
DESCRIPTION 'Printer Setup Sample'

CODE     MOVEABLE DISCARDABLE
DATA     MOVEABLE MULTIPLE

HEAPSIZE      512
STACKSIZE    5000

EXPORTS
    PrSetupWndProc
    PrSetupDialog
```

Although there is a lot of code in PRSETUP, the important thing to keep in mind is that its entire purpose is to retrieve *four* data items, which are the four parameters to **CreateDC**: the driver name, the device name, the port (or filename), and driver initialization data. This last item is only available for drivers that have been updated for Windows 3 and which support the **ExtDeviceMode** function. For drivers that don't support this function, only the first three items are available.

Next, we're going to look at the steps involved in printing. The sample program that we present will not have all the bells and whistles of PRSETUP, but rather it prints on the default printer using default printer settings. You may find this the easiest approach to take as you begin to explore printing under Windows. Let's take a look, then, at what is needed to get output to appear on a printer.

Sending Output to the Printer

As we mentioned earlier, sending output to the printer requires a printer device context. This provides a connection to a printer, a complete set of GDI drawing tools, and access to GDI's drawing routines. Creating a printer DC is a job for the **CreateDC** routine, which we covered earlier.

A few more steps are required to create printer output than was required for display output. For one thing, when outputting to the printer, programs must notify GDI about the beginning and end of a **printer job**, which is defined as a group of pages to be output in sequential order. Programs also must notify GDI when it has finished writing to one page and is ready to begin a new page. All of these tasks are accomplished by a call to the **Escape** routine, which is our first topic of discussion.

We're next going to discuss the need for, and the implementation details surrounding, a print abort function. A key concept in the world of Windows programming revolves around the idea that the user should be able to stop almost any process even after it has begun. This is certainly true of printing, since print jobs can be quite time consuming. Built into the printing process is the ability to define a message loop call-back procedure that allows the user to interact with other programs while a print job is in progress. It also allows the user to interact with a special Abort Print dialog box that we're going to describe. But first, let's take a look at the **Escape** function.

Controlling Printer Output: The Escape Function

Once you have gotten a handle to a printer DC, you're almost ready to draw on a printer. But first, you're going to need to know about the **Escape** function. This GDI routine almost exclusively is used to communicate with printers and plotters (an exception is the GETCOLORTABLE escape, supported by certain non-palette-supporting displays). **Escape** is defined:

```
int Escape (hDC, nEscape, nCount, lpDataIn, lpDataOut)
```

- hDC is a handle to a DC.
- nEscape is an integer that identifies the escape subfunction to be performed.
- nCount is an integer that specifies the number of bytes in the input buffer that is referenced by the lpDataIn parameter.
- lpDataIn is a long pointer to a buffer that certain escape subfunctions use for input data.
- lpDataOut is a long pointer to a buffer that certain escape subfunctions use for output data.

There are 65 escape subfunctions defined in Windows.h. Some of these ask for information from the device driver. For example, the GETPHYSPAGESIZE subfunction returns the width and height of a printed page. Others give an application access to printer capabilities that aren't available in GDI. For example, the BEGIN_PATH and

END_PATH escapes let a program create complex line drawings using the support for paths built into Postscript printers.

The following list of escape codes make up the minimum set required by every printer driver:

Escape Subfunction	Description
ABORTDOC	Abort a print job.
ENDDOC	Marks the end of a print job.
NEWFRAME	Marks the end of page in the current print job.
QUERYESCSUPPORT	Determine whether an escape subfunction is supported.
SETABORTPROC	Define a call-back procedure to connect printing with a message loop.
STARTDOC	Begin a print job.

To signal the beginning of a print job, a program sends the STARTDOC escape. When this escape is sent, the nCount parameter of the **Escape** function contains the length of the job name, and the lpDataIn field points to a character string for the job name itself. Here is an example:

```
cb = lstrlen (achJobName);
err = Escape (hdcPrinter, STARTDOC, cb, achJobName, NULL);
if (err == -1) goto Exit;
```

If **Escape** returns a value of -1, that means an error has occurred and printing cannot continue.

After the STARTDOC escape call, a program starts to output the first page of the document by making GDI drawing calls to the DC. These calls are collected until the program sends the NEWFRAME escape code, which signals the end of a page. This escape takes no other parameters to the **Escape** function:

```
err = Escape (hdcPrinter, NEWFRAME, NULL, NULL, NULL);
```

This continues until all the pages have been sent to the printer, at which time a program indicates the end of a print job by sending the ENDDOC escape code. This signals the end of the print job, after which a program can destroy the printer DC or start another print job. The ENDDOC escape takes no additonal parameters to **Escape**:

```
err = Escape (hdcPrinter, ENDDOC, NULL, NULL, NULL);
```

At any time during the print job, a program can cancel a print job by sending an ABORTDOC escape code. When it is sent, this escape code takes the place of the ENDDOC escape:

```
err = Escape (hdcPrinter, ENDDOC, NULL, NULL, NULL);
```

Another way for a print job to get terminated involves a print abort function, which is defined with the SETABORTPROC escape code. This escape code, and the code required to support an Abort dialog box, are the next topic of our discussion.

Printing, Multitasking, and the Abort Function

When we introduced the ideas behind nonpreemptive multitasking in Chapter 4, we mentioned that Windows is a *nonpreemptive* multitasking system. Windows does not interrupt one program to allow another to run. Instead, programs must interrupt themselves. The driving force behind the operation of this system is the hunger of each application for messages. A program is dependent on messages to run properly, and yet Windows will give a program only one message to process at a time. The multitasking system continues to work because programs continually poll for messages. At such time, Windows may decide to switch away from one program to allow another one to run.

This works well as long as programs continue to ask for messages. But the multitasking system breaks down when a program has a large processing task to do, such as printing a large document. In recognition of this problem, Microsoft provides a facility to allow the printing process to connect to the message system so that some degree of multitasking can occur even when a print job is in progress.

This facility is referred to as an **abort function**, although perhaps a better term would be a printing message loop. In any case, a primary role of this function is to allow user input to be delivered to a program so that it can cancel a print job that is in progress. The abort function is a call-back procedure that you provide in your program. The function itself is defined:

```
BOOL FAR PASCAL AbortFunc (HDC hdc, short code)
```

GDI periodically calls this routine to retrieve whatever messages might be in the print queue. At that time, hdc is the handle to the printer device context. The value of code indicates whether an error has occurred. It can have one of two values: zero if no error has occurred, and SP_OUTOFDISK when disk space is unavailable for spooling.

Here is a sample abort function:

```
BOOL FAR PASCAL AbortLoop (HDC hdc, short code)
    {
    MSG msg;

    while (PeekMessage (&msg, 0, 0, 0, PM_REMOVE))
        {
        TranslateMessage(&msg);
        DispatchMessage(&msg);
        }

    return TRUE;
    }
```

This looks a lot like the message loop of every Windows program. The **PeekMessage** routine is similar to **GetMessage**, except that it returns a value of FALSE when there are no more messages to be processed. The Abort function can be used to abort a print job simply by returning a value of FALSE. The code in this example returns a value of TRUE, which causes GDI to continue printing.

Since GDI calls the abort function, you will probably want to create an instance thunk by calling **MakeProcInstance**. You may recall that you use this routine to set up the data segment register for dialog box procedures. It provides the same service for the abort function. To use it, you start by defining a variable of type FARPROC:

```
FARPROC lpitAbort;
```

This variable will hold the return value for MakeProcInstance. Here is how we might set up an instance thunk for the subroutine we saw earlier:

```
lpitAbort = MakeProcInstance (AbortLoop,hInstance);
```

To install the abort function when printing, you pass GDI a SETABORTPROC escape code, like this:

```
Escape (hdcPrinter, SETABORTPROC, NULL,
        (LPSTR) lpitAbort, NULL)
```

Figure 21.6 *PRINT's display.*

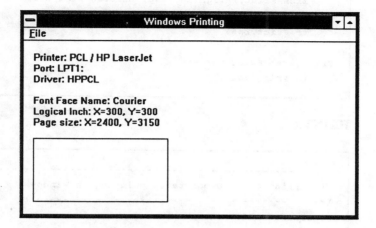

Once this has been done, GDI will periodically call into your function to let some messages flow through the system, so that the printing process does not too severely impact Windows' multitasking.

Next, we're going to look at a sample program which prints out some text and some graphic information onto the printer.

A Sample Program: PRINT

Our next sample program, PRINT, puts together the two printing topics we have just finished discussing: the Escape call and the Abort function. Figure 21.6 shows PRINT's display, which also happens to be the output sent to the printer.

Here is the code to PRINT:

PRINT.MAK

```
Print.res: Print.rc Print.cur Print.ico
    rc -r Print.rc

Print.obj: Print.c
    cl -AM -c -d -Gsw -Od -W2 -Zpi Print.c

Print.exe: Print.obj Print.def
```

```
        link Print,/align:16,/map, mlibcew libw/NOD/NOE/CO,\
             Print.def
        rc Print.res


Print.exe: Print.res
        rc Print.res
```

PRINT.C

```
/*-------------------------------------------------------------*\
|     Print.C  -  Demonstates printing in Windows.             |
\*-------------------------------------------------------------*/
#include <Windows.H>
#include "Print.H"
#include "Abortdlg.H"


/*-------------------------------------------------------------*\
|                    Function Prototypes.                      |
\*-------------------------------------------------------------*/
void NEAR PASCAL PrintOutput (HDC hdc);
void NEAR PASCAL PrintPrint(HWND);
long FAR   PASCAL PrintWndProc (HWND, WORD, WORD, LONG);
BOOL FAR   PASCAL PrintAbortDlg (HWND, WORD, WORD, LONG);
BOOL FAR   PASCAL PrintAbortMsg (HDC, short);
HDC  NEAR PASCAL GetDefPrinterDC (void);


/*-------------------------------------------------------------*\
|                      Static Data.                            |
\*-------------------------------------------------------------*/
BOOL bContinue;        /* Abort printing flag.                 */

char achDriver[80];       /*  Name of printer driver.          */
char achPrinter[32];      /*  Name of printer.                 */
char achPort[12];         /*  Name of port.                    */
char achFont[32];         /*  Printer font face name.          */
char achJobName[] = "Text and Rectangle Print Job.";


FARPROC lpitAbortDlg;     /*  Abort dialog instance thunk.     */
FARPROC lpitAbort;        /*  Abort message loop.              */
```

```
HANDLE hInst;              /* Instance handle.              */
HDC hdcPrinter;           /* Printer DC.                   */
HWND hdlgAbort;           /* Window handle of abort dlg box. */

int  cxPrinterInch;       /* Printer logical inch.         */
int  cyPrinterInch;       /* Printer logical inch.         */

int  cxPageSize;          /* Printer page size.            */
int  cyPageSize;          /* Printer page size.            */

/*------------------------------------------------------------*\
|                    Main Function:  WinMain.                 |
\*------------------------------------------------------------*/
int PASCAL WinMain (HANDLE hInstance,
                    HANDLE hPrevInstance,
                    LPSTR  lpszCmdLine,
                    int    cmdShow)
    {
    HWND     hwnd;
    MSG      msg;
    WNDCLASS wndclass;

    if (!hPrevInstance)
        {
        wndclass.lpszClassName = "Print:MAIN";
        wndclass.hInstance     = hInstance;
        wndclass.lpfnWndProc   = PrintWndProc;
        wndclass.hCursor       = LoadCursor (hInstance, "hand");
        wndclass.hIcon         = LoadIcon (hInstance,"snapshot");
        wndclass.lpszMenuName  = "#1";
        wndclass.hbrBackground = COLOR_WINDOW+1;
        wndclass.style         = NULL;
        wndclass.cbClsExtra    = 0;
        wndclass.cbWndExtra    = 0;

        RegisterClass( &wndclass);
        }

    hInst = hInstance;
```

```
    hwnd = CreateWindow("Print:MAIN",       /* Class name.  */
                        "Windows Printing",  /* Title.       */
                        WS_OVERLAPPEDWINDOW, /* Style bits.  */
                        CW_USEDEFAULT,       /* x - default. */
                        0,                   /* y - default. */
                        CW_USEDEFAULT,       /* cx - default. */
                        0,                   /* cy - default. */
                        NULL,                /* No parent.   */
                        NULL,                /* Class menu.  */
                        hInstance,           /* Creator.     */
                        NULL);               /* Params.      */
    ShowWindow (hwnd, cmdShow);

    lpitAbortDlg = MakeProcInstance (PrintAbortDlg, hInstance);
    lpitAbort    = MakeProcInstance (PrintAbortMsg, hInstance);

    while (GetMessage(&msg, 0, 0, 0))
        {
        TranslateMessage(&msg);          /*  Keyboard input.      */
        DispatchMessage(&msg);
        }
    return 0;
    }

/*------------------------------------------------------------*\
|            Window Procedure:  PrintWndProc.                 |
\*------------------------------------------------------------*/
long FAR PASCAL PrintWndProc (HWND hwnd,   WORD wMsg,
                             WORD wParam, LONG lParam)
    {
    static int cyLine;
    static int cxChar;

    switch (wMsg)
        {
        case WM_CREATE:
            {
            HDC       hdc;
            TEXTMETRIC tm;

            hdcPrinter = GetDefPrinterDC();
```

```
            if (hdcPrinter == 0)
                {
                MessageBox (hwnd,
                            "Unable to create Printer DC.",
                            "Print", MB_OK);
                return -1L;
                }

            /*  Get printer info.                          */
            GetTextFace (hdcPrinter, 32, achFont);
            cxPrinterInch =
                    GetDeviceCaps (hdcPrinter, LOGPIXELSX);
            cyPrinterInch =
                    GetDeviceCaps (hdcPrinter, LOGPIXELSY);

            cxPageSize = GetDeviceCaps (hdcPrinter, HORZRES);
            cyPageSize = GetDeviceCaps (hdcPrinter, VERTRES);

            /*  Get display text metric info.              */
            hdc = GetDC (hwnd);
            GetTextMetrics (hdc, &tm);
            cyLine = tm.tmHeight + tm.tmExternalLeading;
            cxChar = tm.tmAveCharWidth;
            ReleaseDC (hwnd, hdc);
            }
        break;

    case WM_COMMAND:
        switch (wParam)
            {
            case IDM_PRINT:
                PrintPrint(hwnd);
                break;
            case IDM_EXIT:
                DestroyWindow (hwnd);
                break;
            default:
                MessageBox (hwnd,
                            "Command Not Supported.",
                            "Print", MB_OK);
            }
```

```
                break;

        case WM_DESTROY:
            DeleteDC (hdcPrinter);
            PostQuitMessage(0);
            break;

        case WM_PAINT:
            {
            PAINTSTRUCT ps;

            BeginPaint (hwnd, &ps);

            PrintOutput (ps.hdc);

            EndPaint (hwnd, &ps);
            }
            break;

        default:
            return(DefWindowProc(hwnd,wMsg,wParam,lParam));
            break;
        }
    return 0L;
    }

/*-----------------------------------------------------------*\
|  GetDefPrinterDC:  Retrieve DC handle for default printer.  |
\*-----------------------------------------------------------*/
HDC NEAR PASCAL GetDefPrinterDC (void)
    {
    char ach[80];
    HDC  hdc;
    int  cch;
    int  i;
    PSTR pDriver;
    PSTR pPort;
    PSTR pPrinter;

    cch = GetProfileString ("windows", "device", NULL, ach, 80);
    pDriver = pPrinter = &ach[0];
```

```
    for (i=0; i<cch; i++, pDriver++)
        {
        if (*pDriver == ',')
            {
            *pDriver = '\0';
            pDriver++;
            i++;
            break;
            }
        }

    for (pPort=pDriver; i<cch; i++, pPort++)
        {
        if (*pPort == ',')
            {
            *pPort = '\0';
            pPort++;
            break;
            }
        }

    lstrcpy (achDriver, pDriver);
    lstrcpy (achPrinter, pPrinter);
    lstrcpy (achPort, pPort);

    hdc = CreateDC (pDriver, pPrinter, pPort, NULL);
    return (hdc);
    }

/*------------------------------------------------------------*\
|     PrintOutput: Output to display screen or printer.      |
\*------------------------------------------------------------*/
void NEAR PASCAL PrintOutput (HDC hdc)
    {
    char        achBuff[120];
    int         cb;
    int         cxInch;
    int         cyInch;
    int         cyLine;
    int         X, Y;
    TEXTMETRIC  tm;
```

```
/*  Get text measurement information.                      */
GetTextMetrics (hdc, &tm);
X = tm.tmAveCharWidth * 2;
Y = cyLine = tm.tmHeight + tm.tmExternalLeading;

/*  Get local device logical inch.                         */
cxInch = GetDeviceCaps (hdc, LOGPIXELSX);
cyInch = GetDeviceCaps (hdc, LOGPIXELSY);

/*  Display printer name.                                  */
cb = wsprintf (achBuff, "Printer: %s",
                (LPSTR)achPrinter);
TextOut (hdc, X, Y, achBuff, cb);
Y += cyLine;

/*  Display port name.                                     */
cb = wsprintf (achBuff, "Port: %s",
                (LPSTR)achPort);
TextOut (hdc, X, Y, achBuff, cb);
Y += cyLine;

/*  Display driver name.                                   */
cb = wsprintf (achBuff, "Driver: %s",
                (LPSTR)achDriver);
TextOut (hdc, X, Y, achBuff, cb);
Y += cyLine * 2;

/*  Display default printer face name.                     */
cb = wsprintf (achBuff, "Font Face Name: %s",
                (LPSTR)achFont);
TextOut (hdc, X, Y, achBuff, cb);
Y += cyLine;

/*  Display size of logical inch.                          */
cb = wsprintf (achBuff, "Logical Inch: X=%d, Y=%d",
                cxPrinterInch, cyPrinterInch);
TextOut (hdc, X, Y, achBuff, cb);
Y += cyLine;

/*  Display size of printed page in pixels.                */
```

```
        cb = wsprintf (achBuff, "Page size: X=%d, Y=%d",
                        cxPageSize, cyPageSize);
        TextOut (hdc, X, Y, achBuff, cb);
        Y += cyLine * 2;

        /*  Draw a rectangle.                                     */
        Rectangle (hdc, X, Y, X + ( 2*cxInch), Y + cyInch);


        }

/*--------------------------------------------------------------*\
|       PrintPrint:  Print to the printer.                       |
\*--------------------------------------------------------------*/
void NEAR PASCAL PrintPrint(HWND hwnd)
    {
    int  cb;
    int  err;

    /*  Set print continue flag.                                 */
    bContinue = TRUE;
    Escape (hdcPrinter, SETABORTPROC, NULL,
            (LPSTR)lpitAbort, NULL);

    /*  Create abort print dialog box.                           */
    hdlgAbort = CreateDialog (hInst, "#1", hwnd, lpitAbortDlg);

    /*  Disable parent.                                          */
    EnableWindow (hwnd, FALSE);

    /*  Send STARTDOC escape.                                    */
    cb = lstrlen (achJobName);
    err = Escape (hdcPrinter, STARTDOC, cb, achJobName, NULL);
    if (err <= 0) goto Exit;

    /*  Send output to printer.                                  */
    PrintOutput (hdcPrinter);

    /*  Signal next page, or abort printing.                     */
    if (bContinue)
        {
        err = Escape (hdcPrinter, NEWFRAME, NULL, NULL, NULL);
```

```
                if (err < 0) goto Exit;
                }
        else
                Escape (hdcPrinter, ABORTDOC, NULL, NULL, NULL);


        /*  Send ENDDOC escape.                                      */
        err = Escape (hdcPrinter, ENDDOC, NULL, NULL, NULL);

Exit:
    /*  Enable parent.                                               */
    EnableWindow (hwnd, TRUE);

    /*  Remove abort dialog box.                                     */
    DestroyWindow (hdlgAbort);

    if (bContinue && err < 0)
        MessageBox (hwnd, "Unable to print", "Print", MB_OK);
    }



/*------------------------------------------------------------------*\
|     PrintAbortDlg:  Abort Print dialog box procedure.              |
\*------------------------------------------------------------------*/
BOOL FAR  PASCAL PrintAbortDlg (HWND hdlg,      WORD wMsg,
                                    WORD wParam, LONG lParam)

    {
    switch (wMsg)
        {
        case WM_INITDIALOG:
            {
            char ach[50];

            /*  Initialize static text controls.                    */
            SetDlgItemText (hdlg, IDD_JOBNAME, achJobName);
            lstrcpy (ach, achPrinter);
            lstrcat (ach, " on ");
            lstrcat (ach, achPort);
            SetDlgItemText (hdlg, IDD_PRINTER, ach);
            }
            break;
```

```
                /*  User has pushed 'Cancel' button.  Abort printing.  */
                case WM_COMMAND:
                    bContinue = FALSE;
                    return TRUE;


                default:
                    return FALSE;
                }
        }



/*------------------------------------------------------------------*\
 | PrintAbortMsg:  Message loop to monitor abort print dialog.|
 \*------------------------------------------------------------------*/
BOOL FAR PASCAL PrintAbortMsg (HDC hdc, short code)
    {
    MSG msg;

    while (bContinue && PeekMessage (&msg, 0, 0, 0, PM_REMOVE))
        {
        if (!IsDialogMessage (hdlgAbort, &msg))
            {
            TranslateMessage(&msg);
            DispatchMessage(&msg);
            }
        }

    return bContinue;
    }
```

PRINT.H

```
/*------------------------------------------------------------------*\
 |   Print.H  -  Include file for Print.c.                          |
 \*------------------------------------------------------------------*/


#define IDM_NEW     100
#define IDM_OPEN    101
```

```
#define IDM_SAVE    102
#define IDM_SAVEAS  103
#define IDM_PRINT   104
#define IDM_EXIT    105
```

ABORTDLG.H

```
#define IDD_CANCEL   2
#define IDD_JOBNAME  100
#define IDD_PRINTER  101
```

PRINT.RC

```
#include <Windows.H>
#include "Print.H"
#include "Abortdlg.H"

#include "Abort.dlg"

snapshot icon Print.ico

hand   cursor Print.cur


1 MENU
    {
    POPUP "&File"
        {
        MENUITEM "&New",         IDM_NEW
        MENUITEM "&Open...",     IDM_OPEN
        MENUITEM "&Save",        IDM_SAVE
        MENUITEM "Save &As...",  IDM_SAVEAS
        MENUITEM SEPARATOR
        MENUITEM "&Print",       IDM_PRINT
        MENUITEM SEPARATOR
        MENUITEM "E&xit",        IDM_EXIT
        }
    }
```

ABORT.DLG

```
1 DIALOG LOADONCALL MOVEABLE DISCARDABLE 33, 32, 158, 67
CAPTION "Escape  -  Printing"
STYLE WS_BORDER | WS_CAPTION | WS_DLGFRAME | WS_SYSMENU |
      WS_VISIBLE | WS_POPUP
BEGIN
    CONTROL "", IDD_JOBNAME, "static",
            SS_CENTER | WS_CHILD, 0, 10, 158, 8
    CONTROL "", IDD_PRINTER, "static",
            SS_CENTER | WS_CHILD, 0, 25, 158, 8
    CONTROL "Cancel", IDD_CANCEL, "button",
            BS_DEFPUSHBUTTON | WS_TABSTOP | WS_CHILD,
            60, 43, 43, 14
END
```

PRINT.DEF

```
NAME    Print

EXETYPE WINDOWS

DESCRIPTION 'Demonstrates printing in Windows'

CODE    MOVEABLE DISCARDABLE
DATA    MOVEABLE MULTIPLE

HEAPSIZE    512
STACKSIZE   5000

EXPORTS
    PrintWndProc
    PrintAbortDlg
    PrintAbortMsg
```

As shown in Figure 21.7, PRINT creates a modeless dialog box that allows the user to cancel the print job by clicking on the Cancel push button, or by striking the Esc key.

Figure 21.7   *PRINT's abort dialog box*

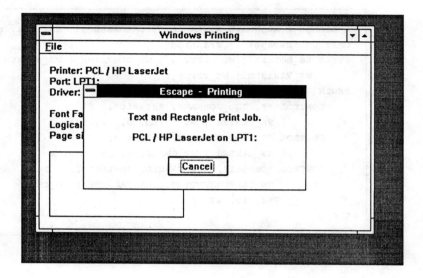

The presence of a modeless dialog box means that the message loop in the Abort function must be changed to include a call to **IsDialogMessage**. As you may recall from our discussion of dialog boxes in Chapter 14, this routine enables the keyboard interface to a modeless dialog box.

The guts of the printing that PRINT performs is found in the routine named PrintPrint. It shows the use of the various escape codes and error handling when printing fails.

Appendix A:
A Taxonomy of Messages

The Eight Types of Messages

Type	Description
Hardware	Mouse and Keyboard Input.
Window Maintenance	Notification, Request for action, Query.
User-Interface Maintenance	Menu, mouse pointer, scroll bar, dialog boxes, MDI.
Termination	Application or system shutdown.
Private	Dialog box controls: edit, button, list box, combobox.
System Resource Notification	Color Changes, fonts, spooler, device modes.
Data Sharing	Clipboard and Dynamic Data Exchange (DDE).
Internal System	Undocumented Messages.

Hardware Messages

Mouse Messages: In a window's client area

WM_LBUTTONDBLCLK	Left button double-click.
WM_LBUTTONDOWN	Left button down.
WM_LBUTTONUP	Left button up.
WM_MBUTTONDBLCLK	Middle button double-click.
WM_MBUTTONDOWN	Middle button down.
WM_MBUTTONUP	Middle button up.

(Continued)

Hardware Messages (continued)

Mouse Messages: In a window's client area

WM_MOUSEMOVE	Mouse move.
WM_RBUTTONDBLCLK	Right button double-click.
WM_RBUTTONDOWN	Right button down.
WM_RBUTTONUP	Right button up.

Mouse Messages: In a window's non-client area

WM_NCLBUTTONDBLCLK	Left button double-click.
WM_NCLBUTTONDOWN	Left button down.
WM_NCLBUTTONUP	Left button up.
WM_NCMBUTTONDBLCLK	Middle button double-click.
WM_NCMBUTTONDOWN	Middle button down.
WM_NCMBUTTONUP	Middle button up.
WM_NCMOUSEMOVE	Mouse move.
WM_NCRBUTTONDBLCLK	Right button double-click.
WM_NCRBUTTONDOWN	Right button down.
WM_NCRBUTTONUP	Right button up.

Keyboard Messages

WM_CHAR	Character input.
WM_DEADCHAR	Dead-character (umlaut, accent, etc.).
WM_KEYDOWN	Key has been depressed.
WM_KEYUP	Key has been released.
WM_SYSCHAR	System character input.
WM_SYSDEADCHAR	System dead-character.
WM_SYSKEYDOWN	System key has been depressed.
WM_SYSKEYUP	System key has been released.

Timer Message

WM_TIMER	Timer has gone off.

Window Maintenance Messages

Window Messages: Notification

WM_ACTIVATE	Window is active.
WM_ACTIVATEAPP	Application is active.
WM_CREATE	Window has been created.
WM_DESTROY	Window has been destroyed.
WM_ENABLE	Input to the window has been enabled.
WM_KILLFOCUS	Window has lost keyboard control.
WM_MOUSEACTIVATE	Notifies a window that it is going to become active because of a mouse click.
WM_MOVE	Window has been moved.
WM_PARENTNOTIFY	A child window has been created, destroyed, or has received a mouse button message.
WM_SETFOCUS	Window has gained keyboard control.
WM_SIZE	Window has changed size.

Window Messages: Request for Action

WM_CLOSE	Close (destroy) window.
WM_ERASEBKGND	Erase background.
WM_ICONERASEBKGND	Erase background of iconic window.
WM_NCACTIVATE	Change title bar to show active state.
WM_NCCREATE	Create non-client area data.
WM_NCDESTROY	Destroy non-client area data.
WM_NCPAINT	Redraw non-client area.
WM_PAINT	Redraw client area.
WM_PAINTICON	Redraw iconic window client area.
WM_SETREDRAW	Inhibit redrawing of window.
WM_SETTEXT	Change window text.
WM_SHOWWINDOW	Change window visibility.

(Continued)

Window Maintenance Messages (continued)

Window Messages: Query

WM_GETMINMAXINFO	What is min/max sizes for window?
WM_GETTEXT	What is the window text?
WM_GETTEXTLENGTH	What is the length of the window text?
WM_NCCALCSIZE	How big should the client area be?
WM_QUERYDRAGICON	For windows that do not have a class cursor: Do you have a cursor to be used as your icon while you are being dragged around the screen?
WM_QUERYNEWPALETTE	Do you have a new palette?
WM_QUERYOPEN	Can iconic window be opened?

User Interface Messages

Menu Messages

WM_COMMAND	Menu item has been selected.
WM_INITMENU	Initialize menu bar menu.
WM_INITMENUPOPUP	Initialize popup menu.
WM_MENUCHAR	Mnemonic key used to select menu.
WM_MENUSELECT	User is browsing through menus.

System Commands: System Menu, Min/Max Buttons, Titlebar, etc.

WM_SYSCOMMAND	A system command has been selected.

Mouse Pointer Messages

WM_NCHITTEST	Query: where is mouse on the window?
WM_SETCURSOR	Request: Change pointer to correct shape.

(Continued)

User Interface Messages (continued)

Scroll Bar Messages

WM_HSCROLL	Horizontal scrollbar has been clicked.
WM_VSCROLL	Vertical scrollbar has been clicked.

Dialog Box and Dialog Box Control Messages

WM_CHARTOITEM	Message sent from a list box to its parent window in response to a WM_CHAR message. Only list boxes with the LBS_WANTKEYBOARDINPUT style send this message. Among other things, it allows a keyboard interface for owner-draw list boxes.
WM_COMMAND	Control communicating with Dialog Box.
WM_COMPAREITEM	Sent to the parent of an owner-draw dialog box control, asking to compare two items for the purpose of sorting.
WM_CTLCOLOR	Control asking for colors to be set.
WM_DELETEITEM	Notification to an owner-draw listbox or an owner-draw combobox that an item has been deleted.
WM_DRAWITEM	Request to the parent of an owner-draw control, or owner-draw menu, to draw.
WM_GETDLGCODE	Query control: want keyboard input?
WM_GETFONT	Query control: what font are you using?
WM_INITDIALOG	Initialize dialog.
WM_MEASUREITEM	Request to the parent of an owner-draw control or an owner-draw item to provide the dimensions of the item that is going to be drawn.

(Continued)

User Interface Messages (continued)

Dialog Box and Dialog Box Control Messages

WM_NEXTDLGCTL	Message sent by a dialog box control to allow the proper handling of the Tab and Return keys for controls that process keyboard input themselves.
WM_SETFONT	Request to control: use this font.
WM_VKEYTOITEM	Message sent from a list box to its parent window in response to a WM_KEYDOWN message. This is only sent by list boxes which have the LBS_WANTKEYBOARDINPUT style set.

Multiple Document Interface Messages

WM_CHILDACTIVATE	Notifies a parent window that a child is active.
WM_MDIACTIVATE	Notifies an MDI child window that it is either gaining or losing activation.
WM_MDICASCADE	Request to arrange the open MDI child windows in a cascading, stair-step fashion.
WM_MDICREATE	Requests an MDI client window to create an MDI child window.
WM_MDIDESTROY	Requests to an MDI client window to destroy an MDI child window.
WM_MDIGETACTIVE	Query an MDI client window for the currently active MDI child window.
WM_MDIICONARRANGE	Request to arrange the iconic MDI child windows in an orderly fashion.
WM_MDIMAXIMIZE	Request to maximize, or zoom, an MDI child window so that it occupies all of its parent's client area.
WM_MDINEXT	Request to activate the next MDI child window.
WM_MDIRESTORE	Request to restore an MDI child window to its previous state—iconic, normal, or zoomed.

(Continued)

User Interface Messages (continued)

Multiple Document Interface Messages

WM_MDISETMENU	Adjusts the menu on an MDI frame window.
WM_MDITILE	Request to arrange the open MDI child windows in a tiled fashion in the MDI parent's client window.

Termination Messages

Application and System Termination

WM_QUIT	Request that a program should terminate.
WM_QUERYENDSESSION	A Query: Ready for system shutdown?
WM_ENDSESSION	Notification of results of shutdown query.

Private Messages

Button Control Messages

BM_GETCHECK	Query whether a button is checked or not.
BM_GETSTATE	Query state of a button.
BM_SETCHECK	Toggles a radio button or a check box.
BM_SETSTATE	Toggles the highlighting in a radio button or check box.
BM_SETSTYLE	Changes the style of an existing button.

Combo Box Control Message

CB_ADDSTRING	Adds a string to the list box of a combo box.
CB_DELETESTRING	Removes a string from the list box of a combo box.

(Continued)

Private Messages (continued)

Combo Box Control Messages

CB_DIR	Adds a list of files from the current directory to the list box of a combo box.
CB_FINDSTRING	Searches the list box in a combo box for a string.
CB_GETCOUNT	Queries the number of items in the list box of a combo box.
CB_GETCURSEL	Queries the index of the currently selected item in the list box of a combo box.
CB_GETEDITSEL	Queries the selected text in the edit control of a combo box.
CB_GETITEMDATA	Queries the item identifier from the list box of a combo box.
CB_GETLBTEXT	Queries a string from the list box of a combo box.
CB_GETLBTEXTLEN	Queries the length of a string in the list box of a combo box.
CB_INSERTSTRING	Inserts a string into the list box of a combo box.
CB_LIMITTEXT	Sets the maximum number of characters that may be entered into the edit control of a combo box.
CB_RESETCONTENT	Removes all items from the list box of a combo box.
CB_SELECTSTRING	Creates a selection in the list box of a combo box.
CB_SETCURSEL	Sets the current selection in the list box of a combo box, and places the text into the edit or static control.
CB_SETEDITSEL	Selects a range of characters in the edit control of a combo box.
CB_SETITEMDATA	Sets the identities for an item in a combo box.

(Continued)

Private Messages (continued)

Combo Box Control Messages

CB_SHOWDROPDOWN	Shows or hides the drop down list box of a combo box.

Dialog Box Messages

DM_GETDEFID	Queries the ID of the default push button in a dialog box.
DM_SETDEFID	Sets the default push button in a dialog box.

Edit Control

EM_CANUNDO	Queries the ability of an edit control to undo a previous edit.
EM_EMPTYUNDOBUFFER	Instructs an edit control to clear its undo buffer.
EM_FMTLINES	Instructs an edit control on how to handle end of line characters.
EM_GETHANDLE	Queries an edit control created with the DS_LOCALEDIT style for the handle of the object allocated from the local heap.
EM_GETLINE	Retrieves a line of text from an edit control.
EM_GETLINECOUNT	Queries the number of lines of text in an edit control.
EM_GETMODIFY	Queries an edit control to determine if the user has entered or changed any text.
EM_GETRECT	Queries an edit control for its display rectangle, which is either its client area or a subset as set by the EM_SETRECT message.
EM_GETSEL	Queries the characters that are included in the current selection.
EM_LIMITTEXT	Sets a limit to the number of characters that may be entered.

(Continued)

Private Messages (continued)

Edit Control

EM_LINEFROMCHAR	Finds the first line that contains a specific character.
EM_LINEINDEX	Queries the number of lines that have been scrolled in a multi-line edit control.
EM_LINELENGTH	Queries the length of a line in an edit control.
EM_LINESCROLL	Scrolls a multi-line edit control.
EM_REPLACESEL	Overwrites the current selection with new text.
EM_SETHANDLE	For edit controls with the DS_LOCALEDIT style, this message instructs the edit control to use a new local memory object for its data.
EM_SETMODIFY	Sets the modify flag for an edit control.
EM_SETPASSWORDCHAR	Sets the character to be displayed when a password is entered in an ES_PASSWORD style edit control.
EM_SETRECT	Sets the display rectangle for a multi-line edit control and causes an immediate repaint to occur.
EM_SETRECTNP	Sets the display rectangle for a multi-line edit control, and postpones painting until later.
EM_SETSEL	Defines a range of characters to display as selected.
EM_SETTABSTOPS	Sets the tab-stops in a multi-line edit control.
EM_SETWORDBREAK	Defines a call-back function to be used for word-break processing in a multi-line edit control.
EM_UNDO	Instructs an edit control to undo the last edit.

(Continued)

Private Messages (continued)

List box Control

LB_ADDSTRING	Inserts a string into a list box.
LB_DELETESTRING	Removes a string for a list box.
LB_DIR	Adds a list of files from the current directory to a list box.
LB_FINDSTRING	Searches a list box for a string.
LB_GETCOUNT	Queries the number of items in a list box.
LB_GETCURSEL	Queries the index of the currently selected item in a list box.
LB_GETHORIZONTALEXTENT	Queries the width in pixels that can be scrolled for a list box with horizontal scroll bars.
LB_GETITEMDATA	Queries the item identifier from a list box.
LB_GETITEMRECT	Queries the dimensions of a rectangle that bounds a list box item.
LB_GETSEL	Queries the selection state of a specific list box item.
LB_GETSELCOUNT	Queries the total number of items that are selected in a list box.
LB_GETSELITEMS	Queries the indices of the selected items in a list box.
LB_GETTEXT	Query the text of a list box item.
LB_GETTEXTLEN	Queries the text length of a list box item.
LB_GETTOPINDEX	Queries the index of the item currently displayed at the top of a list box.
LB_INSERTSTRING	Adds a string to a list box.
LB_RESETCONTENT	Removes all items from a list box.
LB_SELECTSTRING	Selects an item in a list box.
LB_SELITEMRANGE	Selects a range of items in a multi-selection list box.

(Continued)

Private Messages (continued)

List Box Control

LB_SETCOLUMNWIDTH	Sets the column width of multi-column list box.
LB_SETCURSEL	Sets the current selection in a list box.
LB_SETHORIZONTALEXTENT	Sets the horizontal scrolling range of a list box.
LB_SETITEMDATA	Replaces an owner-draw item in a list box.
LB_SETSEL	Highlights a string in a multiple selection list box.
LB_SETTABSTOPS	Sets the tab stop of a list box that was created with the LBS_USETABSTOPS style.
LB_SETTOPINDEX	Scrolls a list box to place a specific item at the top of the list box.

System Private Messages

WM_CANCELMODE	Request by system to cancel a mode, such as a mouse capture.
WM_ENTERIDLE	Notification that the system is in an idling state, because the user is browsing a menu or a dialog box.

System Resource Notification Messages

System Resources Notification Messages

WM_COMPACTING	Notification that system memory is low, and that the Memory Manager is trying to free up some memory.
WM_DEVMODECHANGE	Printer setup has changed.
WM_FONTCHANGE	Installed fonts in the system have changed.

(Continued)

System Resource Notification Messages (continued)
System Resources Notification Messages

WM_PALETTECHANGED	Hardware color palette has changed.
WM_SPOOLERSTATUS	Job has been removed from spooler queue.
WM_SYSCOLORCHANGE	One or more system colors has changed.
WM_TIMECHANGE	System time has changed.
WM_WININICHANGE	Initialization file, WIN.INI, changed.

Data Sharing Messages
Clipboard Messages

WM_ASKCBFORMATNAME	Asks for the name of a Clipboard format.
WM_CHANGECBCHAIN	Notification of a change in the viewing chain.
WM_DESTROYCLIPBOARD	Clipboard contents are being destroyed.
WM_DRAWCLIPBOARD	Clipboard contents have changed.
WM_HSCROLLCLIPBOARD	Horizonal scrolling of owner-draw clipboard item.
WM_PAINTCLIPBOARD	Requests drawing of an owner-draw clipboard item.
WM_RENDERALLFORMATS	Request to provide the data for all clipboard formats that have been promised.
WM_RENDERFORMAT	Request to provide data for a single clipboard format that has been promised.
WM_SIZECLIPBOARD	Notification to the owner of owner-draw clipboard data that the size of the Clipboard viewer window has changed.
WM_VSCROLLCLIPBOARD	Vertical scrolling of an owner-draw clipboard item.

(Continued)

Data Sharing Messages (continued)

Dynamic Data Exchange (DDE) Messages

WM_DDE_ACK	Acknowledgment.
WM_DDE_ADVISE	Request from a DDE client to establish a permanent data link.
WM_DDE_DATA	Send a data item from a DDE server to a DDE client.
WM_DDE_EXECUTE	Request a DDE server to execute a series of commands.
WM_DDE_INITIATE	Logon to a DDE server.
WM_DDE_POKE	Request by a client for a server to update a specific data item.
WM_DDE_REQUEST	One-time request by a DDE client for a piece of information.
WM_DDE_TERMINATE	Logoff from a DDE server.
WM_DDE_UNADVISE	Terminate a permanent data link that was initiated with the WM_DDE_ADVISE message.

Appendix B:
The Default Window Procedure

For your convenience, here is a listing of the default window procedure that Microsoft provided in the Windows software development kit. To see the latest revision of this code, please refer to the sample source diskettes which Microsoft provides as part of the SDK. And here is a list of the messages to which DefWindowProc responds:

WM_NCACTIVATE	WM_ERASEBKGND
WM_NCHITTEST	WM_QUERYOPEN
WM_NCCALCSIZE	WM_QUERYENDSESSION
WM_NCLBUTTONDOWN	WM_SYSCOMMAND
WM_NCMOUSEMOVE	WM_SYSKEYDOWN
WM_NCLBUTTONUP	WM_KEYUP
WM_NCLBUTTONDBLCLK	WM_SYSKEYUP
WM_CANCELMODE	WM_SYSCHAR
WM_NCCREATE	WM_CHARTOITEM
WM_NCDESTROY	WM_VKEYTOITEM
WM_NCPAINT	WM_ACTIVATE
WM_SETTEXT	WM_SETREDRAW
WM_GETTEXT	WM_SHOWWINDOW
WM_GETTEXTLENGTH	WM_CTLCOLOR
WM_CLOSE	WM_SETCURSOR
WM_PAINT	WM_MOUSEACTIVATE
WM_PAINTICON	WM_DRAWITEM
WM_ICONERASEBKGNE	

```
/*------------------------------------------------------------*/
/*                                                            */
/*  DefWindowProc() -                                         */
/*                                                            */
/*------------------------------------------------------------*/
                                                              /

LONG FAR PASCAL DefWindowProc(hwnd, message, wParam, lParam)

register HWND hwnd;
         WORD message;
register WORD wParam;
         LONG lParam;

{
  int        i;
  HDC        hdc;
  PAINTSTRUCT ps;
  HICON      hIcon;
  RECT       rc;
  HANDLE     hCurs;
  HBRUSH     hbr;
  HWND       hwndT;

  if (!CheckHwnd(hwnd))
    return((DWORD)FALSE);

  switch (message)
    {
      case WM_NCACTIVATE:
        if (wParam != 0)
          SetWF(hwnd, WFFRAMEON);
        else
          ClrWF(hwnd, WFFRAMEON);

        if (TestWF(hwnd, WFVISIBLE) && !TestWF(hwnd,
                                             WFNONCPAINT))

          {
            hdc = GetWindowDC(hwnd);
            DrawCaption(hwnd, hdc, TRUE, TestWF(hwnd,
                                             WFFRAMEON));

            InternalReleaseDC(hdc);
```

```
            if (TestWF(hwnd,WFMINIMIZED))
                RedrawIconTitle(hwnd);
        }
    return(TRUE);


case WM_NCHITTEST:
    return(FindNCHit(hwnd, lParam));


case WM_NCCALCSIZE:
    CalcClientRect(hwnd, (LPRECT)lParam);
    break;


case WM_NCLBUTTONDOWN:
{
    WORD      cmd;
    RECT      rcWindow;
    RECT      rcCapt;
    RECT      rcInvert;
    RECT      rcWindowSave;

    cmd = 0;

    switch(wParam)
        {
        case HTZOOM:
        case HTREDUCE:
            GetWindowRect(hwnd, (LPRECT)&rcWindow);
            CopyRect((LPRECT)&rcWindowSave, (LPRECT)&rcWindow);

            if (TestWF(hwnd, WFSIZEBOX))
                InflateRect((LPRECT)&rcWindow,
                            -cxSzBorderPlus1, -cySzBorderPlus1);
            else
                InflateRect((LPRECT)&rcWindow,
                            -cxBorder, -cyBorder);

            rcCapt.right = rcWindow.right + cxBorder;
            rcCapt.left = rcWindow.right - oemInfo.bmReduce.cx-
                            cxBorder;

            if (wParam == HTREDUCE)
```

```
      cmd = SC_MINIMIZE;
    else if (TestWF(hwnd, WFMAXIMIZED))
      cmd = SC_RESTORE;
    else
      cmd = SC_MAXIMIZE;

    if (wParam == HTREDUCE && TestWF(hwnd, WFMAXBOX))
      OffsetRect((LPRECT)&rcCapt,
                 -oemInfo.bmReduce.cx, 0);
    rcCapt.top = rcWindow.top;
    rcCapt.bottom = rcCapt.top + cyCaption;

    CopyRect((LPRECT)&rcInvert, (LPRECT)&rcCapt);
    InflateRect((LPRECT)&rcInvert,
                -cxBorder, -cyBorder);

    rcInvert.right += cxBorder;
    rcInvert.left += cxBorder;

    /* Converting to window coordinates. */
    OffsetRect((LPRECT)&rcInvert,
            -(rcWindowSave.left + cxBorder),
            -(rcWindowSave.top + cyBorder));
    /* Wait for the BUTTONUP message and see if cursor
     *  is still in the Minimize or Maximize box.
     *
     * NOTE: rcInvert is in window coords, rcCapt is
     * in screen coords
     */
    if (!DepressTitleButton(hwnd, rcCapt,
                            rcInvert, wParam))
      cmd = 0;

    break;

  default:
    if (wParam >= HTSIZEFIRST && wParam <= HTSIZELAST)
      /* Change HT into a MV command. */
      cmd = SC_SIZE +
            (wParam - HTSIZEFIRST + MVSIZEFIRST);
}
```

```
        if (cmd != 0)
          {
            /* For SysCommands on system menu,
             * don't do if menu item is disabled.
             */
            if (TestWF(hwnd, WFSYSMENU))
              {
                /* don't check old app child windows
                 */
                if (LOWORD(GetExpWinVer(hwnd->hInstance)) >= VER
                    || !TestwndChild(hwnd))
                  {
                    SetSysMenu(hwnd);
                    if (GetMenuState(GetSysMenuHandle(hwnd),
                                     cmd & 0xFFF0,
                                     MF_BYCOMMAND)
                        & (MF_DISABLED | MF_GRAYED))
                      break;
                  }
              }
            SendMessage(hwnd, WM_SYSCOMMAND, cmd, lParam);
            break;
          }
      /*** FALL THRU ***/
      }

    case WM_NCMOUSEMOVE:
    case WM_NCLBUTTONUP:
    case WM_NCLBUTTONDBLCLK:
      HandleNCMouseGuys(hwnd, message, wParam, lParam);
      break;

    case WM_CANCELMODE:
      if (hwndCapture == hwnd && pfnSB != NULL)
        EndScroll(hwnd, TRUE);

        if (fMenu && hwndMenu == hwnd)
          EndMenu();

      /* If the capture is still set, just release at
```

```
         * this point.  Can put other End functions in later.
         */
      if (hwnd == hwndCapture)
        ReleaseCapture();
      break;

   case WM_NCCREATE:
      if (TestWF(hwnd, (WFHSCROLL | WFVSCROLL)))
        if (InitPwSB(hwnd) == NULL)
           return((LONG)FALSE);

      return((LONG)DefSetText(hwnd,
                     ((LPCREATESTRUCT)lParam)->lpszName));
   case WM_NCDESTROY:
      if (hwnd->hName)
         hwnd->hName = TextFree(hwnd->hName);
      break;

   case WM_NCPAINT:
      /* Force the drawing of the menu. */
      SetWF(hwnd, WFMENUDRAW);
      DrawWindowFrame(hwnd, (HRGN)wParam);
      ClrWF(hwnd, WFMENUDRAW);
      break;

   case WM_SETTEXT:
      DefSetText(hwnd, (LPSTR)lParam);
      if (TestWF(hwnd, WFVISIBLE))
        {
           if (TestWF(hwnd,WFMINIMIZED))
             {
                ShowIconTitle(hwnd,FALSE);
                ShowIconTitle(hwnd,TRUE);
             }
           else if (TestWF(hwnd, WFBORDERMASK) ==
                   (BYTE)LOBYTE(WFCAPTION))
             {
                hdc = GetWindowDC(hwnd);
                DrawCaption(hwnd,
                         hdc,
                         FALSE,
```

```
                          TestWF(hwnd, WFFRAMEON));
                InternalReleaseDC(hdc);
            }
        }
    break;

case WM_GETTEXT:
    if (wParam)
        {
        if (hwnd->hName)
            return (DWORD)TextCopy(hwnd->hName,
                                    (LPSTR)lParam,
                                    wParam);

        /* else Null terminate the text buffer since
         * there is no text.
         */
        ((LPSTR)lParam)[0] = NULL;
        }
    return (0L);


case WM_GETTEXTLENGTH:
    if (hwnd->hName)
        return(lstrlen(TextPointer(hwnd->hName)));

    /* else */
    return(0L);

case WM_CLOSE:
    DestroyWindow(hwnd);
    break;

case WM_PAINT:
    BeginPaint(hwnd, (LPPAINTSTRUCT)&ps);
    EndPaint(hwnd, (LPPAINTSTRUCT)&ps);
    break;

case WM_PAINTICON:
    /* Draw the icon through the window DC if app used
     * own DC. If own DC is used the mapping mode may
```

```
    * not be MM_TEXT.
    */
   BeginPaint(hwnd, (LPPAINTSTRUCT)&ps);
   if (TestCF(hwnd, CFOWNDC) || TestCF(hwnd, CFCLASSDC))
     {
        /* If owndc, do the end paint now so that the
         * erasebackgrounds/validate regions go through
         * properly. Then we get a clean window dc to
         * draw the icon into.
         */
        InternalEndPaint(hwnd, (LPPAINTSTRUCT)&ps, TRUE);
        hdc = GetWindowDC(hwnd);
     }
   else
     {
        hdc = ps.hdc;
     }
   /* wParam is TRUE to draw icon, FALSE to ignore paint. */
   if (wParam)
     {
        hIcon = (HICON)(PCLS)(hwnd->pcls)->hIcon;
        GetClientRect(hwnd, (LPRECT)&rc);

        rc.left = (rc.right - rgwSysMet[SM_CXICON]) >> 1;
        rc.top = (rc.bottom - rgwSysMet[SM_CYICON]) >> 1;

        DrawIcon(hdc, rc.left, rc.top, hIcon);
     }

   /* Delete the update region. */
     if (TestCF(hwnd, CFOWNDC) || TestCF(hwnd, CFCLASSDC))
       {
          InternalReleaseDC(hdc);
          /* ValidateRect(hwnd, NULL); */
       }
     else
        InternalEndPaint(hwnd, (LPPAINTSTRUCT)&ps, TRUE);
   break;


case WM_ICONERASEBKGND:
   /* Erase the icon through the window DC if app used
```

```
       * own DC. If own DC is used the mapping mode may not
       * be MM_TEXT.
       */
      if (TestCF(hwnd, CFOWNDC) || TestCF(hwnd, CFCLASSDC))
        hdc = GetWindowDC(hwnd);
      else
        hdc = (HDC)wParam;

      if (TestWF(hwnd, WFCHILD))      /* for MDI child icons */
        {
          if ((hbr = GetBackBrush(hwnd->hwndParent)) == NULL)
            {
              /* No brush, punt. */
              goto AbortIconEraseBkGnd;
            }
          else
              goto ICantBelieveIUsedAGoToStatement;
        }


      if (hbmWallpaper)
        {
          /* Since desktop bitmaps are done on a wm_paint
           * message (and not erasebkgnd), we need to call
           * the paint proc with our dc.
           */
          PaintDesktop(hdc);
          /* SendMessage(hwndDesktop,WM_ERASEBKGND,hdc,0L);*/
        }
      else
        {
          hbr = sysClrObjects.hbrDesktop;
ICantBelieveIUsedAGoToStatement:
          FillWindow(hwnd->hwndParent,hwnd,hdc,hbr);
        }

AbortIconEraseBkGnd:
      if (TestCF(hwnd, CFOWNDC) || TestCF(hwnd, CFCLASSDC))
        InternalReleaseDC(hdc);

      return((LONG)TRUE);
```

```
case WM_ERASEBKGND:
  if ((hbr = GetBackBrush(hwnd)) != NULL)
    {
       FillWindow(hwnd, hwnd, (HDC)wParam, hbr);
       return((LONG)TRUE);
    }
  break;

case WM_QUERYOPEN:
case WM_QUERYENDSESSION:
  return((LONG)TRUE);

case WM_SYSCOMMAND:
  SysCommand(hwnd, wParam, lParam);
  break;

case WM_KEYDOWN:
  if (wParam == VK_F10)
    fF10Status = TRUE;
  break;
case WM_SYSKEYDOWN:
  /* Is the ALT key down? */
  if (HIWORD(lParam) & SYS_ALTERNATE)
    {
      /* Toggle the fMenuStatus iff this is NOT a
       * repeat KEYDOWN message;  Only if the prev key
       * state was 0, then this is the first KEYDOWN
       * message and then we consider toggling menu
       * status.
       */
      if((HIWORD(lParam) & SYS_PREVKEYSTATE) == 0)
        {
          /* Don't have to lock hwndActive because it's
           * processing this key.
           */
          if ((wParam == VK_MENU) && (!fMenuStatus))
            fMenuStatus = TRUE;
          else
            fMenuStatus = FALSE;
        }
```

```
            fF10Status = FALSE;

            DWP_ProcessVirtKey(wParam);
        }
    else
        {
        if (wParam == VK_F10)
            fF10Status = TRUE;
        else
            {
            if (wParam == VK_ESCAPE)
                {
                    if(GetKeyState(VK_SHIFT) < 0)
                        SendMessage(hwnd,
                                    WM_SYSCOMMAND,
                                    SC_KEYMENU,
                                    (DWORD)MENUSYSMENU);
                }
            }
        }
    break;

case WM_KEYUP:
case WM_SYSKEYUP:
    /* Press and release F10 or ALT.
     * Send this only to top-level windows, otherwise MDI
     * gets confused.  The fix in which DefMDIChildProc()
     * passed up the message was insufficient in case
     * a child window of the MDI child had the focus.
     */
    if ((wParam == VK_MENU && (fMenuStatus == TRUE)) ||
        (wParam == VK_F10 && fF10Status) )
        SendMessage(GetTopLevelWindow(hwnd),
                    WM_SYSCOMMAND,
                    SC_KEYMENU,
                    (DWORD)0);

    fF10Status = fMenuStatus = FALSE;
    break;

case WM_SYSCHAR:
```

```
         /* If syskey is down and we have a char... */
         fMenuStatus = FALSE;
         if ((HIWORD(lParam) & SYS_ALTERNATE) && wParam)
           {
             if (wParam == VK_TAB || wParam == VK_ESCAPE)
               break;

             /* Send ALT-SPACE only to top-level windows. */
             if ((wParam == MENUSYSMENU) && (TestwndChild(hwnd)))
               SendMessage(hwnd->hwndParent,
                            message,
                            wParam,
                            lParam);
             else
               SendMessage(hwnd,
                            WM_SYSCOMMAND,
                            SC_KEYMENU,
                            (DWORD)wParam);
           }
         else
           /* Ctrl-Esc produces a WM_SYSCHAR,
            * But should not beep;
            */
           if (wParam != VK_ESCAPE)
             MessageBeep(0);
         break;

case WM_CHARTOITEM:
case WM_VKEYTOITEM:
  /* Do default processing for keystrokes into
   * owner draw listboxes.
   */
  return(-1);

case WM_ACTIVATE:
  if (wParam)
    SetFocus(hwnd);
  break;

case WM_SETREDRAW:
  DWP_SetRedraw(hwnd, wParam);
```

```
        break;

case WM_SHOWWINDOW:
  /* Non null descriptor implies popup hide or show. */
  /* We should check whether it is a popup window
   * or Owned window
   */
  if (LOWORD(lParam) != 0 &&
      (TestwndPopup(hwnd) || hwnd -> hwndOwner))
    {
      /* IF NOT(showing, invisible, and not set as hidden)
       * AND NOT(hiding and not visible)
       */
      if (!(wParam != 0 && !TestWF(hwnd, WFVISIBLE) &&
            !TestWF(hwnd, WFHIDDENPOPUP)) &&
          !(wParam == 0 && !TestWF(hwnd, WFVISIBLE)))
        {
          /* Are we showing? */
          if (wParam)
            /* Yes, clear the hidden popup flag. */
            ClrWF(hwnd, WFHIDDENPOPUP);
          else
            /* No, Set the hidden popup flag. */
            SetWF(hwnd, WFHIDDENPOPUP);

          ShowWindow(hwnd,
              (wParam ? SHOW_OPENNOACTIVATE : HIDE_WINDOW));
        }
    }
  break;

case WM_CTLCOLOR:
  if (HIWORD(lParam) != CTLCOLOR_SCROLLBAR)
    {
      SetBkColor((HDC)wParam, sysColors.clrWindow);
      SetTextColor((HDC)wParam, sysColors.clrWindowText);
      hbr = sysClrObjects.hbrWindow;
    }
  else
    {
      SetBkColor((HDC)wParam, 0x00ffffff);
```

```
            SetTextColor((HDC)wParam, (LONG)0x00000000);
            hbr = sysClrObjects.hbrScrollbar;
            UnrealizeObject(hbr);
        }

    return((DWORD)hbr);

case WM_SETCURSOR:
 /* wParam  == hwnd that cursor is over
  * lParamL == Hit test area code (result of WM_NCHITTEST)
  * lParamH == Mouse message number
  */
 if (HIWORD(lParam) != 0 &&
     LOWORD(lParam) >= HTSIZEFIRST &&
     LOWORD(lParam) <= HTSIZELAST)
   {
     SetCursor(rghCursor[LOWORD(lParam)
              - HTSIZEFIRST + MVSIZEFIRST]);
     break;
   }

 if ((hwndT = GetChildParent(hwnd)) != NULL &&
     (BOOL)SendMessage(hwndT,
                     WM_SETCURSOR,
                     wParam,
                     lParam))
   return((LONG)TRUE);
 if (HIWORD(lParam) == 0)
   {
     hCurs = hCursNormal;
     SetCursor(hCurs);
   }
 else
   {
     switch (LOWORD(lParam))
       {
       case HTCLIENT:
         if (((HWND)wParam)->pcls->hCursor != NULL)
           SetCursor(((HWND)wParam)->pcls->hCursor);
         break;
```

```
            case HTERROR:
              switch (HIWORD(lParam))
              {
                case WM_LBUTTONDOWN:
                  if ((hwndT = DWP_GetEnabledPopup(hwnd)) !=
                       NULL)
                    {
                      if (hwndT != hwndDesktop->hwndChild)
                        {
                          SetWindowPos(hwnd, NULL,
                                       0, 0, 0, 0,
                                       SWP_NOMOVE |
                                       SWP_NOSIZE |
                                       SWP_NOACTIVATE);
                          SetActiveWindow(hwndT);
                          break;
                        }
                    }

                  /*** FALL THRU ***/

                case WM_RBUTTONDOWN:
                case WM_MBUTTONDOWN:
                  MessageBeep(0);
                  break;
                }
                /*** FALL THRU ***/

              default:
                SetCursor(hCursNormal);
            }
        }

    return((LONG)FALSE);

case WM_MOUSEACTIVATE:
    if ((hwndT = GetChildParent(hwnd)) != NULL &&
        (i = (int)SendMessage(hwndT,
                              WM_MOUSEACTIVATE,
                              wParam,
```

```
                                        lParam)) != 0)
              return((LONG)i);

          /* Moving, sizing or minimizing?
           * Activate AFTER we take action.
           */
          if (LOWORD(lParam) == HTCAPTION)
            return((LONG)MA_NOACTIVATE);
          else
            return((LONG)MA_ACTIVATE);


        case WM_DRAWITEM:
          if (((LPDRAWITEMSTRUCT)lParam)->CtlType == ODT_LISTBOX)
              LBDefaultListboxDrawItem((LPDRAWITEMSTRUCT)lParam);
          break;

      }


    return(0L);
}
```

Appendix C:
Glossary of Terms

__AHINCR__ This is a global symbol that can be used by an application program to increment the segment selector to address memory objects that occupy more than a single segment.

32-Bit Addressing This refers to the capability in the Intel 80386 and later CPUs to use 32-bit offset to address memory. This allows the creation of memory segments that are as large as one megabyte. When running in 386-Enhanced Mode, Windows uses this type of addressing internally, but does not make it directly available to application programs. However, Microsoft does provide support for 32-bit addressing in a dynamic link library that is included with the Windows software development kit called WINMEM32.

Accelerator see Keyboard Accelerator.

Active Window The Active window is a top-level window belonging to the active application. The active application is the application given the highest priority by the user. When a user clicks the mouse on any window owned by an application, selects one of the application's top-level windows from Windows' Task List, or selects the application using keystroke combinations, then the application becomes active. The caption and border of the active application change color to indicate their state to the user. In addition, the windows of the active application are positioned on top of the windows belonging to other applications.

ANSI American National Standards Institute.

ANSI Character Set A standard that defines how character glyphs, or images, are stored as numeric character codes. According to the ANSI standard, the values 0 to 31 (1Fh) are reserved for control codes, the values 32 (20h) to 127 (7Fh) are for a standard set of printed characters, and the values 128 (80h) to 255 (FFh) define a range in which vendors can define their own character sequences. The IBM family of personal computers define a set of code pages that use upper range for line-drawing character, Greek letters, and accented characters. Windows defines a more complete set of accented characters that allows Windows programs to more easily be written for support in non-English-speaking countries.

ASCII American Standard Code for Information Interchange.

Application Message Queue When a Windows application is running, Windows allocates a buffer that is used to store the messages that are posted (using the **PostMessage** routine) to a program. The messages wait in the queue until a program makes a call to **GetMessage** or to **PeekMessage**. By default, a message queue can hold up to 8 messages. Programs that need a larger message queue can request this by calling **SetMessageQueue**.

Aspect Ratio The aspect ratio describes the ratio between the height of a pixel and its width. Another way to think about it is in terms of the relative "squareness" of pixels on a device. CGA displays have an aspect ratio of 2 to 1; EGA displays have a ratio of 1.33 to 1; VGA displays have an aspect ratio of 1 to 1.

Background Color The background color is a DC attribute that is used for drawing text, styled (non-solid) lines, and hatched brushes. It is controlled by the setting of the background mode, another DC attribute.

Background Mode   The background mode is a toggle switch controlling whether the background color is used or not. When set to OPAQUE, the background color is turned on. Setting the background mode to TRANSPARENT turns off the background color.

BitBlt   An acronym for "BIT-boundary BLock Transfer." This GDI function copies rectangular patterns of bits from one location to another. The most obvious use of BitBlt is for moving windows on the display screen. But BitBlts are also used to make menus appear and disappear quickly. Application programs commonly use the BitBlt function to move images stored in bitmaps to an output device like the display screen or a printer. A program can also copy an image from a display screen to a bitmap.

Bitmap   Bitmaps are one of two pseudo-devices that GDI uses to store pictures (the other type is a metafile). Bitmaps use RAM to store rectangular picture images. Bitmaps are created by requesting GDI to allocate the RAM for the picture storage. Once allocated, a bitmap provides an invisible drawing surface on which a program can draw by calling any of the GDI drawing routines. Bitmaps are also a type of resource that allow a program to store a graphic image inside its executable file. The third type of bitmaps are device-independent bitmaps (DIBs), which provide a device-independent way to store color information.

Brush   A brush is a GDI drawing object used to fill areas. There are three types of brushes: solid, pattern, and hatched. Every DC contains a brush that is used for area filling when on of the filled figure routines is called (**Rectangle, Ellipse, Polygon**, etc.). Another function which makes use of

the brush is the **BitBlt** routine, which can use the brush in the destination DC to alter the effect of the bit-blt operation.

Call-back Functions   A call-back function provides a way for Windows to communicate with a program by calling it directly into a program subroutine.

Call thunk   A call thunk is a tiny piece of code that is used by Windows in real mode as a bridge to far functions in a moveable or discardable code segment.

Capture   see Mouse Capture.

Caret   A caret is a user interface object that serves as a keyboard pointer, in much the same way that the cursor serves as a mouse pointer. A caret is a blinking bitmap that notifies the user of the window that has the keyboard focus, and also provides feedback on the location of the current position in a window.

Casting   Refers to the ability of the C compiler to convert one data type into another data type. In the following example, a variable of type int, i, is set equal to the value of a long variable, lValue:

```
long lValue;
int i;

lValue = 1245;
i = (int)lValue
```

Casting overrides the default conversion that the compiler provides, and avoids the warning messages that compilers often generate in such situations. Nevertheless, Windows programmers can omit certains types of casting which were required for older versions of the C compiler. For example, in response to the WM_PAINT message, here is an outdated but still commonly encountered construction:

```
PAINTSTRUCT ps;

BeginPaint
```

```
(hwnd, (LPPAINTSTRUCT)&ps);
.
.
.
EndPaint
(hwnd, (LPPAINTSTRUCT)&ps);
```

While it is harmless enough in this example, explicit casting is not required and can hide certain types of problems. For example, if the programmer had omitted the "&" in the previous example, the compiler would not be able to see the error because of the casting:

```
PAINTSTRUCT ps;
BeginPaint
(hwnd, (LPPAINTSTRUCT)ps);
```

CDECL Calling Convention The CDECL calling convention describes the way that parameters are passed on the stack to a subroutine (right to left), and also assigned the calling routine with the responsibility for clearing parameters from the stack. The CDECL calling convention allows routines to be defined with a variable number of parameters, with the disadvantage of creating slightly larger and slower code than the alternative PASCAL calling convention.

Class see Window Class.

Class Database Refers to the collection of window classes that have been registered in the system with **RegisterClass**.

Client Area Coordinates describe a coordinate system that has its origin (0,0) at the upper-left corner of a window. Client area coordinate units are equal to pixels.

Clipping Region A clipping region defines a closed area used for clipping. Inside the clipping region, drawing is allowed. Outside the clipping region, drawing is not allowed. Clipping regions in Windows are always described in terms of rectangles or groups of rectangles.

Clipping Clipping describes the behavior of GDI drawing routines in the way they recognize arbitrary borders that are defined. Clipping is defined in terms of closed areas: Inside the clipping region, drawing is allowed. Outside the clipping region, no drawing is allowed.

Clipboard The Clipboard provides user-operated data sharing services between programs. Items on the Edit menu ordinarily serve as the primary user interface for the Clipboard, and provide Cut, Copy, and Paste options. In addition, a standard set of accelerator keys has been defined for Clipboard commands.

Code Page A code page defines a character set. The code page determines the set of glyphs, or character images, that will be used to draw a particular character. For example, code page 437 is the standard character set for the United States version of the IBM-PC.

Common User Access (CUA) Refers to the element of IBM's Systems Application Architecture (SAA) that covers the standards that have been developed for the user interfaces part of application and system software.

Compiler Memory Model Refers to the set of defaults that the compiler sets for addressing both code and data.

Coordinate Transformation A coordinate transformation refers to the way that drawing coordinates are interpreted in a graphics output environment. The three basic types of coordinate transformation include translation, scaling, and rotation. In Windows, GDI's coordinate transformations are limited to translation and scaling.

Cursor A cursor is a bitmap that moves in response to the movement of a mouse.

Debug Version of Windows Describes Windows when running with special copies of the KERNEL.EXE (KRNL286.EXE, KRNL386.EXE), USER.EXE and GDI.EXE dynamic link libraries.

Default Window Procedure   A Windows library routine that processes non-client area messages, system commands, system keystrokes, and other messages that window procedures do not process.

Desktop Window   Refers to the window that covers the entire display screen and sits behind every other window in the system.

Device Capability Bits   Refers to a set of flags that are provided by a GDI display or printer driver to describe the native capabilities of the device. GDI uses these flags to determine whether to send a high-level drawing request directly to a device driver, or to simulate the request in software and send the device driver a series of low-level drawing requests.

Device Context (DC)   A data structure created and maintained by GDI in support of device independent drawing operations on displays, printers, metafiles, and bitmaps. A device context is three things rolled into one: It is a toolbox containing a set of drawing attributes or drawing tools, it is a connection to a specific device, and it is a permission slip that allows a program to draw on a device.

Device Independent Bitmap (DIB)   A device-independent bitmap provides a standard format for storing color bitmap information. DIBs come in four formats: one-bit per pixel (monochrome), four bits per pixel (16 color), eight bits per pixel (256 color) and 24 bits per pixel (16 million colors).

Dialog Box   A dialog box is a window, inside of which are other windows that are commonly referred to as dialog box controls. A dialog box is typically used to gather additional information from the user required to complete a command.

Dialog Box Control   A dialog box control is a window that rests inside a dialog box and provides a specific set of services. Among the window classes that have been defined for dialog box controls are button, combo box, edit, listbox, scroll bar, and static.

Dialog Box Coordinates   Dialog box coordinates provide a device-independent way to specify the layout of a dialog box. Dialog box units are relative to the system font, or to whatever font has been defined for the dialog box.

Dialog Box Editor   The dialog box editor is a graphic layout tool for designing the look of a dialog box and the style of each dialog box controls. Microsoft provides the dialog box editor as part of its Software Development Kit (SDK).

Disabled Window   A disabled window is one that is prevented from receiving mouse and keyboard input. For example, the parent window of a modal dialog box is disabled.

Discardable Memory   A discardable memory object is one that, when unlocked, can be purged from memory by the memory manager when available system memory is otherwise unavailable. Windows uses a least recently used algorithm to determine the segment to discard next.

Drawing Attribute   A drawing attribute is a setting or a drawing object inside a device context that can change the appearance of the output produced by different GDI drawing routines. Some examples of drawing attributes include pens, brushes, fonts, mapping mode, and text color.

Dynamic Data Exchange (DDE)   A data exchange mechanism that is built on top of Windows' message passing mechanism. A DDE interaction is called a conversation. There are always two participants in a DDE conversation, one called the client and the other called the server. There are several types of DDE converstions: ongoing data exchange, one-time data exchange, command execution, and poke of data back into the server's database.

Dynamic Link Library   A dynamic link library is a file containing code or data that can be shared by different application programs at run-time. For example, the core components that make up Windows itself are a collection of dynamic link libraries and include KERNEL.EXE, USER.EXE and GDI.EXE, as well as a set of device drivers. Fonts are an example of dynamic link libraries that contain no code, but only data to be shared between programs.

Dynamic Linking   Dynamic linking refers to the process by which different code and data of different modules—application programs and dynamic link libraries—are connected at run time.

Event-driven   Event-driven software is structured to process external events that do not necessarily occur in a sequential manner. Traditionally, interrupt-handling code in an operating system or in a device driver has been the primary domain of event driven software. But the development of personal computers and interactive software has made this a concern of application programmers. Graphical User Interfaces (GUIs) provide a programming environment which assists in the creation of event driven application software.

Expanded Memory Specification (EMS)   The expanded memory specification refers to a protocol that was first introduced in 1984 by Lotus, Intel, and Microsoft to ease the memory crunch that was caused by the 640K memory limitation of real-mode operation. Windows 1.x used EMS memory to cache DOS applications that were dormant; Windows 2.x provided enhanced EMS support to Windows applications that increased the address space of each application in a manner that was transparent to the application programmer. Windows 3.x continues EMS support, although Windows itself only uses EMS in real mode. In the other modes of operation, a Windows program can access EMS memory, but Windows itself does not use EMS because of the

greater flexibility that is available with extended memory.

Extended Memory   Extended memory refers to the memory that is not ordinarily accessible from real mode, but requires protect-mode operation. Extended memory allows the address space of a machine to go beyond the one-megabyte boundary of real mode and to access up to 16 megabytes with an 80286 processor and up to 4 gigabytes with an 80386 processor.

Extended Memory Specification (XMS)   The extended memory specification defines an interface for using the memory areas above the 640K line. This includes the upper memory blocks (UMBs) between 640 and 1024K, the high-memory area (HMA) from 1024 to 1088K, and the extended memory blocks (EMBs) above the 1088K line.

File Manager   One of the desktop accessories that Microsoft has bundled with Windows 3.0.

Fixed Memory   A fixed memory object is one whose logical address does not change. However, in protect mode, the physical address of a fixed memory block can change unless the memory has been fixed, which is done by calling **GlobalFix**. In addtion, in 386 Enhanced Mode, a fixed memory object can also be paged to disk unless it has been page-locked, which is accomplished by calling **GlobalPageLock**.

Focus   see Keyboard Focus.

Font   also see Logical Font.

Function Prototype   Function prototypes provide a means by which the C Compiler can perform some automatic error checking, including check for proper use of the return value and the correct number and type of parameters. Here is an example of a function prototype taken from Window.h:

```
BOOL FAR PASCAL TextOut (HDC,
int, int, LPSTR, int);
```

Global Descriptor Table (GDT) A global descriptor table is one of two data areas used by the Intel 80286 and higher CPUs in protect mode. A global descriptor table allows the CPU to convert segment identifier values (also known as segment selectors) into the physical addresses of segments. Intel designed the GDT to provide a shared data area accessible from all processes. However, Windows does not use a GDT for any of its memory management, but uses the other data area, the local descriptor table (LDT) instead.

Global Heap The global heap refers to the total memory available to Windows itself, to Windows applications, and to other components like device drivers.

Global Memory Object A global memory object is an object allocated from the global heap. In Intel memory architecture terms, a global memory object is a segment.

Granularity In the context of memory allocation, granularity refers to the increments by which memory is actually allocated. The global heap manager uses a granularity of 32 bytes. The local heap manager uses a granularity of 4 bytes.

Graphic Device Interface (GDI) GDI is Windows' device-independent graphics output library.

Graphical User Interface (GUI) Refers to a type of operating system or operating environment that displays output on a bitmapped graphical display screen. Another characteristic of GUI systems is that they are event-driven, which means a different programming model is necessary besides the traditional, sequence oriented programming model that was originally developed for batch oriented systems. Microsoft Windows is an example of a GUI system. Other examples include the Apple Macintosh, the OS/2 Presentation Manager, which was jointly developed by IBM and Microsoft, and Digital Research

Corporation's GEM. The various X-Windows systems deserve to be in this last as well, and they include the Open System Foundation's Motif, and Sun Microsystem's Open Look and Digital Equipment Corporation's DEC-Windows.

GUI an acronym for Graphical User Interface.

Handle A handle is a 16-bit, unsigned integer that identifies an object. In most cases, the meaning of a handle is only known to the subroutine library that issued the handle. A program can modify an object by providing the handle to the subroutine library, which then acts on the objects on behalf of the program.

Hardware Event Queue A buffer maintained by Windows to hold keyboard and mouse events that are waiting to be retrieved by application programs.

High Memory Area (HMA) The high memory area refers to the 64 K-bytes located immediately above the one-megabyte address line on 80286 and 80386 processors. Intel designed this space as the first 64K of extended memory, which was not meant to be part of the real mode address space. However, an XMS (eXtended Memory Specification) driver, like HIMEM.SYS, is able to trick the 80286 and higher chips into allowing access into this data area.

Hit-Test Code Refers to a code returned by the default window procedure in reponse to the WM_NCHITTEST message, which identifies the area of a window where the mouse is located. Hit-test codes are used to help the window manager to install the correct mouse cursor.

Hook A hook is a subroutine that is called by Windows' message handling mechanism to allow the monitoring and modification of message traffic in the system. Hooks are installed on a system-wide basis, and therefore care should be taken when using them to avoid disrupting the normal operation of other programs, and to avoid slowing the system down.

Hungarian naming   Hungarian naming is a convention for creating variable and function names that provide a quick way to compose short but useful identifiers.

Huge Memory Object   A huge memory object is a memory object in the global heap that is larger than 64K. Windows allocates huge memory objects by allocating two or more segments. To access the second and subsequent segments, huge pointer arithmetic is required. This involves updating the segment portion of the address as well as the offset portion. The segment portion is modified by changing the segment value using the __AHINCR update value. This value is added to the segment address to access the next segment in a huge object segment chain.

Icon   An icon is a graphic symbol that serves to remind the user of the presence of a program, file, or data object that is presently closed, but available for future access.

Import Library   An import library provides the linker with information about the exported entry points of a dynamic link library. An import library allows the linker to create a relocation record in a program's .EXE file so that Windows' dynamic link mechanism can provide the required fix-up to the calling code at program execution time.

Instance   An instance of a program refers to a copy of a program in memory. Windows allows several copies of a single program to run simultaneously. Each instance has its own, private data segment, but shares code and resource segments with every other instance of the program.

Instance Thunk   An instance thunk is a tiny piece of code that is created in a program's task database (TDB) to assist in the fix-up of the data segment

for an exported call-back function. An instance thunk is created by **MakeProcInstance**, and freed by **FreeProcInstance**. With the exception of window procedures, every call-back procedure requires an instance thunk. This includes dialog box procedure, enumeration procedures, notification procedures, and certain subclass procedures. No instance thunk is required for any of these procedures when they reside in the code segment of a dynamic link library.

Interrupt Descriptor Table   An interrupt descriptor table (IDT) is a lookup table used by the higher end Intel-86 chips (80286 and above) in protect mode to hold an array of interrupts.

Keyboard Accelerator   A keyboard accelerator provides a means to define key-strokes that are interpreted as commands. Keyboard accelerators mimic menu selection messages, to minimize special processing that would otherwise be required to support a program's command keys.

Keyboard Focus   The keyboard focus tells Windows the window that should receive keyboard input. When a program receives the keyboard focus, it is notified with a WM_SETFOCUS message. When it loses the focus, it is notified with a WM_KILLFOCUS message.

Keyboard Scan Code   A keyboard scan code is a numeric value sent from the keyboard hardware as a notification that a key was pressed, released, or is being held down. Application programs do not ordinarily handle scan codes, since they represent a hardware dependent key code. In Windows, scan codes undergo two translation before they appear in a program as ASCII characters. The first translation is from scan code to virtual key codes. The second translation is from virtual key codes to ASCII characters.

KERNEL   The KERNEL is one of the three core components of Windows, and is responsible for memory management, dynamic linking, resources, atom tables, module managment, interface to DOS, and other operating system services that are available to Windows programs.

Load On Call segment   A load on call segment is a code or resource segment that is loaded into memory when it is referenced.

Local Descriptor Table (LDT)   A local descriptor table is one of two data areas used by the Intel 80286 and higher CPUs in protect mode. A local descriptor table allows the CPU to convert segment identifier values (also known as segment selectors) into the physical addresses of segments. Intel designed the LDT to provide a process with a private address space. In Windows 3.0, a single LDT is used by all application programs. However, a future version of Windows will provide one LDT per application program.

Local Heap   Refers to the heap that is created in a module's default data segment. The automatic startup code automatically initializes the local heap of an application program by calling the **LocalInit** routine. Dynamic link libraries that wish to use a local heap must explicitly call **Local-Init** themselves.

Logical Drawing Object   A logical drawing object is a GDI description of a pen, brush, font, or color. It provides a device-independent way to describe the drawing attributes that are installed in a DC.

Logical Font   A logical font is a description of a font that GDI's font mapper uses to select a font for drawing text. A logical font description can be created using the LOGFONT data structure.

Logical Pen   A logical pen describes the color, width, and style of lines requested by a program.

Mapping Mode   A mapping mode is a DC drawing attribute that describes how drawing coordinates that are given to GDI drawing routines are interpreted. For example, the default mapping mode, MM_TEXT, interprets coordinates as pixels. The other mapping modes can be used to scale coordinates into fractions of an inch, fractions of a centimeter, or scale to arbitrary ratios.

Marker   A marker is a graphic primitive that is guaranteed to be centered on the specified location. Although GDI itself does not directly implement markers, it is a simple matter to build a set of marker subroutines that draw using GDI drawing routines. See Chapter 7.

Message   A message is a 16-bit, unsigned value that notifies a window procedure that an event of interest has occurred. Windows' predefined messages are identified in Windows.H with symbolic constants whose names start with a WM_ prefix. For example, the WM_CREATE message is sent to a window procedure to notify it that a window of that class has been created.

Metafile   A metafile is a pseudo-device that GDI can create for the purpose of storing graphic images. A GDI metafile is a data structure containing a list of calls to be made to GDI routines to reconstruct a picture, along with the parameters to provide those calls.

Module   A module is a specific type of entity in Windows, which reflects the way that code and data is organized on disk. Windows recognizes two types of modules: executable application (.EXE) program files, and dynamic link libraries, which can have an extension of .EXE, .DRV, .DLL, or .FON, to name just a few.

Module Database   A module database is a memory resident image of the file header of an application program or a dynamic link library. The Windows loader uses the module database to load code and resources from disk when they are needed.

Module Definition File An ASCII text file that contains program definition and memory use information. A module definition file normally has an extension of .DEF. At program creation time, the module definition file is given to the linker as part of the bulding of a .EXE or .DLL file.

Mouse Capture Ordinarily, mouse messages are sent to the window lying under the mouse cursor. However, a program can restrict the flow of mouse messages to a single window by setting the mouse capture. This is done by calling **SetCapture**. To free mouse messages, a program calls **ReleaseCapture**.

Moveable Memory Moveable memory objects are an artifact of real mode Windows. In real mode, a moveable object will only move when it is not locked by a program. In protect mode, segments can move at any time, since the physical address is hidden from application software. The protect mode memory management hardware converts logical addresses—which is how application software references memory—into physical addresses by means of a descriptor table. The Windows memory manager can move objects in physical memory without changing their logical addresses, which means that in protect mode, memory movement is transparent to application softare.

Multiple Document Interface or MDI, describes a user-interface standard that opens a new window for each new file or document that is opened in a program.

Nonpreemptive Scheduling Describes the way that a multitasking system schedules programs to run. In a nonpreemptively scheduled system, the operating system does not interrupt programs

OEM Character Set Refers to the set of characters native to a machine. For IBM-compatible computers built for sale in United States, this means code page 437.

Page Locking Page locking refers to a process by which memory in 386-Enhanced Mode is prevented from being swapped to disk. This is accomplished by calling the **GlobalPageLock** routine and is primarily intended for the use of time-critical device drivers that must stay memory resident.

Paragraph When the Intel-86 processors operate in real mode, a paragraph is the smallest memory unit that can be allocated. A paragraph is 16 bytes. Windows' memory manager allocates segments in two-paragraph increments, which means the granularity of the global memory manager is 32 bytes.

Paintbrush One of the desktop accessories that is included with Windows 3.0.

Palette (PAL) A palette provides two services: It describes the colors that are stored in a device-independent bitmap (DIB), and it allows a program to request changes to the physical palette of display devices that support palettes.

PASCAL Calling Convention The PASCAL calling convention describes the way that parameters are passed on the stack to a subroutine (left to right), and also assigns the called routine with the responsibility for cleaning the parameters from the stack. Routines that are defined as PASCAL must have a fixed number of parameters, but this results in slightly smaller and faster code than the alternative CDECL calling convention.

Pen A pen is a DC attribute that describes the color, style, and width of lines. See Logical Pen.

Preemptive Scheduling Describes the way that a multitasking system schedules programs to run. In a preemptively scheduled system, the operating system will interrupt one program to allow another one to run.

Preload Segments A code or resource segment that is marked as preload is moved into memory before a program starts running.

Private Window Class A private window class is reserved for the use of a single program. In contrast are global window classes, which are available for use by any program in the system.

Process Database (PDB) A data structure created by Windows to maintain DOS related per-process data. Windows adds its own elements to this data structure.

Profiler see Swap Kernel.

Program Manager Refers to the main program window in Windows 3.0.

Program Segment Prefix (PSP) see Process Database.

Protect Mode Protect mode refers to an operating mode of Intel 80286 chips and later. Protect mode is characterized by an addressing scheme that prevents programs from illegal access to unowned memory areas. On the 80286, protect mode operation allows a physical address space of 16 megabytes. On the 80386 and 80486, protect mode allows access to a 4 gigabyte address space.

Pull-Model Processing Refers to a style of interaction between the operating system and application software. Pull-model processing places the application software in the active role, in which it polls the system for available input. This is the traditional way that interactive application software has been written, and is how Windows' handles mouse and keyboard input. Also, messages that are transmitted to a window procedure using the PostMessage routine are delivered in a pull-model manner, that is, via the GetMessage or PeekMessage routines. See also push-model processing.

Push-Model Processing Refers to a style of interaction between the operating system and application software. Push-model processing places the operating system software in the active role, in which it calls subroutines in the application software to perform the necessary tasks. Most of the non-hardware related messages in Windows are delivered in a push-model manner. For example, when a program calls the CreateWindow routine to create a window, a WM_CREATE message is pushed into the window procedure of the newly created window. Messages that are transmitted to a window procedure using the **SendMessage** routine are delivered in a push-model manner, which bypasses the pull-model **GetMessage** routine, and calls a window procedure directly.

Raster Operation A raster operation is a logical operation or combination of logical operations that describe how two or more inputs combine to produce a given output. One type of raster operation is the ROP2 codes, which are a DC attribute that describe how pixels, lines, and areas combine with a drawing surface. Another type of raster operation, sometimes known as ROP3 codes, are provided as parameters to the BitBlt and PatBlt functions, to describe how a source bitmap, a destination bitmap, and a brush are to combine.

Return Thunks A return thunk is a tiny piece of code that real mode Windows uses to bridge a function return when the code segment containing the calling routine is discarded from memory.

Resource A resource is a read-only data object that is bound into an executable file at program creation time. From a memory management point of view, resources can be discarded and reread when needed. From the point of view of the Windows user interface, resources define dialog boxes, menus, cursors, icons, bitmaps, to name just a few.

Real Mode Real Mode refers to an operating mode of the Intel-86 family of processors. Real mode is characterized by a one-megabyte address space. Programs have access to the real, physical address of memory, which is how the mode gets its name.

Scan Code see Keyboard Scan Code.

Scanner A graphic scanner reads a graphic image on paper and converts it into a digital form suitable for creating GDI bitmaps.

Segment Selector When the Intel-86 family of processors are running in protect mode, a segment identifier is referred to as a segment selector. Part of a segment selector is an index into a table of descriptors in either an LDT (local descriptor table) or a GDT (global descriptor table), from which is read the physical location of a memory segment.

Segmented Addressing The Intel-86 family of CPUs address memory using a segmented addressing scheme. Segmented addressing requires two pieces in a memory address: a segment identifier and an offset.

Software Development Kit (SDK) The Windows Software Development Kit is a product that Microsoft provides for the purpose of assisting software developers to create Windows programs.

Software Migration Kit (SMK) The Software Migration Kit is a product that Microsoft provides to assist software developers in porting Windows programs to run in OS/2, version 1.2 and later.

Stack Patching Stack patching refers to the process by which the real mode Windows Kernel updates stack references to code segments that have moved or been discarded.

Standard Mode Refers to an operating mode of Windows in which protect mode addressing is enabled to allow Windows to take advantage of features of the Intel family of processors that are available on the 80286 and higher CPUs.

Swap Kernel The swap kernel is a special version of the Windows kernel that runs in real mode only and provides information about the segment loading and discarding of a program. It can be used to fine tune the segment working sets of a program to minimize the program's required memory.

Systems Application Architecture (SAA) A collection of standards created by IBM to provide software consistency that extends from personal computers to mini-computers on up to mainframes. Aspects of application software that will be affected include the user interface, and application programming interface (API). The user interface standards are described in a standard that is part of SAA and is called Common User Access (CUA).

Task Database (TDB) A task database is a memory object created by the Window scheduler to keep track of the things that are owned by a task. This includes file handles, the current MS-DOS disk and directory, information about a task's private interrupts, and a pointer to the DOS program database, also known as a program segment prefix (PSP).

Text Alignment The text alignment is a DC attribute that describes the placement of a line of text relative to a control point.

Text Color The text color is a DC attribute that describes the color for drawing text. Only pure, undithered colors are actually used for text, which means that GDI maps the requested color into the closest available device color.

Thunk A thunk is a tiny piece of code that serves as a dynamic code link (in real mode Windows)

Tiled Windows Tiled windows refers to the placement of windows so that no two windows overlap. Windows 1.x had built-in support for automatic tiling. This support was removed in versions 2.0 and later.

Top-Level Window A top-level window is an overlapping window (WS_OVERLAP) or a popup window (WS_POPUP) which has no parent. All top-level windows are referenced in Windows' Task List that appears in response to the Ctrl + Esc key combination.

Unexpected Application Error (UAE)   An error that causes an application to terminate. Some of the causes of unexpected application errors include general protection faults, unexpected paging fault, and unexpected interrupt.

Viewport Origin   The viewport origin is a DC attribute that defines the coordinate translation to take place after the scaling for the various GDI mapping modes.

Viewport Extent   The viewport extent is a DC attribute that provides a pair of X and Y values that are used to define the ratios for GDI's isotropic and anisotropic mapping modes.

Virtual Key Code   A virtual key code is a value that represents keystroke information as raw keyboard input. Raw keyboard input does not distinguish, for example, between upper and lower-case letters, and does not take into account the state of shift keys like Ctrl, Shift, and Alt. Nor do virtual key codes take into account the state of the various keyboard toggle keys, like Num Lock, Caps Lock, or Scroll Lock. Virtual key codes represent an intermediate step between scan code information, which is hardware-de-

pendent keyboard input, and ASCII characters, which are device-independent representations of ASCII characters.

Window Class   A window class is a template for creating a window. Window classes are created by calling Register-Class and supplying a pointer to a WNDCLASS structure with the class definition information.

Window Extent   The window extent is a DC attribute that provides a pair of X and Y values that are used to define the ratios for GDI's isotropic and anisotropic mapping modes.

Window Origin   The window origin is a DC attribute that defines the translation that is to take place in the world coordinate space before the scaling transformation of any of GDI's mapping modes.

Window Procedure   A function associated with a window class that processes the messages associated with a given window.

Windows Sandwich   A window sandwich describes a code construction made up of three parts: two slices of bread and some filling in between. The top slice of bread borrows a system resource, the filling uses the resource, and the bottom slice of bread returns the resource to the owner.

Appendix D:
Contents of a Device Context

Drawing Attribute	Default Value	Lines	Filled Areas	Text	Raster	Comments
Background Color	White	x	x	x		styled pen, hatch brush
Background Mode	OPAQUE	x	x	x		On/Off switch
Brush Handle	White Brush		x		x	Filled areas
Brush Origin	(0, 0)		x		x	hatch & dithered brushes
Clipping Region Handle	Entire Surface	x	x	x	x	
Color Palette Handle	Default Palette	x	x	x		
Current Pen Position	(0 , 0)	x				For LineTo routine
Drawing Mode	R2_COPYPEN	x	x			Boolean mixing
Font Handle	System Font			x		
Intercharacter Spacing	0			x		
Mapping Mode	MM_TEXT	x	x	x	x	One unit = 1 pixel
Pen Handle	Black Pen	x	x			
Polygon-Filling Mode	Alternate		x			For Polygon routine
Stretching Mode	Black on White				x	For StretchBlt routine
Text Alignment	Left & Top			x		
Text Color	Black			x		

(continued)

Drawing Attribute	Default Value	Lines	Filled Areas	Text	Raster	Comments
Viewport Extent	(1 , 1)	x	x	x	x	Coordinate mapping
Viewport Origin	(0 , 0)	x	x	x	x	Coordinate mapping
Window Extent	(1 , 1)	x	x	x	x	Coordinate mapping
Window Origin	(0 , 0)	x	x	x	x	Coordinate mapping

Appendix E: ANSI and OEM Character Sets

Figure E.1 *Ansi Character Set (Code Page 1004)*

ANSI Character Set - Code Page 1004

	0-	1-	2-	3-	4-	5-	6-	7-	8-	9-	A-	B-	C-	D-	E-	F-
-0	I	I		0	@	P	`	p	I	I		°	À	Ð	à	ð
-1	I	I	!	1	A	Q	a	q	I	´	¡	±	Á	Ñ	á	ñ
-2	I	I	"	2	B	R	b	r	I	·	¢	²	Â	Ò	â	ò
-3	I	I	#	3	C	S	c	s	I	I	£	³	Ã	Ó	ã	ó
-4	I	I	$	4	D	T	d	t	I	I	¤	´	Ä	Ô	ä	ô
-5	I	I	%	5	E	U	e	u	I	I	¥	µ	Å	Õ	å	õ
-6	I	I	&	6	F	V	f	v	I	I	¦	¶	Æ	Ö	æ	ö
-7	I	I	'	7	G	W	g	w	I	I	§	·	Ç	×	ç	÷
-8	I	I	(	8	H	X	h	x	I	I	¨	¸	È	Ø	è	ø
-9	I	I	)	9	I	Y	i	y	I	I	©	¹	É	Ù	é	ù
-A	I	I	*	:	J	Z	j	z	I	I	ª	º	Ê	Ú	ê	ú
-B	I	I	+	;	K	[	k	{	I	I	«	»	Ë	Û	ë	û
-C	I	I	,	<	L	\	l	|	I	I	¬	¼	Ì	Ü	ì	ü
-D	I	I	-	=	M	]	m	}	I	I	-	½	Í	Ý	í	ý
-E	I	I	.	>	N	^	n	~	I	I	®	¾	Î	þ	î	þ
-F	I	I	/	?	O	_	o	I	I	I	¯	¿	Ï	ß	ï	ÿ

Figure E.2 *OEM Character Set (Code Page 437)*

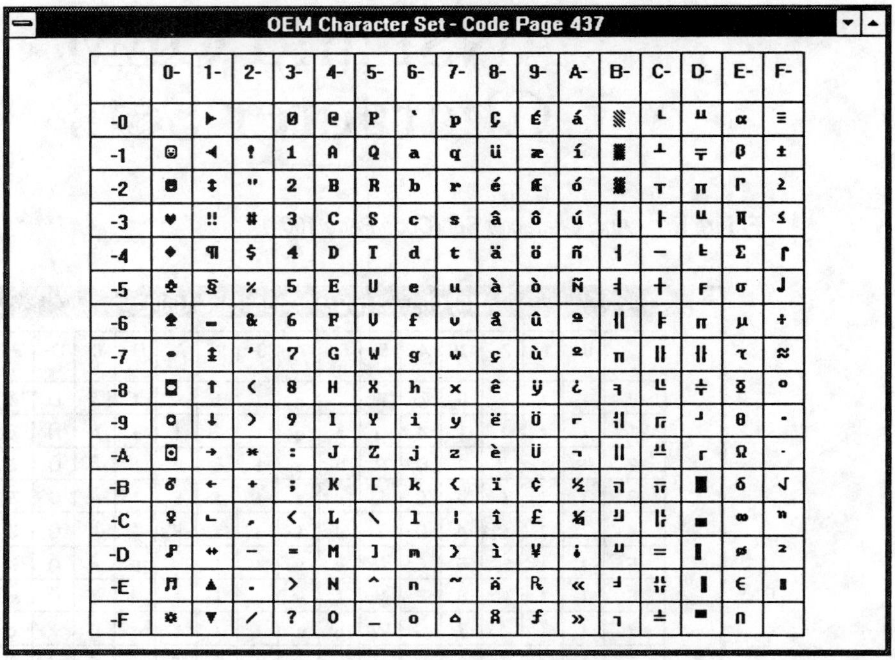

OEM Character Set - Code Page 437

	0-	1-	2-	3-	4-	5-	6-	7-	8-	9-	A-	B-	C-	D-	E-	F-
-0		►		0	@	P	`	p	Ç	É	á	░	└	╨	α	≡
-1	☺	◄	!	1	A	Q	a	q	ü	æ	í	▒	┴	╤	ß	±
-2	☻	↕	"	2	B	R	b	r	é	Æ	ó	▓	┬	╥	Γ	≥
-3	♥	‼	#	3	C	S	c	s	â	ô	ú	│	├	╙	π	≤
-4	♦	¶	$	4	D	T	d	t	ä	ö	ñ	┤	─	╘	Σ	⌠
-5	♣	§	%	5	E	U	e	u	à	ò	Ñ	╡	┼	╒	σ	⌡
-6	♠	▬	&	6	F	V	f	v	å	û	ª	╢	╞	╓	µ	÷
-7	•	↨	'	7	G	W	g	w	ç	ù	º	╖	╟	╫	τ	≈
-8	◘	↑	(	8	H	X	h	x	ê	ÿ	¿	╕	╚	╪	Φ	°
-9	○	↓	)	9	I	Y	i	y	ë	Ö	⌐	╣	╔	┘	Θ	∙
-A	◙	→	*	:	J	Z	j	z	è	Ü	¬	║	╩	┌	Ω	·
-B	♂	←	+	;	K	[	k	{	ï	¢	½	╗	╦	█	δ	√
-C	♀	∟	,	<	L	\	l	|	î	£	¼	╝	╠	▄	∞	ⁿ
-D	♪	↔	-	=	M	]	m	}	ì	¥	¡	╜	═	▌	φ	²
-E	♫	▲	.	>	N	^	n	~	Ä	₧	«	╛	╬	▐	ε	■
-F	☼	▼	/	?	O	_	o	⌂	Å	ƒ	»	┐	╧	▀	∩	

Appendix F:
The Windows Virtual Key Codes

(hex)	(dec)	Symbolic Name	Key Pressed (US English 101/102 Kbd)
1	1	VK_LBUTTON	
2	2	VK_RBUTTON	
3	3	VK_CANCEL	Ctrl-Break
4	4	VK_MBUTTON	
8	8	VK_BACK	Backspace
9	9	VK_TAB	Tab
C	12	VK_CLEAR	5 on Numeric keypad w/Num Lock OFF
D	13	VK_RETURN	Enter
10	16	VK_SHIFT	Shift
11	17	VK_CONTROL	Ctrl
12	18	VK_MENU	Alt
13	19	VK_PAUSE	Pause (or Ctrl-Num Lock)
14	20	VK_CAPITAL	Caps Lock
1B	27	VK_ESCAPE	Esc
20	32	VK_SPACE	Spacebar
21	33	VK_PRIOR	Page Up
22	34	VK_NEXT	Page Down
23	35	VK_END	End
24	36	VK_HOME	Home
25	37	VK_LEFT	Left Arrow
26	38	VK_UP	Up Arrow
27	39	VK_RIGHT	Right Arrow
28	40	VK_DOWN	Down Arrow
29	41	VK_SELECT	<unused>
2A	42	VK_PRINT	<unused>
2B	43	VK_EXECUTE	<unused>
2C	44	VK_SNAPSHOT	Print Screen

(continued)

919

(hex)	(dec)	Symbolic Name	Key Pressed (US English 101/102 Kbd)
2D	45	VK_INSERT	Ins
2E	46	VK_DELETE	Del
2F	47	VK_HELP	<unused>
30-39	48-57	VK_0 to VK_9	0 to 9 above letter keys
41-5A	65-90	VK_A to VK_Z	A to Z
60	96	VK_NUMPAD0	0 on Numeric keypad w/Num Lock ON
61	97	VK_NUMPAD1	1 on Numeric keypad w/Num Lock ON
62	98	VK_NUMPAD2	2 on Numeric keypad w/Num Lock ON
63	99	VK_NUMPAD3	3 on Numeric keypad w/Num Lock ON
64	100	VK_NUMPAD4	4 on Numeric keypad w/Num Lock ON
65	101	VK_NUMPAD5	5 on Numeric keypad w/Num Lock ON
66	102	VK_NUMPAD6	6 on Numeric keypad w/Num Lock ON
67	103	VK_NUMPAD7	7 on Numeric keypad w/Num Lock ON
68	104	VK_NUMPAD8	8 on Numeric keypad w/Num Lock ON
69	105	VK_NUMPAD9	9 on Numeric keypad w/Num Lock ON
6A	106	VK_MULTIPLY	* on Numeric keypad
6B	107	VK_ADD	+ on Numeric keypad
6C	108	VK_SEPARATOR	<unused>
6D	109	VK_SUBTRACT	- on Numeric keypad
6E	110	VK_DECIMAL	. on Numeric keypad w/Num Lock ON
6F	111	VK_DIVIDE	/ on Numeric keypad
70	112	VK_F1	F1 function key
71	113	VK_F2	F2 function key
72	114	VK_F3	F3 function key
73	115	VK_F4	F4 function key
74	116	VK_F5	F5 function key

(continued)

(hex)	(dec)	Symbolic Name	Key Pressed (US English 101/102 Kbd)
75	117	VK_F6	F6 function key
76	118	VK_F7	F7 function key
77	119	VK_F8	F8 function key
78	120	VK_F9	F9 function key
79	121	VK_F10	F10 function key
7A	122	VK_F11	F11 function key
7B	123	VK_F12	F12 function key
7C	124	VK_F13	
7D	125	VK_F14	
7E	126	VK_F15	
7F	127	VK_F16	
90	144	VK_NUMLOCK	Num Lock
91	145		Scroll Lock

The following code apply to US keyboards only

BA	186		colon/semi-colon
BB	187		plus/equal
BC	188		less than/comma
BD	189		underscore/hyphen
BE	190		greater than/period
BF	191		question/slash
C0	192		tilde/back accent
DB	219		left squiggle brace/left square brace
DC	220		horizontal bar/backslash
DD	221		right squiggle brace/right square brace
DE	222		double quote/single quote

Index

International Systems Design
is pleased to offer A Companion Diskette to
Windows 3.0 Power Programming Techniques

Why type? This Companion saves your valuable time by
providing all the Power Programs in the book.

All for only $15.95!
Shipping and Handling Included
(Washington State Residents add 8.1% for tax)

Check or Money Order, MasterCard, Visa

BY PHONE	**BY MAIL**	**BY FAX**
(206) 828-6402	International Systems Design	1-206-828-6312
MC or Visa Only	1075 Bellevue Way, Suite 300	
	Bellevue, Washington 98004	

If you are ordering by mail or by fax and paying by credit
card, be sure to include the following:

Your Name as it Appears on the Card
Your Account Number
The Expiration Date on the Card

Please allow 4–6 weeks for processing.
Ask about our overnight service.